T0178651

Lecture Notes in Computer Science 14446

Founding Editors

Gerhard Goos
Juris Hartmanis

Editorial Board Members

The series Lecture Notes in Computer Science (LNCS), including its subseries Lecture Notes in Artificial Intelligence (LNAI) and Lecture Notes in Bioinformatics (LNBI), has established itself as a medium for the publication of new developments in computer science and information technology research, teaching, and education.

LNCS enjoys close cooperation with the computer science R & D community, the series counts many renowned academics among its volume editors and paper authors, and collaborates with prestigious societies. Its mission is to serve this international community by providing an invaluable service, mainly focused on the publication of conference and workshop proceedings and postproceedings. LNCS commenced publication in 1973.

Erika Ábrahám · Clemens Dubslaff ·
Silvia Lizeth Tapia Tarifa
Editors

Theoretical Aspects of Computing – ICTAC 2023

20th International Colloquium
Lima, Peru, December 4–8, 2023
Proceedings

 Springer

Editors
Erika Ábrahám 🄳
RWTH Aachen University
Aachen, Germany

Clemens Dubslaff 🄳
Eindhoven University of Technology
Eindhoven, The Netherlands

Silvia Lizeth Tapia Tarifa 🄳
University of Oslo
Oslo, Norway

ISSN 0302-9743   ISSN 1611-3349 (electronic)
Lecture Notes in Computer Science
ISBN 978-3-031-47962-5   ISBN 978-3-031-47963-2 (eBook)
https://doi.org/10.1007/978-3-031-47963-2

This Springer imprint is published by the registered company Springer Nature Switzerland AG
The registered company address is: Gewerbestrasse 11, 6330 Cham, Switzerland

Paper in this product is recyclable.

Preface

This volume contains the papers presented at the 20th International Colloquium on Theoretical Aspects of Computing (ICTAC 2023) held during December 4–8, 2023 in Lima, Peru.

The International Colloquia on Theoretical Aspects of Computing (ICTAC) is a series of annual events founded in 2003 by the United Nations University International Institute for Software Technology. Its purpose is to bring together practitioners and researchers from academia, industry, and government to present research results and exchange experience and ideas. Beyond these scholarly goals, another main purpose is to promote cooperation in research and education between participants and their institutions from developing and industrial regions.

ICTAC 2023 received 39 submissions (including 36 regular papers, two short papers, and one tool paper) from authors in 27 different countries. All papers received at least three single-blind reviews. Based on the reviews and extensive discussions, the Program Committee decided to accept 22 papers. This volume contains the revised versions of these 22 papers, which cover a wide variety of topics.

We were honored to have three distinguished guests as invited speakers. Marijn J.H. Heule (Carnegie Mellon University, USA) presented exciting recent developments from the area of SAT solving, Ana Cavalcanti (University of York, UK) talked about the RoboStar framework to support the development of control software for robotics applications, and Pedro R. D'Argenio (National University of Cordoba, Argentina) discussed optimal route synthesis in space delay-tolerant networks. Full papers for the first two invited talks as well as an extended abstract for the third talk are included in this volume.

In addition, five tutorials were given at ICTAC 2023 by Shaukat Ali (Simula Research Laboratory, Norway) and Mahsa Varshosaz (IT University of Copenhagen, Denmark) on testing cyber-physical systems, Ina Schaefer (Karlsruhe IT, Germany) and Maximilian Kodetzki (Karlsruhe IT, Germany) on a correct-by-construction approach to programming using CorC, Maurice H. ter Beek (Istituto di Scienza e Tecnologie dell'Informazione, Italy) on formal methods and tools for software product lines, Einar Broch Johnsen (University of Oslo, Norway) on semantically lifted digital twins, and Martin Leucker (University of Lübeck, Germany) on automata learning with an application to learn and verify recurrent neural networks.

ICTAC 2023 continued the tradition of previous ICTAC conferences in holding a training school. The ICTAC 2023 Training School on Applied Formal Methods aimed at introducing Master's students, Ph.D. students, and early-stage researchers to some important topics in theoretical aspects of computing. Christian Colombo (University of Malta, Malta) gave a lecture on the theory and practice of runtime verification, Pedro R. D'Argenio (National University of Cordoba, Argentina) on probabilistic model checking, Ana Cavalcanti (University of York, UK) together with Ziggy Attala (University of York, UK) and Jim Woodcock (University of York, UK) on software engineering in robotics, and Marijn J.H. Heule (Carnegie Mellon University, USA) on satisfiability checking.

Many colleagues and friends contributed to making ICTAC 2023 a great event. First of all, we thank all authors who submitted their work to ICTAC 2023. We thank also all members of the Program Committee and the external reviewers for their excellent work, providing timely, insightful, and constructive reviews.

We are grateful to our invited speakers for giving such inspiring talks, tutorials, and lectures. We are indebted to the General Chairs, the Publicity Chairs, and the Training School Chairs for their hard work to organize the conference and the school, and to attract submissions. We also acknowledge our gratitude to the Steering Committee for their constant support.

We are indebted to UTEC (University of Engineering and Technology, Lima - Peru) for hosting the conference, and to EasyChair, which greatly simplified the assignment and reviewing of the submissions as well as the production of the material for the proceedings. Finally, we thank Springer for their cooperation in publishing the proceedings and sponsoring the Best Paper Award. We also thank FME (Formal Methods Europe) and SIGSOFT (the ACM Special Interest Group on Software Engineering) for their financial support to cover the costs of invited talks and tutorials at the conference and the operational costs of the ICTAC 2023 Training School on Applied Formal Methods.

December 2023   Erika Ábrahám
                                                      Clemens Dubslaff
                                              Silvia Lizeth Tapia Tarifa

Organization

General Chairs

Jesús Bellido   University of Engineering and Technology, Peru
Silvia Lizeth Tapia Tarifa   University of Oslo, Norway

Program Chairs

Erika Ábrahám   RWTH Aachen, Germany
Clemens Dubslaff   Eindhoven University of Technology,
         The Netherlands
Silvia Lizeth Tapia Tarifa   University of Oslo, Norway

Program Committee

Wolfgang Ahrendt	Chalmers University of Technology, Sweden
S. Akshay	IIT Bombay, India
Elvira Albert	Universidad Complutense de Madrid, Spain
Kyungmin Bae	Pohang University of Science and Technology (POSTECH), South Korea
Ezio Bartocci	TU Wien, Austria
Marcello Bonsangue	Leiden University, The Netherlands
Deepak D'Souza	Indian Institute of Science, India
Besik Dundua	Kutaisi International University, Georgia
Kim Guldstrand	Larsen Aalborg University, Denmark
Jane Hillston	University of Edinburgh, UK
Jana Hofmann	Azure Research, Microsoft, UK
Zoltán Horváth	Eötvös Loránd University, Hungary
Sebastian Junges	Radboud University, The Netherlands
Patrick Koopmann	Vrije Universiteit Amsterdam, The Netherlands
Jan Kretinsky	Technical University of Munich, Germany
Slawomir Lasota	University of Warsaw, Poland
Mircea Marin	West University of Timişoara, Romania
Mieke Massink	CNR-ISTI, Italy
Stefan Mitsch	Carnegie Mellon University, USA
Eugenio Moggi	University of Genoa, Italy

Rosemary Monahan	Maynooth University, Ireland
Joel Oaknine	Max Planck Institute for Software Systems, Germany
Corina Pasareanu	CMU, NASA, KBR, USA
José Proença	CISTER-ISEP and HASLab-INESC TEC, Portugal
Violet Ka I Pun	Western Norway University of Applied Sciences, Norway
Stefan Ratschan	Czech Academy of Sciences, Czech Republic
Mikheil Rukhaia	Tbilisi State University, Georgia
Gwen Salaün	Grenoble Alpes University, France
Augusto Sampaio	Federal University of Pernambuco, Brazil
Cesar Sanchez	IMDEA Software Institute, Spain
Gerardo Schneider	Chalmers University of Gothenburg, Sweden
Martina Seidl	Johannes Kepler University Linz, Austria
Tarmo Uustalu	Reykjavik University, Iceland
Heike Wehrheim	University of Oldenburg, Germany

Additional Reviewers

Muqsit Azeem	Konstantinos Mamouras
Lara Bargmann	Dylan McDermott
Henning Basold	Stefan Milius
István Bozó	Giann Nandi
Martin Ceresa	Dalia Papuc
Francesco Dagnino	Maximilian Prokop
Daniil Frumin	Ricardo Prudencio
Samir Genaim	Gabriel Reder
Pablo Gordillo	Christophe Reutenauer
R. Govind	Cedric Richter
Kush Grover	Jurriaan Rot
Jan Haltermann	Giorgi Rukhaia
Hossein Hojjat	Sylvain Salvati
Ambrus Kaposi	Wolfgang Schreiner
Tobias Kappé	Wendelin Serwe
Johannes Lenfers	Chukri Soueidi
Benjamin Lion	Patrick Stünkel
Dániel Lukács	Nicola Thoben
Hendrik Maarand	Davide Trotta
Dara MacConville	Chana Weil-Kennedy

Contents

Optimal Route Synthesis in Space DTN Using Markov Decision Processes 1
  Pedro R. D'Argenio

Without Loss of Satisfaction 4
  Marijn J. H. Heule

Modelling and Verifying Robotic Software that Uses Neural Networks 15
  Ziggy Attala, Ana Cavalcanti, and Jim Woodcock

A Game-Theoretic Approach to Indistinguishability of Winning Objectives
as User Privacy 36
  Rindo Nakanishi, Yoshiaki Takata, and Hiroyuki Seki

Learning Attack Trees by Genetic Algorithms 55
  Florian Dorfhuber, Julia Eisentraut, and Jan Křetínský

The Landscape of Computing Symmetric n-Variable Functions
with $2n$ Cards 74
  Suthee Ruangwises

On the Complexity of Reasoning in Kleene Algebra with Commutativity
Conditions 83
  Stepan L. Kuznetsov

Towards the Complexity Analysis of Programming Language Proof
Methods 100
  Matteo Cimini

A Dynamic Temporal Logic for Quality of Service in Choreographic
Models 119
  Carlos G. Lopez Pombo, Agustín E. Martinez Suñé, and Emilio Tuosto

Interactive Matching Logic Proofs in Coq 139
  Jan Tušil, Péter Bereczky, and Dániel Horpácsi

An Autonomous Data Language 158
  Tom T. P. Franken, Thomas Neele, and Jan Friso Groote

Formal Language Semantics for Triggered Enable Statecharts
with a Run-to-Completion Scheduling 178
    Karla Vanessa Morris Wright, Thai Son Hoang, Colin Snook,
    and Michael Butler

Strong Call-by-Value and Multi Types 196
    Beniamino Accattoli, Giulio Guerrieri, and Maico Leberle

Algorithms for Checking Intersection Non-emptiness of Regular
Expressions 216
    Weihao Su, Rongchen Li, Chengyao Peng, and Haiming Chen

Realisability of Global Models of Interaction 236
    Maurice H. ter Beek, Rolf Hennicker, and José Proença

Efficient Reactive Synthesis Using Mode Decomposition 256
    Matías Brizzio and César Sánchez

A Categorical Approach to Synthetic Chemistry 276
    Ella Gale, Leo Lobski, and Fabio Zanasi

Closure and Decision Properties for Higher-Dimensional Automata 295
    Amazigh Amrane, Hugo Bazille, Uli Fahrenberg,
    and Krzysztof Ziemiański

Robustness in Metric Spaces over Continuous Quantales
and the Hausdorff-Smyth Monad 313
    Francesco Dagnino, Amin Farjudian, and Eugenio Moggi

Synchronous Agents, Verification, and Blame—A Deontic View 332
    Karam Kharraz, Shaun Azzopardi, Gerardo Schneider,
    and Martin Leucker

Store Locally, Prove Globally 351
    Nadine Karsten and Uwe Nestmann

Denotational Semantics for Symbolic Execution 370
    Erik Voogd, Åsmund Aqissiaq Arild Kløvstad, and Einar Broch Johnsen

TeSSLa-ROS-Bridge – Runtime Verification of Robotic Systems 388
    Marian Johannes Begemann, Hannes Kallwies, Martin Leucker,
    and Malte Schmitz

Simplifying Process Parameters by Unfolding Algebraic Data Types 399
    Anna Stramaglia, Jeroen J. A. Keiren, and Thomas Neele

Modular Soundness Checking of Feature Model Evolution Plans 417
  Ida Sandberg Motzfeldt, Ingrid Chieh Yu, Crystal Chang Din,
  Violet Ka I Pun, and Volker Stolz

Author Index 439

Optimal Route Synthesis in Space DTN Using Markov Decision Processes

Pedro R. D'Argenio[✉][iD]

Universidad Nacional de Córdoba & CONICET, Córdoba, Argentina
pedro.dargenio@unc.edu.ar

Delay-tolerant networks (DTN) are time evolving networks which do not provide continuous and instantaneous end-to-end communication [5,9]. Instead, the topological configuration of DTN changes continuously: connections are available only during some time intervals and thus the network may suffer from frequent partitions and high delay. In this sense, the DTN paradigm is fundamental to understand deep-space [3] and near-Earth communications [4]. A particular characteristic of space networks is that, due to the orbital and periodic behavior of the different agents (e.g. satellites and terrestrial or lunar stations), contact times and durations between nodes can be accurately predicted. This type of DTNs are called *scheduled* and expected contacts can be imprinted in a *contact plan* that exhaustively describes the future network connectivity [10].

Scheduled routing algorithms such as the Contract Graph Routing (CGR) assumes that the future topologies of the network are highly accurate and that communication between nodes are perfect [1]. That is, it disregards transient or permanent faults of nodes, antenna pointing inaccuracies or unexpected interferences. The likelihood of these communication failures can normally be quantified *a priori* and hence included in the contact plan. Thus, the addition of this new information gives rise to a new type of DTN called *uncertain* DTN [12,13].

The behavior of the contact plan with probability failures on contacts yields a Markov decision process (MDP) where the non-determinism corresponds precisely to the routing decisions. With this model at hand, we have developed and studied several off-line techniques for deriving optimal and near-optimal routing solutions that ensure maximum likelihood of end-to-end message delivery. In particular, we have devised an analytical solution that exhaustively explores the MDP very much like probabilistic model checking does. This technique, which we called *routing under uncertain contact plans* (RUCoP), was reported in [13]. As the exhaustive solution is memory and time demanding, we have also explored in [6] simulation based techniques using *lightweight scheduler sampling* (LSS) [8] which has been implemented in the MODES statistical model checker [2] within the Modest toolset [11]. We have also studied variations of these approaches with communication redundancy in order to increase reliability by allowing a network-wide bounded number of message copies. In addition, an exhaustive comparison of these and existing techniques were reported in [7].

Supported by SeCyT-UNC 33620180100354CB (ARES) and EU Grant agreement ID: 101008233 (MISSION).

E. Ábrahám et al. (Eds.): ICTAC 2023, LNCS 14446, pp. 1–3, 2023.
https://doi.org/10.1007/978-3-031-47963-2_1

The objective of this presentation is to report this research as well as current ongoing developments for multi-objective routing optimization on space DTN.

References

1. Araniti, G., et al.: Contact graph routing in DTN space networks: overview, enhancements and performance. IEEE Commun. Mag. **53**(3), 38–46 (2015). https://doi.org/10.1109/MCOM.2015.7060480
2. Budde, C.E., D'Argenio, P.R., Hartmanns, A., Sedwards, S.: An efficient statistical model checker for nondeterminism and rare events. Int. J. Softw. Tools Technol. Transf. **22**(6), 759–780 (2020). https://doi.org/10.1007/s10009-020-00563-2
3. Burleigh, S.C., et al.: Delay-tolerant networking: an approach to interplanetary internet. IEEE Commun. Mag. **41**(6), 128–136 (2003). https://doi.org/10.1109/MCOM.2003.1204759
4. Caini, C., Cruickshank, H.S., Farrell, S., Marchese, M.: Delay- and disruption-tolerant networking (DTN): an alternative solution for future satellite networking applications. Proc. IEEE **99**(11), 1980–1997 (2011). https://doi.org/10.1109/JPROC.2011.2158378
5. Cerf, V.G., et al.: Delay-tolerant networking architecture. RFC **4838**, 1–35 (2007). https://doi.org/10.17487/RFC4838
6. D'Argenio, P.R., Fraire, J.A., Hartmanns, A.: Sampling distributed schedulers for resilient space communication. In: Lee, R., Jha, S., Mavridou, A., Giannakopoulou, D. (eds.) NFM 2020. LNCS, vol. 12229, pp. 291–310. Springer, Cham (2020). https://doi.org/10.1007/978-3-030-55754-6_17
7. D'Argenio, P.R., Fraire, J.A., Hartmanns, A., Raverta, F.D.: Comparing statistical and analytical routing approaches for delay-tolerant networks. In: Ábrahám, E., Paolieri, M. (eds.) QEST 2022. LNCS, vol. 13479, pp. 337–355. Springer, Cham (2022). https://doi.org/10.1007/978-3-031-16336-4_17
8. D'Argenio, P.R., Legay, A., Sedwards, S., Traonouez, L.: Smart sampling for lightweight verification of Markov decision processes. Int. J. Softw. Tools Technol. Transf. **17**(4), 469–484 (2015). https://doi.org/10.1007/s10009-015-0383-0
9. Fall, K.R.: A delay-tolerant network architecture for challenged internets. In: Feldmann, A., Zitterbart, M., Crowcroft, J., Wetherall, D. (eds.) Proceedings of the ACM SIGCOMM 2003 Conference on Applications, Technologies, Architectures, and Protocols for Computer Communication, 25–29 August 2003, Karlsruhe, Germany, pp. 27–34. ACM (2003). https://doi.org/10.1145/863955.863960
10. Fraire, J.A., Finochietto, J.M.: Design challenges in contact plans for disruption-tolerant satellite networks. IEEE Commun. Mag. **53**(5), 163–169 (2015). https://doi.org/10.1109/MCOM.2015.7105656
11. Hartmanns, A., Hermanns, H.: The modest toolset: an integrated environment for quantitative modelling and verification. In: Ábrahám, E., Havelund, K. (eds.) TACAS 2014. LNCS, vol. 8413, pp. 593–598. Springer, Heidelberg (2014). https://doi.org/10.1007/978-3-642-54862-8_51

12. Raverta, F.D., Demasi, R., Madoery, P.G., Fraire, J.A., Finochietto, J.M., D'Argenio, P.R.: A Markov decision process for routing in space DTNs with uncertain contact plans. In: 6th IEEE International Conference on Wireless for Space and Extreme Environments, WiSEE 2018, Huntsville, AL, USA, 11–13 December 2018, pp. 189–194. IEEE (2018). https://doi.org/10.1109/WiSEE.2018.8637330
13. Raverta, F.D., Fraire, J.A., Madoery, P.G., Demasi, R.A., Finochietto, J.M., D'Argenio, P.R.: Routing in delay-tolerant networks under uncertain contact plans. Ad Hoc Netw. **123**, 102663 (2021). https://doi.org/10.1016/j.adhoc.2021.102663

Without Loss of Satisfaction

Marijn J. H. Heule

Carnegie Mellon University, Pittsburgh, PA, USA
marijn@cmu.edu

Abstract. The success of automated reasoning presents us with an interesting peculiarity: while modern solving tools can handle gigantic real-world instances, they often fail miserably on supposedly easy problems. Their poor performance is frequently caused by using reasoning techniques that can only learn logically implied facts. In recent years, a couple of new proof systems have been proposed to overcome this issue by allowing to learn facts that are not logically implied, but preserve satisfaction. Moreover, these systems are surprisingly strong, even without the introduction of new definitions, which is a key feature of short proofs presented in the proof-complexity literature.

We demonstrate the effectiveness of reasoning "without loss of satisfaction" using three problems that are hard for automated-reasoning approaches. First, we present short proofs of mutilated chessboard problems that are completely different than the classical argument. We can produce these proofs automatically and they are understandable. Second, our proofs of the chromatic number of Mycielski graphs show that these proof systems can compactly express arguments that go beyond symmetry breaking. Finally, we illustrate the impact on the proof size using Ramsey number problems. Resolution proofs of Ramsey number four consist of about a billion resolution steps. In contrast, our "without loss of satisfaction" proof uses just 38 steps. None of these proofs introduce new variables.

1 Introduction

A commonly used proof method in mathematics is called "without loss of generality". For example, given three objects, which are colored either red or blue, we can assume without loss of generality that two of the three objects have the same color. This proof method is very useful, but it is challenging to apply to many representations that are suitable for automated reasoning: The objects and colors tend to have specific names in these representations, which makes it hard to detect that they are interchangeable. Moreover, in the popular resolution proof system, this cannot be expressed at all. To overcome this issue we need proof systems that facilitate similar reasoning capabilities.

Many relevant constraint satisfaction problems, from artificial intelligence to combinatorics, explore large search spaces to determine the presence or absence of a certain object. For these problems we are only interested in a single object or,

E. Ábrahám et al. (Eds.): ICTAC 2023, LNCS 14446, pp. 4–14, 2023.
https://doi.org/10.1007/978-3-031-47963-2_2

equivalently, an assignment that satisfies all constraints. Existing learning techniques shrink the search space by pruning parts that may contain no satisfying assignments. The recent proof systems PR (Propagation Redundancy) [12] and SR (Substitution Redundancy) [4] remove this limitation and facilitates pruning parts that contain satisfying assignments. Note that this is only allowed if at least one satisfying assignment remains. We therefore refer to this reasoning as *Without Loss of Satisfaction* (WLoS): Any possible shrinking method is allowed as long as satisfaction is preserved. This reasoning is only restricted in the following way: Validation of each step much be computable in polynomial time using a certificate that demonstrates WLoS.

Solving satisfiability (SAT) problems is at the heart of many reasoning and verification tasks throughout the computer industry. It is essential in electronic design automation in the context of bounded model checking. In recent years, SAT solving has been applied successfully to mathematics as well, including solving Erdős' Discrepancy Problem [19] and the Boolean Pythagorean Triples Problem [16] and Keller's conjecture [3]. The solutions of these problems received global media coverage, mostly due to the enormous size of the proofs (up to many terabytes), although this is actually not particularly interesting and mainly shows that SAT techniques can scale. A shorter proof of these problems would have been much more elegant. However, there is reason to believe that no short proof exists for these problems in the resolution proof system, which is used for reasoning in state-of-the-art SAT solvers. This is why we need to go beyond resolution to find short proofs for these and many other hard problems. We believe that WLoS reasoning can make a big difference here.

Conflict-Driven Clause Learning (CDCL) [21] is the most successful paradigm for solving SAT problems. However, at its core, CDCL is based on the resolution proof system, which means that the same limitations that apply to resolution also apply to CDCL. There exist only exponentially large resolution proofs for several seemingly easy problems [10, 26], implying that CDCL solvers require exponential time to solve these problems. Our approach to break this exponential barrier is the *Satisfaction-Driven Clause Learning* (SDCL) paradigm [14], which can automatically find short proofs for pigeonhole formulas in the PR proof system [12]. SDCL extends CDCL by pruning the search space of truth assignments more aggressively. While a pure CDCL solver learns only clauses that can be efficiently derived via resolution, an SDCL solver can also learn stronger clauses. The initial approach to learn these clauses is based on the so-called *positive reduct*: Given a formula and an assignment, the positive reduct is a simple propositional formula that encodes the question whether the assignment can be safely pruned from the search space. To perform the pruning, the solver learns the clause that *blocks* the partial assignment.Thus, while solving a single hard formula, SDCL solves several simple formulas to improve overall efficiency.

In this paper, we demonstrate the potential of learning PR or SR clauses to reduce the size of proofs. The focus is on three challenging problems for automated reasoning tools: mutilated chessboards, the chromatic number of Mycielski graphs, and Ramsey numbers.

2   Background

We briefly review background concepts: Boolean satisfiability, unit propagation, clausal proof systems, and in particular the PR and SR proof systems.

Boolean satisfiability. For a Boolean variable x, there are two *literals*, the positive literal, denoted by x, and the negative literal, denoted by $\bar{x}$. A *clause* is a finite disjunction of literals, and a *conjunctive normal form (CNF) formula* (or simply *formula*) is a finite conjunction of clauses. A truth assignment for a CNF formula F is a partial function τ that maps literals l in F to $\{\mathbf{t}, \mathbf{f}\}$. If $\tau(l) = v$, then $\tau(\bar{l}) = \neg v$, where $\neg\mathbf{t} = \mathbf{f}$ and $\neg\mathbf{f} = \mathbf{t}$. An assignment can also be thought of as a conjunction of literals. Furthermore, given an assignment τ:

- A clause C is *satisfied* by τ if $\tau(l) = \mathbf{t}$ for some $l \in C$.
- A clause C is *falsified* by τ if $\tau(l) = \mathbf{f}$ for all $l \in C$.
- A formula F is *satisfied* by τ if $\tau(C) = \mathbf{t}$ for all $C \in F$.
- A formula F is *falsified* by τ if $\tau(C) = \mathbf{f}$ for some $C \in F$.

The Boolean satisfiability problem (SAT in short) stands at the crossroads of logic, mathematics, computer science and engineering and addresses the question of whether a CNF formula contains at least one satisfying assignment (or solution). A CNF formula with a satisfying assignment is called *satisfiable*, while a CNF formula without satisfying assignments is called *unsatisfiable*.

As the first and best-known problem which was shown to be NP-complete [5], SAT represents the theoretical cornerstone of the expectation that no efficient algorithm can be made to solve hard combinatorial problems. However, during the last two decades, the performance of tools designed to find solutions for CNF formulas, called SAT solvers, has improved enormously. As a consequence, many applications can now be solved efficiently by translating them into SAT, either to obtain a solution using a SAT solver or to show no solution exists. This approach has been highly successful in applications such as hardware and software verification and solving hard-combinatorial problems.

Unit Propagation. We refer to the empty clause by $\bot$ and to the satisfied clause by $\top$. Given an assignment τ and a clause C, we define $C|_\tau = \top$ if τ satisfies C; otherwise, $C|_\tau$ denotes the result of removing from C all the literals falsified by τ. For a formula F, we define $F|_\tau = \{C|_\tau \mid C \in F \text{ and } C|_\tau \neq \top\}$. Given an assignment τ, the clause $\{x \mid \tau(x) = \mathbf{f}\} \cup \{\bar{x} \mid \tau(x) = \mathbf{t}\}$ is the clause that *blocks* τ. A *unit clause* is a clause with only one literal. The result of applying the *unit clause rule* to a formula F is the formula $F|_l$ where (l) is a unit clause in F. The iterated application of the unit clause rule to a formula F, until no unit clauses are left, is called *unit propagation*. If unit propagation yields the empty clause $\bot$, we say that unit propagation applied to F derived a *conflict*.

Example 1. Given the formula $F = (a \vee b \vee c) \wedge (a \vee \bar{b})$ and the assignment $\bar{a}$. $F|_{\bar{a}} = (b \vee c) \wedge (\bar{b})$. Notice that $F|_{\bar{a}}$ contains a unit clause, applying the unit clause rule results in $F|_{\bar{a}\bar{b}} = c$. Applying the unit clause rule again results in the empty formula $F|_{\bar{a}\bar{b}c} = \top$ (which is trivially satisfiable).

Two formulas are *logically equivalent* if they are satisfied by the same assignments. Two formulas are *satisfiability equivalent* if they are either both satisfiable or both unsatisfiable. For a clause $C = (l_1 \vee \cdots \vee l_k)$, $\neg C$ denotes the units clauses $(\bar{l}_1) \wedge \cdots \wedge (\bar{l}_k)$. Furthermore, by $F \vdash_1 G$ we denote that for every clause $C \in G$, unit propagation applied to $F \wedge \neg C$ derives a conflict. If $F \vdash_1 G$, we say that F implies G via unit propagation.

Clausal Proof Systems. Here, we introduce a formal notion of clause redundancy and demonstrate how it provides the basis for clausal proof systems.

Definition 1. *A clause C is* redundant *w.r.t. a formula F if F and $F \cup \{C\}$ are satisfiability equivalent.*

For instance, the clause $C = (x \vee y)$ is redundant w.r.t. $F = (\bar{x} \vee \bar{y})$ since F and $F \cup \{C\}$ are satisfiability equivalent (although they are not logically equivalent). This notion of redundancy allows us to add redundant clauses to a formula without loss of satisfaction. It also give rise to clausal proof systems.

Clause redundancy can also be expressed as an implication [13]:

Theorem 1. *A clause C is* redundant *w.r.t. a formula F if there exists an assignment τ such that $F \wedge \neg C \vDash (F \wedge C)|\tau$.*

Since entailment ($\vDash$) is not computable in polynomial time, we need to restrict it in practice. The proof system PR, defined below, will use a natural restriction.

Definition 2. *For $n \in \mathbb{N}$ a* derivation *of a formula F_n from a formula F_0 is a sequence of n triples $(d_1, C_1, \tau_1), \ldots, (d_n, C_n, \tau_n)$, where each clause C_i for $1 \leq i \leq n$ is redundant w.r.t. $F_{i-1} \setminus \{C_i\}$ with $F_i = F_{i-1} \cup \{C_i\}$ if $d_i = 0$ and $F_i = F_{i-1} \setminus \{C_i\}$ if $d_i = 1$. The assignment τ_i acts as (arbitrary) witness of the redundancy of C_i w.r.t. F_{i-1} and we call the number n of steps also the* length *of the derivation. A derivation is a* proof of refutation *(or simply proof) of F_0 if $d_n = 0$ and $C_n = \bot$. A derivation is a* proof of satisfaction *of F_0 if F_n equals the empty formula.*

If there exists such a derivation of a formula F' from a formula F, then F and F' are satisfiability equivalent. A refutation of a formula F, as defined above, obviously certifies the unsatisfiability of F since any F' containing the empty clause is unsatisfiable. Note that at this point these τ_i are still place-holders used in refinements, i.e., in the PR proof system defined below (and other clausal proof systems), where these τ_i are witnesses for the redundancy of C_i w.r.t. F_{i-1}. In these specialized proof systems this redundancy can be *checked efficiently*, i.e., in polynomial time w.r.t. the size of C_i, F_{i-1} and τ_i.

By specifying in detail which kind of redundant clauses—and corresponding witnesses—one uses in a derivation, we obtain concrete proof systems. This is usually done by defining an efficiently checkable syntactic criterion that guarantees that clauses fulfilling this criterion are redundant.

Most clauses derived by SAT solvers are known as *reverse unit propagation* (RUP) clauses: A clause C has RUP w.r.t. F if and only if $F \vdash_1 C$, or equivalently if $F \wedge \neg C \vdash \bot$. A RUP proof is a clausal proof in which each clause addition step ($d_i = 0$) is RUP w.r.t. the current formula F_i. Notice that RUP derivations do not use a witness. Also, RUP proofs cannot express any WLoS reasoning.

Example 2. Consider the formula $F = (a \vee b) \wedge (a \vee \overline{b}) \vee (\overline{a} \vee b) \wedge (\overline{a} \vee \overline{b})$. Notice that F implies (a) by unit propagation: in $F \wedge (\overline{a})$, clause $(a \vee b)$ becomes unit (b) and now the assignment $\neg a\, b$ falsifies clause $(a \vee \overline{b})$. Moreover, the RUP derivation $(0, (a), \emptyset), (0, \bot, \emptyset)$ is a proof of refutation of F.

The PR *proof system.* The addition of PR clauses (short for *propagation-redundant clauses*, PR is defined below) to a formula can lead to short proofs for hard formulas without the introduction of new variables. Although PR clauses are not necessarily implied by the formula, their addition preserves satisfiability [12]. The intuitive reason for this is that the addition of a PR clause prunes the search space of possible assignments in such a way that there still remain assignments under which the formula is as satisfiable as under the pruned assignments.

Definition 3. *Let F be a formula and C a non-empty clause. Then, C is propagation redundant* (PR) *with respect to F if there exists an assignment τ such that $F \wedge \neg C \vdash (F \wedge C)|\tau$.*

The clause C can be seen as a constraint that "prunes" from the search space all assignments that extend $\neg C$. Note again, that in our setting assignments are in general partial functions. Since $F \wedge \neg C$ implies $(F \wedge C)|\tau$, every assignment that satisfies $F \wedge \neg C$ also satisfies $(F \wedge C)|\tau$. We refer to τ as the *witness*, since it witnesses the propagation-redundancy of the clause. Consider the following example:

Example 3. Let $F = (x \vee y) \wedge (\overline{x} \vee y) \wedge (\overline{x} \vee z)$, $C = (x)$, and let $\tau = x\, z$ be an assignment. Then, $\neg C = \overline{x}$. Now, consider $F \wedge \neg C$, which simplifies to (y), and $(F \wedge C)|\tau = (y)$. Clearly, unit propagation on $F \wedge \neg C \wedge (\overline{y})$ derives a conflict. Thus, $F \wedge \neg C \vdash (F \wedge C)|\tau$ and C is propagation redundant w.r.t. F.

Most known types of redundant clauses are PR clauses [12], including blocked clauses [20], set-blocked clauses [18], resolution asymmetric tautologies, etc.

Given a formula F and a clause C, the problem to determine whether C is a PR clause w.r.t. F is NP-complete [14]. However, one can efficiently check whether C is a PR clause w.r.t. F using a given witnessing assignment τ as $F \wedge \neg C \vdash (F \wedge C)|\tau$ is computable in polynomial time (with τ being the smallest assignment that falsifies C).

The SR proof system [4] generalizes PR by allowing τ to be a substitution instead of just a truth assignment. This generalization can further reduce the size of proofs. For example, it can compactly express symmetry-breaking in graph existence problems without new variables. To the best of our knowledge, the is not possible with PR.

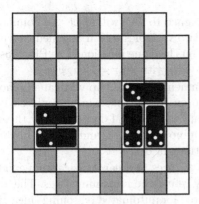 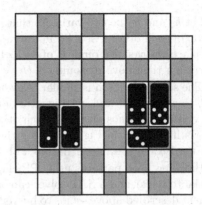

Fig. 1. Two equivalent placements of five dominos on a mutilated chessboard.

3   Mutilated chessboards

A well-known family of problems on which traditional reasoning approaches fail are the *mutilated chessboard problems*. Given a chessboard of size $n \times n$ from which two opposite corner squares have been removed (see Figure 1), a mutilated chessboard problem asks if the remaining squares can be fully covered with dominos (i.e., with stones that cover exactly two squares). The answer is *no*, based on a simple argument: Assume to the contrary that a mutilated chessboard can be fully covered with dominos. Then, since every domino covers exactly one black square and one white square, the number of covered black squares must equal the number of covered white squares. But the number of black squares on a mutilated chessboard is different from the number of white squares since opposite corner squares (of which two were removed) are of the same color.

Automated-reasoning methods on various representations have severe difficulties finding this argument because they do not have colored squares, so they need to come up with this abstraction themselves in order to use a similar argument. John McCarthy has called the mutilated chessboard problems a "tough nut to crack" for automated reasoning [22], and it has been shown that these problems admit only proofs of exponential size within the propositional resolution proof system [1,6].

However, the PR proof system facilitates a completely different but equally short argument for solving mutilated chessboard problems [23]. The new argument rules out possible patterns for the dominos by generalizing—*without loss of satisfaction*—from certain specific patterns that are similar to them.

The first pattern rules out every occurrence of two horizontal dominos on top of each other. The reasoning is as follows: assume that we can cover a region such that there exists two horizontal dominos on top of each other, then there exists another cover the same region without two horizontal dominos on top of each other. The latter can be arranged by replacing every pair of horizontal dominos on top of each other by two vertical dominos next to each other that cover the same space. Figure 1 shows this reasoning using the dominos with 1 and 2 dots.

Let h_1 and h_2 be two variables that if assigned to true will place two dominos on top of each other. Also, let v_1 and v_2 be two variables that if assigned to true will place two vertical on next of each other on the same location. The PR clause expressing the above reasoning is $(\overline{h}_1 \vee \overline{h}_2)$ with witness $\tau = \overline{h}_1 \overline{h}_2 v_1 v_2$.

The second pattern is similar. Any assignment that has two vertical dominos next to each other and a horizontal domino on top of that can be replaced by two vertical dominos on top of each other and a horizontal domino below them. This is illustrated in Figure 1 using the dominos with 3, 4, and 5 dots. In this case the PR clauses have length 3 and a witness of 6 literals.

Blocking both patterns using PR clauses reduces the search space from exponential to linear and a SAT solver can easily refute the remaining cases. The argument described above seems to be well suited for automated reasoning since we discovered it when analyzing PR proofs that were found by our SDCL solver [15]. We argue that the key to automatically solving the mutilated chessboard problems and many other hard problems is not to simulate human thinking but to equip computers with capabilities to find their own short arguments. Moreover, this example demonstrates that automated-reasoning tools cannot only provide us with simple yes/no answers but that they can also help us gain further insights into the nature of a problem.

4 Mycielski graphs

Mycielski graphs are a family of triangle-free graphs with arbitrarily high chromatic number. For each Mycielski graph there is a short informal proof of this chromatic number, yet finding proofs of it via automated reasoning techniques has proved to be a challenging task.

Let $G = (V, E)$ be a graph. The construction of *Mycielski graph* $\mu(G)$ is as follows. We start with a graph $G = (V, E)$. G is a subgraph of $\mu(G)$. For each vertex $v_i \in V$, add a new vertex u_i that is connected to all the neighbors of v_i in G. Finally, add a vertex w that is connected to each u_i.

Unless G has a triangle $\mu(G)$ does not have a triangle, and $\mu(G)$ has chromatic number one higher than G. We denote the chromatic number of G by $\chi(G)$. Starting with $M_2 = K_2$ (the complete graph on 2 vertices) and applying $M_k = \mu(M_{k-1})$ repeatedly, we obtain triangle-free graphs with arbitrarily large chromatic number. We call M_k the *kth Mycielski graph*. Since $\chi(M_2) = 2$ and μ increases the chromatic number by one, we have $\chi(M_k) = k$. Figure 2 shows the graphs M_2, M_3, and M_4.

Computing the chromatic number of Mycielski graphs is hard for automated-reasoning tools. These graphs are also part of the graph coloring challenge suite [17]. Most SAT solvers can determine $\chi(M_6) \geq 6$ in about and hour, but showing that $\chi(M_7) \geq 7$ cannot be done in reasonable time [25]. The runtime and proof size increase exponentially in k. However, there exist short, sublinear-size PR proofs of $\chi(M_k) \geq k$ [27] and finding a satisfying assignment showing that $\chi(M_k) \leq k$ is typically easy.

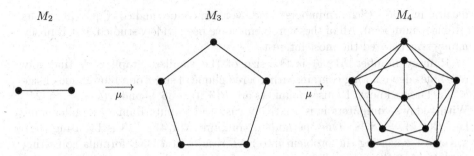

Fig. 2. The first few graphs in the sequence of Mycielski graphs.

The PR clauses forbid assignments where vertex v_i gets color c, another color c' is given to vertex u_i, while w does not have color c. The reason why we can add these PR clauses is as follows: if there exists a satisfying assignment with such a coloring, then there exists another satisfying assignment with v_i and u_i both assigned color c, while w does not have color c. Figure 3 illustrates the reasoning. This copies colors from vertex v_i to u_i. In turn, the solver can deduce edges between vertices u_i and u_j if there exist edges in between v_i and v_j.

After adding these clauses for each u_i and for all pairs of colors c and c', there exist short resolution proofs showing that $\chi(M_k) \geq k$. The PR clauses do not use any new variables and the reasoning does not use a symmetry-breaking argument.

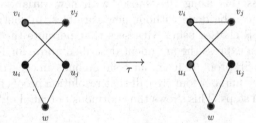

Fig. 3. Schematic form of the argument for the PR inference. With $c = $ Red and $c' = $ Blue, the above diagram shows the transformation we can apply to a solution to obtain another valid solution. A vertex colored black on the inside means that it does not have the outer color, i.e. w has some color other than red. Unit propagation implies that v_j is not colored red.

5   Ramsey numbers

Ramsey Theory [7] involves patterns that cannot be avoided indefinitely, such as avoiding arithmetic progressions while partitioning the natural numbers (Van Der Waerden numbers), avoiding the sum of two elements while partitioning the natural numbers (Schur numbers), and avoiding cliques and co-cliques in graphs (Ramsey numbers). All of these problems have been widely studied, but Ramsey numbers generated the most interest.

Ramsey number $R(r, b)$ is the size of the smallest graph such that any red/blue edge-coloring contains either a red clique of size r or a blue clique of size b. The largest known Ramsey numbers are $R(3, 9) = 36$ [9] and $R(4, 5) = 25$ [24]. With today's computers it is relatively easy to compute Ramsey number four, i.e., $R(4, 4) = 18$ [8]. One method to compute $R(4, 4) = 18$ is by using SAT solvers. Translating the problem into SAT results in a CNF formula consisting of $\binom{18}{2} = 513$ Boolean variables (i.e., the number of edges in the fully-connected undirected graph with 18 vertices) and $2 \cdot \binom{18}{4} = 6120$ clauses. The SAT solver Kissat [2], arguably the most powerful SAT solver at the moment, cannot solve this problem in a day without symmetry-breaking predicates. Earlier experiments with CDCL solver suggested that the produced resolution proof has about a billion resolution steps.

With symmetry breaking, computing the first four Ramsey numbers using SAT is easy. The first and most important step of the symmetry breaking is the sorting of the edges for the first vertex v_1. Let $e_{i,j}$ denote whether the edge between vertex i and j is blue. The sorted edges clauses are $(e_{1,j} \vee \overline{e}_{1,j+1})$ for $j \in \{2 \ldots, |V| - 1\}$. With the sorted edges, the argument for Ramsey number three is short as shown in Figure 4: If we assume that the edge between v_1 and v_4 is blue, then this must also be the case for the edges v_1–v_2 and v_1–v_3. This forces a red triangle by unit propagation. If the edge v_1–v_4 is assigned to red, a similar conflict emerges via unit propagation.

One can express this using PR clauses with new variables [11], but it is unclear whether it can be done without new variables. In contrast, the sorted edges clauses are SR clauses using witnesses that permute the variables. As a consequence, we can express the argument described above for Ramsey number three as a 7-clauses SR proof. In a similar fashion, one can construct a 38-clauses SR proof for Ramsey number four. Recall that resolution proofs for this problem are around a billion steps. This shows the enormous potential of SR to construct short proofs.

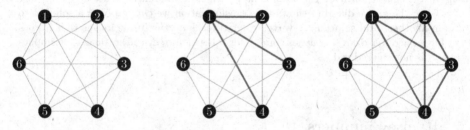

Fig. 4. A fully connected graph with six vertices (left); if we color all edges either red or blue, then without loss of generality we can color a claw (three edges connected by the same vertex) blue (middle); and now avoiding a blue triangle, results in a red triangle (right).

References

1. Alekhnovich, M.: Mutilated chessboard problem is exponentially hard for resolution. Theoretical Computer Science **310**(1-3), 513–525 (2004)
2. Biere, A., Fazekas, K., Fleury, M., Heisinger, M.: CaDiCaL, Kissat, Paracooba, Plingeling and Treengeling entering the SAT Competition 2020. In: Balyo, T., Froleyks, N., Heule, M., Iser, M., Järvisalo, M., Suda, M. (eds.) Proc. of SAT Competition 2020 – Solver and Benchmark Descriptions. Department of Computer Science Report Series B, vol. B-2020-1, pp. 51–53. University of Helsinki (2020)
3. Brakensiek, J., Heule, M., Mackey, J., Narváez, D.: The resolution of keller's conjecture. In: Peltier, N., Sofronie-Stokkermans, V. (eds.) Automated Reasoning. pp. 48–65. Springer International Publishing, Cham (2020)
4. Buss, S., Thapen, N.: DRAT and propagation redundancy proofs without new variables. Log. Methods Comput. Sci. **17**(2) (2021), https://lmcs.episciences.org/7400
5. Cook, S.A.: The complexity of theorem-proving procedures. In: Proceedings of the Third Annual ACM Symposium on Theory of Computing. pp. 151–158. STOC '71, ACM, New York, NY, USA (1971)
6. Dantchev, S.S., Riis, S.: "Planar" tautologies hard for resolution. In: Proc. of the 42nd Annual Symposium on Foundations of Computer Science (FOCS 2001). pp. 220–229. IEEE Computer Society (2001)
7. Graham, R.L., Rothschild, B.L., Spencer, J.H.: Ramsey Theory. A Wiley-Interscience publication, Wiley (1990)
8. Greenwood, R.E., Gleason, A.M.: Combinatorial relations and chromatic graphs. Canadian Journal of Mathematics **7**, 1–7 (1955)
9. Grinstead, C.M., Roberts, S.M.: On the Ramsey numbers r(3, 8) and r(3, 9). Journal of Combinatorial Theory, Series B **33**(1), 27 – 51 (1982)
10. Haken, A.: The intractability of resolution. Theoretical Computer Science **39**, 297–308 (1985)
11. Heule, M.J.H., Hunt, W.A., Wetzler, N.: Expressing symmetry breaking in drat proofs. In: Felty, A.P., Middeldorp, A. (eds.) Automated Deduction - CADE-25. pp. 591–606. Springer International Publishing, Cham (2015)
12. Heule, M.J.H., Kiesl, B., Biere, A.: Short proofs without new variables. In: Proc. of the 26th Int. Conference on Automated Deduction (CADE-26). LNCS, vol. 10395, pp. 130–147. Springer (2017)
13. Heule, M.J.H., Kiesl, B., Biere, A.: Strong extension-free proof systems. Journal of Automated Reasoning **64**(3), 533–554 (2020)
14. Heule, M.J.H., Kiesl, B., Seidl, M., Biere, A.: PRuning through satisfaction. In: In Haifa Verification Conference - HVC. LNCS, vol. 10629, pp. 179–194. Springer (2017)
15. Heule, M.J.H., Kiesl, B., Seidl, M., Biere, A.: PRuning through satisfaction. In: Proc. of the 13th Haifa Verification Conference (HVC 2017). LNCS, vol. 10629, pp. 179–194. Springer (2017). https://doi.org/10.1007/978-3-319-70389-3_12
16. Heule, M.J.H., Kullmann, O., Marek, V.W.: Solving and verifying the Boolean Pythagorean Triples problem via Cube-and-Conquer. In: Proceedings SAT 2016. LNCS, vol. 9710, pp. 228–245. Springer (2016)
17. Johnson, D.J., Trick, M.A.: Cliques, Coloring, and Satisfiability: Second DIMACS Implementation Challenge, Workshop, October 11-13, 1993. American Mathematical Society, USA (1996)

18. Kiesl, B., Seidl, M., Tompits, H., Biere, A.: Super-blocked clauses. In: Proc. of the 8th Int. Joint Conference on Automated Reasoning (IJCAR 2016). LNCS, vol. 9706, pp. 45–61. Springer, Cham (2016)

19. Konev, B., Lisitsa, A.: A sat attack on the erdos discrepancy conjecture. In: Sinz, C., Egly, U. (eds.) Theory and Applications of Satisfiability Testing — SAT 2014, Lecture Notes in Computer Science, vol. 8561, pp. 219–226. Springer International Publishing (2014)

20. Kullmann, O.: On a generalization of extended resolution. Discrete Applied Mathematics **96-97**, 149–176 (1999)

21. Marques-Silva, J., Lynce, I., Malik, S.: Conflict-driven clause learning sat solvers. In: Handbook of Satisfiability, pp. 131–153. IOS Press (2009)

22. McCarthy, J.: A tough nut for proof procedures. Stanford Artifical Intelligence Project **Memo 16** (1964)

23. McCarthy, J.: A tough nut for proof procedures. Memo 16, Stanford Artificial Intelligence Project (July 1964)

24. McKay, B.D., Radziszowski, S.P.: R(4, 5) = 25. Journal of Graph Theory **19**(3), 309–322 (1995)

25. Schaafsma, B., Heule, M.J.H., van Maaren, H.: Dynamic symmetry breaking by simulating zykov contraction. In: Kullmann, O. (ed.) Theory and Applications of Satisfiability Testing - SAT 2009. pp. 223–236. Springer Berlin Heidelberg, Berlin, Heidelberg (2009)

26. Urquhart, A.: Hard examples for resolution. J. ACM **34**(1), 209–219 (Jan 1987)

27. Yolcu, E., Wu, X., Heule, M.J.H.: Mycielski graphs and pr proofs. In: Pulina, L., Seidl, M. (eds.) Theory and Applications of Satisfiability Testing – SAT 2020. pp. 201–217. Springer International Publishing, Cham (2020)

Modelling and Verifying Robotic Software that Uses Neural Networks

Ziggy Attala, Ana Cavalcanti$^{(\boxtimes)}$, and Jim Woodcock

University of York, York, UK
Ana.Cavalcanti@york.ac.uk

Abstract. Verifying learning robotic systems is challenging. Existing techniques and tools for verification of an artificial neural network (ANN) are concerned with component-level properties. Here, we deal with robotic systems whose control software uses ANN components, and with properties of that software that may depend on all components. Our focus is on trained fully connected ReLU neural networks for control. We present an approach to (1) modelling ANN components as part of behavioural models for control software and (2) verification using traditional and ANN-specific verification tools. We describe our results in the context of RoboChart, a domain-specific modelling language for robotics with support for formal verification. We describe our modelling notation and a strategy for automated proof using Isabelle and Marabou, for example.

Keywords: verification · CSP · theorem proving · Isabelle · Marabou

1 Introduction

Artificial neural networks (ANN) are effective, powerful, and widely used [19]. They have been proposed for use in control software for robotic systems, performing various tasks such as collision detection [1,2], and path finding [15]. When ANN components are used instead of non-ML components, they can increase time and space efficiency [19]. In addition, ANN-based systems are highly adaptable to new data and environments [7]. On the other hand, the behaviour of an ANN is highly dependent on the training data used in its development. There is, therefore, great interest in several forms of verification to ensure that an ANN-based system satisfies key properties of concern.

Existing formal-verification work focuses on ANN components. The other components are either considered informally to generate a specification [6,18], or not at all. Here, we define a framework to model and verify the entire control software; we refer to such properties as module-level properties.

Several domain-specific languages support model-based software engineering in robotics [26]. Most, however, are not focused on verification. RoboChart [24] is distinctive in its support for verification by model checking and theorem proving. Our framework uses a denotational process-algebraic semantics for ANN components that integrates with the RoboChart semantics. We use it to enable verification mechanised using Isabelle/UTP [9] and Marabou [21], for instance.

© The Author(s), under exclusive license to Springer Nature Switzerland AG 2023
E. Ábrahám et al. (Eds.): ICTAC 2023, LNCS 14446, pp. 15–35, 2023.
https://doi.org/10.1007/978-3-031-47963-2_3

The semantics of RoboChart is described in the CSP process algebra [31]. CSP enables verification via model checking [12], but is also a front-end to a predicative alphabetised relational theory described using the Unifying Theories of Programming [13] (UTP) for theorem proving.

We introduce novel ANN components in RoboChart, giving them a CSP semantics. To support tractable verification, we model fully connected ReLU pre-trained ANNs [27]. Our semantics, however, supports any activation function, allowing additional tool integration. For proof, we use the UTP encoding of CSP.

In summary, our contributions are as follows. First, we describe a (RoboChart) ANN component with formal semantics. Second, we present an approach to verification that can be mechanised using Isabelle/UTP and Marabou in combination. In a recent survey [4], we have found that Marabou proved a collection of properties we identified twice as fast when compared with 13 other tools. To cater for numerical uncertainty, we use a new notion of conformance with a precision parameter defined in terms of refinement.

Next, in Sect. 2, we provide the background to our work. Section 3 presents our ANN components in RoboChart. Section 4 describes a semantics, and Sect. 5 discusses verification. Section 6 concludes and considers related and future work.

2 Background

We introduce in this section two concepts essential to our work. Section 2.1 briefly introduces ANNs, and Sect. 2.2 introduces CSP and UTP.

2.1 ANNs

An ANN is an abstraction of a nervous system of interconnected neurons: cells with multiple forms and components in biological neural networks. Information is stored at synapses: contact points between different neurons. The basic function of a neuron is to receive several electrical signals from other neurons through dendrites and then to produce an output signal to send to other neurons through an *axon*. The neuron's body determines the output signal sent by the axon.

ANN's approximate biological neurons through nodes (artificial neurons), graphically represented in Fig. 1. Dendrites are modelled by input channels from other nodes. Synapses are modelled by assigning a separate weighting for each node connection. The axon is modelled by a single output value from the nodes. The cell body is modelled by a function assigned to each node, referred to as an activation function, which models the output value decision-making.

In a deep neural network, nodes are arranged in layers. Each node is also assigned a value referred to as a bias. The weights and the biases are parameters of the ANN learnt from training data. Figure 2 shows the overall structure of an ANN, with each line representing a connection from the left to the right layer. The weights of each layer can be represented as a matrix, with one value for the connection of a node in the layer to a node in the previous layer. The bias of a layer can be represented as a vector, with a value for each node.

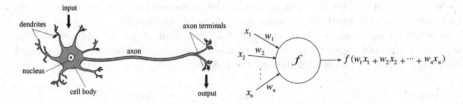

Fig. 1. A basic biological neuron from [25] and a basic node from [30]; w represents the synapses, the input connections represent the dendrites, f represents the cell body, and the output connection represents the axon.

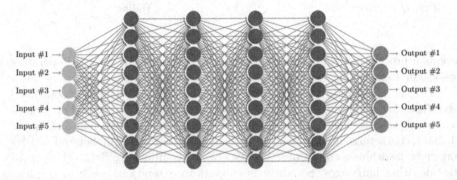

Fig. 2. An abstract neural network from [20].

We can consider an ANN as the definition of a function $F : \mathbb{R}^n \rightarrow \mathbb{R}^m$ based on training data. (Any training process can be used.) Every node takes the weighted sum of the outputs of nodes of the previous layer and applies a bias and a non-linear activation function to this result. This work considers only the ReLU activation function: $f(x) = max(0, x)$.

The ReLU activation function is faster to train, easier to optimise, and performs and generalises well [27]. ReLU is also piecewise linear, which can be viewed as the composition of multiple linear functions. Piecewise linearity has positive implications in implementation, optimisation and verification as opposed to fully non-linear functions such as sigmoid or tanh. Furthermore, ReLU can eliminate the vanishing gradient problem (preventing the weight from changing value), is widely used, and can achieve state-of-the-art results [22].

2.2 CSP and UTP

Communicating Sequential Processes (CSP) [14] is a notation for modelling, validating, and verifying reactive programs via refinement.

A CSP model describes a set of processes defining interaction patterns of a mechanism. Processes interact with each other and their environment via atomic and instantaneous events representing channel communications. The set of all

Table 1. CSP Operators. Here, we use P and Q as metavariables to stand for processes, cs to stand for a channel set, defining a set of events potentially based on channels, e to stand for an event, i for an index, and T for a finite type. In addition, for the replicated (iterated) operators, $a(i)$ stands a set of events identified by an index, and similarly, $P(i)$ is a process identified by the index i.

Symbol	Name	Symbol	Name
$Skip$	Skip	$e \rightarrow P$	Prefix
$P \,\|[cs]\|\, Q$	Parallel Composition	$\|\| \, i : T \bullet [a(i)]P(i)$	Replicated Parallel
$P \,\|\|\|\, Q$	Interleaving	$\|\|\| \, i : T \bullet P(i)$	Replicated Interleaving
$P \Theta_{cs} Q$	Exception	$P \setminus cs$	Hiding

events a process can engage in is named Σ [32]. We present the CSP operators we use in Table 1; they are further described as we use them.

UTP is a semantic framework to describe concepts to give denotational semantics to a wide range of computational paradigms. UTP is based on a predicative alphabetised relational calculus. In UTP, a theory describes a semantic domain, characterising relations by predicates with a given alphabet and satisfying given healthiness conditions. Theories can be combined to define the semantics of richer languages. So, there is support to extend our work to consider languages other than RoboChart that define reactive behaviours, but perhaps also include notions of continuous time [9] and probability [38], for instance.

All UTP theories describe relations between observations of variables. The change in an observation x is captured by the relation between the before value of the observation (named x) and its after value (named x').

We use the UTP theory of reactive contracts [10], which gives semantics to state-rich CSP processes and has a large set of algebraic laws for verification. The observational variables of this theory are st, st', ok, ok', $wait$, $wait'$, tt, ref, and ref'. The variables st and st' record the programming state of the process: its variables. The Boolean variables ok and ok' record the process's stability. The Boolean variables $wait$ and $wait'$ identify when the process is waiting for interaction with the environment. So, ok' and $\neg\, wait'$ indicate termination.

The sequence tt describes the trace of events in the life of the process up to the moment of observation: it is the difference between the trace of all events at the moment of observation and the trace as it was at the initiation of the current process. There is no tt' because tt is defined as $tr' - tr$, where tr and tr' record the traces of the process. The set ref' records the events that the process cannot perform when it next makes visible progress. This set is known as the process's refusals. A healthiness condition makes the value of ref irrelevant, as a process cannot depend on what was being refused before it started.

Reactive contracts take the form $[\, R_1[tt, st] \vdash R_2[tt, st, ref'] \mid R_3[tt, st, st'] \,]$. The square brackets define the observational variables to which each predicate can refer. The precondition, R_1, describes conditions on the pre-state st and the trace tt. The postcondition R_3 describes a condition on the state st, the state update st', and the final value of tt. In addition, we have a third predicate $R2$, which is called a periodcondition. It captures the observations that can be made of a process when in a quiescent but not final state, that is, when it awaits its environment's interaction. The periodcondition defines a condition on the pre-state st, the value of the trace tt, and which events are refused by referring to ref'.

Here, in defining reactive contracts, we use operators $\mathcal{E}[t, E]$ and $\Phi[t]$, which are simplified versions of those in Def. 4.6 from [11], where we consider that a CSP process does not have state variables. With $\mathcal{E}[t, E]$, we can construct a periodcondition stating that t has been observed and the events in E are not refused. On the other hand, $\Phi[t]$ constructs a postcondition, stating that the final trace observed is characterised by t. Finally, we use $\{| \ c \ |\}$ to denote the set of all events for the channel c, communicating values according to type of c.

Next, we introduce our novel ANN components in RoboChart.

3   Modelling ANN Components in RoboChart

RoboChart is a diagrammatic modelling language that can be used to define a simple component model and behaviour of control software for robotics. In RoboChart, the overall software of is represented by a module block, which identifies one or more controllers interacting with a robotic platform. The block for a robotic platform specifies an abstraction of the hardware and its embedded software via events and operations representing services provided by the robot and used by the software. A controller block defines a thread of control, engaging in events, calling platform operations, and communicating with other controllers. One or more (parallel) state machines define the behaviour of a controller.

In our work, we extend RoboChart with a new form of controller defined by an ANN block. In Fig. 3, we present a RoboChart module for a Segway robot that includes an ANN component AnglePIDANN. This module, called Segway, contains a robotic platform SegwayRP, a standard controller SegwayController, and an ANN controller AnglePIDANN. SegwayRP has events representing data provided by the segway sensors and operations to control movement via the segway motors. SegwayController describes the behaviour of this system, defined through three state machines: BalanceSTM, RotationPID and SpeedPID.

As shown in Fig. 3, the block SegwayController has three blocks that represent references to its state machines, which are omitted here, but are available in [3]. SegwayController has a cyclic behaviour defined by BalanceSTM, which updates the motor speeds using the outputs of the PID machines and of the AnglePIDANN controller to keep the segway upright. In the original version of this example, there is a third state machine AnglePID. In our version here, we have an ANN instead, with the same interface. Just like AnglePID, the ANN component AnglePIDANN accepts as input the events anewError and adiff and communicates its output through the event angleOutputE.

The block for an ANN component (marked using the symbol ⚛) has its behaviour defined by the following parameters. First, we have the ANN's input and output sizes, representing the sizes of the vector the ANN is trained on

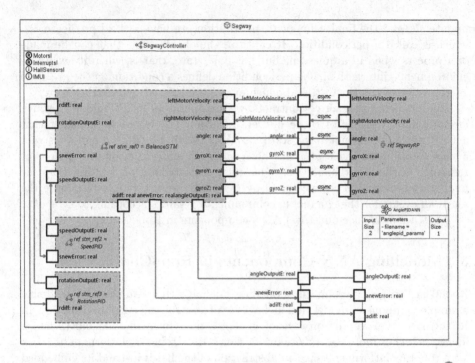

Fig. 3. A parallel version of the Segway model with an ANN component. Legend: ⚙ : Module, ⋘ : controller definition, → : connection, π : constant, ♟ : robotic platform reference, ⚿ : state machine reference, ⚛ : ANN component.

for input and output. Next, we specify a parameter file that defines the layer structure, giving, for each layer, the weights and bias, and the activation function.

An ANN controller operates as a slave component. It can communicate with other controllers via events. The types of the events are restricted: they can either contain one event for every input and output, providing a scalar representation of the ANN, or precisely two events, capturing a vector representation for the inputs and outputs. In our example, we define multiple events (that communicate scalar values) to represent the inputs and output, as our ANN is low-dimensional. We declare two input events anewError and adiff, as the Input Size of AnglePIDANN is 2, and one output event angleOutputE, as the Output Size is 1.

The metamodel for our RoboChart extension is very simple; details are given in [3]. Principally, we have a class ANNController to represent a controller defined using an ANN. It defines the parameters of an ANN so that we have specifications for the values of six properties: insize, the input size of the ANN; outsize, the output size of the ANN; layerstructure, defining the size of each layer, and weights and biases, defining the weights and biases of the ANN. RoboChart's type system is based on Z [34,37]. Hence, we can represent real numbers using the approach in [29]. Although different layers of an ANN can use different functions, we assume all layers use just one function. Extending our work to consider additional functions and different functions in different layers is straightforward.

The following section discusses the semantics of ANNControllers.

4 CSP Semantics

Our semantics defines constants to capture the metamodel. They are $insize : \mathbb{N}$, $outsize : \mathbb{N}$, and $layerstructure : \text{seq}\,\mathbb{N}$. In addition, $layerNo : \mathbb{N}$ and $maxSize : \mathbb{N}$ record properties of $layerstructure$: its length, and its largest element. Finally, we have $weights : \text{seq}(\text{seq}(\text{seq}(Value)))$ and $biases : \text{seq}(\text{seq}(Value))$.

$Value$ is a type that represents the data communicated by our ANN. This is defined based on the types used in the ANN component in RoboChart. Some examples of the types that can be used are floating-point, integer, or binary values. If there are various ANN components, there is a definition of a type $Value$ for each of them. Equally, constants such as $layerstructure$, $maxSize$, and the others mentioned here are defined for each component.

The semantics of an ANN component is a process presented in Fig. 4. It is defined by parallel composition of processes representing nodes and layers.

We use two channels. The first $layerRes : \{0 \mathinner{.\,.} layerNo\}.\{1 \mathinner{.\,.} maxSize\}.Value$ is used to communicate with other processes in the RoboChart semantics and for inter-layer communications. An event $layerRes.l.n.v$ represents the communication of a value v to or from the process for the nth node in the process for the lth layer. The channel $nodeOut : \{1 \mathinner{.\,.} layerNo\}.\{1 \mathinner{.\,.} maxSize\}.\{1 \mathinner{.\,.} maxSize\}.Value$ is for intra-node communication; $nodeOut.l.n.i.v$ refers to the layer, node and value as for $layerRes$. The additional index value i identifies the node in the following layer (of index $l + 1$) that receives this communication.

In our semantics, we treat inputs to the ANN process as events on the channel $layerRes$, with 0 as the first argument's value. In this way, events $layerRes.0$ represent inputs to the ANN process from other components in the RoboChart model. All other communications on $layerRes$ represent results from layer processes. Events $layerRes.layerNo$ represent the outputs of the ANN.

Figure 4 presents the specification of a process ANN, defining the semantics for an ANNController. It terminates ($Skip$) on the occurrence of a special event end, as determined using the exception operator Θ_{end}. This is an event raised by other controllers when all state machines terminate. An ANN does not terminate in any other way, so termination is determined by the other controllers.

The operator $P \, \| [\, cs \,] \| \, Q$ describes the process whose behaviour is defined by those of P and Q, synchronising on all events in the set cs. Also, $P \setminus cs$ defines a process that behaves as P, but its events from the set cs are hidden. ANN composes in parallel the processes $HiddenLayers$ and $OutputLayer$, then repeats via a recursive call. Since the $OutputLayer$ communicates only with the last hidden layer, these processes synchronise on the events $layerRes.(layerNo - 1)$.

All events in $ANNHiddenEvts$ are hidden. This includes all events (Σ), except those of $layerRes.0$, representing inputs, $layerRes.layerNo$, representing outputs, and end. These define the visible behaviour of an ANNController.

$ANN =$
$\quad ((HiddenLayers \,|[\,\{|\ layerRes.(layerNo-1)\ |\}\,]|\ OutputLayer) \setminus ANNHiddenEvts$
$\quad \Theta_{end}\ Skip);$
$\quad ANN$

$ANNHiddenEvts = \Sigma \setminus \{|\ layerRes.0, layerRes.layerNo, end\ |\}$

$HiddenLayers = \underset{}{\big\|}\ i:1\,..\,layerNo-1 \bullet [\,\{|\ layerRes.(i-1), layerRes.i\ |\}\,]$
$\qquad\qquad HiddenLayer(i, layerSize(i), layerSize(i-1))$

$HiddenLayer(l, s, inpSize) = \underset{}{\big\|}\ i:1\,..\,s \bullet [\{|\ layerRes.(l-1)\ |\}]Node(l, i, inpSize)$

$Node(l, n, inpSize) =$
$\quad ((\underset{}{\big\|\big\|\big\|}\ i:1\,..\,inpSize \bullet NodeIn(l, n, i))$
$\qquad |[\ \{|\ nodeOut.l.n\ |\}\ ]|$
$\quad Collator(l, n, inpSize)\,) \setminus \{|\ nodeOut\ |\}$

$NodeIn(l, n, i) = layerRes.(l-1).n?x \to nodeOut.l.n.i!(x * weight) \to Skip$

$Collator(l, n, inpSize) = \textbf{let}$
$\qquad C(l, n, 0, sum) = layerRes.l.n!(ReLU(sum + bias)) \to Skip$
$\qquad C(l, n, i, sum) = nodeOut.l.n.i?x \to C(l, n, (i-1), (sum+x))$
$\quad \textbf{within}$
$\qquad C(l, n, inpSize, 0)$

$OutputLayer = \underset{}{\big\|}\ i:1\,..\,layerSize(layerNo) \bullet [\,\{|\ layerRes.(layerNo-1)\ |\}\,]$
$\qquad\qquad Node(layerNo, i, layerSize(layerNo-1))$

Fig. 4. CSP ANN Semantics - General.

We define the process *HiddenLayers* via an iterated alphabetised parallel composition ($\|$) over an index i for hidden layers ranging from 1 to $layerNo - 1$. For each i, the layer-process $HiddenLayer(i, layerSize(i), layerSize(i-1))$ for the ith layer is associated with the alphabet containing the set of events on $layerRes.(i-1)$ and $layerRes.i$. In an iterated alphabetised parallelism, the parallel processes synchronise on the intersection of their alphabets. So, a layer-process *HiddenLayers* synchronises with the process for the previous layer on $layerRes.(i-1)$ and the process for the following layer on $layerRes.i$. So, the output events of each layer are used as the input events for the next layer.

The second argument $layerSize(i)$ passed to a layer process is the value of the i-th element of *layerstructure*, that is, the number of nodes in the i-th layer if i is greater than 0, and *insize* when i is 0. Similarly, the third argument $layerSize(i-1)$ concerns the layer $i-1$. In our example, $layerNo-1$ is 1, and there is a single *HiddenLayer* process, instantiated with arguments 1, 1, and 2. These are the values of *insize* and *layerstructure*(1) for the example.

$HiddenLayer(l, s, inpSize)$ is also defined by an iterated alphabetised parallelism: over an index i ranging from 1 to s, to compose s node processes $Node(l, i, inpSize)$ interacting via events in $\{|\ layerRes.(layer-1)\ |\}$. This set contains all events the previous layer's node processes use for output because a node process requires the outputs from all nodes in the previous layer.

The $Node(l, n, inpSize)$ process represents the nth node in the layer l, which has $inpSize$ inputs. We define $Node(l, n, inpSize)$ as the parallel composition of interleaved $NodeIn(l, n, i)$ processes, with i ranging over 1 to $inpSize$, and a $Collator(l, n, inpSize)$ process. Interleaved processes ($|||$) do not synchronise.

$NodeIn(l, n, i)$ captures a weight application to an input. A $NodeIn$ process receives inputs via $layerRes.(l-1).n$ and communicates its output through $nodeOut.l.n.i$. The output of $NodeIn(l, n, i)$ is its input weighted by the constant $weight$, which is given by the expression $weights\, l\, n\, i$. After engaging in this output event, $NodeIn$ terminates ($Skip$).

An input of a value x via a channel c can be specified in CSP using the prefixing construct $c?x \rightarrow P$, which defines the process that engages in an event $c.x$ and behaves like P. This process accepts inputs x over the channel c's type. The output prefix $c!v \rightarrow P$ is a process that outputs (synchronises) on the specific event $c.v$ and then behaves like P. $Collator(l, n, inpSize)$ sums all values output by the $NodeIn$ processes and applies the $bias$ value, given by $biases\, l\, n$. The output of $Collator(l, n, inpSize)$ on $layerRes$ is the output of the node process. The definition of $Collator(l, n, inpSize)$ uses a local recursive process $C(l, n, i, sum)$; its extra argument is the accumulated sum of the outputs. In the base case $C(layer, node, 0, sum)$, we have an output sum, with the $bias$ term applied, subject to the activation function $ReLU$. In the recursive case $C(layer, node, i, sum)$, we get an input x via $nodeOut.l.n.i$, and a recursive call whose arguments are a descending index $i-1$, and the sum of x and sum.

Finally, the definition of $OutputLayer$ is similar to that of $HiddenLayer$.

The visible events of an ANN process are used to define its connection to other components of the RoboChart semantics and for defining termination. In our example, these are the events $layerRes.0$, $layerRes.2$, and end. We rename the visible events of our ANN semantics to match the CSP events used to represent the events defined in the RoboChart model. For our example, as mentioned in Sect. 3, these events are anewError, adiff, and angleOutputE.

The RoboChart semantics defines a CSP process for the module by composing processes for each controller, each state machine, and memory, holding values for local variables. The semantics of an ANN component fits in the semantics of a RoboChart module as that of a controller process. With this semantics, we can prove the properties of the RoboChart module in terms of the events and operations of the robotic platform rather than just the inputs of the ANN.

For a primary validation of our semantics, we have used a CSP model checker to compare the semantics of the AnglePIDANN to that of the machine AnglePID of the original version of the segway model. For the latter, we have used the semantics automatically generated by the RoboChart tool[1]. We have used a discretised neural network to make model checking feasible. In this setting, we have been able to show refinement (in both directions) automatically. Further validation has been provided by implementing our semantics in Java using the

---

[1] Available at robostar.cs.york.ac.uk/robotool/.

JCSP package [28]. This has enabled simulation and assertion-based reasoning via JML in a setting where values are floating-point numbers.[2]

In general, however, we require a proof approach that caters for use of real numbers. Next, we describe our proof approach based on UTP.

5 Automated Verification Using UTP

In this section, we define UTP reactive contracts that capture the semantics of our ANN components presented in Sect. 4 and an approach to verification. In Sect. 5.1, we describe a general pattern of UTP reactive contracts for ANN components. In Sect. 5.2, we present a pattern for the semantics of standard RoboChart controllers that we use as specification. Finally, in Sect. 5.3, we present our notion of conformance for ANN components, a verification conditions to prove properties combining Isabelle/UTP and Marabou, for example.

5.1 General Pattern

Definition 1 below provides a pattern for contracts corresponding to an optimised version of the CSP process *ANN* in Fig. 4. The pattern is for the process defining one iteration of the *ANN*: the parallelism between *HiddenLayers* and *OutputLayer*. So, we consider one application of the ANN. With that, compositional reasoning allows us to make direct deductions about the overall *ANN* process.

To optimise reasoning, we eliminate the interleavings that allow inputs and outputs to be received and offered in any order, and internal computations among and inside the layers to occur in any order. Our highly parallel semantics captures the common use of parallelisation to optimise the performance of implementations of ANNs. We have proved, however, that the different interleavings produce equivalent outputs once the internal events are hidden.

First, the model of the ANN is deterministic, and hiding the events representing the communications between the nodes (and the layers) introduces no nondeterminism. This means that the internal order of computation (as signalled by the events) in the layers and their nodes is irrelevant. Second, if we add a wrapper process that keeps that responsiveness for the inputs but feeds them to *ANN* in a fixed order, the values and responsiveness of outputs are maintained. With this, we have rigorous evidence that parallelisation is a valid implementation strategy and that we can use a simpler model for reasoning.

For brevity, in Definition 1, the contract is defined using a sequence *input* containing only the events representing inputs extracted from the trace *tt*. Formally, $input = tt \upharpoonright \{| \ layerRes.0 \ |\}$. (We use $\upharpoonright$ for sequence filtering.)

---

[2] All the artefacts related to this validation work are available at github.com/UoY-RoboStar/robochart-ann-components/.

Definition 1 (ANN Component General Contract).

$GeneralANNContract \; \widehat{=}$
$\quad [\;\; true_r$
$\quad \vdash \#input < insize \land \mathcal{E}[input, \{|\; layerRes.0.(\#input + 1) \;|\}]$
$\quad\quad \lor$
$\quad\quad \#input = insize \land$
$\quad\quad \exists\, l : 1 \,..\, layerNo \bullet \exists\, n : 1 \,..\, layerSize(l) \bullet$
$\quad\quad\quad \mathcal{E}[front \circ layeroutput(l, n), \{\; last \circ layeroutput(l, n) \;\}]$
$\quad\quad | \;\; \#input = insize \land \Phi[layeroutput(layerNo, layerSize(layerNo))]$
$\quad]$

The pattern in Definition 1 is for contracts that require that the process does not diverge: the precondition is $true_r$. This is appropriate as no ANN diverges.

To define the pericondition and the postcondition, we specify the valid observations using the predicate operators $\mathcal{E}$ and Φ. The pericondition characterises the stable intermediate states of the ANN where some or all inputs have been received. We identify these states by considering the size of $inputs$. When some of the inputs are available ($\#input < insize$), the trace is $input$, and the next input event $layerRes.0.(\#input + 1)$ is not refused.

When all inputs are available ($\#input = size$), we specify the trace of $layerRes$ interactions up to where $layerRes.l.n$ has occurred using a function $layeroutput(l, n)$, where l and n are layer and node indices. In the pericondition, we consider all layer indices l and all node indices n in l, from 1 to $layerSize(l)$. The function $layeroutput(l, n)$ encodes the specification of the ANN, in terms of its structure, into a trace-based specification. For instance, for an ANN with input size 2, with two nodes in its first layer, like in our example, if tt defines the $input$ sequence as $\langle layerRes.0.1.1, layerRes.0.2.1 \rangle$, then $layeroutput(1, 2)$ is $\langle layerRes.0.1.1, layerRes.0.2.1, layerRes.1.1.(1.75), layerRes.1.2.(1.80) \rangle$. This reflects the fact that the inputs are taken first, and then the output of each node is the weighted sum of these inputs. Here, we consider all weights to be 0.5, the bias value of the first node to be 0.75, and of the second node to be 0.8. The output of the first node is captured by the event $layerRes.1.1.(1.75)$, where the value 1.75 communicated is the result of the calculation $((1 * 0.5) + (1 * 0.5)) + 0.75$; the output 1.8 for the second node results from considering the bias 0.8.

With $layeroutput(l, n)$, we define the entire trace up to and including the result of the calculation of the node n on the layer l, which is the last element of $layeroutput(l, n)$. Therefore, the trace in the case $\#input = size$, where all inputs have been received, includes all elements in $layeroutput(l, n)$ but the last, denoted using the $front$ function. We define the set of accepted events as the singleton containing the event $last \circ layeroutput(l, n)$.

To specify the postcondition, we use $layeroutput(layerNo, layerSize(layerNo))$ for when the trace for the last node (that of index $layerSize(layerNo)$) of the last layer (that of index $layerNo$) has occurred.

For conciseness, we omit here the definition of *layeroutput*. It can be found in [3], along with all other definitions and proofs omitted here.

Using laws of reactive contracts and the definition of the CSP operators [10], we can prove that the pattern in Definition 1 captures the RoboChart ANN semantics.

5.2 Cyclic Memoryless RoboChart Controllers

An ANN cannot implement reactive behaviour, where events are interspersed according to environmental interactions. So, we consider specifications that define a cyclic controller, whose events can be classified as inputs or outputs, and whose control flow alternates between taking inputs and producing outputs, never terminating and without memory across cycles. (This is the flow of simulations, for example.) For such controllers, the RoboChart semantics of one iteration can be captured by a reactive design of a particular format. A reactive design defines a relation via just a precondition and a postcondition, which, however, specifies both intermediate final observations. In other words, a reactive design combines the pericondition and the postcondition in a single predicate.

In the case of the segway, as already mentioned, the inputs of the AnglePID are anewError and adiff, and the output is angleOutputE as indicated by the connections to the SegwayController (see Fig. 3). The reactive design for AnglePID captures the behaviour of one iteration of the state machine: it receives inputs *anewError* and *adiff* and produces an output via *angleOutputE*. It has precondition $true_r$ and the following postcondition, where the local variables of the RoboChart model are quantified and defined according to that model in terms of constants P and D. (In spite of its name, AnglePID is a PD controller).

$$\exists\, currNewError, currDiff, currAngleOut : Value \mid$$
$$currAngleOut = P * currNewError + D * currDiff \bullet$$
$$wait' \wedge (\,(tt = \langle\rangle \wedge anewError.currNewError \notin ref') \vee$$
$$(tt = \langle anewError.currNewError\rangle \wedge adiff.currDiff \notin ref') \vee$$
$$(tt = \langle anewError.currNewError, adiff.in.currDiff\rangle \wedge$$
$$angleOutputE.currAngleOut \notin ref')\,)$$
$$\vee$$
$$\neg\, wait' \wedge tt = \langle anewError.currNewError, adiff.currDiff,$$
$$angleOutputE.currAngleOut\rangle$$

The postcondition comprises two parts: either the process is waiting on interaction (*wait'*), or not (¬ *wait'*). When *wait'* holds, there are three cases distinguished by the trace contribution *tt*: no input events have happened, just *anewError* has been provided, or both *anewError* and *adiff* have been provided. In each case, the next event is not refused, that is, it does belong to *ref'*. When *wait'* is false, *tt* contains all inputs and the output. In this case, the value of *ref'* is irrelevant and not specified, since the process has terminated.

The design for the AnglePID follows the pattern defined below for a cyclic controller, where we consider *inp* and *out* to be the lists of input and output events. For every event, we have a quantified variable: x_1 to $x_{\#inp}$ for inputs, and y_1 to $y_{\#out}$ for outputs. We also consider a predicate p to capture the permissible values these variables can take, according to the RoboChart model.

Definition 2 (Cyclic RoboChart Controller Pattern).

$$
\begin{aligned}
&Cyclic\_RC\_Controller \,\widehat{=}\\
&\quad [\ true_r\\
&\quad \vdash\\
&\qquad \exists\, x_1, \ldots, x_{\#inp};\ y_1, \ldots, y_{\#out} : Value \mid p \,\bullet\\
&\qquad\quad wait' \wedge (\exists\, i : \mathrm{dom}\,inp \,\bullet\, tt = {}^\frown\!/\, j : 1..(i-1) \,\bullet\, \langle inp(j).x_j\rangle\ \wedge\\
&\qquad\qquad\qquad\qquad\qquad inp(i).x_i \notin ref')\\
&\qquad\qquad \vee\\
&\qquad\qquad (\exists\, i : \mathrm{dom}\,out \,\bullet\, tt = {}^\frown\!/\, n : \mathrm{dom}\,inp \,\bullet\, \langle inp(n).x_n\rangle^\frown\\
&\qquad\qquad\qquad\qquad\qquad {}^\frown\!/\, j : 1..(i-1) \,\bullet\, \langle out(j).y_j\rangle\ \wedge\\
&\qquad\qquad\qquad\qquad out(i).y_i \notin ref')\\
&\qquad\quad \vee\\
&\qquad\quad \neg\, wait' \wedge\\
&\qquad\quad tt = {}^\frown\!/\, i : \mathrm{dom}\,inp \,\bullet\, \langle inp(i).x_i\rangle\ {}^\frown\ {}^\frown\!/\, j : \mathrm{dom}\,out \,\bullet\, \langle out(j).y_j\rangle\\
&\quad]
\end{aligned}
$$

The reactive design for AnglePID is an instance of $Cyclic\_RC\_Controller$ above, where we have two inputs: x_1 is $currNewError$ and x_2 is $currDiff$. The output y_1 is $currAngleOut$. So, dom inp is $\{1,2\}$, and dom out is $\{1\}$. The predicate p characterises values for the outputs in terms of local variables x_i and y_i.

In Definition 2, in the $wait'$ case, we have a disjunction of two existential quantifications. In the first, the quantification on i ranges over dom inp, and we define a value for tt in terms of a distributed concatenation $({}^\frown\!/)$, that is, the concatenation of a sequence of sequences. The concatenation comprises singleton sequences $\langle inp(j).x_j\rangle$, with j ranging over $1..(i-1)$. These represent all input events before the i-th input given by the event $inp(i).x_i$. So we get $tt = \langle\rangle$ for $i = 1$, or $tt = \langle anewError.currNewError\rangle$ for $i = 2$ and $j = 1$. For the definition of ref', we specify that the input event $inp(i).x_i$, which is either $anewError.currNewError$ or $adiff.currDiff$, is not refused. This corresponds to the first two disjuncts in the $wait'$ case of the postcondition for AnglePID.

The second quantification is on i from dom out, with tt formed of two distributed concatenations. The first is of sequences $\langle inp(n).x_n\rangle$, like in the first quantification, but now n ranges over the whole dom inp, so we get all input events. The second is of sequences $\langle out(j).y_j\rangle$, representing proper prefixes of the sequences of all output events. Our example has one output, so this sequence resolves to the empty trace. The refusal does not include the following output. For our example, we accept $out(i).y_i$, which is $angleOutputE.currAngleOut$.

In the terminating case, that is, $\neg\, wait'$, we define tt as the concatenation of all input events followed by all output events. In our example, we get the trace $\langle anewError.currNewError, adiff.currDiff, angleOutputE.currAngleOut\rangle$.

A reactive design that instantiates the pattern in Definition 2 defines one iteration of a cyclic RoboChart controller. In the full model of the controller, that design is the body of a loop with the weakest fixed-point semantics. Since the precondition is $true_r$, the weakest fixed-point operator transfers to the post-condition [10].

Besides structural differences in the patterns in Definitions 1 and 2, we have a substantial difference in how outputs are defined regarding the inputs. In an ANN contract, the results are determined by a deterministic function based on the parameters of an ANN. In the pattern for a cyclic controller, the inputs and outputs are related by the predicate p. We can, for example, define even nondeterministic behaviour with this predicate. Finally, the alphabet of events in the patterns is different: one is based on the *layerRes* events and the other on RoboChart application-specific events to represent inputs and outputs.

We next consider how to verify an ANN component against a cyclic controller.

5.3 Conformance

In our approach to verification, we take a RoboChart standard controller as the specification for an ANN component. So, our goal is to prove that the ANN is correct with respect to the RoboChart controller. ANN components, however, contain numerical imprecision, so we allow an error tolerance on the values communicated by the output events of an ANN component. Formally, we define a conformance relation $Q\ conf(\epsilon)\ P$ that holds if, and only if, Q is a refinement of P, where the value of P's outputs can vary by at most ϵ as formalised below.

Definition 3 (Conformance Relation).

$Q\ conf(\epsilon)\ P \Leftrightarrow$
$\quad \exists s : seq\ Event;\ a : \mathbb{P}\ Event \mid tt\ seqapprox(\epsilon)\ s \wedge (\alpha P \setminus ref')\ setapprox(\epsilon)\ a \bullet$
$\quad\quad P[s, (\alpha P \setminus a)/tt, ref'] \sqsubseteq Q$

We say that $Q\ conf(\epsilon)\ P$ if, and only if, Q is a refinement of $P[s, \alpha P \setminus a/tt, ref']$, that is, we accept P as a specification that restricts the trace s and the refusals $\alpha P \setminus a$, instead of tt and ref', where s and a are approximations of tt and the set a of acceptances as captured by relations $seqapprox(\epsilon)$ and $setapprox(\epsilon)$. Here, αP is the set of events used in P, and $\setminus$ is the set difference operator, so that $\alpha P \setminus ref'$ is the set of events that P is not refusing, that is, its acceptances. Moreover, $s_1\ seqapprox(\epsilon)\ s_2$ relates sequences s_1 and s_2 if, and only if, s_1 differs from s_2 just in that its output values are within ϵ of those of s_2. Similarly, $A_1\ setapprox(\epsilon)\ A_2$ if, and only if, their input events are the same, but although the output events are the same the communicated values differ by at most ϵ.

Our verification approach starts with an abstract RoboChart model. That model can be refined using the structural rules of RoboChart justified by its CSP semantics and refinement relation. (These rules are out of scope here, but we refer to [23] for examples of the kinds of laws of interest.) In particular, refinement may need to be used to derive the specification of a cyclic controller for implementation using an ANN. In our example, we have used refinement to justify transformations to extract the AnglePID state machine out of the SegwayController where it was originally and obtain the Segway module in Fig. 3.

With a refined model, we can identify a controller to be implemented by an ANN and prove conformance according to $conf(\epsilon)$. The following result justifies the joint use of refinement (nondeterminism reduction) and $conf(\epsilon)$.

Theorem 1. $P \sqsubseteq Q \wedge R$ $conf(\epsilon)$ $Q \Rightarrow R$ $conf(\epsilon)$ P

This ensures that the ANN conforms to the original specification. So, the ANN may have removed nondeterminism present in the original controller, and exhibit some numeric imprecision bounded by ϵ, but that is all.

The following theorem identifies verification conditions that are sufficient to prove conformance for instances of our patterns. In Theorem 3, we further instantiate the verification conditions to consider conformance proofs using the semantics of standard and ANN controllers in RoboChart.

Theorem 2. Q $conf(\epsilon)$ P $provided$

$$[Q_2 \Rightarrow \exists s : seq\ Event;\ a : \mathbb{P}\ Event \mid tt\ seqapprox(\epsilon)\ s \wedge (\alpha P \setminus ref')\ setapprox\ a \bullet$$
$$P_2[s, \alpha P \setminus a/tt, ref']]$$

and

$$[Q_3 \Rightarrow \exists s : seq\ Event \mid tt\ seqapprox(\epsilon)\ s \bullet P_3[s/tt]]$$

$where$ Q and P are $instances$ of the $patterns$ in $Definitions$ 1 and $2.$

In short, Theorem 2 gives two verification conditions that distribute conformance over the pericondition and postcondition of Q. For any reactive contract RC, we use RC_2 and RC_3 to refer to its pericondition and to its postcondition. The first verification condition requires the periconditions P_2 and Q_2 to be related by $conf(\epsilon)$. The second condition makes the same requirement of the postconditions P_3 and Q_3 and is simpler because postconditions do not restrict ref'.

In the context of our work, the proof of conformance is in the following form.

$$(Q \setminus ANNHiddenEvts)[inp/layerRes.0, out/layerRes.layerNo]\ conf(\epsilon)\ P \quad (1)$$

Here, Q is a reactive contract that instantiates the pattern in Definition 1, and P captures the semantics of a cyclic controller described using the pattern in Definition 2. As said, our general contract for ANN components does not capture the hiding in the CSP semantics (Fig. 4), so we add it to Q above. Moreover, the pattern is concerned with $layerRes$ events and the specification with RoboChart events. So, we substitute $layerRes.0$ and $layerRes.layerNo$ with the inputs and outputs.

For our example, the conformance requirement is based on $AnglePIDANN$, the reactive contract for AnglePIDANN. Besides hiding the $layerRes.1$ events, we rename *layerRes.0.1* and *layerRes.0.2* to *currNewError* and *layerRes.0.2* to *curradiff*, and *layerRes.2.1* to *currangleOutput*. With this, we can discharge the verification conditions identified in Theorem 2 using Isabelle and the laws of UTP to prove the properties of the segway. For instance, we have proved that *"when P is non-zero, other PID constants are 0, and values greater than or equal to -maxAngle and less than or equal to maxAngle are communicated by the event angle, the values set by setLeftMotorSpeed() and setRightMotorSpeed() are equal to the value communicated by angle multiplied by P"*, using the original model of the segway with the AnglePID state machine. With our proof of (1), we can obtain the same result for the version of the segway software that uses AnglePIDANN, although we need to accept a tolerance for the values set.

For the particular case where the conformance that is being proved is of the form (1) above, the following theorem maps both conditions to set reachability conditions that can be discharged by ANN verification tools and, in particular, by Marabou. The compromise is that while we can carry out proofs for any input values in Isabelle, Marabou does not have facilities for dealing with universal quantification over real-valued sets. So, we approximate the input range with intervals and form properties based on these intervals.

Theorem 3.

$$\neg \, \exists \, x_1, .., x_{insize} : Value \bullet \exists \, y_1, .., y_{outsize} : Value \mid p \bullet \exists \, i : 1 .. outsize \bullet$$
$$\{annoutput(layerNo, i, \langle x_1, .., x_{insize} \rangle)\} \cap \{x : \mathbb{R} \mid |x - y_i| < \epsilon\} = \emptyset$$
$$\Rightarrow [(Q_2 \setminus_{peri} ANNHiddenEvts)[inp/layerRes.0, out/layerRes.layerNo] \Rightarrow$$
$$\exists \, s : seq \, Event; \; a : \mathbb{P} \, Event \mid tt \, seqapprox(\epsilon) \, s \wedge (\alpha P \setminus ref') \, setapprox(\epsilon) \, a \bullet$$
$$P_2[s, (\alpha P \setminus a)/tt, ref']]$$
$$\wedge$$
$$[(Q_3 \setminus_{post} ANNHiddenEvts)[inp/layerRes.0, out/layerRes.layerNo] \Rightarrow$$
$$\exists \, s \mid tt \, seqapprox(\epsilon) \, s \bullet P_3[s/tt]]$$

provided Q_2 is an ANN's pericondition, Q_3 is its postcondition, P_2 is a cyclic RoboChart controller's pericondition, P_3 is its postcondition, and inp and out are sequences of events with $\#inp = insize$ and $\#out = outsize$.

Theorem 3 states that if we show that there is no combination of input and output values for which there is an output y_i whose error, as defined by comparison to $annoutput(layerNo, i, \langle x_1, .., x_{insize} \rangle)$, is greater than ϵ, then our verification conditions are discharged. By requiring that the intersection between the singleton set $\{annoutput(layerNo, i, \langle x_1, .., x_{insize} \rangle)\}$ and $\{x : \mathbb{R} \mid |x - y_i| \leqslant \epsilon\}$ is empty, we require the output y_i to be in range. The error refers to the difference between the ANN's output $annoutput(l, n, \langle x_1, .., x_{insize} \rangle)$ and the cyclic RoboChart controller's output, captured by the variables y_i and the predicate p. The ANN's output value is characterised using $annoutput(l, n, in)$, which determines the value communicated by the output event of the n-th node of layer l, given a sequence in of inputs to the ANN.

We provide an example below of the reachability conditions we obtain using Theorem 3, based on our AnglePID example.

Example 1. The antecedent of Theorem 3 for our example is the following verification condition. (Here, i takes just the value 1).

$$\neg \; \exists \; currNewError, currDiff : Value \bullet$$
$$\exists \; currAngleOut \mid currAngleOut = P * currNewError + D * currDiff \bullet$$
$$\{ annoutput(layerNo, 1, \langle currNewError, currDiff \rangle) \} \cap$$
$$\{ x : \mathbb{R} \mid |x - currAngleOut| < \epsilon \} = \emptyset$$

The verification condition can be encoded as a set of reachability conditions if we define *Value* to be a set *MValue* defined in terms of a minimal value *min* and a natural number c as: $\bigcup \{ n : 0 .. c \bullet [min + n \times c, min + (n + 1) \times c] \}$. Given these constants, we can obtain finite conditions to prove in Marabou if we accept this limitation, as illustrated by the lemma below.

Lemma 1. *The antecedent of Theorem 3 for AnglePIDANN is as follows.*

$$\neg \; \exists \; n_1, n_2 : 0 .. c \bullet \exists \; currNewError, currDiff : \mathbb{R} \bullet$$
$$min + n_1 \times c \leqslant currNewError \leqslant min + (n_1 + 1) \times c \wedge$$
$$min + n_2 \times c \leqslant currDiff \leqslant min + (n_2 + 1) \times c \wedge$$
$$annoutput(layerNo, 1, \langle currNewError, currDiff \rangle) \leqslant$$
$$(P * (min + n_1 \times c) + D * min + n_2 \times c) - \epsilon$$
$$\vee$$
$$min + n_1 \times c \leqslant currNewError \leqslant min + (n_1 + 1) \times c \wedge$$
$$min + n_2 \times c \leqslant currDiff \leqslant min + (n_2 + 1) \times c \wedge$$
$$annoutput(layerNo, 1, \langle currNewError, currDiff \rangle) \geqslant$$
$$(P * (min + (n_1 + 1) \times c) + D * min + (n_2 + 1) \times c) + \epsilon$$

This verification condition amounts to proving $(c + 1) \times (c + 1)$ conditions: one for each value of n_1 and n_2. If any of these conditions fail, Marabou produces a counterexample, where we identify the assignment of input variables x_i that causes the error. This tells us exactly where the failure is, and the ANN can be retrained using this counterexample, using a similar approach to that in [7]. We choose the value of ϵ based on the needs of the system. So, even though Marabou cannot find a least upper bound for ϵ, in our work, this is not necessary.

Lemma 1's constraints form a hyper-rectangle in the domain of an ANN, and form a convex polytope, in inequality form, in the range. We can use these sets to specify properties in other tools [33, 35] as well as in Marabou as we have done. In particular, we can use tools that are able to handle non-linear activation functions, such as tanh and sigmoid, as well as ReLU.

6   Conclusions

As far as we know, we have proposed the first verification technique for robotic software in which an ANN is viewed as a white-box component whose reliability can and should be established. We guarantee properties, specified by state machines, of software that is implemented using instead trained, feed-forward, fully connected ReLU ANNs of any size or shape.

We have defined an ANN as a controller-like component in RoboChart and have validated the semantics via model checking using FDR [36], for discretised versions of the ANN, and via simulation using JCSP [28]. We have also presented a refinement-based method to prove ANN properties. We cater for an ANN component's numerical instability and provide a notion of conformance that can be used to justify replacing an existing RoboChart controller with an ANN if the error bound is accepted. We have identified sufficient verification conditions to establish conformance and shown how to combine ANN-specific (Marabou) and general theorem-proving tools (Isabelle) to discharge them. For illustration, we have applied our technique to a PID controller.

The work by Brucker and Stell in [5] is closely related to ours: they use Isabelle/HOL to verify the properties of feed-forward ANNs. They use their framework to demonstrate the properties of image-classification networks not considered here. Their goal, however, is component-level verification. It is feasible to use their results instead of Marabou to automate our proofs using only Isabelle and avoid input and output value restrictions.

Dupont et al. [8] define approximate notions of refinement for continuous systems. Their work considers two different views of conformance: upwards approximation, where an approximated system is refined to an exact system, and downwards approximation, the inverse. Our approach uses upward approximation: we refine an approximate system into an exact system. We, however, are concerned with ANN outputs, not trajectories of a continuous system.

An immediate goal is to generalise the ANN components. Our metamodel and semantics can easily accommodate several activation functions and can be extended to cater for convolutional neural networks with minor changes. Various tools and techniques remain applicable because the layer function is piecewise linear. Recurrent neural networks require more changes; fewer techniques and tools are available, although some are emerging [17].

Our second future goal is to define a toolchain of ANN-specific tools, so that, instead of relying on discharging our proof obligations using just a single tool, we have a collection of tools available. This requires techniques to reduce the search space and prove properties using complete techniques. This toolchain would allow us to verify more extensive and complex ANNs.

Finally, another future goal is to consider use of an ANN for perception, where the availability of a specification is not immediate. Developing meaningful specifications for such components is challenging, but there is a growing body of relevant work to address this [16] that we plan to consider.

Acknowledgements. This work has been funded by the UK EPSRC Grants EP/R025479/1, and EP/V026801/2, and by the UK Royal Academy of Engineering Grant No CiET1718/45.

References

1. Ahn, J.-H., Rhee, K., You, Y.: A study on the collision avoidance of a ship using neural networks and fuzzy logic. Appl. Ocean Res. **37**, 162–173 (2012)
2. An, P.E., Harris, C.J., Tribe, R., Clarke, N.: Aspects of neural networks in intelligent collision avoidance systems for prometheus. In: Joint Framework for Information Technology, pp. 129–135 (1993)
3. Attala, Z.: Verification of RoboChart models with ANN components. Technical report, University of York (2023). https://robostar.cs.york.ac.uk/publications/reports/Ziggy_Attala_Draft_Thesis.pdf
4. Attala, Z., Cavalcanti, A.L.C., Woodcock, J.C.P.: A comparison of neural network tools for the verification of linear specifications of ReLU networks. In: Albarghouthi, A., Katz, G., Narodytska, N. (eds.) 3rd Workshop on Formal Methods for ML-Enabled Autonomous System, pp. 22–33 (2020)
5. Brucker, A.D., Stell, A.: Verifying feedforward neural networks for classification in Isabelle/HOL. In: Chechik, M., Katoen, J.P., Leucker, M. (eds.) FM 2023. LNCS, vol. 14000, pp. 427–444. Springer, Cham (2023). https://doi.org/10.1007/978-3-031-27481-7_24
6. Clavière, A., Asselin, E., Garion, C., Pagetti, C.: Safety verification of neural network controlled systems. CoRR, abs/2011.05174 (2020)
7. Dreossi, T., et al.: Counterexample-guided data augmentation. arXiv:1805.06962 (2018)
8. Dupont, G., Aït-Ameur, Y., Pantel, M., Singh, N.K.: Event-B refinement for continuous behaviours approximation. In: Hou, Z., Ganesh, V. (eds.) ATVA 2021. LNCS, vol. 12971, pp. 320–336. Springer, Cham (2021). https://doi.org/10.1007/978-3-030-88885-5_21
9. Foster, S., Baxter, J., Cavalcanti, A.L.C., Woodcock, J.C.P., Zeyda, F.: Unifying semantic foundations for automated verification tools in Isabelle/UTP. Sci. Comput. Program. **197**, 102510 (2020)
10. Foster, S., et al.: Unifying theories of reactive design contracts. CoRR, abs/1712.10233 (2017)
11. Foster, S., et al.: Automated verification of reactive and concurrent programs by calculation. CoRR, abs/2007.13529 (2020)
12. Gibson-Robinson, T., Armstrong, P., Boulgakov, A., Roscoe, A.W.: FDR3—a modern refinement checker for CSP. In: Ábrahám, E., Havelund, K. (eds.) TACAS 2014. LNCS, vol. 8413, pp. 187–201. Springer, Heidelberg (2014). https://doi.org/10.1007/978-3-642-54862-8_13
13. Hoare, C.A.R., Jifeng, H.: Unifying Theories of Programming. Prentice-Hall, Englewood Cliff (1998)
14. Hoare, C.A.R.: Communicating Sequential Processes. Prentice Hall International, Englewood Cliff (1985)
15. Hodge, V.J., Hawkins, R., Alexander, R.: Deep reinforcement learning for drone navigation using sensor data. Neural Comput. Appl. **33**, 2015–2033 (2020). https://doi.org/10.1007/s00521-020-05097-x
16. Hu, B.C., et al.: If a human can see it, so should your system. In: Proceedings of the 44th International Conference on Software Engineering. ACM (2022)
17. Jacoby, Y., Barrett, C.W., Katz, G.: Verifying recurrent neural networks using invariant inference. CoRR, abs/2004.02462 (2020)
18. Julian, K.D., Kochenderfer, M.J.: Guaranteeing safety for neural network-based aircraft collision avoidance systems. In: 2019 IEEE/AIAA 38th Digital Avionics Systems Conference (DASC). IEEE (2019)

19. Julian, K.D., Kochenderfer, M.J., Owen, M.P.: Deep neural network compression for aircraft collision avoidance systems. J. Guid. Control. Dyn. **42**(3), 598–608 (2019)

20. Katz, G., Barrett, C., Dill, D.L., Julian, K., Kochenderfer, M.J.: Reluplex: an efficient SMT solver for verifying deep neural networks. In: Majumdar, R., Kunčak, V. (eds.) CAV 2017. LNCS, vol. 10426, pp. 97–117. Springer, Cham (2017). https://doi.org/10.1007/978-3-319-63387-9_5

21. Katz, G., et al.: The marabou framework for verification and analysis of deep neural networks. In: Dillig, I., Tasiran, S. (eds.) CAV 2019. LNCS, vol. 11561, pp. 443–452. Springer, Cham (2019). https://doi.org/10.1007/978-3-030-25540-4_26

22. LeCun, Y., Bengio, Y., Hinton, G.: Deep learning. Nature **521**, 436–444 (2015). https://doi.org/10.1038/nature14539

23. Miyazawa, A., Cavalcanti, A.: Formal refinement in SysML. In: Albert, E., Sekerinski, E. (eds.) IFM 2014. LNCS, vol. 8739, pp. 155–170. Springer, Cham (2014). https://doi.org/10.1007/978-3-319-10181-1_10

24. Miyazawa, A., Ribeiro, P., Li, W., Cavalcanti, A., Timmis, J., Woodcock, J.: RoboChart: modelling and verification of the functional behaviour of robotic applications. Softw. Syst. Model. **18**, 3097–3149 (2019)

25. Neves, A.C., González, I., Leander, J., Karoumi, R.: A new approach to damage detection in bridges using machine learning. In: Conte, J.P., Astroza, R., Benzoni, G., Feltrin, G., Loh, K.J., Moaveni, B. (eds.) EVACES 2017. LNCE, vol. 5, pp. 73–84. Springer, Cham (2018). https://doi.org/10.1007/978-3-319-67443-8_5

26. Nordmann, A., Hochgeschwender, N., Wrede, S.: A survey on domain-specific languages in robotics. In: Brugali, D., Broenink, J.F., Kroeger, T., MacDonald, B.A. (eds.) SIMPAR 2014. LNCS (LNAI), vol. 8810, pp. 195–206. Springer, Cham (2014). https://doi.org/10.1007/978-3-319-11900-7_17

27. Nwankpa, C., et al.: Activation functions: comparison of trends in practice and research for deep learning. arXiv:1811.03378 (2018)

28. Austin, P.D., Welch, P.H.: CSP for JavaTM (JCSP) 1.1-RC4 API specification (2008). https://www.cs.kent.ac.uk/projects/ofa/jcsp/jcsp-1.1-rc4/jcsp-doc/

29. ProofPower-Z reference manual (2006)

30. Rojas, R.: Neural Networks – A Systematic Introduction, chap. 7. Springer, Heidelberg (1996). https://doi.org/10.1007/978-3-642-61068-4

31. Roscoe, A.W.: Understanding Concurrent Systems. Texts in Computer Science. Springer, London (2011). https://doi.org/10.1007/978-1-84882-258-0

32. Roscoe, A.W.: The Theory and Practice of Concurrency. Prentice-Hall, Englewood Cliff (1997)

33. Singh, G., Gehr, T., Mirman, M., Püschel, M., Vechev, M.: Fast and effective robustness certification. In: Bengio, S., Wallach, H., Larochelle, H., Grauman, K., Cesa-Bianchi, N., Garnett, R. (eds.) Advances in Neural Information Processing Systems, vol. 31, pp. 10802–10813. Curran Associates Inc. (2018)

34. Spivey, J.M.: The Z Notation: A Reference Manual. Prentice-Hall, Englewood Cliff (1992)

35. Tran, H.-D., et al.: Star-based reachability analysis of deep neural networks. In: ter Beek, M.H., McIver, A., Oliveira, J.N. (eds.) FM 2019. LNCS, vol. 11800, pp. 670–686. Springer, Cham (2019). https://doi.org/10.1007/978-3-030-30942-8_39

36. University of Oxford. FDR Manual, May 2020. Release 4.2.7. dl.cocotec.io/fdr/fdr-manual.pdf. Accessed 31 May 2020

37. Woodcock, J., Davies, J.: Using Z. Prentice Hall, Englewood Cliff (1996)

38. Ye, K., Foster, S., Woodcock, J.: Automated reasoning for probabilistic sequential programs with theorem proving. In: Fahrenberg, U., Gehrke, M., Santocanale, L., Winter, M. (eds.) RAMiCS 2021. LNCS, vol. 13027, pp. 465–482. Springer, Cham (2021). https://doi.org/10.1007/978-3-030-88701-8_28

A Game-Theoretic Approach to Indistinguishability of Winning Objectives as User Privacy

Rindo Nakanishi[1(✉)], Yoshiaki Takata[2], and Hiroyuki Seki[1]

[1] Graduate School of Informatics, Nagoya University, Furo-cho, Chikusa, Nagoya 464-8601, Japan
{rindo,seki}@sqlab.jp
[2] School of Informatics, Kochi University of Technology, Tosayamada, Kami City, Kochi 782-8502, Japan
takata.yoshiaki@kochi-tech.ac.jp

Abstract. Game theory on graphs is a basic tool in computer science. In this paper, we propose a new game-theoretic framework for studying the privacy protection of a user who interactively uses a software service. Our framework is based on the idea that an objective of a user using software services should not be known to an adversary because the objective is often closely related to personal information of the user. We propose two new notions, $\mathcal{O}$-indistinguishable strategy ($\mathcal{O}$-IS) and objective-indistinguishability equilibrium (OIE). For a given game and a subset $\mathcal{O}$ of winning objectives (or objectives in short), a strategy of a player is $\mathcal{O}$-indistinguishable if an adversary cannot shrink $\mathcal{O}$ by excluding any objective from $\mathcal{O}$ as an impossible objective. A strategy profile, which is a tuple of strategies of all players, is an OIE if the profile is locally maximal in the sense that no player can expand her set of objectives indistinguishable from her real objective from the viewpoint of an adversary. We show that for a given multiplayer game with Muller objectives, both of the existence of an $\mathcal{O}$-IS and that of OIE are decidable.

Keywords: graph game · Muller objective · $\mathcal{O}$-indistinguishable strategy · objective-indistinguishability equilibrium

1 Introduction

Indistinguishability is a basic concept in security and privacy, meaning that anyone who does not have the access right to secret information cannot distinguish between a target secret data and other data. For example, a cryptographic protocol may be considered secure if the answer from an adversary who tries to attack the protocol is indistinguishable from a random sequence [23]. In the database community, k-anonymity has been frequently used as a criterion on privacy of a user's record in a database; a database is k-anonymous if we cannot distinguish a target record from at least $k - 1$ records whose public attribute values are the same as those of the target record [32].

E. Ábrahám et al. (Eds.): ICTAC 2023, LNCS 14446, pp. 36–54, 2023.
https://doi.org/10.1007/978-3-031-47963-2_4

In this paper, we apply indistinguishability to defining and solving problems on privacyof a user who interacts with other users and/or software tools. Our basic framework is a multiplayer non-zero-sum game played on a game arena, which is a finite directed graph with the initial vertex [6,8]. A game has been used as the framework of reactive synthesis problem [21,27]. A play in a game arena is an infinite string of vertices starting with the initial vertex and along edges in the game arena. To determine the result (or payoff) of a play, a winning objective O_p is specified for each player p. If the play satisfies O_p, then we say that the player p wins in this play. Otherwise, the player p loses. A play is uniquely determined when all players choose their own strategies in the game. A strategy σ of a player p is called a winning strategy if the player p always wins by using σ, i.e., any play consistent with the strategy σ satisfies her winning objective regardless of the other players' strategies. One of the main concerns in game theory is to decide whether there is a winning strategy for a given player p and if so, to construct a winning strategy for p. Note that there may be more than one winning strategies for a player; she can choose any one among such winning strategies. In the literatures, a winning objective is *a priori* given as a component of a game. In this study, we regard a winning objective of a player is her private information because objectives of a user of software services are closely related to her private information. For example, users of e-commerce websites may select products to purchase depending on their preference, income, health condition, etc., which are related to private information of the users. Hence, it is natural for a player to choose a winning strategy that maximizes the indistinguishability of her winning objective from the viewpoint of an adversary who may observe the play and recognize which players win the game. For a subset $\mathcal{O}$ of winning objectives which a player p wants to be indistinguishable from one another, we say that a strategy of p is $\mathcal{O}$-indistinguishable if an adversary cannot make $\mathcal{O}$ smaller as the candidate set of winning objectives. The paper discusses the decidability of some problems related to $\mathcal{O}$-indistinguishability.

Another important problem in game theory is to find a good combination of strategies of all players, which provides a locally optimal play. A well-known criterion is Nash equilibrium. A combination of strategies (called a strategy profile) is a Nash equilibrium if any player losing the game in that strategy profile cannot make herself a winner by changing her strategy alone. This paper introduces objective-indistinguishability equilibrium (OIE) as a criterion of local optimality of a strategy profile; a strategy profile is OIE if and only if no player can extend the indistinguishable set of winning objectives by changing her strategy alone. The paper also provides the decidability results on OIE.

Example 1. Figure 1 shows a 1-player game arena with a Büchi objective. The player is a spy. Alice is her buddy. The player wants to communicate with Alice many times and she does not want an adversary to find out that Alice is her buddy. In this game, the objective of the player is to visit the accepting vertex Alice infinitely often. Visiting a vertex corresponds to communicating with the person written on that vertex.

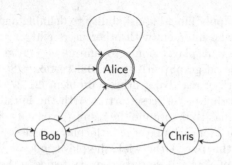

Fig. 1. 1-player game arena with a Büchi objective

We assume that an adversary knows the game arena, the play and whether the player wins. We also assume that an adversary knows the objective of the player is a Büchi objective. We examine the following three strategies of the player, all of which result in the player's winning.

1. Always choose Alice as the next vertex, i.e., the play will be Alice Alice Alice····. In this case, the player wins because she visits Alice infinitely often. An adversary knows that at least Alice is an accepting vertex because the player won and she visited only Alice infinitely often.
2. Choose Bob as the next vertex when the player is in Alice, and Alice when the player is in Bob, i.e., the play will be Alice Bob Alice Bob····. In this case, the player wins and an adversary knows that at least one of Alice and Bob is an accepting vertex. Compared to the case 1, the vertex Bob is added to the candidate set of accepting vertices.
3. Choose Bob as the next vertex when the player is in Alice, Chris when the player is in Bob, and Alice when the player is in Chris, i.e., the play will be Alice Bob Chris Alice····. In this case, the player wins and an adversary knows that at least one of Alice, Bob and Chris is an accepting vertex. Compared to the case 2, the vertex Chris is added to the candidate set of accepting vertices.

Related Work. There is a generalization of games where each player can only know partial information on the game, which is called an imperfect information game [2,5,7,11,12]. While the indistinguishability proposed in this paper shares such restricted observation with imperfect information games, the large difference is that we consider an adversary who is not a player but an individual who observes partial information on the game while players themselves may obtain only partial information in imperfect information games.

Among a variety of privacy notions, k-anonymity is well-known. A database D is k-*anonymous* [28,32] if for any record r in D, there are at least $k-1$ records different from r such that the values of quasi-identifiers of r and these records are the same. Here, a set of quasi-identifiers is a subset of attributes that can 'almost' identify the record such as {zip-code, birthday, income}. Hence, if D is k-anonymous, an adversary knowing the quasi-identifiers of some user u cannot identify the record of u in D among the k records with the same values of the quasi-identifiers. Methods for transforming a database to the one satisfying k-anonymity have been investigated [4, 9]. Refined notions have been proposed by considering the statistical distribution of the attribute values [25, 26].

However, these notions suffer from so called non-structured zero and mosaic effect. Actually, it is known that there is no way of protecting perfect privacy from an adversary who can use an arbitrary external information except the target privacy itself. The notion of ε-differential privacy where $\varepsilon > 0$ was proposed to overcome the weakness of the classical notions of privacy. A query Q to a database D is ε-differentially private (abbreviated as ε-DP) [17, 19] if for any person u, the probability that we can infer whether the information on u is contained in D or not by observing the result of $Q(D)$ is negligible (very small) in terms of ε. (Also see [18, 20].) As the privacy protection of individual information used in data mining and machine learning is becoming a serious social problem [30], methods of data publishing that guarantees ε-DP have been extensively studied [1, 3, 22, 29, 30].

Quantitative information flow (abbreviated as QIF) [15, 31] is another way of formalizing privacy protection or information leakage. QIF of a program P is the mutual information of the secret input X and the public output Y of the program P in the sense of Shannon theory where the channel between X and Y is a program which has logical semantics. Hence, QIF analysis uses not only the calculation of probabilities but also program analysis [16].

We have mentioned a few well-known approaches to formally modeling privacy protection in software systems; however, these privacy notions, even QIF that is based on the logical semantics of a program, share the assumption that private information is a static value or a distribution of values. In contrast, our approach assumes that privacy is a purpose of a user's behavior. The protection of this kind of privacy has not been studied to the best of our knowledge. In [24], the following synthesis problem of privacy preserving systems is discussed: For given multivalued LTL formulas representing secrets as well as an LTL formula representing a specification, decide whether there is a reactive program that satisfies the specification while keeping the values of the formulas representing secrets unknown. The paper [24] treats the secrets as values as in the previous studies, and the approach is very different from ours.

There are criteria other than Nash equilibrium for local optimality of strategy profiles, namely, secure equilibrium (SE) [14] and doomsday equilibrium (DE) [13]. For example, SE is a strategy profile such that no player can improve her payoff or punish any other player without loss of her own payoff by changing only her strategy. SE and DE are secure in the sense that no player is punished by other player(s) and not directly related to user privacy.

2   Preliminaries

Definition 1. *A game arena is a tuple $G = (P, V, (V_p)_{p \in P}, v_0, E)$, where P is a finite set of players, V is a finite set of vertices, $(V_p)_{p \in P}$ is a partition of V, namely, $V_i \cap V_j = \varnothing$ for all $i \neq j$ $(i, j \in P)$ and $\bigcup_{p \in P} V_p = V$, $v_0 \in V$ is the initial vertex, and $E \subseteq V \times V$ is a set of edges.*

As defined later, a vertex in V_p is controlled by a player p, i.e., when a play is at a vertex in V_p, the next vertex is selected by player p. This type of games is called *turn-based*. There are other types of games, concurrent and stochastic games. In a concurrent game [2], each vertex may be controlled by more than one (or all) players. In a stochastic game [10,33,34], each vertex is controlled by a player or a special entity *nature* who selects next nodes according to a probabilistic distribution for next nodes given as a part of a game arena. Moreover, a strategy of a player selects a next node stochastically. In this paper, we consider only deterministic turn-based games.

Play and History. An infinite string of vertices $v_0 v_1 v_2 \cdots$ $(v_i \in V, i \geq 0)$ starting from the initial vertex v_0 is a *play* if $(v_i, v_{i+1}) \in E$ for all $i \geq 0$. A *history* is a non-empty (finite) prefix of a play. The set of all plays is denoted by *Play* and the set of all histories is denoted by *Hist*. We often write a history as hv where $h \in Hist \cup \{\varepsilon\}$ and $v \in V$. For a player $p \in P$, let $Hist_p = \{hv \in Hist \mid v \in V_p\}$. That is, $Hist_p$ is the set of histories ending with a vertex controlled by player p. For a play $\rho = v_0 v_1 v_2 \cdots \in Play$, we define $Inf(\rho) = \{v \in V \mid \forall i \geq 0. \exists j \geq i. v_j = v\}$.

Strategy. For a player $p \in P$, a *strategy* of p is a function $\sigma_p : Hist_p \to V$ such that $(v, \sigma_p(hv)) \in E$ for all $hv \in Hist_p$. At a vertex $v \in V_p$, player p chooses $\sigma_p(hv)$ as the next vertex according to her strategy σ_p. Note that because the domain of σ_p is $Hist_p$, the next vertex may depend on the whole history in general. Let Σ_G^p denote the set of all strategies of p. A *strategy profile* is a tuple $\boldsymbol{\sigma} = (\sigma_p)_{p \in P}$ of strategies of all players, namely $\sigma_p \in \Sigma_G^p$ for all $p \in P$. Let Σ_G denote the set of all strategy profiles. For a strategy profile $\boldsymbol{\sigma} \in \Sigma_G$ and a strategy $\sigma_p' \in \Sigma_G^p$ of a player $p \in P$, let $\boldsymbol{\sigma}[p \mapsto \sigma_p']$ denote the strategy profile obtained from $\boldsymbol{\sigma}$ by replacing the strategy of p in $\boldsymbol{\sigma}$ with σ_p'. We define the function $out_G : \Sigma_G \to Play$ as $out_G((\sigma_p)_{p \in P}) = v_0 v_1 v_2 \cdots$ where $v_{i+1} = \sigma_p(v_0 \cdots v_i)$ for all $i \geq 0$ and for $p \in P$ with $v_i \in V_p$. We call the play $out_G(\boldsymbol{\sigma})$ the *outcome* of $\boldsymbol{\sigma}$. We also define the function $out_G^p : \Sigma_G^p \to 2^{Play}$ for each $p \in P$ as $out_G^p(\sigma_p) = \{v_0 v_1 v_2 \cdots \in Play \mid v_i \in V_p \Rightarrow v_{i+1} = \sigma_p(v_0 \cdots v_i)$ for all $i \geq 0\}$. A play $\rho \in out_G^p(\sigma_p)$ is called a play consistent with the strategy σ_p of player p. By definition, for a strategy profile $\boldsymbol{\sigma} = (\sigma_p)_{p \in P} \in \Sigma_G$, it holds that $\bigcap_{p \in P} out_G^p(\sigma_p) = \{out_G(\boldsymbol{\sigma})\}$.

Objective. In this paper, we assume that the result that a player obtains from a play is either a winning or a losing. Since we are considering non-zero-sum games, one player's winning does not mean other players' losing. Each player has her own winning condition over plays, and we model the condition as a subset O of plays; i.e., the player wins if the play belongs to the subset O. We call the subset $O \subseteq Play$ the *objective* of that player. In this paper, we focus on the following important classes of objectives:

Definition 2. *Let $U \subseteq V$ be a subset of vertices and $\mathcal{F} \subseteq 2^V$ be a subset of subsets of vertices. We will use U and $\mathcal{F}$ as finite representations for specifying objectives as follows:*

- *Büchi objective:* $\text{Büchi}(U) = \{\rho \in Play \mid Inf(\rho) \cap U \neq \varnothing\}.$
- *Muller objective:* $\text{Muller}(\mathcal{F}) = \{\rho \in Play \mid Inf(\rho) \in \mathcal{F}\}.$

Note that a Büchi objective defined in Definition 2 is also a Muller objective: For any $U \subseteq V$, $\text{Büchi}(U) = \text{Muller}(\{I \subseteq V \mid I \cap U \neq \varnothing\})$. We define the description length of a Muller objective $\text{Muller}(\mathcal{F})$ for $\mathcal{F} \subseteq 2^V$ is $|V| \cdot |\mathcal{F}|$, because each element of $\mathcal{F}$, which is a subset of V, can be represented by a bit vector of length $|V|$.[1] By $\Omega \subseteq 2^{Play}$, we refer to a certain class of objectives. For example, $\Omega = \{ \text{Büchi}(U) \mid U \subseteq V \} \subseteq 2^{Play}$ is the class of Büchi objectives.

An *objective profile* is a tuple $\boldsymbol{\alpha} = (O_p)_{p \in P}$ of objectives of all players, namely $O_p \subseteq Play$ for all $p \in P$. For a strategy profile $\boldsymbol{\sigma} \in \Sigma_{\mathcal{G}}$ and an objective profile $\boldsymbol{\alpha} = (O_p)_{p \in P}$, we define the set $\text{Win}_{\mathcal{G}}(\boldsymbol{\sigma}, \boldsymbol{\alpha}) \subseteq P$ of winners as $\text{Win}_{\mathcal{G}}(\boldsymbol{\sigma}, \boldsymbol{\alpha}) = \{p \in P \mid \text{out}_{\mathcal{G}}(\boldsymbol{\sigma}) \in O_p\}$. That is, a player p is a winner if and only if $\text{out}_{\mathcal{G}}(\boldsymbol{\sigma})$ belongs to the objective O_p of p. If $p \in \text{Win}_{\mathcal{G}}(\boldsymbol{\sigma}, \boldsymbol{\alpha})$, we also say that p wins the game $\mathcal{G}$ with $\boldsymbol{\alpha}$ (by the strategy profile $\boldsymbol{\sigma}$). Note that it is possible that there is no player who wins the game or all the players win the game. In this sense, a game is non-zero-sum. We abbreviate $\Sigma_{\mathcal{G}}^p, \Sigma_{\mathcal{G}}, \text{out}_{\mathcal{G}}^p, \text{out}_{\mathcal{G}}$ and $\text{Win}_{\mathcal{G}}$ as $\Sigma^p, \Sigma, \text{out}^p, \text{out}$ and Win, respectively, if $\mathcal{G}$ is clear from the context.

Winning Strategy. For a game arena $\mathcal{G}$, a player $p \in P$ and an objective $O_p \subseteq Play$, a strategy $\sigma_p \in \Sigma^p$ of p such that $\text{out}^p(\sigma_p) \subseteq O_p$ is called a *winning strategy* of p for $\mathcal{G}$ and O_p because if p takes σ_p as her strategy then she wins against any combination of strategies of the other players. (Recall that $\text{out}^p(\sigma_p)$ is the set of all plays consistent with σ_p.) For a game arena $\mathcal{G}$ and a player $p \in P$, we define the set $\text{Winnable}_{\mathcal{G}}^p$ of objectives permitting a winning strategy as $\text{Winnable}_{\mathcal{G}}^p = \{O \mid \exists \sigma_p \in \Sigma_{\mathcal{G}}^p . \text{out}_{\mathcal{G}}^p(\sigma_p) \subseteq O\}$. For a player p, $O \in \text{Winnable}_{\mathcal{G}}^p$ means that p has a winning strategy for $\mathcal{G}$ and O. We have the following theorem on the existence of a winning strategy for a Muller objective.

Theorem 1. *Let $\mathcal{G} = (P, V, (V_p)_{p \in P}, v_0, E)$ be a game arena and $O_p \subseteq Play$ be a Muller objective of $p \in P$. Deciding whether there exists a winning strategy of p for O_p is P-complete.*

Proof. Theorem 21 in [8] states that in a two player zero-sum game, deciding whether there exists a winning strategy for a Muller objective is P-complete. We can apply Theorem 21 to multiplayer non-zero-sum games by regarding a multiplayer non-zero-sum game as a two player zero-sum game as follows: for a

---

[1] Translating a representation of a Büchi objective into that of a Muller objective may cause an exponential blowup in the description length.

player $p \in P$ in a multiplayer non-zero-sum game, we let the other player $-p$ be the coalition of the players $q \in P \setminus \{p\}$ whose objective is the complement of the objective of p.   □

Nash Equilibrium. For non-zero-sum multiplayer games, besides a winning strategy of each player, we often use Nash equilibrium, defined below, as a criterion for a strategy profile (a tuple of strategies of all players) to be locally optimal. Let $\sigma \in \Sigma$ be a strategy profile and $\alpha = (O_p)_{p \in P}$ be an objective profile. A strategy profile σ is called a *Nash equilibrium* (NE) for α if it holds that $\forall p \in P. \, \forall \sigma_p \in \Sigma^p. \, p \in \mathrm{Win}(\sigma[p \mapsto \sigma_p], \alpha) \Rightarrow p \in \mathrm{Win}(\sigma, \alpha)$. Intuitively, σ is a NE if every player p cannot improve the result (from losing to winning) by changing her strategy alone. For a strategy profile $\sigma \in \Sigma$, we call a strategy $\sigma_p \in \Sigma^p$ such that $p \notin \mathrm{Win}(\sigma, \alpha) \wedge p \in \mathrm{Win}(\sigma[p \mapsto \sigma_p], \alpha)$ a *profitable deviation* of p from σ. Hence, σ is a NE if and only if no player has a profitable deviation from σ. Because $p \in \mathrm{Win}(\sigma, \alpha)$ is equivalent to $\mathrm{out}(\sigma) \in O_p$, a strategy profile $\sigma \in \Sigma$ is a NE for α if and only if $\forall p \in P. \, \forall \sigma_p \in \Sigma^p. \, \mathrm{out}(\sigma[p \mapsto \sigma_p]) \in O_p \Rightarrow \mathrm{out}(\sigma) \in O_p$. We write this condition as $\mathrm{Nash}(\sigma, \alpha)$.

3   Multiple Nash Equilibrium

In this section, we define an extension of NE that is a single strategy profile simultaneously satisfying the condition of NE for more than one objective profiles. We can prove that the existence of this extended NE is decidable (Theorem 2), and later we will reduce some problems to the existence checking of this type of NE.

Definition 3. *For a game arena* $\mathcal{G} = (P, V, (V_p)_{p \in P}, v_0, E)$ *and objective profiles* $\alpha_1, \ldots, \alpha_n$, *a strategy profile* $\sigma \in \Sigma$ *is called an* $(\alpha_1, \ldots, \alpha_n)$-*Nash equilibrium if* $\mathrm{Nash}(\sigma, \alpha_j)$ *for all* $1 \leq j \leq n$.

An objective $O \subseteq 2^{Play}$ is *prefix-independent* if $\rho \in O \Leftrightarrow h\rho \in O$ for every play $\rho \in O$ and history $h \in Hist$. The objectives defined in Definition 2 are prefix-independent because $Inf(\rho) = Inf(h\rho)$ for every play ρ and history h. For a game arena $\mathcal{G} = (P, V, (V_p)_{p \in P}, v_0, E)$ and $v \in V$, let $(\mathcal{G}, v) = (P, V, (V_p)_{p \in P}, v, E)$ be the game arena obtained from $\mathcal{G}$ by replacing the initial vertex v_0 of $\mathcal{G}$ with v.

For a game arena $\mathcal{G} = (P, V, (V_p)_{p \in P}, v_0, E)$ with an objective profile $\alpha = (O_p)_{p \in P}$, we define the game arena $\mathcal{G}_p = (\{p, -p\}, V, (V_p, \overline{V_p}), v_0, E)$ with the objective profile $(O_p, \overline{O_p})$ for each $p \in P$. The game arena $\mathcal{G}_p$ with the objective profile $(O_p, \overline{O_p})$ is a 2-player zero-sum game such that vertices and edges are the same as $\mathcal{G}$ and the player $-p$ is formed by the *coalition* of all the players in $P \setminus \{p\}$. The following proposition is a variant of [8, Proposition 28] adjusted to the settings of this paper.

Proposition 1. *Let* $\mathcal{G} = (P, V, (V_p)_{p \in P}, v_0, E)$ *be a game arena and* $\alpha = (O_p)_{p \in P}$ *be an objective profile such that* O_p *is prefix-independent for all* p. *Then, a play* $\rho = v_0 v_1 v_2 \cdots \in Play$ *is the outcome of some NE* $\sigma \in \Sigma$ *for* α, *i.e.,* $\rho = \mathrm{out}(\sigma)$, *if and only if* $\forall p \in P. \, \forall i \geq 0. \, (v_i \in V_p \wedge O_p \in \mathrm{Winnable}^p_{(\mathcal{G}, v_i)}) \Rightarrow v_i v_{i+1} v_{i+2} \cdots \in O_p$.

Proof. We prove the only-if part by contradiction. Assume that a play $\rho = v_0v_1v_2\cdots \in Play$ is the outcome of a NE $\boldsymbol{\sigma} = (\sigma_p)_{p\in P} \in \Sigma$ for $\boldsymbol{\alpha}$ and there exist $p \in p$ and $i \geq 0$ with $v_i \in V_p \wedge O_p \in \text{Winnable}^p_{(\mathcal{G},v_i)}$ such that $v_iv_{i+1}v_{i+2}\cdots \notin O_p$. By the prefix-independence of O_p, $\rho = \text{out}(\boldsymbol{\sigma}) = v_0v_1v_2\cdots \notin O_p$ and thus $p \notin \text{Win}_{\mathcal{G}}(\boldsymbol{\sigma},\boldsymbol{\alpha})$. Since $O_p \in \text{Winnable}^p_{(\mathcal{G},v_i)}$, there exists a winning strategy τ_p of $p \in (\mathcal{G},v_i)$. Let σ'_p be the strategy obtained from σ_p and τ_p as follows: Until producing $v_0v_1\cdots v_i$, σ'_p is the same as σ_p. From v_i, σ'_p behaves as the same as τ_p. Therefore, $\text{out}(\boldsymbol{\sigma}[p \mapsto \sigma'_p])$ equals $v_0v_1\cdots v_{i-1}\pi$ for some play π of $(\mathcal{G},v_i)$, and $\pi \in O_p$ because τ_p is a winning strategy of p in $(\mathcal{G},v_i)$. From prefix-independence of O_p it follows that $\text{out}(\boldsymbol{\sigma}[p \mapsto \sigma'_p]) \in O_p$. This contradicts the assumption that $\boldsymbol{\sigma}$ is an NE.

We omit the opposite direction due to the space limitation. □

Corollary 1. *Let $\mathcal{G} = (P,V,(V_p)_{p\in P},v_0,E)$ be a game arena and $\boldsymbol{\alpha}_j = (O^j_p)_{p\in P}$ ($1 \leq j \leq n$) be objective profiles such that $O^j_p \subseteq Play$ is prefix-independent for all $p \in P$ and $1 \leq j \leq n$. Then, a play $\rho = v_0v_1v_2\cdots \in Play$ is the outcome of some $(\boldsymbol{\alpha}_1,\ldots,\boldsymbol{\alpha}_n)$-NE $\boldsymbol{\sigma} \in \Sigma$, i.e., $\rho = \text{out}(\boldsymbol{\sigma})$, if and only if*

$$\forall p \in P. \ \forall i \geq 0. \ 1 \leq \forall j \leq n.$$
$$(v_i \in V_p \wedge O^j_p \in \text{Winnable}^p_{(\mathcal{G},v_i)}) \Rightarrow v_iv_{i+1}v_{i+2}\cdots \in O^j_p. \tag{1}$$

Proof. If a play $\rho = v_0v_1v_2\cdots \in Play$ is the outcome of a $(\boldsymbol{\alpha}_1,\ldots,\boldsymbol{\alpha}_n)$-NE $\boldsymbol{\sigma} \in \Sigma$, then ρ satisfies $\forall p \in P. \ \forall i \geq 0. \ (v_i \in V_p \wedge O^j_p \in \text{Winnable}^p_{(\mathcal{G},v_i)}) \Rightarrow v_iv_{i+1}v_{i+2}\cdots \in O^j_p$ for all $1 \leq j \leq n$ by Proposition (1). Therefore, ρ satisfies condition (1). If a play $\rho = v_0v_1v_2\cdots \in Play$ satisfies condition (1), then ρ is the outcome of the strategy profile $\boldsymbol{\sigma} \in \Sigma$ that is an NE for all $\boldsymbol{\alpha}_1,\ldots,\boldsymbol{\alpha}_n$ by Proposition (1). Therefore, ρ is the outcome of the $(\boldsymbol{\alpha}_1,\ldots,\boldsymbol{\alpha}_n)$-NE $\boldsymbol{\sigma}$ by Definition 3. □

Theorem 2. *Let $\mathcal{G} = (P,V,(V_p)_{p\in P},v_0,E)$ be a game arena and $\boldsymbol{\alpha}_j = (O^j_p)_{p\in P}$ ($1 \leq j \leq n$) be objective profiles over Muller objectives. Deciding whether there exists an $(\boldsymbol{\alpha}_1,\ldots,\boldsymbol{\alpha}_n)$-NE is decidable.*

Proof. By Corollary 1, there exists a $(\boldsymbol{\alpha}_1,\ldots,\boldsymbol{\alpha}_n)$-NE if and only if there exists a play $\rho = v_0v_1v_2\cdots \in Play$ satisfying Condition (1). Algorithm 1 decides the existence of a play satisfying Condition (1). In Algorithm 1, we call a game arena $\mathcal{G}_{V'} = (\{1\},V',(V'),v_0,E')$ satisfying $V' \subseteq V, v_0 \in V'$ and $E' = \{(v,v') \in E \mid v,v' \in V'\}$ a 1-player subgame arena of $\mathcal{G}$ (induced by V').

Showing the correctness of Algorithm 1 is straightforward. □

4   Indistinguishable Strategy and Related Equilibrium

In this section, we propose two new notions concerning on the privacy of a player: indistinguishable strategy and objective-indistinguishability equilibrium. We first define the set of possible objectives of a player in the viewpoint of an

---

Algorithm 1.

Input: a game arena $\mathcal{G} = (P, V, (V_p)_{p \in P}, v_0, E)$ and objective profiles $\alpha_j = (O_p^j)_{p \in P}$ $(1 \leq j \leq n)$.

1: **for all** $v \in V$ **do**
2:     Let $p \in P$ be the player such that $v \in V_p$.
3:         $O_v := \bigcap_{O_p^j \in \mathrm{Winnable}_{(\mathcal{G},v)}^p, 1 \leq j \leq n} O_p^j$.
4: **end for**
5: Nondeterministically select a set of vertices $V' \subseteq V$ and construct a 1-player subgame arena $\mathcal{G}_{V'} = (\{1\}, V', (V'), v_0, E')$ of $\mathcal{G}$.
6: $O_{\mathcal{G}_{V'}} := \bigcap_{v \in V'} O_v$.
7: **if** Player 1 has a winning strategy $\sigma_1 \in \Sigma_{\mathcal{G}_{V'}}^1$ for $\mathcal{G}_{V'}$ and $O_{\mathcal{G}_{V'}}$ **then**
8:     **return** Yes with σ_1
9: **else**
10:     **return** No
11: **end if**

---

adversary that can observe restricted information on a game, a play and its result (i.e., which players win).

We assume that an adversary guesses objectives of players from the three types of information: a play (p), a game arena (g) and a set of winners (w) of the play. We use a word $knw \in \{\mathsf{pw}, \mathsf{gw}, \mathsf{pg}, \mathsf{pgw}\}$ to represent a type of information that an adversary can use. For example, an adversary guesses objectives from a play and winners when $knw = \mathsf{pw}$. In either case, we implicitly assume that an adversary knows the set V of vertices of the game arena and the class Ω of objectives of players. We do not consider the cases where knw is a singleton by the following reason. An adversary cannot guess anything about objectives when $knw = \mathsf{g}$ or $knw = \mathsf{p}$. When $knw = \mathsf{w}$, he only knows that the objective of a winner is not empty and that of a loser is not the universal set. Let $p \in P$ be a player and $O_p \subseteq Play$ be an objective of p. We define the function $\mathrm{Obj}_{\Omega, knw}^{p, O_p} : \Sigma \to 2^\Omega$ as follows, which maps a strategy profile $\sigma \in \Sigma$ to the set of objectives of p that an adversary guesses. Note that $p \in \mathrm{Win}(\sigma, \alpha)$ is equivalent to $\mathrm{out}(\sigma) \in O_p$ and hence we let $\mathrm{Obj}_{\Omega, knw}^{p, O_p}$ have a parameter O_p instead of α.

$$\mathrm{Obj}_{\Omega, \mathsf{pw}}^{p, O_p}(\sigma) = \{O \subseteq V^\omega \mid (\mathrm{out}(\sigma) \in O \wedge p \in \mathrm{Win}(\sigma, \alpha)) \vee$$
$$(\mathrm{out}(\sigma) \notin O \wedge p \notin \mathrm{Win}(\sigma, \alpha))\},$$

$$\mathrm{Obj}_{\Omega, \mathsf{gw}}^{p, O_p}(\sigma) = \{O \in \Omega \mid (p \in \mathrm{Win}(\sigma, \alpha) \wedge O \neq \varnothing) \vee$$
$$(p \notin \mathrm{Win}(\sigma, \alpha) \wedge O \notin \mathrm{Winnable}^p)\},$$

$$\mathrm{Obj}_{\Omega, \mathsf{pg}}^{p, O_p}(\sigma) = \{O \in \Omega \mid \mathrm{out}(\sigma) \in O \vee (\mathrm{out}(\sigma) \notin O \wedge O \notin \mathrm{Winnable}^p)\},$$

$$\mathrm{Obj}_{\Omega, \mathsf{pgw}}^{p, O_p}(\sigma) = \{O \in \Omega \mid (\mathrm{out}(\sigma) \in O \wedge p \in \mathrm{Win}(\sigma, \alpha)) \vee$$
$$(\mathrm{out}(\sigma) \notin O \wedge p \notin \mathrm{Win}(\sigma, \alpha) \wedge O \notin \mathrm{Winnable}^p)\},$$

where α is any objective profile in which the objective of p is O_p. (Note that for a given σ whether $p \in \text{Win}(\sigma, \alpha)$ or not does not depend on objectives of the players other than p and hence we can use an arbitrary α containing O_p.)

The definitions of $\text{Obj}_{\Omega,knw}^{p,O_p}$ are based on the following ideas. When $knw = $ pw, we assume that an adversary can observe the play and the set of winners but he does not know the game arena. The adversary can infer that the play $\text{out}(\sigma)$ he observed belongs to the objective of a player p if the adversary knows that p is a winner, and $\text{out}(\sigma)$ does not belong to the objective of p if p is not a winner. Note that the adversary does not know the real objective O_p of player p. For the adversary, any $O \subseteq V^\omega$ satisfying $\text{out}(\sigma) \in O$ is a candidate of the objective of player p when p is a winner. Similarly, any $O \subseteq V^\omega$ satisfying $\text{out}(\sigma) \notin O$ is a candidate objective of p when p is not a winner. An adversary does not know the game arena because $knw = $ pw, that is, he does not know the set of edges in the arena. Therefore, the candidate objective O cannot be restricted to a subset of plays (i.e., infinite strings of vertices along the edges in the game arena), but O can be an arbitrary set of infinite strings of the vertices consistent with the information obtained by the adversary.

When $knw = $ gw, an adversary cannot observe the play, but he knows the game arena and can observe the set of winners. If p is a winner, the adversary can infer that p has a strategy σ_p such that $\text{out}^p(\sigma_p) \cap O_p \neq \varnothing$. Because there exists such a strategy σ_p for all O_p other than $\varnothing$, he can remove only $\varnothing$ from the set of candidates for p's objective. On the other hand, if p is a loser, the adversary can infer that p has no winning strategy for O_p because we assume that every player takes a winning strategy for her objective when one exists. Therefore, when p loses, the adversary can narrow down the set of candidates for p's objective to the set of objectives without a winning strategy.

The definition where $knw = $ pg can be interpreted in a similar way. Note that we have $\text{Obj}_{\Omega,pgw}^{p,O_p}(\sigma) = \text{Obj}_{\Omega,pw}^{p,O_p}(\sigma) \cap \text{Obj}_{\Omega,gw}^{p,O_p} \cap \text{Obj}_{\Omega,pg}^{p,O_p}$.

Since $p \in \text{Win}(\sigma, \alpha)$ is equivalent to $\text{out}(\sigma) \in O_p$ as mentioned before, the above definitions can be rephrased as follows:

$$\text{Obj}_{\Omega,pw}^{p,O_p}(\sigma) = \{O \subseteq V^\omega \mid \text{out}(\sigma) \in (O \cap O_p) \cup (\overline{O} \cap \overline{O_p})\},$$

$$\text{Obj}_{\Omega,gw}^{p,O_p}(\sigma) = \{O \in \Omega \mid (O \in \text{Winnable}^p \Rightarrow \text{out}(\sigma) \in O_p) \wedge$$
$$(O = \varnothing \Rightarrow \text{out}(\sigma) \notin O_p)\},$$

$$\text{Obj}_{\Omega,pg}^{p,O_p}(\sigma) = \{O \in \Omega \mid O \in \text{Winnable}^p \Rightarrow \text{out}(\sigma) \in O\},$$

$$\text{Obj}_{\Omega,pgw}^{p,O_p}(\sigma) = \{O \in \Omega \mid \text{out}(\sigma) \in (O \cap O_p) \cup (\overline{O} \cap \overline{O_p}) \wedge$$
$$(O \in \text{Winnable}^p \Rightarrow \text{out}(\sigma) \in O \cap O_p)\}.$$

The reader may wonder why O_p appears in this (alternative) definition in spite of the assumption that the adversary does not know O_p. The condition $\text{out}(\sigma) \in O_p$ (or $\notin O_p$) only means that the adversary knows whether p is a winner (or a loser) without knowing O_p itself.

Example 2. Figure 2 shows a 1-player game arena $\mathcal{G} = (\{1\}, V, (V), v_0, E)$ where $V = \{v_0, v_1, v_2\}$ and $E = \{(v_0, v_1), (v_0, v_2), (v_1, v_1), (v_2, v_2)\}$. We specify a Büchi objective by a set of accepting states, e.g., let $\langle v_1 \rangle$ denote Büchi($\{v_1\}$) = $\{\rho \in V^\omega \mid Inf(\rho) \cap \{v_1\} \neq \varnothing\}$. In this example, we assume the objective of player 1 is $\langle\rangle = \varnothing \subseteq Play$. Therefore, player 1 always loses regardless of her strategy. There are only two strategies σ_1 and σ_2 of player 1. The strategy σ_1 takes the vertex v_1 as the next vertex at the initial vertex v_0 and then keeps looping in v_1. On the other hand, the strategy σ_2 takes v_2 at v_0 and then keeps looping in v_2. Let σ_1 be the strategy player 1 chooses. We have the play $\rho = \text{out}(\sigma_1) = v_0 v_1 v_1 v_1 \cdots$.

We assume that an adversary knows that the objective of player 1 is a Büchi objective. Then, for each type of information $knw \in \{\text{pw}, \text{gw}, \text{pg}, \text{pgw}\}$, $\text{Obj}^{1,\varnothing}_{\text{Büchi}, knw}(\sigma_1)$ becomes as follows:

- If $knw = \text{pw}$, then an adversary can deduce that v_1 is not an accepting state because he knows that $Inf(v_0 v_1 v_1 \cdots) = \{v_1\}$ and player 1 loses. Therefore, we have $\text{Obj}^{1,\varnothing}_{\text{Büchi}, \text{pw}}(\sigma_1) = \{\langle\rangle, \langle v_0 \rangle, \langle v_2 \rangle, \langle v_0, v_2 \rangle\}$. Note that in this game arena, there is no play passing v_0 infinitely often, and thus $\langle\rangle$ and $\langle v_0 \rangle$ (resp. $\langle v_2 \rangle$ and $\langle v_0, v_2 \rangle$) are equivalent actually. However, because an adversary does not know the game arena when $knw = \text{pw}$, he should consider every infinite string over V would be a play and thus $\langle\rangle$ and $\langle v_0 \rangle$ are different for him when $knw = \text{pw}$. In the other cases where an adversary knows the game arena, he also knows e.g. $\langle\rangle$ and $\langle v_0 \rangle$ are equivalent and thus he would consider $\Omega = \{\langle\rangle, \langle v_1 \rangle, \langle v_2 \rangle, \langle v_1, v_2 \rangle\}$.
- If $knw = \text{gw}$, then an adversary can deduce that neither v_1 nor v_2 is an accepting state because player 1 loses in spite of the fact that there are strategies that pass through v_1 or v_2 infinitely often. Therefore, $\text{Obj}^{1,\varnothing}_{\text{Büchi}, \text{gw}}(\sigma_1) = \{\langle\rangle\}$. That is, an adversary can infer the complete information.
- If $knw = \text{pg}$, then an adversary can deduce that $\langle v_2 \rangle$ does not belong to $\text{Obj}^{1,\varnothing}_{\text{Büchi}, \text{pg}}(\sigma_1)$ because player 1 did not take σ_2 to pass through v_2 infinitely often. That is, if $\langle v_2 \rangle$ were the objective of player 1, then it meant she chose losing strategy σ_1 instead of winning strategy σ_2, which is unlikely to happen. Therefore, we have $\text{Obj}^{1,\varnothing}_{\text{Büchi}, \text{pg}}(\sigma_1) = \{\langle\rangle, \langle v_1 \rangle, \langle v_1, v_2 \rangle\}$.
- If $knw = \text{pgw}$, we have

$$\text{Obj}^{1,\varnothing}_{\text{Büchi}, \text{pgw}}(\sigma_1) = \bigcap_{knw \in \{\text{pw}, \text{gw}, \text{pg}\}} \text{Obj}^{1,\varnothing}_{\text{Büchi}, knw}(\sigma_1) = \{\langle\rangle\}.$$

$\mathcal{O}$-indistinguishable strategy.

Definition 4. *Let $\mathcal{G} = (P, V, (V_p)_{p \in P}, v_0, E)$ be a game arena, $\sigma_p \in \Sigma^p$ be a strategy of $p \in P$, $\Omega \subseteq 2^{Play}$ be one of the classes of objectives defined in Definition 2, $O_p \in \Omega$ be an objective of p and $knw \in \{\text{pw}, \text{gw}, \text{pg}, \text{pgw}\}$ be a type of information that an adversary can use. For any set $\mathcal{O} \subseteq 2^{Play}$ of objectives such that $\mathcal{O} \subseteq \bigcap_{\sigma \in \Sigma} \text{Obj}^{p, O_p}_{\Omega, knw}(\sigma[p \mapsto \sigma_p])$, we call σ_p an $\mathcal{O}$-indistinguishable strategy ($\mathcal{O}$-IS) of p (for O_p and knw).*

Intuitively, when a player takes an $\mathcal{O}$-IS as her strategy, an adversary cannot narrow down the set of candidates of p's objective from $\mathcal{O}$ by the following reason. By definition, any objective O belonging to $\mathcal{O}$ also belongs to $\text{Obj}^{p, O_p}_{\Omega, knw}(\boldsymbol{\sigma}[p \mapsto$

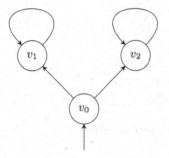
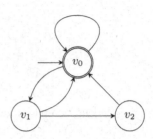

Fig. 2. 1-player game arena with a Büchi objective

Fig. 3. 1-player game arena a with Büchi objective

$\sigma_p]$) for the combination of σ_p and any strategies of the players other than p. This means that such an objective O is possible as the objective of p from the viewpoint of the adversary who can use a type of information specified by knw. If an $\mathcal{O}$-IS $\sigma_p \in \Sigma^p$ is a winning strategy of p, then we call σ_p a *winning $\mathcal{O}$-IS* of p.

Example 3. Figure 3 shows a 1-player game arena $\mathcal{G} = (\{1\}, V, (V), v_0, E)$ where $V = \{v_0, v_1, v_2\}$ and $E = \{(v_0, v_0), (v_0, v_1), (v_1, v_0), (v_1, v_2), (v_2, v_0)\}$. We use the same notation of Büchi objectives as Example 2, and in this example the objective of player 1 is $\langle v_0 \rangle \subseteq Play$. We assume that an adversary knows that the objective of player 1 is a Büchi objective. In this example, we focus on $knw = \mathsf{pw}$. We examine the following three strategies of player 1, all of which result in player 1's winning.

- Let $\sigma_1 \in \Sigma^1$ be a strategy of player 1 such that $\mathrm{out}(\sigma_1) = v_0 v_0 v_0 \cdots$. Since player 1 wins, an adversary can deduce that v_0 must be an accepting state. Therefore, $\mathrm{Obj}_{\mathrm{Büchi,pw}}^{1,\langle v_0 \rangle}(\sigma_1) = \{\langle v_0 \rangle, \langle v_0, v_1 \rangle, \langle v_0, v_2 \rangle, \langle v_0, v_1, v_2 \rangle\}$. For all $\mathcal{O} \subseteq \mathrm{Obj}_{\mathrm{Büchi,pw}}^{1,\langle v_0 \rangle}(\sigma_1)$, σ_1 is an $\mathcal{O}$-IS (for $\langle v_0 \rangle$ and $knw = \mathsf{pw}$).
- Let $\sigma_2 \in \Sigma^1$ be a strategy of player 1 such that $\mathrm{out}(\sigma_1) = v_0 v_1 v_0 v_1 \cdots$. In a similar way as the above case, an adversary can deduce that v_0 or v_1 (or both) must be an accepting state. Therefore, $\mathrm{Obj}_{\mathrm{Büchi,pw}}^{1,\langle v_0 \rangle}(\sigma_2) = \{\langle v_0 \rangle, \langle v_1 \rangle, \langle v_0, v_1 \rangle, \langle v_1, v_2 \rangle, \langle v_2, v_0 \rangle, \langle v_0, v_1, v_2 \rangle\}$. For all $\mathcal{O} \subseteq \mathrm{Obj}_{\mathrm{Büchi,pw}}^{1,\langle v_0 \rangle}(\sigma_2)$, σ_2 is an $\mathcal{O}$-IS.
- Let $\sigma_3 \in \Sigma^1$ be a strategy of player 1 such that $\mathrm{out}(\sigma_3) = v_0 v_1 v_2 v_0 v_1 v_2 \cdots$. In a similar way as the above cases, an adversary can deduce that at least one of v_0, v_1, and v_2 must be an accepting state. Therefore, $\mathrm{Obj}_{\mathrm{Büchi,pw}}^{1,\langle v_0 \rangle}(\sigma_3) = \{\langle v_0 \rangle, \langle v_1 \rangle, \langle v_2 \rangle, \langle v_0, v_1 \rangle, \langle v_1, v_2 \rangle, \langle v_2, v_0 \rangle, \langle v_0, v_1, v_2 \rangle\}$. For all $\mathcal{O} \subseteq \mathrm{Obj}_{\mathrm{Büchi,pw}}^{1,\langle v_0 \rangle}(\sigma_3)$, σ_3 is an $\mathcal{O}$-IS.

In the above example, $\mathrm{Obj}_{\mathrm{Büchi,pw}}^{1,\langle v_0 \rangle}(\sigma_1) \subset \mathrm{Obj}_{\mathrm{Büchi,pw}}^{1,\langle v_0 \rangle}(\sigma_2) \subset \mathrm{Obj}_{\mathrm{Büchi,pw}}^{1,\langle v_0 \rangle}(\sigma_3)$. Hence, the strategy σ_3 is the most favorable one for player 1 with regard to her

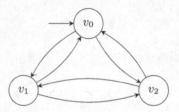

Fig. 4. 3-player game arena with Büchi objectives

privacy protection. This observation motivates us to introduce a new concept of equilibrium defined below.

Objective-Indistinguishability Equilibrium.

Definition 5. *Let $(O_p)_{p \in P}$ be an objective profile and $knw \in \{\mathsf{pw}, \mathsf{gw}, \mathsf{pg}, \mathsf{pgw}\}$ be a type of information that an adversary can use. We call a strategy profile $\sigma \in \Sigma$ such that*

$$\forall p \in P. \ \forall \sigma_p \in \Sigma^p. \ \mathrm{Obj}_{knw}^{p,O_p}(\sigma[p \mapsto \sigma_p]) \subseteq \mathrm{Obj}_{knw}^{p,O_p}(\sigma) \tag{2}$$

an objective-indistinguishability equilibrium *(OIE) for knw.*

If a strategy profile σ is an OIE for *knw*, no player can expand her $\mathrm{Obj}_{knw}^{p,O_p}(\sigma)$ by changing her strategy alone. For a strategy profile $\sigma \in \Sigma$, we call a strategy $\sigma_p \in \Sigma^p$ such that $\mathrm{Obj}_{\Omega,knw}^{p,O_p}(\sigma[p \mapsto \sigma_p]) \not\subseteq \mathrm{Obj}_{\Omega,knw}^{p,O_p}(\sigma)$ a profitable deviation for OIE. In this paper, we think that a set $\mathcal{O}_1 \subseteq 2^{Play}$ of objectives is less indistinguishable than a set $\mathcal{O}_2 \subseteq 2^{Play}$ of objectives when $\mathcal{O}_1 \subset \mathcal{O}_2$, not when $|\mathcal{O}_1| < |\mathcal{O}_2|$ because the latter does not always imply that $\mathcal{O}_1$ is more informative than $\mathcal{O}_2$. If an OIE σ is an NE as well, we call σ an *objective-indistinguishability Nash equilibrium* (OINE). While an OIE is locally optimal with respect only to indistinguishability, an OINE is locally optimal with respect to both indistinguishability and the result (winning or losing) of the game.

Example 4. Figure 4 shows a 3-player game arena $\mathcal{G} = (P, V, (V_p)_{p \in P}, v_0, E)$ where $P = \{0, 1, 2\}$, $V = \{v_0, v_1, v_2\}$, $V_p = \{v_p\}$ $(p \in P)$ and $E = \{(v_i, v_j) \mid i, j \in P, i \neq j\}$. The objective of player $p \in P$ is $\langle v_p \rangle$, and hence the objective profile is $\alpha = (\langle v_0 \rangle, \langle v_1 \rangle, \langle v_2 \rangle)$. Let $\sigma_p \in \Sigma^p$ $(p \in P)$ be the strategies defined as follows: $\sigma_0(hv_0) = v_1$, $\sigma_1(hv_1) = v_0$, and $\sigma_2(hv_2) = v_0$ for every $h \in Hist \cup \{\varepsilon\}$. Let $\sigma = (\sigma_1, \sigma_2, \sigma_3)$. It holds that $\mathrm{out}(\sigma) = v_0 v_1 v_0 v_1 \cdots$ and $\mathrm{Win}(\sigma, \alpha) = \{0, 1\}$.

- For *knw* = pw, σ is not an OIE because there exists a profitable deviation $\sigma_1' \in \Sigma^1$ for OIE such that $\sigma_1'(h) = v_2$ for all $h \in Hist_1$. While $\mathrm{out}(\sigma)$ does not visit v_2, player 1 can make the outcome visit v_2 infinitely often by changing her strategy from σ_1 to σ_1'. As a result, $\mathrm{Obj}_{\mathrm{B\ddot{u}chi},\mathsf{pw}}^{1,\langle v_1 \rangle}(\sigma) = \{\langle v_0 \rangle, \langle v_1 \rangle, \langle v_0, v_1 \rangle, \langle v_1, v_2 \rangle, \langle v_2, v_0 \rangle, \langle v_0, v_1, v_2 \rangle\}$ and $\mathrm{Obj}_{\mathrm{B\ddot{u}chi},\mathsf{pw}}^{1,\langle v_1 \rangle}(\sigma[1 \mapsto \sigma_1']) = \mathrm{Obj}_{\mathrm{B\ddot{u}chi},\mathsf{pw}}^{1,\langle v_1 \rangle}(\sigma) \cup \{\langle v_2 \rangle\}$.

- For $knw = $ gw, σ is an OIE by the following reason: In general, when $knw = $ gw, by definition $\mathrm{Obj}_{\Omega,\mathrm{gw}}^{p,O_p}(\sigma) = \Omega \setminus \{\varnothing\}$ if p wins and $\mathrm{Obj}_{\Omega,\mathrm{gw}}^{p,O_p}(\sigma) = \overline{\mathrm{Winnable}^p}$ otherwise. (That is, an adversary cannot exclude any objective other than $\varnothing$ from candidate objectives of player p when p wins, while he can exclude objectives in $\mathrm{Winnable}^p$ when p loses.) In this example, $\mathrm{Obj}_{\Omega,\mathrm{gw}}^{0,\langle v_0\rangle}(\sigma) = \mathrm{Obj}_{\Omega,\mathrm{gw}}^{1,\langle v_1\rangle}(\sigma) = \Omega \setminus \{\varnothing\}$ since players 0 and 1 are winners. They have no profitable deviation for OIE, because each of them cannot become a loser unless other players change their strategies and thus $\mathrm{Obj}_{\Omega,\mathrm{gw}}^{p,\langle v_p\rangle}(\sigma[p \mapsto \sigma_p'])$ $(p \in \{0,1\})$ still equals $\Omega \setminus \{\varnothing\}$ for any strategy σ_p' $(p \in \{0,1\})$. For player 2, $\mathrm{Obj}_{\Omega,\mathrm{gw}}^{2,\langle v_2\rangle}(\sigma) = \overline{\mathrm{Winnable}^2}$ $(= \{\langle\rangle, \langle v_2\rangle\})$.[2] She also has no profitable deviation for OIE, because she cannot become a winner unless player 0 or 1 changes their strategies and thus $\mathrm{Obj}_{\Omega,\mathrm{gw}}^{2,\langle v_2\rangle}(\sigma[2 \mapsto \sigma_2'])$ still equals $\overline{\mathrm{Winnable}^2}$ for any her strategy σ_2'.
- For $knw = $ pg, σ is not an OIE because for $\sigma_1' \in \Sigma^1$ defined above, $\mathrm{Obj}_{\mathrm{Büchi,pg}}^{1,\langle v_1\rangle}(\sigma) = \{\langle\rangle, \langle v_0\rangle, \langle v_1\rangle, \langle v_0, v_1\rangle, \langle v_1, v_2\rangle, \langle v_2, v_0\rangle, \langle v_0, v_1, v_2\rangle\}$ and $\mathrm{Obj}_{\mathrm{Büchi,pg}}^{1,\langle v_1\rangle}(\sigma[1 \mapsto \sigma_1']) = \mathrm{Obj}_{\mathrm{Büchi,pg}}^{1,\langle v_1\rangle}(\sigma) \cup \{\langle v_2\rangle\}$.
- For $knw = $ pgw, σ is not an OIE because $\sigma_1' \in \Sigma^1$ is again a profitable deviation for OIE.

5 Decidability Results

Theorem 3. *Let $\mathcal{G} = (P, V, (V_p)_{p\in P}, v_0, E)$ be a game arena and $\alpha = (O_p)_{p\in P}$ be an objective profile over Muller objectives. For a subset $\mathcal{O} \subseteq 2^{Play}$ of Muller objectives, whether there exists an $\mathcal{O}$-IS of p for O_p is decidable. Moreover, the problem is decidable in polynomial time when $knw = $ pg or when $knw = $ gw and $\mathcal{O}$ does not contain $\varnothing$.*

Proof. First we consider the case where $knw = $ pgw. We can show that a strategy $\sigma_p \in \Sigma^p$ is an $\mathcal{O}$-IS of p for O_p, i.e. $\mathcal{O} \subseteq \bigcap_{\sigma \in \Sigma} \mathrm{Obj}_{\mathrm{pgw}}^{p,O_p}(\sigma[p \mapsto \sigma_p])$, if and only if

$$\mathrm{out}^p(\sigma_p) \subseteq \bigcap_{O\in\mathcal{O}} \left((O \cap O_p) \cup (\overline{O} \cap \overline{O_p}) \right) \cap \bigcap_{O\in\mathcal{O}\cap\mathrm{Winnable}^p} (O \cap O_p). \quad (3)$$

This can be shown as follows:[3] Assume that $\mathcal{O} \subseteq \bigcap_{\sigma\in\Sigma} \mathrm{Obj}_{\mathrm{pgw}}^{p,O_p}(\sigma[p \mapsto \sigma_p])$. Then, every $O \in \mathcal{O}$ should belong to $\mathrm{Obj}_{\mathrm{pgw}}^{p,O_p}(\sigma[p \mapsto \sigma_p])$ for every $\sigma \in \Sigma$. Then by the definition of $\mathrm{Obj}_{\mathrm{pgw}}^{p,O_p}$, every $O \in \mathcal{O}$ and every $\sigma \in \Sigma$ should satisfy $\mathrm{out}(\sigma[p \mapsto \sigma_p]) \in (O \cap O_p) \cup (\overline{O} \cap \overline{O_p})$ and whenever $O \in \mathrm{Winnable}^p$, $\mathrm{out}(\sigma[p \mapsto $

---

[2] In this example, player 2 can visit v_i $(i = 0, 1)$ infinitely often by choosing v_i as the next vertex at v_2. Therefore, an objective such that v_0 or v_1 is an accepting state is winnable and hence $\mathrm{Winnable}^2 = \Omega \setminus \{\langle\rangle, \langle v_2\rangle\}$.

[3] We have confirmed this equivalence using a proof assistant software Coq. The proof script is available at https://github.com/ytakata69/proof-indistinguishable-objectives.

$\sigma_p]) \in O \cap O_p$. Because $\mathrm{out}^p(\sigma_p) = \{\mathrm{out}(\boldsymbol{\sigma}[p \mapsto \sigma_p]) \mid \boldsymbol{\sigma} \in \Sigma\}$, we have the containment in the above (3). The reverse direction can be proved similarly.

The above expression (3) means that σ_p is a winning strategy of p for the objective equal to the right-hand side of the containment in this expression (3). Because the class of Muller objectives is closed under Boolean operations, the right-hand side of (3) is also a Muller objective. Since deciding the existence of a winning strategy for a Muller objective is decidable as stated in Theorem 1, deciding the existence of an $\mathcal{O}$-IS is also decidable. (In this computation, deciding the existence of a winning strategy is used both for deciding whether $O \in \mathrm{Winnable}^p$, i.e., O has a winning strategy, and for deciding whether the right-hand side of (3) has a winning strategy.)

For the other cases, we can similarly show that $\sigma_p \in \Sigma^p$ is an $\mathcal{O}$-IS of p for O_p if and only if the following inclusions (4), (5), and (6) hold when $knw = \mathsf{pw}, \mathsf{gw}, \mathsf{pg}$, respectively:

$$\mathrm{out}^p(\sigma^p) \subseteq \bigcap_{O \in \mathcal{O}} \left((O \cap O_p) \cup (\overline{O} \cap \overline{O_p}) \right), \tag{4}$$

$$\mathrm{out}^p(\sigma^p) \subseteq \bigcap_{O \in \mathcal{O} \cap \mathrm{Winnable}^p} O_p \cap \bigcap_{O \in \mathcal{O} \cap \{\varnothing\}} \overline{O_p}, \tag{5}$$

$$\mathrm{out}^p(\sigma^p) \subseteq \bigcap_{O \in \mathcal{O} \cap \mathrm{Winnable}^p} O. \tag{6}$$

Therefore in any cases, we can reduce the problem of deciding the existence of an $\mathcal{O}$-IS into the one deciding the existence of a winning strategy for a Muller objective.

Since $\mathrm{Muller}(\mathcal{F}_1) \cap \mathrm{Muller}(\mathcal{F}_2) = \mathrm{Muller}(\mathcal{F}_1 \cap \mathcal{F}_2)$, the description lengths of the right-hand sides of (6) and (5) with $\mathcal{O}$ not containing $\varnothing$ are not greater than the sum of those of $\mathcal{O}$ and O_p.[4] Since deciding the existence of a winning strategy for a Muller objective is solvable in polynomial time by Theorem 1, deciding the existence of an $\mathcal{O}$-IS when $knw = \mathsf{pg}$ or when $knw = \mathsf{gw}$ and $\mathcal{O}$ does not contain $\varnothing$ is also solvable in polynomial time.   □

When $knw = \mathsf{pgw}$ or pw, we cannot guarantee that deciding the existence of an $\mathcal{O}$-IS is solvable in polynomial time because the complementation of a Muller objective in the right-hand sides of (3) and (4) may make the description length of the resultant objective $O(|V| \cdot 2^{|V|})$ even when the description lengths of $\mathcal{O}$ and α are small. Similarly, when $knw = \mathsf{gw}$, $\mathcal{O} \cap \mathrm{Winnable}^p = \varnothing$ and $\varnothing \in \mathcal{O}$, we cannot guarantee that deciding the existence of an $\mathcal{O}$-IS is solvable in polynomial time because the right-hand side of (5) becomes $\overline{O_p}$.

Theorem 4. *Let $\mathcal{G} = (P, V, (V_p)_{p \in P}, v_0, E)$ be a game arena and $\alpha = (O_p)_{p \in P}$ be an objective profile over Muller objectives. For a subset $\mathcal{O} \subseteq 2^{Play}$ of Muller*

---

[4] As an exception, if $\mathcal{O} \cap \mathrm{Winnable}^p = \varnothing$ (resp. $\mathcal{O} \cap (\mathrm{Winnable}^p \cup \{\varnothing\}) = \varnothing$), then the right-hand side of (6) (resp. (5)) equals the set of all plays, which equals $\mathrm{Muller}(2^V)$. In these cases, every strategy satisfies (5) and (6) and thus we can trivially decide the existence of an $\mathcal{O}$-IS.

objectives, whether there exists a winning $\mathcal{O}$-IS of p for O_p is decidable in polynomial time.

Proof. By definition, $\sigma_p \in \Sigma^p$ is a winning strategy of p for O_p if and only if $\text{out}^p(\sigma_p) \subseteq O_p$. Therefore, by replacing the right-hand side of each of (3)–(6) with the intersection of it and O_p, we can decide the existence of a winning $\mathcal{O}$-IS in the same way as the proof of Theorem 3. Namely, σ_p is a winning $\mathcal{O}$-IS of p for O_p if and only if

$$\text{out}^p(\sigma^p) \subseteq O_p \cap \bigcap_{O \in \mathcal{O}} O \qquad \text{(when } knw = \text{pgw or pw)}, \qquad (7)$$

$$\text{out}^p(\sigma^p) \subseteq O_p \cap \bigcap_{O \in \mathcal{O} \cap \{\varnothing\}} \overline{O_p} \qquad \text{(when } knw = \text{gw)}, \qquad (8)$$

$$\text{out}^p(\sigma^p) \subseteq O_p \cap \bigcap_{O \in \mathcal{O} \cap \text{Winnable}^p} O \qquad \text{(when } knw = \text{pg)}. \qquad (9)$$

When $knw = \text{pgw}, \text{pw}$ or pg, since the right-hand sides of (7) and (9) do not require complementation, the description lengths of them are not greater than the sum of the description lengths of $\mathcal{O}$ and O_p. When $knw = \text{gw}$, the right-hand side of (8) is $O_p \cap \overline{O_p} = \varnothing$ if $\varnothing \in \mathcal{O}$, and O_p otherwise, and hence the description length of it is not greater than the description length of O_p. Therefore, in the same way as the cases where $knw = \text{pg}$ or $knw = \text{gw}$ and $\varnothing \notin \mathcal{O}$ in Theorem 3, deciding the existence of a winning $\mathcal{O}$-IS is also solvable in polynomial time for any $knw \in \{\text{pw}, \text{gw}, \text{pg}, \text{pgw}\}$. $\qquad \Box$

Theorem 5. *For a game arena $\mathcal{G}$ and an objective profile $\alpha = (O_p)_{p \in P}$ over Muller objectives, whether there exists an OIE for $\mathcal{G}$ and α is decidable.*

Proof. Condition (2) in Definition 5 is equivalent to the following condition:

$$\forall p \in P. \ \forall \sigma_p \in \Sigma^p. \ \forall O \in \Omega. \ O \in \text{Obj}^{p,O_p}_{\Omega,knw}(\sigma[p \mapsto \sigma_p]) \Rightarrow O \in \text{Obj}^{p,O_p}_{\Omega,knw}(\sigma). \tag{10}$$

First we consider the case where $knw = \text{pgw}$. By the definition of $\text{Obj}^{p,O_p}_{\Omega,\text{pgw}}$, Condition (10) for $knw = \text{pgw}$ is equivalent to the following condition:

$\forall p \in P. \ \forall \sigma_p \in \Sigma^p. \ \forall O \in \Omega.$

if $O \in \text{Winnable}^p$, then $(\text{out}(\sigma[p \mapsto \sigma_p]) \in O \cap O_p \Rightarrow \text{out}(\sigma) \in O \cap O_p)$;

otherwise, $(\text{out}(\sigma[p \mapsto \sigma_p]) \in (O \cap O_p) \cup (\overline{O} \cap \overline{O_p}) \Rightarrow \text{out}(\sigma) \in (O \cap O_p) \cup (\overline{O} \cap \overline{O_p}))$. $\tag{11}$

For $O \in \mathcal{O}$ and $p \in P$, let R^O_p be the objective defined as follows: If $O \in \text{Winnable}^p$, $R^O_p = O \cap O_p$. Otherwise, $R^O_p = (O \cap O_p) \cup (\overline{O} \cap \overline{O_p})$. Let $\alpha_O = (R^O_p)_{p \in P}$ be the objective profile consisting of these objectives. Then, Condition (11) can be written as $\forall O \in \mathcal{O}. \ \text{Nash}(\sigma, \alpha_O)$. Therefore, this theorem holds by Theorem 2.

For the other cases, the implication inside the scope of the three universal quantifiers in Condition (10) is equivalent to the following implications:

when $knw = \mathsf{pw}$

$\mathrm{out}(\boldsymbol{\sigma}[p \mapsto \sigma_p]) \in (O \cap O_p) \cup (\overline{O} \cap \overline{O_p}) \Rightarrow \mathrm{out}(\boldsymbol{\sigma}) \in (O \cap O_p) \cup (\overline{O} \cap \overline{O_p})$,

when $knw = \mathsf{gw}$

if $O \in \mathrm{Winnable}^p$, then $\mathrm{out}(\boldsymbol{\sigma}[p \mapsto \sigma_p]) \in O_p \Rightarrow \mathrm{out}(\boldsymbol{\sigma}) \in O_p$;

if $O = \varnothing$, then $\mathrm{out}(\boldsymbol{\sigma}[p \mapsto \sigma_p]) \in \overline{O_p} \Rightarrow \mathrm{out}(\boldsymbol{\sigma}) \in \overline{O_p}$,

when $knw = \mathsf{pg}$

if $O \in \mathrm{Winnable}^p$, then $\mathrm{out}(\boldsymbol{\sigma}[p \mapsto \sigma_p]) \in O \Rightarrow \mathrm{out}(\boldsymbol{\sigma}) \in O$.

These conditions can be written as the combination of NE in the same way as the case where $knw = \mathsf{pgw}$. Therefore, this theorem also holds for $knw \in \{\mathsf{pw}, \mathsf{gw}, \mathsf{pg}\}$ by Theorem 2. $\qquad\square$

Theorem 6. *For a game arena $\mathcal{G}$ and an objective profile $\boldsymbol{\alpha} = (O_p)_{p \in P}$ over Muller objectives, whether there exists an OINE for $\mathcal{G}$ and $\boldsymbol{\alpha}$ is decidable.*

Proof. By the proof of Theorem 5, an OINE $\boldsymbol{\sigma} \in \Sigma$ must satisfy the condition $\forall O \in \mathcal{O}. \mathrm{Nash}(\boldsymbol{\sigma}, \boldsymbol{\alpha}_O)$. Moreover, $\boldsymbol{\sigma}$ must also satisfy $\mathrm{Nash}(\boldsymbol{\sigma}, \boldsymbol{\alpha})$ because $\boldsymbol{\sigma}$ is a NE. Therefore, $\boldsymbol{\sigma}$ is an $((\boldsymbol{\alpha}_O)_{O \in \mathcal{O}}, \boldsymbol{\alpha})$-NE and thus, this theorem holds by Theorem 2. $\qquad\square$

6   Conclusion

We proposed two new notions $\mathcal{O}$-indistinguishable strategy ($\mathcal{O}$-IS) and objective-indistinguishability equilibrium (OIE). Then, we proved that whether there exists an $\mathcal{O}$-IS and an OIE over Muller objectives are both decidable. To prove this, we defined an $(\boldsymbol{\alpha}_1, \ldots, \boldsymbol{\alpha}_n)$-Nash equilibrium as a strategy profile which is simultaneously a nash equilibrium for all objective profiles $\boldsymbol{\alpha}_1, \ldots, \boldsymbol{\alpha}_n$. We proved that whether there exists an $(\boldsymbol{\alpha}_1, \ldots, \boldsymbol{\alpha}_n)$-Nash equilibrium is decidable in the full version of this paper.

In this paper, we assume that an adversary is not a player but an individual who observes partial information on the game. He cannot directly affect the outcome of the game by choosing next vertices. We can consider another setting where an adversary is also a player. His objective is minimizing the set $\mathrm{Obj}_{\Omega, knw}^{p, O_p}$ of candidate objectives of other players and he takes a strategy for achieving the objective. Considering a framework on this setting, by extending the results shown in this paper, is future work.

References

1. Abadi, M., et al.: Deep learning with differential privacy. In: ACM CCS (2016)

2. Almagor, S., Guendelman, S.: Concurrent games with multiple topologies. arXiv:2207.02596
3. Andrés, M.E., Bordenabe, N.E., Chatzikokolakis, K., Palamidessi, C.: Geo-indistinguishability: differential privacy for location based systems. In: ACM CCS (2013)
4. Bayardo, R.J., Agrawal, R.: Data privacy through optimal k-anonymization. In: ICDE, pp. 217–228 (2005)
5. Berthon, R., Maubert, B., Murano, A., Rubin, S., Vardi, M.Y.: Strategy logic with imperfect information. ACM Trans. Comput. Logic **22**(1), 1–51 (2021)
6. Bloem, R., Chatterjee, K., Jobstmann, B.: Graph games and reactive synthesis. In: Clarke, E., Henzinger, T., Veith, H., Bloem, R. (eds.) Handbook of Model Checking, pp. 921–962. Springer, Cham (2018). https://doi.org/10.1007/978-3-319-10575-8_27
7. Bouyer, P., Markey, N., Vester, S.: Nash equilibria in symmetric graph games with partial observation. Inf. Comput. **254**, 238–258 (2017)
8. Bruyère, V.: Computer aided synthesis: a game-theoretic approach. In: Charlier, É., Leroy, J., Rigo, M. (eds.) DLT 2017. LNCS, vol. 10396, pp. 3–35. Springer, Cham (2017). https://doi.org/10.1007/978-3-319-62809-7_1
9. Byun, J.-W., Kamra, A., Bertino, E., Li, N.: Efficient k-anonymization using clustering techniques. In: Kotagiri, R., Krishna, P.R., Mohania, M., Nantajeewarawat, E. (eds.) DASFAA 2007. LNCS, vol. 4443, pp. 188–200. Springer, Heidelberg (2007). https://doi.org/10.1007/978-3-540-71703-4_18
10. Chatterjee, K., de Alfaro, L., Henzinger, T.A.: The complexity of stochastic Rabin and Streett games. In: Caires, L., Italiano, G.F., Monteiro, L., Palamidessi, C., Yung, M. (eds.) ICALP 2005. LNCS, vol. 3580, pp. 878–890. Springer, Heidelberg (2005). https://doi.org/10.1007/11523468_71
11. Chatterjee, K., Doyen, L.: The complexity of partial-observation parity games. In: Fermüller, C.G., Voronkov, A. (eds.) LPAR 2010. LNCS, vol. 6397, pp. 1–14. Springer, Heidelberg (2010). https://doi.org/10.1007/978-3-642-16242-8_1
12. Chatterjee, K., Doyen, L.: Games with a weak adversary. In: Esparza, J., Fraigniaud, P., Husfeldt, T., Koutsoupias, E. (eds.) ICALP 2014. LNCS, vol. 8573, pp. 110–121. Springer, Heidelberg (2014). https://doi.org/10.1007/978-3-662-43951-7_10
13. Chatterjee, K., Doyen, L., Filiot, E., Raskin, J.-F.: Doomsday equilibria for omega-regular games. Inf. Comput. **254**, 296–315 (2017)
14. Chatterjee, K., Henzinger, T.A., Jurdziński, M.: Games with secure equilibria. Theor. Comput. Sci. **365**, 67–82 (2006)
15. Chatzikokolakis, K., Palamidessi, C., Panangaden, P.: Anonymity protocols as noisy channels. Inf. Comput. **206**(2–4), 378–401 (2008)
16. Clark, D., Hunt, S., Malacaria, P.: A static analysis for quantifying information flow in a simple imperative language. J. Comput. Secur. **15**, 321–371 (2007)
17. Dwork, C.: Differential privacy. In: Bugliesi, M., Preneel, B., Sassone, V., Wegener, I. (eds.) ICALP 2006. LNCS, vol. 4052, pp. 1–12. Springer, Heidelberg (2006). https://doi.org/10.1007/11787006_1
18. Dwork, C.: Differential privacy: a survey of results. In: Agrawal, M., Du, D., Duan, Z., Li, A. (eds.) TAMC 2008. LNCS, vol. 4978, pp. 1–19. Springer, Heidelberg (2008). https://doi.org/10.1007/978-3-540-79228-4_1
19. Dwork, C., McSherry, F., Nissim, K., Smith, A.: Calibrating noise to sensitivity in private data analysis. In: Halevi, S., Rabin, T. (eds.) TCC 2006. LNCS, vol. 3876, pp. 265–284. Springer, Heidelberg (2006). https://doi.org/10.1007/11681878_14

20. Dwork, C., Roth, A.: The algorithmic foundations of differential privacy. Found. Trends Theor. Comput. Sci. **9**, 3–4 (2013)
21. Fisman, D., Kupferman, O., Lustig, Y.: Rational synthesis. In: Esparza, J., Majumdar, R. (eds.) TACAS 2010. LNCS, vol. 6015, pp. 190–204. Springer, Heidelberg (2010). https://doi.org/10.1007/978-3-642-12002-2_16
22. Fung, B.C.M., Wang, K., Chen, R., Yu, P.S.: Privacy-preserving data publishing: a survey of recent developments. ACM Comput. Surv. **42**(4), 14:1–14:53 (2010)
23. Goldreich, O.: Foundations of Cryptography, volume I: Basic Tools. Cambridge University Press, Cambridge (2001)
24. Kupferman, O., Leshkowitz, O.: Synthesis of privacy-preserving systems. In: FSTCS, pp. 42:1–21 (2022)
25. Li, N., Li, T., Venkatasubramanian, S.: t-closeness: privacy beyond k-anonymity and ℓ-diversity. In: ICDE, pp. 106–115 (2007)
26. Machanavajjhala, A., Gehrke, J., Kifer, D.: ℓ-diversity: privacy beyond k-anonymity. In: ICDE, vol. 24 (2006). also in TKDD **1**(1) (2007)
27. Pnueli, A., Rosner, R.: On the synthesis of a reactive module. In: ACM POPL, pp. 179–190 (1989)
28. Samarati, P.: Protecting respondents' identities in microdata release. IEEE Trans. Knowl. Data Eng. **13**(6), 1010–1027 (2001)
29. Shokri, R., Shmatikov, V.: Privacy-preserving deep learning. In: ACM CCS (2015)
30. Shokri, R., Stronati, M., Song, C., Shmatikov, V.: Membership inference attacks against machine learning models. In: IEEE Symposium Security and Privacy (2017)
31. Smith, G.: On the foundations of quantitative information flow. In: de Alfaro, L. (ed.) FoSSaCS 2009. LNCS, vol. 5504, pp. 288–302. Springer, Heidelberg (2009). https://doi.org/10.1007/978-3-642-00596-1_21
32. Sweeney, L.: k-anonymity: a model for protecting privacy. Int. J. Uncertainty Fuzziness Knowl.-Based Syst. **10**(5), 557–570 (2002)
33. Ummels, M.: The complexity of Nash equilibria in infinite multiplayer games. In: Amadio, R. (ed.) FoSSaCS 2008. LNCS, vol. 4962, pp. 20–34. Springer, Heidelberg (2008). https://doi.org/10.1007/978-3-540-78499-9_3
34. Ummels, M., Wojtczak, D.: The complexity of Nash equilibria in stochastic multiplayer games. Logical Methods Comput. Sci. **7**(3) (2011)

Learning Attack Trees by Genetic Algorithms

Florian Dorfhuber[1,2(✉)], Julia Eisentraut[1], and Jan Křetínský[1,2]

[1] Technical University of Munich, Munich, Germany
florian.dorfhuber@in.tum.de, julia.eisentraut@posteo.de,
xkretins@fi.muni.cz
[2] Masaryk University Brno, Brno, Czech Republic

Abstract. Attack trees are a graphical formalism for security assessment. They are particularly valued for their explainability and high accessibility without security or formal methods expertise. They can be used, for instance, to quantify the global insecurity of a system arising from the unreliability of its parts, graphically explain security bottlenecks, or identify additional vulnerabilities through their systematic decomposition. However, in most cases, the main hindrance in the practical deployment is the need for a domain expert to construct the tree manually or using further models. This paper demonstrates how to learn attack trees from logs, i.e., sets of traces, typically stored abundantly in many application domains. To this end, we design a genetic algorithm and apply it to classes of trees with different expressive power. Our experiments on real data show that comparably simple yet highly accurate trees can be learned efficiently, even from small data sets.

1 Introduction

The security of real-world applications depends on various factors. Both physical aspects and the IT infrastructure play a crucial role. Additionally, all humans who interact with the system need to use it securely. Consequently, rigorous threat modeling should provide insights and formal arguments to system designers and security *experts* as well as allow for easy communication of the findings to *everyday users* and all stakeholders without computer-science background. *Attack trees* [36] and their extensions [14, 18, 24, 25] are valued for combining both aspects and, as a result, have seen an increasing number of applications recently [9, 22, 34, 35]. In particular, to identify vulnerabilities earlier, modeling methodologies [38] often include attack trees as recommended, e.g., by *OWASP CISO AppSec Guide*[1], or by NATO's *Improving Common Security Risk Analysis* report [29].

Automated generation of attack trees has been recognized as the **major gap** between the needs of practitioners and the current state-of-the-art tools [10] since manual construction is tedious and error-prone. In recent years, some approaches to overcome this issue have been provided. However, none of them

---

[1] https://www.owasp.org/index.php/CISO_AppSec_Guide:_Criteria_for_Managing_Application_Security_Risks.

© The Author(s), under exclusive license to Springer Nature Switzerland AG 2023
E. Ábrahám et al. (Eds.): ICTAC 2023, LNCS 14446, pp. 55–73, 2023.
https://doi.org/10.1007/978-3-031-47963-2_5

are automated, in particular, due to relying on (i) another system model to be given [5,10,17,31,32,39] or (ii) a library of models or refinement rules [5,19,31–33], which defers the workload rather than reduces it. All these approaches have in common that they construct an attack tree representing exactly the attacks given on input, not inferring other likely attacks but relying on the completeness of their description.

In contrast, in this work, for the first time, we *learn* an attack tree from a set of *sequential descriptions (traces)*, regarding the attack tree as a classifier of traces into successful and unsuccessful attacks. This has two advantages. Firstly, traces can be obtained not only by running other existing system models or by expert knowledge but also simply from *logs* of system behavior and attacks, which are often abundantly collected in many application domains. Moreover, these heterogeneous sources can also be combined, another valuable consequence of our weak assumption. Secondly, we only require these traces to be labeled as successful or unsuccessful attacks, but they *do not need to be consistent or complete*. In real-world systems, this liberty is an essential property since (hopefully) not every possible attack on the system has already been recorded, third-party software might not allow inspecting all necessary details or experts might disagree on possible attacks.

As the basis for our learning approach, we use *genetic algorithms*, randomized optimization algorithms inspired by the process of natural selection. Our algorithm maintains a set of attack tree models and optimizes them over a fixed number of *generations*. In each generation, models are altered (*mutation*) or combined (*crossover*) into new models, using simple editing operations on trees. Both our mutations and our crossovers only modify the structure of the attack tree (e.g., exchanging subtrees containing the same basic events or switching the position of basic events) but do not need any domain knowledge. Only the fittest models among the new ones (w.r.t. a *fitness function*) are transferred to the next generation. As the fitness function, we choose a weighted sum of the *sensitivity* and the *specificity* of the prediction quality of our attack tree models.

To evaluate our approach, we use both synthetic and real data. To measure the performance, we create sets of labeled traces from the attack trees and learn trees from those traces. We provide experimental evidence of the following claims, arguing for the usability of this first automatic approach, and observations giving insights into the nature of the problem and the data:

- Sanity check: Our approach can learn models perfectly predicting attacks if all successful attacks are given.
- Checking for overfitting: We run k-fold cross-validation to show that overfitting is a minor problem for the algorithm.
- For comparison (given that there are no automatic competitors), we also implement *logistic regression* to solve the task because it is known to perform well on binary classification tasks; however, logistic regression does not provide any graphical model, which is our main aim. Regarding *accuracy*, our genetic algorithms for attack trees are on par with logistic regression, and, in contrast to the latter, our algorithm provides a **simple graphical model**.

- The learned trees are essentially as simple as the original trees used to generate the traces. In particular, for attack trees, the learned ones are of the same size. Note that this small size is crucial to ensure the *explainability* of the automatically constructed model.
- We show that the number of generations is the most relevant hyper-parameter regarding fitness.
- Interestingly, for our algorithm to learn accurate models, even a few traces of successful attacks are sufficient.

In summary, the approach is the first to generate attack trees automatically. The trees are very accurate, given our inputs are only sampled data. Moreover, surprisingly and fortunately, it comes at **no extra cost for the graphicality** compared to classification by logistic regression, where no graphical model is produced. (An explanation of why decision trees are not suited for the task is discussed in Subsect. 2.2).

Our contribution can be summarized as follows:

- We provide a genetic algorithm to learn attack trees and their extensions from labeled sets of traces, the **first to automatically generate these graphical models**. For comparison, we also implement logistic regression.
- In a series of detailed experiments, we show the feasibility of our approach, also on real benchmarks from the military domain.
- We provide an implementation and visualization of all algorithms in a tool that links to standard verification tools for attack trees. The output models can be directly analyzed using tools such as ADTool [11] or displayed using Graphviz[2]. This unleashes the power of the verification tools to attack tree users, eliminating the manual step of model construction.

Organization. We present related work in Subsect. 1.1. In Sect. 2, we recall the most important features of genetic algorithms and attack trees. We show how to define mutations and crossovers to learn attack trees in Sect. 3 and evaluate our algorithms in Sect. 4. Furthermore, we provide a real-world demonstration on the KDD Cup 1999 dataset in Sect. 4.7. In Sect. 5, we conclude the paper and present several ideas for future work.

1.1 Related Work

This section briefly presents the most recent literature on attack tree synthesis and the use of genetic algorithms in attack model generation and security in general. A recent overview on the *analysis of attack trees using formal methods* can be found in [40]. We refer the interested reader to [23] for a *broad overview on different extensions of attack trees*. A recent survey on using *genetic algorithm for multi-label classification* can be found in [12].

---

[2] https://graphviz.org/.

Genetic Algorithms in Attack Model Generation and Security. Genetic algorithms have seen some applications in security. To the best of our knowledge, there is no approach to attack tree synthesis based on genetic algorithms. In this section, we present the applications which are closest to our application. In [26], the authors add an attacker profile (which can be seen as a set of constraints) to the attack tree analysis. An attack is only successful in its setting if it satisfies all constraints of the attacker profile. The authors use a genetic algorithm to simplify the search for attacks satisfying the attacker profile, but a system designer constructs the attack tree itself. Similarly, genetic algorithms have been used in [13] to find a strategy to reduce the system vulnerability with as little cost as possible. Also, [21] uses genetic algorithms to approximate the maximum outcome for the attacker on a given attack tree. On attack graphs [37], genetic algorithms have been used to find minimum cut sets [2]. Another more prominent application of genetic algorithms in security is the generation of intrusion detection systems [28,30]. While these approaches often also take a set of sequential behavior descriptions as inputs, learning an understandable model plays a very minor role.

Linard et al. [27] propose a genetic algorithm to generate fault trees. It also uses data generated by a system with labels for system failure. This approach performed well in a benchmark with up to 24 nodes. Their data sets use between 9000 and 230k data points. Recently, [20] expanded the idea to a multi-objective approach. Compared to these publications, our algorithm needs less data with a few successful attacks to perform the task. Also, the KDD example in Sect. 4.7 includes more than twice the number of basic events in the largest model used in their experiments or a case study [6].

Generation of Attack Trees. We present the last decade of research on attack tree synthesis.

In [15], Hong et al. present an approach to automatically construct attack trees from a set of sequential descriptions of attacks. In the first step, an exhaustive model as disjunction over all given traces is built. Consecutively, the model is simplified by collapsing similar nodes without changing the logical meaning. In contrast to [15], we use both successful and unsuccessful attacks as inputs, which prevents our approach from overfitting to a certain extent. Hence, their approach needs all successful attacks to build a complete model, while our algorithm is likely to predict future attacks not explicitly given. In [39], Vigo et al. provide a generation method to synthesize attack trees from processes specified in value-passing quality calculus (a derivation of π-calculus). The authors define an attack as a set of channels an attacker needs to know to reach a certain location in the system. The attack specifications and the processes are then translated to propositional logic formulae interpreted as attack trees.

In [31,32], Pinchinat et al. present an approach to sequential attack tree synthesis from a library, a formal description of the system and an attack graph. While the attack graph is automatically constructed from model checking, the formal description consisting of a set of actions assigned to different abstraction levels and a set of refinement rules of higher-level actions into combinations of lower-level actions need to be specified by the system designer. Although reusing libraries is possible, it is necessary to specify them manually at some point. This approach does not support the operator AND.

The synthesis approach presented in [17] by Ivanova et al. also transforms a system model into an attack tree. The method requires a graph-based model annotated with policies as input. We could not find a publicly available implementation. In [10], Gadyatskaya et al. present an approach to sequential attack tree synthesis that requires a specification of the expected behavior (called semantics) and a refinement specification as input[3]. Again, this approach does not feature the operator AND. Both the semantics (in the form of series-parallel graphs) and the refinement specifications are not automatically constructed in [10].

The approach presented in [19] by Jhawar et al. requires an expert to interact with the overall construction process of an attack tree to such an extent that it cannot be considered an automated generation method in comparison to the other approaches presented in this section. An attack tree, at least rudimentarily describing attacks on a given system and annotations to the nodes in the form of preconditions and postconditions need to be given to the approach. Using the annotations, the attack tree can then be automatically refined using a given library of annotated attack trees.

In [5], Bryans et al. give a synthesis approach for sequential attack trees from a network model consisting of nodes and connectivity information and a library of attack tree templates. Both the network model and the library are constructed manually. In [33], Pinchinat et al. show that the complexity of the synthesis problem for sequential attack trees equipped with trace semantics is NP-complete. More specifically, their attack synthesis problem takes a trace and a library (basically a set of context-free grammar rules) as input and decides whether a sequential attack tree exists such that the given trace complies with the semantics (and provides the attack tree, too). An implementation is provided.

With one exception, all approaches rely on a library of already built models or another preexisting formal model of the system. The one approach uses all possible successful attacks, which are not commonly available in secure systems. We present a first approach to use a comparatively small amount of mostly non-attack data without needing preexisting system knowledge.

2 Background

2.1 Attack Trees

Attack-defense trees (for example, see Fig. 1) are labeled trees that allow refining major attack goals into smaller steps until no refinement is possible anymore. The atomic steps are called *basic events*. Each inner node of the tree represents a *composed event*. The operator attached to an inner node determines how its children need to succeed for the composed event to succeed as well.

In Fig. 1, we present an attack tree that models an attack on an IoT device from [3]. The attack tree represents the following attacks: The root represents

---

[3] We interpret the refinement specification as library similar to [33].

the goal of getting access to the IoT device and exploiting it. This goal is refined using the operator SAND, which requires all its inputs (in this case another composed event labeled with AND and the two basic events *run malicious script* and *exploit software vulnerability in IoT device*) to succeed in the given order (here, events need to succeed from left to right). The first input refines the intermediate goal *get access to IoT device* again into smaller steps. AND and OR here are the standard logical operations, i.e., AND represents a conjunctive and OR a disjunctive refinement. Thus, the leftmost subtree of the root specifies that the basic event *get credentials* needs to succeed for this subtree to succeed. Additionally, either the basic events *MAC address spoofing* and *finding a LAN access port* or the basic events *breaking WPA keys* and *finding WLAN access to the IoT device* need to succeed.

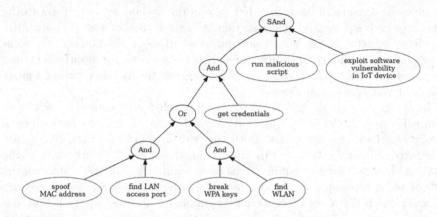

Fig. 1. A sequential attack tree from [3] representing an attacked IoT device.

We define the set of all operators $O = \{AND, OR, NOT\}$ and use Definition 1 of [14] restricted to those operations. Intuitively, the operators are the standard logic operations. An *attack-defense tree* is a tuple $ADT = (V, E, t)$, where (V, E) form a tree with all leaves being *basic events* (BE) and all inner nodes being *gates*. The gates are assigned their operator by the *type function* t.

A *trace* is a finite (ordered) sequence of basic events such that every basic event occurs at most once. The signature of a node v of an attack-defense tree ADT is the set of basic events that occur in the subtree rooted in v.

The level of detail introduced in this section is sufficient for the further development of this paper.

2.2 Attack Trees vs Decision Trees

We use attack trees and their extensions over decision trees, as decision trees are designed to generate high information gain and are thus likely to ignore very rare events. This is a problem especially concerning imbalanced data sets,

Table 1. The used hyperparameter in the algorithm with the abbreviations used in the paper.

Abbreviation	Description
ϵ	Number of new random models per generation
PSize	The size of the population preserved for the next generation
w_1	Weight for sensitivity in the fitness function
mutr	The ratio of mutations over crossovers
Act	Number of actions (e.g., mutations) per model in a generation
Gen	Number of generations until the algorithm terminates
trainr	Training rate. The portion of all traces in the training set

which we expect to deal with. It may be for instance solvable with specific sampling methods, but this step requires more work and is dependent on the context [8]. In addition, the graphical representation of decision trees might not be helpful for system designers to gain insights into the composition of successful and unsuccessful attacks since leaves are annotated by the result of the attack rather than the basic attack steps. Attack-defense trees allow synthesis based on sub-goals, naturally starting with the simplest action. Further, while decision trees can include information on time sequences, additional decision nodes are required for every relevant order of events. This results in a potential blowup of the model and a reduction in readability. Finally, attack-tree analysis can easily use information on already happened events to update the likelihood of successful attacks based on prior events. Thus, our models are valuable for the real-time surveillance of systems.

3 Genetic Algorithm for Learning *ADT*

This section presents our approach to learning attack trees from traces using genetic algorithms. In our genetic algorithm, the population of candidate solutions consists of attack-defense trees. Each attack-defense tree consists of composed and basic events, and the way they are linked are the chromosomes of the candidate attack-defense trees. In this section, we first define the fitness function to evaluate the fitness of every individual in the population. Then, we define mutation and crossovers. Note that the algorithm starts with completely random models and introduces a number ϵ of new random models to each generation to reduce the risk of premature convergence. An overview of all hyperparameters is listed in Table 1.

3.1 Fitness Function

To evaluate the fitness, we check how many log traces our attack-defense trees can correctly separate into successful or unsuccessful attacks. For a finite set $\mathcal{X}$, we denote its size by $\|\mathcal{X}\|$. To this end, let $\mathsf{ADT} = (\mathsf{V}, \mathsf{E}, \mathsf{t})$ be an attack-defense tree, Tr be a set of traces and $\mathsf{c} \colon \mathsf{Tr} \to \{\mathsf{tt}, \mathsf{ff}\}$ be a labeling function, which assigns each trace its output value and $\mathsf{ADT}(\mathsf{tr})$ computes the label on a given ADT, where tt represents a successful attack and ff an unsuccessful attack. A straightforward definition of the fitness function using our labeled data set is the prediction accuracy of the attack-defense tree.

However, we assume that successful traces are less common than unsuccessful traces since, in a real-world application, one hopefully observes the system more often in its normal behavior than after a successful attack. Using the prediction accuracy as a fitness function in such a setting may result in an algorithm always returning false having a good accuracy. Therefore, we use a multi-objective approach including the *sensitivity* Sens and the *specificity* Spec of the prediction as follows:

$$\mathsf{Sens}(\mathsf{ADT}) = \frac{\#\mathsf{Tr}\text{ correctly labeled as }\mathsf{tt}}{\#\mathsf{Tr}\text{ in test set labeled as }\mathsf{tt}} = \frac{\|\{\mathsf{tr} \in \mathsf{Tr} \mid \mathsf{ADT}(\mathsf{tr}) = \mathsf{tt} \wedge \mathsf{c}(\mathsf{tr}) = \mathsf{tt}\}\|}{\|\{\mathsf{tr} \in \mathsf{Tr} \mid \mathsf{c}(\mathsf{tr}) = \mathsf{tt}\}\|}$$

$$\mathsf{Spec}(\mathsf{ADT}) = \frac{\#\mathsf{Tr}\text{ correctly labeled as }\mathsf{ff}}{\#\mathsf{Tr}\text{ in test set labeled as }\mathsf{ff}} = \frac{\|\{\mathsf{tr} \in \mathsf{Tr} \mid \mathsf{ADT}(\mathsf{tr}) = \mathsf{ff} \wedge \mathsf{c}(\mathsf{tr}) = \mathsf{ff}\}\|}{\|\{\mathsf{tr} \in \mathsf{Tr} \mid \mathsf{c}(\mathsf{tr}) = \mathsf{ff}\}\|}$$

Let $\mathsf{w}_1, \mathsf{w}_2$ be weights such that $0 \le \mathsf{w}_1, \mathsf{w}_2 \le 1; \mathsf{w}_1 + \mathsf{w}_2 = 1$. Then, we define the fitness function F for an attack-defense tree ADT as[4]

$$\mathsf{F}(\mathsf{ADT}) = \mathsf{w}_1 \cdot \mathsf{Sens}(\mathsf{ADT}) + \mathsf{w}_2 \cdot \mathsf{Spec}(\mathsf{ADT}).$$

This definition ensures F being smooth for

$$\|\{\mathsf{tr} \in \mathsf{Tr} \mid \mathsf{c}(\mathsf{tr}) = \mathsf{ff}\}\|, \|\{\mathsf{tr} \in \mathsf{Tr} \mid \mathsf{c}(\mathsf{tr}) = \mathsf{tt}\}\| \ge 1$$

Additionally, we define the *positive predictive value* PPV as the probability that for a trace tr and a prediction $\mathsf{ADT}(\mathsf{tr}) = \mathsf{tt}$ we actually have $\mathsf{c}(\mathsf{tr}) = \mathsf{tt}$.

$$\mathsf{PPV}(\mathsf{ADT}) = \frac{\|\{\mathsf{tr} \in \mathsf{Tr} \mid \mathsf{ADT}(\mathsf{tr}) = \mathsf{tt} = \mathsf{c}(\mathsf{tr})\}\|}{\|\{\mathsf{tr} \in \mathsf{Tr} \mid \mathsf{ADT}(\mathsf{tr}) = \mathsf{tt} = \mathsf{c}(\mathsf{tr}) \vee \mathsf{ADT}(\mathsf{tr}) = \mathsf{tt} \ne \mathsf{c}(\mathsf{tr})\}\|}.$$

If we report the fitness, the specificity, or the sensitivity, we use the result of the test set for each model to report the *mean* μ $\pm$ *standard deviation* σ according to their canonical definition for a set of models.

3.2   Mutations and Crossovers for Attack Trees

While mutations change labels of composed or basic events of the attack tree, crossovers change the position of subtrees within the tree. In this section, we restrict ourselves to attack trees, i.e., all inner nodes are either labeled with AND or OR. Our input data consists of a set of traces Tr, and their corresponding value is $\mathsf{c} \colon \mathsf{Tr} \to \{\mathsf{tt}, \mathsf{ff}\}$. We consider the following expectable *mutations*:

---

[4] There is no optimal combination for the weights. Hence, we explore different weights and how they influence the overall fitness in Sect. 4.

1. SWITCH to switch the position of any two basic events
2. CHANGE the label of an inner node v from AND to OR or vice versa

While mutations can be applied at every node of an attack tree, we have to ensure that *crossovers* do not violate the model's integrity, i.e., after a crossover, the model must still include every basic event exactly once. Thus, we only use swapping of subtrees containing the same basic events as crossover operations. Therefore, the amount of possible crossovers is smaller than that of mutations. This can result in no possible crossover between two models (except the root), especially in small models. In this case, the operation will be skipped.

3.3   Extension to Attack-Defense Trees

In contrast to many attack-defense tree models [24], we do not assign a player to inner nodes. Hence, we also cannot and do not assign a different semantics to these inner nodes based on the player controlling it.

To include defense actions in our learning approach, we only need to split the set of basic events BE into two disjoint sets (a set of basic events BE_A controlled by the attacker and a set of basic events BE_D controlled by the defender such that $BE = BE_A \cup BE_D$). Intuitively speaking, the borders of nodes in BE_D are colored green, while elements in BE_A have a red border. After learning the tree using our approach, we assign each basic event its respective player. The learning algorithm does not need to be changed; thus, the fitness does not change. Hence, we only perform experiments on attack trees.

4   Experiments

This section evaluates our approach experimentally. Firstly, we demonstrate that our algorithm is capable of synthesizing attack trees classifying all traces correctly for data sets containing all possible traces over a fixed set of basic events. Secondly, we run k-fold cross-validation to show that the selection of traces for the test and training sets does have a minor influence on the outcome. Thirdly, we compare our approach to logistic regression which allows us to assess the adequacy of our genetic algorithm in comparison to other learning approaches. Fourthly, we explore how to choose the weight parameters for specificity and sensitivity and how many successful traces are necessary to reach a high accuracy. Fifthly, we analyze different hyperparameter constellations to show their relevance to the outcome. Finally, we use the algorithm on the real KDD-Cup 1999 data set to demonstrate, that it could already be deployed for real-world systems. All experiments are executed on a machine with Intel ®Core ^{TM}i7 CPU and 15 GiB RAM running a VM image with 4 GiB RAM and one Core.[5] If not stated otherwise, the algorithm can use the operators AND, OR and NOT.

---

[5] The artifact can be found at https://doi.org/10.5281/zenodo.8352279.

4.1 Generating Input Datasets

Generating Data. Let $\mathsf{ADT} = (\mathsf{V}, \mathsf{E}, \mathsf{t})$ be an attack-defense tree over the set of basic events BE. We generate traces of basic events randomly (without using any information of the structure of the tree) and then, compute the valuation of the trace w.r.t. the attack-defense tree $\mathsf{ADT}(\mathsf{tr})$ to obtain the label function $\mathsf{c}: \mathsf{Tr} \rightarrow \{\mathsf{tt}, \mathsf{ff}\}$. A trace ends if all be were attempted or if the root of the tree evaluates to tt.

Each basic event can only occur once in a trace. Hence, for an *ADT* with n basic events there are $\frac{n!}{(n-m)!}$ traces of length m. So, there is a total of $\sum_{m=1}^{n} \frac{n!}{(n-m)!}$ traces[6].

Since the number of possible traces grows rapidly and in a real-world system, we may also only have a limited amount of data available, we restrict ourselves to a fixed number of traces in each experiment.

Splitting Data. Given a set of traces Tr and a corresponding labeling function c the dataset is split into a training and a test set. Our algorithm only uses the training set to learn an attack tree. The test set is used for the final evaluation of the fitness of the learned model. The sets are split with the *training rate* trainr preserving the ratio between tt and ff labeled traces.

4.2 Sanity Check: Perfect Fitting for Small Models

First, we demonstrate that our algorithm is potentially able to lead to an optimal outcome w.r.t. the given fitness function F_c (see Subsect. 3.1).

Setup. We use 80 randomly generated models with nine nodes and five basic events each. All inner nodes are labeled with either AND or OR (i.e. we restrict ourselves to attack trees here). We use all existing traces for these models as input for both training and testing. While this setup results in overfitting the dataset, this is acceptable in this situation since we know there are no further traces (not contained in the dataset). We use the following configuration for the hyperparameters: number of generations $\mathsf{Gen} = 120$, population size $\mathsf{PSize} = 140$, mutation rate $\mathsf{mutr} = 0.8$, and number of actions $\mathsf{Act} = 1$. Act is set to 1 to get an intuition on how many actions on the models are needed for the result.

Results. All models were learned with 100 % accuracy in the given generations limit. The mean time until termination was 2.5 s.

Observation 1. *Small models can be learned to 100% accuracy if all existing traces are given as input.*

The high number of iterations needed to achieve the goal suggests that the genetic algorithm is able to learn the corresponding models, but may not be the best choice to learn accurate attack-defense trees if the dataset is small enough

---

[6] We already have about one million distinct traces with $n = 9$. However, this is only an upper bound since we stop the traces as soon as the root turns tt.

to apply exact solutions. This is due to the unsystematic search. For instance, a mutation can simply undo the previous mutation, which will keep the better model unchanged for the next generation. Thus, we are not guaranteed to make progress during a generation.

4.3   Crossvalidation: No Overfitting of Models

Setup. To further validate the algorithm, we perform k-fold crossvalidation with $k = 10$, i.e. training the model on nine of ten random subsets and validating it on the remaining one. To check if the algorithm is over fitting the data, we used 35 attack trees and generated a training set of 800 traces on each. The experiment used the following hyperparameters: number of generations Gen $= 60$, population size PSize $= 40$, mutation rate mutr $= 0.8$, number of actions Act $= 3$.

Results. The cross validation showed only minor deviations between the folds and the performance on the evaluation set, i.e. the left out fold. Overall the mean of the standard deviation in Fitness over all datasets was 0.003 ± 0.002.

Observation 2. *Our genetic algorithm is, in this setting, robust to overfitting due to sampling.*

4.4   Comparison to Logistic Regression

Attack trees can be seen as *Boolean functions*. *Logistic Regression* is a viable competitor for learning Boolean functions since it is optimized to predict binary endpoints from labeled data sets [16].

Setup. To be able to compare both approaches, we chose datasets consisting of 1000 traces in a way that about $50 \pm 1\%$ of the traces are labeled with tt. This was done to have a balanced relation in accuracy. Having 96% ff labeled traces as in Subsect. 4.5 in these experiments leads to classifiers always returning false having an accuracy of 96%, which does not provide any information on attacks. Due to the high frequency of attacks, this setup is unlikely in a real-world scenario. We use setups with fewer attacks in the following sections.

Creating equally sized sets of tt and ff labeled traces implies the necessity to choose an attack tree with a mix of both operators since more nodes labeled with AND reduce the quantity of possible tt labeled traces and nodes labeled with OR cause the opposite. Thus, for these experiments, we selected only attack trees of which the algorithm was able to produce enough traces for both labels.

The fitness function for our genetic algorithm was set to the overall accuracy (i.e. F_c in Subsect. 3.1). We learned the logistic LR using R version 3.6.3 and indicator variables for every basic event showing if the event is present in a trace. In attack trees, the order of basic events does not matter. Hence, we only allowed traces that could not be reordered in each other (i.e. no permutations). Overall, we used 35 attack trees ranging from 31 to 53 nodes (and 16 to 26 basic events). We used the following configuration for the hyperparameters: number of generations Gen $= 60$, population size PSize $= 40$, mutation rate mutr $= 0.8$, number of actions Act $= 3$ and training rate trainr $= 0.8$.

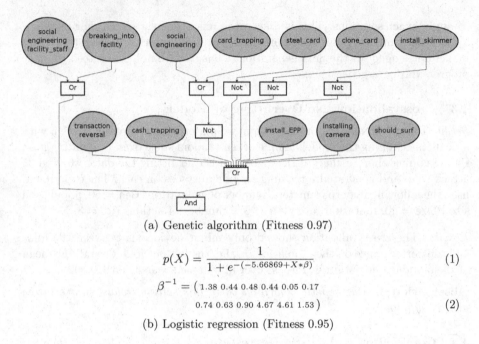

(a) Genetic algorithm (Fitness 0.97)

$$p(X) = \frac{1}{1 + e^{-(-5.66869 + X*\beta)}} \tag{1}$$

$$\beta^{-1} = (\ 1.38\ 0.44\ 0.48\ 0.44\ 0.05\ 0.17$$
$$0.74\ 0.63\ 0.90\ 4.67\ 4.61\ 1.53\ ) \tag{2}$$

(b) Logistic regression (Fitness 0.95)

Fig. 2. The resulting models for the tree from [7]. The model in (a) was simplified manually, by collapsing subsequent operators of the same kind into one. The equation in (b) displays the corresponding logistic regression model.

Results. The accuracy is measured according to the fitness function F_c (see Subsect. 3.1) for every single of the 35 models on the test set containing 200 traces and after training on 800 traces each.

Observation 3. *Our genetic algorithm approach performs comparable to logistic regression with a mean difference of only 0.04 (standard deviation 0.01) but, in contrast, results in a graphical, interpretable model.*

In more detail, our approach yielded a mean accuracy of 0.82 (with a standard deviation 0.08), and the logistic regression produced 0.86±0.08 (mean±standard deviation). We show a real-world example in Fig. 2. The slight inferiority of our algorithm is due to logistic regression being optimized for this specific setting. However, it is only a suitable competitor in this specific setting. An expansion to non-binary labels, e.g. undecided for an unknown system status, would make a comparison with multi-label classification algorithms necessary. Also, results will differ in specific fields or data settings. Additionally, introducing time-dependent features results in a massive increase in independent variables, which results in a higher standard error and unstable results [16]. Furthermore, logistic regression obviously does not directly create an attack tree, which is one main goal of this paper. Decision trees as an alternative have been discussed in Subsect. 2.2.

4.5 Learning Attack Trees

Here we analyze the performance of the genetic algorithm for attack trees (see Subsect. 3.2).

Setup. We use 35 datasets as described in Subsect. 4.4 using subsets with different ratios of traces labeled as unsuccessful to successful in our experiments. Our goal is to estimate which proportion of traces labeled tt is needed to generate fit models in real-world systems. More specifically, we create datasets with 1000 traces where 5, 10, 20, 40, 80, 160, 320, or 500 of the 1000 overall traces are labeled tt. For each dataset, we experiment with weight w_1 from 0.1 to 0.9 in steps of size 0.1 (and set $w_2 = 1 - w_1$ accordingly). The other parameters are equal to the last experiment, i.e. number of generations Gen = 60, population size PSize = 40, mutation rate mutr = 0.8, number of actions Act = 3 and training rate trainr = 0.8.

Results. We report the sensitivity and specificity of all final models on the test set in a 3D-Plot[7]. Parts of the results are listed in Fig. 3.

Observation 4. *Only about 4% of all traces in the dataset need to be successful attacks to learn fit functions with a mean sensitivity of up to 95%, or specificity of up to 99%.*

The mean of sensitivity and specificity show a positive correlation to their weights with *Pearson's correlation coefficient* $r_{Pearson} = 0.778$ ($p :< 0.001$) and $r_{Pearson} = 0.887$ ($p :< 0.001$) for sensitivity and specificity, respectively. Additionally, there is no significant correlation between sensitivity and the number of tt traces with $r_{Pearson} = 0.317$ ($p : 0.007$), the same seems to be true for specificity $r_{Pearson} = -0.200$ ($p : 0.092$). These results suggest that the impact of choosing the weight is bigger than of choosing the number of successful attack traces.

This seems promising for real-world scenarios since there may only be small amount of successful attacks but an abundant amount of unsuccessful or incomplete ones to learn attack trees from. In terms of runtime, it took about 10–12 minutes for each execution of the algorithm on all models. The average execution time for a single prompt was about 20–30 s. More information on runtimes can be found at Subsect. 4.6.

Our results show that the weights of the sensitivity and the specificity need to be chosen appropriately within the application scenario. A high-risk security infrastructure might rely on a high sensitivity to spot all ongoing attacks. On the other hand, a low specificity may lead to many false positives, especially, if we have only a small number of attack traces. For instance, with 20 attack traces (traces labeled tt), we have a sensitivity of 82.7% and specificity of 67.2% at $w_1 = 0.7$. Given this information, that means that there were 321 false positives per 1000 traces and a positive predictive value PPV of about 4.9%. Hence, 95.1%

---

[7] https://www.model.in.tum.de/~kraemerj/upload/3dplots/.

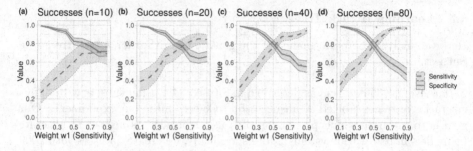

Fig. 3. Sensitivity and specificity are depicted as mean with 95% confidence interval depending on the weight w_1 for sensitivity in the fitness function. n specifies the number of successful attacks among the 1000 traces in the dataset.

of all predictions on our full dataset are false alarms. Favoring specificity with $w_1 = 0.3$ would result in a PPV of about 18.6%.

Therefore, we cannot give a general recommendation regarding the weight w_1, as it is highly dependent on the security needs and possible damages.

4.6   Hyperparameter Optimization

The previous sections were dedicated to optimizing the parameters of the weight w and the number of attack traces n. In this section, we optimize the parameters inherent to genetic algorithms: the number of generations Gen, the population size PSize, the mutation rate mutr and the number of actions Act.

Setup. We learn attack trees from the 35 datasets from Subsect. 4.5 on a fixed set of hyperparameters only changing one parameter at once. Each parameter was set to multiple values while both sensitivity and specificity were recorded as dependent variables. The base setting was $n = 80$, $w_1 = 0.5$, Gen = 60, PSize = 40, mutr = 0.8, Act = 3 and trainr = 0.8.

For line-searching Gen We used metadata provided by the previous experiment Subsect. 4.5. It contains the fitness of each model after each generation. Thus, we used 60 data points each. For search the PSize was altered in steps of 10 between 10 and 100. The mutr was between 0.1 and 0.9 and increased in steps of 0.1. Lastly, Act was checked in a range from 1 up to 10 increasing in steps of 1.

We created a mixed linear model as described in [4]. This model is needed as performance varies depending on the dataset and therefore, the different settings cannot be treated as independent.

Results. Estimates for the mixed linear model after altering one parameter of the standard setup are shown in Table 2. All given runtime Data below is with regard to a full run over all 35 models. Except for the number of generations Gen (and for specificity Spec on the number of actions Act), none of the results is statistically significant, leading to:

Table 2. Slopes in the mixed linear model after altering one parameter of the standard setup. Except for the estimates for the number of generations Gen and for the specificity Spec on the number of actions Act, none of the results is statistically significant suggesting a low impact on algorithm performance.

	Estimate for Sens	Estimate for Spec
# Generations	$0.002\ (t : < 0.001)$	$< 0.001\ (t : < 0.001)$
Population Size	$< 0.001\ (t : 0.882)$	$< 0.001\ (t : 0.354)$
Mutation Rate	$< 0.001\ (t : 0.717)$	$0.014\ (t : 0.560)$
# Actions	$0.004\ (t : 0.268)$	$< 0.001\ (t : 0.955)$

Observation 5. *Choosing a sufficiently high number of generations suffices for a good learning result in our experiments. The other hyperparameters only have a minor impact on the fitness of the learned models.*

4.7   Real-World Demonstration: KDD Cup 1999 Dataset

Finally, we validate our algorithm on the *KDD Cup 1999 Dataset*[8] generated in a simulated military network environment. In this dataset, every entry denotes a summary of one single connection to a server, which is either an intrusion or a normal connection. The dataset consists of 4.9 and 0.3 million entries in the training and test set, respectively. Our goal is to learn an attack-defense tree to distinguish intrusions from normal connections. Note in contrast to previous experiments, no attack tree is used to generate the traces.

Setup. We interpret every column as a single event. However, some columns in the dataset are continuous. Thus, we split the values at a given *quantile* q and see every value equal or greater than it as an attempted event of this column. Additionally, our algorithm currently only supports attack-defense trees using a single root node. Hence, we change the different attack labels e.g. *guess_passwd* to one single label. The label is tt if any of the attack labels is tt otherwise we interpret the trace as an unsuccessful attack. We use the hyperparameters Gen = 100, PSize = 60, mutr = 0.8, Act = 3. Weight w_1 and quantile q are changed by 0.1 between 0.1 and 0.9 in every run. We then record the best resulting model and the corresponding Sens and Spec.

Results. We present the results for the best models in Fig. 4. Please note that the fallout is simply $1 - \text{Spec}$. The point with the lowest Euclidean distance to the optimum, i.e. $(0, 1)$, is the combination of $w_1 = 0.9$ and $q = 0.4$ with Sens = 0.968 and Spec = 0.994 on the test set. Interestingly, the high values of weight w_1 produced the best result, although only 19.9% of the entries are normal. We suspect this may be due to the higher stability of the specificity Spec reported

---

[8] https://kdd.ics.uci.edu/databases/kddcup99/kddcup99.html.

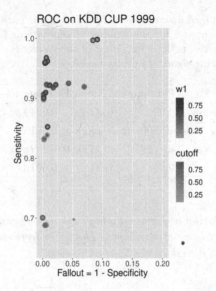

Fig. 4. ROC-Curve of setups with w_1 and q ranging between 0.1 and 0.9. 14 points with Spec < 0.2 or Sens < 0.5 were removed for better readability. The best point uses $w_1 = 0.9$ and q $= 0.4$ resulting in Sens $= 0.968$ and Spec $= 0.994$.

in the earlier experiments. While the Performance of our model is similar to the one reported by [1] using a decision-tree-based approach, our setup uses a less complex set of labels than their approach does.

5 Conclusion and Future Work

We have presented the first algorithm to learn attack trees from sets of traces labeled as successful or unsuccessful attacks. To this end, we have used genetic algorithms. We consider this a step forward to *bridging the gap* between real-world applications and their respective analysis since such traces are often collected anyway in many application domains in the form of logs. Consequently, the attack trees can be created automatically, eliminating the burden of manual involvement of domain experts in other approaches. Our experiments have shown that (i) the accuracy of our graphical models is comparable to (non-graphical) logistic regression while (ii) producing **small and straightforward graphical models**, and (iii) that only a **small amount of attack traces** among all traces are necessary to learn accurate models. Additionally, the algorithm was able to classify data from the preexisting KDD CUP 1999 data set with a performance that is comparable with existing models but in contrast with **no human intervention** required. Surprisingly, compared to the previous approaches on fault trees, our algorithms seem to need far fewer traces to generate usable models.

Future Work. Our algorithm can be extended in various ways. Firstly, it would be worthwhile to test whether including prior knowledge in generation 0 leads to fitter models. Secondly, one can experiment with richer sets of mutations and crossovers to include domain knowledge or existing attack tree models. Thirdly, including additional types of inner nodes could overcome the condition of a basic event only occurring once per trace. Using more real-world data the choice of hyperparameters could be better justified or tested with different tuners. Additionally, extensions to the algorithm like using multi-objective approaches for fitness, may improve the performance. Setting a baseline for future solutions with this algorithm may help compare this approach with options from other fields e.g. SMT.

Acknowledgement. The work was partially supported by the MUNI Award in Science and Humanities (MUNI/I/1757/2021) of the Grant Agency of Masaryk University.

References

1. Jalil, K.A., Kamarudin, M.H., Masrek, M.N.: Comparison of machine learning algorithms performance in detecting network intrusion. In: 2010 International Conference on Networking and Information Technology, pp. 221–226. IEEE (2010)
2. Alhomidi, M., Reed, M.: Finding the minimum cut set in attack graphs using genetic algorithms. In: 2013 International Conference on Computer Applications Technology (ICCAT), pp. 1–6. IEEE (2013)
3. André, É., et al.: Parametric analyses of attack-fault trees. In: 2019 19th International Conference on Application of Concurrency to System Design (ACSD), pp. 33–42. IEEE (2019)
4. Bates, D., et al.: Fitting linear mixed-effects models using lme4 (2014)
5. Bryans, J., et al.: A template-based method for the generation of attack trees. In: Laurent, M., Giannetsos, T. (eds.) WISTP 2019. LNCS, vol. 12024, pp. 155–165. Springer, Cham (2020). https://doi.org/10.1007/978-3-030-41702-4_10
6. Budde, C.E., Bucur, D., Verkuil, B.: Automated fault tree learning from continuous-valued sensor data. Int. J. Prognostics Health Manag. **13**(2) (2022). https://doi.org/10.36001/ijphm.2022.v13i2.3160. ISSN 2153-2648
7. Buldas, A., et al.: Attribute evaluation on attack trees with incomplete information. Comput. Secur. **88**, 101630 (2020)
8. Chawla, N.V.: C4. 5 and imbalanced data sets: investigating the effect of sampling method, probabilistic estimate, and decision tree structure. In: Proceedings of the ICML, Toronto, ON, Canada, vol. 3, p. 66. CIBC (2003)
9. Fila, B., Wideł, W.: Attack–defense trees for abusing optical power meters: a case study and the OSEAD tool experience report. In: Albanese, M., Horne, R., Probst, C.W. (eds.) GraMSec 2019. LNCS, vol. 11720, pp. 95–125. Springer, Cham (2019). https://doi.org/10.1007/978-3-030-36537-0_6
10. Gadyatskaya, O., Trujillo-Rasua, R.: New directions in attack tree research: catching up with industrial needs. In: Liu, P., Mauw, S., Stølen, K. (eds.) GraMSec 2017. LNCS, vol. 10744, pp. 115–126. Springer, Cham (2018). https://doi.org/10.1007/978-3-319-74860-3_9
11. Gadyatskaya, O., et al.: Attack trees for practical security assessment: ranking of attack scenarios with ADTool 2.0. In: Agha, G., Van Houdt, B. (eds.) QEST 2016. LNCS, vol. 9826, pp. 159–162. Springer, Cham (2016). https://doi.org/10.1007/978-3-319-43425-4_10

12. Gonçalves, E.C., Freitas, A.A., Plastino, A.: A survey of genetic algorithms for multi-label classification. In: 2018 IEEE Congress on Evolutionary Computation (CEC), pp. 1–8 (2018)
13. Gupta, M., et al.: Matching information security vulnerabilities to organizational security profiles: a genetic algorithm approach. Decis. Support Syst. **41**(3), 592–603 (2006)
14. Hermanns, H., et al.: The value of attack-defence diagrams. In: Piessens, F., Viganò, L. (eds.) POST 2016. LNCS, vol. 9635, pp. 163–185. Springer, Heidelberg (2016). https://doi.org/10.1007/978-3-662-49635-0_9
15. Hong, J.B., Kim, D.S., Takaoka, T.: Scalable attack representation model using logic reduction techniques. In: 2013 12th IEEE International Conference on Trust, Security and Privacy in Computing and Communications, pp. 404–411. IEEE (2013)
16. Hosmer, D.W., Jr., Lemeshow, S., Sturdivant, R.X.: Applied Logistic Regression, vol. 398. Wiley, Hoboken (2013)
17. Ivanova, M.G., et al.: Attack tree generation by policy invalidation. In: Akram, R.N., Jajodia, S. (eds.) WISTP 2015. LNCS, vol. 9311, pp. 249–259. Springer, Cham (2015). https://doi.org/10.1007/978-3-319-24018-3_16
18. Jhawar, R., et al.: Attack trees with sequential conjunction. In: Federrath, H., Gollmann, D. (eds.) SEC 2015. IAICT, vol. 455, pp. 339–353. Springer, Cham (2015). https://doi.org/10.1007/978-3-319-18467-8_23
19. Jhawar, R., et al.: Semi-automatically augmenting attack trees using an annotated attack tree library. In: Katsikas, S.K., Alcaraz, C. (eds.) STM 2018. LNCS, vol. 11091, pp. 85–101. Springer, Cham (2018). https://doi.org/10.1007/978-3-030-01141-3_6
20. Jimenez-Roa, L.A., et al.: Automatic inference of fault tree models via multi-objective evolutionary algorithms. IEEE Trans. Dependable Secure Comput. **20**(4), 3317–3327 (2023). https://doi.org/10.1109/tdsc.2022.3203805. ISSN 1545-5971
21. Jürgenson, A., Willemson, J.: On fast and approximate attack tree computations. In: Kwak, J., Deng, R.H., Won, Y., Wang, G. (eds.) ISPEC 2010. LNCS, vol. 6047, pp. 56–66. Springer, Heidelberg (2010). https://doi.org/10.1007/978-3-642-12827-1_5
22. Kim, D., Choi, J., Han, K.: Risk management-based security evaluation model for telemedicine systems. BMC Med. Inform. Decis. Mak. **20**(1), 1–14 (2020)
23. Kordy, B., Pietre-Cambacedes, L., Schweitzer, P.: DAG-based attack and defense modeling: don't miss the forest for the attack trees. CoRR, abs/1303.7397 (2013). http://arxiv.org/abs/1303.7397
24. Kordy, B., et al.: Foundations of attack-defense trees. In: Degano, P., Etalle, S., Guttman, J. (eds.) FAST 2010. LNCS, vol. 6561, pp. 80–95. Springer, Heidelberg (2011). https://doi.org/10.1007/978-3-642-19751-2_6 ISBN 978-3-642-19750-5
25. Kumar, R., Stoelinga, M.: Quantitative security and safety analysis with attack-fault trees. In: High Assurance Systems Engineering (HASE), pp. 25–32 (2017). https://doi.org/10.1109/HASE.2017.12
26. Lenin, A., Willemson, J., Sari, D.P.: Attacker profiling in quantitative security assessment based on attack trees. In: Bernsmed, K., Fischer-Hübner, S. (eds.) NordSec 2014. LNCS, vol. 8788, pp. 199–212. Springer, Cham (2014). https://doi.org/10.1007/978-3-319-11599-3_12
27. Linard, A., Bucur, D., Stoelinga, M.: Fault trees from data: efficient learning with an evolutionary algorithm. In: Guan, N., Katoen, J.-P., Sun, J. (eds.) SETTA 2019. LNCS, vol. 11951, pp. 19–37. Springer, Cham (2019). https://doi.org/10.1007/978-3-030-35540-1_2

28. Majeed, P.G., Kumar, S.: Genetic algorithms in intrusion detection systems: a survey. Int. J. Innov. Appl. Stud. **5**(3), 233 (2014)
29. RTO NATO. Improving common security risk analysis. Technical report, RTO Technical Report TR-IST-049, Research and Technology Organisation of NATO (2008)
30. Pawar, S.N.: Intrusion detection in computer network using genetic algorithm approach: a survey. Int. J. Adv. Eng. Technol. **6**(2), 730 (2013)
31. Pinchinat, S., Acher, M., Vojtisek, D.: ATSyRa: an integrated environment for synthesizing attack trees. In: Mauw, S., Kordy, B., Jajodia, S. (eds.) GraMSec 2015. LNCS, vol. 9390, pp. 97–101. Springer, Cham (2016). https://doi.org/10. 1007/978-3-319-29968-6_7
32. Pinchinat, S., Acher, M., Vojtisek, D.: Towards synthesis of attack trees for supporting computer-aided risk analysis. In: Canal, C., Idani, A. (eds.) SEFM 2014. LNCS, vol. 8938, pp. 363–375. Springer, Cham (2015). https://doi.org/10.1007/ 978-3-319-15201-1_24
33. Pinchinat, S., Schwarzentruber, F., Lê Cong, S.: Library-based attack tree synthesis. In: Eades III, H., Gadyatskaya, O. (eds.) GraMSec 2020. LNCS, vol. 12419, pp. 24–44. Springer, Cham (2020). https://doi.org/10.1007/978-3-030-62230-5_2
34. Ramos, J.L.H., Skarmeta, A.: Assessing vulnerabilities in IoT-based ambient assisted living systems. Secur. Privacy Internet Things Challenges Solutions **27**, 94 (2020)
35. Rosmansyah, Y., Hendarto, I., Pratama, D.: Impersonation attack-defense tree. Int. J. Emerg. Technol. Learn. (iJET) **15**(19), 239–246 (2020)
36. Schneier, B.: Secrets & Lies: Digital Security in a Networked World, 1st edn. Wiley, New York (2000). ISBN 0471253111
37. Sheyner, O., et al.: Automated generation and analysis of attack graphs. In: Proceedings of the 2002 IEEE Symposium on Security and Privacy, SP 2002, Washington, DC, USA, p. 273. IEEE Computer Society (2002). http://dl.acm.org/citation. cfm?id=829514.830526. ISBN 0-7695-1543-6
38. Shostack, A.: Threat Modeling: Designing for Security. Wiley, Hoboken (2014)
39. Vigo, R., Nielson, F., Nielson, H.R.: Automated generation of attack trees. In: 2014 IEEE 27th Computer Security Foundations Symposium, pp. 337–350. IEEE (2014)
40. Widel, W., et al.: Beyond 2014: formal methods for attack tree-based security modeling. ACM Comput. Surv. (CSUR) **52**(4), 1–36 (2019)

The Landscape of Computing Symmetric n-Variable Functions with $2n$ Cards

Suthee Ruangwises[✉]

Department of Informatics, The University of Electro-Communications, Tokyo, Japan
ruangwises@gmail.com

Abstract. Secure multi-party computation using a physical deck of cards, often called card-based cryptography, has been extensively studied during the past decade. Card-based protocols to compute various Boolean functions have been developed. As each input bit is typically encoded by two cards, computing an n-variable Boolean function requires at least $2n$ cards. We are interested in optimal protocols that use exactly $2n$ cards. In particular, we focus on symmetric functions. In this paper, we formulate the problem of developing $2n$-card protocols to compute n-variable symmetric Boolean functions by classifying all such functions into several NPN-equivalence classes. We then summarize existing protocols that can compute some representative functions from these classes, and also solve some open problems in the cases $n = 4$, 5, 6, and 7. In particular, we develop a protocol to compute a function kMod3, which determines whether the sum of all inputs is congruent to k modulo 3 ($k \in \{0, 1, 2\}$).

Keywords: card-based cryptography · secure multi-party computation · symmetric function

1 Introduction

Secure multi-party computation involves computing the output value of a particular function with inputs from different parties, while keeping the input values secret. Secure multi-party computation using a physical deck of cards, often called *card-based cryptography*, has been a subject of research since the *five-card trick* was introduced by den Boer [1] in 1989. This area has gained interest from researchers and has been extensively studied during the past decade [3].

Typically, each input bit is encoded by an order of a black card ♣ and a red card ♡; a bit 0 is represented by a *commitment* ♣♡, and bit 1 by a commitment ♡♣. The five-card trick can compute a logical AND function of two input bits using five cards: two cards for a commitment of each bit, and one additional helping card. Later, Mizuki et al. [6] showed that the two-variable AND function can be computed with only four cards, using no helping card.

Besides the AND function, protocols to compute various other Boolean functions have also been developed. As each input bit is encoded by two cards, computing an n-variable Boolean function requires at least $2n$ cards. A challenging work is to develop card-minimal protocols that use exactly $2n$ cards.

E. Ábrahám et al. (Eds.): ICTAC 2023, LNCS 14446, pp. 74–82, 2023.
https://doi.org/10.1007/978-3-031-47963-2_6

2   Symmetric Boolean Functions

We focus on *symmetric* functions where each party is treated equally. A Boolean function $f : \{0,1\}^n \rightarrow \{0,1\}$ is called symmetric if

$$f(x_1, x_2, ..., x_n) = f(x_{\sigma(1)}, x_{\sigma(2)}, ..., x_{\sigma(n)})$$

for any $x_1, x_2, ..., x_n$ and any permutation $(\sigma(1), \sigma(2), ..., \sigma(n))$ of $(1, 2, ..., n)$. Note that for a symmetric Boolean function f, the value of $f(x_1, x_2, ..., x_n)$ only depends on the sum $\sum_{i=1}^{n} x_i$.

We denote an n-variable symmetric Boolean function by S_X^n for some $X \subseteq \{0, 1, ..., n\}$. A function S_X^n is defined by

$$S_X^n(x_1, x_2, ..., x_n) = \begin{cases} 1, & \text{if } \sum_{i=1}^{n} x_i \in X; \\ 0, & \text{otherwise.} \end{cases}$$

For example, a function $x_1 \wedge x_2 \wedge ... \wedge x_n$ is denoted by $S_{\{n\}}^n$, and a function $x_1 \oplus x_2 \oplus ... \oplus x_n$ is denoted by $S_{\{1,3,5,...,2\lfloor \frac{n-1}{2} \rfloor + 1\}}^n$.

In general, observe that if a function f is computable by some number of cards, functions derived from f by (1) negating variables, (2) permuting variables, and (3) negating the output, are also computable by the same number of cards. Hence, we can classify all n-variable symmetric Boolean functions into several classes called *Negation-Permutation-Negation (NPN)-equivalence classes* [10], where all functions in the same class can be computed by essentially the same protocol, so it is sufficient to consider only one representative function from each class. Note that S_X^n is always in the same class as $S_{\{n-x|x\in X\}}^n$ (negating all variables) and $S_{\{1,2,...,n\}-X}^n$ (negating f).

3   Existing Protocols

In 2015, Nishida et al. [8] showed that any n-variable symmetric Boolean function can be computed with $2n + 2$ cards, providing an upper bound for the number of required cards. However, we are mainly interested in $2n$-card protocols.

3.1   Two Variables

For $n = 2$, all eight functions can be classified into three classes, as shown in Table 1. A four-card XOR protocol was developed by Mizuki and Sone [7] in 2009, and a four-card AND protocol was developed by Mizuki et al. [6] in 2012.

A protocol is called *committed-format* if the output is encoded in the same format as the inputs. While committed-format is a desirable property (so that the output can be used as the input in other protocols), it has been proved [4] that there is no four-card committed-format AND protocol with a guaranteed finite number of shuffles[1], so the protocol of Mizuki et al. [6] is the optimal one in this sense.

---

[1] The number of shuffles is defined to be the number of times we perform shuffling operations described in Sect. 4.1.

Table 1. Four-card protocols to compute symmetric two-variable functions

Function	Name	Protocol	Committed?	#Shuffles	Other Functions in the Same Class
$S^2_\emptyset$	Constant	trivial			$S^2_{\{0,1,2\}}$
$S^2_{\{1\}}$	XOR	Mizuki-Sone [7], 2009	yes	1	$S^2_{\{0,2\}}$
$S^2_{\{2\}}$	AND	Mizuki et al. [6], 2012	no	2	$S^2_{\{0\}}, S^2_{\{0,1\}}, S^2_{\{1,2\}}$

Table 2. Six-card protocols to compute symmetric three-variable functions

Function	Name	Protocol	Committed?	#Shuffles	Other Functions in the Same Class
$S^3_\emptyset$	Constant	trivial			$S^3_{\{0,1,2,3\}}$
$S^3_{\{1,3\}}$	XOR	Mizuki-Sone [7], 2009	yes	2	$S^3_{\{0,2\}}$
$S^3_{\{3\}}$	AND	Mizuki [5], 2016	no	5	$S^3_{\{0\}}, S^3_{\{0,1,2\}}, S^3_{\{1,2,3\}}$
		Isuzugawa et al. [2], 2021	no	2	
$S^3_{\{0,3\}}$	Equality	Shinagawa-Mizuki [13], 2019	no	1	$S^3_{\{1,2\}}$
		Ruangwises-Itoh [9], 2021	yes	2	
$S^3_{\{2,3\}}$	Majority	Toyoda et al. [15], 2021	no	2	$S^3_{\{0,1\}}$
$S^3_{\{1\}}$	1Mod3	Shikata et al. [11], 2023	no	3	$S^3_{\{2\}}, S^3_{\{0,1,3\}}, S^3_{\{0,2,3\}}$

3.2 Three Variables

For $n = 3$, all 16 functions can be classified into six classes, as shown in Table 2. Several researchers independently developed protocols to compute different functions. First, as the XOR protocol of Mizuki and Sone [7] is committed-format, it can be repeatedly applied to any number of variables without requiring helping cards. In 2016, Mizuki [5] developed a card-minimal protocol to compute the AND function with any number of variables. Isuzugawa et al. [2] later improved the performance of the three-variable AND protocol to use only two shuffles.

In 2019, Shinagawa and Mizuki [13] constructed a six-card protocol to compute the equality function $S^3_{\{0,3\}}$ that uses only a single shuffle. Later, Ruangwises and Itoh [9] developed a card-minimal protocol for the same function (with any number of variables) that uses more shuffles but is committed-format. They also introduced a general technique to compute any n-variable *doubly symmetric*[2] Boolean function with $2n$ cards. In 2021, Toyoda et al. [15] proposed a six-card protocol to compute the majority function $S^3_{\{2,3\}}$.

Very recently, in 2023, Shikata et al. [11] introduced a six-card protocol to compute any three-variable function S^n_X such that $0 \in X$ if and only if $3 \in X$. This solved the only remaining non-trivial class (the one containing $S^3_{\{1\}}$) in the case $n = 3$, finally making the problem settled for this case.

---

[2] A doubly symmetric function is a function S^n_X such that $x \in X$ if and only if $n - x \in X$ for every $x \in \{0, 1, ..., n\}$.

3.3 Four Variables

Table 3. Eight-card protocols to compute symmetric four-variable functions (An asterisk denotes the expected number of shuffles in Las Vegas protocols).

Function	Name	Protocol	Committed?	#Shuffles	Other Functions in the Same Class
$S_\emptyset^4$	Constant	trivial			$S_{\{0,1,2,3,4\}}^4$
$S_{\{1,3\}}^4$	XOR	Mizuki-Sone [7], 2009	yes	3	$S_{\{0,2,4\}}^4$
$S_{\{4\}}^4$	AND	Mizuki [5], 2016	no	5	$S_{\{0\}}^4$, $S_{\{0,1,2,3\}}^4$, $S_{\{1,2,3,4\}}^4$
$S_{\{0,4\}}^4$	Equality	Ruangwises-Itoh [9], 2021	yes	3	$S_{\{1,2,3\}}^4$
$S_{\{2\}}^4$	2Mod3		no	3	$S_{\{0,1,3,4\}}^4$
$S_{\{1\}}^4$	–	Shikata et al. [11], 2023	no	$\approx 7^*$	$S_{\{3\}}^4$, $S_{\{0,1,2,4\}}^4$, $S_{\{0,2,3,4\}}^4$
$S_{\{1,2\}}^4$	–		no	$\approx 8^*$	$S_{\{2,3\}}^4$, $S_{\{0,1,4\}}^4$, $S_{\{0,3,4\}}^4$
$S_{\{0,3\}}^4$	0Mod3	**Ours (Sect. 4)**	no	4	$S_{\{1,4\}}^4$, $S_{\{0,2,3\}}^4$, $S_{\{1,2,4\}}^4$
$S_{\{3,4\}}^4$	Majority	open problem			$S_{\{0,1\}}^4$, $S_{\{0,1,2\}}^4$, $S_{\{2,3,4\}}^4$
$S_{\{0,2\}}^4$	–				$S_{\{2,4\}}^4$, $S_{\{0,1,3\}}^4$, $S_{\{1,3,4\}}^4$

For $n = 4$, all 32 functions can be classified into ten classes, as shown in Table 3. The aforementioned XOR protocol [7], AND protocol [5], and equality protocol [9] can compute respective functions with eight cards. Also, function $S_{\{2\}}^3$ is doubly symmetric and thus can be computed by the technique of Ruangwises and Itoh [9].

Functions $S_{\{1\}}^3$ and $S_{\{1,2\}}^3$ can be computed with eight cards by protocols of Shikata et al. [11]. However, their protocols are Las Vegas[3].

The remaining three classes still lack a card-minimal protocol, leaving open problems of whether there exist such protocols. In Sect. 4, we propose an eight-card protocol to compute the 0Mod3 function $S_{\{0,3\}}^3$, solving one of the three open problems.

3.4 More Than Four Variables

In 2022, Shikata et al. [12] proved that there exists a $2n$-card protocol to compute any n-variable symmetric Boolean function for $n \geq 8$. This limits the open problems to only $n = 5$, 6, and 7, where there are 64, 128, and 256 functions that can be classified into 20, 36, and 72 classes, respectively.

For $n = 5$, five non-trivial classes of functions can be computed by existing protocols. Our protocol in Sect. 4 can compute the 0Mod3 function $S_{\{0,3\}}^5$, leaving 13 non-trivial classes as open problems.

For $n = 6$, eight non-trivial classes of functions can be computed by existing protocols. Our protocol in Sect. 4 can compute the 1Mod3 function $S_{\{1,4\}}^6$, leaving 26 non-trivial classes as open problems.

---

[3] A Las Vegas protocol is a protocol that does not guarantee a finite number of shuffles, but has a finite expected number of shuffles.

For $n = 7$, 12 non-trivial classes of functions can be computed by existing protocols. Our protocol in Sect. 4 can compute the 0Mod3 function $S^7_{\{0,3,6\}}$, leaving 58 non-trivial classes as open problems.

4 Our Protocol for kMod3 Function

For $k \in \{0, 1, 2\}$, the kMod3 function determines whether the sum of all inputs is congruent to k modulo 3. Formally, it is defined by

$$k\mathrm{Mod}3(x_1, x_2, ..., x_n) = \begin{cases} 1, & \text{if } \sum_{i=1}^n x_i \equiv k \pmod 3; \\ 0, & \text{otherwise.} \end{cases}$$

In this section, we will briefly describe the necessary subprotocols, then we will introduce our kMod3 protocol that uses $2n$ cards for any $n \geq 3$.

4.1 Preliminaries

We use two types of cards in our protocol: ♣ and ♡. All cards have indistinguishable back sides. As per convention, we encoded 0 by a commitment ♣♡, and 1 by a commitment ♡♣.

All of the randomness in our protocol is generated by the following two shuffling operations, which are jointly executed by all parties. (For other operations that do not involve randomness, the operations can be executed by any party while being observed by other parties).

Random Cut. Given a sequence S of n cards, a *random cut* shifts S by a uniformly random cyclic shift unknown to all parties. It can be implemented by letting all parties take turns to apply *Hindu cuts* (taking several card from the bottom of the pile and putting them on the top) to S.

Random k-Section Cut. Given a sequence S of kn cards, a *random k-section cut* [14] divides S into k blocks, each consisting of n consecutive cards, then shifts the blocks by a uniformly random cyclic shift unknown to all parties. It can be implemented by putting all cards in each block into an envelopes and applying the random cut to the sequence of envelopes.

4.2 Encoding Integers in $\mathbb{Z}/3\mathbb{Z}$

For $i \in \{0, 1, 2\}$, define $E_3^{\clubsuit}(i)$ to be a sequence of three cards, all of them being ♡s except the $(i+1)$-th card from the left being a ♣, e.g. $E_3^{\clubsuit}(1)$ is ♡♣♡. Conversely, define $E_3^{\heartsuit}(i)$ to be a sequence of three cards, all of them being ♣s except the $(i+1)$-th card from the left being a ♡, e.g. $E_3^{\heartsuit}(0)$ is ♡♣♣.

4.3   Adding Two Commitments in $\mathbb{Z}/3\mathbb{Z}$

Given two commitments of bits $a, b \in \{0,1\}$, this subprotocol produces either $E_3^\clubsuit(a+b)$ or $E_3^\heartsuit(a+b)$, each with probability $1/2$, without using any helping card. It was developed by Shikata et al. [12].

1. Arrange the commitments of a and b as a sequence in this order from left to right.
2. Apply a random 2-section cut on the sequence. Then, apply a random cut on the middle two cards.
3. Let (c_1, c_2, c_3, c_4) be the obtained sequence in this order from left to right. Turn over c_2.
   - If it is a ♣, then (c_1, c_3, c_4) will be $E_3^\clubsuit(a+b)$.
   - If it is a ♡, then (c_4, c_3, c_1) will be $E_3^\heartsuit(a+b)$.

4.4   Adding Two Integers in $\mathbb{Z}/3\mathbb{Z}$

Given two sequences $E_3^\clubsuit(a) = (a_0, a_1, a_2)$ and $E_3^\heartsuit(b) = (b_0, b_1, b_2)$, this subprotocol produces a sequence $E_3^\clubsuit(a + b \bmod 3)$ without using any helping card. It was developed by Ruangwises and Itoh [9].

1. Rearrange the cards as a sequence $(a_0, b_2, a_1, b_1, a_2, b_0)$.
2. Apply a random 3-section cut on the sequence, transforming it into $(a_r, b_{2-r}, a_{r+1}, b_{1-r}, a_{r+2}, b_{-r})$ for a uniformly random $r \in \mathbb{Z}/3\mathbb{Z}$, where the indices are taken modulo 3.
3. Rearrange the cards back as they were before. We now have two sequences $E_3^\clubsuit(a - r \bmod 3) = (a_r, a_{r+1}, a_{r+2})$ and $E_3^\heartsuit(b + r \bmod 3) = (b_{-r}, b_{1-r}, b_{2-r})$, where the indices are taken modulo 3.
4. Turn over the sequence $E_3^\heartsuit(b + r \bmod 3)$ to reveal $s = b + r \bmod 3$. Then, shift the sequence $E_3^\clubsuit(a - r)$ cyclically to the right by s positions, transforming it into $E_3^\clubsuit(a - r + s \bmod 3) = E_3^\clubsuit(a + b \bmod 3)$ as desired.

4.5   Main Protocol

We use an idea similar to the one in [11], but extends their idea further to the case of n variable for any $n \geq 3$.

1. Apply the subprotocol in Sect. 4.3 on the commitments of x_1 and x_2 to obtain either $E_3^\clubsuit(x_1 + x_2)$ or $E_3^\heartsuit(x_1 + x_2)$.
2. If we get an $E_3^\clubsuit(x_1 + x_2)$, use a free ♣ and the commitment of x_3 to create $E_3^\heartsuit(x_3)$. Then, apply the subprotocol in Sect. 4.4 on $E_3^\clubsuit(x_1 + x_2)$ and $E_3^\heartsuit(x_3)$ to obtain $E_3^\clubsuit(x_1 + x_2 + x_3 \bmod 3)$. Conversely, if we get an $E_3^\heartsuit(x_1 + x_2)$, use a free ♡ and the commitment of x_3 to create $E_3^\clubsuit(x_3)$. Then, apply the subprotocol in Sect. 4.4 on $E_3^\clubsuit(x_3)$ and $E_3^\heartsuit(x_1 + x_2)$ to obtain $E_3^\clubsuit(x_1 + x_2 + x_3 \bmod 3)$.

3. Use a free ♣ and the commitment of x_4 to create $E_3^\heartsuit(x_4)$. Then, apply the subprotocol in Sect. 4.4 on $E_3^\clubsuit(x_1 + x_2 + x_3)$ and $E_3^\heartsuit(x_4)$ to obtain $E_3^\clubsuit(x_1 + x_2 + x_3 + x_4 \bmod 3)$. Repeatedly perform this step for the rest of inputs until we obtain $E_3^\clubsuit(x_1 + x_2 + ... + x_n \bmod 3)$.
4. Turn over the $(k+1)$-th leftmost card. If it is a ♣, return 1; otherwise, return 0.

4.6 Proof of Correctness and Security

Our main protocol largely depends on the subprotocols in Sects. 4.3 and 4.4. Proofs of correctness and security of these two subprotocols are shown in [12, §3.1] and [9, §A.1], respectively. The proofs consist of drawing a structure called *KWH-tree*, which iterates all possible states and their probabilities of the sequence of cards after each operation. By observing the conditional probability of each state, one can verify that (1) the resulting sequence is always correct, and (2) turning some cards face-up during the protocol does not reveal any probabilistic information of the inputs.

Assuming the correctness and security of both subprotocols, it is easy to show that our main protocol is also correct and secure.

In Step 1, the probability of getting $E_3^\clubsuit(x_1 + x_2)$ or $E_3^\heartsuit(x_1 + x_2)$ is 1/2 each, regardless of the inputs [12, §3.1]. Therefore, one cannot deduct any information of x_1 and x_2 upon getting $E_3^\clubsuit(x_1 + x_2)$ or $E_3^\heartsuit(x_1 + x_2)$.

Steps 2 and 3 are straightforward applications of the subprotocol in Sect. 4.4, and thus are correct and secure.

In Step 4, the resulting sequence is $E_3^\clubsuit(x_1+x_2+...+x_n \bmod 3)$, which is either ♣♡♡, ♡♣♡, or ♡♡♣. Turning over the $(k+1)$-th leftmost card reveals whether $x_1+x_2+...+x_n \equiv k \pmod 3$ (if the card is a ♣, then $x_1+x_2+...+x_n \equiv k \pmod 3$; if the card is a ♡, then $x_1 + x_2 + ... + x_n \not\equiv k \pmod 3$) without revealing any other information of the inputs. Hence, our main protocol is correct and secure.

4.7 Analysis

Table 4. Properties of protocols to compute the kMod3 function

Protocol	#Cards	#Shuffles	Committed?
Nishida et al. [8], 2015	$2n + 2$	$O(n \lg n)$	yes
Ruangwises-Itoh [9], 2021	$2n + 2$	n	no
Ours	$2n$	n	no

Our protocol is the first card-minimal protocol for the kMod3 function. There are several existing protocols that can compute the function using more than $2n$

cards, e.g. the protocol of Nishida et al. [8] which uses $2n + 2$ cards and $O(n \lg n)$ shuffles, and the protocol of Ruangwises-Itoh [9] which uses $2n + 2$ cards and n shuffles. See Table 4. Therefore, our protocol is also optimal in terms of number of shuffles.

For each $n \geq 3$, our protocol can compute six functions (0Mod3, 1Mod3, 2Mod3, and their negations), which are from two different NPN-equivalence classes (for $n \equiv 0 \pmod 3$, 1Mod3 and 2Mod3 are in the same class; for $n \equiv 1 \pmod 3$, 0Mod3 and 1Mod3 are in the same class; for $n \equiv 2 \pmod 3$, 0Mod3 and 2Mod3 are in the same class).

5 Future Work

We formulated the problem of developing $2n$-card protocols to compute n-variable symmetric Boolean functions, and also proposed protocols for some classes of these functions. It remains an open problem to construct card-minimal protocols, or to prove that none exists, for the remaining classes in the cases $n = 4, 5, 6$, and 7.

Another possible consideration is the property of a protocol. For example, if we restrict the protocols to be the ones with a guaranteed finite number of shuffles, functions $S^4_{\{1\}}$ and $S^4_{\{1,2\}}$ still lack a card-minimal finite protocol, leaving four classes unsolved in the case $n = 4$. Also, most of the existing protocols are not committed-format. It is a challenging work to construct card-minimal committed-format protocols to compute more functions, or to prove that none exists for some functions, similar to the proof of non-existence of a four-card committed-format finite AND protocol in [4].

Acknowledgement. The author would like to thank Daiki Miyahara for a valuable discussion on this research.

References

1. Boer, B.: More efficient match-making and satisfiability *the five card trick*. In: Quisquater, J.-J., Vandewalle, J. (eds.) EUROCRYPT 1989. LNCS, vol. 434, pp. 208–217. Springer, Heidelberg (1990). https://doi.org/10.1007/3-540-46885-4_23
2. Isuzugawa, R., Toyoda, K., Sasaki, Yu., Miyahara, D., Mizuki, T.: A card-minimal three-input AND protocol using two shuffles. In: Chen, C.-Y., Hon, W.-K., Hung, L.-J., Lee, C.-W. (eds.) COCOON 2021. LNCS, vol. 13025, pp. 668–679. Springer, Cham (2021). https://doi.org/10.1007/978-3-030-89543-3_55
3. Koch, A.: The landscape of optimal card-based protocols. Math. Cryptol. **1**(2), 115–131 (2021)
4. Koch, A., Walzer, S., Härtel, K.: Card-based cryptographic protocols using a minimal number of cards. In: Iwata, T., Cheon, J.H. (eds.) ASIACRYPT 2015. LNCS, vol. 9452, pp. 783–807. Springer, Heidelberg (2015). https://doi.org/10.1007/978-3-662-48797-6_32
5. Mizuki, T.: Card-based protocols for securely computing the conjunction of multiple variables. Theoret. Comput. Sci. **622**, 34–44 (2016)

6. Mizuki, T., Kumamoto, M., Sone, H.: The five-card trick can be done with four cards. In: Wang, X., Sako, K. (eds.) ASIACRYPT 2012. LNCS, vol. 7658, pp. 598–606. Springer, Heidelberg (2012). https://doi.org/10.1007/978-3-642-34961-4_36

7. Mizuki, T., Sone, H.: Six-card secure AND and four-card secure XOR. In: Deng, X., Hopcroft, J.E., Xue, J. (eds.) FAW 2009. LNCS, vol. 5598, pp. 358–369. Springer, Heidelberg (2009). https://doi.org/10.1007/978-3-642-02270-8_36

8. Nishida, T., Hayashi, Y., Mizuki, T., Sone, H.: Card-based protocols for any Boolean function. In: Jain, R., Jain, S., Stephan, F. (eds.) TAMC 2015. LNCS, vol. 9076, pp. 110–121. Springer, Cham (2015). https://doi.org/10.1007/978-3-319-17142-5_11

9. Ruangwises, S., Itoh, T.: Securely computing the n-variable equality function with $2n$ cards. Theoret. Comput. Sci. **887**, 99–100 (2021)

10. Sasao, T.: Switching Theory for Logic Synthesis, 1st edn. Kluwer Academic Publishers, Norwell (1999)

11. Shikata, H., Miyahara, D., Mizuki, T.: Few-helping-card protocols for some wider class of symmetric Boolean functions with arbitrary ranges. In: Proceedings of the 10th ACM International Workshop on ASIA Public-Key Cryptography (APKC), pp. 33–41 (2023)

12. Shikata, H., Miyahara, D., Toyoda, K., Mizuki, T.: Card-minimal protocols for symmetric Boolean functions of more than seven inputs. In: Seidl, H., Liu, Z., Pasareanu, C.S. (eds.) ICTAC 2022. LNCS, vol. 13572, pp. 388–406. Springer, Cham (2022). https://doi.org/10.1007/978-3-031-17715-6_25

13. Shinagawa, K., Mizuki, T.: The six-card trick: secure computation of three-input equality. In: Lee, K. (ed.) ICISC 2018. LNCS, vol. 11396, pp. 123–131. Springer, Cham (2019). https://doi.org/10.1007/978-3-030-12146-4_8

14. Shinagawa, K., et al.: Card-based protocols using regular polygon cards. IEICE Trans. Fundam. Electron. Commun. Comput. Sci. **E100.A**(9), 1900–1909 (2017)

15. Toyoda, K., Miyahara, D., Mizuki, T.: Another use of the five-card trick: card-minimal secure three-input majority function evaluation. In: Adhikari, A., Küsters, R., Preneel, B. (eds.) INDOCRYPT 2021. LNCS, vol. 13143, pp. 536–555. Springer, Cham (2021). https://doi.org/10.1007/978-3-030-92518-5_24

On the Complexity of Reasoning
in Kleene Algebra with Commutativity
Conditions

Stepan L. Kuznetsov[(✉)]

Steklov Mathematical Institute of RAS, Moscow, Russia
sk@mi-ras.ru

Abstract. Kleene algebras are one of the basic algebraic structures used in computer science, involving iteration, or Kleene star. An important subclass of Kleene algebras is formed by $*$-continuous ones. In his 2002 paper, Dexter Kozen pinpointed complexity of various logical theories for Kleene algebras, both in the general and in the $*$-continuous case. Those complexity results range from equational theories to Horn theories, or reasoning from hypotheses. In the middle, there are fragments of Horn theories, with restrictions on hypotheses. For the case when the hypotheses are commutativity conditions, i.e., commutation equations for designated pairs of atoms, however, Kozen mentioned the complexity result (Π_1^0-completeness) only for the $*$-continuous case, while the general case remained an open question. This was the only gap in Kozen's table of results, and the present paper fills this gap. Namely, we prove that reasoning from commutativity conditions on the class of all Kleene algebras is Σ_1^0-complete. In particular, this problem is undecidable.

Keywords: Kleene algebra · commutativity conditions · algorithmic complexity

1   Introduction

Kleene algebra is an abstract algebraic construction generalizing the algebra of regular expressions which is widely used in programming. The most interesting operation in Kleene algebras is iteration, or Kleene star. There are two ways of defining iteration. The stronger one, called the $*$-continuous definition, is infinitary and defines Kleene star as the supremum of powers. The weaker definition is an inductive-style one: iteration is defined as a least fixpoint.

While most of the natural examples of Kleene algebras, like the algebra of regular languages or the algebra of binary relations, are $*$-continuous, the fixpoint definition is much simpler from the algorithmic point of view. Namely, the logical theories for generic (not necessarily $*$-continuous) Kleene algebras enjoy recursive axiomatisation, and therefore are recursively enumerable. In contrast, theories of $*$-continuous Kleene algebras typically allow only infinitary axiomatisations, and their complexity can rise up to Π_1^1-completeness (see below).

Before formulating the result of the present paper, let us recall the basic definitions.

E. Ábrahám et al. (Eds.): ICTAC 2023, LNCS 14446, pp. 83–99, 2023.
https://doi.org/10.1007/978-3-031-47963-2_7

Definition 1. *A Kleene algebra is an algebraic structure* $\mathbf{K} = (K, +, \cdot, {}^*, 0, 1)$, *where the following holds for any* $a, b, c \in K$ *(as usual, we omit* $\cdot$; *the priority of operations is, in ascending order, as follows:* $+$, $\cdot$, *):

$$a + (b + c) = (a + b) + c \qquad\qquad a(b + c) = ab + ac$$
$$a + b = b + a \qquad\qquad (a + b)c = ac + bc$$
$$a + 0 = a + \overset{.}{a} = a \qquad\qquad 1 + aa^* \le a^*$$
$$a(bc) = (ab)c \qquad\qquad 1 + a^*a \le a^*$$
$$1a = a1 = a \qquad\qquad \text{if } ab \le b, \text{ then } a^*b \le b$$
$$0a = a0 = 0 \qquad\qquad \text{if } ba \le b, \text{ then } ba^* \le b$$

Here and further $a \le b$ *means* $a + b = b$.

In other words, $(K, +, \cdot, 0, 1)$ is an idempotent semiring and a^* should be simultaneously the least fixpoint of two operators: $x \mapsto 1 + ax$ and $x \mapsto 1 + xa$.

We shall use the notation a^+ (positive iteration) for aa^*. We shall also make use of several well-known properties of Kleene algebra:

– transitivity: if $a \le b$ and $b \le c$, then $a \le c$;
– monotonicity: if $a \le b$, then $ac \le bc$, $ca \le cb$, and $a^* \le b^*$;
– semilattice structure: $a + b$ is the smallest upper bound for $\{a, b\}$, that is, $a \le a + b$, $b \le a + b$, and if $a \le c$ and $b \le c$, then $a + b \le c$.

Definition 2. *A Kleene algebra* $\mathbf{K}$ *is* $*$-*continuous, if*

$$ba^*c = \sup\{ba^nc \mid n \ge 0\}$$

for any $a, b, c \in K$.

Now let us define the logical language used for reasoning in Kleene algebras. *Terms* are built in a standard way: starting from (a countable set of) *variables* and constants 0 and 1, using two binary operations $+$ and $\cdot$ and one unary operation *:

A particular case of a term is a *word*, which is built from variables using only $\cdot$ (since $\cdot$ is an associative operation, we may ignore bracketing).

Throughout this paper, we shall use notational conventions which are close to the ones used in [8]:

objects	letters
elements of K	a, b, c
variables	p, q
words	U, V, X, Y, Z
terms	other capital letters

The letters used may also be decorated by super- or subscripts. Kozen [8] uses small letters (x, y, s, t) for terms also. For clarification, we use capital letters instead. In particular, U, V, X, Y, Z are reserved for words, and other capital letters, like S and T (but not K, which has already been used before), denote arbitrary terms.

Atomic formulae (equations) are expressions of the form $A = B$, where A and B are terms. Inequations of the form $A \leq B$ are regarded as shorthands for $A + B = B$, that is, they are a particular case of atomic formulae.

As we wish to consider reasoning from hypotheses, we define *Horn formulae* as expressions of the form $\mathcal{H} \to A = B$, where $\mathcal{H}$ is a finite set of atomic formulae. An atomic formula may be also considered as a Horn formula, with $\mathcal{H} = \varnothing$.

Validity (general truth) of a Horn formula on a class of Kleene algebras is defined in a standard manner. Let us fix a Kleene algebra **K** and an interpretation of variables on **K**, i.e., a function ν from the set of variables to K. The interpretation is propagated to terms in a natural way (structural induction).

Definition 3. *An atomic formula $A = B$ is true under a given interpretation on* **K**, *if the interpretations of A and B coincide.*

The formal definition of the interpretation is given as follows. For each term A we define its valuation $\bar{\nu}(A) \in K$ by recursion on the structure of A: $\bar{\nu}(x) = \nu(x)$ for each variable x, $\bar{\nu}(0) = 0$, $\bar{\nu}(1) = 1$, $\bar{\nu}(A + B) = \bar{\nu}(A) + \bar{\nu}(B)$, $\bar{\nu}(A \cdot B) = \bar{\nu}(A) \cdot \bar{\nu}(B)$, $\bar{\nu}(A^*) = (\bar{\nu}(A))^*$. An atomic formula is true under on **K** under interpretation ν if $\bar{\nu}(A) = \bar{\nu}(B)$. This fact is denoted by $\mathbf{K}, \nu \vDash A = B$.

Definition 4. *A Horn formula $\mathcal{H} \to A = B$ is valid on a given class of Kleene algebras, if for each interpretation ν on an algebra* **K** *from this class, under which all formulae from $\mathcal{H}$ are true, formula $A = B$ is also true.*

Symbolically: $(\forall \mathbf{K}, \nu) \left((\forall (C = D) \in \mathcal{H}) \, \mathbf{K}, \nu \vDash C = D \right) \Rightarrow \mathbf{K}, \nu \vDash A = B$.

We consider two classes of Kleene algebras: all Kleene algebras and $*$-continuous Kleene algebras. Complexity of reasoning from *unrestricted* hypotheses is the complexity of the set of all Horn formulae which are valid on the given class of Kleene algebras. This set is also called the Horn theory of the given class. One may also impose restrictions on the sets of hypotheses, that is, consider only Horn formulae with sets $\mathcal{H}$ of a given shape. This yields *fragments* of the Horn theory, which potentially could have smaller complexity.

Kozen [9] gives the following complexity table for reasoning from hypotheses (restricted or unrestricted) on the two classes of Kleene algebras. This table summarises Kozen's own and previously known results.

	all Kleene algebras	$*$-continuous Kleene algebras
no hypotheses (equational theory)	PSPACE-complete	
commutativity conditions: hypotheses of the form $pq = qp$, where $p, q \in \mathrm{Var}$	$\circledast$	Π_1^0-complete
monoid equations: hypotheses of the form $U = V$, where $U, V \in \mathrm{Var}^*$	Σ_1^0-complete	Π_2^0-complete
unrestricted hypotheses	Σ_1^0-complete	Π_1^1-complete

Notice that the lowermost line can be extended from Horn theories to much more powerful first-order theories, with arbitrary combinations of Boolean operations and quantifiers for elements of the algebra. Indeed, Definition 1 gives a finite axiomatisation of this theory, which is sound and complete by Gödel's completeness theorem. This gives the Σ_1^0 upper bound; the lower bound comes from the Horn fragment. For the *-continuous case, a calculus with the ω-rule may be provided, reflecting Definition 2. A general argument (see [13]) gives a Π_1^1 upper bound. The lower bound, again, comes from the Horn theory.

The cell marked with ⊛, that is, complexity of reasoning on the class of *all* Kleene algebras from commutativity conditions, was left in [9] as an open question. The best known lower bound was EXPSPACE-hardness. This lower bound follows from the corresponding result for commutative monoids [15], i.e., its proof does not essentially use the Kleene star. The trivial upper bound for ⊛ is Σ_1^0.

In this paper, we solve ⊛ by proving undecidability:

Theorem 1. *Reasoning from commutativity conditions on the class of all Kleene algebras is Σ_1^0-complete.*

The proof of Theorem 1, presented is this paper, follows roughly the same idea as used an earlier article of the author [12]. That article considers *action algebras,* which are Kleene algebras extended with residuals, defined by Pratt [18]. Kozen [7] posed the question of complexity for the equational theory of the class of all action algebras. Buszkowski [2] proved Π_1^0-hardness for its *-continuous (infinitary) variant. (The corresponding upper bound was proved by Palka [17].)

Buszkowski's proof encoded the *non-halting* problem for Turing machines, via totality of context-free grammars. Such an inverted ('negative') encoding yields Π_1^0-hardness: a Turing machine M does not halt on input α if and only if the corresponding encoding formula is generally true on all *-continuous action algebras.

In [12], this construction is shifted from the *-continuous to the general case. Namely, it happens that if machine M does not halt on α for a trivial reason, by reaching a designated 'capturing' state c, from which it cannot move, then a slightly modified version of Buszkowski's encoding formula is generally true already on the class of all action algebras, not necessarily *-continuous. Such behavior of a machine is called trivial cycling, or c-looping.

Unfortunately, this is not an "if and only if" statement. However, the class of pairs (M, α) for which the encoding formula is valid on all action algebras lies between c-looping and non-halting. By a folklore fact, c-looping and halting are recursively inseparable, which gives undecidability for this class, and therefore for the equational theory of action algebras. A more fine-grained technique of effective inseparability allows to pinpoint exact complexity: Σ_1^0-completeness, and thus answer Kozen's question.

The argument presented in this article follows the same lines. We start with the Π_1^0-hardness proof for reasoning from commutativity conditions on the class of *-continuous Kleene algebras, presented in [8]. This proof again encodes non-halting of Turing machines, via non-solvability for Post's Correspondence Problem. Again, a slight modification of the construction allows handling of c-looping:

if machine M c-loops on input α, then the (modified) Horn formula is valid on all Kleene algebras. This puts reasoning from commutativity conditions between c-looping and non-halting, and the same arguments, as sketched above, give Σ_1^0-completeness.

It is important to notice that the aforementioned undecidability results (both for the general and the $*$-continuous case) hold only for reasoning from specific commutativity conditions, that is, for "partially commutative" Kleene algebras. The equational theory of commutative Kleene algebras (in which all possible commutativity conditions are imposed) is the same for the general and for the $*$-continuous case. An axiomatisation of this theory was given by Redko [19]. This theory is decidable by Post's theorem, as it belongs both to Σ_1^0 and Π_1^0. The complexity estimation for the equational theory of commutative Kleene algebras was given by Haase and Hofman [6]: this theory is CONEXP-complete (thus, it is harder than its non-commutative counterpart).

Besides Kozen's table of complexity results presented above, let us briefly mention other closely related works. Cohen [3] proved decidability for reasoning in Kleene algebras (including the $*$-continuous case) from hypotheses of specific forms: $A = 0$ (where A is a term) and $x \leq 1$ (where x is a variable). Kozen et al. [10,11] handled the cases of hypotheses of the form $1 = U$ or $x = U$, where $x \in \mathrm{Var}$ and $U \in \mathrm{Var}^*$. The decidability problem for derivability from hypotheses of the form $1 = x_1 + \ldots + x_n$ ($x_i \in \mathrm{Var}$) was posed as an open question by Cohen [3], and it was solved positively by Doumane et al. [4]. We also mention the work of Maarand and Uustalu [14], who established a derivability results with commutativity conditions of a very specific form. This discussion of related work shows that algorithmic problems closely related to reasoning from (arbitrary) commutativity conditions often happen to be decidable, which makes the undecidability result an interesting one.

This also suggests an area of future research: what other simple specific forms of hypotheses will lead to undecidability, both in the general and in the $*$-continuous case? A more specific question is as follows: does there exist a restriction on the set of hypotheses such that the corresponding fragment of the Horn theory is undecidable in the $*$-continuous case and decidable in the general one (or vice versa)? To the best of the author's knowledge, the answer is unknown.

2   Proof Idea

Before going into the details, let us explain the general ideas behind the proof of Theorem 1. The interesting part is, of course, the lower bound.

Our starting point will be the proof of Π_1^0-hardness for the $*$-continuous version of the problem in question:

Theorem 2 (E. Cohen, 1994, and others). *Reasoning from commutativity conditions on the class of $*$-continuous Kleene algebras is Π_1^0-hard.*

We shall use the proof which Kozen attributes to unpublished work of Ernie Cohen and which is presented in Kozen's paper [8]. For other proofs, Kozen cites Berstel [1] and Gibbons and Rytter [5].

This proof uses a negative encoding of *Post's Correspondence Problem* (PCP). Namely, validity of the Horn formula constructed from a given PCP instance is equivalent to the fact that the PCP does *not* have a solution.

The construction starts with a fixed set of commutativity conditions $\mathcal{H}$ and a term T. Then, for each PCP Π, a term S_Π is constructed, such that Π does not have a solution if and only if the Horn formula $\mathcal{H} \to S_\Pi \leq T$ is valid on the class of *-continuous Kleene algebras.

Instances of Post's Correspondence Problem, in turn, encode arbitrary Turing computations (see, e.g., Sipser's textbook [21, § 5.2]). For a Turing machine M and its input value α there exists a PCP $\Pi(\text{M}, \alpha)$ such that M halts on input x if and only if $\Pi(\text{M}, \alpha)$ has a solution. In the further constructions, we shall dive into the details of Turing machine executions (pinpointing the c-looping case). For this reason, we cannot use the well-known undecidability result for PCP as a black box, and have to explicitly discuss the reduction from Turing computations to PCP solutions.

Combining these two encodings, one obtains the following argument for Theorem 2. For a Turing machine M and its input value α, the following statements are equivalent:

1. Machine M does not halt on α.
2. PCP $\Pi(\text{M}, \alpha)$ does not have a solution.
3. Horn formula $\mathcal{H} \to S_{\Pi(\text{M},\alpha)} \leq T$ is valid on the class of *-continuous Kleene algebras.

Next, we adapt this argument to prove Theorem 1. This modification uses the same idea as used earlier in [12]. In that article, Buszkowski's [2] proof of Π_1^0-hardness of infinitary action logic (the equational theory of *residuated* *-continuous Kleene algebras) was modified to prove Σ_1^0-hardness of action logic (the equational theory of all action algebras [18], i.e., residuated Kleene algebras).

We show that the weaker logic of reasoning from commutativity conditions on all (not necessarily *-continuous) Kleene algebras is still capable of encoding certain trivial kinds of non-halting of Turing machines. We suppose that each Turing machine has a special 'capturing' state c with the following property. If the machine reaches state c, it stays in this state forever. Thus, c is not a final state, and, moreover, reaching c guarantees non-halting. We shall denote this trivial case of non-halting as c-*looping*.[1]

Let us emphasize the fact that the capturing state c, together with the rules which guarantee that the machine gets stuck when it reaches c, is fixed in the definition of the machine. The only thing which depends on runtime is whether the machine reaches this state or not.

---

[1] Such a specific term is used in order to avoid confusion with other sorts of looping or cyclic behaviour, e.g., getting stuck at a state other than c or going into non-trivial infinite loops.

After a modification of the encoding, namely, replacing T with its variation $\widetilde{T}_{\mathtt{M}}$ (which takes care of c-looping),[2] we manage to prove the following implications (Lemma 5 and Lemma 6 below):

1. If machine $\mathtt{M}$ c-loops on input α, then $\mathcal{H} \to S_{\Pi(\mathtt{M},\alpha)} \leq \widetilde{T}_{\mathtt{M}}$ is valid on the class of *all* Kleene algebras.
2. If $\mathcal{H} \to S_{\Pi(\mathtt{M},\alpha)} \leq \widetilde{T}_{\mathtt{M}}$ is valid on the class of *-*continuous* Kleene algebras, then $\mathtt{M}$ does not halt on α.

Notice that there is a gap: the first statement talks about c-looping and arbitrary Kleene algebras, while the second one considers arbitrary non-halting and only *-continuous Kleene algebras. Thus, these two statements do not constitute an equivalence which would give a direct reduction of c-looping of $\mathtt{M}$ on α to validity of $\mathcal{H} \to S_{\Pi(\mathtt{M},\alpha)} \leq \widetilde{T}_{\mathtt{M}}$ on all Kleene algebras.

However, the desired undecidability result is obtained using the notion of *inseparability*. Namely, the sets $\{(\mathtt{M},\alpha) \mid \mathtt{M} \text{ c-loops on } \alpha\}$ and $\{(\mathtt{M},\alpha) \mid \mathtt{M} \text{ halts on } \alpha\}$ are recursively inseparable (an accurate proof of that is given in [12], see Proposition 8 below, but the fact itself is folklore), that is, there is no decidable set which includes the first set and is disjoint with the second one. As one can easily see from the statements above, the set

$$\{(\mathtt{M},\alpha) \mid \mathcal{H} \to S_{\Pi(\mathtt{M},\alpha)} \leq \widetilde{T}_{\mathtt{M}} \text{ is valid on all Kleene algebras}\}$$

is such a separating set. Therefore, it is undecidable, whence so is reasoning from commutativity conditions on the class of all Kleene algebras. A more fine-grained technique of *effective inseparability* shows that it is in fact Σ_1^0-complete.

In the next two sections, we give a detailed presentation of the argument sketched above.

3 Encoding of Looping

In this section, we shall prove the principal technical lemmata on the encoding of c-looping (resp., non-halting) of Turing machines using commutativity conditions on all (resp., *-continuous) Kleene algebras. The proof of Theorem 1 is given in the next section.

Let us recall the definition of an instance of Post's Correspondence Problem (PCP). A PCP Π is a finite set of pairs of words over a given alphabet, denoted in the following way

$$\begin{bmatrix} X_1 \\ Y_1 \end{bmatrix}, \ldots, \begin{bmatrix} X_k \\ Y_k \end{bmatrix}.$$

A *solution* of Π is a word X such that there exist numbers $i_1, \ldots, i_m \in \{1, \ldots, k\}$, where $m > 0$, such that $X = X_{i_1} \ldots X_{i_m} = Y_{i_1} \ldots Y_{i_m}$.

---

[2] For technical reasons, now the right-hand side also depends on the machine being encoded.

As noticed above, a standard construction yields $\Pi(\mathsf{M}, \alpha)$, the PCP which represents a Turing machine M together with its input value α. Let us recall this construction, following [21], with necessary modifications.

Throughout this paper, we consider only deterministic Turing machines. We define a Turing machine as a tuple $\mathsf{M} = (\mathcal{Q}, \Gamma, \Delta, q_0, q_F, \mathsf{c})$. Here $\mathcal{Q}$ is the set of states, q_0 is the initial state and q_F is the final accepting state. For simplicity, we do not add a rejecting state: unsuccessful executions could either be infinite or abort when a command cannot be executed (see below). As usual, Γ is the tape alphabet of the machine, and Δ is the set of commands. The sets $\mathcal{Q}$, Γ, and Δ are disjoint.

We do not designate a special input alphabet: any letter from the tape alphabet may be used in the input word. The tape alphabet Γ includes a specific 'blank' symbol $\sqcup$, which is added when the machine reaches the right end of the tape to extend it. Extending the tape to the left is disallowed.

Commands of M are of the form (q, a, r, b, d), where $q, r \in \mathcal{Q}$, $a, b \in \Gamma$, and $d \in \{R, L, N\}$ ('right,' 'left,' or 'no move'). For each pair (q, a), where $q \neq q_F$, there exists exactly one command of this form (determinism). For $q = q_F$ there is no such command. Command (q, a, r, b, d) means the following: being in state q and observing letter a on the tape, change the state to r, replace a with b, and perform one step in direction d.

Commands for state $q = \mathsf{c}$ are required to be the following: $(\mathsf{c}, a, \mathsf{c}, a, N)$ for each $a \in \Gamma$. This guarantees that c is the capturing state.

We distinguish three possible behaviours of M on a given input α:

- M halts on input α, that is, it reaches state q_F;
- M c-loops on input α, that is, it reaches the capturing state c and stays in this state forever; this is a special case of non-halting;
- M does not halt on input α for another reason: either it goes into infinite computation, but not at state c, or crashes by trying to execute a command with $d = L$ while observing the leftmost cell of the tape.

Now we recall the construction [21, §5.2] of $\Pi(\mathsf{M}, \alpha)$, which is the PCP corresponding to the execution of machine M on input α.[3] Consider an extended alphabet $\Sigma = \mathcal{Q} \cup \Gamma \cup \{\#, \star, \diamond\}$. Extra symbols $\#$, $\star$, $\diamond$ will be used for delimiting purposes.

The *configuration* of M when it is in state q, with word $a_1 \ldots a_n$ on the tape, and observing letter a_i, is encoded by the following string:

$$\kappa = \star a_1 \star a_2 \ldots \star a_{i-1} \star q \star a_i \ldots \star a_n.$$

Next, we define the *halting protocol* of M on the input word α, denoted by $\pi(\mathsf{M}, \alpha)$. The halting protocol is the complete transcript of execution of M on input α, starting from the initial configuration and ending in a final one. Thus, $\pi(\mathsf{M}, \alpha)$ should encode the sequence of configurations $\kappa_1, \ldots, \kappa_m$, where:

---

[3] Sipser [21] uses a two-step construction, which first defines an MPCP ("modified PCP") and then transforming it into a PCP. We construct the PCP directly.

1. κ_1 is the code of the initial configuration: if the input word α is $a_1 \ldots a_n$, then $\kappa_1 = \star q_0 \star a_1 \ldots \star a_n$;
2. each κ_{i+1} is the code of the configuration which immediately follows κ_i in the execution process of M;
3. κ_m encodes a final configuration, i.e., the state in κ_m is q_F.

The configurations in $\pi(\mathsf{M}, \alpha)$ are separated by $\star\#$ delimiters; the end of the protocol is marked by the combination $\star\#\diamond$.

For technical reasons, however, it will be necessary to perform "*garbage collection*" at the end of the protocol, so that the last element in the configuration sequence is just $\star q_F$, with no symbols in the tape. This is obtained by adding "pseudo-configurations" of the form described below (informally: allowing q_F to absorb the tape symbols). Let $\kappa_m = \star a_1 \star a_2 \ldots \star a_{i-1} \star q_F \star a_i \ldots \star a_n$. Then we introduce the following pseudo-configurations:

$$\lambda_k = \star a_1 \ldots \star a_{i-k} \star q_F \star a_i \ldots \star a_n \qquad \text{for } k = 2, \ldots, i;$$
$$\mu_k = \star q_F \star a_{i+k} \ldots \star a_n \qquad \text{for } k = 1, \ldots, (n-i+1).$$

In particular, $\lambda_i = \star q_F \star a_i \ldots \star a_n$ and $\mu_{n-i+1} = \star q_F$.

Using this notation, we define the halting protocol as the following string:

$$\pi(\mathsf{M}, \alpha) = \star\#\kappa_1 \star\# \ldots \star\#\kappa_m \star\#\lambda_2 \star\# \ldots \star\#\lambda_i \star\#\mu_1 \star\# \ldots \star\#\mu_{n-i+1} \star\#\star\#\star\diamond,$$

(Recall that $\mu_{n-i+1} = \star q_F$.) Note that the halting protocol, if it exists, is unique. Indeed, for the real computation phase, the sequence $\kappa_1, \ldots, \kappa_m$ is unique due to determinism. The garbage collection phase, $\lambda_2, \ldots, \mu_{n-i+1}$, is also performed in a deterministic manner: first absorb all letters to the left of q_F, then all letters to the right. Since there is no command starting from q_F, the start of the garbage collection phase is also determined uniquely.

In the case where M runs infinitely long on input α, we shall use the notion of *infinite protocol*, defined as follows:

$$\star\#\kappa_1 \star\#\kappa_2 \star\# \ldots \star\#\kappa_k \ldots$$

The infinite protocol is an infinitary word (ω-word), and we shall consider finite words which are prefixes of the infinite protocol.

Now let us define the PCP $\Pi(\mathsf{M}, \alpha)$ as a PCP including the following pairs:

1. the initial pair:
$$\begin{bmatrix} \star\# \\ \star\#\kappa_1 \star\#\star \end{bmatrix}$$

2. for each command $(q, a, r, b, R) \in \Delta$ and each $c \in \Sigma$, the following pairs:
$$\begin{bmatrix} \star q \star a \star c \\ b \star r \star c \star \end{bmatrix} \quad \text{and} \quad \begin{bmatrix} \star q \star a \star\# \\ b \star r \star_{\textvisiblespace} \star\#\star \end{bmatrix}$$

3. for each command $(q, a, r, b, L) \in \Delta$ and each $c \in \Sigma$, the following pair:

$$\begin{bmatrix} \star c \star q \star a \\ r \star c \star b \star \end{bmatrix}$$

4. for each command $(q, a, r, b, N) \in \Delta,$[4]

$$\begin{bmatrix} \star q \star a \\ r \star b \star \end{bmatrix}$$

5. for every $a \in \Gamma$, the following pair:

$$\begin{bmatrix} \star a \\ a \star \end{bmatrix}$$

6. the pair

$$\begin{bmatrix} \star \# \\ \# \star \end{bmatrix}$$

7. for every $a \in \Gamma$, the following garbage collection pairs:[5]

$$\begin{bmatrix} \star a \star q_F \\ q_F \star \end{bmatrix} \quad \text{and} \quad \begin{bmatrix} \star \# \star q_F \star a \\ \# \star q_F \star \end{bmatrix}$$

8. the final pairs:

$$\begin{bmatrix} \star q_F \star \# \star \# \\ \# \star \end{bmatrix} \quad \text{and} \quad \begin{bmatrix} \star \diamond \\ \diamond \end{bmatrix}$$

The main property of this construction is formulated in the following proposition (see [21, proof of Thm. 5.15]):

Proposition 3. *Let* M *be a Turing machine and let* $\alpha \in \Gamma^*$ *be its input value. Then the PCP* $\Pi(M, \alpha)$, *as constructed above, has the following properties.*

1. *If* M *does not halt on input* α, *then* $\Pi(M, \alpha)$ *has no solution.*
2. *If* M *halts on input* α, *then* $\Pi(M, \alpha)$ *has a solution. Moreover, in this case solutions of* $\Pi(M, \alpha)$ *are exactly concatenations of several (one or more) copies of* $\pi(M, \alpha)$.
3. *Each word in* $\Pi(M, \alpha)$ *is non-empty.*

---

[4] Sipser [21] does not use 'no move' commands, but we need them for the capturing state.

[5] The second type of pairs includes $\#$, which guarantees that the μ-phase of garbage collection is started only when there are no letters to the left of q_F.

In particular, as the capturing state c may never appear in a halting protocol of M, no solution of $\Pi(\mathsf{M}, \alpha)$ includes c as a letter.

In order to make the construction closer to Kozen's presentation [8], we shall transform $\Pi(\mathsf{M}, \alpha)$ into a PCP over a 2-letter alphabet $\Sigma_2 = \{p, q\}$. This is done by replacing each symbol a from Σ by a binary string $\hat{a}$ of a fixed length, namely $2\lceil \log_2 |\Sigma| \rceil + 4$. This is done in the following way. First, we encode a as a 'byte' (binary string) $b_1 \ldots b_k$, where $k = \lceil \log_2 |\Sigma| \rceil$ and $b_1, \ldots, b_k \in \{p, q\}$. Next, let

$$\hat{a} = ppqb_1qb_2\ldots qb_kqq.$$

The homomorphic image of a word $\gamma \in \Sigma^*$ under this translation will be denoted by $\hat{\gamma}$. It is easy to see that solutions of the new PCP, which we shall denote by $\hat{\Pi}(\mathsf{M}, x)$, are in one-to-one correspondence with solutions of $\Pi(\mathsf{M}, x)$, given by the function $\hat{\cdot}: \Sigma^* \to \Sigma_2^*$.

In particular, the translation of letter $c \in \mathcal{Q} \subseteq \Sigma$ is a binary word $\hat{c} \in \Sigma_2^*$. It is important to notice that $\hat{c}$ is a 'forbidden word' for $\hat{\Pi}(\mathsf{M}, x)$, due to the following lemma:

Lemma 1. *A word $\gamma \in \Sigma^*$ includes c (as a letter) if and only if its translation $\hat{\gamma} \in \Sigma_2^*$ includes $\hat{c}$ (as a subword).*

Proof. The "only if" direction is trivial. The "if" direction is a bit trickier, and this is the reason why we could not have used just a standard binary encoding of letters. Let $\gamma = a_1 \ldots a_n$ and let $\hat{\gamma} = \hat{a}_1 \ldots \hat{a}_n$ include $\hat{c}$. We claim that $\hat{c}$ is $\hat{a}_i$ for some i. Indeed, $\hat{c}$ starts with pp, and the only place where this combination may appear in $\hat{\gamma}$ is at the beginning of one of the $\hat{a}_i$'s. Hence, $c = a_i$ is a letter of γ. $\qquad \square$

This gives the following corollary: no solution of $\hat{\Pi}(\mathsf{M}, \alpha)$ may include $\hat{c}$ as a subword. Indeed, if $\hat{c}$ is a subword of a solution, then c is a letter of a solution of the original PCP $\Pi(\mathsf{M}, \alpha)$. By Proposition 3, item 2, this means that then c appears in the halting protocol of M on α. The latter is impossible, since c is the capturing state of M.

Now let us recall Cohen's construction for Theorem 2, as presented by Kozen [8]. We consider the following alphabets: $\Sigma_2 = \{p, q\}$, $\Sigma_2' = \{p', q'\}$, $\Sigma_4 = \Sigma_2 \cup \Sigma_2'$. For a word $Y \in \Sigma_2^*$, by Y' we denote its image in $\Sigma_2'^*$ under the following homomorphism: $p \mapsto p'$, $q \mapsto q'$.

Let $\hat{\Pi}(\mathsf{M}, \alpha)$ be the following PCP:

$$\begin{bmatrix} X_1 \\ Y_1 \end{bmatrix}, \ldots, \begin{bmatrix} X_k \\ Y_k \end{bmatrix}.$$

(Here X_i, Y_i are words over Σ_2.)

The following (fixed) set of commutativity conditions will be used:

$$\mathcal{H} = \{pp' = p'p, \quad pq' = q'p, \quad qp' = p'q, \quad qq' = q'q\}$$

and the following two terms $S = S_{\hat{\Pi}(M,\alpha)}$ and T are defined:

$$S = (X_1 Y_1' + X_2 Y_2' + \ldots + X_k Y_k')^+,$$
$$T = (pp' + qq')^* \big((p+q)^+ + (p'+q')^+ + (pq' + qp')(p+q+p'+q')^* \big).$$

The informal idea behind this construction is as follows. Thanks to commutativity conditions from $\mathcal{H}$, the order matters only for letters from the same alphabet (Σ_2 or Σ_2'). Thus, each word from the combined alphabet Σ_4 can be separated as XY', where $X, Y \in \Sigma_2$. The term S generates all such pairs of words X and Y, which can be obtained using our PCP (X on the top, Y on the bottom). In particular, it will include XX', if X is a solution of the PCP. The term T, conversely, is used to avoid pairs of this form, generating only pairs XY' such that $X \neq Y$. This means that solvability of the PCP invalidates $S \leq T$ (in the presence of $\mathcal{H}$), and the other way round: if the PCP has no solution, then $\mathcal{H} \to S \leq T$ is generally true.

In order to handle c-looping, we modify the definition of T and obtain a new term $\widetilde{T} = \widetilde{T}_M$ in the following way:

$$\widetilde{T} = (pp' + qq')^* \big((p+q)^+ + (p'+q')^+ + (pq' + qp' + \hat{c})(p+q+p'+q')^* \big).$$

In the proof of Theorem 2, the main lemma states that $\mathcal{H} \to S \leq T$ is valid on all $*$-continuous Kleene algebras if and only if M does not halt on input α [8]. Notice that by distributivity

$$\widetilde{T} = T + (pp' + qq')^* \, \hat{c} \, (p+q+p'+q')^*,$$

therefore $\widetilde{T} \geq T$. This means that the modified Horn formula, $\mathcal{H} \to S \leq \widetilde{T}$, is weaker than $\mathcal{H} \to S \leq T$.

Therefore, we have to modify both directions of the main lemma of Theorem 2.

1. We shall prove (Lemma 6 below) that M does not halt on α already if the weaker Horn formula $\mathcal{H} \to S \leq \widetilde{T}$ is valid on all $*$-continuous Kleene algebras.
2. We shall prove (Lemma 5) that if M c-loops on α, then $\mathcal{H} \to S \leq \widetilde{T}$ is valid on all Kleene algebras, not only $*$-continuous ones.

Before going further, let us prove a technical lemma, which is called the "long rule" in [12]:

Lemma 4. If $\mathcal{H} \to A \leq B$, $\mathcal{H} \to A^2 \leq B$, ..., $\mathcal{H} \to A^n \leq B$, and $\mathcal{H} \to A^n A^+ \leq B$ are valid on all Kleene algebras, then so is $\mathcal{H} \to A^+ \leq B$. (cf. [12, Lemma 3])

Proof. Induction on n. For $n = 0$ the statement is trivial. For induction step, we use the equality $A^+ = A + AA^+$, which is valid on all Kleene algebras. By monotonicity, we get $A^n A^+ = A^{n+1} + A^{n+1} A^+$. Thus, given $\mathcal{H} \to A^{n+1} \leq B$ and $\mathcal{H} \to A^{n+1} A^+ \leq B$, we get $\mathcal{H} \to A^n A^+ \leq B$. Together with $\mathcal{H} \to A \leq B$, ..., $\mathcal{H} \to A^n \leq B$, this yields $\mathcal{H} \to A^+ \leq B$ by induction.

Now we are ready to prove the main lemmata.

Lemma 5. *If* M *c-loops on input* α, *then* $\mathcal{H} \to S \leq \tilde{T}$ *is valid on all Kleene algebras.*

Proof. Let M c-loop on α. Consider the infinite protocol of this computation, after translating to the binary alphabet Σ_2, and let n be the length of a prefix of this protocol which already contains $\hat{c}$. Indeed, since M c-loops, its computation at some point reaches the capturing state c.

Since S is of the form A^+, we may use Lemma 4. Now it is sufficient to prove validity of $\mathcal{H} \to A^m \leq B$ for $m \in \{1, \ldots, n\}$ and of $\mathcal{H} \to A^n A^+ \leq B$.

Let us start with the first one, and establish a stronger, since $T \leq \tilde{T}$, Horn formula:

$$\mathcal{H} \to (X_1 Y_1' + \ldots + X_k Y_k')^m \leq T.$$

In order to establish this, by distributivity, it is sufficient to prove that $\mathcal{H}$ entails the following atomic formulae:

$$X_{i_1} Y_{i_1}' X_{i_2} Y_{i_2}' \ldots X_{i_m} Y_{i_m}' \leq T$$

for all $i_1, \ldots, i_m \in \{1, \ldots, k\}$.

Let $X = X_{i_1} \ldots X_{i_m}$ and $Y' = Y_{i_1}' \ldots Y_{i_m}'$. By commutativity conditions from $\mathcal{H}$, we may replace $X_{i_1} Y_{i_1}' X_{i_2} Y_{i_2}' \ldots X_{i_m} Y_{i_m}'$ with XY'. Now we have to prove $XY' \leq T$.

We know that $\hat{\Pi}(\text{M}, \alpha)$ has no solution, because M does not halt on α. In particular, this means, for given $i_1, \ldots, i_m$, that $X \neq Y$ (as words over Σ_2).

This may happen in one of the following two cases:

1. for some j, the j-th letter of X is p and the j-th letter of Y is q, or vice versa (X and Y *disagree* at position j);
2. Y is a proper prefix of X, or vice versa.

Using commutativity conditions from $\mathcal{H}$, let us rearrange letters in XY' such that letters from Σ_2 interleave with letters from Σ_2' (e.g., $pp'qq'pq'\ldots$). If X and Y have different length, then in the end we have a tail of letters only from Σ_2 or from Σ_2'. Denote the resulting word by Z.

For the first case, let j be the smallest position with the given property. Then Z falls under the regular expression $(pp' + qq')^*(pq' + qp')(p + q + p' + q')^*$. Therefore, $\mathcal{H}$ entails $Z \leq T$ on the class of all Kleene algebras. More precisely, we can prove $Z \leq (pp' + qq')^{j-1}(pq' + qp')(p + q + p' + q')^{\ell}$ for some ℓ, and then use monotonicity and the fact that $A^n \leq A^*$ is true in all Kleene algebras.

The second case is similar: if ℓ is the length of Y, which is a proper prefix of X, we get $Z \leq (pp' + qq')^{\ell}(p + q)^+ \leq T$. The case where X is a proper prefix of Y is analogous.

This argument is essentially the same as the one from the proof of Theorem 2. The more interesting Horn formula is

$$\mathcal{H} \to (X_1 Y_1' + \ldots + X_k Y_k')^n (X_1 Y_1' + \ldots + X_k Y_k')^+ \leq \tilde{T},$$

where c-looping comes into play. Again, it is sufficient to establish

$$\mathcal{H} \to X_{i_1} Y'_{i_1} \ldots X_{i_n} Y'_{i_n} (X_1 Y'_1 + \ldots + X_k Y'_k)^+ \leq \widetilde{T}$$

for arbitrary $i_1, \ldots, i_n \in \{1, \ldots, k\}$. Let us replace, using $\mathcal{H}$, $X_{i_1} Y'_{i_1} \ldots X_{i_n} Y'_{i_n}$ with XY', where $X = X_{i_1} \ldots X_{i_n}$ and $Y' = Y'_{i_1} \ldots Y'_{i_n}$.

Now we have the following two cases:

1. X and Y disagree at a position j;
2. X includes the 'forbidden word' $\hat{c}$ as a subword.

Indeed, the first situation happens when X is not even a prefix of the infinite protocol of M on α. If it is, however, it should include $\hat{c}$, because all X_i's are non-empty, and therefore the length of X is greater or equal to n.

Let j be either the smallest number of a position where X and Y disagree, or the position of the first letter of $\hat{c}$ in X.

In both situations, we derive (rearranging letters in XY')

$$\mathcal{H} \to XY' \leq (pp' + qq')^{j-1} (pq' + qp' + \hat{c})(p + q + p' + q')^*.$$

Recalling that $X_1 Y'_1 + \ldots + X_k Y'_k \leq (p + q + p' + q')^*$, we get

$$\mathcal{H} \to XY'(X_1 Y'_1 + \ldots + X_k Y'_k)^+ \leq (pp' + qq')^{j-1}(pq' + qp' + \hat{c})(p + q + p' + q')^* \leq \widetilde{T},$$

which is the desired goal. (Here we have used $A^*(A^*)^+ \leq A^*$, which is generally true in Kleene algebras, and monotonicity.)

Lemma 6. *If $\mathcal{H} \to S \leq \widetilde{T}$ is valid on $*$-continuous Kleene algebras, then M does not halt on α.*

Proof. Suppose the contrary: let M halt on α. Let us construct a $*$-continuous Kleene algebra which falsifies $\mathcal{H} \to S \leq \widetilde{T}$.[6]

We take $K = \mathcal{P}(\Sigma_1^* \times \Sigma_2'^*) = \mathcal{P}(\{(U, V') \mid U, V \in \Sigma_2^*\})$. For $a, b \in K$ let

$$ab = \{(U_1 U_2, V'_1 V'_2) \mid (U_1, V'_1) \in a, (U_2, V'_2) \in b\}$$
$$a + b = a \cup b$$
$$a^* = \{(U_1 \ldots U_n, V'_1 \ldots V'_n) \mid (U_1, V'_1), \ldots, (U_n, V'_n) \in a\}$$
$$0 = \varnothing$$
$$1 = \{(\varepsilon, \varepsilon)\}$$

It is easy to see that $\mathbf{K} = (K, +, \cdot, {}^*, 0, 1)$ is a $*$-continuous Kleene algebra.

Let us interpret variables p, q, p', q' as $\{(p, \varepsilon)\}$, $\{(q, \varepsilon)\}$, $\{(\varepsilon, p')\}$, $\{(\varepsilon, q')\}$ respectively. This interpretation obeys the set of conditions $\mathcal{H}$.

Each pair (U, V') in the interpretation of $\widetilde{T}$ has at least one of the following properties:

---

[6] Our construction is based on language algebras, which differs from the one from [8], where relational algebra is used.

1. $U \neq V$ (they have either different length, or different letters at the same position);
2. U includes $\hat{c}$ as a subword.

Since M halts on α (as we have supposed), $\Pi(\text{M}, \alpha)$ has a solution X_0, which is the halting protocol of M on α (Proposition 3). Since c is a 'capturing' state, it cannot appear in a terminating computation. Therefore, as shown above (Lemma 1), $\hat{c}$ is not a subword of X_0.

The interpretation of S includes every pair of the form (X, X') where X is a solution of $\Pi(\text{M}, \alpha)$. In particular, this set includes (X_0, X_0'). This pair is neither of the form of the form (U, V') with $U \neq V$, nor does X_0 include $\hat{c}$ is a subword. Hence, (X_0, X_0') does not belong to the interpretation of $\widetilde{T}$.

Therefore, $S \leq \widetilde{T}$ is false under the given interpretation. Since this intepretation satisfies $\mathcal{H}$, this falsifies $\mathcal{H} \rightarrow S \leq \widetilde{T}$

4   Effective Inseparability Argument

Proving undecidability of reasoning from commutativity conditions (and even from the fixed set $\mathcal{H}$ of those) is now simple and performed as sketched in Sect. 2. The set

$$\mathscr{K} = \{(\text{M}, \alpha) \mid \mathcal{H} \rightarrow S_{\Pi(\text{M},\alpha)} \leq \widetilde{T}_\text{M} \text{ is valid on all Kleene algebras}\}$$

includes the set $\mathscr{L} = \{(\text{M}, \alpha) \mid \text{M c-loops on } \alpha\}$ and is disjoint with $\mathscr{H} = \{(\text{M}, \alpha) \mid \text{M halts on } \alpha\}$. Indeed, $\mathscr{L} \subseteq \mathscr{K}$ by Lemma 5 and $\mathscr{K} \cap \mathscr{H} = \varnothing$ by Lemma 6.

Since these two sets are known to be recursively inseparable, $\mathscr{K}$ is undecidable, and therefore so is the problem of reasoning from $\mathcal{H}$ on all Kleene algebras.

Theorem 1, however, claims more than just undecidability: we need to prove Σ_1^0-completeness. This is done by using a more fine-grained technique of effective inseparability (cf. [12, 22]). Let us recall the basic definitions and results. By $\mathcal{W}_u$ we denote the recursively enumerable set of index u (i.e., enumerated by a Turing machine whose code is u).

Definition 5. *Two sets of natural numbers, $\mathscr{A}$ and $\mathscr{B}$, are effectively inseparable, if they are disjoint and there exists a partial computable function f of two arguments such that if $\mathscr{A} \subseteq \mathcal{W}_u$, $\mathscr{B} \subseteq \mathcal{W}_v$, and $\mathcal{W}_u$ and $\mathcal{W}_v$ are disjoint, then $f(u, v)$ is defined and $f(u, v) \notin \mathcal{W}_u \cup \mathcal{W}_v$.*

The informal idea is that f provides a constructive counterexample to any attempt to separate $\mathscr{A}$ and $\mathscr{B}$ by a decidable set. By Post's theorem, a decidable set is an enumerable set $\mathcal{W}_u$ whose complement is also an enumerable set $\mathcal{W}_v$, thus $\mathcal{W}_u \cup \mathcal{W}_v$ is $\mathbb{N}$. The element $f(u, v)$ witnesses that this is not the case.

Proposition 7. *If two sets are effectively inseparable, and both are recursively enumerable, then they are both Σ_1^0-complete.*

This statement is an easy corollary of a theorem by Myhill [16], see [20, Exercise 11-14] or [12, Corollary 2].

Proposition 8. *The sets $\mathscr{L}$ and $\mathscr{H}$ (where we tacitly encode pairs (M, α) as natural numbers) are effectively inseparable.*

This fact is folklore, see [20, Exercise 7-55d] or [12, Proposition 3].

Proposition 9. *If $\mathscr{A}$ and $\mathscr{B}$ are effectively inseparable, $\mathscr{A}' \supseteq \mathscr{A}$ and $\mathscr{A}' \cap \mathscr{B} = \varnothing$, then $\mathscr{A}'$ and $\mathscr{B}$ are also effectively inseparable.*

This is also folklore.

Proof. Take the same function f. Let $\mathscr{A}' \subseteq \mathcal{W}_u$ and $\mathscr{B} \subseteq \mathcal{W}_v$. Indeed, we have also $\mathscr{A} \subseteq \mathcal{W}_u$, and therefore $f(u,v) \notin \mathcal{W}_u \cup \mathcal{W}_v$.

Now everything is ready to prove Theorem 1. Indeed, $\mathscr{L} \subseteq \mathscr{K}$, $\mathscr{K} \cap \mathscr{H} = \varnothing$. By Proposition 8, $\mathscr{L}$ and $\mathscr{H}$ are effectively inseparable. By Proposition 9, so are $\mathscr{K}$ and $\mathscr{H}$. By Proposition 7, $\mathscr{K}$ is Σ_1^0-complete. This yields Σ_1^0-hardness of reasoning from $\mathcal{H}$ on the class of all Kleene algebras. The upper Σ_1^0 bound follows from a finitary axiomatisation.

This finishes the proof of Theorem 1, and thus fills the only cell left empty in Kozen's complexity table [9].

Acknowledgments. The author is grateful to the reviewers for valuable comments and suggestions which helped to improve the paper significantly.

References

1. Berstel, J.: Transductions and Context-Free Languages. Teubner, Stuttgart (1979). https://doi.org/10.1007/978-3-663-09367-1
2. Buszkowski, W.: On action logic: equational theories of action algebras. J. Log. Comput. **17**(1), 199–217 (2007). https://doi.org/10.1093/logcom/exl036
3. Cohen, E.: Hypotheses in Kleene algebra. Technical report, Bellcore (1994)
4. Doumane, A., Kuperberg, D., Pous, D., Pradic, P.: Kleene algebra with hypotheses. In: Bojańczyk, M., Simpson, A. (eds.) FoSSaCS 2019. LNCS, vol. 11425, pp. 207–223. Springer, Cham (2019). https://doi.org/10.1007/978-3-030-17127-8_12
5. Gibbons, A., Rytter, W.: On the decidability of some problems about rational subsets of free partially commutative monoids. Theoret. Comput. Sci. **48**, 329–337 (1986). https://doi.org/10.1016/0304-3975(86)90101-5
6. Haase, C., Hofman, P.: Tightening the complexity of equivalence problems for commutative grammars. In: 33rd Symposium on Theoretical Aspects of Computer Science (STACS 2016), vol. 47 of Leibniz International Proceedings in Informatics (LIPIcs), pp. 41:1–41:14. Schloss Dagstuhl–Leibniz-Zentrum für Informatik (2016). https://doi.org/10.4230/LIPIcs.STACS.2016.41
7. Kozen, D.: On action algebras. In: van Eijck, J., Visser, A. (ed.) Logic and Information Flow, pp. 78–88. MIT Press (1994)
8. Kozen, D.: Kleene algebra with tests and commutativity conditions. In: Margaria, T., Steffen, B. (eds.) TACAS 1996. LNCS, vol. 1055, pp. 14–33. Springer, Heidelberg (1996). https://doi.org/10.1007/3-540-61042-1_35
9. Kozen, D.: On the complexity of reasoning in Kleene algebra. Inf. Comput. **179**, 152–162 (2002). https://doi.org/10.1006/inco.2001.2960

10. Kozen, D., Mamouras, K.: Kleene algebra with equations. In: Esparza, J., Fraigniaud, P., Husfeldt, T., Koutsoupias, E. (eds.) ICALP 2014. LNCS, vol. 8573, pp. 280–292. Springer, Heidelberg (2014). https://doi.org/10.1007/978-3-662-43951-7_24

11. Kozen, D., Patron, M.-C.: Certification of compiler optimizations using Kleene algebra with tests. In: Lloyd, J., et al. (eds.) CL 2000. LNCS (LNAI), vol. 1861, pp. 568–582. Springer, Heidelberg (2000). https://doi.org/10.1007/3-540-44957-4_38

12. Kuznetsov, S.: Action logic is undecidable. ACM Trans. Comput. Logic **22**(2), 1–26 (2021). https://doi.org/10.1145/3445810

13. Kuznetsov, S.L., Speranski, S.O.: Infinitary action logic with exponentiation. Ann. Pure Appl. Logic **173**(2), 103057 (2022). https://doi.org/10.1016/j.apal.2021.103057

14. Maarand, H., Uustalu, T.: Reordering derivatives on trace closures of regular languages. In: 30th International Conference on Concurrency Theory (CONCUR 2019), vol. 140 of Leibniz International Proceedings in Informatics (LIPIcs), pp. 40:1–40:16. Schloss Dagstuhl–Leibniz-Zentrum für Informatik (2019). https://doi.org/10.4230/LIPIcs.CONCUR.2019.40

15. Mayr, E.W., Meyer, A.R.: The complexity of the word problems for commutative semigroups and polynomial ideals. Adv. Math. **46**(3), 305–329 (1982). https://doi.org/10.1016/0001-8708(82)90048-2

16. Myhill, J.: Creative sets. Z. Math. Logik Grundlagen Math. **1**, 97–108 (1955). https://doi.org/10.1002/malq.19550010205

17. Palka, E.: An infinitary sequent system for the equational theory of *-continuous action lattices. Fund. Inform. **78**(2), 295–309 (2007)

18. Pratt, V.: Action logic and pure induction. In: van Eijck, J. (ed.) JELIA 1990. LNCS, vol. 478, pp. 97–120. Springer, Heidelberg (1991). https://doi.org/10.1007/BFb0018436

19. Redko, V.N.: On the algebra of commutative events. Ukrainskiĭ Matematicheskiĭ Zhurnal **16**(2), 185–195 (1964). In Russian

20. Rogers, H.: Theory of Recursive Functions and Effective Computability. MIT Press, Cambridge (1987)

21. Sipser, M.: Introduction to the Theory of Computation. Cengage Learning. 3rd edn (2012)

22. Speranski, S.O.: A note on hereditarily Π_1^0- and Σ_1^0-complete sets of sentences. J. Log. Comput. **26**(5), 1729–1741 (2016). https://doi.org/10.1093/logcom/exu066

Towards the Complexity Analysis
of Programming Language Proof Methods

Matteo Cimini[✉] [iD]

University of Massachusetts Lowell, Lowell, MA 01854, USA
matteo_cimini@uml.edu

Abstract. Numerous proof methods have been proposed to establish
language properties such as type soundness, confluence, strong normalization, and others. However, literature does not provide a study of the
complexity of carrying out these proof methods.

This paper provides an investigation on the complexity of carrying out
the "syntactic approach" to type soundness (progress theorem and type
preservation theorem) for a class of functional languages, and characterizes the complexity of its proofs as a function of the number of expression
constructors, number of typing rules, reduction rules, and other common
quantities of operational semantics. Although we do not claim to provide
the complexity of this approach, this paper provides the first example of
complexity analysis of a programming language proof method.

Keywords: Type soundness · Complexity analysis · Functional
languages

1 Introduction

Language verification is an important part of the development of programming
languages. Once we have created a programming language, there are many questions that are interesting to investigate: Is the language type sound? Is it strongly
normalizing? Is it free of data races? Since the very beginning of programming
language theory, numerous proof methods have been developed in order to establish these and other language properties.

Some proof methods are lengthy to carry out and such lengthiness may
depend on the specifics of the operational semantics at hand such as the number
of type constructors, the number of reduction rules, as well as other semantics
quantities. However, literature does not provide a study of the complexity of carrying out programming language proof methods. In this paper, we provide an
example of such complexity analysis for the "syntactic approach" to type soundness [27] for a class of functional languages. Type soundness is one of the most
important properties in programming languages theory [13,21]. Milner proposed
this property in order to establish (an aspect of) the correctness of programming languages [18]. Wright and Felleisen have developed a syntactic approach

E. Ábrahám et al. (Eds.): ICTAC 2023, LNCS 14446, pp. 100–118, 2023.
https://doi.org/10.1007/978-3-031-47963-2_8

1. Theorem *progress* : $\forall e, T.$ *Main* : $\vdash\ e : T \Rightarrow e$ *is value* $\lor e$ *is error* $\lor \exists e'.e \longrightarrow e'$.

2. Proof

3. *induction on Main.*

4. *apply inductive hypothesis on the typing of the arg. (e of* (**head** e) *and* (**fst** e)).

5. *case analysis on the progress of that argument.*

(a) **head** e

6. *apply canonical-form-list.*

7. *appeal to existence of red. rule for nil.*

8. *appeal to existence of red. rule for cons*

9. *appeal to existence of an error context.*

10. *appeal to existence of an eval context.*

(b) **fst** e

6. *apply canonical-form-×. (product)*

7. *appeal to existence of r. rule for* $\langle v, v \rangle$.

8. *appeal to existence of an error context.*

9. *appeal to existence of an eval context.*

Fig. 1. Part of a proof for the progress theorem

to type soundness [27], which Harper has later adapted in its well-known formulation that is based on the progress theorem and type preservation theorem [13]. Since then, proving type soundness with this method has become widespread in research papers, an essential part of programming languages theory, and a staple element of courses such as Software Foundations[1] and others [13,16,21].

What is the complexity of carrying out this proof method? To give an idea of what we mean: Since there is a canonical form lemma for each type constructor of the language at hand, we expect its complexity to be *at least* $\Theta(|\mathsf{Type}|)$ where $|\mathsf{Type}|$ denotes the number of productions of the grammar Type of types.

The motivation for analyzing the complexity of proof methods is largely theoretical. However, detecting lengthy proof methods inspires researchers to develop better proofs. Comparing the complexity of proof methods is also interesting. For example, in the future we would like to compare the complexity of the method of Volpano et al. for noninterference [26] to that of Pottier and Simonet's [22], which reduces this property to type soundness as proved with the syntactic approach.

Our Approach: Analysis of Language-parametrized Proofs. In prior work [8], we have proposed an approach to express *language-parametrized proofs*, that is, proofs that can be applied to classes of languages rather than one single language. To make an example, consider the progress theorem. The proof that resolves the progress theorem for **head** e (head of a list) is analogous to that of **fst** e (first of a pair) and several other operations. Fig 1 shows the beginning of such a proof in Line 1-5. For a language with **head**, this proof continues as in column (a). For a language with **fst**, this proof continues as in column (b). However, whether the operation is **head** or **fst** a pattern applies nonetheless and [8] develops a domain-specific language called LANG-N-PROVE for expressing such patterns. For example, LANG-N-PROVE can generate Line 6 of both column (a) and (b) with code that expresses "if the operation at hand is an elimination form of type constructor c, apply the canonical form for type c". Having computed c, LANG-N-PROVE can also generate Line 7-8 for (a) and Line 7 for (b) with code

---

[1] https://softwarefoundations.cis.upenn.edu/.

that expresses "for all values of c, appeal to the existence of a reduction rule". (The canonical forms of lists are the empty list and cons-constructor, while there is only the canonical form for building pairs for the product type.)

LANG-N-PROVE has been used in [8] to express the syntactic approach to type soundness, and in particular it provides language-parametrized proofs for the canonical form lemmas, the progress theorem, and the type preservation theorem (though substitution lemmas must be manually provided) for a class of languages that is described in [8] as *pure harmonious functional languages with derived operators and error handlers*. (We describe these languages in Sect. 2.) This class includes common types and operators such as pairs, option types, sum types, universal and recursive types, exceptions, list operations such as map, filter, range and reverse, as well as others.

In this paper, we study the complexity of the language-parametrized proofs of [8]. These algorithms may be regarded as a pseudocode version of the syntactic approach to type soundness when applied to our intended class of functional languages. We characterize the complexity of these proofs as a function of the number of expression constructors, number of typing rules, reduction rules, and other common quantities of operational semantics. Our concluding section comfortably summarizes our findings in a table for our readers (Sect. 8, Fig. 7). It is to notice that [8] does not provide a proof for the substitution lemmas, which are used only in the type preservation theorem in our context. Therefore, the complexity that we offer for type preservation is parametrized by the complexity of substitution lemmas that is left unspecified. Why do we not fill the gap of [8] here and provide language-parametrized proofs for substitution lemmas? Such lemmas are strongly dependent on the representation of binders (de Bruijn indices, higher-order abstract syntax, locally nameless, and so on). We believe that a subsequent paper should specifically address the language-parametrized proofs for all these binding approaches and the study of their complexity.

Threat to Validity. To recall, our question is: What is the complexity of carrying out the syntactic approach to type soundness for our intended class of functional languages? We certainly acknowledge that it is in the eye of the beholder to reckon whether the algorithms in [8] describe this proof method accurately. We do not claim to answer this question definitely, hence "*Towards*" in our title, which stresses that this paper offers a first example of this kind of analysis.

The paper is organized as follows. Section 2 reviews the main elements of operational semantics and provides some definitions that we will use in our complexity analysis. Section 3 provides our analysis of canonical form lemmas. Section 4 analyzes the progress theorem. Section 5 analyzes the type preservation theorem. Section 6 discusses some limitations of our analysis. Section 7 discusses related work and Sect. 8 concludes the paper.

2   Operational Semantics and Complexity Definitions

We begin with a review of operational semantics. Figure 2 shows a λ-calculus with lists, pairs, let-declarations, an error and a (simple) `try` error handler. We call this language `fl` (as in "functional language").

A language has a grammar and an inference rule system. The latter defines relations such as a typing relation and a reduction relation. A grammar consists of a series of *grammar rules*, each of which defines a *syntactic category*, such as Type and Expression. Each syntactic category has a metavariable, such as T and e in Fig. 2, and a series of *grammar productions*, such as Int, $T \rightarrow T$, and List T of Type. The elements that can be derived by a grammar are *terms*, ranged over by t. Terms can contain metavariables. Terms can use unary binding $(X)t$ [6], denoting that the variable X is bound in t, and the capture-avoiding substitution $t[t/X]$. As LANG-N-PROVE needs to access terms uniformly, terms are handled in abstract syntax tree, for example we have $(\times \ T_1 \ T_2)$ rather than $T_1 \times T_2$. Each inference rule has a series of formulae called *premises* and one formula called *conclusion*. For example, $\Gamma \vdash e_1 : T_1 \rightarrow T_2$ and $\Gamma \vdash e_2 : T_1$ are premises of rule (T-APP), and $\Gamma \vdash e_1 \ e_2 : T_2$ is its conclusion. Inference rules whose conclusion can derive a $\vdash$-formula are called *typing rules*, whereas those that derive a $\longrightarrow$-formula are called *reduction rules*. `fl` makes use of evaluation contexts, which define which arguments of an operator can be evaluated. Error contexts specify in which contexts the occurrence of the error can be detected so that the overall computation can fail.

Some Definitions for Complexity Analysis. The following definitions will be useful in our analysis. Given a language definition, $|cname|$ is the number of grammar productions of the syntactic category *cname* of the language. For example, $|\text{Type}| = 4$ and $|\text{Expression}| = 13$ for `fl`. Notation $|rel|$ denotes the number of inference rules whose conclusion derives a formula for the relation *rel*. For example, $|\vdash| = 13$ and $|\longrightarrow| = 10$ for `fl`. We also define $|rules| = |\longrightarrow| + |\vdash|$. Notation `max-arity`(*cname*) denotes the maximum number of arguments that a single constructor has in *cname*. For example, `max-arity`(Expression) $= 2$ because `cons`, abstraction (with arguments T and $(x)e$), application, pairs, `let`, and `try` have two arguments and that is the maximum.

We make the following assumption: The maximum number of arguments of operators is small and negligible compared to other quantities such as the number of rules, expressions, and so on. For `fl`, for example, we have that `max-arity`(Expression) $= 2$ while $|\vdash| = 13$. Then, we remove `max-arity`-terms in our calculations in terms such as (`max-arity`(Expression) $* |\vdash|$) as $|\vdash|$ is dominant but we still keep `max-arity`-terms when they have a higher order, as in (`max-arity`(Expression)$^2 * |\vdash|$). This assumption occurs pervasively in practice and simplifies our calculations.

We shall see that the type preservation proof needs to detect whether a substitution is used in the targets of reduction rules. That is, we need to traverse the nodes of the abstract syntax tree of e' of $e \longrightarrow e'$ to see whether a substitution occurs. This complexity needs to be taken into account. We then define

Type $T ::= \texttt{Int} \mid T \to T \mid \texttt{List } T \mid T \times T$

Expression $e ::= n \mid x \mid \lambda x : T.e \mid (e\ e) \mid \texttt{nil} \mid \texttt{cons } e\ e \mid \texttt{head } e$
$\mid \langle e, e \rangle \mid \texttt{fst } e \mid \texttt{snd } e \mid \texttt{let } x = e \texttt{ in } e \mid \texttt{error} \mid \texttt{try } e \texttt{ with } e$

Value $v ::= n \mid \lambda x : T.e \mid \texttt{nil} \mid \texttt{cons } v\ v \mid \langle v, v \rangle$

EvalCtx $E ::= \Box \mid (E\ e) \mid (v\ E) \mid \texttt{cons } E\ e \mid \texttt{cons } v\ E \mid \texttt{head } E \mid \langle E, e \rangle \mid \langle v, E \rangle$
$\mid \texttt{fst } E \mid \texttt{snd } E \mid \texttt{let } x = E \texttt{ in } e \mid \texttt{try } E \texttt{ with } e$

ErrorCtx $F ::= \text{all evaluation contexts } E \text{ except } \texttt{try } E \texttt{ with } e$

$$\Gamma \vdash n : \texttt{Int}$$
$$\Gamma, x : T \vdash x : T$$

$$\frac{\Gamma, x : T_1 \vdash e : T_2}{\Gamma \vdash \lambda x : T_1.e : T_1 \to T_2}$$

(T-APP)
$$\frac{\Gamma \vdash e_1 : T_1 \to T_2 \qquad \Gamma \vdash e_2 : T_1}{\Gamma \vdash (e_1\ e_2) : T_2}$$

(T-NIL)
$$\Gamma \vdash \texttt{nil} : \texttt{List } T$$

$$\frac{\Gamma \vdash e_1 : T \qquad \Gamma \vdash e_2 : \texttt{List } T}{\Gamma \vdash \texttt{cons } e_1\ e_2 : \texttt{List } T}$$

(T-HEAD)
$$\frac{\Gamma \vdash e : \texttt{List } T}{\Gamma \vdash \texttt{head } e : T}$$

$$\frac{\Gamma \vdash e_1 : T_1 \qquad \Gamma \vdash e_2 : T_2}{\Gamma \vdash \langle e_1, e_2 \rangle : T_1 \times T_2}$$

$$\frac{\Gamma \vdash e : T_1 \times T_2}{\Gamma \vdash \texttt{fst } e : T_1}$$

$$\frac{\Gamma \vdash e : T_1 \times T_2}{\Gamma \vdash \texttt{snd } e : T_2}$$

$$\frac{\Gamma \vdash e_1 : T_1 \qquad \Gamma, x : T_1 \vdash e_2 : T_2}{\Gamma \vdash \texttt{let } x = e_1 \texttt{ in } e_2 : T_2}$$

$$\Gamma \vdash \texttt{error} : T$$

$$\frac{\Gamma \vdash e_1 : T \qquad \Gamma \vdash e_2 : T}{\Gamma \vdash \texttt{try } e_1 \texttt{ with } e_2 : T}$$

$$
\begin{aligned}
((\lambda x : T.e)\ v) &\longrightarrow e[v/x] \\
\texttt{head nil} &\longrightarrow \texttt{error} \\
\texttt{head (cons } v_1\ v_2) &\longrightarrow v_1 \\
\texttt{fst } \langle v_1, v_2 \rangle &\longrightarrow v_1 \\
\texttt{snd } \langle v_1, v_2 \rangle &\longrightarrow v_2 \\
\texttt{let } x = v \texttt{ in } e &\longrightarrow e[v/x]
\end{aligned}
$$

$$\texttt{try } v \texttt{ with } e \longrightarrow v$$
$$\texttt{try error with } e \longrightarrow e$$

$$\frac{e \longrightarrow e'}{E[e] \longrightarrow E[e']}$$

$$F[\texttt{error}] \longrightarrow \texttt{error}$$

Fig. 2. Language definition of fl. (Integers only serve as base values.)

nodesInTargets as the maximum number of nodes of the abstract syntax tree of the targets of reduction rules. For example, nodesInTargets = 5 in fl because the target $e[v/x]$ of the β-reduction rule has 5 nodes (top-level constructor for the substitution operation and children e, v, and a variable-node with x as its only child) and that is the maximum.

Our Intended Class of Functional Languages. The language-parametrized proofs of [8] do not apply to every language. Their application is limited to a restricted class of languages that [8] describes as 1) pure functional, i.e., computation solely proceeds by rewriting expressions (and therefore there is no state), 2) harmonious [11,19], i.e., operators can be classified in elimination forms (application, head, fst and snd in fl) and introduction forms (n, λ, nil, cons and pairs), and 3) to which we can add derived operators (such as let), an error and error handlers. (The work in [8] considers the presence of one error only or none.) These characteristics entail some constraints on language definitions. For example, the reduction relation must be $e \longrightarrow e'$ and we handle the usual typing relation $\Gamma \vdash e : T$ with a standard type environment (map from variables to types).

Other constraints apply but due to lack of space we cannot review them and we refer the reader to the paragraph "What Languages Do We Target in This Paper?" of Sect. 2 of [8], and the paragraph "Limitations" of Sect. 9 of that paper. The following constraints are not explicitly stated in [8] and we use them:

- *Grammar productions are "skeletons" or metavariables.* We define *skeleton* as a constructor name applied to metavariables as its arguments. For example, $(e\ e)$ is a skeleton in Expression. In inference rules, a term is a skeleton whenever its metavariables are also distinct, as $(e_1\ e_2)$ in (T-APP).
- *There is exactly one typing rule per constructor of* Expression, *which applies to a skeleton.* This also entails that $|\text{Expression}| = |\vdash|$ holds for our languages.

This prevents languages from having terms such as $(e_1\ (\text{cons}\ e_2\ e_3))$ as grammar productions of, say, Expression, or as subjects of typing rules. (They would not make inductive reasoning immediately available.) These restrictions also make some operations simpler. For example, given a term $(op\ e_1\ e_2)$ from Expression, and given a typing rule, we have a quick means to check whether the latter is a typing rule of that expression. Indeed, since both the expression and the subject of the typing rule are skeletons, it is sufficient to check that their top-level constructor name is equal. We will make use of these considerations during our analysis. Our readers are invited to see that f1 of Fig. 2 adheres to the constraints stated above and that these characteristics are, indeed, quite common in functional languages. (Languages that do not respect them may still be type sound but the language-parametrized proofs of [8] would not prove that.)

3   Analysis of Canonical Form Lemmas

LANG-N-PROVE provides a proof language for expressing proofs. We do not repeat its syntax from [8] and we shall describe its relevant parts as we encounter them. All the language-parametrized proofs that we analyze in this paper are presented and described in [8] and we shall review them before their complexity analysis. We refer our readers to [8] for their original description. Language-parametrized proofs are algorithms for generating proofs when a language definition is given as input. Therefore, we shall use phrases such as "Line n generates such lemma" and "Line n emits such a formula" in our analysis.

Figure 3 shows the language-parametrized proof for canonical form lemmas of [8]. These lemmas establish the shape of values for types. Line 1 generates a lemma for each type constructor in the grammar of types. Therefore, the overall complexity is that of Line 2-11 multiplied by |Type|. Line 2-4 generate the statement of one canonical form lemma. We have highlighted some parts of Fig. 3 with colors. The figure also shows some examples of statements, which use those colors to indicate which instructions have generated them.

Intuition on how Fig. 3 generates one statement follows. (Review of [8].) The variable ty is a type from the grammar of types. As ty may contain variables (as List T or $\times\ T_1\ T_2$), we universally quantify these variables with $\forall_{\text{vars}}(ty)$. We generate a series of or-formulae with $\bigvee$. Each formula says that e can be one

1. for each ty in $Type$, Theorem $canonical\text{-}form\text{-}\_(ty)$:
2. $\forall e.\ \forall_{vars}(ty).\ Main : \vdash e : ty \Rightarrow ValHyp : (e\ is\ value) \Rightarrow$
3. $\quad\quad \bigvee_{(v\ in\ valuesOf(ty))}$.
4. $\quad\quad\quad (\ \exists_{vars}(v).\ e = v\ \wedge\ \bigwedge_{(arg\ in\ valueArgs(v))}.(arg\ is\ value)).$
5. Proof. intros. case $Main$.
6. for each e in $Expression$:
7. if $ty = \text{ofType}(e)$ or $\text{isVar}(\text{ofType}(e))$
8. then if e in $Value$ then search
9.   else if e may be $Value$ then case $ValHyp$. search
10.   else case $ValHyp$
11. else noOp

Examples of theorem statements:
Theorem $canonical\text{-}form\text{-}list : \forall e,\ T\ .\ Main : \vdash e : (\text{List}\ T) \Rightarrow ValHyp : (e\ is\ value) \Rightarrow$
$e = \text{nil}\ \vee\ (\ \exists v_1, v_2\ .\ e = (\text{cons}\ v_1\ v_2)\ \wedge\ (v_1\ is\ value)\ \wedge\ (v_2\ is\ value)$

Theorem $canonical\text{-}form\text{-}\times : \forall e,\ T_1, T_2\ .\ Main : \vdash e : (\times\ T_1\ T_2) \Rightarrow$
$ValHyp : (e\ is\ value) \Rightarrow (\ \exists v_1, v_2\ .\ e = \langle v_1, v_2 \rangle\ \wedge\ (v_1\ is\ value)\ \wedge\ (v_2\ is\ value)$

Fig. 3. Language-parametrized proof of [8] for canonical form lemmas

of the values of ty. We compute all the values of ty with $\text{valuesOf}(ty)$. These values may contain variables (as $\langle v_1, v_2 \rangle$) and we existentially quantify them with $\exists_{vars}(v)$. Furthermore, some of these variables must be values themselves (as v_1 and v_2 of $\langle v_1, v_2 \rangle$) and so we create and-formulae with $\bigwedge$ that state that they are values.

Complexity analysis follows. The complexity of generating one statement is the sum of the complexity of 1) $\forall_{vars}(ty)$, 2) $\text{valuesOf}(ty)$, 3) $\exists_{vars}(v)$, repeated for as many values of ty, that is, $O(|\text{Value}|)$ times, and 4) $\text{valueArgs}(v)$ repeated $O(|\text{Value}|)$ times for the same reason. Notice that Line 2 emits "$\forall e$", which is $O(1)$. Generally speaking, emitting fixed parts of formulae and proofs is $O(1)$ and we shall omit including the lines that do just that from our calculations.

In $\forall_{vars}(ty)$, we have that ty is a skeleton from Type (top-level constructor applied to metavariables). Its arguments are the variables to quantify over. Therefore, the complexity of $\forall_{vars}(ty)$ is $\text{max-arity}(\text{Type})$. The $\text{valuesOf}(ty)$ expression iterates over the terms v in the grammar Value in $O(|\text{Value}|)$. For each, we return the output of its typing rule by scanning the typing rules in $O(|\vdash|)$, and checking if its conclusion applies to v. This latter check is $O(1)$ because we can simply compare two top-level constructors thanks to the fact that the two are skeletons. Therefore, the complexity of $\text{valuesOf}(ty)$ is $O(|\text{Value}| * |\vdash|)$. The complexity of $\exists_{vars}(v)$ is analogous to $\forall_{vars}(\cdot)$ and is $O(\text{max-arity}(\text{Value}))$. In $\text{valueArgs}(v)$, v is a skeleton from Value and so we scan its arguments in $O(\text{max-arity}(\text{Value}))$ to check whether they are a value variable in $O(1)$. The complexity of one lemma statement is then the sum of:

$O(\text{max-arity}(\mathtt{Type}))$ $\forall_{\text{vars}}(ty)$

$O(|\mathsf{Value}| * |\vdash|)$ $\mathtt{valuesOf}(ty)$

$O(|\mathsf{Value}| * \text{max-arity}(\mathsf{Value}))$ $\exists_{\text{vars}}(v)., O(|\mathsf{Value}|)$ *times*

$O(|\mathsf{Value}| * \text{max-arity}(\mathsf{Value}))$ $\mathtt{valueArgs}(v), O(|\mathsf{Value}|)$ *times*

That is $O(|\mathsf{Value}| * |\vdash|)$.

Intuition on how Fig. 3 generates one proof follows. (Review of [8].) intros introduces the proviso of the theorem, and case performs a case analysis on a given hypothesis. The case analysis of Line 5 is on how the expression has been typed. Line 6 iterates over expression forms (except object vars x, by default). For each, we compute the type assigned by its typing rule with $\mathtt{ofType}(e)$. It is helpful to make examples with *canonical-form-list* to see this proof. For example, $\mathtt{ofType}(\mathtt{nil}) = \mathtt{List}\ T$ because of (T-NIL) of Fig. 2. In this case, nil succeeds the condition $ty = \mathtt{ofType}(e)$ at Line 7. nil also succeeds the condition e in *Value* at Line 8, which checks that nil is derived by the grammar Value. We then conclude the proof case with search. The search instruction denotes that we have everything we need to prove the current goal. At this point, search concludes the proof because nil must be in the or-formula built by the statement of the lemma. Another example is (cons e_1 e_2). Line 7 succeeds because $\mathtt{ofType}(\mathtt{cons}\ e_1\ e_2) = \mathtt{List}\ T$ but Line 8 does not because (cons e_1 e_2) in *Value* does not hold since Value contains (cons v_1 v_2), instead. The condition (cons e_1 e_2) may be *Value* at Line 9 succeeds, however, as it checks that cons is among the grammar productions of Value. In this case, we do a case analysis on *ValHyp*, which says that (cons e_1 e_2) is a value and therefore must be (cons v_1 v_2). Then, we conclude with search. Another example is (head e). We have $\mathtt{ofType}(\mathtt{head}\ e) = T$ because of (T-HEAD), and so it is not List T. However, Line 7 succeeds because of isVar, which checks that T is a metavariable. The other conditions do not succeed and we end up in the else-branch at Line 10. This is a case analysis on how head is a value, but head is not a value and so this proof case is discharged by contradiction. Another example is expression n with $\mathtt{ofType}(n) = \mathtt{Int}$. None of the conditions of Line 7 succeed and we end up in the else-branch at Line 11. noOp does not generate any proof. Indeed, the lemma says *Main* : $\vdash e$: List T and a case analysis on it does not even propose the case for n.

Complexity analysis follows. The complexity for generating one proof is the sum of the complexity of the operations above. The $\mathtt{ofType}(e)$ operation scans the typing rules in $O(|\vdash|)$ and detects whether the typing rule applies to the selected e in $O(1)$ (because it compares top-level constructors, thanks to having two skeletons). Equality "$=$" of Line 7 is shallow and compares the top-level constructors of the two terms in input in $O(1)$. (We use a different notation with $=$, may be, and in than in [8].) isVar is $O(1)$, as well. The e in *Value* test scans all the productions of the grammar Value in $O(|\mathsf{Value}|)$ and for each it checks their equality to e. This time around also the arguments are compared because, we recall, this is the check that rejects (cons e_1 e_2) for not matching (cons v_1 v_2). This is done in $O(\texttt{max-arity}(\textsf{Value}))$. The e may be *Value* test is similar to e in *Value* except that it matches only top-level constructors in $O(1)$.

The complexity of generating one proof is therefore:

$$O(|\textsf{Expression}|) \ast \textit{(but recall from Section 2 that } |\textsf{Expression}| = |\vdash|)$$
$$(\ O(|\vdash|) \qquad\qquad\qquad\qquad\qquad \texttt{ofType}(e)$$
$$+ O(|\textsf{Value}| \ast \texttt{max-arity}(\textsf{Value})) \qquad e \text{ in } \textit{Value}$$
$$+ O(|\textsf{Value}|) \ ) \qquad\qquad\qquad\quad e \text{ may be } \textit{Value}.$$

As $|\textsf{Expr.}| = |\vdash|$, this is $O(|\vdash| \ast (|\vdash| + |\textsf{Value}|)) = O(|\vdash|^2 + (|\textsf{Value}| \ast |\vdash|))$, which is simply $O(|\vdash|^2)$.

The overall complexity is: For each type, statement + proof, given below.

$$O(|\textsf{Type}| \ \ast \ (|\textsf{Value}| \ast |\vdash| \ + \ |\vdash|^2)) = O(|\textsf{Type}| \ast |\vdash|^2).$$

The intuition behind this complexity is that there is a lemma for each type constructor (hence $|\textsf{Type}| \ast \ldots$), each of which requires a case analysis of the typing rules (hence a first $\ast |\vdash|$), but then each of these cases entails operations such as $\texttt{ofType}(e)$ that, too, iterate over the typing rules (hence another $\ast |\vdash|$).

---

1. **Theorem** *progress* : $\forall e, T. \ Main : \ \vdash e : T \Rightarrow e \ progresses$.
2. **Proof.** *Typ* : **induction on** *Main*.
3. **for each** e **in** *Expression* :
4.   **for each** i **in** $\texttt{contextualArgs}(e)$: **apply** *IH* **to** $Typ\_(i)$.
5.   **backchain** $progress\text{-}\_(e)$.

Fig. 4. Language-parametrized proof of [8] for the progress theorem

---

4   Analysis of the Progress Theorem

The proof of the progress theorem is divided into two parts. The first part is the main theorem. Figure 4 shows its language-parametrized proof of [8]. The formula "*e progresses*" holds whenever e is a value, e is an error, or $e \longrightarrow e'$, for some e'. (We use a different notation for it and for $\vdash$-formulae than in [8].)

4.1   Analysis of the Main Theorem

Intuition on the proof of the progress theorem in Fig. 4 follows. (Review of [8].) The proof is by induction. Line 2 shows that sometimes instructions are prefixed with a name. This name is used to store the formulae that are derived after performing that instruction. For example, *Typ* : **induction on** *Main* stores derived formulae as hypotheses *Typ0*, *Typ1*, and so on. (Example for **head** e: after induction, *Typ0* is the premise $\Gamma \vdash e : \textsf{List } T$ of (T-HEAD) of Fig. 2). The proof continues as follows. For each operator, we invoke the inductive hypothesis to derive that its evaluated arguments "progress". Then, an operator-specific progress theorem concludes the proof. To make an example, consider the application $(e_1\ e_2)$. The inductive hypothesis derives that both e_1 and e_2 "progress", then the theorem *progress-app* of Fig. 5 proves that the whole $(e_1\ e_2)$ "progresses". (backchain applies the lemma to conclude the proof.)

Complexity analysis follows. The complexity of the main theorem in Fig. 4 is characterized by Line 4 repeated |Expression| times. The contextualArgs(e) operation computes the evaluated arguments of the operator of e by scanning the grammar EvalCtx in $O(|\text{EvalCtx}|)$. For each grammar production, we match its top-level operator with that of e in $O(1)$. Then, we scan the arguments in $O(\text{max-arity}(\text{EvalCtx}))$ to find E, that is, the position that is contextual. Then, contextualArgs returns a list of indexes. The number of positions that are returned by contextualArgs(e) is $O(\text{max-arity}(\text{EvalCtx}))$. Therefore, the apply at Line 4 is emitted (in $O(1)$) $O(\text{max-arity}(\text{EvalCtx}))$ times.

The complexity of the proof of the progress theorem is the following.

$$O(|\text{Expression}| * ((|\text{EvalCtx}| * \text{max-arity}(\text{EvalCtx})) + \text{max-arity}(\text{EvalCtx}))),$$

which is $O(|\text{Expression}| * |\text{EvalCtx}|)$.

The intuition behind this complexity is that for each expression constructor we have to call the inductive hypothesis on all its contextual arguments before applying the finishing lemma, and computing the contextual arguments for an expression constructor entails scanning the grammar EvalCtx (hence $* |\text{EvalCtx}|$).

4.2   Analysis of Operator-Specific Progress Theorems

Figure 5 shows the language-parametrized proof for operator-specific progress theorems of [8]. Line 1 generates a proof for each expression constructor. Therefore, the complexity of this proof is that of Line 2-16 multiplied by |Expression|.

Intuition on how Fig. 5 generates one statement follows. (Review of [8].) The expression selected by the iteration at Line 1 may contain variables, which we universally quantify with $\forall_{\text{vars}}(e)$. The $\Longrightarrow$ operation creates a premise for each evaluated argument. We compute them with evaluationOrder(e), which is similar to contextualArgs(e) except that it returns indexes in the order of evaluation. We create premises such as e_1 *progresses* and e_2 *progresses* using getArg(e, i), which returns the i-th argument of e as in getArg$((e_1\ e_2), 0) = e_1$.

Complexity analysis follows. The complexity for generating one statement is the sum of 1) $\forall_{\text{vars}}(e)$, 2) evaluationOrder(e), and 3) getArg(e, i) repeated for as many evaluated arguments of e, that is, $O(\text{max-arity}(\text{EvalCtx}))$ times. As discussed in Sect. 3, $\forall_{\text{vars}}(e)$ is $O(\text{max-arity}(\text{Expression}))$. The operation getArg$(e, i)$ accesses the argument in array-style and is $O(1)$. We explain evaluationOrder(e) with an example similar to that of [8], which cites [10] for using this method. Consider an operator op with five arguments, $(\text{op}\ e\ e\ e\ e\ e)$, and let us evaluate its arguments from right to left. evaluationOrder(e) scans the grammar EvalCtx of evaluation contexts and creates the graph $\{(0 \mapsto 1), (0 \mapsto 2), (0 \mapsto 3), (0 \mapsto 4), (1 \mapsto 2), (1 \mapsto 3), (1 \mapsto 4), (2 \mapsto 3), (2 \mapsto 4), (3 \mapsto 4)\}$, which summarizes the arguments' dependencies. For each evaluation context, the graph

1. for each e in *Expression*, Theorem *progress-_(e)* :

2. $\forall T.\ \forall_{\text{vars}}(e).\ \ Main : \vdash e : T \Rightarrow$

3. $\Rightarrow_{(i\ \text{in}\ \text{evaluationOrder}(e))}.PrgE\_(i) :$ **getArg**(e, i) *progresses* $\Rightarrow e$ *progresses*

4. Proof. intros.

5. for each i in evaluationOrder(e) : *ProgressHyp_(i)* : case *PrgsE_(i)*.

6. if isEliminationForm(e)

7. then *Typ* : case *Main*.

8. *Canonical* : apply *canonical-form-_*(getArgType$(e, 0)$) to *Typ0 ProgressHyp0*.

9. case *Canonical*.

10. for each v in valuesOf(getArgType$(e, 0)$) : search.

11. for each i in evaluationOrder(e) : search. search.

12. else if isErrorHandler(e)

13. then

14. search. case *ProgressHyp0*. search. search.

15. for each i in evaluationOrder(e) : if $i = 0$ then noOp else search. search.

16. else search. for each i in evaluationOrder(e) : search. search.

Examples of theorem statements:

progress-app: $\forall T,\ \boxed{e_1, e_2}$.

$\vdash (e_1\ e_2) : T \Rightarrow PrgE_1 : \boxed{e_1}\ progresses \Rightarrow PrgE_2 : \boxed{e_2}\ progresses \Rightarrow (e_1\ e_2)\ progresses$

progress-head: $\forall T,\ \boxed{e}$. $\vdash (\textbf{head}\ e) : T \Rightarrow PrgE_1 : \boxed{e}\ progresses \Rightarrow (\textbf{head}\ e)\ progresses$

Fig. 5. Language-parametrized proof of [8] for operator-specific progress theorems

contains pairs from the position of E to each of the v positions. For example, the evaluation context (op e E v v v) creates the pairs $(1 \mapsto 2)$, $(1 \mapsto 3)$, and $(1 \mapsto 4)$ of that graph. Scanning EvalCtx is $O(|\text{EvalCtx}|)$ and generating the pairs is $O(\texttt{max-arity}(\text{EvalCtx}))$ for each context because we scan the arguments in search of E and v. Afterwards, evaluationOrder computes the topological sort of this graph, which returns the arguments in their evaluation order, which is $[4, 3, 2, 1, 0]$ in the example above. The complexity of topological sort is $O(|V| + |E|)$. Here, the set of vertices V is the number of evaluated arguments of an operator, that is, $|V| = O(\texttt{max-arity}(\text{EvalCtx}))$. The number of edges (set E) is the number of pairs like the ones above ($\{(0 \mapsto 1), (0 \mapsto 2), (0 \mapsto 3), \ldots\}$), which are constrained by the fact that [8] imposes that contexts have no circular dependencies. Therefore, the first evaluated argument does not depend on other arguments. The second evaluated argument depends at most on the first. The third evaluated argument depends at most on the first and the second, and so on. The number of pairs in E is then at most $1 + 2 + 3 + \ldots + k$ for an operator with k evaluated arguments. The maximum value for k is $\texttt{max-arity}(\text{EvalCtx})$. This summation can be described with the Gaussian formula $|E| = 1/2 * (\texttt{max-arity}(\text{EvalCtx})) * (\texttt{max-arity}(\text{EvalCtx}) + 1)$, which is essentially $O(\texttt{max-arity}(\text{EvalCtx})^2)$. Then $O(|V| + |E|)$ is $O(\texttt{max-arity}(\text{EvalCtx})^2)$.

The complexity for generating one theorem statement is the sum of:

$O(\text{max-arity}(\text{Expression}))$ $\forall_{\text{vars}}(e)$

$O(1) * O(\text{max-arity}(\text{EvalCtx}))$ $\text{getArg}(e, i)$, *for each element of* $\Rightarrow$

$O(\text{max-arity}(\text{EvalCtx})^2)$ $\text{evaluationOrder}(e)$

That is $O(\text{max-arity}(\text{EvalCtx})^2)$.

Intuition on how Fig. 5 generates one proof follows. (Review of [8].) In our setting, an operator can be an elimination form, an introduction form, an error, an error handler or a derived operator. We review the explanation of [8] insofar elimination forms is concerned because it is the worst case scenario. We refer our readers to [8] for the other cases.

Line 5 performs case analyses on the progress premises in the order of evaluation. To see why, let us consider an elimination form with three arguments arg_1, arg_2, and arg_3 that are evaluated from left to right. A case analysis on the progress of arg_1 creates a tree of proof cases with three children: 1) it is a value, 2) it is an error, and 3) it takes a step. Then, it operates in case 1) from which we do a case analysis on the progress of arg_2. This creates a subtree in case 1) of arg_1 with its three cases for arg_2. Then, it operates in case 1) of arg_2 from which we do a case analysis for arg_3, which creates a subtree in case 1) of arg_2 with its three cases for arg_3. (Fig. 11 of [8] shows this type of tree. Due to lack of space, we could not draw a tree here.) After all the case analyses, we operate in the proof case 1) of the last evaluated argument, that is, all evaluated arguments are values in this case. Therefore, the elimination form has a chance to apply a reduction rule, as the needed arguments have been evaluated. We apply the canonical form lemma at Line 8. To invoke the correct lemma, we need the type that the elimination form eliminates. (If it is head we need List, if it is fst we need ×, and so on). We compute this type with $\text{getArgType}(e, 0)$. Without loss of generality, [8] fixes that the *principal argument* [13], i.e., the argument that resolves the behavior of an elimination form, is the first, hence index 0. The $\text{getArgType}(e, 0)$ operation retrieves the type of the first argument of the elimination form according to its typing rule. For example, according to (T-HEAD), the type of e in (head e) is List. Next, Line 9 opens a proof case for each canonical form of such type. For each, we appeal to the existence of a reduction rule (with search at Line 10). This concludes case 1) of the last evaluated argument, say, arg_3 above. Then, the remaining cases are 2) for arg_3, for which we appeal to the existence of an error context with search, and 3) for arg_3, for which we appeal to the existence of an evaluation context with search. Concluding this subtree completes case 1) for arg_2, for which cases 2) and 3) remains to be proved with the same searchs. Line 11 generalizes and emits two searchs for each evaluated argument to prove cases 2) and 3) for each of them.

Complexity Analysis. The complexity of generating one proof is given by the sum of 1) $\text{evaluationOrder}(e)$, 2) valuesOf, 3) $\text{isEliminationForm}(e)$, 4) $\text{getArgType}(e, 0)$, 5) emitting "search" $O(|\text{Value}|)$ times at Line 10, and 6) emitting "search. search" $O(\text{max-arity}(\text{EvalCtx}))$ times at Line 11. As we have already discussed 1) and 2), we discuss the rest. In isEliminationForm(e), e is from Expression and is a skeleton, say, of an operator op. We scan all the reduction rules that define a step for op in $O(|\longrightarrow|)$. (Checking that the top-level operator of a source of a reduction rule is op is $O(1)$). For each of these rules we check that the principal argument is in Value. As previously discussed, this check is $O(|\mathsf{Value}| * \mathtt{max\text{-}arity}(\mathsf{Value}))$. The getArgType($e, 0$) operation retrieves the typing rule of e in $O(|\vdash|)$. Then, it retrieves the first premise and returns the output type of this premise. These are $O(1)$ array-style accesses.

The complexity for generating one theorem proof is then the sum of:

$O(\mathtt{max\text{-}arity}(\mathsf{EvalCtx})^2)$	evaluationOrder(e)
$O(|\longrightarrow| * |\mathsf{Value}| * \mathtt{max\text{-}arity}(\mathsf{Value}))$	isEliminationForm(e)
$O(|\vdash|)$	getArgType($e, 0$)
$O(|\mathsf{Value}| * |\vdash|)$	valuesOf(ty)
$O(|\mathsf{Value}|)$	search $iterated$ at $Line$ 10
$O(\mathtt{max\text{-}arity}(\mathsf{EvalCtx}))$	search. search $iterated$ at $Line$ 11.

That is $O(\mathtt{max\text{-}arity}(\mathsf{EvalCtx})^2 + (|\longrightarrow| * |\mathsf{Value}|) + (|\mathsf{Value}| * |\vdash|))$, which is $O(\mathtt{max\text{-}arity}(\mathsf{EvalCtx})^2 + (|rules| * |\mathsf{Value}|))$.

The overall complexity is: For each expression, statement + proof:

(We mention the term $\mathtt{max\text{-}arity}(\mathsf{EvalCtx})^2$ *only once)*
$O(|\mathsf{Expression}| * (\mathtt{max\text{-}arity}(\mathsf{EvalCtx})^2 + (|rules| * |\mathsf{Value}|)))$
$= O(((|\mathsf{Expression}| * \mathtt{max\text{-}arity}(\mathsf{EvalCtx})^2) + (|\mathsf{Expr.}| * |rules| * |\mathsf{Value}|)).$

The intuition behind this complexity is that for each expression constructor we need to compute the evaluation order of its evaluated arguments with a topological sort (hence $|\mathsf{Expression}| * \mathtt{max\text{-}arity}(\mathsf{EvalCtx})^2$). Furthermore, to carry out the proof, each expression constructor needs us to perform operations with two nested loops that iterate over the rules and over the values (hence $|\mathsf{Expression}| * |rules| * |\mathsf{Value}|$). For example, isEliminationForm(e) iterates over the reduction rules, besides the values, and valuesOf(ty) iterates over the typing rules, besides the values.

5   Analysis of the Type Preservation Theorem

Figure 6 shows the language-parametrized proof for the type preservation theorem of [8]. This theorem establishes that, for each step $e \longrightarrow e'$, the type of e and the type of e' coincide. (We use a different notation for $\longrightarrow$-formulae than in [8].) Line 1 creates the statement of the theorem in $O(1)$.

Intuition on how Fig. 6 generates the proof follows. (Review of [8].) The proof is by induction on $\vdash e : T$. For each expression e, we perform a case analysis on the reduction steps that e can take (Line 4). This case analysis fails for values, proving the case by contradiction. Otherwise, all the steps of e are proved in the following order: (1) the reduction steps that are specific of e are handled at Line 5 and 6, (2) contextual steps (such as head $e \longrightarrow$ head e' when $e \longrightarrow e'$) are

1. **Theorem** *type-preservation* : $\forall e, e', T$. *Main* : $\vdash e : T \Rightarrow Step : e \longrightarrow e' \Rightarrow \vdash e' : T$
2. **Proof** *Typ* : **induction on** *Main*.
3. **for each** e **in** *Expression* :
4. *StepOfSubExp* : **case** *Step*.
5. **for each** tg **in** stepsWithoutPM(e) : **if** containsSubst(tg) **then** □ **else** search.
6. **for each** tg **in** stepsWithPM(e) : **if** ctnsSbst(tg) **then** □ **else case** *Typ0*. search.
7. **for each** i **in** contextualArgs(e) : **apply** *IH* **to** *Typ_(i) StepOfSubExp*. search.
8. **for each** i **in** contextualArgs(e) : **if** isErrorHandler(e) **and** $i = 0$
9.   **then** noOp **else** backchain *error-types-all*

(At Line 6, ctnsSbst abbreviates containsSubst.)

Fig. 6. Language-parametrized proof of [8] for the type preservation theorem

handled at Line 7, and (3) the error steps (such as head error $\longrightarrow$ error) are handled at Line 8 and 9. The cases of contextual steps (2) are proved thanks to the inductive hypothesis. Error steps (3) are proved by appealing to the lemma *error-types-all*: $\forall err, T_1, T_2. \vdash err : T_1 \Rightarrow \vdash err : T_2$ whose proof is trivial and can be simply emitted in $O(1)$. (Appendix B of [8] shows this trivial proof. Notice that [8] imposes that the error must be typed at any type.) Case (3) also goes differently for error handlers when the error occurs as principal argument ($i = 0$ at Line 8). Such a case is handled as case (1) rather than (3). Case (1) distinguishes two cases: (i) Line 5 handles rules such as let $x = v$ in $e \longrightarrow e[v/x]$ which fire for every value, and (ii) Line 6 handles the rules for elimination forms such as head (cons v_1 v_2) $\longrightarrow v_1$, which pattern-match the principal argument. As (i) and (ii) are similar cases, we cover (ii) in some detail and refer our readers to [8] for case (i). The case analysis spawn by the induction at Line 2 provides the type of the arguments of head and so gives the type of (cons v_1 v_2) as List T at hypothesis *Typ0* (i.e., the principal argument, which is always the first argument by convention). However, we do not have yet the types of v_1 and v_2, therefore we perform a case analysis on *Typ0* to acquire them and to type check the target v_1 to see if it has the same type of the source. (Although other rules like the β-reduction rule would need to apply a substitution lemma, the types of all the metavariables of the source are known after the case analysis on *Typ0*.) This schema applies to all elimination forms of our setting. The stepsWithPM(e) operation returns the targets of all the reduction rules of type (ii) (such as v_1 above). The stepsWithoutPM(e) operation of Line 5 returns the targets of the reduction rules of type (i) (such as $e[v/x]$ above). Notice that Line 5 and 6 also detect occurrences of substitutions in targets with containsSubst(tg), so that a substitution lemma can be applied. This case is left unspecified as □.

Complexity Analysis. The complexity of carrying out this proof is characterized by the iteration over all expressions at Line 3. Therefore, the overall complexity is that of Line 4-9 multiplied by |Expression|. We notice that stepsWithoutPM(e) and stepsWithPM(e) perform the same test (which we describe shortly) and thus have the same complexity. We then analyze Line 6 only among 5 and 6. We also notice that Line 8-9 have worst complexity than Line 7. Therefore the complexity of Line 4-9 is characterized by Line 6 and Line 8-9. Line 6: stepsWithPM(e) scans all the reduction rules in $O(|\longrightarrow|)$ and checks if the rule is for the top-level constructor of e in $O(1)$ and whether its principal argument is a complex value in $O(1)$, i.e., built itself with a top-level constructor. Line 6 iterates over the targets provided by stepsWithPM(e), that is, $O(|\longrightarrow|)$ times. The containsSubst(tg) operation traverses the term tg to detect the use of substitution in $O(\text{nodesInTargets})$ (defined in Sect. 2). The worst case scenario is when containsSubst(tg) succeeds and code for applying a substitution lemma is needed. As [8] does not provide these lemmas, we leave their complexity unspecified and denote it with $\mathcal{C}(Subst)$. The complexity of Line 6 is then $O(|\longrightarrow|) + O(|\longrightarrow|*(\text{nodesInTargets}+\mathcal{C}(Subst)))$. Line 8-9 depend on contextualArgs(e) and isErrorHandler(e). We have analyzed contextualArgs(e) in Sect. 4.1. The complexity of isErrorHandler(e) is that of isEliminationForm(e), which we have analyzed in Sect. 4.2, except that it scans the grammar Error rather than Value and is therefore $O(|\longrightarrow| * \text{max-arity}(\text{Error}))$. Then, Line 8-9 is $O(\text{max-arity}(\text{EvalCtx}) + (\text{max-arity}(\text{EvalCtx}) * |\longrightarrow| * \text{max-arity}(\text{Error})))$.

The overall complexity for the type preservation theorem is:

$$O(|\text{Expression}|) *$$
$$(\quad O(|\longrightarrow| * (\text{nodesInTargets} + \mathcal{C}(Subst))) \qquad\qquad Line\ 6$$
$$+\ O(\text{max-arity}(\text{EvalCtx}) * |\longrightarrow| * \text{max-arity}(\text{Error}))\ )\quad Line\ 8\ and\ 9$$

That is $O((\text{nodesInTargets} + \mathcal{C}(Subst)) * |\longrightarrow| * |\text{Expression}|)$.

The intuition behind this complexity is that for each expression constructor we have to extract its reduction rules by iterating over all the reduction rules. For each of these rules, the dominant complexity is that of detecting the presence of substitution and use substitution lemmas.

6   Limitations of Our Analysis

Our analysis presents some limitations that we would like to discuss.

This paper focuses on complexity upper bounds only. It would be interesting, instead, to explore lower bounds as they may provide useful insights into the way the proofs that we have addressed are carried out.

Proofs are λ-terms in several type theories and proof assistants, and λ-terms do have a notion of size. We did not attempt to connect such a size with the complexity given in this paper. It would be interesting to explore that venue.

This paper does not address the space complexity of carrying out proofs. It would be interesting to do so. A subtle scenario may occur when proofs require to evaluate λ-terms, which may lead to unexpected space costs [1]. However, those cases do not occur in the proofs of this paper because we never fully evaluate λ-terms. The closest task to evaluating λ-terms occurs within the progress theorem but such a task is limited to derive one step from an expression. Furthermore, such derivations act on inference rules with a simple form, as the reduction rules of our intended class of functional languages do not have any premises or they have at most one recursive call on a subexpression (see Fig. 2, for an example).

We have handled the complexity of search as constant time. Alternatively, we could include the complexity of performing search. We can explain the difference between the two approaches with an example outside of the realm of language proofs. Let us suppose that a proof case concludes with search because $1*2*3 = 6$. A high-level view on the proof method being analyzed would say that we simply appeal to the fact that the two numbers are equal. In this case, the work to carry out this proof case is minimal and is $O(1)$. A low-level view would instead include the complexity of multiplication. We have opted for the former view but we acknowledge that the latter view is a valid alternative.

Works such as [10] checks whether language definitions belong to our intended class and whether they have all in order so that type soundness is guaranteed to hold. Once this property is established there would not be a need for generating a proof. Most of the checks of [10] have also been implemented in [9] in the form of database queries. It would be interesting to study the complexity of performing the checks of these works.

7   Related Work

Automated Proving of Type Soundness. The proof language of LANG-N-PROVE is inspired by that of the Abella proof assistant [4]. In addition to express language-parametrized proofs, the LANG-N-PROVE tool also takes a language definition as input and generates machine-checked proofs in Abella. The work in [8] reports that LANG-N-PROVE has been applied to a plethora of functional languages with common types and operations. (See Sect. 9 of [8] for a list of these languages.) That paper also reports generating, for all these languages, the mechanized proof that fully machine checks type soundness when the correct code for substitution lemmas is provided. (We believe that this provides some evidence that the algorithms of [8] capture the intended proof method with some accuracy.)

There are other works that automate type soundness. For example, Veritas [12] gives theorems as input to a first-order automated prover and, for some functional languages, Twelf [20] can prove these theorems at once with high automation in higher-order logic programming. However, these works do not aim at *describing* the syntactic approach to type soundness. In some sense, the complexity of mechanizing type soundness is different from that of a proof method because mechanized proofs can be short thanks to proof automation. The complexity of Veritas and Twelf ultimately depends on the complexity of automated theorem provers and of logic programming machinery, which does not inform about the complexity of the syntactic approach of type soundness.

Complexity of Type Sound Interpreters. The intrinsic typing approach [7] leverages on the meta-theoretic properties of a type theory. In this approach, an interpreter is written in such a way that if it type checks then the language is guaranteed to be type sound. This approach has been applied extensively

[2,3,14,23,25]. The complexity of type checking may be known for several type theories. This may be a means to establish a bound on the complexity of certifying type soundness. However, such a bound is general to all sorts of programs that can be written within the type theory at hand and does not provide the specific complexity of the syntactic approach to type soundness.

Similarly, Implicit Computational Complexity [5,15,17] is a remarkable research area on the cost analysis of reductions in λ-calculi and type theories. However, such work does not characterize the complexity in terms of language elements such as the number of expression constructors, number of typing rules, reduction rules, and other common operational semantics quantities of a language being implemented within them, which is instead the goal of this paper.

8   Conclusion

Our question was: What is the complexity of carrying out the syntactic approach to type soundness for our intended class of functional languages? We have analyzed the complexity of the language-parametrized proofs of [8], which algorithmically describe such approach and have been applied to a plethora of functional languages in that prior work.

Figure 7 summarizes our analysis. We refrain to claim to have answered the question above definitely, as it is in the eye of the beholder to reckon whether the algorithms in [8] describe this proof method accurately. Nonetheless, this paper offers an example of analysis that strives to tackle this question.

In the future, we would like to address the limitations that we have discussed in Sect. 6. We also plan on systematically developing language-parametrized proofs of substitution lemmas for the major approaches to binders (de Bruijn

Theorem	Complexity
Canonical form lemma (one statement)	$O(|\mathsf{Value}| * |\vdash|)$
Canonical form lemma (one proof)	$O(|\vdash|^2)$
Canonical form lemmas (all statements and proofs)	$O(|\mathsf{Type}| * |\vdash|^2)$
Progress theorem (statement)	$O(1)$
Progress theorem (proof)	$O(|\mathsf{Expression}| * |\mathsf{EvalCtx}|)$
Op. progress theorem (one statement)	$O(\texttt{max-arity}(\mathsf{EvalCtx})^2)$
Op. progress theorem (one proof)	$O(\genfrac{}{}{0pt}{}{\texttt{max-arity}(\mathsf{EvalCtx})^2}{+ (|rules| * |\mathsf{Value}|)})$
Op. progress theorems (all statements and proofs)	$O(\genfrac{}{}{0pt}{}{(|\mathsf{Expression}| * \texttt{max-arity}(\mathsf{EvalCtx})^2)}{+ (|\mathsf{Expression}| * |rules| * |\mathsf{Value}|)})$
Type preservation theorem (statement)	$O(1)$
Type preservation theorem (proof)	$O(\genfrac{}{}{0pt}{}{\texttt{nodesInTargets} + \mathcal{C}(Subst))}{* |\longrightarrow| * |\mathsf{Expression}|})$

Fig. 7. Summary of our complexity analysis. "Op." abbreviates "Operator-specific".

indices, locally nameless, and higher-order abstract syntax, among others) and studying their complexity. We also would like to extend the proofs of [8] to work in the presence of subtyping. Finally, we would like to address noninterference as we have mentioned in Sect. 1, and also develop a language-parametrized proof of strong normalization based on Tait's method with logical relations [24].

References

1. Accattoli, B., Dal Lago, U., Vanoni, G.: The (in)efficiency of interaction. Proc. ACM Program. Lang. (PACMPL) **5**(POPL), 1–33 (2021). https://doi.org/10.1145/3434332
2. Altenkirch, T., Reus, B.: Monadic presentations of lambda terms using generalized inductive types. In: Flum, J., Rodriguez-Artalejo, M. (eds.) CSL 1999. LNCS, vol. 1683, pp. 453–468. Springer, Heidelberg (1999). https://doi.org/10.1007/3-540-48168-0_32
3. Bach Poulsen, C., Rouvoet, A., Tolmach, A., Krebbers, R., Visser, E.: Intrinsically-typed definitional interpreters for imperative languages. Proc. ACM Programm. Lang. (PACMPL) **2**(POPL), 1–34 (2017). https://doi.org/10.1145/3158104
4. Baelde, D., et al.: Abella: a system for reasoning about relational specifications. J. Formalized Reason. **7**(2), 1–89 (2014). https://doi.org/10.6092/issn.1972-5787/4650
5. Bellantoni, S.J., Cook, S.A.: A new recursion-theoretic characterization of the poly-time functions (extended abstract). In: Proceedings of the Twenty-Fourth Annual ACM Symposium on Theory of Computing, pp. 283–293. STOC 1992, Association for Computing Machinery, New York, NY, USA (1992). https://doi.org/10.1145/129712.129740
6. Cheney, J.: Toward a general theory of names: binding and scope. In: Pollack, R. (ed.) Proceedings of the 3rd ACM SIGPLAN Workshop on Mechanized Reasoning about Languages with Variable Binding, pp. 33–40. MERLIN 2005, Association for Computing Machinery, New York, NY, USA (2005). https://doi.org/10.1145/1088454.1088459
7. Church, A.: A formulation of the simple theory of types. J. Symb. Log. **5**, 56–68 (1940). https://doi.org/10.2307/2266170
8. Cimini, M.: Lang-n-prove: a DSL for language proofs. In: Proceedings of the 15th ACM SIGPLAN International Conference on Software Language Engineering, pp. 16–29. SLE 2022, Association for Computing Machinery, New York, NY, USA (2022). https://doi.org/10.1145/3567512.3567514
9. Cimini, M.: A query language for language analysis. In: Schlingloff, B.H., Chai, M. (eds.) SEFM 2022. LNCS, vol. 13550, pp. 57–73. Springer, Cham (2022). https://doi.org/10.1007/978-3-031-17108-6_4
10. Cimini, M., Miller, D., Siek, J.G.: Extrinsically typed operational semantics for functional languages. In: Lämmel, R., Tratt, L., de Lara, J. (eds.) Proceedings of the 13th ACM SIGPLAN International Conference on Software Language Engineering, SLE 2020, Virtual Event, USA, 16–17 November 2020, pp. 108–125. ACM (2020). https://doi.org/10.1145/3426425.3426936
11. Dummett, M.: Frege: Philosophy of Language, 2nd edn. Harvard University Press, Cambridge (1993)

12. Grewe, S., Erdweg, S., Wittmann, P., Mezini, M.: Type systems for the masses: deriving soundness proofs and efficient checkers. In: Murphy, G.C., Steele Jr., G.L. (eds.) 2015 ACM International Symposium on New Ideas, New Paradigms, and Reflections on Programming and Software (Onward!), pp. 137–150. Onward! 2015, ACM, New York, NY, USA (2015). https://doi.org/10.1145/2814228.2814239

13. Harper, R.: Practical Foundations for Programming Languages. 2 edn. Cambridge University Press, Cambridge (2016). https://doi.org/10.1017/CBO9781316576892

14. Harper, R., Stone, C.: A type-theoretic interpretation of standard ML. In: Plotkin, G., Stirling, C., Tofte, M. (eds.) Proof, Language, and Interaction: Essays in Honor of Robin Milner. MIT Press (2000). https://doi.org/10.5555/345868.345906

15. Jones, N.D.: LOGSPACE and PTIME characterized by programming languages. Theor. Comput. Sci. **228**(1–2), 151–174 (1999). https://doi.org/10.1016/S0304-3975(98)00357-0

16. Kokke, W., Siek, J.G., Wadler, P.: Programming language foundations in Agda. Sci. Comput. Program. **194**, 102440 (2020). https://doi.org/10.1016/j.scico.2020.102440

17. Leivant, D., Marion, J.-Y.: Lambda calculus characterizations of poly-time. In: Bezem, M., Groote, J.F. (eds.) TLCA 1993. LNCS, vol. 664, pp. 274–288. Springer, Heidelberg (1993). https://doi.org/10.1007/BFb0037112

18. Milner, R.: A theory of type polymorphism in programming. J. Comput. Syst. Sci. **17**(3), 348–375 (1978). https://doi.org/10.1016/0022-0000(78)90014-4

19. Pfenning, F.: Lecture notes on harmony (lecture 3) 15–317: constructive logic (2009). https://www.cs.cmu.edu/~fp/courses/15317-f09/lectures/03-harmony.pdf

20. Pfenning, F., Schürmann, C.: System description: Twelf — a meta-logical framework for deductive systems. In: CADE 1999. LNCS (LNAI), vol. 1632, pp. 202–206. Springer, Heidelberg (1999). https://doi.org/10.1007/3-540-48660-7_14

21. Pierce, B.C.: Types and Programming Languages. MIT Press, Cambridge (2002)

22. Pottier, F., Simonet, V.: Information flow inference for ML. In: Proceedings of the 29th ACM SIGPLAN-SIGACT Symposium on Principles of Programming Languages, pp. 319–330. POPL 2002, Association for Computing Machinery, New York, NY, USA (2002). https://doi.org/10.1145/503272.503302

23. van der Rest, C., Poulsen, C.B., Rouvoet, A., Visser, E., Mosses, P.: Intrinsically-typed definitional interpreters à la carte. Proc. ACM Program. Lang. (PACMPL) **6**(OOPSLA2), 1903–1932 (2022). https://doi.org/10.1145/3563355

24. Tait, W.W.: Intensional interpretations of functionals of finite type I. J. Symb. Log. **32**(2), 198–212 (1967). https://doi.org/10.2307/2271658

25. Thiemann, P.: Intrinsically-typed mechanized semantics for session types. In: Komendantskaya, E. (ed.) Proceedings of the 21st International Symposium on Principles and Practice of Declarative Programming, pp. 19:1–19:15. PPDP 2019, Association for Computing Machinery, New York, NY, USA (2019). https://doi.org/10.1145/3354166.3354184

26. Volpano, D., Irvine, C., Smith, G.: A sound type system for secure flow analysis. J. Comput. Secur. **4**(2–3), 167–187 (1996). https://doi.org/10.3233/JCS-1996-42-304

27. Wright, A.K., Felleisen, M.: A syntactic approach to type soundness. Inf. Comput. **115**(1), 38–94 (1994). https://doi.org/10.1006/inco.1994.1093

A Dynamic Temporal Logic for Quality of Service in Choreographic Models

Carlos G. Lopez Pombo[1], Agustín E. Martinez Suñé[2,3]([⊠]), and Emilio Tuosto[4]

[1] Centro Interdisciplinario de Telecomunicaciones, Electrónica, Computación Y Ciencia Aplicada - CITECCA, Universidad Nacional de Río Negro - Sede Andina, San Carlos de Bariloche, Argentina
cglopezpombo@unrn.edu.ar
[2] CONICET-Universidad de Buenos Aires. Instituto de Ciencias de la Computación, Buenos Aires, Argentina
[3] Universidad de Buenos Aires, Facultad de Ciencias Exactas y Naturales. Departamento de Computación, Buenos Aires, Argentina
aemartinez@dc.uba.ar
[4] Gran Sasso Science Institute, L'Aquila, Italy
emilio.tuosto@gssi.it

Abstract. We propose a framework for expressing and analyzing the *Quality of Service* (QoS) of message-passing systems using a choreographic model that consists of *g-choreographies* and *Communicating Finite State machines* (CFSMs). The following are our three main contributions: (I) an extension of CFSMs with non-functional contracts to specify quantitative constraints of local computations, (II) a dynamic temporal logic capable of expressing QoS, properties of systems relative to the g-choreography that specifies the communication protocol, (III) the semi-decidability of our logic which enables a bounded model-checking approach to verify QoS property of communicating systems.

1 Introduction

Over the past two decades, software has steadily changed from monolithic applications to distributed cooperating components. Choreographic approaches are gaining momentum in industry (e.g. [1–3,5]) which, increasingly, conceives applications as components interacting over existing communication infrastructures.

Research partly supported by the EU H2020 RISE programme under the Marie Sk lodowska-Curie grant agreement No 778233. Research partly supported by the PRO3 MUR project Software Quality, and PNRR MUR project VITALITY (ECS00000041), Spoke 2 ASTRA - Advanced Space Technologies and Research Alliance. Carlos G. Lopez Pombos research is partly supported by Universidad de Buenos Aires by grant UBACyT 20020170100544BA and Agencia Nacional de Promoción de la Investigación, el Desarrollo Tecnológico y la Innovación Científica through grant PICT-2019-2019-01793.
The authors thank the anonymous reviewers for their constructive comments.
C. G. L. Pombo—On leave from Instituto de Ciencias de la computación CONICET–UBA and Departamento de Computación, Facultad de Ciencias Exactas y Naturales, Universidad de Buenos Aires.

© The Author(s), under exclusive license to Springer Nature Switzerland AG 2023
E. Ábrahám et al. (Eds.): ICTAC 2023, LNCS 14446, pp. 119–138, 2023.
https://doi.org/10.1007/978-3-031-47963-2_9

Among other models, choreographies stand out for a neat separation of concerns: choreographic models abstract away local computations from communications among participants. In fact, since their introduction [6], choreographies advocate for a separation between a *global view* and a *local view* of communication. The former is a high-level description of (distributed) interactions. The latter view is a description of each component in isolation. This is the distinctive feature of choreographies that we exploit here to reason about quantitative properties of applications. The basic idea is to specify the values of quality attributes of local states of components and then *aggregate* those attributes along runs involving communications. A simple example can illustrate this. Suppose that a component A sends another component B a message m and we want to consider two quality attributes: monetary cost (c) and memory consumption (mem). This behaviour can be abstracted away with the finite-state machines below

behaviour of A:

$$\{c \leq 5, mem = 0\} \qquad\qquad \{5 \leq c \leq 10, \ mem < 3\}$$
$$q_0 \xrightarrow{\quad\text{A B!m}\quad} q_1$$

behaviour of B:

$$\{c = 0, mem = 0\} \qquad\qquad \{10 \leq mem \leq 50, \ c = 0.01 \cdot mem\}$$
$$q_0' \xrightarrow{\quad\text{A B?m}\quad} q_1' \tag{1}$$

where A B!m and A B?m respectively denote the output and input communication actions, and each state is decorated with a specification predicating over the quality attributes in the local states of A and B. For instance, both A and B allocate no memory in their initial states, computation in A may cost up to five monetary units before executing the output, and B has no cost since it's just waiting to execute the input ($c = 0$). Likewise, after the communication actions, the local computations of A and B are specified by the formulae associated to states q_1 and q_1'.

The interaction between A and B depends on the communication infrastructure; e.g., asynchronous message-passing yields a run like

$$\pi : \quad s_0 \xrightarrow{\quad\text{A B!m}\quad} s_1 \xrightarrow{\quad\text{A B?m}\quad} s_2$$

where first the message is sent by A and then it is eventually received by B.

We are interested in analyzing quality properties that admit a measurement, thus assuming that the QoS attributes are *quantitative*. These properties encompass both quantitative attributes at the application level as well as resource consumption metrics. For instance, we could be interested in analyzing the monetary cost or the number of messages retrieved in a messaging system; but we could also be interested in analyzing its memory usage or CPU time. It's important to emphasize that our framework is designed to be agnostic and adaptable, allowing for the consideration of any quantifiable attribute, regardless of its specific nature. Furthermore, our framework is specifically designed to enable analysis of how quantitative properties of local computations influence the system-wide properties. Hence, we envisage the quality constraints as *contracts* that the local computations of components should honour. For instance, the specifications in (1) tell the cost of local computations in A and B, they do not predicate on the QoS of the communication infrastructure.

Once these quality constraints on local computations are fixed, natural questions to ask are e.g., "is the memory consumption of B along run π within a given range?" or "is the overall ry cost below a given threshold?". Answers to such questions require checking that the *aggregation* of the values of the quality attributes along the run π entails the properties. Interestingly, how to aggregate those values depends on the quality attributes. For instance, the aggregation of memory consumption can be computed by taking the maximum, while the aggregation of monetary cost can be computed as the sum. We work under the hypothesis that developers have no control over communication infrastructure. More precisely, QoS aspects related to how communications are realised are not under the control of applications' designers. Instead, designers have control over local computations, thus suggesting that QoS constraints are naturally associated to states of components. Indeed, we rely on behavioural types (such as [9–13]) which abstract away low level details.

Contributions. We propose a framework for the design and analysis of QoS-aware distributed systems, enabled by the following technical contributions:

Models for QoS attributes. Section 4 presents a straightforward extension of communicating finite-state machines (CFSMs [14]; reviewed in Sect. 3) to express QoS aspects of components. Basically, we assign to each state of CFSMs a QoS specification as in (1). We adopt real-closed fields (RCFs, cf. Sect. 3) to abstractly represent QoS values; besides being a complete and decidable abstract formalisation of the first-order theory of the real numbers, RCFs are instrumental for a smooth definition of our framework.

A dynamic temporal logic for QoS. Section 5 introduces a logic, dubbed $\mathcal{QL}$, to express QoS properties. Taking inspiration from *Propositional Dynamic Linear Temporal Logic* (DLTL) [15], $\mathcal{QL}$ indexes temporal modalities with *global choreographies* [16] (g-choreographies, Sect. 3), a model of global views of choregraphies, in order to predicate over QoS properties of the whole system. This is a distinct characteristic of $\mathcal{QL}$ that we comment in Sect. 2.

A semi-decision procedure for $\mathcal{QL}$. Section 6 proves $\mathcal{QL}$ to be semi-decidable by providing a k-bounded semi-decision procedure and relying on the decidability of the theory of real-closed fields [17] to check QoS constraints in atomic formulae. A distinctive aspect of the procedure is that it can be used as a bounded model-checking procedure of $\mathcal{QL}$ formulae.

Section 7 draws some conclusions and points out some further lines of research.

2   Related Work

The relevance of the problem addressed here has been already highlighted by other researchers [7,8]. There is a vast literature on QoS, spanning a wide range of contexts and methods [18,19]. This paper can be positioned in the category of general application-level QoS. The combination of RCFs and our behavioural types aims to capture essential aspects for applications' quantitative analysis while striving for generality. In this vein, a proof-of-concept methodology based on behavioural types has been proposed in [20] for client-server systems. To the best of our knowledge, our is the first work blending behavioural types with QoS and offering a decision procedure for multiparty protocols.

In order to abstractly capture QoS (instead of focusing on specific attributes) we adopt RCFs. Other abstract models of QoS such as quantales [21] or c-semirings [22–24] have been proposed. We opted for RCFs due to their inherent decidability, which is crucial for ensuring the decidability of our logic. Moreover, RCFs offer practical advantages as they can be readily employed in modern SMT (satisfiability modulo theories) solvers [39, Chapter 33].

Theory presentations over QoS attributes are used in [25] to enable the automatic analysis of QoS properties with a specification language that only considers convex polytopes; this restriction is not present in our language. Also, the approach in [25] can be thought as "monolithic", in the sense that specifications are given considering the system as a black box. We instead assign QoS contracts to states of components and then aggregate them in order to analyze properties along executions of the behavior emerging from interactions.

The use of choreographic methods for non-functional analysis yields other advantages. For instance, QoS contracts of components are derived from global specifications [7]. These contracts can then be used for run-time prediction, adaptive composition, or compliance checking, similarly to what is done in [8]. This top-down approach can be transferred to behavioural types as well similarly to what has been done in [11, 26] for qualitative properties. The framework proposed in [27] uses CFSMs as a dynamic binding mechanism of services but only considers the communicational aspects of the software component. Such a framework could be extended to include QoS attributes as well by leveraging the results presented in this paper.

Our $\mathcal{QL}$ logic takes inspiration from *dynamic linear temporal logic* (*DLTL*) [15] which blends trace semantics (akin *linear temporal logic* [28]) and regular expressions over a set of atomic actions (akin programs in *propositional dynamic logic* [29]). Intuitively a key difference is that, unlike *DLTL*, $\mathcal{QL}$ does not predicate about the behaviour of sequential programs; rather $\mathcal{QL}$ describes properties of asynchronous message-passing systems. This requires a modification of the syntax of *DLTL*; in fact, the syntax of $\mathcal{QL}$ is essentially the same of *DLTL* barred for the indexes of modalities, which become choreographies of interactions. This straightforward modification has deep impact on the semantics which requires a complete redefinition (see Sect. 5 for further details). Another key difference is that, while *DLTL* is propositional, $\mathcal{QL}$'s atomic formulae are first order formulae on QoS attributes. As a consequence, not only $\mathcal{QL}$ can express usual temporal properties, such as safety and liveness ones, but temporal properties constraining the value of QoS attributes. These points of comparison with *DLTL* apply in the same way to a similar logic called *linear dynamic logic* (LDL), introduced first in [30] and later formalized for finite traces in [31].

3 Preliminaries

This section surveys background material underpinning our work. We first describe the protocol used as a running example, then we review our choreographic model and we briefly recall *real-closed fields*.

A Running Example. Through the paper we will use a (simplified variant) of the POP protocol [32]. This protocol allows mail clients to access a remote mailbox and retrieve e-mails. In the POP protocol a client starts the communication by sending a message of type helo to a POP server (note that protocol specifications are oblivious of messages' payload).[1] The server replies with the number of unread messages in the mailbox using a message of type int. At this point the client can either halt the protocol or read one of the e-mails. These options are selected by sending a message of type quit or of type read respectively. In the former case, the server acknowledges with a message of type bye and the protocol ends. In the latter case, the server sends the client the number of bytes of the current unread message in a message of type size. Next, the client has again a choice between quitting the protocol (as before) or receiving the email (selected in the read message) by sending the server a message of type retr. In the latter case the server sends the email with a message of type msg, the client answers with a message of type ack and the reading process starts again.

A Choreographic Model. We use *global choreographies* [16] to specify the global view of communicating systems whose local view are rendered as *communicating finite state machines* [14].

Hereafter, we fix a set $\mathcal{P}$ of *participants* and a set $\mathcal{M}$ of (types of) *messages* such that $\mathcal{P} \cap \mathcal{M} = \varnothing$. We start by surveying the definition of g-choreographies.

Definition 1 (Global choreographies [16]). *A global choreography over $\mathcal{P}$ and $\mathcal{M}$ (*g-choreography *for short) is a term* G *that can be derived in*

$$\mathsf{G} ::= \mathbf{0} \mid \mathsf{A} {\to} \mathsf{B} : \mathsf{m} \mid \mathsf{G}; \mathsf{G}' \mid \mathsf{G} \mid \mathsf{G}' \mid \mathsf{G} + \mathsf{G}' \mid \mathsf{G}^*$$

where $\mathsf{A}, \mathsf{B} \in \mathcal{P}$, $\mathsf{A} \neq \mathsf{B}$ *and* $\mathsf{m} \in \mathcal{M}$.

Intuitively, a g-choreography specifies the communication protocol of participants. The basic g-choreography is the empty one $\mathbf{0}$, which specifies that no communications should happen. An *interaction* $\mathsf{A} {\to} \mathsf{B} : \mathsf{m}$ specifies that participants A and B (are expected to) exchange a message of type m; it is worth remarking that we assume asynchronous communication where the sender A does not wait for B to consume m to continue its execution. Moreover, g-choreographies can be composed sequentially $(\mathsf{G}; \mathsf{G}')$, in parallel $(\mathsf{G} \mid \mathsf{G}')$, and in non-deterministic

---

[1] Our framework can handle multiparty protocols; however, our examples are two-party for simplicity. Also, we stick to the types of messages as carefully described in the protocol specifications [32].

choices $(G + G')$; we assume that $\mathbf{0}$ is the neutral element of $\_;\_$, $\_|\_$, and $\_+\_$. Note that, due to asynchrony in the communication, in a sequential composition $G; G'$, outputs in G' can occur before G is fully executed; for instance, the distributed execution of $A{\to}B$: m; $C{\to}B$: m' allows the output from C to happen before the one from A. Finally, a g-choreography may be iterated (G^*).

Example 1 (A g-choreography for POP). Our running example can be expressed as the g-choreography $G_{pop} = C{\to}S$: helo; $G_{start} + G_{quit}$ where

$$G_{start} = S{\to}C: \text{int}; (G_{read} + G_{read}; G_{retr})^*; G_{quit} \quad G_{read} = C{\to}S: \text{read}; S{\to}C: \text{size}$$
$$G_{retr} = C{\to}S: \text{retr}; S{\to}C: \text{msg}; C{\to}S: \text{ack} \quad G_{quit} = C{\to}S: \text{quit}; S{\to}C: \text{bye}$$

$(\_;\_$ takes precedence over $\_+\_)$. ◇

The participants of a communicating system interact through *channels* borrowed from the set $\mathcal{C} = \{ (A, B) \in \mathcal{P} \times \mathcal{P} \mid A \neq B \}$. A channel $(A, B) \in \mathcal{C}$ (written AB for short) allows A to asynchronously send messages to B through an unbounded FIFO buffer associated to AB. The set of *communication actions* is $\mathcal{L} = \mathcal{L}^! \cup \mathcal{L}^?$ where $\mathcal{L}^! = \{AB!m \mid AB \in \mathcal{C} \text{ and } m \in \mathcal{M}\}$ and $\mathcal{L}^? = \{AB?m \mid AB \in \mathcal{C} \text{ and } m \in \mathcal{M}\}$ are respectively the set of *output* and *input* actions. The *language* $\mathcal{L}[G]$ of a g-choreography G is essentially the set of all possible sequences in $\mathcal{L}$ compatible with the causal relation induced by G. Since $\mathcal{L}[G]$ is prefix-closed, we write $\hat{\mathcal{L}}[G]$ for the set of sequences in $\mathcal{L}[G]$ that are not proper prefixes of any other sequence in $\mathcal{L}[G]$. The technical definition of $\mathcal{L}[G]$, immaterial here, can be found in [16]. We will adapt CFSM [14] to model the QoS-aware *local view* of a system.

Definition 2 (Communicating systems [14]). *A communicating finite-state machine (CFSM) is a finite transition system $M = (Q, q_0, \to)$ where*

- *Q is a finite set of states with $q_0 \in Q$ the initial state, and*
- *$\to \subseteq Q \times \mathcal{L} \times Q$; we write $q \xrightarrow{\ell} q'$ for $(q, \ell, q') \in \to$.*

For $AB!m \in \mathcal{L}$ (resp. $AB?m \in \mathcal{L}$), let $sbj(AB!m) = A$ (resp. $sbj(AB?m) = B$). Given $A \in \mathcal{P}$, M is A-local if $sbj(\ell) = A$ for each $q \xrightarrow{\ell} q'$. A (communicating) system is a map $S = (M_A)_{A \in \mathcal{P}}$ assigning a A-local CFSM M_A to each $A \in \mathcal{P}$.

Example 2 (Communicating system for POP). The following CFSM exhibits a behaviour of a POP client compatible with the protocol in Example 1 because its executions yield a subset of the client's execution specified there.

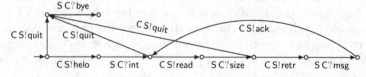

For a POP server, being a two-party protocol, we can use a dual CFSM obtained by replacing send actions with corresponding receive actions and vice versa. ◇

The asynchronous communication between participants is formalised by a labelled transition system (LTS) tracking the (local) state of each CFSM and the content of each buffer (i.e. communication channel) in the system. A *configuration* of a communicating system S is a pair $s = \langle q \,;\, b \rangle$ where q and b respectively map participants to states and channels to sequences of messages; state $q(A)$ keeps track of the state of the machine M_A and buffer $b(AB)$ yields the messages sent from A to B and not yet consumed. The *initial* configuration s_0 is the one where, for all $A \in \mathcal{P}$, $q(A)$ is the initial state of the corresponding CFSM and $b(AB)$ is the empty sequence for all $AB \in \mathcal{C}$.

A configuration $s' = \langle q' \,;\, b' \rangle$ is *reachable* from another configuration $s = \langle q \,;\, b \rangle$ by *firing a transition* ℓ, written $s \overset{\ell}{\Rightarrow} s'$, if there is a message $m \in \mathcal{M}$ such that either (1) or (2) below holds:

1. $\ell = AB!m$ with $q(A) \overset{\ell}{\to}_A q'$ and

   a. $q' = q[A \mapsto q']$
   b. $b' = b[AB \mapsto b(AB).m]$

2. $\ell = AB?m$ with $q(B) \overset{\ell}{\to}_B q'$ and

   a. $q' = q[B \mapsto q']$ and
   b. $b = b'[AB \mapsto m.b'(AB)]$.

Condition (1) puts m on channel AB, while (2) gets m from channel AB. In both cases, any machine or buffer not involved in the transition is left unchanged in the new configuration s'.

Example 3 (Semantics of CFSMs). For the run π of the communicating system in (1) (cf. Sect. 1) we have, for $i \in \{0, 1, 2\}$, $s_i = \langle q_i \,;\, b_i \rangle$, where $q_0 = \{A \mapsto q_0, B \mapsto q_0'\}$, $b_0 = \{AB \mapsto \epsilon, BA \mapsto \epsilon\}$, $q_1 = \{A \mapsto q_1, B \mapsto q_0'\}$, $b_1 = \{AB \mapsto m, BA \mapsto \epsilon\}$, and $q_2 = \{A \mapsto q_1, B \mapsto q_1'\}$, $b_2 = b_0$.   ◇

Let S be a communicating system. A sequence $\pi = (s_i, \ell_i, s_{i+1})_{i \in I}$ where I is an initial segment of natural numbers (i.e., $i - 1 \in I$ for each $0 < i \in I$) is a run of S if $s_i \overset{\ell_i}{\Rightarrow} s_{i+1}$ is a transition of S for all $i \in I$. The set of runs of S is denoted as Δ_S^∞ and the set of runs of length k is denoted as Δ_S^k. Note that Δ_S^∞ may contain runs of infinite length, the set of finite runs of S is the union of all Δ_S^k and will be denoted as Δ_S. Given a run π, we define $\mathcal{L}[\pi]$ to be the sequence of labels $(\ell_i)_{i \in I}$. The *language* of S is the set $\mathcal{L}[S] = \{\mathcal{L}[\pi] \mid \pi \in \Delta_S^\infty\}$. Finally, $prf : \Delta_S^\infty \to 2^{\Delta_S}$ maps each run $\pi \in \Delta_S^\infty$ to its set of finite prefixes. As usual, for all $\pi \in \Delta_S^\infty$, the empty prefix ϵ belongs to $prf(\pi)$. For convenience, we will occasionally write $s_0 \overset{\ell_0}{\Rightarrow} s_1 \ldots s_n \overset{\ell_n}{\Rightarrow} s_{n+1}$ for finite sequences.

Real-Closed Fields. Real numbers are natural candidates to express quantitative attributes of a software artifact. We adopt *real-closed fields* (RCFs), which is the formalisation of the first-order theory of the real numbers, as a foundation for QoS values. Let Σ_{field} denote the first-order signature $\langle \{0, 1\}, \{+, \cdot\}, \{<\} \rangle$. An ordered field is a first-order theory presentation $\langle \Sigma_{\text{field}}, \Gamma_{\text{field}} \rangle$, where Γ_{field} consists of the *field* axioms as well as the axioms defining $<$ as a strict total order relation. Real-closed fields are ordered fields whose non-empty subsets all have a supremum. Tarski's axiomatization of real-closed fields, denoted here as

$\langle \Sigma_{\text{RCF}}, \Gamma_{\text{RCF}} \rangle$, was introduced in [17]. Tarski further demonstrated the existence of a decision procedure for this first-order theory of real numbers in [17, Thm. 37]. Thus, the main reason for selecting RCFs as the foundation for QoS lies in the fact that first-order theories extending them using elementary operations are decidable, providing effective means for analysis.

4   Quality of Service of Communicating Systems

In this section we extend CFSMs with QoS specifications in order to express QoS contracts of components in message-passing systems. Basically, each state of CFSMs is assigned a QoS contract specifying the usage of computational resources. We formalise QoS contracts as *QoS specifications* which are theory presentations over the RCFs, noted as $\langle \Sigma, \Gamma \rangle$, paired up with *aggregation operators*, noted as $\oplus^a$, to define how each QoS attribute accumulates along a communicating system. These aggregation operators will be essential to formally define the notion of aggregation along a run, as shown later in Example 9.

Definition 3. *A QoS specification $\langle \Sigma, \Gamma \rangle$ is a (first-order) theory presentation extending $\langle \Sigma_{\text{RCF}}, \Gamma_{\text{RCF}} \rangle$ as follows:*

1. *$\Sigma = \langle \{0,1\} \cup Q, \{+, \cdot\} \cup \{\oplus^a\}_{a \in Q}, \{<\} \rangle$, where Q is a finite set of constant symbols (other that 0 and 1) representing the* quantitative attributes *(from now on referred to as QoS attributes) and, for each $a \in Q$, $\oplus^a$ is an associative algebraic binary operator and*
2. *$\Gamma = \Gamma_{\text{RCF}} \cup \Gamma'$, being Γ' a finite set of first-order formulae formalising specific constraints over the QoS attributes in Q.*

The class of QoS specifications will be denoted as $\mathcal{C}(Q)$.

In order to preserve decidability of QoS properties, we only consider QoS specifications involving additional constant symbols representing the QoS attributes of components. Aggregation operators are required to be algebraic because the extension of the theory must be kept in the first-order fragment (uninterpreted function or predicate symbols must be avoided to preserve decidability). It is worth noticing that aggregation operators strongly depend on the nature of each specific attribute; for example, natural aggregation operators for memory and time are the maximum function and sum respectively.

Example 4 (QoS specification). With reference to Example 2, possible quantitative attributes of interest in an implementation of POP are $Q = \{t, c, m\}$ representing CPU *t*ime, monetary *c*ost, and *m*emory usage, respectively. Then a QoS specification that characterises low computational costs, where no internal process consumes significant amount of resources, can be written according to Definition 3 as follows:

$$\Sigma = \langle \{0,1\} \cup \{t, c, m\}, \{+, \cdot\} \cup \{\oplus^t, \oplus^c, \oplus^m\}, \{<\} \rangle$$
$$\Gamma = \Gamma_{\text{RCF}} \cup \Gamma'_{\text{Low}}$$

where $\oplus^t = +$, $\oplus^c = +$, $\oplus^m = max$, and $\Gamma'_{\text{Low}} = \{t \leq .01, c \leq .01, m \leq .01\}$ ◇

From now on, we fix a set of constant symbols Q which we omit from the set of *QoS specifications*, that will be referred to just as $\mathcal{C}$. It is worth noting that, when Q is fixed, a QoS specification $\langle \Sigma, \Gamma_{\mathrm{RCF}} \cup \Gamma' \rangle$, is completely determined by Γ'. Therefore, we can unambiguously refer to a QoS specification using its set of formulas Γ'. Thus, the QoS specification in Example 4 is Γ'_{Low}.

Example 5 (QoS for POP). The following QoS specifications formalise the costs associated to different activities in the POP protocol of Example 2.

$$\Gamma'_{\mathrm{Chk}} = \{t \leq 5, c = 0.5, m = 0\}$$
$$\Gamma'_{\mathrm{Mem}} = \{1 \leq t \leq 6, c = 0, m \leq 64\}$$
$$\Gamma'_{\mathrm{DB}} = \{t \leq 3 \implies (\exists x)(0.5 \leq x \leq 1 \wedge c = t \cdot x), t > 3 \implies c = 10, m \leq 5\}$$

Basically, Γ'_{Chk} formalizes the costs associated to the activity of integrity checking a message, Γ'_{Mem} to the activity of a server receiving a message, and Γ'_{DB} to establishing that the monetary cost is fixed if the insertion takes more than three time-units and it is a fraction of the execution time, otherwise.   ◇

We now extend communicating systems (cf. Sect. 3) with QoS-specifications.

Definition 4 (QoS-extended CFSMs). *A* QoS-extended CFSM *is a tuple* $M^{QoS} = \langle M, F, qos \rangle$ *where:*

- $M = \langle Q, q_0, \rightarrow \rangle$ *is a CFSM,*
- $F \subseteq Q$ *is a set of final states of M, and*
- $qos : Q \rightarrow \mathcal{C}$ *maps states of M to QoS specifications.*

A QoS-extended communicating system S^{QoS} *is a map* $(M_{\mathsf{A}}^{QoS})_{\mathsf{A} \in \mathcal{P}}$ *assigning an A-local QoS-extended CFSM M_{A}^{QoS} to each $\mathsf{A} \in \mathcal{P}$. A configuration $\langle \mathsf{q} \, ; \, \mathsf{b} \rangle$ of S^{QoS} is a final configuration if $\mathsf{q}(\mathsf{A}) \in F_{\mathsf{A}}$ for every $\mathsf{A} \in \mathcal{P}$.*

Example 6 (QoS-extended CFSMs). An extended CFSM of the POP client in Example 2 with the QoS specifications of Example 5 is as follows:

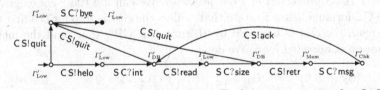

where the filled state is the only final state. Each state is assigned a QoS specification given in Example 5 according to the following idea. States where the client performs negligible computations are assigned the QoS specification Γ'_{Low}. The remaining states are assigned QoS specifications as follows. The local states where C performs a database insertion (right after receiving an int or size message) and those where C accesses the memory (right before receiving an unread e-mail) are constrained respectively by Γ'_{DB} and Γ'_{Mem}; finally, Γ'_{Chk} constrains the states where C performs an integrity check (right after receiving an unread e-mail).   ◇

Notice that Definition 4 requires every state of a CFSM to be assigned a QoS specification. However, in most cases, most states will have the same QoS specification, as it is the case of Γ'_{Low} in Example 6; typically one only has to identify the QoS costs specific to few states.

The semantics of QoS-extended communicating systems is defined in the same way as the semantics of communicating systems. This is a consequence of the fact that QoS specifications do not have any effect on communications.

5 $\mathcal{QL}$: A Dynamic Logic for QoS

To describe QoS properties we introduce $\mathcal{QL}$, a logical language akin $DLTL$.

Definition 5 (QoS formulae). *The QoS logic $\mathcal{QL}$ consists of the smallest set of formulae that can be obtained from the following grammar:*

$$\Phi ::= \top \mid \psi \mid \neg\Phi \mid \Phi \vee \Phi \mid \Phi\,\mathcal{U}^{\mathsf{G}}\Phi$$

where ψ is a formula in a theory presentation in $\mathcal{C}$, and G is a g-choreography over $\mathcal{P}$ and $\mathcal{M}$ (see Definition 1).

Atomic formulae express constraints over quantitative attributes. Akin $DLTL$, properties of runs are linear temporal formulae where the until operator is indexed with a global choreography G. In essence, the role of G is to restrict the set of runs to be considered for the satisfiability of the until. Global choreographies are suitable for this purpose because they are a declarative and compact way of characterizing the behaviour of asynchronous message-passing systems. The possibility modality $\langle\mathsf{G}\rangle\Phi$ is defined as $\top\mathcal{U}^{\mathsf{G}}\Phi$ and the necessity modality $[\mathsf{G}]\Phi$ is defined (dually) as $\neg\langle\mathsf{G}\rangle\neg\Phi$. Finally, propositional connectives $\wedge$ and $\implies$ are defined as usual.

The following example shows how to express non-functional properties of specific runs of the system in $\mathcal{QL}$.

Example 7 (QoS properties of POP protocol). We can use the g-choreographies and the $\mathcal{QL}$ formula below to state that, unless the cost is zero for the first three e-mails read, the cost is bounded by 10 times the CPU time, and the memory consumption is bounded by 5. We define

$$\Phi \equiv [\mathsf{G}_3](c > 0) \implies [\mathsf{G}_3; \mathsf{G}_{\mathsf{msg}}{}^*]((c \leq t \cdot 10) \wedge (m \leq 5)) \qquad \text{where}$$
$$\mathsf{G}_3 = \mathsf{C}\!\rightarrow\!\mathsf{S}: \mathsf{helo}; \mathsf{S}\!\rightarrow\!\mathsf{C}: \mathsf{int}; \mathsf{G}_{\mathsf{msg}}; \mathsf{G}_{\mathsf{msg}}; \mathsf{G}_{\mathsf{msg}} \qquad \text{and}$$
$$\mathsf{G}_{\mathsf{msg}} = \mathsf{C}\!\rightarrow\!\mathsf{S}: \mathsf{read}; \mathsf{S}\!\rightarrow\!\mathsf{C}: \mathsf{size}; \mathsf{C}\!\rightarrow\!\mathsf{S}: \mathsf{retr}; \mathsf{S}\!\rightarrow\!\mathsf{C}: \mathsf{msg}; \mathsf{S}\!\rightarrow\!\mathsf{C}: \mathsf{ack}$$

Intuitively, for Φ to hold, either the first three message retrievals must have zero cost in any run of the system, or on every subsequent message retrieval, the total cost and memory consumption fall within the specified bounds.   ◇

A $\mathcal{QL}$ formula (like Φ in Example 7) can be used in quantitative analyses by *aggregating* the values of the QoS attributes along the runs of the system.

More precisely, given a run π, our interpretation is that, for each transition $s_i \overset{\ell_i}{\Rightarrow} s_{i+1}$ of π, the obligations stated in the QoS specification of s_i are met after aggregating QoS information along π from state s_0 up to state s_i. Therefore, a central notion in our framework is that of *aggregation function*. Given a QoS-extended communicating system S, an *aggregation function* $\text{agg}_S : \Delta_S \to \mathcal{C}$ yields a QoS specification capturing the cumulative QoS attributes along a run $\pi \in \Delta_S$ by "summing-up" QoS specifications of participants' local states.

Example 8 (Aggregation). Recall the run π (1) from Sect. 1:

$$
\begin{array}{llll}
 & \{c \le 5, m = 0\} & \{5 \le c \le 10,\ m < 3\} & \\
A: & q_0 & \xrightarrow{\ \ A\,B!m\ \ } & q_1
\end{array}
$$

$$
\begin{array}{llll}
 & \{c = 0, m = 0\} & \{10 \le m \le 50,\ c = 0.01 \cdot m\} & \\
B: & q_0' & \xrightarrow{\ \ A\,B?m\ \ } & q_1'
\end{array}
$$

$$
\pi: \quad s_0 \xrightarrow{\ \ A\,B!m\ \ } s_1 \xrightarrow{\ \ A\,B?m\ \ } s_2
$$

Let c_A^q (resp. c_B^q) denote the value of the QoS attribute c in the state q of participant A (resp. B) and likewise for the attribute m. After π, we expect $\max\{m_A^{q_0}, m_A^{q_1}, m_B^{q_0'}, m_B^{q_1'}\}$ and $c_A^{q_0} + c_A^{q_1} + c_B^{q_0'} + c_B^{q_1'}$ to respectively be the memory consumption and the overall monetary cost in s_2. This boils down to aggregate the QoS attributes c and m using the maximization and addition operations, respectively. $\diamond$

Essentially, the aggregation in this case is obtained by (1) instantiating the QoS specification associated to the local state of participants (this is done by renaming attributes as in Example 8); and (2) adding an equation combining all the instances of QoS specifications. The following formula captures this intuition and exemplifies one way in which the aggregation function could be defined.

Example 9 (Aggregation). Let $S = (\langle M_A, \text{qos}_A \rangle)_{A \in \mathcal{P}}$, we define the aggregation function $\text{agg}_S : \Delta_S \to \mathcal{C}$ to be $\text{agg}_S(\pi) = f(\pi) \cup g(\pi)$ where

$$
f(\pi) = \bigcup_{\substack{A \in \mathcal{P} \\ 0 \le i \le n}} \text{qos}_A(q_i(A))_A^{q_i(A)} \quad \text{and} \quad g(\epsilon) = \left\{ a = \left(\bigoplus_{A \in \mathcal{P}}^{a} a_A^{q_0(A)} \right) \ \middle|\ a \in Q \right\}
$$

$$
g(\pi) = \left\{ a = \left(\bigoplus_{\substack{0 \le i < n \\ A = \text{sbj}(\ell_i)}}^{a} a_A^{q_i(A)} \right) \oplus^a \left(\bigoplus_{A \in \mathcal{P}}^{a} a_A^{q_n(A)} \right) \ \middle|\ a \in Q \right\} \qquad \text{if } \pi \ne \epsilon
$$

where $\pi = \langle q_0 ; b_0 \rangle \overset{\ell_0}{\Rightarrow} \ldots \overset{\ell_{n-1}}{\Rightarrow} \langle q_n ; b_n \rangle \in \Delta_S$, and $\Pi_A^q = \{\psi_A^q \mid \psi \in \Pi\}$ for a set of $\mathcal{QL}$ formulae Π, and ψ_A^q is obtained by replacing each QoS attribute c with the symbol c_A^q in the atomic formula ψ. The intuition is that $f(\pi)$ collects all the QoS specifications of the local states of the participants along the run π, and $g(\pi)$ uses the aggregation operators to calculate the aggregated values of the QoS attributes in the run π. If we apply this aggregation function to the run π in Example 8, we obtain the following:

$$f(\pi) = \{c_A^{q_0} \leq 5, m_A^{q_0} = 0\} \cup \{5 \leq c_A^{q_1} \leq 10, \ m_A^{q_1} < 3\}$$
$$\cup \{c_B^{q_0'} = 0, m_B^{q_0'} = 0\} \cup \{10 \leq m_B^{q_1'} \leq 50, \ c_B^{q_1'} = 0.01 \cdot m_B^{q_1'}\}$$
$$g(\pi) = \left\{ m = \max\{m_A^{q_0}, m_A^{q_1}, m_B^{q_0'}, m_B^{q_1'}\}, c = c_A^{q_0} + c_A^{q_1} + c_B^{q_0'} + c_B^{q_1'} \right\} \qquad \diamond$$

It is important to emphasize that, in our conception, an aggregation function relies on a run of the system as its input. This run inherently encompasses a specific sequential ordering of the actions carried out by the participants. The aggregation operators max and $+$ used in Example 8 follow this interpration. As will become clear in Definition 6, this interpretation is sufficient for the purposes of this paper, since it enables $\mathcal{QL}$ to specify temporal QoS properties about runs of the system. However, one might be interested in a different kind of aggregation that is aware of local states that are executed in parallel. This may require some care and possibly to exploit truly-concurrent models, such as pomsets; this is left for future work.

The semantics of our logic is defined in terms of QoS-extended communicating systems.

Definition 6 ($\mathcal{QL}$ semantics). *Given a QoS-extended communicating system S, an S-model for a QoS property Φ is a pair $\langle \pi, \pi' \rangle$, where $\pi \in \Delta_S^\infty$ contains a final configuration (see Definition 4) and $\pi' \in prf(\pi)$ up to such configuration such that $\langle \pi, \pi' \rangle \models_S \Phi$ where the relation $\models_S$ is defined as follows:*

$$\langle \pi, \pi' \rangle \models_S \Phi \quad \text{iff} \quad \mathsf{aggs}(\pi') \vdash_{RCF} \Phi \quad \textit{if } \Phi \textit{ is an atomic formula}$$
$$\langle \pi, \pi' \rangle \models_S \neg\Phi \quad \text{iff} \quad \langle \pi, \pi' \rangle \models_S \Phi \textit{ does not hold}$$
$$\langle \pi, \pi' \rangle \models_S \Phi_1 \vee \Phi_2 \quad \text{iff} \quad \langle \pi, \pi' \rangle \models_S \Phi_1 \textit{ or } \langle \pi, \pi' \rangle \models_S \Phi_2$$
$$\langle \pi, \pi' \rangle \models_S \Phi_1 \, \mathcal{U}^G \, \Phi_2 \quad \text{iff} \quad \textit{there exists } \pi'' \textit{ such that } \mathcal{L}[\pi''] \in \hat{\mathcal{L}}[G],$$
$$\pi'\pi'' \in prf(\pi) \textit{ up to a final configuration in } \pi,$$
$$\langle \pi, \pi'\pi'' \rangle \models_S \Phi_2 \textit{ and, for all } \pi''' \in prf(\pi''),$$
$$\textit{if } \pi''' \neq \pi'' \textit{ then } \langle \pi, \pi'\pi''' \rangle \models_S \Phi_1.$$

A QoS property Φ is satisfiable in S if there exists a run $\pi \in \Delta_S^\infty$ such that $\langle \pi, \epsilon \rangle \models_S \Phi$, and it is valid (denoted as $\models_S \Phi$) if, for all runs $\pi \in \Delta_S^\infty$ that contain a final configuration, $\langle \pi, \epsilon \rangle \models_S \Phi$.

Negation and disjunction are handled in the standard way. The definition of the until operator is similar to the standard operator: Φ_2 must hold at some point in the future, i.e., $\pi'\pi''$ and Φ_1 must hold up to that point; the key difference is that the satisfaction of Φ_2 is restricted to runs where the extension π'' is in $\hat{\mathcal{L}}[G]$. Finally, atomic formulae are handled by obtaining the aggregated QoS of the accumulated run π' and using the entailment relation of RCFs.

6   A Semidecision Procedure for $\mathcal{QL}$

We now establish the semi-decidability of $\mathcal{QL}$ by presenting a k-bounded semidecision procedure relying on three algorithms: qSAT, qMODELS, and qUNTIL. The qSAT algorithm is the main algorithm of the procedure and determines whether a given formula is satisfiable in a given system. It relies on qMODELS to check if there is a run that satisfies the formula which, in turn, uses qUNTIL to handle the $\mathcal{U}$ operator. Let us start by looking at qSAT defined as:

```
1  qSAT(Φ, S, k):
2      i = 0
3      while i ≤ k do
4          foreach π ∈ Δ^i_S do
5              if the last configuration of π is final and qMODELS(Φ, S, π, ε) then
6                  ⊢ return true
7          i = i + 1
8      return false
```

Basically, qSAT enumerates all the runs of S up to a given bound k and checks whether any of them satisfies Φ (recall that Δ^i_S is the set of all runs of S with length i). Let us now focus on the algorithm qMODELS:

```
1  qMODELS(Φ, S, π, π′):
2      switch Φ do
3          case ⊤ do
4              ⊢ return true
5          case ψ do
6              ⊢ return whether aggs(π′) ⊢_RCF ψ
7          case ¬Φ_1 do
8              ⊢ return not qMODELS(Φ_1, S, π, π′)
9          case Φ_1 ∨ Φ_2 do
10             ⊢ return qMODELS(Φ_1, S, π, π′) or qMODELS(Φ_2, S, π, π′)
11         case Φ_1 U^G Φ_2 do
12             ⊢ return qUNTIL(Φ_1, G, Φ_2, S, π, π′, ε)
```

Following Definition 6, qMODELS recursively inspects the $\mathcal{QL}$ formula. It invokes qUNTIL to handle the $\mathcal{U}$ operator and the decision procedure of the theory of real-closed fields to check the atomic formulae. Let us now look at the algorithm qUNTIL:

```
1  qUNTIL(Φ_1, G, Φ_2, S, π, π′, π″):
2      if L[π″] ∈ L̂[G] and qMODELS(Φ_2, S, π, π′π″) then
3          ⊢ return true
4      else if not qMODELS(Φ_1, S, π, π′π″) then
5          ⊢ return false
6      else
7          Let ⇒ q be the transition such that π′π″ ⇒ q ∈ prf(π)
                (takes the first transition in π if π′π″ = ε,
                and it is not defined if π′π″ = π)
8          if π′π″ = π or L[π″ ⇒ q] ∉ L[G] then
9              ⊢ return false
10         else
11             ⊢ return qUNTIL(Φ_1, G, Φ_2, S, π, π′, π″ ⇒ q)
```

This procedure takes care of searching for a witness of the existential in the semantics of $\mathcal{U}$ by starting in the current prefix π' and following the transitions of π. According to Definition 6, qUNTIL searches for a witness of the existential part of $\mathcal{U}$. It takes as parameters the complete run π, the prefix π' at which the $\mathcal{U}$ is being evaluated, and the current extension π'' that is used to search for the witness. If π'' is enough to reach a verdict, the algorithm returns true or false accordingly (Lines 3 and 5). Otherwise, it tries to extend π'' by borrowing the next transition of π (Line 7). If such extension exists and is a candidate for being in the language of G, the algorithm recursively calls itself with the extended prefix (Line 11). Hereafter, we fix a QoS-extended communicating system S.

Theorem 1 (qSAT is sound and k-bounded complete). *Given a QoS formula $\Phi \in \mathcal{QL}$ and a bound k, qSAT(Φ, S, k) returns **true** iff there exists $\pi \in \Delta_S^i$ such that $\langle \pi, \epsilon \rangle \models_S \Phi$, for some $i \leq k$.*

The soundness of qSAT immediately follows from the soundness of qMODELS (established in Lemma 1 below) which, in turn, relies on the soundness and completeness of qUNTIL (cf. Lemmas 2 and 3, respectively). This guarantees that the call to qMODELS in Line 5 of qSAT returns true iff the run π satisfies Φ. Note that qSAT is not guaranteed to be complete due to the bound k.

Lemma 1 (qMODELS is sound and complete). *Given a QoS formula $\Phi \in \mathcal{QL}$ and runs $\pi, \pi' \in \Delta_S$, where $\pi' \in prf(\pi)$, qMODELS(Φ, S, π, π') returns **true** iff $\langle \pi, \pi' \rangle \models_S \Phi$.*

Proof. By structural induction on Φ. If Φ is $\top$, the result follows trivially. If Φ is an atomic formula, the algorithm computes the aggregation over the run π' (Line 6) and invokes the decision procedure of RCFs to check whether $\mathrm{agg}_S(\pi')$ entails Φ in the theory of real closed fields. If Φ is $\Phi_1 \vee \Phi_2$, the algorithm perform two recursive calls and returns true iff either $\langle \pi, \pi' \rangle \models_S \Phi_1$ or $\langle \pi, \pi' \rangle \models_S \Phi_2$. If Φ is $\Phi_1 \, \mathcal{U}^G \, \Phi_2$, the algorithm returns true iff qUNTIL$(\Phi_1, G, \Phi_2, S, \pi, \pi', \epsilon)$ returns true. By Lemmas 2 and 3 this is equivalent to $\langle \pi, \pi' \rangle \models_S \Phi_1 \, \mathcal{U}^G \, \Phi_2$. $\qquad\square$

We now prove the soundness and completeness of qUNTIL.

Lemma 2 (qUNTIL is sound). *Given a QoS formula $\Phi_1, \Phi_2 \in \mathcal{QL}$, a g-choreography G, and runs π, π', π'' such that*

a) $\pi'\pi'' \in prf(\pi)$ and $\pi \in \Delta_S$, and
b) for all $\pi''' \in prf(\pi'')$, if $\pi''' \neq \pi''$ then $\langle \pi, \pi'\pi''' \rangle \models_S \Phi_1$

*if qUNTIL$(\Phi_1, G, \Phi_2, S, \pi, \pi', \pi'')$ returns **true** then $\langle \pi, \pi' \rangle \models_S \Phi_1 \, \mathcal{U}^G \, \Phi_2$.*

Proof. The call to qUNTIL$(\Phi_1, G, \Phi_2, S, \pi, \pi', \pi'')$ either reaches Lines 3 or it reaches Line 11 and the recursive call returns true. In the first case, we know $\mathcal{L}[\pi''] \in \hat{\mathcal{L}}[G]$ and that qMODELS$(\Phi_2, S, \pi, \pi'\pi'')$ returned true. By Lemma 1 it follows that $\langle \pi, \pi'\pi'' \rangle \models_S \Phi_2$. Together with hypotheses a) and b) the conditions of the semantics of the formula $\Phi_1 \, \mathcal{U}^G \, \Phi_2$ (see Definition 6) are met. In the case of reaching Line 11 we know the recursive call qUNTIL$(\Phi_1, G, \Phi_2, S, \pi, \pi', \pi'' \overset{\ell}{\Rightarrow} q)$ returned true. Conditions a) and b) applied to the input of the recursive call holds because of the way transition $\overset{\ell}{\Rightarrow} q$ was chosen and the fact that condition on Line 4 returned false. Therefore, we can take the output of the recursive call to satisfy Lemma 2 as an inductive hypothesis and conclude $\langle \pi, \pi' \rangle \models_S \Phi_1 \, \mathcal{U}^G \, \Phi_2$.

$\qquad\square$

Lemma 3 (qUntil is complete). *Given a QoS formula $\Phi_1, \Phi_2 \in \mathcal{QL}$, a g-choreography G, and runs π, π', π'' such that*

a) $\pi'\pi'' \in prf(\pi)$ *and* $\pi \in \Delta_S$, *and*
b) for all $\pi''' \in prf(\pi'')$, *if* $\pi''' \neq \pi''$ *then either* $\mathcal{L}[\pi'''] \notin \hat{\mathcal{L}}[G]$ *or* $\langle \pi, \pi'\pi''' \rangle \nvDash_S \Phi_2$

if qUntil$(\Phi_1, G, \Phi_2, S, \pi, \pi', \pi'')$ *returns **false** then* $\langle \pi, \pi' \rangle \nvDash_S \Phi_1 \, \mathcal{U}^G \, \Phi_2$

Proof. The call to qUntil$(\Phi_1, G, \Phi_2, S, \pi, \pi', \pi'')$ reaches either Line 5, Line 9 or it reaches Line 11 and the recursive call returns false. In all cases, by condition b) we know that no prefix of π'' could be witness of the existential in the semantics of $\Phi_1 \, \mathcal{U}^G \, \Phi_2$ (see Definition 6) because it would need to both be in $\hat{\mathcal{L}}[G]$ and satisfy Φ_2. Run π'' itself cannot be the witness for the same reasons due to the fact that condition in Line 2 was not met. Which means either $\mathcal{L}[\pi''] \notin \hat{\mathcal{L}}[G]$ or qMODELS$(\Phi_2, S, \pi, \pi'\pi'')$ returned false, therefore, using Lemma 1, either $\mathcal{L}[\pi''] \notin \hat{\mathcal{L}}[G]$ or $\langle \pi, \pi'\pi'' \rangle \nvDash_S \Phi_2$. The only remaining possibility is for the witness to be a $\pi^\star$ such that $\pi'' \in prf(\pi^\star)$ and $\pi^\star \neq \pi''$. In the case of reaching Line 5, we know that qMODELS$(\Phi_1, S, \pi, \pi'\pi'')$ returned false. By Lemma 1 it follows that $\langle \pi, \pi'\pi'' \rangle \nvDash_S \Phi_1$. Therefore, extension $\pi^\star$ couldn't be a witness for the existential in the semantics of $\Phi_1 \, \mathcal{U}^G \, \Phi_2$. In the case of reaching Line 9, candidate extension $\pi^\star$ does not exist or it is not in $\hat{\mathcal{L}}[G]$. In the case of reaching Line 11, we know that qUntil$(\Phi_1, G, \Phi_2, S, \pi, \pi', \pi'' \xrightarrow{\,\ell\,} q)$ returned false. Notice that conditions a) and b) applied to the input of the recursive calls holds because of the way transition $\xrightarrow{\,\ell\,} q$ was chosen and that condition in Line 2 was not met. Therefore, we can take the output of the recursive calls to satisfy Lemma 3 as an inductive hypothesis and conclude that $\langle \pi, \pi' \rangle \nvDash \Phi_1 \, \mathcal{U}^G \, \Phi_2$.   □

Notice that the proof for Lemma 1 uses Lemma 3 and Lemma 2, and that the proofs for Lemma 3 and Lemma 2 use Lemma 1. This does not undermine the soundness of the proofs because the lemmas are always (inductively) applied on smaller $\mathcal{QL}$ formulas. Now that the soundness and completeness of qMODELS and qUntil is established, it remains to show their termination. Termination follows from the fact that both the number of logical operators in Φ and the number of transitions in π are finite. The first guarantees qMODELS eventually reaches a base case and the second guarantees qUntil eventually reaches a base case. Finally, the base case in qMODELS, computing aggregation and checking entailment in the theory of real closed fields, terminates due to the decidability of RCFs [17].

6.1   A Bounded Model-Checking Approach for $\mathcal{QL}$

Previous results allow for a straightforward bounded model-checking approach for $\mathcal{QL}$. Like for other model-checking procedures for a language that admits negation, qSat can be used to check validity of a $\mathcal{QL}$ formula in a system S by checking the satisfiability of the negated formula. This constitutes a counterexample-finding procedure for $\mathcal{QL}$. The caveat is that qSat is a k-bounded semidecision procedure rather than a decision procedure. However, restricting to $\mathcal{QL}^-$, namely $\mathcal{QL}$ formulae that do not contain the $*$ operator in their choregraphies, we can find finite models of satisfiable formulae of $\mathcal{QL}^-$ (cf. Theorem 2).

Theorem 2 (Finite model property of $\mathcal{QL}^-$). *Given a QoS formula $\Phi \in \mathcal{QL}^-$, and runs $\pi \in \Delta_S^\infty$, $\pi' \in \Delta_S$ such that $\pi' \in prf(\pi)$. If $\langle \pi, \pi' \rangle \models_S \Phi$ then there exists a finite run $\pi^- \in \Delta_S$ such that $\pi^- \in prf(\pi)$ and $\langle \pi^-, \pi' \rangle \models_S \Phi$.*

Proof. By structural induction on Φ. If Φ is $\top$ or an atomic formula, take $\pi^- = \pi'$. If Φ is $\Phi_1 \vee \Phi_2$, we have that either $\langle \pi, \pi' \rangle \models_S \Phi_1$ or $\langle \pi, \pi' \rangle \models_S \Phi_2$. By inductive hypothesis, either $\langle \pi_1^-, \pi' \rangle \models_S \Phi_1$ or $\langle \pi_2^-, \pi' \rangle \models_S \Phi_2$ for some finite $\pi_1^-, \pi_2^- \in prf(\pi)$. Therefore, either $\langle \pi_1^-, \pi' \rangle \models_S \Phi_1 \vee \Phi_2$ or $\langle \pi_2^-, \pi' \rangle \models_S \Phi_1 \vee \Phi_2$.

If Φ is $\Phi_1 \, \mathcal{U}^{\mathsf{G}} \, \Phi_2$, by Definition 6 we have there exists π'' such that $\mathcal{L}[\pi''] \in \mathcal{L}[\mathsf{G}]$, $\pi'\pi'' \in prf(\pi)$ up to a final configuration with $\langle \pi, \pi'\pi'' \rangle \models_S \Phi_2$, and for all $\pi''' \in prf(\pi'')$, if $\pi''' \neq \pi''$ then $\langle \pi, \pi'\pi''' \rangle \models_S \Phi_1$. If we apply the inductive hypothesis to Φ_1 and Φ_2, we have there exists π'' such that $\mathcal{L}[\pi''] \in \mathcal{L}[\mathsf{G}]$, $\pi'\pi'' \in prf(\pi)$ up to a final configuration with $\langle \pi_2^-, \pi'\pi'' \rangle \models_S \Phi_2$ for some $\pi_2^- \in \Delta_S$ such that $\pi_2^- \in prf(\pi)$, and for all $\pi''' \in prf(\pi'')$, if $\pi''' \neq \pi''$ then $\langle \pi_1^-, \pi'\pi''' \rangle \models_S \Phi_1$ for some $\pi_1^- \in \Delta_S$ such that $\pi_1^- \in prf(\pi)$. Notice that since G is $*$-free, run π'' in the language $\mathcal{L}[\mathsf{G}]$ is necessarily finite and so is the number of quantified runs π'''. Therefore, the number of runs π_1^- involved in the previous statement is finite, and there is a maximum among their lengths, so we can take π^- as the longest between π_2^- and runs π_1^-. Since π_2^- and all the π_1^- are prefixes of π, then they will also be prefixes of π^-, and therefore we have the conditions to conclude $\langle \pi^-, \pi' \rangle \models_S \Phi_1 \, \mathcal{U}^{\mathsf{G}} \, \Phi_2$.

If the outermost operator in Φ is $\neg$, we need to consider al the possible cases for the immediate subformula of Φ. If Φ is $\neg\psi$ with ψ atomic formula, we have that $\langle \pi, \pi' \rangle \nvDash_S \psi$. Take $\pi^- \in prf(\pi)$ an extension of π' whose last configuration is final. If Φ is $\neg(\Phi_1 \vee \Phi_2)$, we have that $\langle \pi, \pi' \rangle \nvDash_S \Phi_1 \vee \Phi_2$. It follows that $\langle \pi, \pi' \rangle \nvDash_S \Phi_1$ and $\langle \pi, \pi' \rangle \nvDash_S \Phi_2$. By inductive hypothesis, there exists $\pi_1^- \in \Delta_S$ such that $\pi_1^- \in prf(\pi)$ and $\langle \pi_1^-, \pi' \rangle \nvDash_S \Phi_1$ and there exists $\pi_2^- \in \Delta_S$ such that $\pi_2^- \in prf(\pi)$ and $\langle \pi_2^-, \pi' \rangle \nvDash_S \Phi_2$. It is enough to take π^- as the longest between π_1^- and π_2^-. If Φ is $\neg(\Phi_1 \, \mathcal{U}^{\mathsf{G}} \, \Phi_2)$, we have that $\langle \pi, \pi' \rangle \nvDash_S \Phi_1 \, \mathcal{U}^{\mathsf{G}} \, \Phi_2$. Therefore, for all π'' such that $\pi'\pi'' \in prf(\pi)$ up to a final configuration of π, if $\mathcal{L}[\pi''] \in \mathcal{L}[\mathsf{G}]$, and $\langle \pi, \pi'\pi'' \rangle \models_S \Phi_2$, then there exists $\pi''' \in prf(\pi'')$, with $\pi''' \neq \pi''$ such that $\langle \pi, \pi'\pi''' \rangle \models_S \neg\Phi_1$. If we apply the inductive hypothesis to Φ_2 and $\neg\Phi_1$, we have that for all π'' such that $\pi'\pi'' \in prf(\pi)$ up to a final configuration of π, if $\mathcal{L}[\pi''] \in \mathcal{L}[\mathsf{G}]$, and $\langle \pi_2^-, \pi'\pi'' \rangle \models_S \Phi_2$ for some $\pi_2^- \in \Delta_S$ with $\pi_2^- \in prf(\pi)$, then there exists $\pi''' \in prf(\pi'')$, with $\pi''' \neq \pi''$ such that $\langle \pi_1^-, \pi'\pi''' \rangle \models_S \neg\Phi_1$ for some $\pi_1^- \in \Delta_S$ with $\pi_1^- \in prf(\pi)$. Notice that since G is $*$-free, any run in the language $\mathcal{L}[\mathsf{G}]$ is necessarily finite. Therefore, there is a maximum among the lengths of the runs π_2^-, and we can take π^- as the longest between π_2^- and π_1^-. $\square$

The proof of Theoream 2 hints that the length of the run π^- constitutes a suitable bound for qSAT; which would turn qSAT into a decision procedure for $\mathcal{QL}^-$ if one could compute such bound. Searching for counterexamples of an arbitrary formula $\Phi \in \mathcal{QL}$ up to a bounded number of unfoldings of $*$ is equivalent to searching for counterexamples in a formula $\hat{\Phi}$ in $\mathcal{QL}^-$ where each $*$ has been replaced by a finite number of unfoldings. Which means that the bounded procedure for searching models of formulae in $\mathcal{QL}^-$ could be used to search for counterexamples of formulae in $\mathcal{QL}$. Notice that QSAT can be easily extended to return the run that satisfies the formula, if there is one. Such run can be used to identify the source of QoS formula violations when QSAT is used as a counterexample-finding procedure.

7   Conclusions

We presented a framework for the design and analysis of QoS-aware distributed message-passing systems using choreographies and a general model of QoS. We tackle this problem by: 1) abstractly representing QoS attributes as symbols denoting real values, whose behaviour is completely captured by a decidable RCFs theory, 2) extending the choreographic model of CFSM by associating QoS specifications to each state of the machine, 3) introducing $\mathcal{QL}$, a logic based on $DLTL$, for expressing QoS properties with a straightforward satisfaction relation based on runs of communicating systems, and 4) giving a semi-decision procedure for $\mathcal{QL}$ and defining a fragment $\mathcal{QL}^-$ that allowed us to give a bounded model-checking procedure for the full logic. A prototype implementation of our procedure is under development. It relies on the SMT solver Z3 [33] for the satisfiability of the QoS constraints in atomic formulae and on ChorGram [34, 35] for the semantics of g-choreographies and CFSMs. An interesting by-product of our framework is that it could be used for the monitoring of local computations to check at run-time if they stay in the constraint of QoS specifications. If static guarantees on QoS specifications are not possible, run-time monitors can be easily attained by adapting techniques for monitor generation from behavioural types [36, 37].

We identify two further main future research directions. On the one hand, there is the theoretical question of whether $\mathcal{QL}$ is decidable or not. In this respect, the similarity of $\mathcal{QL}$ with $DLTL$ (cf. Sect. 2) hints towards an affirmative answer suggesting that the problem can be translated to checking emptyness of Büchi automata [38] corresponding to $\mathcal{QL}$ formulae. However, the decidability of QL is not so easy to attain. In general, a communicating system may yield an infinite state space due to many reasons so satisfaction might not be possible in a finite number of steps. For instance, due to potentially infinite instantiations of QoS attributes or that no final configuration might be reachable. On the other hand, the usability of the framework could be improved through two extensions of $\mathcal{QL}$ and a less demanding way of modeling QoS-extended communicating systems. The first extension of $\mathcal{QL}$ are *selective* aggregation, enabling the aggregation of QoS attributes only for some specific states of runs. This can be done by extending the grammar of g-choreographies given in Definition 1 with an extra production of the shape G $::= \cdots \mid \lceil$G$\rfloor$, "bracketing" the part of the choreography relevant for the aggregation. Notice that the run still has to match the whole choreography. A second extension of $\mathcal{QL}$ is the introduction of *wildcards* as a mechanism to "ignore" a subchoreography. Syntactically, it can be represented by, once again, extending the grammar given in Definition 1 with an extra production, with shape $\mathsf{G} ::= \cdots \mid \_$, where $\_$ is interpreted as a wildcard and plays the role of matching any possible g-choreography. In this case, the shape of the part of the run that matches the wildcard is disregarded but attributes are aggregated along the whole run. Finally, a less demanding way of modeling QoS-extended systems could be achieved by extending g-choreographies with QoS specifications annotating specific interactions and extending the projection of g-choregraphies into CFSMs taking into account such annotations.

References

1. Obj. Mgmt. Group: Business Process Model and Notation. http://www.bpmn.org
2. Bonér, J.: Reactive Microsystems - The Evolution Of Microservices At Scale. O'Reilly, Newton (2018)
3. Frittelli, L., Maldonado, F., Melgratti, H.C., Tuosto, E.: A choreography-driven approach to apis: the opendxl case study. In: [4], 107–124 (2020)
4. Bliudze, S., Bocchi, L. (eds.): COORDINATION 2020. LNCS, vol. 12134. Springer, Cham (2020). https://doi.org/10.1007/978-3-030-50029-0
5. Autili, M., Inverardi, P., Tivoli, M.: Automated synthesis of service choreographies. IEEE Softw. **32**(1), 50–57 (2015)
6. World Wide Web Consortium: Web services description language (wsdl) version 2.0 part 1: Core language. https://www.w3.org/TR/wsdl20/
7. Ivanović, D., Carro, M., Hermenegildo, M.V.: A constraint-based approach to quality assurance in service choreographies. In: Liu, C., et al. (eds.) Proceedings of SOC, pp. 252–267 (2012)
8. Kattepur, A., Georgantas, N., Issarny, V.: QoS analysis in heterogeneous choreography interactions. In: Basu, S., et al. (eds.) Proceedings of SOC, pp. 23–38 (2013)
9. Güdemann, M., Poizat, P., Salaün, G., Ye, L.: VerChor: a framework for the design and verification of choreographies. IEEE Trans. Serv. Comput. **9**(4), 647–660 (2016)
10. Autili, M., Di Salle, A., Gallo, F., Pompilio, C., Tivoli, M.: CHOReVOLUTION: automating the realization of highly–collaborative distributed applications. In: Riis Nielson, H., Tuosto, E. (eds.) COORDINATION 2019. LNCS, vol. 11533, pp. 92–108. Springer, Cham (2019). https://doi.org/10.1007/978-3-030-22397-7_6
11. Bocchi, L., Melgratti, H.C., Tuosto, E.: On resolving non-determinism in choreographies. Log. Methods Comput. Sci. **16**(3) (2020)
12. Basu, S., Bultan, T., Ouederni, M.: Deciding choreography realizability. In: Field, J., et al. (eds.) Proceedings of the 39th ACM SIGPLAN-SIGACT POPL 2012, pp. 191–202. ACM (2012)
13. Hüttel, H., et al.: Foundations of session types and behavioural contracts. ACM Comput. Surv. **49**(1), 3:1–3:36 (2016)
14. Brand, D., Zafiropulo, P.: On communicating finite-state machines. J. ACM **30**(2), 323–342 (1983)
15. Henriksen, J.G., Thiagarajan, P.: Dynamic linear time temporal logic. Ann. Pure Appl. Logic **96**(1–3), 187–207 (1999)
16. Tuosto, E., Guanciale, R.: Semantics of global view of choreographies. J. Logical Algebr. Methods Program. **95**, 17–40 (2018)

17. Tarski, A.: A decision method for elementary algebra and geometry. Memorandum RM-109, RAND Corporation (1951)

18. Aleti, A., Buhnova, B., Grunske, L., Koziolek, A., Meedeniya, I.: Software architecture optimization methods: a systematic literature review. IEEE Trans. Softw. Eng. **39**, 658–683 (2013)

19. Hayyolalam, V., Pourhaji Kazem, A.A.: A systematic literature review on QoS-aware service composition and selection in cloud environment. J. Netw. Comput. Appl. **110**, 52–74 (2018)

20. Giachino, E., de Gouw, S., Laneve, C., Nobakht, B.: Statically and dynamically verifiable SLA metrics. In: Ábrahám, E., Bonsangue, M., Johnsen, E.B. (eds.) Theory and Practice of Formal Methods. LNCS, vol. 9660, pp. 211–225. Springer, Cham (2016). https://doi.org/10.1007/978-3-319-30734-3_15

21. Rosenthal, K.: Quantales and Their Applications, vol. 234 of Pitman Research Notes in Mathematics Series. Longman Scientific & Technical (1990)

22. Buscemi, M.G., Montanari, U.: CC-Pi: a constraint-based language for specifying service level agreements. In: De Nicola, R. (ed.) ESOP 2007. LNCS, vol. 4421, pp. 18–32. Springer, Heidelberg (2007). https://doi.org/10.1007/978-3-540-71316-6_3

23. Lluch-Lafuente, A., Montanari, U.: Quantitative μ-calculus and CTL based on constraint semirings. Electron. Notes Theor. Comp. Sci. **112**, 37–59 (2005)

24. De Nicola, R., Ferrari, G., Montanari, U., Pugliese, R., Tuosto, E.: A process calculus for QoS-aware applications. In: Jacquet, J.-M., Picco, G.P. (eds.) COORDINATION 2005. LNCS, vol. 3454, pp. 33–48. Springer, Heidelberg (2005). https://doi.org/10.1007/11417019_3

25. Martinez Suñé, A.E., Lopez Pombo, C.G.: Automatic quality-of-service evaluation in service-oriented computing. In: Riis Nielson, H., Tuosto, E. (eds.) COORDINATION 2019. LNCS, vol. 11533, pp. 221–236. Springer, Cham (2019). https://doi.org/10.1007/978-3-030-22397-7_13

26. Bocchi, L., Honda, K., Tuosto, E., Yoshida, N.: A theory of design-by-contract for distributed multiparty interactions. In: Gastin, P., Laroussinie, F. (eds.) CONCUR 2010. LNCS, vol. 6269, pp. 162–176. Springer, Heidelberg (2010). https://doi.org/10.1007/978-3-642-15375-4_12

27. Vissani, I., Lopez Pombo, C.G., Tuosto, E.: Communicating machines as a dynamic binding mechanism of services. In: Gay, D., et al. (eds.) Proceedings of PLACES, vol. 203 of Electronics Proceedings in Theoretical Computer Science, pp. 85–98 (2016)

28. Pnueli, A.: The temporal semantics of concurrent programs. Theor. Comp. Sci. **13**(1), 45–60 (1981)

29. Pratt, V.R.: Semantical consideration on floyd-hoare logic. In Carlyle, et al. (eds.) Proceedings of 17th SFCS, pp. 109–121. IEEE Computer Society (1976)

30. Vardi, M.Y.: The rise and fall of LTL: invited talk at the 2nd. Games, automata, logics and formal verification. Electron. Proc. Theor. Comp. Sci. **54** (2011)

31. De Giacomo, G., Vardi, M.Y.: Linear temporal logic and linear dynamic logic on finite traces. In: Proceedings of 23rd IJCAI, 2013, pp. 854–860. AAAI Press (2013)

32. Post Office Protocol: Version 2. RFC 937 (1985)

33. de Moura, L., Bjørner, N.: Z3: an efficient SMT solver. In: Ramakrishnan, C.R., Rehof, J. (eds.) TACAS 2008. LNCS, vol. 4963, pp. 337–340. Springer, Heidelberg (2008). https://doi.org/10.1007/978-3-540-78800-3_24

34. Coto, A., Guanciale, R., Tuosto, E.: Choreographic development of message-passing applications - a tutorial. In: [4], pp. 20–36 (2020)

35. Coto, A., Guanciale, R., Lange, J., Tuosto, E.: **ChorGram**: tool support for choreographic deveelopment. https://bitbucket.org/eMgssi/chorgram/src/master/ (2015)
36. Francalanza, A., Mezzina, C.A., Tuosto, E.: Towards choreographic-based monitoring. In: Ulidowski, I., Lanese, I., Schultz, U.P., Ferreira, C. (eds.) RC 2020. LNCS, vol. 12070, pp. 128–150. Springer, Cham (2020). https://doi.org/10.1007/978-3-030-47361-7_6
37. Bocchi, L., Chen, T., Demangeon, R., Honda, K., Yoshida, N.: Monitoring networks through multiparty session types. Theor. Comput. Sci. **669**, 33–58 (2017)
38. Büchi, J.R.: On a decision method in restricted second order arithmetic. In: Proceedings of the International Congress on Logic, Method, and Philosophy of Science, pp. 1–11. Stanford University, Stanford University Press, Stanford (1962)
39. Biere, A., Heule, M., Van Maaren, H., Walsh, T. (eds.): Handbook of Satisfiability, 2nd edn. IOS Press, Amsterdam (2021)

Interactive Matching Logic Proofs in Coq

Jan Tušil[1,3]($\boxtimes$) [iD], Péter Bereczky[2] [iD], and Dániel Horpácsi[2] [iD]

[1] Masaryk University, Brno, Czech Republic
jan.tusil@mail.muni.cz
[2] Eötvös Loránd University, Budapest, Hungary
berpeti@inf.elte.hu, daniel-h@elte.hu
[3] Runtime Verification Inc., Chicago, USA

Abstract. Matching logic (ML) is a formalism for specifying and reasoning about mathematical structures by means of patterns and pattern matching. Previously, it has been used to capture a number of other logics, e.g., separation logic with recursive definitions and linear temporal logic. ML has also been formalized in the Coq Proof Assistant, and the soundness of its Hilbert-style proof system has been mechanized.

However, using a Hilbert-style system for interactive reasoning is challenging—even more so in ML, which lacks a general deduction theorem. Therefore, we propose a single-conclusion sequent calculus for ML that is more amenable to interactive proving. Based on this sequent calculus, we implement a *proof mode* for interactive reasoning in ML, which significantly simplifies the construction of ML proofs in Coq. The proof mode is a mechanism for displaying intermediate proof states and an extensible set of proof tactics that implement the rules of the sequent calculus. We evaluate our proof mode on a collection of examples, showing a substantial improvement in proof script size and readability.

Keywords: Matching logic · Sequent calculus · Coq · Interactive reasoning

1 Introduction

Matching logic [11, 27] (ML) is a simple but expressive logic designed mainly for reasoning about programs and programming language semantics. It can capture reasoning in first-order logic (FOL) [27], in modal μ-calculus and reachability logic [13], and serves as the logical foundation of the $\mathbb{K}$ framework [9]. Matching logic's Hilbert-style *proofs* can be checked using a simple checker [9].

Although $\mathbb{K}$ is based on matching logic, it does *not* provide support for general ML reasoning. For program verification, $\mathbb{K}$ implements automated reasoning based on *reachability logic* [28] and its ML embedding [13]. When verification engineers need some lemmas to finish a proof, they prove them on paper and add them as trusted lemmas to the specification. Since these lemmas are essentially ML theorems, they could be proven using a proof assistant, and the resulting proof objects could be combined with the ones generated by $\mathbb{K}$.

E. Ábrahám et al. (Eds.): ICTAC 2023, LNCS 14446, pp. 139–157, 2023.
https://doi.org/10.1007/978-3-031-47963-2_10

Recently, matching logic has been formalized [4] in Coq [29]. This implementation covers the syntax, semantics, and Hilbert-style proof system of ML, with a mechanized proof of soundness. Furthermore, the formalization enables users to define their own ML theories and formally reason about their models, as well as about provability. Therefore, the Coq embedding of the proof system of ML can be used to formalize and check paper-based proofs.

Yet using this system (or any Hilbert-style proof system in general [2]) is not intuitive for *constructing* proofs by humans. In addition, the fact that a general deduction theorem does not hold in ML [14] further complicates reasoning with the Hilbert-style system. For example, the proof of $\varphi \to \varphi$ in a Hilbert system (which contains axioms of propositional logic) is presented in Fig. 1a. In contrast, using a sequent calculus [2], the same theorem can be proved more naturally just in two steps (as in Fig. 1b).

$$(\text{P2}): \frac{(\varphi \to ((\varphi \to \varphi) \to \varphi)) \to}{((\varphi \to (\varphi \to \varphi)) \to (\varphi \to \varphi))} \qquad (1)$$

$$(\text{P1}): \varphi \to ((\varphi \to \varphi) \to \varphi) \qquad (2)$$

$$(\text{MP}) \text{ on } 1, 2: (\varphi \to (\varphi \to \varphi)) \to (\varphi \to \varphi) \qquad (3)$$

$$(\text{P1}): \varphi \to (\varphi \to \varphi) \qquad (4)$$

$$(\text{MP}) \text{ on } 3, 4: \varphi \to \varphi \qquad (5)$$

$$\frac{\dfrac{}{\varphi \vdash \varphi} \; hyp}{\vdash \varphi \to \varphi} \vdash \to$$

(a) Hilbert-style proof of $\varphi \to \varphi$

(b) Proof of $\varphi \to \varphi$ using a sequent calculus

Fig. 1. Proofs of $\varphi \to \varphi$

Therefore we propose a sequent calculus for ML (focusing on the first-order fragment), on which we re-base the *proof mode* (called MLPM) of [4]; we also significantly extend MLPM, and highlight some details on its implementation. MLPM provides a number of high-level proof tactics for ML that mirror the behavior of similarly-named Coq tactics, while it is also responsible for displaying the *proof state* in a readable way[1]. Moreover, proofs written with MLPM are also (automatically) converted to proofs in the original proof system of ML. Usually, the converted proof is larger than a hand-crafted Hilbert-style proof of the same theorem, but the proof script written with our proof mode is significantly smaller.

Contributions. In this paper we make the following contributions:

- a *sound sequent calculus* for the first-order fragment of ML with equality;
- a principled implementation [1] of a *Coq proof mode for ML* (MLPM) utilizing a shallow embedding of the sequent calculus on top of the mechanized Hilbert-style proof system[2];

---

[1] This is done without modifications to Coq. In particular, MLPM is *not* a Coq plugin.

[2] We expand on the preliminary implementation reported in [4].

– an *evaluation* of MLPM, showing a significant reduction of proof script size (in comparison to a direct use of the embedded Hilbert-style proof system).

The paper is structured as follows. Section 2 introduces matching logic; Sect. 3 describes the proposed sequent calculus; Sect. 4 discusses how the calculus was implemented as the core of MLPM; Sect. 5 contains an evaluation of MLPM; Sect. 6 summarizes related work; and Sect. 7 concludes.

2   Matching Logic

Matching logic is being actively studied [10,15,30] and used for expressing programming language semantics [9,21]. In this paper we use the applicative variant of ML [11] (as formalized in [4]). This section summarises its syntax, semantics, and proof system. Some results in the literature we refer to were proved for a different variant of ML [13,14]: these were adapted to the applicative variant either by us or by the authors of [4]. We annotate the definitions, lemmas, theorems with references to the corresponding code parts in the formalization.

2.1   Matching Logic Syntax

Definition 1 ([1, Signature.v, Pattern.v]).
A signature is a triple (EV, SV, Σ), *where*

– *EV is a countably infinite set of* element variables, *denoted* x, y, $\ldots$;
– *SV is a countably infinite set of* set variables, *denoted* X, Y, $\ldots$;
– Σ *is a countable set of* (constant) symbols, *denoted* σ, f, g, $\ldots$.

EV, SV, and Σ *are pairwise disjoint. When EV and SV are understood from the context, we use* Σ *to denote the whole signature. Given a signature* Σ, *the set of matching logic formulas (aka* patterns*) is inductively defined by the grammar*

$$\varphi ::= x \mid X \mid \sigma \mid \varphi_1 \varphi_2 \mid \bot \mid \varphi_1 \to \varphi_2 \mid \exists x . \varphi \mid \mu X . \varphi \quad \text{where } \varphi \text{ is positive in } X.$$

The syntax elements are, in order, *element* and *set variables*, *symbols*, *application of patterns* (left-associative), *bottom*, *implication* (right-associative), *existential quantification*, and *least fixpoint binder*. Other connectives of FOL are defined as notations in the usual way. We use the notation $\varphi[\psi/x]$ for capture-avoiding substitution, and let $FV(\varphi)$ denote the set of free (element or set) variables of φ.

Definition 2 ([1, PatternContext.v, ApplicationContext.v]).
A (pattern) context C *is a pattern with a distinguished variable denoted by* $\square$. *We denote by* $C[\psi]$ *the substitution of* $\square$ *with* ψ *in* C. *We call a context* $C^{\$}$ *an* application context *if from the root of* $C^{\$}$ *to* $\square$ *there are only applications; that is, if* C *is constructed with one of the following rules:*

– $C^{\$}$ *is* $\square$ *itself, called the identity context; or*
– $C^{\$} \equiv C_1^{\$} \varphi$, *where* $C_1^{\$}$ *is an application context; or*
– $C^{\$} \equiv \varphi C_2^{\$}$, *where* $C_2^{\$}$ *is an application context.*

We extend the notation $FV(\varphi)$ for contexts (C) and list of patterns (Δ): $FV(C)$ denotes the set of free variables of the context C, while $FV(\Delta)$ denotes the union of $FV(\varphi)$ for all $\varphi \in \Delta$.

2.2   Matching Logic Semantics

Here we give some intuition to the *semantics* of matching logic; we refer to [11] for more details. Intuitively, matching logic has a *pattern matching semantics* - a pattern (formula) is interpreted as the (often singleton) *set* of model elements that *match* the pattern in the given valuation. For example, when using matching logic to reason about a small-step semantics of a programming language as done in the $\mathbb{K}$ framework [9], the pattern

$$state\ (\texttt{incr i})\ (map\ \texttt{i}\ x)$$

will, in the right model and the valuation ρ, match exactly the program state consisting of the program $\texttt{incr i}$ (that is to be executed) and a memory that maps the program variable $\texttt{i}$ (represented by a symbol $\texttt{i} \in \Sigma$) to the value $\rho(x)$ (where $x \in EV$). Formally, a Σ-*model* is a triple $\mathcal{M} = (M, \cdot_M, \{\sigma_M\}_{\sigma \in \Sigma})$ where:

- M is a nonempty carrier set;
- $\_\ \cdot_M\ \_ : M \times M \rightarrow \mathcal{P}(M)$ is a binary application function, where $\mathcal{P}(M)$ denotes the powerset of M;
- $\sigma_M \subseteq M$ is the interpretation of σ, for each $\sigma \in \Sigma$.

Application from the model is extended to any subsets of the model in the pointwise manner: application of two *sets* is defined as the union of application of pairs from the Cartesian product of the two sets: $A \cdot_M B := \bigcup_{(a,b) \in A \times B} a \cdot_M b$. Then, the semantics $|\varphi_1\ \varphi_2|_\rho$ of matching logic application $\varphi_1\ \varphi_2$ is defined using this pointwise extension, to be $|\varphi_1|_\rho \cdot_M |\varphi_2|_\rho$. In practice, φ_1 is often either a symbol (which is interpreted exactly as prescribed by the model), or a symbol applied to other patterns (as e.g., $map\ \texttt{i}$ in $(map\ \texttt{i}\ x)$). However, one can also write patterns such as $even\ (3 \vee 4)$, which is equivalent to $(even\ 3) \vee (even\ 4)$, and $(even \vee odd)\ 3$, equivalent to $(even\ 3) \vee (odd\ 3)$ (where $even$, odd are symbols from the signature). Boolean connectives are interpreted as the corresponding set operations; e.g., conjunction as intersection, negation as complement, bottom as an empty set. Variables (element and set) are interpreted as prescribed by the valuation, to (in the case of element variable, singleton) sets of model elements.

2.3   Definedness, Totality, Equality

One can define a construct called *definedness* - a symbol $\lceil\_\rceil$ that, when applied to a pattern φ (usually written as $\lceil\varphi\rceil$), matches either all model elements (if φ is *defined* - i.e., matches something) or none (if φ matches nothing). Patterns that match all elements or none are known as *predicate patterns*. One can also define the dual of definedness, called *totality* ($\lfloor\varphi\rfloor \overset{\text{def}}{=} \neg\lceil\neg\varphi\rceil$) which is a predicate pattern and matches all model elements iff φ matches them all (otherwise matches none). *Equality* can be defined using totality ($\varphi_1 = \varphi_2 \overset{\text{def}}{=} \lfloor\varphi_1 \leftrightarrow \varphi_2\rfloor$), and has the property that the pattern $\varphi_1 = \varphi_2$ is predicate matched by all model elements iff φ_1 and φ_2 are matched by the same model elements. Definedness, totality, and equality are axiomatized by a (finite) theory Γ^{DEF}, which we treat as a black box in this paper; we refer an interested reader to [27] for an in-depth description.

Table 1. Hilbert-style proof system for matching logic ([1, ProofSystem.v])

FOL reasoning

(P1)	$\varphi \to (\psi \to \varphi)$	(P2)	$\begin{aligned}(\varphi \to (\psi \to \xi)) \to \\ (\varphi \to \psi) \to (\varphi \to \xi)\end{aligned}$
(P3)	$((\varphi \to \bot) \to \bot) \to \varphi$	(MP)	$\dfrac{\varphi \quad \varphi \to \psi}{\psi}$
($\exists$-Quan)	$\varphi[y/x] \to \exists x . \varphi$	($\exists$-Gen)	$\dfrac{\varphi \to \psi}{(\exists x . \varphi) \to \psi}$ if $x \notin FV(\psi)$

Frame reasoning

(Prop$\bot$)	$C^{\$}[\bot] \to \bot$	(Prop$\vee$)	$C^{\$}[\varphi \vee \psi] \to C^{\$}[\varphi] \vee C^{\$}[\psi]$
(Prop$\exists$)	$\begin{aligned}C^{\$}[\exists x . \varphi] \to \exists x . C^{\$}[\varphi] \\ \text{if } x \notin FV(C^{\$})\end{aligned}$	(Framing)	$\dfrac{\varphi \to \psi}{C^{\$}[\varphi] \to C^{\$}[\psi]}$

Fixpoint reasoning

(Subst)	$\dfrac{\varphi}{\varphi[\psi/X]}$	(Pre-Fixp)	$\varphi[(\mu X . \varphi)/X] \to \mu X . \varphi$
(KT)	$\dfrac{\varphi[\psi/X] \to \psi}{(\mu X . \varphi) \to \psi}$		

Technical rules

(Existence)	$\exists x . x$	(Singleton)	$\neg(C_1^{\$}[x \wedge \varphi] \wedge C_2^{\$}[x \wedge \neg\varphi])$

2.4 The Hilbert-Style Proof System

We present the Hilbert-style proof system of matching logic [11] in Table 1 and denote it with $\vdash_{\mathcal{H}}$. The proof rules can be divided into four categories:

- **FOL reasoning** contains standard Hilbert-style proof as in FOL. In ($\exists$-Quan), only element variables are substituted, *not* arbitrary patterns.
- **Frame reasoning** consists of three propagation rules and a framing rule that allow one to propagate formal reasoning through an application context. (These rules are equivalent[3] to the ones in [4].)
- **Fixpoint reasoning** contains fixpoint rules as in modal μ-calculi [7];
- **Technical rules** which are important for various results in [14].

We denote the provability relation with $\Gamma \vdash_{\mathcal{H}} \varphi$ and highlight a meta-theorem mechanized in [4] that allows one to replace equivalent patterns in any context.

Lemma 1 ([1, `ProofMode/Misc.v: prf_equiv_congruence`]).
$\Gamma \vdash_{\mathcal{H}} \varphi_1 \leftrightarrow \varphi_2$ *implies* $\Gamma \vdash_{\mathcal{H}} C[\varphi_1] \leftrightarrow C[\varphi_2]$

A FOL-style deduction theorem does not hold in ML [13], but the following variant (which uses totality) holds.

---

[3] [1, `ProofMode/Misc.v`: Prop_bot_ctx, Framing, prf_prop_ex_iff, prf_prop_or_iff].

Theorem 1 ([1, `Definedness_ProofSystem.v: deduction_theorem_noKT`]).   *Let* $\Gamma^{\mathsf{DEF}} \subseteq \Gamma$. *If a proof of* $\Gamma \cup \{\psi\} \vdash_{\mathcal{H}} \varphi$ *does not use (∃-Gen) and (Subst) with* $FV(\psi)$ *and does not use (KT), then* $\Gamma \vdash_{\mathcal{H}} \lfloor \psi \rfloor \to \varphi$.

As in [13], Thoerem 1 is used together with Lemma 1 (recall $\varphi_1 = \varphi_2 \overset{\text{def}}{=} \lfloor \varphi_1 \leftrightarrow \varphi_2 \rfloor$ from Sect. 2.3) to prove Lemma 2.

Lemma 2 ([1, `Definedness_ProofSystem.v: equality_elimination_basic_ar`]).
For any pattern context C *in which* $\square$ *does not appear inside any* μ *binders,* $\Gamma \vdash_{\mathcal{H}} (\varphi_1 = \varphi_2) \to (C[\varphi_1] \leftrightarrow C[\varphi_2])$, *assuming that* $\Gamma^{\mathsf{DEF}} \subseteq \Gamma$.

This lemma justifies the $(=\vdash)$ rule of our sequent calculus (Sect. 3), which forms the basis of the `mlRewriteBy` proof mode tactic (Sect. 4).

3   A Single-Conclusion Sequent Calculus

As noted already in [2], Hilbert-style proof systems are not particularly intuitive for constructing proofs. Therefore, we define an alternative, *single-conclusion sequent calculus* $\vdash_{\mathcal{S}}$, which we mechanize to implement an intuitive, interactive prover for matching logic. This calculus is inspired by the family of *sequent natural deduction* calculi [6,25], and is shown to be equivalent to $\vdash_{\mathcal{H}}$ (using Gentzen's definition of equivalence [2]). Before presenting the calculus, we introduce the notion of *proof constraint* used by our formalization of Theorem 1.

3.1   Proof Constraints

The deduction theorem (Theorem 1) has three essential side conditions that constrain the rules usable in the proof of the premise. Unlike the Hilbert-style proof system $\vdash_{\mathcal{H}}$, the proposed sequent calculus allows these conditions to be checked without inspecting the proof. In particular, we trace the availability of proof rules by using the notion of *proof constraints*. This allows us to rephrase the deduction theorem such that it only checks the constraint instead of inspecting the proof. We define the syntax of constraints and tie them to proofs as follows.

Definition 3 ([1, `ProofInfo.v: ProofInfo`]).   *The set* $\mathcal{C}$ *of* proof constraints *(or simply* constraints*) is defined by* $\mathcal{C} \overset{\text{def}}{=} \mathcal{P}(EV) \times \mathcal{P}(SV) \times \{true, false\}$. *The notations* c^{eg}, c^{sub}, *and* c^{kt} *are used for the first, second, and third components, respectively, of a constraint* $c \in \mathcal{C}$. *We let* $\top_{\mathcal{C}} \overset{\text{def}}{=} (EV, SV, true)$ *and* $\bot_{\mathcal{C}} \overset{\text{def}}{=} (\emptyset, \emptyset, false)$.

Definition 4 ([1, `ProofInfo.v: ProofInfoMeaning`]).   *A proof* p *of* $\vdash_{\mathcal{H}}$ *satisfies a constraint* $c \in \mathcal{C}$, *if*

- *every* $x \in EV$ *used in some (∃-Gen) step in* p *satisfies* $x \in c^{eg}$;
- *every* $X \in SV$ *used in some (Subst) step in* p *satisfies* $X \in c^{sub}$;
- *if (KT) was used in* p, *then* c^{kt} *is true.*

We write $\Gamma \vdash_{\mathcal{H}}^{c} \varphi$ *to mean that* φ *has a proof from* Γ *in* $\vdash_{\mathcal{H}}$ *that satisfies* c.

$$\frac{\Gamma \vdash_{\mathcal{H}}^c \psi}{\Gamma \blacktriangleright_c [\,] \vdash_{\mathcal{S}} \psi} \text{ INHERIT} \qquad \frac{\Gamma \blacktriangleright_c \Delta_1, \Delta_2 \vdash_{\mathcal{S}} \psi}{\Gamma \blacktriangleright_c \Delta_1, \varphi, \Delta_2 \vdash_{\mathcal{S}} \psi} \text{ WEAKEN}$$

$$\frac{\Gamma \blacktriangleright_{c'} \Delta \vdash_{\mathcal{S}} \psi \quad c' \sqsubseteq c}{\Gamma \blacktriangleright_c \Delta \vdash_{\mathcal{S}} \psi} \text{ RELAX}_\sqsubseteq \qquad \frac{\Gamma \blacktriangleright_c \Delta_1 \vdash_{\mathcal{S}} \varphi \quad \Gamma \blacktriangleright_c \Delta_1, \varphi, \Delta_2 \vdash_{\mathcal{S}} \psi}{\Gamma \blacktriangleright_c \Delta_1, \Delta_2 \vdash_{\mathcal{S}} \psi} \text{ CUT}$$

(a) Technical inference rules   (b) Structural inference rules

Fig. 2. Technical and structural inference rules

Next, we define the ordering $\sqsubseteq$ between proof constraints component-wise.

Definition 5 ([1, `ProofInfo.v: ProofInfoLe`]).
$$c_1 \sqsubseteq c_2 \overset{def}{=} c_1^{eg} \subseteq c_2^{eg} \wedge c_1^{sub} \subseteq c_2^{sub} \wedge (c_1^{kt} \implies c_2^{kt})$$

Naturally, a constraint of a ML proof can be relaxed.

Lemma 3 ([1, `ProofInfo.v: ProofInfoLe_ProofLe`]). *If $c_1 \sqsubseteq c_2$, then any proof satisfying c_1 also satisfies c_2.*

3.2 Sequents

Now we define single-conclusion sequents and introduce the calculus $\vdash_{\mathcal{S}}$.

Definition 6 ([1, `ProofMode/Basics.v: MLGoal`]). *A* sequent *is a quadruple* $\Gamma \blacktriangleright_c \Delta \vdash_{\mathcal{S}} \psi$, *where*

- Γ *is a (possibly infinite) set of ML patterns, called a* theory;
- Δ *is a finite (comma-separated) list of ML patterns, called* antecedent *or* local context;
- ψ *is a ML pattern, called* succedent *or* conclusion;
- c *is a proof constraint from the set $\mathcal{C}$.*

We reuse the standard notations for the antecedents [2,6], except for the empty antecedent denoted by []; we also use lists instead of sets (for technical reasons). We also introduce the notation of $\Gamma \vdash_{\mathcal{S}} \psi$, which means $\Gamma \blacktriangleright_{\top_c} [\,] \vdash_{\mathcal{S}} \psi$. We use the notion of inference rules and derivability in the usual way [2]. We define the rules of $\vdash_{\mathcal{S}}$ in the following figures:

- Figure 2 contains (a) technical inference rules and for relaxing proof constraints and a fallback mechanism for reasoning outside the explicitly supported fragment, and (b) structural inference rules.
- Figure 3 contains the inference rules needed to carry out reasoning in the first-order fragment of matching logic. These rules are similar to the rules in other calculi for first-order logic [2,6,17].
- Figure 4 contains rules related to definedness and equality.

$$\frac{}{\Gamma \blacktriangleright_c \Delta_1, \varphi, \Delta_2 \vdash_S \varphi} \text{ Hyp} \qquad\qquad \frac{}{\Gamma \blacktriangleright_c \Delta_1, \bot, \Delta_2 \vdash_S \psi} (\vdash \bot)$$

$$\frac{\Gamma \blacktriangleright_c \Delta_1, \Delta_2 \vdash_S \varphi_1 \quad \Gamma \blacktriangleright_c \Delta_1, \varphi_2, \Delta_2 \vdash_S \psi}{\Gamma \blacktriangleright_c \Delta_1, \varphi_1 \to \varphi_2, \Delta_2 \vdash_S \psi} (\to\vdash) \qquad \frac{\Gamma \blacktriangleright_c \Delta, \varphi \vdash_S \psi}{\Gamma \blacktriangleright_c \Delta \vdash_S \varphi \to \psi} (\vdash\to)$$

$$\frac{\Gamma \blacktriangleright_c \Delta_1, \varphi_1, \varphi_2, \Delta_2 \vdash_S \psi}{\Gamma \blacktriangleright_c \Delta_1, \varphi_1 \wedge \varphi_2, \Delta_2 \vdash_S \psi} (\wedge\vdash) \qquad \frac{\Gamma \blacktriangleright_c \Delta \vdash_S \psi_1 \quad \Gamma \blacktriangleright_c \Delta \vdash_S \psi_2}{\Gamma \blacktriangleright_c \Delta \vdash_S \psi_1 \wedge \psi_2} (\vdash \wedge)$$

$$\frac{\Gamma \blacktriangleright_c \Delta \vdash_S \psi_1}{\Gamma \blacktriangleright_c \Delta \vdash_S \psi_1 \vee \psi_2} (\vdash \vee_L)$$

$$\frac{\Gamma \blacktriangleright_c \Delta_1, \varphi_1, \Delta_2 \vdash_S \psi \quad \Gamma \blacktriangleright_c \Delta_1, \varphi_2, \Delta_2 \vdash_S \psi}{\Gamma \blacktriangleright_c \Delta_1, \varphi_1 \vee \varphi_2, \Delta_2 \vdash_S \psi} (\vee\vdash)$$

$$\frac{\Gamma \blacktriangleright_c \Delta \vdash_S \psi_2}{\Gamma \blacktriangleright_c \Delta \vdash_S \psi_1 \vee \psi_2} (\vdash \vee_R)$$

$$\frac{\Gamma \blacktriangleright_c \Delta_1, \varphi[y/x], \Delta_2 \vdash_S \psi}{\Gamma \blacktriangleright_c \Delta_1, \forall x. \varphi, \Delta_2 \vdash_S \psi} (\forall\vdash) \qquad \frac{\Gamma \blacktriangleright_c \Delta \vdash_S \psi[y/x] \quad y \in c^{eg} \quad y \notin FV(\Delta, \forall x.\psi)}{\Gamma \blacktriangleright_c \Delta \vdash_S \forall x. \psi} (\vdash \forall)$$

$$\frac{\Gamma \blacktriangleright_c \Delta_1, \varphi[y/x], \Delta_2 \vdash_S \psi \quad y \in c^{eg} \quad y \notin FV(\Delta, \exists x.\varphi, \psi)}{\Gamma \blacktriangleright_c \Delta_1, \exists x. \varphi, \Delta_2 \vdash_S \psi} (\exists\vdash)$$

$$\frac{\Gamma \blacktriangleright_c \Delta \vdash_S \psi[y/x]}{\Gamma \blacktriangleright_c \Delta \vdash_S \exists x. \psi} (\vdash \exists)$$

Fig. 3. Inference rules for first-order reasoning

A discussion of the proof rules follows. We use INHERIT of Fig. 2 to lift proofs from $\vdash_{\mathcal{H}}$ into $\vdash_S$. This rule increases the usability of the system, since existing proofs in $\vdash_{\mathcal{H}}$ do not need to be repeated in $\vdash_S$. Moreover, it ensures relative completeness of $\vdash_S$ (Lemma 5). Currently[4], this rule provides the only way for fixpoint or frame reasoning in $\vdash_S$: perform the reasoning in $\vdash_{\mathcal{H}}$ and then lift it. Rules WEAKEN and CUT are standard in sequent calculi [2]; they are used for removing and adding patterns from and to the antecedent. The rule RELAX$_\sqsubseteq$ corresponds to Lemma 3. Rules CUT, WEAKEN, and HYP can be use to derive the usual *Interchange* rule [2] which changes the order of the patterns in the antecedent.

Figure 3 contains the usual introduction and elimination rules of sequent calculi [2,6]. The rules in Figs. 2 and 3 do not assume anything about the theory Γ; for the rules in Fig. 4, we assume that $\Gamma^{\mathsf{DEF}} \subseteq \Gamma$. We use $mu\_free(C)$ to denote the fact that $\Box$ does not occur inside any μ binders in C. DEDUCTION captures a variant of the deduction theorem for matching logic, while $(\vdash=)$ and $(=\vdash)$ capture the axioms of the theory of equality [18].

---

[4] We plan to extend $\vdash_S$ with fixpoint and frame reasoning capabilities in the future.

$$\frac{\Gamma \cup \{\varphi\} \blacktriangleright_c \Delta \vdash_S \psi \quad c^{eg} \cap FV(\varphi) = \emptyset \quad c^{sub} \cap FV(\varphi) = \emptyset \quad c^{kt} = false}{\Gamma \blacktriangleright_{\top_c} \lfloor \varphi \rfloor, \Delta \vdash_S \psi} \text{ DEDUCTION}$$

$$\frac{}{\Gamma \blacktriangleright_{\top_c} \Delta \vdash_S \psi = \psi} \; (\vdash=) \qquad \frac{\Gamma \blacktriangleright_{\top_c} \Delta_1, \varphi_1 = \varphi_2, \Delta_2 \vdash_S C[\varphi_2] \quad mu\_free(C)}{\Gamma \blacktriangleright_{\top_c} \Delta_1, \varphi_1 = \varphi_2, \Delta_2 \vdash_S C[\varphi_1]} \; (=\vdash)$$

Fig. 4. Deduction; and rules about equality. These rules assume that $\Gamma^{\mathsf{DEF}} \subseteq \Gamma$.

3.3   Meta-properties of $\vdash_S$

We proved the equivalence between $\vdash_{\mathcal{H}}$ and $\vdash_S$. Unlike in [2], in our interpretation of the sequent, the patterns in the antecedent are not connected with conjunction, but they form a chain of implications leading to the conclusion. We opted for this approach because unlike conjunction, implication is a primitive construct in matching logic and in $\vdash_{\mathcal{H}}$, and is thus easier to reason about. Specifically, we prove the following lemma.

Lemma 4 (Correspondence).

$$\Gamma \blacktriangleright_c \varphi_1, \ldots, \varphi_k \vdash_S \psi \iff \Gamma \vdash_{\mathcal{H}}^c \varphi_1 \to \ldots \to \varphi_k \to \psi$$

Proof. For the $\Longrightarrow$ direction, we refer to the formalization [1, ProofMode subdirectory] and Sect. 4. One can also follow the references from Figs. 2, 2b, 3 and 4. To prove the other ($\Longleftarrow$) direction, we can first use INHERIT and then ($\vdash\to$) k times.

Thus, we obtain the equivalence of the two systems.

Lemma 5 (Equivalence of $\vdash_S$ and $\vdash_{\mathcal{H}}$). *The relation $\vdash_S$ is sound and complete with respect to $\vdash_{\mathcal{H}}$, meaning that $\Gamma \vdash_S \psi \iff \Gamma \vdash_{\mathcal{H}} \psi$.*

Proof. Completeness follows from the INHERIT proof rule, soundness from Lemma 4.

Combining Lemma 4 and the soundness of the $\vdash_{\mathcal{H}}$ [4], we obtain:

Theorem 2 (Soundness of $\vdash_S$). *The sequent calculus $\vdash_S$ is sound with respect to the semantics of matching logic described in [4].*

We can strengthen our completeness claim about the first-order fragment.

Theorem 3 (Completeness of the first-order fragment of $\vdash_S$). *All the axioms and inference rules in the first-order section of Table 1 are derivable in $\vdash_S$ using only the rules in Fig. 2b (i.e., excluding INHERIT and RELAX$_\sqsubseteq$) and Fig. 3.*

Proof. Formalized in [1, Tests/TEST_ProofMode_relative_completeness.v] as a collection of lemmas.

One novelty of $\vdash_S$ is in the notion of proof constraints, which provide a formal and compositional way to treat and ensure the side-conditions of Theorem 1. We explain this in more detail in Sect. 4.3. Moreover, $\vdash_{\mathcal{S}}$ is compatible with $\vdash_{\mathcal{H}}$ due to INHERIT.

Another well-known question is whether $\vdash_{\mathcal{S}}$ admits cut elimination. For now, we have not investigated this question; however, it is of future interest.

4   Implementation of the Proof Mode

In this section we describe the *Coq proof mode for matching logic* (MLPM) which we made available as [1]. The core of MLPM consists of a shallow embedding of $\vdash_{\mathcal{S}}$ into $\vdash_{\mathcal{H}}$, which itself is deeply embedded in Coq. Therefore, we start with a brief review of the embedding of $\vdash_{\mathcal{H}}$ in Coq as described in [4]. Next, we introduce our running example, on which we illustrate various concepts of MLPM. We conclude the section with a discussion on the architecture of MLPM.

4.1   Matching Logic Proof System in Coq

We base our work on the mechanization of matching logic described in [4], where the authors develop a *deep embedding* of ML patterns, models, and a Hilbert-style proof system equivalent[5] to $\vdash_{\mathcal{H}}$, into Coq. There, a *locally nameless* encoding [8] of binders is used, which means that bound variables are represented by *indices* (that is, natural numbers) and free variables by *names* (typically strings); additionally, a *well-formedness* predicate is used to filter out representations that do not correspond to any pattern. Reasoning about well-formedness of patterns presents a difficulty from the usability point of view, since most rules of the embedded proof system require the involved patterns to be well-formed. We discuss two ways in which we overcome this difficulty in Sect. 4.4.

The price we pay for using a deeply embedded proof system [4] is that we cannot easily reuse Coq's handling of propositional and first-order connectives. However, we argue that a deep embedding of the matching logic from [4] is appropriate for our purposes. First, the calculus contains a rule for elimination of equality ($=\vdash$), which is based on its Hilbert-style counterpart from [12]. This rule relies on the deduction theorem of matching logic, which is proved by induction on the structure of the input proof—which is easier to do when one treats proofs as deeply-embedded, inductively-defined data. Another advantage of a deep embedding is that it will allow us to extract proofs from Coq using its built-in extraction mechanism, as we plan to do in the future.

4.2   Example Interactive Proof

We demonstrate various aspects of MLPM on Fig. 5. The frames represent Coq's *proof state*; everything below the full line is *Coq goal*; everything above the full line is *Coq context* (which we omit in all cases but the first one). When inside MLPM, the Coq goal corresponds to a sequent (Definition 6). The goal is divided

---

[5] The application context of the framing rules are decomposed into two separate rules in [4].

```
Σ: Signature      defsyntax: definedness_syntax      Γ: Theory
HΓ: definedness_theory ⊆ Γ      x: evar      p, φ₁, φ₂: Pattern
mff: mu_free p      wff: well_formed p      wfφ₁: well_formed (ex , φ₁)
wfφ₂: well_formed (ex , φ₂)

Γ
⊢ (all , φ₂ =ml φ₁) and p $ φ₁^{evar:0↦x} --->
  (ex , p $ φ₂)

   (* 1 *) mlIntro "H".

Γ ⊢
"H" : (all , φ₂ =ml φ₁) and p $ φ₁^{evar:0↦x},
---------------------------------------
ex , p $ φ₂

   (* 2 *) mlDestructAnd "H" as "H1" "H2".
   (* 3 *) mlSpecialize "H1" with x.

Γ ⊢
"H1" : (φ₂ =ml φ₁)^{evar:0↦x},
"H2" : p $ φ₁^{evar:0↦x},
---------------------------------------
ex , p $ φ₂

   (* 4 *) mlExists x.
           mlSimpl. rewrite [p^{evar:0↦x}]evar_open_closed;[wf_auto2|].

Γ ⊢
"H1" : φ₂^{evar:0↦x} =ml φ₁^{evar:0↦x},
"H2" : p $ φ₁^{evar:0↦x},
---------------------------------------
p $ φ₂^{evar:0↦x}

   (* 5 *) mlRewriteBy "H1" at 1;[auto|(
           apply mu_free_in_path;cbn;by rewrite mff)|].

Γ ⊢
"H1" : φ₂^{evar:0↦x} =ml φ₁^{evar:0↦x},
"H2" : p $ φ₁^{evar:0↦x},
---------------------------------------
p $ φ₁^{evar:0↦x}

   (* 6 *) mlExact "H2".
```

Fig. 5. An example interactive ML proof. The notation $\phi^{\{evar:n \mapsto \psi\}}$ means ϕ with substituted pattern ψ for the de Bruijn index n representing a bound variable; =ml denotes the ML equality (Sect. 2.4). The notations all, $, and denote universal quantification, application and conjunction, respectively.

by the ⊢ symbol and a dashed line into three parts: the matching logic theory
Γ, which is a (possibly infinite) set of patterns; the *local context*, which is a
list of *named hypotheses*; and the *conclusion*. For example, the goal after proof
step *(* 1 *)* corresponds to the sequent $\Gamma \blacktriangleright_{\top_C} (\forall y.\phi_2 = \phi_1) \wedge p(\phi_1[x/y]) \vdash_S$
$\exists y.(p \, \phi_2)$. In this example, the proof constraint is $\top_C$ throughout the execution
of the whole proof script, and is therefore automatically hidden. However, it is
checked at step *(* 5 *)* when rewriting using equality (as in the rule $(=\vdash)$); the
proof step would fail if the constraint were too strict.

We use automation for discharging *freshness* (non-occurrence of a variable in
a pattern) proof obligations; similarly, we use the tactic wf_auto2 for discharging
well-formedness proof obligations generated when applying certain lemmas (such
as evar_open_closed). However, most MLPM tactics do not require proving well-
formedness, as well-formedness is preserved by the tactics.

All the names of MLPM tactics have the prefix ml and resemble names of Coq
tactics with similar behavior. Tactics outside MLPM (not having the ml prefix)
are used to further simplify the goal and to discharge technical proof obligations.
We refer an interested reader to the proof mode tutorial[6] of the formalization [1].

4.3   Proof Constraints

When using Theorem 1 on paper, one has to be careful not to forget checking
the theorem's side conditions. When using it in Coq, the proof assistant automatically generates the corresponding proof obligations. But how to prove such
obligations? Since we have formalized the concepts in the side-conditions of the
deduction theorem as computable, bool-valued predicates on the type of matching logic proofs, one can try to discharge the obligations by simple computation.

However, we quickly ran into issues when using this approach. First, for larger
proofs, the computation can be slow. Second, this approach is not compositional:
when a theorem T is applied after using the deduction theorem, its proof has to
be examined despite the possibility that it has already been examined before—
and with this approach, subproofs do not "remember" whether they have been
examined or not. Third, we usually do not work with concrete theorems about
concrete patterns, but with meta-theorems that are *parameterized* by patterns.
This means that some function or theorem applications that occur in matching
logic proofs cannot be fully reduced to constructor terms. Typically, the symbolic
computation gets stuck on a dependent pattern matching.

Therefore we resort to a different approach. In our development, we annotate
every theorem of $\vdash_{\mathcal{H}}$, including its proofs rules, with a *proof constraint*[7] as in
Sect. 3.1, which represents an overapproximation of the proof rules used in the
proof of the theorem. Annotated theorems carry with them a Coq proof ensuring
that the ML proof satisfies the constraint. The formalization of Theorem 1 then
consumes such annotated proofs, and is then used to prove the soundness of
$(=\vdash)$.

---

[6] examples/02_proofmode/theories/tutorial.v.

[7] In the implementation we allow only (co-)finite sets of variables for the components
of a constraint.

```
Lemma prf_conj_split
  {Σ : Signature} Γ a b l:
  well_formed a ->
  well_formed b ->
  Pattern.wf l ->
  Γ ⊢i (foldr patt_imp a l) --->
       (foldr patt_imp b l) --->
       (foldr patt_imp (a and b) l)
  using BasicReasoning.
```

(a) A layer (1) lemma

```
Lemma MLGoal_splitAnd
  {Σ : Signature} Γ a b l i:
  of_MLGoal (mkMLGoal Σ Γ l a i) ->
  of_MLGoal (mkMLGoal Σ Γ l b i) ->
  of_MLGoal (mkMLGoal Σ Γ l (a and b) i).
```

(b) A layer (2) lemma

```
Ltac mlSplitAnd :=
  _ensureProofMode;
  apply MLGoal_splitAnd.
```

(c) A layer (3) tactic

Fig. 6. The architecture of $(\vdash \wedge)$ ([1, `ProofMode/Propositional.v`]).

```
Coercion of_MLGoal {Σ : Signature} (MG : MLGoal) : Type :=
  let ψ := (mlConclusion MG) in let φs := (patterns_of (mlHypotheses MG)) in
  well_formed ψ -> Pattern.wf φs ->
  (mlTheory MG) ⊢i (fold_right patt_imp ψ φs) using (mlInfo MG).
```

Fig. 7. A coercion from sequents to $\vdash_{\mathcal{H}}$ ([1, `ProofMode/Basics.v`]). The `fold_right` _ _ _ part represents the chain of implications of Lemma 4.

4.4   Architecture of the Proof Mode

Conceptually, we recognize three layers in which MLPM is organized: (1) annotated admissible rules of $\vdash_{\mathcal{H}}$, (2) proof state transforming theorems, and (3) user-facing tactics. Typically, the tactics of layer (3) apply theorems of layer (2), which are based on layer (1) theorems, which are proved using already existing tactics of layer (3). For example, consider the `mlSplitAnd` tactic (Fig. 6), which implements the $(\vdash \wedge)$ rule. In layer (1), we have the lemma `prf_conj_split` (Fig. 6a), which is proved by induction on l and repeated applications of $(\vdash \rightarrow)$, HYP, WEAKEN, and CUT (which are already defined at that point in the development). In layer (2), we have the lemma `MLGoal_splitAnd` (Fig. 6b), which is proved using `prf_conj_split`. Here, `mkMLGoal` is the constructor of the type `MLGoal` representing sequents, and is coerced by a function named `of_MLGoal` (Fig. 7) to a corresponding (in the sense of Lemma 4) proof obligation about $\vdash_{\mathcal{H}}$. The lemma `MLGoal_splitAnd` thus justifies the soundness of the rule $(\vdash \wedge)$ by transforming $\vdash_{\mathcal{H}}$ proofs corresponding to premises of the rule to a $\vdash_{\mathcal{H}}$ proof corresponding to its conclusion. This way, we do not have one global theorem of soundness of $\vdash_{\mathcal{S}}$; rather, rules of $\vdash_{\mathcal{S}}$ are justified by the corresponding lemmas from layer (2). This design allows us to implement the rules incrementally.

Figure 6 also illustrates another aspect of MLPM: its goals are *shallowly* embedded into Coq goals. The tactic `mlSplitAnd`, when invoked, generates two Coq goals, with a single MLPM goal (i.e., sequent) in each of them. This means that we reuse Coq's infrastructure for managing goals; that is, goal selectors, shelving, etc. Overall, our layered architecture with the coercion from the type of the sequent resembles that of Iris Proof Mode [20].

Table 2. Results of first-order examples

	$\vdash_{\mathcal{H}}$	MLPM 1	MLPM 2	Ltac
Proof size	103	2129	6279	-
Steps	34	10	4	4
Length	1212	224	65	31
Subproofs	43	1	0	0
Patterns	36	1	0	0

(a) Results of Example 6

	$\vdash_{\mathcal{H}}$	FOL MLPM	MLPM	Ltac
Proof size	488	574	1696	-
Steps	6	6	6	5
Length	810	244	138	75
Subproofs	18	3	0	0
Patterns	5	1	0	0

(b) Results of Example 7

5   Evaluation

In this section we evaluate MLPM using a number of example patterns and their proofs. We use the following goals as our case study:

$$\Gamma \vdash_{\mathcal{H}}^{\perp c} \varphi \to \psi \to \varphi \wedge \psi \tag{6}$$

$$\Gamma \vdash_{\mathcal{H}}^{\top c} (\exists x.\, \varphi_1 \wedge \varphi_2) \to \exists x.\, \varphi_1 \tag{7}$$

$$\Gamma \vdash_{\mathcal{H}}^{\top c} \varphi_2\, \varphi_3 \leftrightarrow \varphi_4 \; implies \; \Gamma \vdash_{\mathcal{H}}^{\top c} \varphi_1\, \varphi_2\, \varphi_3 \to \varphi_1\, \varphi_4 \tag{8}$$

$$\Gamma \vdash_{\mathcal{H}}^{\top c} (\forall x.\, \varphi_2 = \varphi_1 \wedge p\, \varphi_1) \to (\exists x.\, p\, \varphi_2) \tag{9}$$

From our experience, these examples are representative of the kind of subgoals one needs to solve in practice. Examples 6 and 8 also demonstrate how hand-crafted $\vdash_{\mathcal{H}}$-proofs can exploit the structure of the particular patterns. We proved these theorems in multiple different ways, and compared the results with respect the following aspects:

- *Proof size*: the number of proof rules (of $\vdash_{\mathcal{H}}$) used in the resulting proof.
- *Steps*: the number of high-level steps used in the proof script, which does not include solving technical side conditions (e.g., well-formedness, freshness proof of variables). These steps include the use of MLPM tactics, application of existing theorems, or proof rules.
- *Length*: the total character count of the proof script (not considering leading white-spaces, comments).
- *Subproofs*: the number of subproofs that are explicitly written in the script to solve constraints about well-formedness, variable freshness, and replacing equal patterns (unfolding definitions, simplifying substitutions).
- *Patterns*: the number of matching logic patterns that have been manually specified as parameters during the proof.

5.1   First-Order Proofs

First, we present the details about the propositional proof of Example 6 in Table 2a [1, `Evaluation/Propositional.v`]. This theorem corresponds to $(\vdash \wedge)$ in our sequent calculus. We proved this theorem in three different ways, and we also inspected the same proof in Coq formalized as **Prop**-based statements:

Table 3. Results of Example 8

	(Framing)	Congruence	MLPM	Ltac
Proof size	534	6005	42889	–
Steps	4	4	3	4
Length	132	418	59	81
Subproofs	3	10	0	0
Patterns	1	1	0	0

- $\vdash_{\mathcal{H}}$: only rules of $\vdash_{\mathcal{H}}$ and lemmas proved with $\vdash_{\mathcal{H}}$ were used;
- **MLPM 1**: MLPM was used without the tactic mlSplitAnd;
- **MLPM 2**: there was no restriction on the used MLPM tactics;
- **Ltac**: a proof of the same propositional statement embedded in Coq's logic, proved using Coq's own tactic language Ltac.

The use of MLPM results in smaller proof script (comparable to the equivalent Ltac proof) with fewer proof steps and fewer side conditions remaining to be proved manually. The user only rarely needs to write matching logic patterns. The downside of using MLPM is that the generated proof terms are larger.

Example 7 in Table 2b [1, Evaluation/Firstorder.v] requires reasoning about quantifiers. The $\vdash_{\mathcal{H}}$ and **Ltac** columns have the same meaning as in Table 2a; **FOL MLPM** is MLPM without propositional tactics (only tactics manipulating quantifiers were used); **MLPM** is full MLPM. The situation is similar as in Table 2a. The number of the proof steps is the same in all three proofs, since helper lemmas were used in the $\vdash_{\mathcal{H}}$ proofs. Interestingly, the first-order tactics of MLPM increase the size of the generated proof term only slightly. This is because the first-order rules of $\vdash_{\mathcal{S}}$ (on which the first-order MLPM tactics are based) are more direct consequences of the first-order $\vdash_{\mathcal{H}}$ proof rules (($\exists$-Quan) and ($\exists$-Gen)) than the propositional ones of the propositional rules.

5.2   Rewriting-Based Proofs

Table 3 shows results of three proofs of Example 8 [1, Evaluation/Rewrite.v], which is focused on the use of mlRewrite. The individual proofs are:

- **(Framing)**: (Framing) was used directly in the proof;
- **Congruence**: the congruence lemma (Lemma 1) was used;
- **MLPM**: no restriction on MLPM tactics (the mlRewrite tactic was used); and
- **Ltac**: the corresponding Coq proof, written with Ltac.

Using Lemma 1 directly results in more complex proof scripts and larger proof terms than using (Framing); on the other hand, (Framing) can be used only for application contexts without other connectives. In the **Congruence** case, Lemma 1 was used manually with explicitly specified context $C := \varphi_1\, x$ (with a fresh name x), while in the **MLPM** case, the mlRewrite tactic applied Lemma

Table 4. Results of Example 9 (same as in Figure 5)

	$\vdash_{\mathcal{H}}$ proof	MLPM proof
Proof size	10650557	10653299
Steps	10	7
Length	926	252
Subproofs	35	4
Patterns	1	1

1 with C automatically inferred as $\varphi_1 x \rightarrow \varphi_1 \varphi_4$. Again, the **MLPM** proof is shorter than the manual ones. Interestingly, it is even shorter than the **Ltac** proof, because the latter one has to explicitly use the axiom of propositional extensionality to turn the assumed equivalence into equality.

5.3   Complex Proofs

For a complex proof, we present the data for our running example (Fig. 5) in Table 4 [1, `Evaluation/Complex.v`]. With the hand-crafted $\vdash_{\mathcal{H}}$ proof we followed the same proof strategy as in the MLPM case, using formalized Hilbert-style theorems. Therefore, the resulting proof terms have very similar size. However, when using MLPM, the proof script is smaller, with fewer subproofs. We also proved the following theorems using MLPM, thus demonstrating its ability to handle real-world examples. These theorems correspond to the FOL-style ($\vdash \exists$) and ($\forall \vdash$), where the condition $\exists y. \psi = y$ ensures that ψ represents a term.

Theorem 4 (Functional substitution [1, `Evaluation/Complex.v`]).
If $\Gamma^{\mathsf{DEF}} \subseteq \Gamma$, and φ does not contain μ binders, then

$$\Gamma \vdash_{\mathcal{H}}^{\mathsf{T}c} \varphi[\psi/x] \wedge (\exists y. \psi = y) \rightarrow \exists x.\varphi, \text{ and } \quad \Gamma \vdash_{\mathcal{H}}^{\mathsf{T}c} \forall x.\varphi \wedge (\exists y. \psi = y) \rightarrow \varphi[\psi/x]$$

6   Related Work

In general, reasoning with a Hilbert system differs from how proofs are explained in practice [2]. To bridge this gap between Hilbert proofs and mathematical deduction, Gentzen developed new formal calculi (natural deduction and sequent calculus) [2] that are equivalent to the Hilbert system. Afterward, many different versions of these calculi emerged; among these, we highlight [6,17] that contain single-conclusion sequent calculi on which we based our system for matching logic.

When implementing interactive reasoning for a logic, one has basically two options: either to write a standalone tool for it (e.g., in [6] Bornat and Sufrin implement a proof calculator), or to embed their logic to an existing proof assistant and develop a "proof mode" for the logic, as is the example of Iris Proof Mode [20] for a variant of concurrent separation logic. Other works from this second category include, for example, [26,31] for (focused) linear logic, [16] for linear temporal logic, [5] for differential dynamic logic, and [3,19,22] for various separation logic dialects. The main difference between [20] and our work is, besides the fact that the target logic is different, that our work is based on a deep embedding of the target logic, as explained in Sect. 4. However, the work on Iris Proof Mode was a major source of inspiration for us.

Various proof systems of propositional logics have been formalized in [24]. A Metamath-based [23] formalization of $\vdash_{\mathcal{H}}$ together with an interactive theorem prover for ML is given in [9]. There, the authors also work with Γ^{DEF}; however, they do not prove (Lemma 2) but rather assume it. We believe that this is because in their shallow embedding, Theorem 1 (on which Lemma 2 depends) is not expressible.

7   Conclusion

Deep embedding of expressive domain logic in proof assistants for interactive proof construction is a challenging engineering problem; nevertheless, it comes with benefits: deep embedding allows one to do induction on the syntax and the proofs, supporting, amongst others, proof extraction and proving meta-theorems. On the other hand, proving object-level theorems becomes more tedious because the proof assistant's capabilities are not directly applicable to reasoning about object-level judgements. We argue that this can be observed as an opportunity for creating a custom-made proof mode for the embedded logic, theoretically backed by a sound alternative proof calculus.

In this paper, we introduced a sequent calculus for matching logic, for now focusing on its first-order fragment, and we proved that on this fragment, the sequent calculus is sound and complete w.r.t. the existing Hilbert system. Sequents in our approach are annotated with proof constraints that can be checked—statically, without traversing the proof—by proof-transforming functions (such as the deduction theorem, Theorem 1). Proofs in our sequent calculus can be translated into the Hilbert system, and unlike other approaches in the literature, the translation does not rely on the existence of a general deduction theorem for the logic. Lastly, we described a shallow embedding of the calculus into a matching logic formalization in Coq; the shallow embedding serves as the core of a practical and extensible proof mode for matching logic. The use of this proof mode significantly eases interactive development of matching logic proofs: proofs are shorter and easier to comprehend than the corresponding hand-crafted Hilbert-style proofs. The work presented here improves on the preliminary work of [4] by (1) adding a support for first-order reasoning, (2) extending the list of user-facing tactics, (3) giving a proof-theoretical foundation to the proof mode by means of the sequent calculus, and (4) giving the notion of proof constraints to aid the use of the deduction theorem.

Acknowledgements. We warmly thank Runtime Verification Inc. for their generous funding support.

References

1. Matching logic formalization. https://github.com/harp-project/AML-Formalization/releases/tag/v1.0.15. Accessed 27 June 2023
2. Investigations into logical deduction. In: Szabo, M. (ed.) The Collected Papers of Gerhard Gentzen. Studies in Logic and the Foundations of Mathematics. Elsevier (1969). https://doi.org/10.1016/S0049-237X(08)70822-X
3. Appel, A.W., Blazy, S.: Separation logic for small-step CMINOR. In: Schneider, K., Brandt, J. (eds.) TPHOLs 2007. LNCS, vol. 4732, pp. 5–21. Springer, Heidelberg (2007). https://doi.org/10.1007/978-3-540-74591-4_3
4. Bereczky, P., Chen, X., Horpácsi, D., Peña, L., Tušil, J.: Mechanizing matching logic in Coq. Electronic Proceedings in Theoretical Computer Science (2022). https://doi.org/10.4204/eptcs.369.2
5. Bohrer, R., Rahli, V., Vukotic, I., Völp, M., Platzer, A.: Formally verified differential dynamic logic. In: Proceedings of the 6th ACM SIGPLAN Conference on Certified Programs and Proofs, CPP 2017. Association for Computing Machinery (2017). https://doi.org/10.1145/3018610.3018616
6. Bornat, R., Sufrin, B.: Animating formal proof at the surface: the Jape Proof Calculator. Comput. J. (1999). https://doi.org/10.1093/comjnl/42.3.177
7. Bradfield, J., Stirling, C.: Modal mu-calculi. In: Handbook of Modal Logic. Studies in Logic and Practical Reasoning. Elsevier (2007). https://doi.org/10.1016/S1570-2464(07)80015-2
8. Charguéraud, A.: The locally nameless representation. J. Autom. Reason. (2012). https://doi.org/10.1007/s10817-011-9225-2
9. Chen, X., Lin, Z., Trinh, M.-T., Roşu, G.: Towards a trustworthy semantics-based language framework via proof generation. In: Silva, A., Leino, K.R.M. (eds.) CAV 2021. LNCS, vol. 12760, pp. 477–499. Springer, Cham (2021). https://doi.org/10.1007/978-3-030-81688-9_23
10. Chen, X., Lucanu, D., Rosu, G.: Capturing constrained constructor patterns in matching logic. J. Log. Algebraic Methods Program. (2023). https://doi.org/10.1016/j.jlamp.2022.100810
11. Chen, X., Lucanu, D., Roşu, G.: Matching logic explained. J. Logical Algebraic Methods Program. (2021). https://doi.org/10.1016/j.jlamp.2021.100638
12. Chen, X., Roşu, G.: Applicative matching logic: semantics of K. Technical report, University of Illinois at Urbana-Champaign (2019). http://hdl.handle.net/2142/104616
13. Chen, X., Roşu, G.: Matching μ-logic. In: 34th Annual ACM/IEEE Symposium on Logic in Computer Science, LICS 2019, Vancouver, BC, Canada, 24–27 June 2019. IEEE (2019). https://doi.org/10.1109/LICS.2019.8785675
14. Chen, X., Roşu, G.: Matching mu-logic. Technical report, University of Illinois at Urbana-Champaign (2019). http://hdl.handle.net/2142/102281. Accessed 16 Feb 2023
15. Cheney, J., Fernandez, M.: Nominal matching logic. In: Proceedings of the 24th International Symposium on Principles and Practice of Declarative Programming, PPDP 2022. Association for Computing Machinery (2022). https://doi.org/10.1145/3551357.3551375
16. Coupet-Grimal, S.: An axiomatization of linear temporal logic in the Calculus of Inductive Constructions. J. Log. Comput. (2003). https://doi.org/10.1093/logcom/13.6.801

17. Dyckhoff, R.: Contraction-free sequent calculi for intuitionistic logic. J. Symb. Logic (1992). https://doi.org/10.2307/2275431
18. Fitting, M.: First-Order Logic and Automated Theorem Proving. Springer, New York (1996). https://doi.org/10.1007/978-1-4612-2360-3
19. Krebbers, R., et al.: MoSeL: a general, extensible modal framework for interactive proofs in separation logic. Proc. ACM Program. Lang. (2018). https://doi.org/10.1145/3236772
20. Krebbers, R., Timany, A., Birkedal, L.: Interactive proofs in higher-order concurrent separation logic. In: Proceedings of the 44th ACM SIGPLAN Symposium on Principles of Programming Languages, POPL 2017, Paris, France, 18–20 January 2017. ACM (2017). https://doi.org/10.1145/3009837.3009855
21. Lungu, A.I., Lucanu, D.: A matching logic foundation for Alk. In: Seidl, H., Liu, Z., Pasareanu, C.S. (eds.) ICTAC 2022. LNCS, vol. 13572, pp. 290–304. Springer, Cham (2022). https://doi.org/10.1007/978-3-031-17715-6_19
22. McCreight, A.: Practical tactics for separation logic. In: Berghofer, S., Nipkow, T., Urban, C., Wenzel, M. (eds.) TPHOLs 2009. LNCS, vol. 5674, pp. 343–358. Springer, Heidelberg (2009). https://doi.org/10.1007/978-3-642-03359-9_24
23. Megill, N., Wheeler, D.A.: Metamath: a computer language for mathematical proofs. http://us.metamath.org. Accessed 16 Feb 2023
24. Michaelis, J., Nipkow, T.: Formalized proof systems for propositional logic. In: 23rd International Conference on Types for Proofs and Programs, TYPES 2017, Budapest, Hungary, 29 May–1 June 2017. LIPIcs, Schloss Dagstuhl - Leibniz-Zentrum für Informatik (2017). https://doi.org/10.4230/LIPIcs.TYPES.2017.5
25. Pelletier, F.J., Hazen, A.: Natural deduction systems in logic. In: The Stanford Encyclopedia of Philosophy. Metaphysics Research Lab, Stanford University (2022)
26. Power, J.F., Webster, C.: Working with linear logic in Coq (1999). https://mural.maynoothuniversity.ie/6461/1/JP-Working-Linear-Logic.pdf. Accessed 16 Feb 2023
27. Roşu, G.: Matching logic. Log. Methods Comput. Sci. (2017). https://doi.org/10.23638/LMCS-13(4:28)2017
28. Stefanescu, A., Park, D., Yuwen, S., Li, Y., Rosu, G.: Semantics-based program verifiers for all languages. In: Proceedings of the 2016 ACM SIGPLAN International Conference on Object-Oriented Programming, Systems, Languages, and Applications, OOPSLA 2016, Part of SPLASH 2016, Amsterdam, The Netherlands, 30 October–4 November 2016. ACM (2016). https://doi.org/10.1145/2983990.2984027
29. The Coq Development Team: The coq proof assistant (2022). https://doi.org/10.5281/zenodo.7313584
30. Wang, S.B., Dong, W.Y.: Matching logic for concurrent programs based on rely/guarantee and abstract patterns. Int. J. Softw. Eng. Knowl. Eng. (2022)
31. Wiedijk, F.: Encoding the HOL Light logic in Coq (2007). https://www.cs.ru.nl/~freek/notes/holl2coq.pdf. Accessed 30 June 2023

An Autonomous Data Language

Tom T. P. Franken$^{(\boxtimes)}$, Thomas Neele , and Jan Friso Groote

Eindhoven University of Technology, Eindhoven, The Netherlands
{t.t.p.franken,t.s.neele,j.f.groote}@tue.nl

Abstract. Nowadays, the main advances in computational power are
due to parallelism. However, most parallel languages have been designed
with a focus on processors and threads. This makes dealing with data
and memory in programs hard, which distances the implementation from
its original algorithm. We propose a new paradigm for parallel programming, the *data-autonomous* paradigm, where computation is performed
by autonomous data elements. Programs in this paradigm are focused on
making the data collaborate in a highly parallel fashion. We furthermore
present AuDaLa, the first data autonomous programming language, and
include an operational semantics. Programming in AuDaLa is very natural, as illustrated by examples, albeit in a style very different from
sequential and contemporary parallel programming.

Keywords: Data-Autonomous · Programming Language ·
Operational Semantics

1 Introduction

As increasing the speed of sequential processing becomes more difficult [28],
exploiting parallelism has become one of the main means of obtaining further performance improvements in computing. Thus, languages and frameworks aimed at
parallel programming play an increasingly important role in computation. Many
existing parallel languages use a *task-parallel* or a *data-parallel* paradigm [14].

Task-parallelism mostly focuses on the computation carried out by individual
threads, scheduling tasks to threads depending on which threads are idle. In
data-parallelism, threads execute the same function but are distributed over the
data, thus performing a parallel computation on the collection of all data.

In a shared memory setting, programs in both paradigms require careful
design of memory layout, memory access and movement of data to facilitate the
threads used by the program. Examples of this are the use of barriers and data
access based on thread id's, as well as access protocols. Not only is extensive
data movement costly and hinders some performance optimizations [20,22], the
memory handling necessary throughout the entire program due to the focus on
threads only widens the gap between algorithms and implementation as noted
by for instance Leiserson *et al.* [28]. Therefore, to promote memory locality and
more algorithmic code, a new data-focused paradigm is in order.

E. Ábrahám et al. (Eds.): ICTAC 2023, LNCS 14446, pp. 158–177, 2023.
https://doi.org/10.1007/978-3-031-47963-2_11

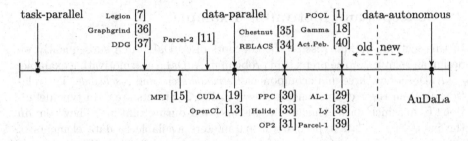

Fig. 1. Approximate placement of related work on an axis from process-focused (left) to data-focused (right) paradigms.

In this paper, we propose the new *data-autonomous* paradigm, where *data elements* not only locally store data and references, but also execute their own computations. Computations are always carried out in parallel by all data elements; this is governed by a *schedule*. Data elements can cooperate through stored references. The paradigm completely abstracts away from processors and memory and is fully focused on data, compared to task- and data-parallelism (see Fig. 1).

This provides several benefits. First, it results in a *separation of concerns*: code concerning data structures, algorithms and orchestration is properly separated. Furthermore, parallelism is encouraged by always running computations concurrently on groups of data elements. Finally, the paradigm promotes a bottom-up design process, from data structure to computations to schedule.

Contributions. As a first step towards developing the data-autonomous paradigm, we present *AuDaLa (Autonomous Data Language)*, the first data-autonomous programming language. In AuDaLa, *structs*, *steps* and a *schedule* are responsible for data, computation and orchestration, respectively. We illustrate our thought process behind AuDaLa by means of a motivating example. We introduce AuDaLa programs for a few standard problems. Compared to programs taken from literature, our AuDaLa programs require less memory management and clearly separate data flow and orchestration.

In this work, we focus on providing a solid theoretical foundation of AuDaLa. Thus, we completely formalise AuDaLa's behaviour in an operational semantics, enabled by its compact syntax. Though we have a prototype compiler of AuDaLa to CUDA, discussing it is out of the scope of this paper.

Overview. We first present a motivating example and show the concepts of AuDaLa in Sect. 2. We then give the syntax of AuDaLa in Sect. 3 and a semantics in Sect. 4. We discuss more examples in Sect. 5. Lastly, we review related work in Sect. 6 and conclude in Sect. 7.

2   Concepts and Motivating Example

In this section, we first discuss the concepts of AuDaLa, and subsequently we design a program for the prefix sum problem in AuDaLa as a motivating example.

AuDaLa has three main components: *structs*, *steps* and a *schedule*. The relation between these components is shown in Fig. 2. Structs are data type definitions from which data elements are instantiated during runtime. They contain the name of the data type and the parameters available to data elements of that type. See Listing 1.3 for an example of a struct definition. When starting an AuDaLa program, every struct gets a special *null*-instance, a data element representing the undefined instance of that struct. The parameters of this *null*-instance cannot be changed, but they otherwise function like normal data elements. A *null*-instance can be used for initialisation (since it already exists when launching the program) or as special value, for example to indicate the end of a list.

Each struct contains zero or more *steps*, which represent operations a data element instantiated from that struct can do. A step contains simple, algorithmic code, consisting of conditions and assignments, without loops. This makes steps easy to reason about. Within a step, it is possible to access the parameters of the surrounding struct and also to follow references stored in those parameters. Since these access patterns are known at compile-time, we can increase memory locality by grouping struct instances in a suitable manner.

The *schedule* prescribes an execution order on the steps. It contains step references and fixpoint operators (*Fix*). The occurrences of step references and fixpoint operators are separated by synchronization barriers ('<'). Execution only proceeds past a barrier when all computations that precede the barrier have concluded. Whenever a step occurs in the schedule, it is executed in parallel by all data elements which contain that step, although it is also possible to invoke a step for data elements of a specific type. AuDaLa programs are thus inherently parallel.

We do not make assumptions about a global execution order of statements executed in parallel. In particular, code is not executed by multiple struct instances in *lock-step*. Furthermore, we allow the occurrence of data races within one step, see also Sect. 5. Thus, barriers (and implicit barriers, see below) are the main method of synchronisation.

Iterative behaviour is achieved through a fixpoint operator, which executes its body repeatedly until an iteration occurs in which no data is changed. At this point, a fixpoint is reached and the schedule continues past the fixpoint operator. Between the iterations of a fixpoint, there is an implicit synchronisation barrier. For an example schedule, see Listing 1.4.

To give an example of these components in action, we consider the *prefix sum* problem: given a sequence of integers $x_1, \ldots, x_n$, we compute for each position $1 \leq k \leq n$ the sum $\Sigma_{i=1}^{k} x_i$. We have included OpenCL and CUDA implementations of the problem that previously occurred in the literature [13,24], see Listings 1.1 and 1.2. Here, we omit the initialization to focus on the kernels. Both kernels require synchronization barriers in their algorithmic code, as well

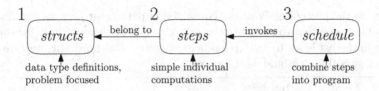

Fig. 2. The three main components of an AuDaLa program.

as an offset variable to check which data needs to be operated on, against which the thread ids need to be checked multiple times per execution.

```
1  kernel void koggeStone(const local T *in, local T *out) {
2    out[tid] = in[tid];
3    barrier();
4    for (unsigned offset = 1; offset < n; offset *= 2){
5      T temp;
6      if (tid ≥ offset) temp = out[tid  offset];
7      barrier();
8      if (tid ≥ offset) out[tid] = temp ⊕ out[tid];
9      barrier();
10 }}
```

Listing 1.1. OpenCL kernel for Prefix Sum (from [13])

```
1  __global__ void scan(float *g_odata, float *g_idata, int n){
2    extern __shared__ float temp[];
3    int thid = threadIdx.x;
4    int pout = 0, pin = 1;
5    temp[pout*n + thid] = (thid > 0) ? g_idata[thid1] : 0;
6    __syncthreads();
7    for (int offset = 1; offset < n; offset *= 2){
8      pout = 1  pout; // swap double buffer indices
9      pin = 1  pout;
10     if (thid >= offset)
11       temp[pout*n+thid] += temp[pin*n+thid  offset];
12     else
13       temp[pout*n+thid] = temp[pin*n+thid]
14     __syncthreads();
15   }
16   g_odata[thid] = temp[pout*n+thid];
17 }
```

Listing 1.2. CUDA kernel for Prefix Sum (or Scan) (from [24])

To design a corresponding AuDaLa program, we follow the design structure suggested in Fig. 2. As before, we omit the initialization. In the prefix sum problem, the input is a sequence of integers. We model an element of this sequence with a struct *Position* containing a value *val*. We also give every *Position* a

reference to the preceding *Position*, contained in parameter *prev*, as seen in Listing 1.3. This is needed to compute the prefix sum. The value of *prev* for the first
position in the list is set to *null*, referencing the *null-Position*. This *null*-instance
has the values 0 for *val* and *null* for *prev*.

```
  struct Position(val: Int, prev: Position){ [...] }
```

Listing 1.3. Partial AuDaLa code for the structs for Prefix Sum

In Listing 1.4 the steps *read* and *write* of the *Position* struct are shown. These
steps are based on the method for computing prefix sum in parallel shown in
Fig. 3, which was introduced by Hillis and Steele [27]. Every *Position* first reads
prev.prev and *prev.val* from their predecessor in the step *read*, and after synchronisation, every position updates their *prev* to *prev.prev* and their *val* to *prev.val*
in the step *write*. As the scope of local variables in AuDaLa does not exceed a
step, the use of additional parameters *auxprev* and *auxval* in the *read* step is
required to recover the value in the *write* step. The steps do not need an *offset*
variable like the CUDA and OpenCL kernels, as *Positions* which reached the
beginning of the list have a *null*-instance as predecessor and can still execute
the steps.

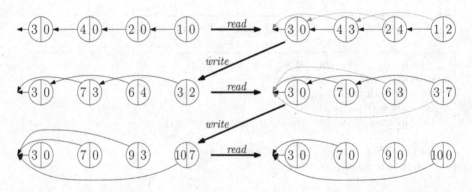

Fig. 3. Execution of Prefix Sum on a small list. The left side of a list element holds the
parameter *val*, while the right side holds the parameter *auxval*. The parameter *prev* is
shown as unmarked black arrows, while the parameter *auxprev* is shown as unmarked
grey arrows.

```
1   struct Position(val: Int, prev: Position, auxval: Int, auxprev: Position){
2     read {                                                    /*step definition*/
3       auxval := prev.val;
4       auxprev := prev.prev;
5     }
6     write {                                                   /*step definition*/
7       val := val + auxval;
8       prev := auxprev;
9   }}
10
11  Fix(read < write)                                           /*schedule*/
```

Listing 1.4. AuDaLa code for Prefix Sum with steps and a schedule

For our program schedule, we want to repeat *read* and then *write* until all *Positions* have reached the beginning of the list, which results in the schedule as shown in Listing 1.4. Eventually, all *Positions* will have *null* as their predecessor and no parameters will change further, causing the fixpoint to terminate.

As illustrated by Listing 1.4 and by Fig. 2, AuDaLa has a high *separation of concerns*: structs model data and their attributes, steps contain the algorithmic code and the schedule contains the execution. This approach requires no synchronization barriers in the user code for the steps, no variables to find the right indices for memory access and no offset variables to avoid going out of bounds.

3   Syntax

In this section, we highlight the most important parts of the concrete syntax of AuDaLa. In the definitions below, non-terminals are indicated with $\langle - \rangle$ and symbols with quotes; the empty word is ε. The non-terminal *Id* describes identifiers, and the non-terminal *Type* describes type names, which are either Int, Nat (natural number), Bool, String or an identifier (the name of a struct).

An AuDaLa *Program* consists of a list of definitions of *structs* and a schedule:

$$\langle Program \rangle ::= \langle Defs \rangle \; \langle Sched \rangle$$
$$\langle Defs \rangle ::= \langle Struct \rangle \mid \langle Struct \rangle \; \langle Defs \rangle$$

A *struct* definition gives the struct a type name (*Id*), a list of parameters (*Pars*) and a number of steps (*Steps*):

$$\langle Struct \rangle ::= \text{'struct'} \; \langle Id \rangle \; \text{'('} \; \langle Pars \rangle \; \text{')'} \; \text{'\{'} \; \langle Steps \rangle \; \text{'\}'},$$
$$\langle Pars \rangle ::= \langle Par \rangle \langle ParList \rangle \mid \varepsilon$$
$$\langle ParList \rangle ::= \text{','} \; \langle Par \rangle \langle ParList \rangle \mid \varepsilon$$
$$\langle Par \rangle ::= \langle Id \rangle \; \text{':'} \; \langle Type \rangle$$

Steps are defined with a step name (*Id*) and a list of statements:

$$\langle Steps \rangle ::= \langle Id \rangle \; \text{'\{'} \; \langle Stats \rangle \; \text{'\}'} \; \langle Steps \rangle \mid \varepsilon$$
$$\langle Stats \rangle ::= \langle Stat \rangle \; \langle Stats \rangle \mid \varepsilon$$

A *statement* adheres to the following syntax:

$\langle Stat \rangle ::=$ 'if' $\langle Exp \rangle$ 'then' '{' $\langle Stats \rangle$ '}'   if-then statement
$\quad | \langle Type \rangle \langle Id \rangle$ ':=' $\langle Exp \rangle$ ';'   variable assignment
$\quad | \langle Var \rangle$ ':=' $\langle Exp \rangle$ ';'   variable update
$\quad | \langle Id \rangle$ '(' $\langle Exps \rangle$ ')' ';'   constructor statement

The *Id* in the variable assignment is a variable name. The constructor statement spawns a new data element of the type determined by *Id*, with parameter values determined by the expressions *Exps*. The syntax of *Exps* is similar to that of *Pars*, using *ExpList* and *Exp*. The syntax for a single *expression Exp* is as follows:

$\langle Exp \rangle ::= \langle Exp \rangle \langle BOp \rangle \langle Exp \rangle$ binary operator expression
$\quad | $ '(' $\langle Exp \rangle$ ')'   brackets
$\quad | $ '!' $\langle Exp \rangle$ negation
$\quad | \langle Id \rangle$ '(' $\langle Exps \rangle$ ')'   constructor expression
$\quad | \langle Var \rangle$ variable expression
$\quad | \langle Literal \rangle$ literal expression
$\quad | $ 'null'   null expression
$\quad | $ 'this'   this expression

A *variable* reference follows the syntax:

$$\langle Var \rangle ::= \langle Id \rangle \text{ '.'} \langle Var \rangle \mid \langle Id \rangle,$$

where in the first case the *Id* is the name of a struct. Through the first case, one can access the parameters of parameters. For example, *prev.prev.val* would have been valid AuDaLa in Listing 1.4, and would access the value of the *Position* before the previous *Position* of the current *Position*.

Lastly, the schedule consists of the variants as given in the following syntax:

$\langle Sched \rangle ::= \langle Id \rangle$ step execution
$\quad | \langle Id \rangle$ '.' $\langle Id \rangle$ typed step execution
$\quad | \langle Sched \rangle$ '<' $\langle Sched \rangle$ barrier composition
$\quad | $ 'Fix' '(' $\langle Sched \rangle$ ')'   fixpoint calculation

The *Id* in the step execution is a step name. In the typed step execution, the first *Id* is a type name, while the second is a step name. The typed step execution is used to schedule a step executed by only one specific struct type.

On top of this concrete syntax, we adopt a number of additional requirements for an AuDaLa program to be well-formed. First of all, we have a number of usual sanity requirements, including 'identifiers may not be keywords', 'a step name is declared at most once within each struct definition', 'names of local variables do not overlap with parameter names of the surrounding struct definition', 'local variables are not accessed from outside their surrounding struct definition', and 'local variables are not used before they are declared in a step'. Furthermore, we also assume common rules for well-typedness, so that binary operators are applied to the right types, the types in assignments and variable declarations are equal and constructor calls use the right type of arguments.

4   Semantics

In this section, we present the semantics of AuDaLa. Here, we regularly use lists. List concatenation is denoted with a semicolon, and we identify a singleton list with its only element. The empty list is denoted ε. Schedules are expressed as a list, e.g. the schedule $A < Fix(B)$ is expressed as $A; Fix(B)$.

We define updates for functions as follows. Given a function $f : A \to B$ and $a \in A$ and $b \in B$, then $f[a \mapsto b](a) = b$ and $f[a \mapsto b](x) = f(x)$ for all $x \neq a$. We lift this operation to sets of updates: $f[\{a_1 \mapsto b_1, a_2 \mapsto b_2, \dots\}] = f[a_1 \mapsto b_1][a_2 \mapsto b_2]\dots$. Since the order of applying updates is relevant, this is only well-defined if the left-hand sides $a_1, a_2, \dots$ are pairwise distinct. If B contains tuples, that is, $B = B_1 \times \dots \times B_n$, we can also update a single element of a tuple: if $f(a) = \langle b_1, \dots, b_n \rangle$, then we define $f[a, i \mapsto b](a) = \langle b_1, \dots, b_{i-1}, b, b_{i+1}, \dots, b_n \rangle$ and $f[a, i \mapsto b](x) = f(x)$ for all $x \neq a$.

We assume the existence of a parser and typechecker for the concrete syntax. Henceforth, we work on an *abstract syntax tree* (AST) produced by running the parser and typechecker on a program. We thus do not concern ourselves with operator precedence and parentheses, and we assume that polymorphic elements such as `null` and 42 are labelled with the right type for their context, *viz.*, $null_T$ is the expression *null* of type T.

We have a number of sets containing AST elements: ID is the set of all identifiers, LT is the set of all literals, SC is the set of all schedules, ST is the set of all statements, E contains all expressions and O contains all syntactic binary operators. The set containing all syntactic types is $\mathcal{T} = \{\text{Nat}, \text{Int}, \text{Bool}, \text{String}\} \cup ID$.

In our semantics, *labels* reference concrete instances of structs (as opposed to struct definitions). We assume some sufficiently large set $\mathcal{L}$ containing these labels. We also have the semantic types $\mathbb{N}, \mathbb{Z}, \mathbb{B}$ and *String* corresponding to the natural numbers, the integers, the booleans and the set of all strings, respectively. All semantic values are collected in $\mathcal{V} = \mathcal{L} \cup \mathbb{N} \cup \mathbb{Z} \cup \mathbb{B} \cup String$. The semantic value of a literal $g \in LT$ is $val(g)$.

In addition, we assume for every struct type sL the existence of a *null-label* $\ell^0_{sL} \in \mathcal{L}$, so that we can provide a default value for each syntactical type with the function $defaultVal : \mathcal{T} \to \mathcal{V}$, defined as:

$$defaultVal(T) = \begin{cases} 0 & \text{if } T = \text{Nat or } T = \text{Int} \\ false & \text{if } T = \text{Bool} \\ \varepsilon & \text{if } T = \text{String} \\ \ell^0_T & \text{if } T \in ID \end{cases}.$$

We define the set of all *null*-labels to be $\mathcal{L}^0$, with $\mathcal{L}^0 \subset \mathcal{L}$.

To facilitate conciseness in our operational semantics, we break down statements and expressions into *commands*: atomic actions in the semantics.

Definition 1 (Commands). *A* command *c is constructed according to the following grammar:*

$$c ::= \textbf{push}(val) \mid \textbf{rd}(v) \mid \textbf{wr}(v) \mid \textbf{cons}(v) \mid \textbf{if}(C) \mid \textbf{not} \mid \textbf{op}(o)$$

where val $\in \mathcal{V} \cup \{\mathbf{this}\}$ *is a semantic value or* **this**, *a special value,* $v \in ID$ *is an identifier,* C *is a list of commands, and* $o \in O$ *is an operator. The set of all commands is* $\mathcal{C}$.

Intuitively, **this** is the semantic equivalent to the syntactic this-expression. The precise effect of each command is discussed later in this section when the inference rules are given. Statements and expressions are compiled into a list of commands according to the following recursive interpretation function:

Definition 2 (Interpretation function). *Let* $v, v_1, \ldots, v_n \in ID$ *be variables,* $a, a_1, \ldots, a_m \in E$ *expressions,* $g \in LT$ *a literal,* $sL \in ID$ *a struct type,* $s \in ST$ *a statement,* $S \in ST^*$ *a list of statements,* $T \in \mathcal{T}$ *a type and* op $\in O$ *an operator from the syntax. Let the list* $v_1; \ldots; v_n$ *be the list of* n *variables from* v_1 *to* v_n. *We define the* interpretation function $[\![\cdot]\!] : ST^* \cup E \to \mathcal{C}^*$ *transforming a list of statements into a list of commands:*

$$[\![g]\!] = \mathbf{push}(val(g))$$
$$[\![\mathbf{this}]\!] = \mathbf{push}(\mathbf{this})$$
$$[\![\mathtt{null}_T]\!] = \mathbf{push}(defaultVal(T))$$
$$[\![v_1; \ldots; v_n]\!] = \mathbf{push}(\mathbf{this}); \mathbf{rd}(v_1); \ldots; \mathbf{rd}(v_n)$$
$$[\![!\mathtt{a}]\!] = [\![a]\!]; \mathbf{not}$$
$$[\![\mathtt{a_1\ op\ a_2}]\!] = [\![a_1]\!]; [\![a_2]\!]; \mathbf{op}(\mathrm{op})$$
$$[\![\mathtt{if\ a\ then}\{S\}]\!] = [\![a]\!]; \mathbf{if}([\![S]\!])$$
$$[\![T, \mathtt{v} := \mathtt{a}]\!] = [\![\mathtt{v} := \mathtt{a}]\!]$$
$$[\![\mathtt{v_1}; \ldots; \mathtt{v_n}; \mathtt{v} := \mathtt{a}]\!] = [\![a]\!]; [\![v_1; \ldots; v_n]\!]; \mathbf{wr}(v)$$
$$[\![sL(\mathtt{a_1}; \ldots; \mathtt{a_m})]\!] = [\![a_1]\!]; \ldots; [\![a_m]\!]; \mathbf{cons}(sL)$$
$$[\![\varepsilon]\!] = \varepsilon$$
$$[\![s; S]\!] = [\![s]\!]; [\![S]\!]$$

During the runtime of a program, multiple instances of a struct definition may exist simultaneously. We refer to these as *struct instances*.

Definition 3 (Struct instance). *A struct instance is a tuple* $\langle sL, \gamma, \chi, \xi \rangle$ *where:*

- $sL \in ID$ *is the type of the struct,*
- $\gamma \in \mathcal{C}^*$ *is a list of commands that are to be executed,*
- $\chi \in \mathcal{V}^*$ *is a stack that stores values during the evaluation of an expression,*
- $\xi : ID \to \mathcal{V}$ *is an environment that stores the values of local variables as well as parameters.*

We define $\mathcal{S}$ *as the set of all possible struct instances.*

A state of a program is the combination of a schedule that remains to be executed, a collection with all the struct instances that currently exist and a stack of Boolean values that are required to determine whether a fixpoint has been reached. Note that every label can refer to at most one distinct struct instance.

Definition 4 (State). *A state is a tuple* $\langle Sc, \sigma, s\chi \rangle$, *where:*

- $Sc \in SC$ *is a schedule expressed as a list,*
- $\sigma : \mathcal{L} \to \mathcal{S} \cup \{\bot\}$ *is a struct environment,*
- $s\chi \in \mathbb{B}^*$ *is a stability stack.*

The set of all states is defined as $S_{\mathcal{G}} = SC \times (\mathcal{L} \to \mathcal{S} \cup \{\bot\}) \times \mathbb{B}^*$.

With a notion of states and struct instances, we define *null-instances*:

Definition 5 (Null-instances). *Let* $St = \langle Sc, \sigma, s\chi \rangle \in S_{\mathcal{G}}$ *be a state. Then the set of* null-instances *in state St is defined as* $\{\sigma(\ell) \mid \sigma(\ell) \neq \bot \wedge \ell \in \mathcal{L}^0\}$.

Thus, each struct instance that is labelled with a *null*-label is a *null*-instance.

Henceforth, we fix an AuDaLa program $\mathcal{P}$ and define $SL_{\mathcal{P}} \subseteq ID$ to be the set of all struct types defined in $\mathcal{P}$. The initial variable environment for a struct instance of type sL is ξ_{sL}^0, defined as $\xi_{sL}^0(p) = defaultVal(T)$ for all $p \in Par_{sL}$ where T is the type of p and Par_{sL} refers to the parameters of sL. For other variables $v \in ID$, $\xi_{sL}^0(v)$ is left arbitrary. Recall that $Sc_{\mathcal{P}}$ is the schedule defined in $\mathcal{P}$.

The initial state of a graph machine program depends on which program is going to be executed (The state space does not depend on the program, *cf.* Definition 4):

Definition 6 (Initial state). *The initial state of* $\mathcal{P}$ *is* $P_{\mathcal{P}}^0 = \langle Sc_{\mathcal{P}}, \sigma_{\mathcal{P}}^0, \varepsilon \rangle$, *where* $\sigma_{\mathcal{P}}^0(\ell_{sL}^0) = \langle sL, \varepsilon, \varepsilon, \xi_{sL}^0 \rangle$ *for all* $sL \in SL_{\mathcal{P}}$ *and* $\sigma_{\mathcal{P}}^0(\ell) = \bot$ *for all other labels.*

Intuitively, this definition states that the initial state of a program $\mathcal{P}$ consists of the schedule as found in the program, a struct environment filled with *null*-instances for every struct type declared in $\mathcal{P}$ and an empty stack.

We proceed by defining the transition relation $\Rightarrow$ by means of inference rules. There are rules that define the execution of commands and rules for the execution of a schedule. We start with the former. Command **push**(v) pushes value v on the stack χ, and **push(this)** pushes the label of the structure instance on χ:

$$\textbf{(ComPush)} \; \frac{\sigma(\ell) = \langle sL, \textbf{push}(val); \gamma, \chi, \xi \rangle}{\langle Sc, \sigma, s\chi \rangle \Rightarrow \langle Sc, \sigma[\ell \mapsto \langle sL, \gamma, \chi; val, \xi \rangle], s\chi \rangle}$$

$$\textbf{(ComPushThis)} \; \frac{\sigma(\ell) = \langle sL, \textbf{push(this)}; \gamma, \chi, \xi \rangle}{\langle Sc, \sigma, s\chi \rangle \Rightarrow \langle Sc, \sigma[\ell \mapsto \langle sL, \gamma, \chi; \ell, \xi \rangle], s\chi \rangle}$$

The command **rd**(v) reads the value of variable v from environment ξ' of ℓ' and places it onto the stack:

$$\textbf{(ComRd)} \; \frac{\sigma(\ell) = \langle sL, \textbf{rd}(v); \gamma, \chi; \ell', \xi \rangle \quad \sigma(\ell') = \langle sL', \gamma', \chi', \xi' \rangle}{\langle Sc, \sigma, s\chi \rangle \Rightarrow \langle Sc, \sigma[\ell \mapsto \langle sL, \gamma, \chi; \xi'(v), \xi \rangle], s\chi \rangle}$$

For normal struct instances, $\mathbf{wr}(v)$ takes a label ℓ' and a value val from the stack and writes this to $\xi'(v)$, the environment of the struct instance corresponding to ℓ'. If v is a parameter and writing val changes its value, then any surrounding fixpoint in the schedule becomes unstable. In that case, we set the auxiliary value su (for *stability update*) to false and clear the stability stack by setting it to $s\chi_1 \wedge su; \ldots; s\chi_{|s\chi|} \wedge su$. Note that this leaves the stack unchanged if su is true. Below, in the update "$[\ell', 4 \mapsto \xi'[v \mapsto val]]$", recall that $f[a, i \mapsto b]$ denotes the update of a function that returns a tuple.

$$\sigma(\ell) = \langle sL, \mathbf{wr}(v); \gamma, \chi; val; \ell', \xi \rangle$$
$$\sigma(\ell') = \langle sL', \gamma', \chi', \xi' \rangle$$
$$\ell' \notin \mathcal{L}^0 \vee v \notin Par_{sL'}$$

$$(\mathbf{ComWr}) \frac{su = (v \notin Par_{sL'} \vee \xi'(v) = val)}{\langle Sc, \sigma, s\chi \rangle \Rightarrow \langle Sc, \sigma[\ell \mapsto \langle sL, \gamma, \chi, \xi \rangle][\ell', 4 \mapsto \xi'[v \mapsto val]],}$$
$$s\chi_1 \wedge su; \ldots; s\chi_{|s\chi|} \wedge su \rangle$$

The next rule skips the write if the target is a parameter of a *null*-instance, which ensures that the parameters of a *null*-instance cannot be changed:

$$\sigma(\ell) = \langle sL, \mathbf{wr}(v); \gamma, \chi; val; \ell', \xi \rangle$$
$$\sigma(\ell') = \langle sL', \gamma', \chi', \xi' \rangle$$

$$(\mathbf{ComWrNSkip}) \frac{\ell' \in \mathcal{L}^0 \wedge v \in Par_{sL'}}{\langle Sc, \sigma, s\chi \rangle \Rightarrow \langle Sc, \sigma[\ell \mapsto \langle sL, \gamma, \chi, \xi \rangle], s\chi \rangle}$$

A **not** command negates the top value of the stack χ:

$$(\mathbf{ComNot}) \frac{\sigma(\ell) = \langle sL, \mathbf{not}; \gamma, \chi; b, \xi \rangle}{\langle Sc, \sigma, s\chi \rangle \Rightarrow \langle Sc, \sigma[\ell \mapsto \langle sL, \gamma, \chi; \neg b, \xi \rangle], s\chi \rangle}$$

An $\mathbf{op}(o)$ command applies the semantic equivalent $\circ \in \{=, \neq, \leq, \geq, <, >, *, /, \%, +, -, \hat{}, \wedge, \vee\}$ of the syntactic operator $o \in O$ to the two values at the top of χ, of which the result is put on top of the stack:

$$(\mathbf{ComOp}) \frac{\sigma(\ell) = \langle sL, \mathbf{op}(o); \gamma, \chi; a; b, \xi \rangle}{\langle Sc, \sigma, s\chi \rangle \Rightarrow \langle Sc, \sigma[\ell \mapsto \langle sL, \gamma, \chi; (a \circ b), \xi \rangle], s\chi \rangle}$$

Let sL' be the type of a struct with n parameters. The command $\mathbf{cons}(sL')$ creates a new struct instance of type sL' in the struct environment σ with a fresh label ℓ', and initializes the parameters to the top n values of the stack:

$$\sigma(\ell) = \langle sL, \mathbf{cons}(sL'); \gamma, \chi; p_1; \ldots; p_n, \xi \rangle$$
$$Par_{sL'} = par_1; \ldots; par_n$$
$$\sigma(\ell') = \bot$$

$$(\mathbf{ComCons}) \frac{}{\langle Sc, \sigma, s\chi \rangle \Rightarrow \langle Sc, \sigma[\{\ell \mapsto \langle sL, \gamma, \chi; \ell', \xi \rangle,}$$
$$\ell' \mapsto \langle sL', \varepsilon, \varepsilon, \xi^0_{sL'}[\{par_1 \mapsto p_1, \ldots, par_n \mapsto p_n\}]\})\}], false^{|s\chi|} \rangle$$

The command $\mathbf{if}(C)$ with $C \in \mathcal{C}^*$ adds commands C to the start of γ if the top value of the stack is *true*. If the top value is *false*, the command does nothing:

$$(\mathbf{ComIfT}) \frac{\sigma(\ell) = \langle sL, \mathbf{if}(C); \gamma, \chi; true, \xi \rangle}{\langle Sc, \sigma, s\chi \rangle \Rightarrow \langle Sc, \sigma[\ell \mapsto \langle sL, C; \gamma, \chi, \xi \rangle], s\chi \rangle}$$

$$(\mathbf{ComIfF}) \frac{\sigma(\ell) = \langle sL, \mathbf{if}(C); \gamma, \chi; false, \xi \rangle}{\langle Sc, \sigma, s\chi \rangle \Rightarrow \langle Sc, \sigma[\ell \mapsto \langle sL, \gamma, \chi, \xi \rangle], s\chi \rangle}$$

In the remaining rules, let $Done(\sigma) = \forall \ell.(\sigma(\ell) = \bot \vee \exists sL, \chi, \xi.\sigma(\ell) = \langle sL, \varepsilon, \chi, \xi \rangle)$, and let F_1 be a (possibly empty) schedule. The predicate $Done(\sigma)$ holds when all commands have been executed in all struct instances in σ.

We can initiate steps globally and locally. The global step initiation converts all statements in a step to commands for any structure instance that has that step and adds the commands to γ. Let S_{sL}^F be the statements in a step with name F in a struct instance with type sL. Note that the schedule is expressed as a list in the operational semantics, and is therefore separated by ';' as opposed to '<'.

$$(\mathbf{InitG}) \frac{Done(\sigma)}{\begin{aligned}&\langle F; F_1, \sigma, s\chi \rangle \Rightarrow \\ &\langle F_1, \sigma[\{\ell \mapsto \langle sL_\ell, [\![S_{sL_\ell}^F]\!], \varepsilon, \xi_\ell \rangle \mid \sigma(\ell) = \langle sL_\ell, \gamma_\ell, \chi_\ell, \xi_\ell \rangle\}], s\chi \rangle\end{aligned}}$$

The local step initiation converts the step to commands and adds those commands to γ only for struct instances of a specified struct x:

$$(\mathbf{InitL}) \frac{Done(\sigma)}{\begin{aligned}&\langle x.F; F_1, \sigma, s\chi \rangle \Rightarrow \\ &\langle F_1, \sigma[\{\ell \mapsto \langle x, [\![S_x^F]\!], \varepsilon, \xi_\ell \rangle \mid \sigma(\ell) = \langle x, \gamma_\ell, \chi_\ell, \xi_\ell \rangle\}], s\chi \rangle\end{aligned}}$$

Fixpoints are initiated when first encountered:

$$(\mathbf{FixInit}) \frac{Done(\sigma)}{\langle Fix(F); F_1, \sigma, s\chi \rangle \Rightarrow \langle F; aFix(F); F_1, \sigma, s\chi; true \rangle}$$

The symbol $aFix$ is a semantic symbol used to denote a fixpoint which has been initiated. When an initiated fixpoint is encountered again, the stability stack is used to determine whether the body should be executed again:

$$(\mathbf{FixIter}) \frac{Done(\sigma)}{\langle aFix(F); F_1, \sigma, s\chi; false \rangle \Rightarrow \langle F; aFix(F); F_1, \sigma, s\chi; true \rangle}$$

$$(\mathbf{FixTerm}) \frac{Done(\sigma)}{\langle aFix(F); F_1, \sigma, s\chi; true \rangle \Rightarrow \langle F_1, \sigma, s\chi \rangle}$$

With these rules, we give an operational semantics for AuDaLa:

Definition 7 (Operational semantics). *The semantics of $\mathcal{P}$ is the graph $[\![\mathcal{P}]\!] = \langle S_{\mathcal{G}}, \Rightarrow, P_{\mathcal{P}}^0 \rangle$, where $S_{\mathcal{G}}$ is the set of all states (Definition 4), $\Rightarrow$ is the transition relation as given above and $P_{\mathcal{P}}^0$ is the initial state of $\mathcal{P}$ (Definition 6).*

5   Standard Algorithms

In this section, we provide more intuition on how AuDaLa works in practice by means of two example AuDaLa programs. The first creates a spanning tree and the second is a sorting program.

5.1   Creating a Spanning Tree

Given a connected directed graph $G = (V, E)$ and a root node $u \in V$, we can create a spanning tree of G rooted in u using *breadth-first search*. In this tree, for every node v, the path from u to v is a shortest path in G. We do this by incrementally adding nodes from G with a higher distance to u to the spanning tree.

```
1   struct Node(dist: Int, in: Edge){}
2
3   struct Edge(s: Node, t: Node){
4     linkEdge{
5       if s.dist != 1 && t.dist == 1 then {
6         t.in := this;
7     }}
8     handleEdge {
9       if t.in != null then {
10        if t.in == this then {
11          t.dist := s.dist + 1;
12        }
13        if t.in != this then {
14          s := null;
15          t := null;
16   }}}}
17
18   Fix(linkEdge < handleEdge)
```

Listing 1.5. AuDaLa code for creating a spanning tree

We first sketch our approach. In the ith BFS iteration, the algorithm adds all edges (s, t) to the tree such that the distance from u to s is $i - 1$ and the distance from u to t is still unknown. If multiple such edges lead to the same t, the algorithm uses a *data race* to determine which edge is chosen. As any edge will suffice, this data race is benign. The distance from u to t is then set to i and we continue with the next iteration. The program runs with $O(|V| + |E|)$ data elements in $O(d)$ time, where d is the diameter of the graph.

Contained in Listing 1.5 is an AuDaLa program that implements this approach. The program defines the struct *Node* (line 1) with parameters *dist*, to store the distance from root node u, and *in*, a reference to its incoming spanning tree edge. The struct *Edge* (line 3) has a source s and a target t.

During initialization, the input should be a directed graph, with a root *Node* u with *dist* 0 and with the *dist* parameter of the other *Nodes* set to -1. For every *Node*, the parameter *in* should be *null*.

Both steps in the program belong to *Edge*. The first step, *linkEdge*, first determines whether an *Edge* e from *Node* s to *Node* t is at the frontier of the tree in line 5. This is the case when s is in the tree, but t is not. If so, e nominates itself as the *Edge* connecting t to the tree, *t.in* (line 6). This is a data race won by only one edge for t, the edge which applies the semantic rule **ComWr** last. In the second step, *handleEdge*, if the nomination for t has finished (line 9) and e has won the nomination (line 10), e will update t's distance to the root. If e has lost, it will remove itself from the graph, here coded as setting the source and target parameters to *null* in lines 13 to 16.

To create a full spanning tree, this must be executed until all *Nodes* have a positive *dist* and all *Edges* are either *t.in* for their target *Node* t or have *null* as their source and target. To this end, the schedule (line 18) contains a fixpoint, in which *Edges* first nominate themselves and then update the distances of new *Nodes*. This fixpoint terminates, as *Edges* in the spanning tree will continuously update their targets with the same information and *Edges* which lost their nomination will not get past the first conditions of the two steps, causing the data elements to stabilize after all *Nodes* have received a distance from u. Initialization steps should be placed at the start of the shown schedule. An execution of the program on a small graph is shown in Fig. 4, where the edges and nodes of the graph are modelled by their respective structs.

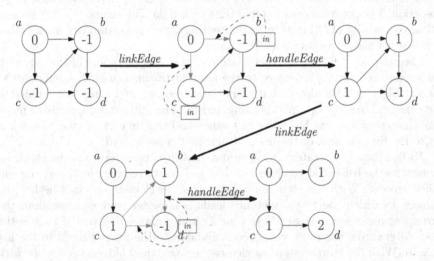

Fig. 4. Execution of Listing 1.5 on a small graph. Every *Edge* newly considered in the current step is grey. Considered *Edges* stay considered, but stable. The dotted arrows denote the possible new values for *t.in* of a target node t. Note that the *Edge* from c to d wins the data race to the reference *d.in*.

5.2   Sorting

```
1   struct ListElem(val: Int, next: ListElem, newNext: ListElem, comp: ListElem){
2     compareElement {
3       if comp != null then {
4         if (comp.val > val && (comp.val < newNext.val || newNext == null))
          then
5           {newNext := comp;}
6           comp := comp.next;
7     }}
8     reorder {
9       next := newNext;
10    }}
11
12    Fix(compareElement) < reorder
```

Listing 1.6. AuDaLa code for sorting

A concise example of an AuDaLa program for sorting a linked list of n elements can be found in Listing 1.6. In it, the elements of the list traverse the list together, during which each element e is looking for its successor in the sorted list. After the traversal, the successor element is saved and the link is updated to the saved element. This reorders the sorted list. See Fig. 5 for a visualization of an execution. The program runs in $O(n)$ time with n data elements. We can achieve a time complexity of $O(\log n)$ by implementing Cole's algorithm [16] in AuDaLa, but that is outside the scope for this paper.

The program defines the struct *ListElem*, modeling the nodes of the list, with parameters *val*, *next*, a reference to the next *ListElem*, *newNext*, a reference to the *ListElem* that should come next in the sorted list, and *comp*, a reference to the current *ListElem newNext* is compared to. The initialization needs to make sure that every element has a distinct value, and that in every element, *comp* is set to the first element of the list and *newNext* is set to *null*.

To facilitate our strategy we give our *ListElem* two steps, one to check an element in the list called *compareElement* and one to reorder the list at the end called *reorder*. With the step *compareElement*, an element checks whether the element to which the *comp* reference leads is a better next element than the current element saved in *newNext* (line 4) and updates *newNext* if that is the case. Afterwards, the *comp* reference is updated to the next element in the list (line 6). With the *reorder* step, an element replaces their old *next* reference with *newNext* (line 9).

To have the program execute our strategy, we call a fixpoint on *compareElement*, such that every element checks all elements in the list. After that is done, the schedule tells the elements to *reorder* (line 12).

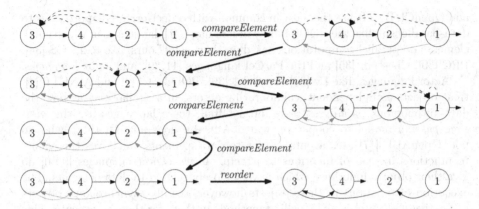

Fig. 5. Execution of Listing 1.6 on a small list. The parameters *next*, *newNext* and *comp* are shown as black, grey and dashed unmarked arrows respectively, and the *null*-references for *newNext* and *comp* are not shown. The nodes corresponding to *ListElems* contain the value of parameter *val*.

6   Related Work

Conceptually, our work is related to the Parallel Pointer Machine (PPM) [23], which models memory as a graph that is traversed by processors. In AuDaLa, on the other hand, processors are implicit and data is the main focus.

The concept of cooperating data elements is present in the Chemical Abstract Machine [8], based on the Γ-language [5,6]. In the data-autonomous paradigm these components are coordinated by a schedule as opposed to the Chemical Abstract Machine, where the data elements float around freely. By extension, AuDaLa is related to the Γ-Calculus Parallel Programming Framework [18].

The data-autonomous paradigm shares the same focus on data as *message passing* languages like Active Pebbles [40], ParCel-2 [11] and AL-1 [29], but differs in using shared variables instead of synchronisation and messages. It also does not allow the use of data as passive elements, like in the messages of MPI [15].

The *specialist-parallel* approach [12] models a problem as a network of relatively autonomous nodes which perform one specified task. In comparison, the data-autonomous paradigm defines their specialists around data instead of tasks and data elements perform multiple or no tasks depending on their steps.

In AuDaLa, the relations between data elements can be viewed as a graph, which is also the case for *graph based* languages, such as DDG [37], a scheduling language, and GraphGrind [36], a graph partitioning language. The Connection Machine [26] uses a graph-based hardware architecture for parallel computation. Similarly, the way data is expressed in Legion [7] and OP2 [31] is similar to AuDaLa. However, these two languages work top down from a main process that calls functions on data, which is unlike the data-autonomous paradigm.

Since the data-autonomous paradigm extends data-parallelism (see Fig. 1), AuDaLa shares concepts with other data-parallel languages like CUDA [19,24] and OpenCL [13]. It has the most in common with object-oriented approaches to data-parallelism, like the POOL family of languages [1], languages in which small elements do parallel computations based on their neighbours, like RELaCS [34], PPC [30], Chestnut [35] and the ParCel languages [11,39], and *actor languages*.

Actor languages, like Ly [38], ParCel-1 [39], PObC++ [32] and A-NETL [4], treat objects as independent, collaborating actors, in a similar way as how the data-autonomous paradigm treats data. Often, these languages use the *message passing* model to cooperate, which AuDaLa does not. Of those who do not, OpenABL [17] uses agents similar to data elements, but gives the agents to functions instead of functions to agents. *Active Object* languages [9,10] do give their objects functions, which is very closely related to data elements. The execution of functions in these objects however, is fully asynchronous: objects can activate other objects by calling methods in them for them to execute. This is less structured than in AuDaLa, in which the functions to be executed are defined in the schedule. As a result, AuDaLa does not use futures, unlike most active object languages.

The use of a schedule in the data-autonomous paradigm relates AuDaLa to some more functional data-parallel languages as well, like Halide [33], which uses a schedule as well, and even Futhark [25], in which the manipulation of an array has some similarity to calling a step in AuDaLa. The schedule can be considered as a coordination language [2] for the paradigm and AuDaLa, but is fully integrated and required for both to function. It also does not need to create channels between components, like for example Reo [3].

Similar to our motivation, ICE [21], which is a framework for implementing PRAM algorithms, sets the goal of bridging the gap between algorithms and implementation. However, as ICE is based on a PRAM, it is not data autonomous.

7   Conclusion

In this paper, we presented the data-autonomous paradigm and introduced it by means of the Autonomous Data Language, by giving examples of standard algorithms and discussing the syntax and semantics.

In the future, we will extend these foundations in multiple directions. First, we plan to perform an extensive practical evaluation of AuDaLa. Currently, we have prototypes of a sequential interpreter and a compiler to CUDA (for parallel execution on GPUs). Using these, we will investigate methods for efficient parallel execution of AuDaLa programs. Based on these experiences we may further extend the language and semantics, for example by introducing variants of the fixpoint operator.

On the theoretical side, one immediate avenue of research is to determine the expressivity of the language, which we have started to investigate. We also plan on creating formal analysis methods for AuDaLa programs, including methods for finding data races in AuDaLa programs and methods for proving functional correctness. For finding the data-races, we have already laid the groundwork in the operational semantics. We may also investigate how extensions to the current semantics impact the design of the envisioned formal analyses.

Acknowledgments. We would like to thank the AVVA project members for their insights and comments and Gijs Leemrijse, Clemens Dubslaff, Erik de Vink and the reviewers for their feedback.

References

1. America, P., van der Linden, F.: A parallel object-oriented language with inheritance and subtyping. SIGPLAN Not. **25**(10), 161–168 (1990). https://doi.org/10.1145/97946.97966
2. Arbab, F., Ciancarini, P., Hankin, C.: Coordination languages for parallel programming. Parallel Comput. **24**(7), 989–1004 (1998). https://doi.org/10.1016/S0167-8191(98)00039-8
3. Arbab, F.: Reo: a channel-based coordination model for component composition. Math. Struct. Comput. Sci. **14**(3), 329–366 (2004). https://doi.org/10.1017/S0960129504004153
4. Baba, T., Yoshinaga, T.: A-NETL: a language for massively parallel object-oriented computing. In: PMMPC Proceedings, pp. 98–105. IEEE (1995). https://doi.org/10.1109/PMMPC.1995.504346
5. Banâtre, J.P., Coutant, A., Le Metayer, D.: A parallel machine for multiset transformation and its programming style. Future Gener. Comput. Syst. **4**(2), 133–144 (1988). https://doi.org/10.1016/0167-739X(88)90012-X
6. Banâtre, J.P., Le Métayer, D.: The gamma model and its discipline of programming. Sci. Comput. Program. **15**(1), 55–77 (1990). https://doi.org/10.1016/0167-6423(90)90044-E
7. Bauer, M., Treichler, S., Slaughter, E., Aiken, A.: Legion: expressing locality and independence with logical regions. In: SC 2012, pp. 1–11 (2012). https://doi.org/10.1109/SC.2012.71
8. Berry, G., Boudol, G.: The chemical abstract machine. Theor. Comput. Sci. **96**(1), 217–248 (1992). https://doi.org/10.1016/0304-3975(92)90185-I
9. de Boer, F., et al.: A survey of active object languages. ACM Comput. Surv. **50**(5), 76:1–76:39 (2017). https://doi.org/10.1145/3122848
10. de Boer, F.S., Clarke, D., Johnsen, E.B.: A complete guide to the future. In: De Nicola, R. (ed.) ESOP 2007. LNCS, vol. 4421, pp. 316–330. Springer, Heidelberg (2007). https://doi.org/10.1007/978-3-540-71316-6_22
11. Cagnard, P.-J.: The ParCeL-2 programming language. In: Bode, A., Ludwig, T., Karl, W., Wismüller, R. (eds.) Euro-Par 2000. LNCS, vol. 1900, pp. 767–770. Springer, Heidelberg (2000). https://doi.org/10.1007/3-540-44520-X_106
12. Carriero, N., Gelernter, D.: How to write parallel programs: a guide to the perplexed. ACM Comput. Surv. **21**(3), 323–357 (1989). https://doi.org/10.1145/72551.72553
13. Chong, N., Donaldson, A.F., Ketema, J.: A sound and complete abstraction for reasoning about parallel prefix sums. SIGPLAN Not. **49**(1), 397–409 (2014). https://doi.org/10.1145/2578855.2535882
14. Ciccozzi, F., et al.: A comprehensive exploration of languages for parallel computing. ACM Comput. Surv. **55**(2), 24:1–24:39 (2022). https://doi.org/10.1145/3485008

15. Clarke, L., Glendinning, I., Hempel, R.: The MPI message passing interface standard. In: Programming Environments for Massively Parallel Distributed Systems, Monte Verità, pp. 213–218. Birkhäuser (1994). https://doi.org/10.1007/978-3-0348-8534-8_21

16. Cole, R.: Parallel merge sort. SIAM J. Comput. **17**, 770–785 (1988). https://doi.org/10.1137/0217049

17. Cosenza, B., et al.: OpenABL: a domain-specific language for parallel and distributed agent-based simulations. In: Aldinucci, M., Padovani, L., Torquati, M. (eds.) Euro-Par 2018. LNCS, vol. 11014, pp. 505–518. Springer, Cham (2018). https://doi.org/10.1007/978-3-319-96983-1_36

18. Gannouni, S.: A Gamma-calculus GPU-based parallel programming framework. In: WSWAN Proceedings, pp. 1–4. IEEE (2015). https://doi.org/10.1109/WSWAN.2015.7210299

19. Garland, M., et al.: Parallel computing experiences with CUDA. IEEE Micro **28**(4), 13–27 (2008). https://doi.org/10.1109/MM.2008.57

20. Geist, A., Reed, D.A.: A survey of high-performance computing scaling challenges. Int. J. High Perform. Comput. Appl. **31**(1), 104–113 (2017). https://doi.org/10.1177/1094342015597083

21. Ghanim, F., Vishkin, U., Barua, R.: Easy PRAM-based high-performance parallel programming with ICE. IEEE Trans. Parallel Distrib. Syst. **29**(2), 377–390 (2018). https://doi.org/10.1109/TPDS.2017.2754376

22. Giles, M.B., Reguly, I.: Trends in high-performance computing for engineering calculations. Phil. Trans. R. Soc. A. **372**(2022) (2014). https://doi.org/10.1098/rsta.2013.0319

23. Goodrich, M.T., Kosaraju, S.R.: Sorting on a parallel pointer machine with applications to set expression evaluation. J. ACM **43**(2), 331–361 (1996). https://doi.org/10.1145/226643.226670

24. Harris, M., Sengupta, S., Owens, J.D.: Parallel prefix sum (scan) with CUDA. GPU Gems **3**(39), 851–876 (2007)

25. Henriksen, T., et al.: Futhark: purely functional GPU-programming with nested parallelism and in-place array updates. In: PLDI 2017, pp. 556–571. ACM (2017). https://doi.org/10.1145/3062341.3062354

26. Hillis, W.D.: The Connection Machine. MIT Press, Cambridge (1989)

27. Hillis, W.D., Steele, G.L.: Data parallel algorithms. Commun. ACM **29**(12), 1170–1183 (1986). https://doi.org/10.1145/7902.7903

28. Leiserson, C.E., et al.: There's plenty of room at the top: what will drive computer performance after Moore's law? Science **368**(6495), eaam9744 (2020). https://doi.org/10.1126/science.aam9744

29. Marcoux, A., Maurel, C., Salle, P.: AL 1: a language for distributed applications. In: FTDCS1990 Workshop Proceedings, pp. 270–276. IEEE (1988). https://doi.org/10.1109/FTDCS.1988.26707

30. Maresca, M., Baglietto, P.: A programming model for reconfigurable mesh based parallel computers. In: PMMPC Workshop Proceedings, pp. 124–133. IEEE (1993). https://doi.org/10.1109/PMMP.1993.315547

31. Mudalige, G., Giles, M., Reguly, I., Bertolli, C., Kelly, P.: OP2: an active library framework for solving unstructured mesh-based applications on multi-core and many-core architectures. In: InPar 2012, pp. 1–12 (2012). https://doi.org/10.1109/InPar.2012.6339594

32. Pinho, E.G., de Carvalho, F.H.: An object-oriented parallel programming language for distributed-memory parallel computing platforms. Sci. Comput. Program. **80**, 65–90 (2014). https://doi.org/10.1016/j.scico.2013.03.014

33. Ragan-Kelley, J., et al.: Halide: decoupling algorithms from schedules for high-performance image processing. Commun. ACM **61**, 106–115 (2017). https://doi.org/10.1145/3150211

34. Raimbault, F., Lavenier, D.: RELACS for systolic programming. In: ASAP Proceedings, pp. 132–135. IEEE (1993). https://doi.org/10.1109/ASAP.1993.397128

35. Stromme, A., Carlson, R., Newhall, T.: Chestnut: a GPU programming language for non-experts. In: PMAM Proceedings, pp. 156–167. ACM (2012). https://doi.org/10.1145/2141702.2141720

36. Sun, J., Vandierendonck, H., Nikolopoulos, D.S.: GraphGrind: addressing load imbalance of graph partitioning. In: ICS Proceedings, pp. 1–10. ACM (2017). https://doi.org/10.1145/3079079.3079097

37. Tran, V., Hluchy, L., Nguyen, G.: Parallel programming with data driven model. In: EMPDP Proceedings, pp. 205–211. IEEE (2000). https://doi.org/10.1109/EMPDP.2000.823413

38. Ungar, D., Adams, S.S.: Harnessing emergence for manycore programming: early experience integrating ensembles, adverbs, and object-based inheritance. In: OOPSLA Proceedings, pp. 19–26. ACM (2010). https://doi.org/10.1145/1869542.1869546

39. Vialle, S., Cornu, T., Lallement, Y.: ParCeL-1: a parallel programming language based on autonomous and synchronous actors. SIGPLAN Not. **31**(8), 43–51 (1996). https://doi.org/10.1145/242903.242945

40. Willcock, J.J., Hoefler, T., Edmonds, N.G., Lumsdaine, A.: Active pebbles: parallel programming for data-driven applications. In: ICS Proceedings, p. 235. ACM (2011). https://doi.org/10.1145/1995896.1995934

Formal Language Semantics for Triggered Enable Statecharts with a Run-to-Completion Scheduling

Karla Vanessa Morris Wright[1]([envelope])[iD], Thai Son Hoang[2][iD], Colin Snook[2][iD], and Michael Butler[2][iD]

[1] Sandia National Laboratories, 7011 East Avenue, Livermore, CA 94550, USA
knmorri@sandia.gov
[2] ECS, University of Southampton, Southampton SO17 1BJ, UK
{t.s.hoang,cfs,m.j.butler}@soton.ac.uk

Abstract. The increased complexity of high-consequence digital system designs with intricate interactions between numerous components has placed a greater need on ensuring that the design satisfies its intended requirements. This digital assurance can only come about through rigorous mathematical analysis of the design. This manuscript provides a detailed description of a formal language semantics that can be used for modeling and verification of systems. We use Event-B to build a formalized semantics that supports the construction of triggered enable statecharts with a run-to-completion scheduling. Rodin has previously been used to develop and analyse models using this semantics.

Keywords: Run-To-Completion · statecharts · Formal Semantics · SCXML · Event-B

1 Introduction

Motivation. Statechart notations, with event-triggered, *'run-to-completion'* semantics [5,6,10], provide an intuitive and visual modelling interface with which engineers can design and communicate. SCXML [15] is an example of such a statechart notation. Formal refinement, as in Event-B [1], provides a safe way to abstract important properties and introduce details in a manageable way. Hence we have proposed the introduction of refinement into SCXML in previous work [11–13]. These case studies presented examples of systems modeled using this proposed semantics. The focus then was on illustrating the incremental model construction process, the support of a divide and conquer approach for the verification of model properties leveraging refinement rules as defined in Event-B, and the translation from SCXML to Event-B. In order to define our proposals for refinement in SCXML more precisely, we first need to formally specify the semantics of SCXML itself. In this paper, we focus on the formalization of SCXML semantics using Event-B. SCXML can be viewed as

© The Author(s), under exclusive license to Springer Nature Switzerland AG 2023
E. Ábrahám et al. (Eds.): ICTAC 2023, LNCS 14446, pp. 178–195, 2023.
https://doi.org/10.1007/978-3-031-47963-2_12

2 superimposed behaviours: a) the underlying behaviour of how the statechart is structured and how it changes its active state and b) the run-to-completion schedule that dictates the order in which enabled transitions should be fired. We approach the formalization by addressing these issues as separate Event-B models and then compose them using the CamilleX extension [9] to obtain the complete formalization of the SCXML semantics.

Contribution. Our contributions are as follows.

- We provide a formalization of the run-to-completion semantics of SCXML statecharts in Event-B. Although we refer to SCXML as an example, we believe that it is typical of other similar statechart notations and we have not relied on specific SCXML definitions.
- The work illustrates how Event-B with its automatic proof obligation generators and theorem provers can be used to define formal semantics of notations. Here we explain the Event-B models and outline the more interesting proofs that required manual intervention.
- The work also illustrates how the composition feature of CamilleX can be used to structure such semantics definitions into more manageable sub-issues.

As far as we know, this is the first tool-supported semantics model for SCXML statecharts supporting features such as parallel regions.

Structure. In Sect. 2, we provide a high-level description of statecharts, and the run-to-completion execution model, as well as, the Event-B modeling method used to formalized the semantics of our triggered statechart modeling language. Section 3 introduces a turnstile running example which will be used in subsequent sections to illustrate the construction and analysis of a system using our formalized semantics. We develop the semantics model of the run-to-completion statecharts in three separate steps: (1) first, we model the semantics the untriggered statecharts (Sect. 4); and (2) we then specify the run-to-completion triggering mechanism (Sect. 5); and (3) we compose the two individual semantics models to construct the triggered statechart semantics (Sect. 6). A summary of our findings and concluding remarks are discussed in Sect. 7.

2   Background

2.1   Statecharts

Statecharts have been used for visual representation in the specification and design of complex systems for several decades. Different statechart formalizations exist depending on the features supported and specific characteristics of the modeled systems [4–6]. These diagrams provide a compact representation for modeling hierarchy, concurrency and communication in a systems design. Statecharts were originally developed to address unbounded modeling complexity in other state diagrams.

2.2   Run-to-Completion and SCXML

State Chart eXtensible Markup Language (SCXML) [3,15] is a general-purpose
event-based statemachine language that combines concepts from Call Control
eXtensible Markup Language (CCXML) and Harel State Tables. Harel State
Tables are included in the Unified Modeling Language (UML). The concrete
syntax for SCXML is based on XML. Hence, SCXML is an XML notation for
UML style statemachines extended with an action language that is intended
for call control features in voice applications. SCXML uses a run-to-completion
semantics, also known as macro-step/micro-step semantics. This means that
trigger events may be needed to enable transitions. Trigger events are queued
when they are raised, and then one is de-queued and consumed by firing all the
transitions that it enables, followed by any (un-triggered) transitions that then
become enabled due to the change of state caused by the initial transition firing.
This is repeated until no transitions are enabled, and then the next trigger is
de-queued and consumed. There are two kinds of triggers: internal triggers are
raised by transitions and external triggers are raised non-deterministically by
the environment. An external trigger may only be consumed when the internal
trigger queue has been emptied. This means that an external trigger is only
consumed when no transition can be taken without doing so.

2.3   Event-B

Event-B [1] is a formal method used to design and model software systems, of
which certain properties must hold, such as safety properties. This method is
useful in modelling safety-critical systems, using mathematical proofs to show
consistency of models in adhering to its specification. Models consist of constructs known as machines and contexts. A *context* is the static part of a model,
such as *carrier sets* (which are conceptually similar to types), *constants*, and
axioms. Axioms are properties of carrier sets and constants which always hold.
A context can *extend* one or more contexts by adding more carrier sets, constants and axioms. The following listing shows the context for a simple systems
with two states.

```
1  context c
2  constants SA SB
3  sets states
4  axioms @def-states: partition(states, {SA}, {SB})
```

Machines describe the dynamic part of the model, that is, how the state
of the model changes. The state is represented by the current values of the
variables, which may change values as the state changes. *Invariants* are declared
in the machine, stating properties of variables which should always be true,
regardless of the state. *Events* in the machine describe state changes. Events
can have *parameters* and *guards* (predicates on variables and event parameters);
the guard must hold true for event execution. Each event has a set of *actions*
which happen simultaneously, changing the values of the variables, and hence

the state. Every machine has an initialisation event which sets initial variable values. The listing below shows a machine example with a single variable st.

```
1  machine m, sees c
2  variables st // state
3  invariants @typeof−st: st ∈ {SA, SB}
4  events
5    event INITIALISATION
6    then @init−st: st := SA
7    end
8    event t1
9    where @source: st = SA  // event t1 guard
10   then @target−st: st := SB // event t1 action
11   end
```

Contexts can be extended and machines can be refined to introduce details of the formal model gradually. Event extensions enable refinement of abstract events, the refined event will implicitly have all the parameters, guards and actions of the abstract event. We utilise context and event extension in this paper. An important set of proof obligations are invariant preservation. They are generated and required to be discharged to show that no event can potentially change the state to one which breaks any invariant, a potentially unsafe state. Event-B is supported by the extensible Rodin platform [2]. Extensions of Event-B and Rodin such as CamilleX [9] facilitate development of complex systems by allowing composition of existing models, and the reuse of modelling and proving efforts. This model composition capability enables machine inclusion with refinement and correct-by-construction proofs [7]. For example, when machine A includes another machine B, A will inherit all the invariants and discharged proofs of B (without the need for reproving). A can only modify the state variables of B by "synchronizing" with B's events. Direct modification of B's variables in A will introduce inconsistencies that result in unprovable proof obligations.

3   Turnstile Example

A turnstile is used to illustrate the construction of a system model under the developed semantics. Figure 1 shows the statechart diagram for the turnstile. The system has two sub-components that manage the operations performed by the gate and card reader in the turnstile. These components are represented by the *GATE* and *CARD_READER* parallel regions, respectively.

The model has two external triggers (*OnOff*, and *CardIn*), which are signals provided by the environment under which the system operates. In addition, there are internal triggers (*CardOk*, *Unblock*, *Block*, and *Reset*) that are raised by the components in the system. Transitions from source to target state are guarded by the specified conditions (i.e., [Unblock], *Unblock* trigger is in the queue). Actions associated with a specific transition are expressed as \raise Trigger, which result in adding the trigger to the queue. In the current model some of the internal triggers are raised non-deterministically (e.g. *CardOk*, *CardError*), as the details

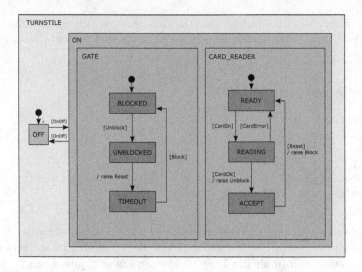

Fig. 1. Design model for a turnstile system

of the actual mechanisms responsible for the generation of the signal are not fully specified. Even in the presence of this non-determinism the system must satisfy certain requirements. Refinement of the abstract model presented in Fig. 1 can be used to incorporate implementation details. For example, a nested statechart could be added to the *READING* state to specify the process by which the aforementioned triggers are raised. This manuscript focuses on formalizing the modeling language semantics for triggered statecharts of this form, and leaves the extensions required for refinement proofs to a future publication.

4   Formalization of Untriggered Statecharts

In this section, we formalize the syntactic elements and semantics of untriggered statecharts. This includes finding sufficient conditions for well-defined untriggered statecharts to guarantee consistent semantic behaviour of such models. The main ideas for our formalization are (1) to use the Event-B *contexts* to capture the *syntactic elements* of the model with axioms ensuring that the model is well-defined (Sect. 4.1), and (2) to use the Event-B *machines* to capture the *semantics* of the models (Sect. 4.2).

4.1   Formalization of the Untriggered Statechart Syntactic Elements

As the syntactic elements of untriggered statecharts are fairly complex, we develop them gradually, together with their well-definedness conditions, using Event-B context extension in the following steps.

1. Model the tree-structure of the states
2. Model the parallel regions
3. Model the transformations between states

Tree-Structure States. The structure of the states of a statechart is represented by the following constants; states (the set of all states), root (the implicit root state), container (the relationship between a child state and its parent container), leaves (the set of leaf states). These constants satisfy an axiom stating that they form a tree-shaped structure (here $\mapsto$ is the notation for specifying tuples).

$$\text{states} \mapsto \text{root} \mapsto \text{container} \mapsto \text{leaves} \in \text{Tree}$$

Where, Tree is a constant, defined using transitive closure, that formalizes the definition of tree-shaped structures. An important derived property of a tree-shaped structured (proved as a theorem) is needed to allow us to prove properties by induction.

Theorem 1 (Tree induction from root). *Consider a property P. If*

1. *The root satisfies P, and*
2. *for every non-root state s, if the container of s, i.e., container(s), satisfies P, then s also satisfies P,*

then every state in the tree satisfies P.

Example 1 (Turnstile Example. Tree-shaped Structure States). Formally, we have the following definitions.

```
1  // All states of the turnstile examples
2  partition(states, {root}, {OFF}, {ON}, {BLOCKED}, {UNBLOCKED}, {TIMEOUT},
3    {READY}, {READING}, {ACCEPT})
4  // The container relationship between states
5  container = {OFF ↦ root, ON ↦ root, BLOCKED ↦ ON, UNBLOCKED ↦ ON,
6    TIMEOUT ↦ ON, READY ↦ ON, READING ↦ ON, ACCEPT ↦ ON}
7  // leaf states
8  leaves = {BLOCKED, UNBLOCKED, TIMEOUT, READY, READING, ACCEPT, OFF}
```

The partition operator defines an enumerated set, states, where all the elements are explicitly given.

Regions. Untriggered statecharts support the parallel composition of two or more nested statechart regions. That is a single state of a statechart may represent several sub components and associate with each component a corresponding region. In the turnsile example, the container state *ON* has two regions *GATE* and *CARD_READER*. We formalizes the notion of regions as partitions of the set of non-root states by using the following axioms to constrain the constant regions.

Axiom 1 (Regions are subsets of states). *Each region is a subset of the statechart's states. (Here $\mathbb{P}$ is the notation for powerset.)*

$$@region\_type: regions \subseteq \mathbb{P}(states)$$

Axiom 2 (Regions are disjoint). *Every pair of distinct regions does not share any states.*

$@region\_disjoint: \forall r1, r2 \cdot r1 \in regions \land r2 \in regions \land r1 \neq r2 \Rightarrow r1 \cap r2 = \varnothing$

Axiom 3 (Regions cover non-root states). *Every non-root state belongs to a region.*

$$@region\_complete: union(regions) = states \ \{root\}$$

Axiom 4 (Region has a unique container). *Every region has a unique container state. Here container[region] is the image of the relation container applying to region.*

$$@region\_same\_parent: \forall region \cdot region \in regions \Rightarrow$$
$$(\exists parent \cdot container[region] = \{parent\})$$

Example 2 (Turnstile Example. Regions). Formally, we have three regions as follows.

```
1 regions = { {ON, OFF}, // TURNSTILE region
2 {BLOCKED, UNBLOCKED, TIMEOUT}, // GATE region
3 {READY, READING, ACCEPT} // CARD_READER region
4 }
```

Note that states ON and OFF implicitly form a region without any sibling parallel region.

Transformations. Unlike the common definitions of transitions, which map a source state to a target state, we define transformations, which give an hierarchical view of the set of all simultaneously enabled transitions of the system, from one *enabling* state configuration to the next configuration. There are different types of transformation including *forking* (starting from a state and ending in one or more states in different parallel regions), *joining* (starting from two or more states in different parallel regions and ending in a state), *parallel* (updating parallel regions at the same time), and any combination of these types. To model all transformation types, we formalize each transformation by three sets of states.

- enabling: A transformation is enabled (i.e., can be executed) if its (non-empty) set of enabling states are active.
- exiting: The (possibly empty) set of states that the transformation will exit upon execution.
- entering: The (possibly empty) set of states the transformation will enter upon execution.

Formally, these notions are formalized as constants as follows.

```
1 enabling ∈ transformations → ℙ₁(states)
2 exiting ∈ transformations → ℙ(states)
3 entering ∈ transformations → ℙ(states)
```

Example 3 (Turnstile Example. Transformation). We give the enabling, exiting, and entering states of the following example transformations.

- Consider the transformation from the BLOCKED state to the UNBLOCKED state, we call this BLOCKED_2_UNBLOCKED. We have

  1 enabling(BLOCKED_2_UNBLOCKED) = {BLOCKED}
  2 exiting(BLOCKED_2_UNBLOCKED) = {BLOCKED}
  3 entering(BLOCKED_2_UNBLOCKED) = {UNBLOCKED}

- Consider the transformation from the OFF state to the ON state, we call this OFF_2_ON. Notice that the transformation will take into account also the transition from the initial states within the two sub-statecharts (regions). As a result, we have

  1 enabling(OFF_2_ON) = {OFF}
  2 exiting(OFF_2_ON) = {OFF}
  3 entering(OFF_2_ON) = {ON, BLOCKED, READY}

- Consider the transformation from the ON state to the OFF state, we call this ON_2_OFF. Notice that the transformation will take into account the non-deterministic exit from the two sub-statecharts (regions). As a result, we have

  1 enabling(ON_2_OFF) = {ON}
  2 exiting(ON_2_OFF) = {ON, BLOCKED, UNBLOCKED, TIMEOUT, READY, READING, ACCEPT}
  3 entering(ON_2_OFF) = {OFF}

There are several additional constraints (well-definedness conditions) relating the enabling, exiting, and entering states for a transformation. We identified some of the constraints directly. For instance, the following axioms related to exiting states.

Axiom 5 (Exiting a contained region). *If the container of a region is an exiting state, there must be an exiting state within that region. Here* container[r], *is the image of the relation container applying to region r.*

1 @exiting−contained_region:
2   $\forall trf, s, r \cdot trf \in transformations \land s \in exiting(trf) \land r \in regions \land container[r] = \{s\}$
3     $\Rightarrow exiting(trf) \cap r \neq \varnothing$

Axiom 6 (Exiting one or all states in a region). *If a region r has an exiting state s then either s is the unique exiting state or all the states in r are exiting states.*

1 @exiting−either_one_or_all_in_a_region:
2   $\forall trf, s, r \cdot trf \in transformations \land s \in exiting(trf) \land r \in regions \land s \in r$
3     $\Rightarrow exiting(trf) \cap r = \{s\} \lor r \subseteq exiting(trf)$

The following axioms linking exiting and enabling states was "discovered" during the proof of the invariant preservation proof obligations (see Theorem 3).

Axiom 7 (Exiting a unique enabling state in a region). *Given a region r and an exiting state s in r, if r has states other than s, s must be the unique enabling state in r.*

1 @exiting−unique_enabling_state_in_a_region:
2   ∀trf, s, r · trf ∈ transformations ∧ r ∈ regions ∧ exiting(trf) ∩ r = {s} ∧ r ≠ {s}
3   ⇒ enabling(trf) ∩ r = {s}

Axiom 8 (Enabling state is the unique exiting state). *Given a region r with some exiting state, an enabling state s in r, s must the unique exiting state in r.*

1 @enabling−unique_exiting_state_in_a_region:
2   ∀trf, s, r · trf ∈ transformations ∧ s ∈ enabling(trf) ∧
3   exiting(trf) ∩ r ≠ ∅ ∧ r ∈ regions ∧ s ∈ r ⇒ exiting(trf) ∩ r = {s}

The following axiom relates entering with enabling and exiting states. It is also discovered during the proof of the invariant preservation proof obligations (see Theorem 3).

Axiom 9 (Transformation stays within a state). *If a transformation enters a region r but not the container of r (called c), then c is not an exiting state and there is an enabling state which is a descendant of c. Here, cl(container) denote the transitive closure of container relationship, hence the inverse of that (i.e., cl(container)∼ is the descendant relationship between states.*

1 @entering−stay_within_state:
2   ∀trf, r, c · trf ∈ transformations ∧ r ∈ regions ∧ container[r] = {c} ∧
3   entering(trf) ∩ r ≠ ∅ ∧ entering(trf) ∩ container[r] = ∅
4   ⇒ enabling(trf) ∩ cl(container)∼[{c}] ≠ ∅ ∧ c ∉ exiting(trf)

4.2   Formalization of the Untriggered Statechart Semantics

Given an untriggered statechart (characterized by the tree-shape structured states, the regions, and the transformation), the semantics of the statechart is characterized by the set of active states during its execution. For instance, consider the turnstile example in Fig. 1, initially, the turnstile has one active state, namely OFF, i.e., the set of active states is {OFF}

- A transformation OFF_2_ON (from OFF to ON) will change the set of active states to {ON, BLOCKED, READY}.
- A transformation BLOCKED_2_UNBLOCKED will change the set of active states to {ON, UNBLOCKED, READY}.
- A transformation ON_2_OFF changes the set of active states to {OFF}.

We can now formalize the semantics of the untriggered statechart in a machine using a single variable active satisfying active ⊆ states . The system's functionality is encoded through one event called transformation that captures how the design transitions from one configuration to the next. Essentially variable active provides a discrete characterization of the information and event transformation represents the operation of the system under analysis.

```
1  event transformation
2  any trf where
3    @typeof−trf: trf ∈ transformations
4    @active−enabling: enabling(trf) ⊆ active
5  then
6    @update−active: active := (active \ exiting(trf)) ∪ entering(trf)
7  end
```

Guard @active−enabling ensures that the chosen transformation trf is enabled and action @update−active first removes the trf's exiting states then adds trf's entering states. Notice that this action also allows a transformation to exit a state and re-enter that state.

An important aspect for the semantics of statecharts is that it can only transform amongst valid configurations. For example, we want to ensure that the turnstile statechart is never in the configuration where both ON and OFF states are active or in a state where BLOCKED is active, but ON is not active. The following constraints on active specify the valid configuration for a statechart, which we encode as 4 invariants for the machine.

Invariant 1 (Container active). *If a non-root state is active then its container is also active.*

$$@container\_active: \forall s \cdot s \in active \setminus root \Rightarrow container(s) \in active$$

Invariant 2 (Content active). *If a container state is active then one of its sub-state must be active.*

$$@content\_active: \forall s \cdot s \in ran(container) \land s \in active \Rightarrow$$
$$container\sim[\{s\}] \cap active \neq \varnothing$$

where ran(container) is the range of the container relation

Invariant 3 (Unique active state within a region). *There can be at most one active state in a region.*

$$@active−region−unique: \forall r, s \cdot r \in regions \land s \in r \cap active \Rightarrow r \cap active \subseteq \{s\}$$

Invariant 4 (Parallel regions are inactive/active at the same time).
All parallel regions are inactive (hence active) at the same time.

$$@active−region−parallel: \forall r1, r2 \cdot r1 \in regions \land r2 \in regions \land$$
$$container[r1] = container[r2] \land r1 \cap active = \varnothing \Rightarrow r2 \cap active = \varnothing$$

As a consequence of Invariant 1, we can prove the following machine theorem. Note that all proofs related to this work were discharged semi-automatically within Rodin using the Proving Perspective. We present the general structure of a selected subset of these proofs.

Theorem 2 (Ancestors active). *If a state s is active then all ancestors of s are also active.*

$$@ancestor\_active{:}\ \forall\, s \cdot s \in active \Rightarrow cl(container)[s] \subseteq active$$

Proof. The proof of the theorem relying on Invariant 1 and the inductive nature of transitive closure. We omit the details here.

We have to prove that event transformation maintains the invariants relying on the well-definedness constraints that we have put as axioms.

Preservation of Invariant @active_container . The proof obligation for ensuring that invariant @active_container is maintained by event @transformation after simplification can be stated as the following theorem.

Theorem 3 (Event transformation maintains @active_container). *Given a non-root state s such that either (1) s is active but non-exiting state, or (2) s is an entering state, then either (G1) container(s) is active but non-exiting state, or (G2) container(s) is an entering state.*

Proof. Since s is a non-root state, there exists a region r containing s (follows from Axiom 3 @region_complete). We continue the proof by considering Cases 1 and Case 2.

Case 1 (s is active but non-exiting state). We discharge (G1) by proving that (G1-1) container(s) is an active state, and (G1-2) container(s) is a non-exiting state.

- *Proof of (G1-1).* According to Invariant 1 (@container_active), since s is an active state, container(s) is an active state.
- *Proof of (G1-2).* We proceed by considering if r contains any exiting states.
  - *Case 1.1 (r does not contain any exiting states)* Using the contraposition of Axiom 5, we can conclude that container(s) (which is also the container of the region r) must not be an exiting state, which conclude the proof of (G1-2).
  - *Case 1.2 (r contains some exiting states)* The proof continue as follows.
    * According to Axiom 8 (@enabling−unique_exiting_state_in_a_region), s cannot be an enabling state since s is a non-exiting state.
    * We prove this by contradiction, i.e., assuming that container(s) is an exiting state.
      · According to Axiom 5 (@exiting−contained_region), there must be an exiting state in the region r since the state containing r (in this case container(s)) is an exiting state, let us call this state x.
      · According to Axiom 6 (@exiting−either_one_or_all_in_a_region, either x is the unique exiting state in r or all states in r are exiting states.
      · Since s is a non-exiting state, x must be r's unique exiting state.
      · From Axiom 7 (@exiting−unique_enabling_state_in_a_region), x is the unique enabling state in r.
      · According to guard @active−enabling of transformation, x (being an enabling state) must be an active state.

· We now have two distinct active states x and s in r, which contradicts Invariant 3 (@active−region−unique).

Case 2 (s is an entering state). In this case, we proceed with the proof by assuming that (G2) does not hold (i.e., container(s) is not a container state) and prove (G1).

- According to Axiom 9, the transformation entering region r but not the container of r (i.e., container(s)), hence container(s) is not an exiting state and has a enabling descendant state, let us call this x.
- According to guard. @active−enabling of transformation, x (being an enabling state) must be an active state.
- According to Theorem 2, container(s) (being an ancestor of x) must be an active state.
- We therefore have container(s) is active but non-exiting state (G1).

$$\square$$

We omit the proof of the preservation of other Invariants 2, 3, and 4 due to limited space. The proofs are done within the Rodin tool utilising several axioms and the tree induction theorem (Theorem 1). Details can be found in [8].

5   Formalization of the Run-to-Completion Schedule

Similar to the previous section, the formalization is done using an Event-B context to capture the syntactic elements (Sect. 5.1) and an Event-B machine to model the semantics (Sect. 5.2).

5.1   Formalization of the Run-to-completion Syntactic Elements

To define run to completion execution we first specify the syntactic elements involved. Triggers are partitioned into either internal or external triggers. We define the internal and external trigger queues as sequences of internal and external triggers respectively. Sequences and their allowed operations (e.g. append trigger, head of sequence) are constructively defined via a series of theorems and axioms which are omitted here.

Figure 2 shows the state machine for the run-to-completion schedule. From the *Ready to de-queue* state, an internal or (if internal queue is empty) external trigger is de-queued from the corresponding queues and the system moves to the *Firing Triggered* state. A trigger step that consumes the dequeued trigger is then fired and the system moves to the *Firing Untriggered* state. From this state, untriggered steps can be fired repeatedly or the system moves back to the *Ready to de-queue* state. Both triggered and untriggered steps can raise more internal triggers, which will need to be handled in the future runs.

The context defining the syntactic elements for a run to completion is shown in Listing 1. An important notion for the run to completion schedule are steps. A triggered step is taken when an internal/external trigger is consumed and a non-deterministic number of untriggered steps may be taken subsequently. We will show how these steps relate to triggered/untriggered transitions later.

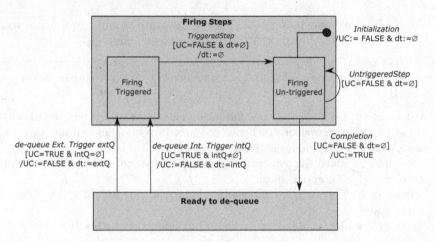

Fig. 2. State diagram for run to completion scheduling

```
1  context r2c_ctx extends r2c_c0_2_dequeue
2  sets Steps
3  constants InternalTriggers ExternalTriggers Triggers StepTrigger StepRaised
4  axioms
5    @typeof_IT: InternalTriggers ⊆ InternalTriggerType
6    @typeof_XT: ExternalTriggers ⊆ ExternalTriggerType
7    @def_T: Triggers = InternalTriggers ∪ ExternalTriggers
8    @typeof_StepTrigger: StepTrigger ∈ Steps ↛ Triggers
9    @typeof_StepRaised: StepRaised ∈ Steps → Seq(InternalTriggers)
10 end
```

Listing 1. Context for Run-to-Completion Semantics

Here StepTrigger (as a partial function) defines the required trigger for a Step (if any), and StepRaised defines the sequence of internal triggers that will be raised for a step (including an empty sequence). Steps that do not have any required trigger will be untriggered steps.

5.2 Formalization of the Run-to-Completion Semantics

Given the syntactic elements defined earlier, the machine defining the semantics for the run-to-completion schedule models the trigger queues in the system according to Fig. 2. The dynamic status of the run-to-completion schedule is represented by the variables int_q, ext_q, dt (dequeue trigger), and completed with the following invariants.

```
1   @int_q: int_q ∈ Seq(InternalTriggers)
2   @ext_q: ext_q ∈ Seq(ExternalTriggers)
3   @dequeue_trigger: dt ∈ DeQueueType
4   @dequeue_triggerwd: dt ⊆ InternalTriggers ∪ ExternalTriggers
5   @firingTriggered: dt ≠ ∅ ⇒ completed=FALSE
```

Where int_q and ext_q represent the sequences of internal and external triggers that need to be handled, dt keeps track of the trigger that has been removed from the queues (de-queue) to be consumed by a *TriggeredStep*. Note that dt is a singleton set of trigger when the system is in the *Firing Triggered* state and empty otherwise (this is also the definition of DeQueueType). Finally, variable completed (denoted as UC in Fig. 2) is TRUE indicates that the system is in the *Ready to de-queue* state.

```
1  event dequeueInternalTrigger
2  any trigger where
3    @grd1: completed = TRUE
4    @grd2: int_q ≠ ∅
5    @grd3: trigger = Seq_head(int_q)
6  then
7    @act1: dt := {trigger}
8    @act2: int_q := Seq_tail(int_q)
9    @act3: completed := FALSE
10 end
```

```
1  event dequeueExternalTrigger
2  any trigger where
3    @grd1: completed = TRUE
4    @grd2: ext_q ≠ ∅
5    @grd3: trigger = Seq_head(ext_q)
6    @grd4: int_q = ∅
7  then
8    @act1: dt := {trigger}
9    @act2: ext_q := Seq_tail(ext_q)
10   @act3: completed := FALSE
11 end
```

Starting from the *Ready to de-queue* state (where completed = TRUE), the system will de-queue an internal/external trigger if there are any. Note that an external trigger is only de-queued when the internal queue is empty. The system then moves to the *Firing triggered* state (where completed = FALSE and dt is not empty).

The behaviour of the *TriggeredStep* and *UntriggeredStep* are formalized by the corresponding events as follows. Both events can raise a sequence of internal triggers which is concatenated to the the internal queue.

```
1  event triggeredStep
2  any Step where
3    @grd1: Step ∈ dom(StepTrigger)
4    @grd2: StepTrigger(Step) ∈ dt
5  then
6    @act1: dt := dt \ {StepTrigger(Step)}
7    @act2: int_q := Seq_concat(int_q ↦
           StepRaised(Step))
8  end
```

```
1  event untriggeredStep
2  any Step where
3    @grd1: Step ∈ Steps \ dom(StepTrigger)
4    @grd2: dt = ∅
5  then
6    @act1: int_q := Seq_concat(int_q ↦
           StepRaised(Step))
7  end
```

While the internal triggers are raised through steps, external triggers can be raised non-deterministically by event raiseExternalTrigger and appended to the external queue. Note that at this stage (without the statemachine), there is a non-determinism between untriggeredStep and completion. When we combine the untriggered statechart and the run-to-completion schedule in the next section, we will distinguish the two cases.

```
1 event raiseExternalTrigger          1 event completion
2 any trigger where                   2 where
3   @grd1: trigger ∈ ExternalTriggers  3   @grd1: dt = ∅
4 then                                 4   @grd2: completed = FALSE
5   @act1: ext_q := Seq_append(ext_q ↦  5 then
      trigger)                         6   @act1: completed := TRUE
6 end                                  7 end
```

The model of the run-to-completion schedule maintains its invariants straightforwardly (relying on operations of sequence manipulation).

6   Formalization of Triggered Statecharts

The triggered statecharts are a unified statechart model representation based on SCXML [15]. To formalize the complete semantics we compose the previous two models, of the untriggered statechart (Sects. 4) and of the run-to-completion schedule (Sect. 5). The composition is performed by, using the inclusion mechanism built into the CamilleX extension [9] of the Rodin platform.

6.1   Triggered Statechart Syntactic Elements

Since a *triggered* statechart is a combination of an *untriggered* one and a run-to-completion schedule, the former is a syntactic extension of the latter (Listing 2). We introduce some syntactic elements *connecting* the sub-context together. Namely, relationships linking untriggered statechart transformations and run-to-completion steps, to form transitions.

```
1 context tstc_ctx extends r2c_ctx utstc_ctx
2 constants transitions discardSteps
3 axioms
4 @typeof−transitions: transitions ∈ transformations ↣↠ Steps \ discardSteps
5 @discardSteps−Triggers: discardSteps ◁ StepTrigger ∈ discardSteps ↣↠ Triggers
6 @discardSteps−Raised: StepRaised[discardSteps] = { ∅ }
7 end
```

Listing 2. Context for Triggered Statechart

At the same time, when we combine the two sub-models, we need to ensure an important aspect of triggered statecharts which is their responsiveness. In particular, if a trigger (internal or external) is de-queued, but no enabled transformation that can consume the trigger, we need to ensure that the system can still progress. More precisely, the system will need to *discard* the problematic trigger in order to continue. Constants discardSteps are introduced to capture the special steps that discarding triggers.

Axiom @typeof−transitions specifies that transitions is a one-to-one correspondence between transformations and non-discarding steps (↣↠ is the symbol for bijective functions). Axioms @discardSteps−Triggers and @discardSteps−Raised ensure that there is a discard step for every trigger and the discard steps do not raise any trigger ($\lhd$ is the symbol for domain restriction, $[..]$ is a relational image, and $\{\varnothing\}$ the singleton set of the empty set).

6.2   Triggered Statechart Semantics

The semantics of a triggered statechart is captured by a machine that includes both the untriggered statechart and the run-to-completion schedule. We also use prefixing mechanism, e.g., **includes** r2c **as** r2c, so that all modelling elements of the included machine are prefixed accordingly.

The following events are *lifted* from the run-to-completion machine (unchanged): raiseExternalTrigger, dequeueExternalTrigger, dequeueInternalTrigger. Essentially, they only concern the management of trigger queues and do not relate to the statechart's status.

```
1 event triggeredTransition
2 synchronises r2c.triggeredStep
3 synchronises utstc.transformation
4 where
5   @grd1: transitions(utstc_trf) =
          r2c_Step
6 end
```

```
1 event untriggeredTransition
2 synchronises r2c.untriggeredStep
3 synchronises utstc.transformation
4 where
5   @grd1: transitions(utstc_trf) =
          r2c_Step
6 end
```

Events to model the transitions (triggeredTransition and untriggeredTransition) *synchronises* with the events from the untriggered statechart and the run-to-complete schedule. The additional guard of the events ensure that the chosen transformation (from the untriggered statechart) and the step (from the run-to-completion model) corresponds with each other.

As discussed before, we need to introduce the events to discard triggers discardTrigger (in the case where triggeredTransition is not available). This condition is formalized as discardTrigger's grd3. We also strengthen the guard of completion to ensure that the system will complete a run only when untriggeredTransition is not available (see completion's grd1).

```
1 event discardTriggered
2 any trigger
3 synchronises r2c.triggeredStep
4 where
5   @grd1: r2c_Step ∈ discardSteps
6   @grd2: trigger = StepTrigger(r2c_Step)
7   @grd3: ∀trf · transitions(trf) ∈
        StepTrigger∼[{trigger}] ⇒ ¬enabling
        (trf) ⊆ utstc_active
8 end
```

```
1 event completion
2 synchronises r2c.completion
3 where
4   @grd1:
5     ∀ r2c_Step · r2c_Step ∈ Steps \
        dom(StepTrigger)
6   ⇒
7     ¬ (enabling(transitions∼(r2c_Step))
        ⊆ utstc_active)
8 end
```

The use of composition as supported by the inclusion mechanism in Rodin results in the triggered statechart semantics inheriting the invariants from the sub-machines without the need to prove them as they are correct-by-construction.

7   Conclusions

We formalize the semantics of SCXML run-to-completion statecharts using Event-B. We formalize the syntactic elements using Event-B contexts and dynamic semantics using Event-B machines. The semantics model is built in a compositional fashion: the semantics of (untriggered) statecharts and run-to-completion schedule is developed independently and composed to create the SCXML statechart's semantics model. This approach allows us to reduce the complexity of the consistency reasoning by focusing on different parts of the models. The combined model inherits the consistency of the sub-models by construction.

In order to ensure the consistency of the semantics, several well-definedness conditions on the syntactic elements have been identified. They are encoded as axioms in the formal models. These well-definedness conditions can be used as the specification of a validation tool to ensure the consistency of SCXML models. Given the semantic models are consistent, any instantiation will inherit this consistency without the need for reproving. For instance, the model of the turnstile example can have consistency about the active states and the triggering mechanism. Often, these consistency checks make up the majority of the proof obligations, only a small number are related to the specific model properties.

We plan to extend this work to formalize the semantics of refinement as described in [11,12]. In particular, we will formalize the syntactic constraints that ensure consistent refinement of SCXML statecharts, proving the consistency of the refinement rules, e.g., in [13]. The consistency of the semantic models focuses on safety properties, expressed as invariants. Furthermore, we model some of the syntactic elements in our formal models at a fairly abstract level, e.g., the notion of enabling, exiting, entering states for transformation. Our abstract semantics supports the majority of typical statechart features such as transitions, hierarchical structure, clustering, concurrency, start and stop states. We do not cover history or timeout mechanisms. Our composition approach means that our untriggered statechart semantics, which is common to most statechart notations, can be reused regardless of their triggering semantics (or lack thereof). E.g. UML-B [14] is untriggered. Furthermore, since SCXML is based on the widely used Harel statechart semantics [5], our run to completion semantics can also be used for such notations and where notations deviate in their run semantics (e.g. [4]), we at least encapsulate the extent of re-work required.

All data supporting this study are openly available from the University of Southampton repository at https://doi.org/10.5258/SOTON/D2791.

Acknowledgements. Sandia National Laboratories is a multimission laboratory managed and operated by National Technology & Engineering Solutions of Sandia, LLC, a wholly owned subsidiary of Honeywell International Inc., for the U.S. Department of Energy's National Nuclear Security Administration under contract DE-NA0003525.

References

1. Abrial, J.-R.: Modeling in Event-B: System and Software Engineering. Cambridge University Press, Cambridge (2010)
2. Abrial, J.-R., Butler, M., Hallerstede, S., Hoang, T.S., Mehta, F., Voisin, L.: Rodin: an open toolset for modelling and reasoning in Event-B. Softw. Tools Technol. Transf. **12**(6), 447–466 (2010)
3. Barnett, J.: Introduction to SCXML. In: Dahl, D.A. (ed.) Multimodal Interaction with W3C Standards, pp. 81–107. Springer, Cham (2017). https://doi.org/10.1007/978-3-319-42816-1_5
4. Eshuis, R.: Reconciling statechart semantics. Sci. Comput. Program. **74**(3), 65–99 (2009)
5. Harel, D.: Statecharts: a visual formalism for complex systems. Sci. Comput. Program. **8**(3), 231–274 (1987)
6. Harel, D., Gery, E.: Executable object modeling with statecharts. In: Proceedings of IEEE 18th International Conference on Software Engineering, pp. 246–257. IEEE (1996)
7. Hoang, T.S., Dghaym, D., Snook, C., Butler, M.: A composition mechanism for refinement-based methods. In: 2017 22nd International Conference on Engineering of Complex Computer Systems (ICECCS), pp. 100–109 (2017)
8. Hoang, T.S., Snook, C., Morris, K., Butler, M.: SCXML semantics model in Event-B (2023). https://doi.org/10.5258/SOTON/D2791
9. Hoang, T.S., Snook, C., Dghaym, D., Fathabadi, A.S., Butler, M.: Building an extensible textual framework for the rodin platform. In: Masci, P., Bernardeschi, C., Graziani, P., Koddenbrock, M., Palmieri, M. (eds.) SEFM 2022. LNCS, vol. 13765, pp. 132–147. Springer, Cham (2023). https://doi.org/10.1007/978-3-031-26236-4_11
10. Lüttgen, G., von der Beeck, M., Cleaveland, R.: A compositional approach to statecharts semantics. SIGSOFT Softw. Eng. Notes **25**(6), 120–129 (2000)
11. Morris, K., Snook, C., Hoang, T.S., Armstrong, R., Butler, M.: Refinement of statecharts with run-to-completion semantics. In: Artho, C., Ölveczky, P.C. (eds.) FTSCS 2018. CCIS, vol. 1008, pp. 121–138. Springer, Cham (2019). https://doi.org/10.1007/978-3-030-12988-0_8
12. Morris, K., Snook, C., Hoang, T.S., Hulette, G., Armstrong, R., Butler, M.: Refinement and verification of responsive control systems. In: Raschke, A., Méry, D., Houdek, F. (eds.) ABZ 2020. LNCS, vol. 12071, pp. 272–277. Springer, Cham (2020). https://doi.org/10.1007/978-3-030-48077-6_23
13. Morris, K., Snook, C.F., Hoang, T.S., Hulette, G.C., Armstrong, R.C., Butler, M.J.: Formal verification and validation of run-to-completion style state charts using Event-B. Innov. Syst. Softw. Eng. **18**(4), 523–541 (2022)
14. Snook, C.F., Butler, M.J., Hoang, T.S., Fathabadi, A.S., Dghaym, D.: Developing the UML-B modelling tools. In: Masci, P., Bernardeschi, C., Graziani, P., Koddenbrock, M., Palmieri, M. (eds.) SEFM 2022. LNCS, vol. 13765, pp. 181–188. Springer, Cham (2023). https://doi.org/10.1007/978-3-031-26236-4_16
15. W3C. SCXML specification website (2015). http://www.w3.org/TR/scxml/

Strong Call-by-Value and Multi Types

Beniamino Accattoli[1], Giulio Guerrieri[2]([✉]), and Maico Leberle[1]

[1] Inria & LIX, École Polytechnique, UMR 7161, Palaiseau, France
{beniamino.accattoli,maico-carlos.leberle}@inria.fr
[2] Aix Marseille Univ, CNRS, LIS UMR 7020, Marseille, France
giulio.guerrieri@lis-lab.fr

Abstract. This paper provides foundations for strong (that is, possibly under abstraction) call-by-value evaluation for the λ-calculus. Recently, Accattoli et al. proposed a form of call-by-value strong evaluation for the λ-calculus, the *external strategy*, and proved it reasonable for time. Here, we study the external strategy using a semantical tool, namely Ehrhard's call-by-value multi types, a variant of intersection types. We show that the external strategy terminates exactly when a term is typable with so-called *shrinking multi types*, mimicking similar results for strong call-by-*name*. Additionally, the external strategy is normalizing in the untyped setting, that is, it reaches the normal form whenever it exists.

We also consider the *call-by-extended-value* approach to strong evaluation shown reasonable for time by Biernacka et al. The two approaches turn out to *not* be equivalent: terms may be externally divergent but terminating for call-by-extended-value.

1   Introduction

Plotkin's call-by-value λ-calculus λ_v [40] is at the heart of programming languages such as OCaml and proof assistants such as Coq. In the study of programming languages, call-by-value (shortened to CbV) evaluation is usually *weak*, that is, it does not reduce under abstractions, and terms are assumed to be *closed*, *i.e.*, without free variables. These constraints give rise to an elegant framework—we call it *Closed CbV*, following Accattoli and Guerrieri [5].

Plotkin did not present the CbV λ-calculus λ_v with these restrictions, and properties such as confluence also hold without the restrictions. As soon as open terms are allowed, however, or evaluation is *strong* (that is, it can reduce under abstractions), the calculus behaves badly at the semantical level. There are at least two issues, first pointed out by Paolini and Ronchi Della Rocca [38,39,41].

1. *False normal forms*: some terms are contextually equivalent to the looping term $\Omega := (\lambda x.xx)(\lambda x.xx)$ and yet they are normal in Plotkin's setting.
2. *Failing of denotational soundness/adequacy beyond the closed case*: denotational models are usually both *sound* (that is, denotations are stable by reduction: if $t \to u$ then $[\![t]\!] = [\![u]\!]$) and *adequate* (that is, the denotation $[\![t]\!]$ is non-empty if and only if the evaluation of t terminates) only for Closed CbV; at least one of the two properties fails in the open/strong case.

E. Ábrahám et al. (Eds.): ICTAC 2023, LNCS 14446, pp. 196–215, 2023.
https://doi.org/10.1007/978-3-031-47963-2_13

Extensions of Plotkin's Call-by-Value. A number of calculi extending Plotkin's λ_v have been proposed. A first line of work studies a related and yet different issue of λ_v, namely the equational incompleteness with respect to continuation-passing translations, pointed out by Plotkin himself in [40]. This issue was solved with categorical tools by Moggi [37], which led to a number of studies, among others [21,24,30,34,42,43], that introduced many proposals of improved calculi for CbV.

A second and more recent line of work, due to Accattoli, Guerrieri, and coauthors, addresses the problem of open terms and strong evaluation directly [1,2,5–8,11,17,29]. It builds on the work of Paolini and Ronchi Della Rocca and on tools and techniques coming from the theory of Girard's linear logic [26].

In [5], they compare four different extensions of Plotkin's calculus in the framework of weak evaluation with possibly open terms. Their result is that the four calculi are all *termination equivalent*: t terminates in one of these extensions if and only if terminates in the other ones. In particular, in these extensions the issue of *false normal forms* is solved because all terms contextually equivalent to Ω do diverge, in contrast to what happens in Plotkin's calculus λ_v. The notion of termination shared by the four calculi is then referred to as *Open CbV* in [5].

One of the aims of this paper is identifying an analogous notion of termination for *strong* CbV evaluation. Perhaps surprisingly, indeed, the termination equivalent calculi of Open CbV do not agree on what such a notion should be.

Two Relevant Extensions. Two Open CbV calculi are relevant here. The first one is a *call-by-extended-values* λ-calculus where the restriction on β-redexes *by value* is weakened to β-redexes having as argument an extended, more general notion of *value*. First used as a nameless technical tool by Paolini and Ronchi Della Rocca [39,41], then rediscovered by Accattoli and Sacerdoti Coen [12] to study cost models, it has some similarities with a calculus introduced by Grégoire and Leroy [27] to study a CbV abstract machine for Coq. In [12], extended values are called *fireballs* (a pun on *fire-able*) and the calculus is called *fireball calculus*.

The second extension is the *value substitution calculus* (shortened to VSC) due to Accattoli and Paolini and related to linear logic proof nets [1,11]. It was introduced to overcome some of the semantical problems of Plotkin's setting, and it is a flexible tool, used in particular to relate the four extensions in [5].

Beyond False Normal Forms. In later works [6,8], Accattoli and Guerrieri show that the termination equivalence of Open CbV does not necessarily solve the other semantical issue of Open CbV, namely *the failing of denotational soundness/adequacy beyond the closed case*. On the one hand, they show that the fireball calculus is adequate but *not sound* with respect to Ehrhard's CbV relational model [25], a paradigmatic model arising from the theory of linear logic and handily presented as a *multi types system* (a variant of intersection types). On the other hand, they show that the open VSC is *both* adequate and sound with respect to that model, suggesting that it is a better setting for Open CbV.

Strong Call-by-Value. The strong case has received less attention. In particular, it is not even clear what is the right notion of termination. The recent literature contains two proposals of strong CbV evaluation, which have been carefully studied from the point of views of abstract machines and reasonable cost models, but not from a semantical point of view. The first one is the *strong fireball calculus*, for which abstract machines have been recently designed in 2020 [14] and 2021 [15] by Biernacka et al., the latter being reasonable for time (defined as the number of β-steps). The second proposal is the strong VSC, and more precisely the *external strategy* of the strong VSC, introduced in 2021 by Accattoli et al. [2], together with a reasonable machine implementing it.

The works [15] and [2] have been developed independently and at the same time, by two distinct groups, who cite each other. They state that both implement *Strong CbV*, but they fail to notice that they implement *different notions of termination*, raising the question of what exactly should be considered as Strong CbV. As we point out here, indeed, some terms are normalizing in the strong fireball calculus but have no normal form with respect to the external strategy.

Strong Call-by-Value and Multi Types. To clarify the situation, we here explore the semantic perspective provided by CbV multi types. For such types, typability coincides with termination of *open* CbV evaluation, as shown by Accattoli and Guerrieri [6, 8, 28], so they do not directly model strong evaluation. A similar mismatch happens in call-by-name (CbN for short), where terms typable with multi types coincide with the *head* (rather than strong) terminating ones. It is well known, however, that the restriction to *shrinking types* (that have no negative occurrences of the empty multiset) does model strong evaluation: in CbN, terms typable with shrinking types coincide with the leftmost(-outermost) terminating ones, and the leftmost strategy is a normalizing strategy of Strong CbN. Such a use of shrinkingness is standard in the theory of intersection and multi types, see Krivine [32], de Carvalho [19], Kesner and Ventura [31], Bucciarelli et al. [16].

Here, we adapt to CbV the shrinking technique as presented by Accattoli et al. for CbN multi types in [4], where the *shrinking* terminology is also introduced. Our main result is the characterization of external termination via shrinking types: a term t is typable with shrinking CbV multi types *if and only if* the external strategy terminates on t. Technically, the result is a smooth adaptation of the technique in [4]. Smoothness is here a *plus*, as it shows that the external strategy is the notion of Strong CbV termination *naturally* validated by CbV multi types, without ad-hoc stretchings of the technique.

Untyped Normalization Theorem. In an untyped setting, not every term normalizes (think of Ω) and in the strong case some terms have both reductions that normalize and reductions that diverge, for instance $(\lambda x.y)(\lambda z.\Omega)$. Thus, it is important to have a strategy that reaches a normal form whenever possible, i.e., that is *normalizing* in an untyped setting. The canonical evaluation strategy in Strong CbN is leftmost reduction and its key property is precisely that it is normalizing. A further contribution of the paper is an *untyped normalization theorem* for the external strategy in the Strong VSC, obtained as an easy corollary of the study via multi types. Such a result gives to the external strategy the same solid status of the leftmost strategy in CbN, and completes the picture.

No Tight Bounds. Multi types can be used to extract *tight bounds* on the length of evaluations and the size of normal forms. Here, we only study termination, not tight bounds, even if in the technical report [9] we also developed the enriched results with tight bounds. A first reason is that the characterization of external termination and the untyped normalization theorem we focus on here do not need the bounds. A second reason is that the enriched results are considerably more technical, while here we aim at a slightly weaker but more accessible treatment.

Proofs. Omitted proofs are in [10], the long version of this paper.

2   Technical Preliminaries

Basic Rewriting Notions. For a relation R on a set of terms, R^* is its reflexive-transitive closure. Given a relation $\to_r$, an *r-evaluation* (or simply evaluation if unambiguous) d is a finite sequence of terms $(t_i)_{0 \leq i \leq n}$ (for some $n \geq 0$) such that $t_i \to_r t_{i+1}$ for all $1 \leq i < n$, and we write $d\colon t \to_r^* u$ if $t_0 = t$ and $t_n = u$. The *length* n of d is noted $|d|$, and $|d|_a$ is the number of *a-steps* (*i.e.* the number of $t_i \to_a t_{i+1}$ for some $1 \leq i \leq n$) in d, for a given subrelation $\to_a$ of $\to_r$.

A term t is r-*normal* if there is no u such that $t \to_r u$. An evaluation $d\colon t \to_r^* u$ is r-*normalizing* if u is r-normal. A term t is *weakly* r-*normalizing* if there is a r-normalizing evaluation $d\colon t \to_r^* u$; and t is *strongly* r-*normalizing* if there no infinite sequence $(t_i)_{i \in \mathbb{N}}$ such that $t_0 = t$ and $t_i \to_r t_{i+1}$ for all $i \in \mathbb{N}$. Clearly, strong r-normalization implies weak r-normalization.

The Diamond Property. Following Dal Lago and Martini [22], we say that a relation $\to_r$ is *diamond* if $u_1 \,_r\!\leftarrow t \to_r u_2$ and $u_1 \neq u_2$ imply $u_1 \to_r s \,_r\!\leftarrow u_2$ for some s. Terminology in the literature is inconsistent: Terese [44, Exercise 1.3.18] dubs this property CR^1, and defines the diamond more restrictively, without requiring $u_1 \neq u_2$ in the hypothesis: u_1 and u_2 have to join even if $u_1 = u_2$.

Dal Lago and Martini show that if $\to_r$ is diamond then:

1. $\to_r$ is confluent, that is, $u_1 \,_r^*\!\leftarrow t \to_r^* u_2$ implies $u_1 \to_r^* s \,_r^*\!\leftarrow u_2$ for some s;
2. all r-evaluations with the same start and r-normal end terms have the same length (*i.e.* if $d\colon t \to_r^* u$ and $d'\colon t \to_r^* u$ with u r-normal, then $|d| = |d'|$);
3. t is weakly r-normalizing if and only if it is strongly r-normalizing.

Properties 2 and 3 are called *length invariance* and *uniform normalization*, respectively. Basically, the diamond captures a more liberal form of determinism.

Contextual Equivalence. The standard of reference for program equivalences is contextual equivalence, that can be defined abstractly as follows.

Definition 1 (Contextual Preorder and Equivalence). *Given a language of terms $\mathcal{T}$ with its associated notion of contexts C and an operational semantics given as a rewriting relation $\to$, we define the associated contextual preorder $\precsim_C$ and contextual equivalence $\simeq_C$ as follows:*

- *$t \precsim_C t'$ if $C\langle t \rangle$ weakly $\to$-normalizing implies $C\langle t' \rangle$ weakly $\to$-normalizing for all contexts C such that $C\langle t \rangle$ and $C\langle t' \rangle$ are closed terms.*
- *$\simeq_C$ is the equivalence relation induced by $\precsim_C\colon t \simeq_C t' \iff t \precsim_C t'$ and $t' \precsim_C t$.*

$$\begin{array}{rl} \text{TERMS} & t, u, s, q ::= x \mid \lambda x.t \mid tu \\ \text{VALUES} & v, v' ::= \lambda x.t \\ \text{EVALUATION CONTEXTS} & E ::= \langle \cdot \rangle \mid tE \mid Et \end{array}$$

$$\begin{array}{cc} \text{RULE AT TOP LEVEL} & \text{CONTEXTUAL CLOSURE} \\ (\lambda x.t)v \;\mapsto_{\beta_v}\; t\{x \leftarrow v\} & E\langle t \rangle \to_{\beta_v} E\langle u \rangle \quad \text{if } t \mapsto_{\beta_v} u \end{array}$$

Fig. 1. Our presentation of Plotkin's calculus λ_v.

3   Call-by-Value and Call-by-Fireball

The call-by-value λ-calculus λ_v was introduced by Plotkin [40] in 1975 as the restriction of the λ-calculus where β-redexes can be fired only when their argument is a *value*, and values are defined as variables and abstractions.

Our Presentation of CbV. In Fig. 1, we present λ_v adopting three specific choices, departing from Plotkin's presentation [40] in inessential details. Firstly, Plotkin also considers constants in the term syntax, with their own reduction rules, which are left unspecified. For simplicity, in our presentation there are no constants.

Secondly, for Plotkin values are variables and abstractions, while here *values are only abstractions*, as it is the case in the papers about Strong CbV motivating our study [12,14,15]. As stressed by Accattoli and Guerrieri [8], removing variables from values provides a better inductive description of normal forms in the open/strong case, without affecting properties such as termination or confluence. For further quantitative benefits, see Accattoli and Sacerdoti Coen [13]. In our paper, variables are not values, but all our results could be restated by considering them as values.

Thirdly, Plotkin defines both a multi-step non-deterministic (and confluent) evaluation relation reducing redexes *everywhere* in the term, and a single-step deterministic reduction (proceeding left-to-right) that is *weak*, that is, it does not reduce under abstractions. We instead adopt the somewhat halfway approach by Dal Lago and Martini [22]: our $\to_{\beta_v}$ is single-step, weak but *non-deterministic*. The idea is that it can evaluate the left and right sub-term of an application in any order (that is, the left sub-term is not forced to be evaluated first as Plotkin does), because (in the weak case) the obtained reduction relation has the *diamond property* (definition in Sect. 2), a relaxed form of determinism. Thus, the obtained notion of reduction slightly generalizes Plotkin's single-step reduction without changing whether a term terminates or not. The non-deterministic version is obtained via the notion of *evaluation context E* defined in Fig. 1.

Problem with Open Terms. It is well known that Plotkin's framework works well only as long as terms are closed. The problem with open terms is that there are *false normal forms* such as $\Omega_l := (\lambda x.\delta)(yy)\delta$ (where $\delta := \lambda x.xx$ is the duplicator) which are β_v-normal, because yy is not a value (and cannot become one), but are *semantically divergent*. Such a divergence can be formalized in various ways, perhaps the simplest of which is that Ω_l is contextually equivalent

TERMS, VALUES, EVALUATION CTXS, and $\to_{\beta_v}$ As for Plotkin's calculus

$$\text{FIREBALLS} \qquad f, f', f'' ::= v \mid i$$

$$\text{INERT TERMS} \qquad i, i', i'' ::= x f_1 \dots f_n \qquad n \geq 0$$

RULE AT TOP LEVEL   CONTEXTUAL CLOSURE

$$(\lambda x.t)i \; \mapsto_{\beta_i} \; t\{x \leftarrow i\} \qquad E\langle t \rangle \to_{\beta_i} E\langle u \rangle \quad \text{if } t \mapsto_{\beta_i} u$$

Fig. 2. The fireball calculus λ_{fire}.

(definition in Sect. 2) to the diverging term $\Omega := \delta\delta$. This problem was first pointed out by Paolini and Ronchi Della Rocca [38,39,41]. It is discussed at length by Accattoli and Guerrieri [5], who analyze various ways of extending Plotkin's calculus to solve the issue, that is, as to make false normal forms such as Ω_l diverge without simply switching to CbN (which, intuitively, amounts to diverge on $(\lambda x.y)\Omega$ as done by CbV but not by CbN), and show their equivalence with respect to termination, referring to them collectively as *Open CbV*.

The Fireball Calculus. The simplest presentation of Open CbV is probably the fireball calculus, defined in Fig. 2. The idea is that the values of the CbV λ-calculus are generalised to *fireballs* (a pun on *fire-able* terms), by adding *inert terms*, which contain in particular variables. Actually fireballs and inert terms are defined by mutual induction (in Fig. 2). For instance, $\lambda x.t$ is a fireball as a value, while x, $y(\lambda x.x)$, xy and $z(\lambda x.x)(zz)(\lambda y.t)$ are fireballs as inert terms.

The main feature of inert terms is that they are open, normal, and that when plugged in a context they cannot create a redex, hence the name. Essentially, they are the *neutral terms* of Open CbV.

Dynamically, β-redexes can also be fired if their argument is an inert term, via $\to_{\beta_i}$. Evaluation is weak, as evaluation contexts do not go under abstractions. Note that Ω_l given above now diverges: $\Omega_l = (\lambda x.\delta)(yy)\delta \to_{\beta_i} \delta\delta \to_{\beta_v} \cdots$

Two relevant properties of the fireball calculus are that its reduction is non-deterministic but diamond and that a term is a normal form if and only if it is a fireball, a property called *harmony* by Accattoli and Guerrieri [5].

Issues with the Fireball Calculus. In later works [6,8], Accattoli and Guerrieri show that, despite the termination equivalence of the various formalisms for Open CbV, they can behave quite differently with respect to semantical notions. In particular, they show that the fireball calculus does not behave well with respect to Ehrhard's multi types [25], which are a notion of type inducing a paradigmatic denotational model of the λ-calculus, the *relational model*, linked to linear logic. Technically, they show that multi types do not satisfy subject reduction with respect to the fireball calculus. The issue can be illustrated without multi types, and amounts to the fact that the fireball calculus allows one to erase and duplicate inert terms. The erasure is particularly problematic. We reformulate here the problem in terms of contextual equivalence, to stress that the issue concerns the fireball calculus independently of multi types.

An expected property of any calculus is what we call here *contextual stability*, that is, the fact that its operational semantics $\rightarrow$ is included in its contextual equivalence $\simeq_C$—in symbols: if $t \rightarrow^* u$ then $t \simeq_C u$. In the fireball calculus, contextual stability fails. Consider $t := (\lambda x.\mathsf{I})(yy)$, where $\mathsf{I} := \lambda z.z$ is the identity combinator, and note that $t \rightarrow_{\beta_i} \mathsf{I}$ because yy is an inert term. Now, consider the closing context $C := (\lambda y.\langle \cdot \rangle)\delta$ and note that $C\langle \mathsf{I} \rangle = (\lambda y.\mathsf{I})\delta \rightarrow_{\beta_v} \mathsf{I}$, while

$$C\langle t \rangle = (\lambda y.((\lambda x.\mathsf{I})(yy)))\delta \rightarrow_{\beta_v} (\lambda x.\mathsf{I})(\delta\delta) \rightarrow_{\beta_v} (\lambda x.\mathsf{I})(\delta\delta) \rightarrow_{\beta_v} \cdots$$

That is, $t \rightarrow_{\beta_i} \mathsf{I}$ but $t \not\simeq_C \mathsf{I}$ because $C\langle t \rangle$ diverges while $C\langle \mathsf{I} \rangle$ terminates.

To overcome false normal forms such as Ω_l, one *has to* work around redexes having inert terms has arguments. But substituting inert terms (thus sometimes erasing them) as done by the fireball calculus is a *brute force* solution. At the open level, it does not alter termination but it deteriorates semantics properties of the calculus such as contextual stability or the relationship with multi types. The alternative presentation of Open CbV given by the value substitution calculus [11], discussed in the next section, does not suffer of these shortcomings.

Issues with the Strong Fireball Calculus. The strong evaluation strategy by Biernacka et al. [14,15] is a deterministic version of the fireball calculus (namely proceeding right-to-left) extended to evaluate under abstractions. We omit the actual definition of its extension under abstractions because it is non-trivial and the issue we want to point out can be explained without detailing them.

At the open level, the issue with the fireball calculus is about the semantics, but not about termination. The semantical issue of the open level, however, induces a termination issue at the strong level. Indeed, the strong fireball calculus suffers of a phenomenon similar to the one of false normal forms, even if no redexes are stuck. Consider the term $u := (\lambda x.\mathsf{I})(y(\lambda z.\Omega))$. In the fireball calculus, one has $u \rightarrow_{\beta_i} \mathsf{I}$ because $y(\lambda z.\Omega)$ is an inert term. That is, u terminates on a strong normal form, namely I. Instead, u is *semantically divergent* at the strong level, as it was the case for Ω_l in Plotkin's calculus. Intuitively, the inert subterm $y(\lambda z.\Omega)$ should be somehow kept, instead of being erased, and evaluated strongly, which would lead to divergence because of the Ω under abstraction.

The non-trivial point is how to bring evidence that this is what should happen in a good definition of strong CbV evaluation. One way to see that something is wrong with the strong fireball calculus is to observe that the step $u \rightarrow_{\beta_i} \mathsf{I}$ provides another breaking of contextual stability. This is detailed in the Appendix of [10], because although interesting it does not involve strong evaluation.

Better evidence is developed along the paper. We adopt the value substitution calculus (VSC) and the external strategy by Accattoli et al. [2] for which t is divergent. Then, we show that, when refining Ehrhard's CbV multi types [25] by adding the machinery for characterizing termination of strong evaluation, one obtains that t above is not typable. That is, t is also semantically diverging.

4   Value Substitution Calculus

Here we present the *value substitution calculus* (VSC for short) introduced by
Accattoli and Paolini [11], and recall some properties. The operational semantics
shall be different from the fireball calculus of the previous section, but we shall
nonetheless exploit the concept of fireball to describe its normal forms.

Terms. The VSC is a CbV λ-calculus extended with let-expressions, similarly to
Moggi's CbV calculus [36,37]. We do however write a let-expression let $x = u$ in t
as a more compact *explicit substitution* $t[x{\leftarrow}u]$ (ES for short), which binds x in
t. Moreover, our let/ES does not fix an order of evaluation between t and u, in
contrast to many papers in the literature (*e.g.* Sabry and Wadler [43] or Levy et
al. [33]) where u is evaluated first. The grammars follow:

$$\text{Values}\quad v ::= \lambda x.t \qquad \text{Terms}\quad t,u,s ::= x \mid v \mid tu \mid t[x{\leftarrow}u]$$

The set of free variables of term t is denoted by $\mathsf{fv}(t)$ and terms are identified
up to α-renaming of bound variables. We use $t\{x{\leftarrow}u\}$ for the capture-avoiding
substitution of u for each free occurrence of the variable x in t.

Contexts. All along the paper, we use (many notions of) *contexts*, *i.e.* terms with
exactly one hole, noted $\langle\cdot\rangle$. For now, we need general contexts and the notion of
substitution contexts L, which are simply lists of ES. The grammars are:

$$\text{(General) Contexts}\quad C ::= \langle\cdot\rangle \mid Ct \mid tC \mid \lambda x.C \mid C[x{\leftarrow}t] \mid t[x{\leftarrow}C]$$
$$\text{Substitution Contexts}\quad L ::= \langle\cdot\rangle \mid L[x{\leftarrow}t]$$

Plugging a term t in a context C is noted $C\langle t\rangle$, possibly capturing variables,
for instance $(\lambda x.\lambda y.\langle\cdot\rangle)\langle xy\rangle = \lambda x.\lambda y.xy$ (while $(\lambda x.\lambda y.z)\{z{\leftarrow}xy\} = \lambda x'.\lambda y'.xy$).
An *answer* is a term of shape $L\langle v\rangle$.

Reduction Rules. The reduction rules of VSC are slightly unusual as they use
contexts both to allow one to reduce redexes located in sub-terms, which is
standard, *and* to define the redexes themselves, which is less standard—this
kind of rule is called *at a distance*. The rewriting rules in fact mimic exactly cut-
elimination on proof nets, via Girard's CbV translation $(A \Rightarrow B)^v = !(A^v \multimap B^v)$
[26] of intuitionistic logic into linear logic, see Accattoli [1].

There are two rewrite rules. Their root cases (that is, before context closure)
follow (the terminology is inherited from linear logic):

$$\text{Multiplicative root rule}\quad L\langle\lambda x.t\rangle u \mapsto_{\mathsf{m}} L\langle t[x{\leftarrow}u]\rangle$$
$$\text{Exponential root rule}\quad t[x{\leftarrow}L\langle v\rangle] \mapsto_{\mathsf{e}} L\langle t\{x{\leftarrow}v\}\rangle$$

Both root rules are *at a distance* in that they involve a substitution context L,
and L does not capture the free variables of u in $\mapsto_{\mathsf{m}}$ (resp. of t in $\mapsto_{\mathsf{e}}$). We shall
consider two variants of the VSC, the open and the strong version. They differ
only in the choice of evaluation contexts for the root rewrite rules.

The Open VSC. We first focus on the open fragment of the VSC, where rewriting is forbidden under abstraction and terms are *possibly* open (but not necessarily). This fragment has a nice inductive description of its normal forms, called *fireballs* and *inert terms* as they are the lifting to the VSC of the respective notions from the fireball calculus. Open contexts and rules are defined as follows.

$$\text{OPEN CONTEXTS} \quad O ::= \langle \cdot \rangle \mid Ot \mid tO \mid O[x \leftarrow t] \mid t[x \leftarrow O]$$

$$\text{OPEN REWRITE RULES:} \quad \frac{t \mapsto_a t'}{O\langle t \rangle \rightarrow_{oa} O\langle t' \rangle} \qquad \text{OPEN REDUCTION:}$$
$$(a \in \{\mathsf{m}, \mathsf{e}\}) \qquad\qquad\qquad\qquad \rightarrow_o := \rightarrow_{om} \cup \rightarrow_{oe}$$

Proposition 1 (Properties of open reduction [8]).

1. *Open reduction $\rightarrow_o$ is diamond.*
2. *A term is o-normal if and only if it is a fireball, where fireballs (and inert terms) are defined by:*

$$\text{INERT TERMS} \quad i, i' ::= x \mid if \mid i[x \leftarrow i'] \qquad \text{FIREBALLS} \quad f ::= v \mid i \mid f[x \leftarrow i]$$

Plotkin vs VSC. The open fragment of the VSC is enough to discuss the relationship with Plotkin's CbV λ-calculus as defined in the previous section. Plotkin's calculus can be easily simulated in the VSC. Indeed, if $(\lambda x.t)v \mapsto_{\beta_v} t\{x \leftarrow v\}$ then $(\lambda x.t)v \mapsto_{\mathsf{m}} t[x \leftarrow v] \mapsto_{\mathsf{e}} t\{x \leftarrow v\}$.

There is no sensible way, instead, to simulate VSC into Plotkin's calculus. Indeed, VSC is a proper extension of Plotkin's: false normal forms of Plotkin's calculus such as $\Omega_l = (\lambda x.\delta)(yy)\delta$ and $\Omega_r := \delta((\lambda x.\delta)(yy))$ are divergent in VSC:

$$\Omega_l \rightarrow_{om} \delta[x \leftarrow yy]\delta \rightarrow_{om} (xx)[x \leftarrow \delta][x \leftarrow yy] \rightarrow_{oe} (\delta\delta)[x \leftarrow yy] \rightarrow_{om} \cdots$$
$$\Omega_r \rightarrow_{om} \delta\delta[x \leftarrow yy] \rightarrow_{om} (xx)[x \leftarrow \delta[x \leftarrow yy]] \rightarrow_{oe} (\delta\delta)[x \leftarrow yy] \rightarrow_{om} \cdots$$

Note that divergence of Ω_l crucially uses distance on $\rightarrow_{\mathsf{m}}$ (in the second step), while divergence of Ω_r crucially uses distance on $\rightarrow_{\mathsf{e}}$ (in the third step).

VSC and Contextual Equivalence. Pleasantly, Plotkin's calculus and the VSC induce the same notion of contextual equivalence on λ-terms without ES, since contextual equivalence is defined with respect to contexts that *close* terms, see Accattoli and Guerrieri [8]. Moreover, the Open VSC is *contextually stable.*

Proposition 2 (Contextual stability [3]). *The Open VSC is contextually stable, that is, if $t \rightarrow_o^* u$ then $t \simeq_c u$.*

The Strong VSC. The Strong VSC is obtained by allowing rewriting rules everywhere, including under abstractions, via a closure by general contexts.

$$\text{STRONG REWRITE RULES:} \quad \frac{t \mapsto_a t'}{C\langle t \rangle \rightarrow_a C\langle t' \rangle} \qquad \text{STRONG REDUCTION:}$$
$$(a \in \{\mathsf{m}, \mathsf{e}\}) \qquad\qquad\qquad\qquad \rightarrow_{vsc} := \rightarrow_{\mathsf{m}} \cup \rightarrow_{\mathsf{e}}$$

Unlike the previous cases, $\rightarrow_{vsc}$ is not diamond: consider all the vsc-evaluations of $(xx)[x \leftarrow \lambda y.\mathsf{II}]$, with $\mathsf{I} := \lambda z.z$.

Proposition 3 (Properties of strong reduction [8,11]).

1. *The reduction* $\rightarrow_{\mathsf{vsc}}$ *is confluent.*
2. *A term is* vsc-*normal if and only if it is a strong fireball, where strong fireballs (and strong inert terms, strong values) are:*

$$\text{STRONG INERT TERMS} \quad i_{\mathsf{s}} ::= x \mid i_{\mathsf{s}}f_{\mathsf{s}} \mid i_{\mathsf{s}}[x{\leftarrow}i_{\mathsf{s}}'] \quad \text{STRONG VALUES} \quad v_{\mathsf{s}} ::= \lambda x.f_{\mathsf{s}}$$
$$\text{STRONG FIREBALLS} \quad f_{\mathsf{s}} ::= i_{\mathsf{s}} \mid v_{\mathsf{s}} \mid f_{\mathsf{s}}[x{\leftarrow}i_{\mathsf{s}}]$$

The notions of strong inert terms and strong fireballs are a generalization of inert terms and fireballs, respectively, by simply iterating the construction under all abstractions. Note that they are similar to normal forms of the (CbN) λ-calculus, but they can have ESs containing strong inert terms.

5 The External Strategy

In this section, we define Accattoli et al.'s (strong) *external* strategy [2], that shall be studied via multi types in Sect. 8. Its role is analogous to the leftmost-outermost strategy of the λ-calculus. A notable difference, however, is that the external strategy is itself non-deterministic, but in a harmless way, because it is diamond. The idea is the same used for Plotkin's calculus, that is, allowing one to reduce sub-terms of applications (and ES) in any order. In a strong setting, however, it is a bit trickier to enforce it.

We need a few notions. Firstly, *rigid terms*, *i.e.* the variation over inert terms where the arguments of the head variable can be whatever term:

$$\text{RIGID TERMS} \quad r, r' ::= x \mid rt \mid r[x{\leftarrow}r']$$

Every (strong) inert term is a rigid term, but the converse does not hold—consider $y(\delta\mathsf{I})$, which is rigid but not inert.

Secondly, we need evaluation contexts for the external strategy $\rightarrow_{\mathsf{x}}$, which is defined on top of open evaluation. The base case is given by the open rewriting rules (themselves defined via a closure by open contexts, see Sect. 4), which are then closed by *external contexts*, defined mutually with *rigid contexts*:

$$\text{EXTERNAL CONTEXTS} \quad X ::= \langle \cdot \rangle \mid \lambda x.X \mid t[x{\leftarrow}R] \mid X[x{\leftarrow}r] \mid R$$
$$\text{RIGID CONTEXTS} \quad R ::= rX \mid Rt \mid R[x{\leftarrow}r] \mid r[x{\leftarrow}R]$$

$$\text{EXTERNAL REWRITE RULES:} \quad \frac{t \rightarrow_{\mathsf{oa}} t'}{X\langle t\rangle \rightarrow_{\mathsf{xa}} X\langle t'\rangle} \qquad \text{EXTERNAL REDUCTION:}$$
$$(a \in \{\mathsf{m}, \mathsf{e}\}) \qquad\qquad\qquad\qquad\qquad \rightarrow_{\mathsf{x}} := \rightarrow_{\mathsf{xm}} \cup \rightarrow_{\mathsf{xe}}$$

Clearly, $\rightarrow_{\mathsf{x}} \subsetneq \rightarrow_{\mathsf{vsc}}$. The strategy diverges on $y(\lambda z.\Omega)$ (as $y\lambda z.\langle\cdot\rangle$ is a rigid—thus external—context) and normalizes the potentially diverging term $(\lambda x.y)(\lambda z.\Omega)$ $\rightarrow_{\mathsf{x}}^{*} y$, because values can be erased even if they diverge under abstraction.

Key example: the external strategy diverges on the term $t = (\lambda x.\mathsf{I})(y(\lambda z.\Omega))$ of Sect. 3 on which the strong fireball calculus terminates, showing that *the two strong settings have different notions of termination*. Indeed, $t \rightarrow_{\mathsf{xm}} \mathsf{I}[x{\leftarrow}y(\lambda z.\Omega)]$

and then the external strategy diverges because $y(\lambda z.\Omega)$ cannot be erased and Ω occurs in the external evaluation context $I[x{\leftarrow}y(\lambda z.\langle\cdot\rangle)]$.

The grammars of external and rigid contexts allow evaluation to enter only inside non-applied abstractions, e.g. $(\lambda x.(II))v \not\to_\mathsf{x} (\lambda x.(y[y{\leftarrow}I]))v$. This is a sort of outside-in order which is neither left-to-right nor right-to-left—we have both $(II)(II) \to_\mathsf{xm} (y[y{\leftarrow}I])(II)$ and $(II)(II) \to_\mathsf{xm} (II)(y[y{\leftarrow}I])$—since open contexts do not impose an order on applications. As just showed, the strategy is non-deterministic: another example is given by $t = x(\lambda y.(II))[x{\leftarrow}x(II)] \to_\mathsf{xm} x(\lambda y.z[z{\leftarrow}I])[x{\leftarrow}x(II)]$, and $t \to_\mathsf{xm} x(\lambda y.(II))[x{\leftarrow}x(z[z{\leftarrow}I])]$. Such a behavior however is only a relaxed form of determinism, as it satisfies the *diamond property*.

Proposition 4 (Properties of external reduction $\to_\mathsf{x}$ [2]).

1. *External reduction $\to_\mathsf{x}$ is diamond.*
2. *Fullness: let t be a VSC term, t is x-normal if and only if t is vsc-normal.*

6   Multi Types by Value

We present here the system of CbV *multi types* that we shall use to characterize the termination of the external strategy in Sect. 8. The system was introduced by Ehrhard [25] for Plotkin's CbV λ-calculus, as the CbV version of de Carvalho's multi types system for CbN [18, 19]. Both systems can be seen as presentations of the relational semantics of linear logic restricted to the CbV/CbN interpretation of the λ-calculus. The CbV multi type system is also used in [3,6,8,17,23,28].

Multi Types. There are two layers of types, *linear* and *multi types*:

$$\begin{array}{lll} \text{LINEAR TYPES} & \mathsf{A,B} ::= \mathsf{G} \mid \mathsf{M} \multimap \mathsf{N} \\ \text{MULTI TYPES} & \mathsf{M,N} ::= [\mathsf{A}_1,\ldots,\mathsf{A}_n] & n \in \mathbb{N} \end{array}$$

where G is an unspecified ground type and $[\mathsf{A}_1,\ldots,\mathsf{A}_n]$ is our notation for finite multisets. The *empty* multi type $[\,]$ obtained by taking $n = 0$ is also denoted by $\mathbf{0}$. When CbV multi types are used to study weak evaluation, they are usually presented without the ground type G, as one can use $\mathbf{0}$ as base case for types. For studying strong evaluation, however, G is mandatory, as we shall see.

A multi type $[\mathsf{A}_1,\ldots,\mathsf{A}_n]$ has to be intended as a conjunction $\mathsf{A}_1 \wedge \cdots \wedge \mathsf{A}_n$ of linear types $\mathsf{A}_1,\ldots,\mathsf{A}_n$, for a commutative, associative, non-idempotent conjunction $\wedge$ (morally a tensor $\otimes$), of neutral element $\mathbf{0}$. Note however that $[\mathsf{A}] \neq \mathsf{A}$.

The intuition is that a linear type corresponds to a single use of a term t, and that t is typed with a multiset M of n linear types if it is going to be used (at most) n times. The meaning of *using a term* (once) is not easy to define precisely. Roughly, it means that if t is part of a larger term u, then a copy of t shall end up in evaluation position during the evaluation of u. More precisely, the copy shall end up in evaluation position where it is applied to some terms.

The derivation rules for the multi types system are in Fig. 3 (explanation follows). The rules are the same as in Ehrhard [25], up to their extension to ESs.

Judgments have shape $\Gamma \vdash t : \mathsf{M}$ or $\Gamma \vdash t : \mathsf{A}$ where t is a term, M is a multi type, A is a linear type, and Γ is a *type context*, that is, a total function from variables to multi types such that $\mathsf{dom}(\Gamma) := \{x \mid \Gamma(x) \neq \mathbf{0}\}$ is finite.

$$\frac{}{x:[\mathsf{A}] \vdash x:\mathsf{A}}\,\mathsf{ax} \qquad \frac{\varGamma \vdash t:[\mathsf{M}\multimap\mathsf{N}] \quad \varDelta \vdash u:\mathsf{M}}{\varGamma \uplus \varDelta \vdash tu:\mathsf{N}}\,@ \qquad \frac{\varGamma,x:\mathsf{M} \vdash t:\mathsf{N}}{\varGamma \vdash \lambda x.t:\mathsf{M}\multimap\mathsf{N}}\,\lambda$$

$$\frac{\varGamma,x:\mathsf{M} \vdash t:\mathsf{N} \quad \varDelta \vdash u:\mathsf{M}}{\varGamma \uplus \varDelta \vdash t[x{\leftarrow}u]:\mathsf{N}}\,\mathsf{es} \qquad \frac{[\varGamma_i \vdash v_t:\mathsf{A}_i]_{i\in I}}{\uplus_{i\in I}\varGamma_i \vdash v_t:[\mathsf{A}_i]_{i\in I}}\,\mathsf{many}$$

Fig. 3. Call-by-value multi type system. In rule many, v_t is a *theoretical value*, *i.e.* a variable or an abstraction, and I is a finite set.

Technicalities About Types. The type context $\varGamma$ is *empty* if $\mathsf{dom}(\varGamma) = \emptyset$. Multiset sum $\uplus$ is extended to type contexts point-wise, *i.e.* $(\varGamma \uplus \varDelta)(x) := \varGamma(x) \uplus \varDelta(x)$ for each variable x. This notion is extended to a finite family of type contexts as expected, in particular $\uplus_{i\in J}\varGamma_i$ is the empty type context if $J = \emptyset$. A type context $\varGamma$ is denoted by $x_1:\mathsf{M}_1,\ldots,x_n:\mathsf{M}_n$ (for some $n \in \mathbb{N}$) if $\mathsf{dom}(\varGamma) \subseteq \{x_1,\ldots,x_n\}$ and $\varGamma(x_i) = \mathsf{M}_i$ for all $1 \le i \le n$. Given two type contexts $\varGamma$ and $\varDelta$ such that $\mathsf{dom}(\varGamma) \cap \mathsf{dom}(\varDelta) = \emptyset$, the type context $\varGamma,\varDelta$ is defined by $(\varGamma,\varDelta)(x) := \varGamma(x)$ if $x \in \mathsf{dom}(\varGamma)$, $(\varGamma,\varDelta)(x) := \varDelta(x)$ if $x \in \mathsf{dom}(\varDelta)$, and $(\varGamma,\varDelta)(x) := \mathbf{0}$ otherwise. Note that $\varGamma,x:\mathbf{0} = \varGamma$, where we implicitly assume $x \notin \mathsf{dom}(\varGamma)$.

We write $\varPhi \rhd \varGamma \vdash t:\mathsf{M}$ if $\varPhi$ is a *(type) derivation* (*i.e.* a tree constructed using the rules in Fig. 3) with conclusion the multi judgment $\varGamma \vdash t:\mathsf{M}$. In particular, we write $\varPhi \rhd \vdash t:\mathsf{M}$ when $\varGamma$ is empty. We write $\varPhi \rhd t$ if $\varPhi \rhd \varGamma \vdash t:\mathsf{M}$ for some type context $\varGamma$ and some multi type M.

We need a notion of size of type derivations, which shall be used as the termination measure for typable terms.

Definition 2 (Derivation size). *Let $\varPhi$ be a type derivation. The* size *$|\varPhi|$ of $\varPhi$ is the number of rule occurrences in $\varPhi$ except for rule* many.

Multisets and Rule many. Rule many plays a crucial role, as it is the only rule introducing multisets on the right-hand side of judgments: it takes as premises a finite multiset of derivations of linear types for a term v_t, and glues them together giving a judgment with the finite multiset of linear types to v_t. The term v_t is a *theoretical value* v_t, that is, a variable or an abstraction—the terminology is taken from Accattoli and Sacerdoti Coen [13]. Rule many is the multi types analogous of the promotion rule of linear logic, which, in the CbV representation of the λ-calculus, is indeed used for typing abstractions and variables. Note that in particular all abstractions are typable with $\mathbf{0}$ via a many rule with no premises.

Subject Reduction and Expansion. The first properties of the type system that we show are subject reduction and expansion, which hold for *every* VSC step, not only external ones. They rely on a substitution lemma (and its inverse for subject expansion) in the Appendix of [10].

Proposition 5 (Qualitative subjects). *Let $t \to_{\mathsf{vsc}} t'$.*

1. Reduction: *if $\varPhi \rhd \varGamma \vdash t:\mathsf{M}$ then there is $\varPhi' \rhd \varGamma \vdash t':\mathsf{M}$ such that $|\varPhi| \ge |\varPhi'|$.*
2. Expansion: *if $\varPhi' \rhd \varGamma \vdash t':\mathsf{M}$ then there is a derivation $\varPhi \rhd \varGamma \vdash t:\mathsf{M}$.*

Note that subject reduction (Proposition 5.1) says also that the derivation size *cannot increase* after a reduction step. It does not say that it *decreases* at every step because, for instance, if $\lambda x.t \to_{\mathsf{vsc}} \lambda x.t'$ and $\lambda x.t$ is typed using a empty many rule (*i.e.* with 0 premises), which is a derivation of size 0, then also $\lambda x.t'$ is typed using a empty many rule, of size 0. Hence, not all typable terms terminate for strong/external evaluation, as for instance $\lambda x.\Omega$ is typable (with **0**).

There are two ways to strengthen subject reduction without changing the type system and recover termination: restricting either the reductions to not take place under abstraction, which is what we shall do in the next section for the open case, or the kind of types taken into account (roughly, as to limit the use of **0**), which is what shall guarantee termination for the external strategy.

7   Multi Types for Open CbV

Here we recall the qualitative part of the relationship between CbV multi types and Open CbV studied by Accattoli and Guerrieri in [8], where they develop also a quantitative study not used here. The reason to recall their result is twofold. Firstly, the external case relies on the open one. Secondly, the open case provides the blueprint for the strong case, allowing us to stress similarities and differences.

The result is that the open evaluation $\to_\mathsf{o}$ of t terminates if and only if t is typable. Since $\to_\mathsf{o}$ does not reduce under abstractions, every abstraction is o-normal and indeed typable, for instance with **0**. As an example, note that $\lambda x.\Omega$ is typable with **0** (rule many with 0 premises), though Ω is not.

Correctness. Open correctness establishes that all typable terms are o-normalizing and it is proved by showing that the size of type derivation decreases with every o-step. Open correctness is proved following a standard scheme, namely proving a quantitative version of open subject reduction, stating that every $\to_\mathsf{o}$ step preserves types and decreases the general size of a derivation.

Proposition 6 (Open quantitative subject reduction). *Let* $\Phi \triangleright \Gamma \vdash t \colon \mathsf{M}$ *be a derivation. If* $t \to_\mathsf{o} t'$ *then there is* $\Phi' \triangleright \Gamma \vdash t' \colon \mathsf{M}$ *with* $|\Phi| > |\Phi'|$.

The size of derivations decreases after any $\to_\mathsf{o}$ step, thus proving $\to_\mathsf{o}$-termination for typable terms. Clearly, the size provides a bound to the number of steps.

Theorem 1 (Open correctness). *Let* $\Phi \triangleright t$ *be a derivation. Then there is a* o*-normalizing evaluation* $d \colon t \to_\mathsf{o}^* f$ *with* $|d| \leq |\Phi|$.

Completeness. Open completeness establishes that every o-normalizing term is typable. Again, the proof technique is standard: a lemma states that every o-normal form is typable, and subject expansion (Proposition 5.2) allows us to pull back typability along $\to_\mathsf{o}$ steps. The lemma about open normal forms says that they are all typable with **0** and relies on a stronger statement about inert terms: they can be assigned whatever multi type M, by tuning the type context Γ accordingly.

RIGHT MULTI TYPE $\mathsf{M^R} ::= [\mathsf{A}_1^\mathsf{R}, \ldots, \mathsf{A}_n^\mathsf{R}]$ $n \geq 1$ RIGHT LINEAR TYPE $\mathsf{A^R} ::= \mathsf{G} \mid \mathsf{M^L} \multimap \mathsf{M^R}$

LEFT MULTI TYPE $\mathsf{M^L} ::= [\mathsf{A}_1^\mathsf{L}, \ldots, \mathsf{A}_n^\mathsf{L}]$ $n \geq 0$ LEFT LINEAR TYPE $\mathsf{A^L} ::= \mathsf{G} \mid \mathsf{M^R} \multimap \mathsf{M^L}$

Fig. 4. Right and left (shrinking) types.

Lemma 1 (Typability of open normal forms).

1. Inert: *for every inert term i and multi type M, there exists a type context Γ and a derivation $\Phi \rhd \Gamma \vdash i : \mathsf{M}$.*
2. Fireball: *for every fireball f there exists a type context Γ and a derivation $\Phi \rhd \Gamma \vdash f : \mathbf{0}$.*

Theorem 2 (Open completeness). *Let $d : t \to_\circ^* f$ be an o-normalizing evaluation. Then there is a derivation $\Phi \rhd \Gamma \vdash t : \mathbf{0}$.*

8 Shrinking Multi Types for the External Strategy

In this section, we restrict the set of judgments as to characterize the typable terms that terminate with respect to the external strategy. The restriction is obtained by adapting to CbV the *shrinking technique* for CbN multi types in Accattoli et al. [4]. At the end of the section, we also obtain the untyped normalization theorem for the external strategy.

The definition of shrinking judgments is standard and not due to [4], see for instance Krivine's book [32], but the proof technique that we shall use is due to [4] and it is different from others in the literature [16,19,31,32]. Its key ingredient is the isolation of a key property of rigid terms (Lemma 2 below).

The Need for Shrinking. As already pointed out at the end of Sect. 6, some terms that diverge with strong evaluation are typable. We have that Ω itself is not typable, but $\lambda y.\Omega$ is typable with $\mathbf{0}$ (via a many rule with 0 premises). It might seem that the problem is being typable with $\mathbf{0}$, but also $x(\lambda y.\Omega)$ is externally divergent and can be typed by assigning $[\mathbf{0} \multimap \mathsf{M}]$ to x (any M works). In this case the problem is that, since $\mathbf{0}$ is on the left of $\multimap$, the argument is meant to be erased, but x cannot actually erase it. This is a problem typical of strong settings, as it occurs also in Strong CbN. The solution is to restrict to type derivations satisfying a predicate that forbids types where $\mathbf{0}$ plays these dangerous tricks; in particular a ground type $\mathsf{G} \neq \mathbf{0}$ is needed. This is unavoidable and standard, see [4,32]. Following [4], the predicate is here called *shrinkingness* because it ensures that the size of type derivations shrinks at each $\to_\times$ step (see Prop. 7 below).

Defining Shrinking. The definition of shrinking forbids the empty multiset $\mathbf{0}$ on the left of some type arrows $\multimap$. We actually need two notions of shrinking types, *left* and *right*. Intuitively, it is because the typing rule λ shifts a type from the left-hand side of a judgment to the left of $\multimap$ on the right-hand side of a judgment. Formally, *left* and *right shrinking* (multi or linear) *types* are defined in Fig. 4 (we omit *shrinking* when referring to left or right types, for brevity), by mutual induction. The key point is that right multi types *cannot be empty* (note $n \geq 1$), thus $\mathbf{0}$ is forbidden on the left of top $\multimap$ for left linear types.

The notions extend to type contexts and to derivations as follows:

- A type context $x_1 : M_1, \ldots, x_n : M_n$ is *left* if each M_i is left;
- A derivation $\Phi \rhd \Gamma \vdash t : M$ is *shrinking* if Γ is left and M is right.

Examples: $[G]$ is both left and right (this fact shall play a role below), while $\mathbf{0}$ is left but not right, and $[\mathbf{0} \multimap [G]]$ is right but not left.

Key Property of Left Shrinking. Shrinkingness is a predicate of derivations depending only on their *final judgment*. For proving properties of shrinking derivations, we have to analyze how shrinking propagates to sub-derivations, to apply the *i.h.* in proofs. The following lemma is specific to *left* shrinkingness, on which the propagation of shrinkingness then builds. It says that for specific terms—typable *rigid* terms—left shrinkingess spreads from the type context to the right-hand multi type in a judgment. It is the key property of the proof technique.

Lemma 2 (Spreading of left shrinkingness on judgments). *Let $\Phi \rhd \Gamma \vdash r : M$ be a derivation and r be a rigid term. If Γ is left then M is left.*

Correctness. Shrinking correctness establishes that all typable terms with a shrinking derivation are externally normalizing. We follow the same pattern as for the open case, but the proof of subject reduction is trickier—this is the delicate point of the proof technique by Accattoli et al. [4]. It crucially uses the key property of left shrinking for rigid terms above (Lemma 2), and it also requires an auxiliary statement with a weaker hypothesis for the induction to go through.

Proposition 7 (Shrinking quantitative subject reduction for $\rightarrow_\times$).

1. Auxiliary statement: *Let Γ be a left context. Suppose that $\Phi \rhd \Gamma \vdash t : M$ and that if t is a answer then M is right. If $t \rightarrow_\times t'$ then there is a derivation $\Phi' \rhd \Gamma \vdash t' : M$ with $|\Phi| > |\Phi'|$.*
2. Actual statement: *Let $\Phi \rhd \Gamma \vdash t : M$ be a shrinking derivation. If $t \rightarrow_\times t'$ then there is a derivation $\Phi' \rhd \Gamma \vdash t' : M$ with $|\Phi| > |\Phi'|$.*

Proof. Note that the auxiliary statement is stronger, because every shrinking derivation (defined as having Γ left and M right) satisfies it: if t is not an answer then M can be whatever, in particular it can be right. For the auxiliary statement, we give two cases, the one motivating the use of the auxiliary statement and one showing the use of the key property for rigid terms. The other cases are in the Appendix of [10]. The proof is by induction on the external context X such that $t = X\langle u \rangle \rightarrow_\times X\langle u' \rangle = t'$ with $u \rightarrow_\circ u'$. The two cases:

- *Rigid context applied to term, i.e.* $X = Rs$. Then, $t = X\langle u \rangle = R\langle u \rangle s \rightarrow_\times R\langle u' \rangle s = X\langle u' \rangle = t'$ with $u \rightarrow_\circ u'$. The derivation Φ has the following shape:

$$\Phi = \frac{\Psi \rhd \Delta \vdash R\langle u\rangle : [\mathsf{N} \multimap \mathsf{M}] \qquad \Theta \rhd \Sigma \vdash s : \mathsf{N}}{\Delta \uplus \Sigma \vdash R\langle u\rangle s : \mathsf{M}} @$$

where $\Gamma = \Delta \uplus \Sigma$ is left by hypothesis, and then so is Δ. By *i.h.* (as $R\langle u\rangle$ is not an answer), there is a derivation $\Psi' \rhd \Delta \vdash R\langle u'\rangle : [\mathsf{N} \multimap \mathsf{M}]$ with $|\Psi'| < |\Psi|$. We can then build the following derivation:

$$\Phi' = \frac{\Psi' \rhd \Delta \vdash R\langle u'\rangle : [\mathsf{N} \multimap \mathsf{M}] \qquad \Theta \rhd \Sigma \vdash s : \mathsf{N}}{\Delta \uplus \Sigma \vdash R\langle u'\rangle s : \mathsf{M}} @$$

where $\Gamma = \Delta \uplus \Sigma$ and $|\Phi'| = |\Psi'| + |\Theta| + 1 < |\Psi| + |\Theta| + 1 = |\Phi|$. Note that in this case we have no hypothesis on N, thus on $[\mathsf{N} \multimap \mathsf{M}]$, which is why we need a weaker statement in order to use the *i.h.*

- *Rigid term applied to external context, i.e.* $X = rX'$. Then, $t = X\langle u\rangle = rX'\langle u\rangle \to_{\times} rX'\langle u'\rangle = X\langle u'\rangle = t'$ with $u \to_{\circ} u'$. The derivation Φ is:

$$\Phi = \frac{\Psi \rhd \Delta \vdash r : [\mathsf{N} \multimap \mathsf{M}] \qquad \Theta \rhd \Sigma \vdash X'\langle u\rangle : \mathsf{N}}{\Delta \uplus \Sigma \vdash rX'\langle u\rangle : \mathsf{M}} @$$

where $\Gamma = \Delta \uplus \Sigma$ is left by hypothesis, and then so are Δ and Σ. According to spreading of left shrinkingness applied to Ψ (Lemma 2, which can be applied because r is a rigid term), $[\mathsf{N} \multimap \mathsf{M}]$ is a left multi type and hence N is a right multi type. Thus, the *i.h.* applied to Θ gives a derivation $\Theta' \rhd \Sigma \vdash X'\langle u'\rangle : \mathsf{N}$ with $|\Theta'| < |\Theta|$. We then build the following derivation:

$$\Phi' = \frac{\Psi \rhd \Delta \vdash r : [\mathsf{N} \multimap \mathsf{M}] \qquad \Theta' \rhd \Sigma \vdash X'\langle u'\rangle : \mathsf{N}}{\Delta \uplus \Sigma \vdash rX'\langle u'\rangle : \mathsf{M}} @$$

where $\Gamma = \Delta \uplus \Sigma$ and $|\Phi'| = |\Psi| + |\Theta'| + 1 < |\Psi| + |\Theta| + 1 = |\Phi|$. $\qquad \square$

Theorem 3 (Shrinking correctness for $\to_{\times}$). *Let* $\Phi \rhd t$ *be a shrinking derivation. Then there is a* $\times$-*normalizing evaluation* $d : t \to_{\times}^{*} f_{\mathsf{s}}$ *with* $|d| \leq |\Phi|$.

Shrinking correctness for $\to_{\times}$ shows that the term $t = (\lambda x.\mathsf{I})(y(\lambda z.\Omega))$ diverging for $\to_{\times}$ but normalizing for the strong fireball calculus is not typable, otherwise it would $\to_{\times}$-terminate. That is, it shows that t is semantically diverging.

Completeness. Shrinking completeness is proven as in the open case, using a lemma about the shrinking typability of strong fireballs. Note that the lemma now has an existential quantification on the type M of strong fireballs, while in the open case the type was simply $\mathbf{0}$; here $\mathbf{0}$ would not work, because it is not right. Note also the part about inert terms, stating that M is *left*: it is not a mistake, it can be seen as an instance of the key properties of rigid terms (Lemma 2, inert terms are rigid), and it gives shrinking derivations when M is instantiated with, say, $[\mathsf{G}]$, which is both left an right.

Lemma 3 (Shrinking typability of normal forms).

1. Inert: *for every strong inert term* i_{s} *and left multi type* M, *there exists a left type context* Γ *and a derivation* $\Phi \rhd \Gamma \vdash i_{\mathsf{s}} : \mathsf{M}$.
2. Fireball: *for every strong fireball* f_{s} *there is a shrinking derivation* $\Phi \rhd f_{\mathsf{s}}$.

Theorem 4 (Shrinking completeness for $\to_{\times}$). *Let* $d : t \to_{\times}^{*} f_{\mathsf{s}}$ *be a* $\times$-*normalizing evaluation. Then there is a shrinking derivation* $\Phi \rhd t$.

Untyped Normalization Theorem. By exploiting an elegant proof technique used by de Carvalho et al. [20] and Mazza et al. [35], we obtain an *untyped normalization* theorem for the external strategy of the VSC, as a corollary of our study of multi types. The key points are subject expansion (Prop. 5.2) for the *whole* reduction $\rightarrow_{\mathsf{vsc}}$, instead that just for the external strategy, and the fact that shrinkingness is a predicate of derivations depending only on their conclusion.

Theorem 5 (Untyped normalization for $\rightarrow_{\mathsf{x}}$). *If there is a* vsc-*normalizing evaluation* $d\colon t \rightarrow^{*}_{\mathsf{vsc}} f_{\mathsf{s}}$, *then* $t \rightarrow^{*}_{\mathsf{x}} f_{\mathsf{s}}$.

Proof. Shrinking typability of normal forms (Lemma 3) gives a shrinking derivation $\varPhi \triangleright \varGamma \vdash f_{\mathsf{s}}\colon \mathsf{M}$. Subject expansion (Prop. 5.2) iterated along $t \rightarrow^{*}_{\mathsf{vsc}} f_{\mathsf{s}}$ gives a shrinking derivation $\varPsi \triangleright \varGamma \vdash t\colon \mathsf{M}$. By shrinking correctness (Thm. 3), $t \rightarrow^{*}_{\mathsf{x}} f'_{\mathsf{s}}$ for a strong fireball f'_{s}. By confluence of the VSC (Prop. 3.1), $f_{\mathsf{s}} = f'_{\mathsf{s}}$. $\square$

Relational Semantics. Multi types induce a denotational model, the *relational semantics*, interpreting a term as the set of its derivable judgments [6,8,18,19, 25,28]. Here we focus on the semantics induced by shrinking derivations. Let t be a term and let $\vec{x} = (x_1, \ldots, x_n)$ be a list of pairwise distinct variables with $n \geq 0$ and $\mathsf{fv}(t) \subseteq \{x_1, \ldots, x_n\}$: the *shrinking semantics* $\llbracket t \rrbracket_{\vec{x}}$ of t for $\vec{x}$ is defined by $\llbracket t \rrbracket_{\vec{x}} := \{((\mathsf{N}_1, \ldots, \mathsf{N}_n), \mathsf{M}) \mid \exists \text{ shrinking } \varPhi \triangleright x_1\colon\mathsf{N}_1, \ldots, x_n\colon\mathsf{N}_n \vdash t\colon\mathsf{M}\}$.

Subject reduction and expansion (Proposition 5) guarantee that $\llbracket t \rrbracket_{\vec{x}}$ is *sound* for $\rightarrow_{\mathsf{vsc}}$: if $t \rightarrow_{\mathsf{vsc}} u$ then $\llbracket t \rrbracket_{\vec{x}} = \llbracket u \rrbracket_{\vec{x}}$. Shrinking correctness (Theorem 3) and completeness (Theorem 4), along with untyped normalization (Theorem 5), guarantee *adequacy* for this semantics, *i.e.*, they give a semantic characterization of normalization in Strong VSC: t is weakly vsc-normalizing if and only if $\llbracket t \rrbracket_{\vec{x}} \neq \emptyset$.

9   Conclusions

This paper studies call-by-value strong evaluation defined as the external strategy $\rightarrow_{\mathsf{x}}$ of the value substitution calculus (VSC). Such a strategy is analyzed using the semantical tool of Ehrhard's multi types, declined in their shrinking variant as it is standard for studying strong evaluation. The main contributions are that $\rightarrow_{\mathsf{x}}$-normalizing terms are exactly those typable with shrinking call-by-value multi types, plus an untyped normalization theorem for $\rightarrow_{\mathsf{x}}$ in the strong VSC. These results mimic faithfully similar results for strong call-by-name.

These contributions are developed to validate the external strategy as the good notion of termination for strong call-by-value, in contrast to the other *non-equivalent* proposal in the literature given by the strong fireball calculus, which we show to terminate on some terms on which the external strategy diverges.

We conjecture that all x-normalizing terms are also normalizing in the strong fireball calculus, but a proof is likely to be very technical.

References

1. Accattoli, B.: Proof nets and the call-by-value λ-calculus. Theor. Comput. Sci. **606**, 2–24 (2015). https://doi.org/10.1016/j.tcs.2015.08.006
2. Accattoli, B., Condoluci, A., Sacerdoti Coen, C.: Strong call-by-value is reasonable, implosively. In: LICS 2021. IEEE (2021). https://doi.org/10.1109/LICS52264.2021.9470630
3. Accattoli, B., Faggian, C., Lancelot, A.: Normal form bisimulations by value. CoRR abs/2303.08161 (2023). https://doi.org/10.48550/arXiv.2303.08161
4. Accattoli, B., Graham-Lengrand, S., Kesner, D.: Tight typings and split bounds. PACMPL **2**(ICFP), 94:1–94:30 (2018). https://doi.org/10.1145/3236789
5. Accattoli, B., Guerrieri, G.: Open call-by-value. In: Igarashi, A. (ed.) APLAS 2016. LNCS, vol. 10017, pp. 206–226. Springer, Cham (2016). https://doi.org/10.1007/978-3-319-47958-3_12
6. Accattoli, B., Guerrieri, G.: Types of fireballs. In: Ryu, S. (ed.) APLAS 2018. LNCS, vol. 11275, pp. 45–66. Springer, Cham (2018). https://doi.org/10.1007/978-3-030-02768-1_3
7. Accattoli, B., Guerrieri, G.: Abstract machines for open call-by-value. Sci. Comput. Program. **184** (2019). https://doi.org/10.1016/j.scico.2019.03.002
8. Accattoli, B., Guerrieri, G.: The theory of call-by-value solvability. Proc. ACM Program. Lang. **6**(ICFP), 855–885 (2022). https://doi.org/10.1145/3547652
9. Accattoli, B., Guerrieri, G., Leberle, M.: Semantic bounds and strong call-by-value normalization. CoRR abs/2104.13979 (2021). https://arxiv.org/abs/2104.13979
10. Accattoli, B., Guerrieri, G., Leberle, M.: Strong call-by-value and multi types (long version). CoRR abs/2309.12261 (2023). https://arxiv.org/abs/2309.12261
11. Accattoli, B., Paolini, L.: Call-by-value solvability, revisited. In: Schrijvers, T., Thiemann, P. (eds.) FLOPS 2012. LNCS, vol. 7294, pp. 4–16. Springer, Heidelberg (2012). https://doi.org/10.1007/978-3-642-29822-6_4
12. Accattoli, B., Sacerdoti Coen, C.: On the relative usefulness of fireballs. In: LICS 2015. IEEE (2015). https://doi.org/10.1109/LICS.2015.23
13. Accattoli, B., Sacerdoti Coen, C.: On the value of variables. Inf. Comput. **255**, 224–242 (2017). https://doi.org/10.1016/j.ic.2017.01.003
14. Biernacka, M., Biernacki, D., Charatonik, W., Drab, T.: An abstract machine for strong call by value. In: APLAS 2020 (2020). https://doi.org/10.1007/978-3-030-64437-6_8
15. Biernacka, M., Charatonik, W., Drab, T.: A derived reasonable abstract machine for strong call by value. In: PPDP 2021. ACM (2021). https://doi.org/10.1145/3479394.3479401
16. Bucciarelli, A., Kesner, D., Ventura, D.: Non-idempotent intersection types for the lambda-calculus. Log. J. IGPL (2017). https://doi.org/10.1093/jigpal/jzx018
17. Carraro, A., Guerrieri, G.: A semantical and operational account of call-by-value solvability. In: Muscholl, A. (ed.) FoSSaCS 2014. LNCS, vol. 8412, pp. 103–118. Springer, Heidelberg (2014). https://doi.org/10.1007/978-3-642-54830-7_7
18. de Carvalho, D.: Sémantiques de la logique linéaire et temps de calcul. Université Aix-Marseille II, Thèse de doctorat (2007)
19. de Carvalho, D.: Execution time of λ-terms via denotational semantics and intersection types. Math. Str. Comput. Sci. **28**(7), 1169–1203 (2018). https://doi.org/10.1017/S0960129516000396
20. de Carvalho, D., Pagani, M., Tortora de Falco, L.: A semantic measure of the execution time in linear logic. Theor. Comput. Sci. **412**(20), 1884–1902 (2011). https://doi.org/10.1016/j.tcs.2010.12.017

21. Curien, P., Herbelin, H.: The duality of computation. In: ICFP 2000 (2000). https://doi.org/10.1145/351240.351262
22. Dal Lago, U., Martini, S.: The weak lambda calculus as a reasonable machine. Theor. Comput. Sci. **398** (2008). https://doi.org/10.1016/j.tcs.2008.01.044
23. Díaz-Caro, A., Manzonetto, G., Pagani, M.: Call-by-value non-determinism in a linear logic type discipline. In: Artemov, S., Nerode, A. (eds.) LFCS 2013. LNCS, vol. 7734, pp. 164–178. Springer, Heidelberg (2013). https://doi.org/10.1007/978-3-642-35722-0_12
24. Dyckhoff, R., Lengrand, S.: Call-by-Value lambda-calculus and LJQ. J. Log. Comput. **17**(6), 1109–1134 (2007). https://doi.org/10.1093/logcom/exm037
25. Ehrhard, T.: Collapsing non-idempotent intersection types. In: CSL 2012, pp. 259–273. Schloss Dagstuhl (2012). https://doi.org/10.4230/LIPIcs.CSL.2012.259
26. Girard, J.Y.: Linear Logic. Theore. Comput. Sci. **50**, 1–102 (1987). https://doi.org/10.1016/0304-3975(87)90045-4
27. Grégoire, B., Leroy, X.: A compiled implementation of strong reduction. In: ICFP 2002, pp. 235–246. ACM (2002). https://doi.org/10.1145/581478.581501
28. Guerrieri, G.: Towards a semantic measure of the execution time in call-by-value λ-calculus. In: DCM/ITRS 2018 (2019). https://doi.org/10.4204/EPTCS.293.5
29. Guerrieri, G., Paolini, L., Ronchi Della Rocca, S.: Standardization and conservativity of a refined call-by-value lambda-calculus. Log. Methods Comput. Sci. **13**(4) (2017). https://doi.org/10.23638/LMCS-13(4:29)2017
30. Herbelin, H., Zimmermann, S.: An operational account of call-by-value minimal and classical λ-calculus in "Natural Deduction" form. In: Curien, P.-L. (ed.) TLCA 2009. LNCS, vol. 5608, pp. 142–156. Springer, Heidelberg (2009). https://doi.org/10.1007/978-3-642-02273-9_12
31. Kesner, D., Ventura, D.: Quantitative types for the linear substitution calculus. In: Diaz, J., Lanese, I., Sangiorgi, D. (eds.) TCS 2014. LNCS, vol. 8705, pp. 296–310. Springer, Heidelberg (2014). https://doi.org/10.1007/978-3-662-44602-7_23
32. Krivine, J.: Lambda-Calculus, Types and Models. Ellis Horwood, New York (1993)
33. Levy, P.B., Power, J., Thielecke, H.: Modelling environments in call-by-value programming languages. Inf. Comput. **185**(2), 182–210 (2003). https://doi.org/10.1016/S0890-5401(03)00088-9
34. Maraist, J., Odersky, M., Turner, D.N., Wadler, P.: Call-by-name, call-by-value, call-by-need and the linear λ-calculus. Theor. Comput. Sci. **228**(1–2), 175–210 (1999). https://doi.org/10.1016/S0304-3975(98)00358-2
35. Mazza, D., Pellissier, L., Vial, P.: Polyadic approximations, fibrations and intersection types. Proc. ACM Program. Lang. **2**(POPL), 6:1–6:28 (2018). https://doi.org/10.1145/3158094
36. Moggi, E.: Computational λ-Calculus and Monads. LFCS report ECS-LFCS-88-66, University of Edinburgh (1988). http://www.lfcs.inf.ed.ac.uk/reports/88/ECS-LFCS-88-66/ECS-LFCS-88-66.pdf
37. Moggi, E.: Computational λ-calculus and monads. In: LICS 1989. IEEE Computer Society (1989). https://doi.org/10.1109/LICS.1989.39155
38. Paolini, L.: Call-by-value separability and computability. In: ICTCS 2001 (2001). https://doi.org/10.1007/3-540-45446-2_5
39. Paolini, L., Ronchi Della Rocca, S.: Call-by-value solvability. RAIRO Theor. Inf. Appl. **33**(6), 507–534 (1999). https://doi.org/10.1051/ita:1999130
40. Plotkin, G.D.: Call-by-name, call-by-value and the lambda-calculus. Theore. Comput. Sci. (1975). https://doi.org/10.1016/0304-3975(75)90017-1

41. Ronchi Della Rocca, S., Paolini, L.: The parametric λ-calculus - a metamodel for computation. In: Texts in Theoretical Computer Science. An EATCS Series. Springer, Heidelberg (2004). https://doi.org/10.1007/978-3-662-10394-4
42. Sabry, A., Felleisen, M.: Reasoning about programs in continuation-passing style. LISP Symb. Comput. **6**(3–4), 289–360 (1993)
43. Sabry, A., Wadler, P.: A reflection on call-by-value. ACM Trans. Program. Lang. Syst. **19**(6), 916–941 (1997). https://doi.org/10.1145/267959.269968
44. Terese: Term Rewriting Systems. Cambridge Tracts in Theoretical Computer Science, vol. 55. Cambridge University Press (2003)

Algorithms for Checking Intersection Non-emptiness of Regular Expressions

Weihao Su[1,2], Rongchen Li[1,2], Chengyao Peng[1,2], and Haiming Chen[1(✉)]

[1] State Key Laboratory of Computer Science, Institute of Software, Chinese Academy of Sciences, Beijing 100190, China
{suwh,lirc,pengcy,chm}@ios.ac.cn
[2] University of Chinese Academy of Sciences, Beijing 101400, China

Abstract. The intersection non-emptiness problem of regular languages is one of the most classical and fundamental decision problems in formal language theory, which plays an important role in many areas. Because of its wide applications, the efficiency of the algorithms becomes particularly crucial. In practice, it is quite common that automata have large numbers of states, therefore the explicit construction of automata may incur significant costs in terms of both time and space, significantly impacting the performance of the related programs. To overcome this challenge, in this paper, we present four efficient algorithms for checking the intersection of regular expressions without the need for automata construction. Our algorithms employ lazy evaluation strategies to simulate intersection non-emptiness checking on automata to avoid constructing automata. They also use automata with fewer states to reduce the state complexity. We conducted experiments and compared our results with seven state-of-the-art tools. The results show significant advantages of our algorithms over existing methods in terms of efficiency and accuracy.

Keywords: Regular Expressions · Intersection Non-emptiness Problem · Online Algorithms

1 Introduction

The intersection non-emptiness problem of regular languages is one of the most classical and fundamental decision problems in formal language theory. The problem has a wide range of applications and has been extensively studied by researchers. Given a set of m regular expressions $E_1, \ldots, E_m$ defined over the alphabet Σ, the problem is to determine whether $\bigcap_{i=1}^{m} L(E_i) \neq \varnothing$, where $\varnothing$ denotes the empty set. In other words, it decides whether there exists a common word in all languages. The algorithms for solving this problem play an important role in various fields such as SMT (Satisfiability Modulo Theories) solvers, model checking tools, artificial intelligence [35], data privacy [24], and ReDoS (Regular expression Denial of Service) vulnerability detection [32]. For instance, SMT string solvers like Z3seq [39], CVC4 [33], and OSTRICH [21] use these

E. Ábrahám et al. (Eds.): ICTAC 2023, LNCS 14446, pp. 216–235, 2023.
https://doi.org/10.1007/978-3-031-47963-2_14

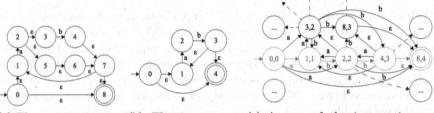

(a) Thompson automa- (b) Thompson au- (c) A part of the intersection au-
ton of E_1 tomaton of E_2 tomaton for illustrating an accepting path from the starting state (0,0)
to the final state (8,4) in the intersection automaton, which indicates
$\bigcap_{i=1}^{2} L(E_i) \neq \varnothing$

* Thompson's construction [34] is one of the most frequently used methods for constructing
automata from regular expressions, for example, [4, 21, 36].

Fig. 1. The classical process for determining $\bigcap_{i=1}^{2} L(E_i) \neq \varnothing$ for $E_1 = (a(b + \epsilon))^*$ and
$E_2 = (ab)^*$.

algorithms to solve regular membership queries. Similarly, model checking tools
like Mona [25] use these algorithms to verify hardware and software systems.

The classical process of determining the intersection non-emptiness of two
regular expressions is illustrated in Fig. 1, which can be solved in polynomial time [27]. The key steps include (1) compiling the expressions into finite
automata, (2) constructing the intersection automaton from the compiled
automata by the cross product algorithm [38], and (3) performing non-emptiness
testing on the intersection automaton. For this example, the path colored in
green in Fig. 1(c) shows an accepting path in the intersection automaton, indicating that the intersection exists between E_1 and E_2, so the process returns
true. The above process can be naturally extended to determine the intersection
non-emptiness of multiple regular expressions, still in polynomial time [37, 42].
When taking the number k of the regular expressions and the maximum number
of states n in the automata from those expressions as parameters, this problem is fixed-parameter tractable [40]. For an unbounded number of inputs, this
problem is PSPACE-complete [29].

Computing the intersection non-emptiness of regular expressions is a common task in various applications, making efficient algorithms particularly important. The aforementioned classical process is based on automata. However, the
above algorithm may incur significant costs in terms of both time and space during automata construction[1], since in practice it is quite common for automata
to have large numbers of states. In particular, the states of the intersection
automaton grow rapidly: for two automata with Q_1 and Q_2 states respectively,
the intersection automaton will have $Q_1 * Q_2$ states. Indeed in our experiments
(see Sect. 5), the automata-based algorithms (i.e. Z3-Trau [1], OSTRICH [21]

---

[1] Consisting of both compiling regular expressions into finite automata and constructing the intersection automaton.

and Brics library [36]) are not sufficiently capable to solve the problem within 20 s. Our key observation is that explicit construction of automata for determining the intersection non-emptiness of regular expressions can significantly impact the performance of related programs, even acting as a bottleneck. For instance, we conducted an experiment with ReDoSHunter [32], which uses the Brics automaton library [36] for automata construction, on regular expressions from the corpus library [15], and the result reveals that intersection checking based on automaton construction occupies 59.26% of the runtime and causes the maximum memory usage of the entire program. In addition, the program often crashes due to the timeout of the intersection checking. This shows the necessity of not constructing the whole automaton explicitly when optimizing program performance.

To address this issue, we use lazy evaluation strategies to simulate intersection non-emptiness checking on automata to avoid constructing automata. It is well known that looking for a reason to fail or finding a reachable path is easy to spot. Also, the number of states in an automaton has a direct impact on the size of the solution space of the intersection non-emptiness problem [26,45]. Thus our algorithms simulate finite automata with fewer states [8,18] to reduce the state complexity of the intersection automata.

Specifically, in this paper, we present four intersection non-emptiness detection algorithms. The first type utilizes the positions of characters in the expressions. In detail, the first algorithm is based on the position sets [22], which can be used to compute transition tables of the position automata [46], resulting in the `Pos_intersect` algorithm. Building on `Pos_intersect`, we further utilize the equivalence relation $\equiv_f$ (detailed in Sect. 3) to obtain the `Follow_intersect` algorithm, which simulates intersection non-emptiness search on the follow automata [28], effectively reducing the size of the solution space. The second type of algorithms employ derivatives: Based on c-continuation, we propose the `CCon_intersect` algorithm for simulating intersection non-emptiness search on the $M_{ccon}(E)/_{=_c}$ automaton. The time and space complexity of c-continuation is lower than partial derivative [13], but the solution space of the algorithm is larger than that of the equation automaton [2]. To reduce the solution space, we develop another algorithm, `Equa_intersect`, based on the equivalence relation $\equiv_c$ (see Sect. 4), which effectively simulates the intersection non-emptiness search on the equation automata.

To validate the efficiency and effectiveness of our algorithms, we compared them to seven state-of-the-art tools which takes regular expressions as input. Our experiments demonstrate that our four algorithms have significant advantages over existing methods in solving the intersection non-emptiness problem of regular expressions. In particular, our approach outperforms the competition in terms of speed and accuracy, highlighting the effectiveness of our methodology. In addition, we have observed the potential for the extensibility of these algorithms (as detailed in Sect. 7): such as the output of a witness for intersection non-emptiness, the addition of extended features in real-world regular expressions, and the use of heuristic search or conflict-driven strategies to optimize these algorithms.

2   Preliminaries

In this section, we briefly recall the necessary definitions in regular languages and automata theory, for further details, we suggest referring to [44].

2.1   Regular Expressions and Deterministic Regular Expressions

Let Σ be an alphabet and Σ^* the set of all possible words over Σ; $|\Sigma|$ denotes the size of Σ, ε denotes the empty word. A *language* over Σ is a subset of Σ^*. A *regular expression* over Σ is either $\varnothing$, ε or $a \in \Sigma$, or is the union $E_1 + E_2$, the concatenation $E_1 E_2$, or the Kleene star E_1^* for regular expressions E_1 and E_2. $\varnothing$ denotes the empty set. The regular language defined by E is denoted by $L(E)$. The size of a regular expression E is denoted by $|E|$ and represents the number of symbols and operators (excluding parentheses) in E when written in postfix. The alphabetic width of E, denoted by $\|E\|$, is the number of symbols occurring in E. Σ_E denotes the symbols occurring in E, i.e., the minimal alphabet of E.

We define $\mathsf{nullable}(E) = true$ if $\varepsilon \in L(E)$, and $false$ otherwise. We mark symbols in E with numerical subscripts to obtain a linearized regular expression $E^{\#}$ over $\Sigma^{\#}$ such that all marked symbols in $E^{\#}$ occur no more than once. For example, let $E = (a + b)(a^* + ba^* + b^*)$, a linearized regular expression is $E^{\#} = (a_1 + b_2)(a_3^* + b_4 a_5^* + b_6^*)$. The reverse of marking, i.e., dropping off the subscripts, is denoted by $E^{\natural}$, then we have $(E^{\#})^{\natural} = E$. We extend the notations for sets of symbols, words and automata in an obvious way.

Deterministic (one-unambiguous) regular expressions were first proposed and formalized by Brüggemann-Klein and Wood [7].

Definition 1. *A regular expression E is deterministic if and only if for all words $uxv, uyw \in L(E^{\#})$ s.t. $|x| = |y| = 1$, if $x \neq y$ then $x^{\natural} \neq y^{\natural}$. A regular language is deterministic if it is denoted by some deterministic expression.*

For example, $b^* a (b^* a)^*$ is deterministic, while its semantically equivalent regular expression $(a + b)^* a$ is not deterministic. Deterministic regular languages are a proper subclass of the regular languages [7].

2.2   Position Automaton and Star Normal Form

A deterministic finite automaton (DFA) is a quintuple $M = (Q, \Sigma, \delta, s, F)$, where Q is the finite set of states, Σ is the alphabet, $\delta \subseteq Q \times \Sigma \to Q$ is the state transition function, $s \in Q$ is the starting (or initial) state, and $F \subseteq Q$ is the set of final states. A non-deterministic automaton (NFA) is a quintuple $M = (Q, \Sigma, \delta, s, F)$ where Q, Σ, s, and F are defined in exactly the same way as a DFA, except that $\delta \subseteq Q \times \Sigma \to 2^Q$ is the state transition function where 2^Q denotes the power set of Q. $L(M)$ denotes the language accepted by the automaton M.

Let $\equiv \subseteq Q \times Q$ be an equivalence relation. For $q \in Q$, $[q]_{\equiv}$ denotes the equivalence class of q w.r.t. $\equiv$ and, for $S \subseteq Q$, $S/_{\equiv}$ denotes the quotient set $S/_{\equiv} = \{[q]_{\equiv} \mid q \in S\}$. We say that $\equiv$ is right invariant w.r.t. M if and only if:

1. $\equiv \subseteq (Q - F)^2 \cup F^2$,
2. $\forall p, q \in Q, a \in A$, if $p \equiv q$, then $\delta(p,a)/_{\equiv} = \delta(q,a)/_{\equiv}$.

If $\equiv$ is right invariant, then the *quotient automaton* $M/_{\equiv}$ is constructed as $M/_{\equiv} = (Q/_{\equiv}, \Sigma, \delta_{\equiv}, [s_0]_{\equiv}, F/_{\equiv})$, where $\delta_{\equiv} = \{([p]_{\equiv}, a, [q]_{\equiv}) \mid (p,a,q) \in \delta\}$; Notice that $L(M/_{\equiv}) = L(M)$. Given two automata $M_1 = (Q_1, \Sigma, \delta_1, s_1, F_1)$ and $M_2 = (Q_2, \Sigma, \delta_2, s_2, F_2)$, denote $M_1 \simeq M_2$ if M_1 and M_2 are isomorphic, i.e. (1). $|Q_1| = |Q_2|$; (2). there exists a bijective function $f : Q_1 \to Q_2$, such that if there exists a transition $q = \delta_1(p,a)$ in M_1, there exists a transition $f(q) = \delta_2(f(p),a)$ in M_2; and (3). $q \in F_1 \Leftrightarrow f(q) \in F_2$.

For a regular expression E over Σ and a symbol $a \in \Sigma$, we define the following sets:

$$\mathsf{first}(E) = \{b \mid bw \in L(E), b \in \Sigma, w \in \Sigma^*\} \tag{1}$$

$$\mathsf{last}(E) = \{b \mid wb \in L(E), b \in \Sigma, w \in \Sigma^*\} \tag{2}$$

$$\mathsf{follow}(E, a) = \{b \mid uabv \in L(E), u, v \in \Sigma^*, b \in \Sigma\} \tag{3}$$

Independently introduced by Glushkov [22] and McNaughton and Yamada [34], the position automaton is considered as the natural presentation of a regular expression [3]. Until now, the deterministic position automaton still serves as the major matching model of Hyperscan [41] and BVA-Scan [30] with extensions. Here we follow [6] and define "the Glushkov NFA" as the position automaton.

Definition 2. *The position automaton $M_{pos}(E)$ of a regular expression E is defined by a 5-tuple $(Q_{pos}, \Sigma, \delta_{pos}, s_{pos}, F_{pos})$ where*
$Q_{pos} = \Sigma^\# \cup \{s_{pos}\}$,
$s_{pos} = 0$,
$\delta_{pos}(s_{pos}, a) = \{x \mid x \in \mathsf{first}(E^\#), x^\natural = a\}$, *for $a \in \Sigma$,*
$\delta_{pos}(x, a) = \{y \mid y \in \mathsf{follow}(E^\#, x), y^\natural = a\}$, *for $x \in \Sigma^\#$ and $a \in \Sigma$,*
$F_{pos} = \begin{cases} last(E^\#) \cup \{s_{pos}\}, & if \ \mathsf{nullable}(E) = true, \\ last(E^\#), & otherwise. \end{cases}$

We assume that 0 is a symbol that is not in $\Sigma_{E\#}$. From the definition we have $\mathsf{follow}(E^\#, 0) = \mathsf{first}(E^\#)$. We also define $\mathsf{last}_0(E^\#)$, which is $\mathsf{last}(E^\#)$ if $\mathsf{nullable}(E) = false$, and $\mathsf{last}(E^\#) \cup \{0\}$ otherwise. We denote $\mathsf{pos}_0(E) = \Sigma^\# \cup \{0\}$. The construction of the position automaton defined above is improved to quadratic time in the size of the expression [6,14,46]. Among these works, Brüggemann-Klein [6] gave a linear-time algorithm to transform an arbitrary regular expression E into star normal form.

Definition 3. *A regular expression E is in star normal form $E^\bullet$, if for each starred subexpression H^* of E, the following conditions hold:*
$\mathsf{follow}(H^\#, a) \cap \mathsf{first}(H^\#) = \varnothing$, *for $a \in \mathsf{last}(H^\#)$,*
$\mathsf{nullable}(H) = false$.

For example, given $E = (a^*b^*)^*$, E can be transformed into the semantically equivalent star normal form $E^\bullet = (a + b)^*$.

Furthermore, from [6] we have:

Proposition 1. *For a deterministic regular expression E, the position automaton $M_{pos}(E)$ can be computed in linear time and $M_{pos}(E)$ is deterministic.*

2.3 Derivatives of Regular Expressions

J. Brzozowski [10] introduced the notion of derivatives of regular expressions. The number of Brzozowski's (total) derivatives may not be finite. When considering similarity of associativity, commutativity and idempotence of $+$, the number of Brzozowski's derivatives can still be exponential in the worst case upon arbitrary regular expressions, e.g. on $(a + b)^* a(a + b)^k$, where k is a positive integer. But for deterministic regular languages, the number of Brzozowski's derivatives has a linear upper bound on the size of the regular expressions [16].

Antimirov [2] generalized Brzozowski's results and introduced the partial derivatives to construct an NFA - the partial derivative automaton, or the equation automaton.

Definition 4. *Given a regular expression E and a symbol a, the partial derivative w.r.t. a, denoted by $\partial_a(E)$, is defined inductively as follows:*

$$\partial_a(\varnothing) \quad = \quad \partial_a(\varepsilon) = \varnothing, \tag{1}$$

$$\partial_a(b) \quad = \quad \begin{cases} \varepsilon, & if\ b = a, \\ \varnothing, & otherwise, \end{cases} \tag{2}$$

$$\partial_a(F + G) \quad = \quad \partial_a(F) \cup \partial_a(G), \tag{3}$$

$$\partial_a(FG) \quad = \quad \begin{cases} \partial_a(F)G, & if\ \mathsf{nullable}(F) = false, \\ \partial_a(F)G \cup \partial_a(G), & otherwise, \end{cases} \tag{4}$$

$$\partial_a(F^*) \quad = \quad \partial_a(F)F^*. \tag{5}$$

The partial derivative w.r.t. a word is computed by: $\partial_\varepsilon(E) = \{E\}$, $\partial_{wa}(E) = \bigcup_{p \in \partial_w(E)} \partial_a(p)$. Denote $PD(E)$ as $\bigcup_{w \in \Sigma^*} \partial_w(E)$ and we have the definition of the equation automaton as follows:

Definition 5. *The equation automaton $M_e(E)$ of a regular expression E is defined by a 5-tuple $(Q_e, \Sigma, \delta_e, s_e, F_e)$, where*
$Q_e = PD(E)$,
$\delta_e(q, a) = \partial_a(q)$, *for $q \in Q_e$ and $a \in \Sigma$,*
$s_e = E$,
$F_e = \{q \in PD(E) \mid \varepsilon \in L(q)\}$.

It was proved in [2] that the size of $PD(E)$ is less than or equal to $\|E\| + 1$. It is known that the equation automaton $M_e(E)$ is isomorphic to a quotient of the position automaton $M_{pos}(E)$ [13, 20, 28].

3   Position-Based Algorithms

In [9], the authors proposed novel position and c-continuation constructions of regular expressions extended with intersection operators. In [19], the authors proposed an M_{E_1}-directed search algorithm on position automata that avoids the explicit construction of complement automata to check inclusion between deterministic regular expressions. These inspired us to develop intersection non-emptiness checking algorithms based on the first, follow, and last sets defined in Sect. 2 without explicit construction of automata. We first propose an algorithm based on simulating the construction of position automata, and further optimize it with another type of automata, the follow automata [28].

Algorithm 1: Pos_intersect

Input: two regular expressions E_1 and E_2.
Output: *true* if $L(E_1) \cap L(E_2) \neq \varnothing$ or *false* otherwise.

1   Pos_intersect :: (Expression E_1, Expression E_2) → Boolean
2   begin
3     $E_1^\bullet \leftarrow snf(E_1)$; $E_2^\bullet \leftarrow snf(E_2)$;
4     $E_1^\# \leftarrow linearize(E_1^\bullet)$; $E_2^\# \leftarrow linearize(E_2^\bullet)$;
5   if nullable($E_1^\#$) = *true* $\wedge$ nullable($E_2^\#$) = *true* then
6   return *true*;
7   else
8   if last($E_1^\natural$) $\cap$ last($E_2^\natural$) = $\varnothing$ then
9   return *false*;
10   else
11   return Pos_recur(first($E_1^\#$), first($E_2^\#$), $\{(s_{pos_1}, s_{pos_2})\}$);

12 Pos_recur :: (Set v_1, Set v_2, Set Q) → Boolean
13 begin
14   if $v_1^\natural \cap v_2^\natural = \varnothing$ then
15   return *false*;
16   forall the $p_1 \in v_1 \wedge p_2 \in v_2 \wedge p_1^\natural = p_2^\natural$ do
17   if $p_1 \in$ last($E_1^\#$) $\wedge$ $p_2 \in$ last($E_2^\#$) then
18   return *true*;
19   if $(p_1, p_2) \notin Q$ then
20   return Pos_recur(follow($E_1^\#, p_1$), follow($E_2^\#, p_2$), $Q \cup \{(p_1, p_2)\}$);
21   else
22   return *false*;

The algorithm Pos_intersect is listed in Algorithm 1, which simulates intersection non-emptiness checking on the position automata. The algorithm first turns regular expressions into star normal form and linearizes them. Then in line 5 and line 8, it checks the nullability and the intersection non-emptiness of their last sets as heuristics to bail out the algorithm earlier, i.e. if both expressions are nullable, then ε is in the intersection, and if all of the last characters between both languages are disjointed, then from Definition 2 we know the final state sets of the position automata of the expressions are disjoint, so the intersection is empty. Next in line 11, it starts the recursive searching procedure with the first sets and the tuple of both the starting states as initial inputs. In the recursive function (from line 12 to line 23), the set v_1 and v_2 are position sets which implies the transition of the position automata and Q is introduced to store the position tuples visited, i.e. states of the intersection of the position automata. The function first performs an intersection non-emptiness check on the symbols of input sets, thus deciding the next positions to search, effectively cumulating transitions that have the same symbols from both the current states in the position automata. For every tuple of positions (p_1, p_2) from v_1 and v_2 that represent the same symbol (i.e., $p_1^\natural = p_2^\natural$), it checks if both of them are in the *last* sets in each expression respectively. If so it returns true. Otherwise, if the position tuple has been reached before, it returns false, otherwise, it memorizes the tuple into the set Q and continues the search with the follow sets of positions, simulating a transition from this state to a next state in both position automata.

Theorem 1. *Given two regular expressions E_1 and E_2,* Pos_intersect *returns true if and only if $L(E_1) \cap L(E_2) \neq \varnothing$.*[2]

Next, we show how the follow automaton [28] can be integrated into Algorithm 1 as an optimization. Ilie and Yu proposed a new quadratic algorithm to construct ε-free NFAs from regular expressions named follow automaton, denoted as $M_f(E)$. The authors proposed a novel constructive method based on removal of ε transitions from a small ε-automaton similar to Thompson's automaton [34]. We refer to [28] for details of the construction.

Definition 6. *The follow automaton $M_f(E)$ of a regular expression E is defined by a 5-tuple $(Q_f, \Sigma, \delta_f, s_f, F_f)$ where*[3]
$Q_f = \{(\mathsf{follow}(E^\#, x), x \in \mathsf{last}_0(E^\#))\}$, *for* $x \in \mathsf{pos}_0(E)$,
$\delta_f(x, a) = \{(\mathsf{follow}(E^\#, y), y \in \mathsf{last}_0(E^\#)) \mid y \in \mathsf{follow}(E^\#, x), y^\natural = a\}$, *for* $x \in \mathsf{pos}_0(E)$ *and* $a \in \Sigma$,
$s_f = (\mathsf{first}(E^\#), 0 \in \mathsf{last}_0(E^\#))$,
$F_f = \{(\mathsf{follow}(E^\#, x), true) \mid x \in \mathsf{last}_0(E^\#)\}$.

We define the right invariant equivalence relation $\equiv_f \subseteq Q_{pos}^2$ [28]:

Definition 7. *Given two states a_1 and a_2 in Q_{pos}, we have:*

$$a_1 \equiv_f a_2 \iff \begin{cases} a_1 \in \mathsf{last}_0(E^\#) \Leftrightarrow a_2 \in \mathsf{last}_0(E^\#), \\ \mathsf{follow}(E^\#, a_1) = \mathsf{follow}(E^\#, a_2). \end{cases} \tag{1}$$

Proposition 2. *(See [28]).* $M_f(E) \simeq M_{pos}(E)/_{\equiv_f}$.

Since the follow automaton is a quotient of its position automaton, then simulating the follow automaton instead of the position automaton in Algorithm 1 can reduce the size of the solution space. This motivated us to

---

[2] Due to space limitation, the details of proofs are shown in our complete version in https://github.com/SuperMaxine/ICTAC2023.
[3] We refer readers to [8] for a similar definition.

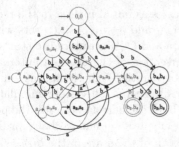
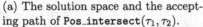

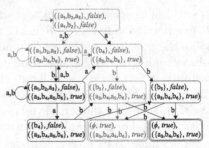

(a) The solution space and the accepting path of Pos_intersect(τ_1, τ_2).

(b) The solution space and the accepting path of Follow_intersect(τ_1, τ_2).

Fig. 2. The solution spaces and the accepting paths of Pos_intersect and Follow_intersect in deciding the non-emptiness of $\tau_1 \cap \tau_2$.

develop a new algorithm Follow_intersect. Specifically, we adapt Algorithm 1 to using the equivalence relation $\equiv_f$, which is mainly achieved by substituting the function in line 11 to Pos_recur(first($E_1^{\#}$), first($E_2^{\#}$), {(first($E_1^{\#}$), $0 \in$ last$_0(E_1)$), (first($E_2^{\#}$), $0 \in$ last$_0(E_2)$))}), the condition in line 19 to ((follow($E_1^{\#}, p_1$), $p_1 \in$ last$_0(E_1)$), (follow($E_2^{\#}, p_2$), $p_2 \in$ last$_0(E_2)$))) $\notin Q$ and the condition in line 20 to Pos_recur(follow($E_1^{\#}, p_1$), follow($E_2^{\#}, p_2$), $Q \cup$ {((follow($E_1^{\#}, p_1$), $p_1 \in$ last$_0(E_1)$), (follow($E_2^{\#}, p_2$), $p_2 \in$ last$_0(E_2)$))}) $= true$. After the substitution, Algorithm 1 starts recursive search with first sets as in Definition 6 and selects the positions whose symbols are identical, combines them pairwise and checks if they are in both last$_0$ sets, i.e. indicating the final states of follow automata, if not, check if their follow sets and the Boolean value of whether they are in the last$_0$ sets are reached before, if not, memorize them into Q and continue to check their follow sets, simulating a transition from the current state to the next state in both follow automata. Overall the search space of the checking algorithm is reduced to simulating the search procedure on the states of the product automaton of two follow automata.

We illustrate our algorithms with two regular expressions $\tau_1 = (a^*b^*)^*abb$ and $\tau_2 = (a+b)(a^* + ba^* + b^*)^*$. After being converted into star normal form and linearized, we have $\tau_1^{\#} = (a_1 + b_2)^*a_3b_4b_5$ and $\tau_2^{\#} = (a_1 + b_2)(a_3 + b_4a_5^* + b_6)^*$. The search spaces and the accepting paths of Pos_intersect and Follow_intersect for $\tau_1^{\#} \cap \tau_2^{\#}$ are shown in Fig. 2, where the solution space of Follow_intersect is smaller than that of Pos_intersect.

Theorem 2. *Given two regular expressions E_1 and E_2, Follow_intersect returns true if and only if $L(E_1) \cap L(E_2) \neq \varnothing$.*

Complexity. The computation of the intersection of two position sets can be done in time $O(\|E_1\| + \|E_2\|)$ with the help of an auxiliary hash table of follow set has $O(\|E_1\|)$. The identification of condition $(p_1, p_2) \notin Q$ takes time $O(\|E_1\|\|E_2\|)$, since the set of position tuples Q has a size of

$O(\|E_1\|\|E_2\|)$. This condition is checked $\|E_1\|\|E_2\|$ times the worst time. Then Pos_intersect have time complexity of $O(\|E_1\|^2\|E_2\|^2)$ and space complexity of $O(\|E_1\|\|E_2\|)$. For the case of Follow_intersect, the intersection of two position sets is computed the same as above. The identification of condition $((\mathsf{follow}(E_1^\#,p_1),p_1 \in \mathsf{last}_0(E_1)),(\mathsf{follow}(E_2^\#,p_2),p_2 \in \mathsf{last}_0(E_2))) \notin Q$ takes time $O(\|E_1\| + \|E_2\|)\|E_1\|\|E_2\|)$ since the set of follow set tuple Q has a size of $O(\|E_1\| + \|E_2\|)\|E_1\|\|E_2\|)$. This condition is checked $\|E_1\|\|E_2\|$ times. Then we have the overall time complexity of $O((\|E_1\| + \|E_2\|)\|E_1\|^2\|E_2\|^2)$ and space complexity of $O((\|E_1\| + \|E_2\|)\|E_1\|\|E_2\|)$. For a deterministic regular expression E, the size of position sets has a upper bound of $|\Sigma_E|$, thus the time complexity of Pos_intersect is $O((|\Sigma_{E_1} \cap \Sigma_{E_2}|)(\|E_1\| + \|E_2\|)\|E_1\|\|E_2\|)$ and the space complexity is $O(\|E_1\|\|E_2\|)$. For Follow_intersect, the time complexity is $O((|\Sigma_{E_1}| + |\Sigma_{E_2}|)|\Sigma_{E_1} \cap \Sigma_{E_2}|(\|E_1\| + \|E_2\|)\|E_1\|\|E_2\|)$ and space complexity is $O((|\Sigma_{E_1}| + |\Sigma_{E_2}|)\|E_1\|\|E_2\|)$.

4   C-Continuation-Based Algorithms

The notion of continuation is developed by Berry and Sethi [3], by Champarnaud and Ziadi [13], by Ilie and Yu [28], and by Chen and Yu [20]. In [21], the author gave a novel construction of derivatives on deterministic regular expressions and proved its linear cardinality. However when arbitrary regular expressions are considered, exponential search space of the algorithm is inevitable. To avoid the exponential blow-up, we exploit the notion of c-continuation proposed in [13] to check the intersection non-emptiness of two regular expressions.

Definition 8. *Given a regular expression E and a symbol a, the c-derivative w.r.t. a, denoted by $d_a(E)$, is defined inductively as follows [13]:*

$$d_a(\varnothing) \;=\; d_a(\varepsilon) = \varnothing, \tag{1}$$

$$d_a(b) \;=\; \begin{cases} \varepsilon, & \text{if } b = a, \\ \varnothing, & \text{otherwise,} \end{cases} \tag{2}$$

$$d_a(F + G) \;=\; \begin{cases} d_a(F), & \text{if } d_a(F) \neq \varnothing, \\ d_a(G), & \text{otherwise,} \end{cases} \tag{3}$$

$$d_a(FG) \;=\; \begin{cases} d_a(F)G, & \text{if } d_a(F) \neq \varnothing, \\ d_a(G), & \text{if } d_a(F) \neq \varnothing \wedge \mathsf{nullable}(F) = true, \\ \varnothing, & \text{otherwise,} \end{cases} \tag{4}$$

$$d_a(F^*) \;=\; d_a(F)F^*. \tag{5}$$

The c-derivative w.r.t. a word is computed by: $d_\varepsilon(E) = E$, $d_{wa} = d_a(d_w(E))$, for $a \in \Sigma$ and $w \in \Sigma^*$.

Lemma 1. *(see [13]). For a linearized regular expression $E^\#$, for every symbol a and every word u, the c-derivative $d_{ua}(E^\#)$ w.r.t the word ua is either $\varnothing$ or unique.*

Definition 9. *Given a linearized regular expression $E^{\#}$ and a symbol $a \in \Sigma_E$, the c-continuation of $E^{\#}$ w.r.t. a, denoted as $c_a(E^{\#})$, is defined inductively as follows:*

$$c_a(a) \quad = \quad \varepsilon \tag{1}$$

$$c_a(F + G) \quad = \quad \begin{cases} c_a(F), & if \ c_a(F) \neq \varnothing, \\ c_a(G), & otherwise, \end{cases} \tag{2}$$

$$c_a(FG) \quad = \quad \begin{cases} c_a(F)G, & if \ c_a(F) \neq \varnothing, \\ c_a(G), & otherwise, \end{cases} \tag{3}$$

$$c_a(F^*) \quad = \quad c_a(F)F^*. \tag{4}$$

Notice that different from Definition 8, c-continuations are defined on linearized regular expressions and non-null. Also we let $c_0(E^{\#}) = d_\varepsilon(E^{\#}) = E^{\#}$.

Proposition 3. *If E is a regular expression in star normal form, then $c_a(E^{\#})$ is in star normal form, for each a in $\Sigma^{\#}$.*

The proof is a straightforward induction on the structure of $c_a(E^{\#})$.

Here, given two states a_1 and a_2 in Q_{pos}, we can define the following equivalence relations $=_c, \equiv_c \subseteq Q_{pos}^2$:

$$a_1 =_c a_2 \iff c_{a_1}(E^{\#}) = c_{a_2}(E^{\#}) \tag{1}$$

$$a_1 \equiv_c a_2 \iff c_{a_1}(E^{\#})^{\natural} = c_{a_2}(E^{\#})^{\natural} \tag{2}$$

It has been shown both $=_c$ and $\equiv_c$ are right-invariant w.r.t. $M_{pos}(E)$ [13]. Using the definition of c-continuation, the c-continuation automaton $M_{ccon}(E)$ can be constructed, and we have the following lemma [13].

Lemma 2. *For a regular expression E, $M_{ccon}(E)$ and $M_{pos}(E)$ are identical.*

Definition 10. *Automaton $M_{ccon}(E)/_{=_c}$ of a regular expression E is defined by a 5-tuple $(Q_{ccon}, \Sigma, \delta_{ccon}, s_{ccon}, F_{ccon})$ where*
  $Q_{ccon} = \{c_x(E^{\#}) \mid x \in \Sigma^{\#} \cup \{0\}\}$,
  $\delta_{ccon}(c_x(E^{\#}), a) = \{d_y(c_x(E^{\#})) \mid y^{\natural} = a\}$, *for* $x \in \Sigma^{\#} \cup \{0\}$ *and* $a \in \Sigma$,
  $s_{ccon} = c_0(E^{\#})$,
  $F_{ccon} = \{c_x(E^{\#}) \mid \text{nullable}(c_x(E^{\#})) = true\}$.

Proposition 4. *For a deterministic regular expression E, $M_{ccon}(E)/_{=_c}$ is deterministic.*

We have the following relations between $M_{ccon}(E)/_{=_c}(E)$ and $M_{pos}(E)$.

Lemma 3. *(See [13]). For any $a \in \Sigma_E$, the following relations hold:* $\text{first}(c_a(E^{\#})) = \text{follow}(E^{\#}, a)$ *and* $a \in \text{last}_0(E^{\#}) \iff \text{nullable}(c_a(E^{\#})) = true$.

Algorithm 2: CCon_intersect

Input: two regular expressions E_1 and E_2.
Output: *true* if $L(E_1) \cap L(E_2) \neq \varnothing$ or *false* otherwise.

1 CCon_intersect :: (Expression E_1, Expression E_2) $\rightarrow$ Boolean
2 **begin**
3       $E_1^{\bullet} \leftarrow snf(E_1)$; $E_2^{\bullet} \leftarrow snf(E_2)$;
4       $E_1^{\#} \leftarrow linearize(E_1^{\bullet})$; $E_2^{\#} \leftarrow linearize(E_2^{\bullet})$;
5   **if** nullable$(E_1^{\#}) = true \wedge$ nullable$(E_2^{\#}) = true$ **then**
6   **return** *true*;
7   **else**
8   **if** last$(E_1^{\natural}) \cap$ last$(E_2^{\natural}) = \varnothing$ **then**
9   **return** *false*;
10   **else**
11   **return** CCon_recur$(E_1^{\#}, E_2^{\#}, \{(E_1^{\#}, E_2^{\#})\})$;

12 CCon_recur :: (Expression $r_1^{\#}$, Expression $r_2^{\#}$, Set C) $\rightarrow$ Boolean
13 **begin**
14   **if** first$(r_1^{\natural}) \cap$ first$(r_2^{\natural}) = \varnothing$ **then**
15   **return** *false*;
16   **forall the** $a_1 \in$ first$(r_1^{\#}) \wedge a_2 \in$ first$(r_2^{\#}) \wedge a_1^{\natural} = a_2^{\natural}$ **do**
17          $c_1 \leftarrow c_{a_1}(r_1^{\#})$; $c_2 \leftarrow c_{a_2}(r_2^{\#})$;
18   **if** nullable$(c_1) = true \wedge$ nullable$(c_2) = true$ **then**
19   **return** *true*;
20   **if** $(c_1, c_2) \notin C$ **then**
21   **return** CCon_recur$(c_1, c_2, C \cup \{(c_1, c_2)\})$;
22   **else**
23   **return** *false*;

While the preprocessing procedure of Algorithm 2 before the recursive search follows the same technique as Algorithm 1, the recursive function starts the search with the linearized expressions and a tuple of them as inputs. The linearized expressions correspond to elements in $CC(E_1)$ and $CC(E_2)$, then the tuples are states of $M_{ccon}(E_1)/_{=c} \cap M_{ccon}(E_2)/_{=c}$, which starts from $(E_1^{\#}, E_2^{\#})$ as in Definition 10, $E^{\#}$ is a starting state of $M_{ccon}(E)/_{=c}$. The recursive search performs an intersection non-emptiness check on the symbols of first sets correspondingly. For a_1 and a_2 in first sets of each expressions that have the same symbol, i.e. $a_1^{\natural} = a_2^{\natural}$, we calculate c-continuations of the input expressions w.r.t the positions and check the nullability of their c-continuations as from Definition 10, a nullable c-continuation corresponds to a final state. If the c-continuations are not nullable simultaneously, we first check if this c-continuation tuple is reached before, we terminate this branch, if not, we memorize the tuple into a set C as a reached state in the intersection automaton and continue the search

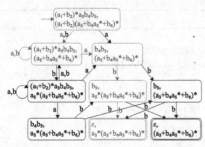
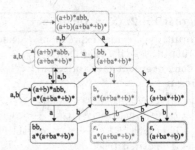

(a) The solution space and the accepting path of CCon_intersect(τ_1, τ_2).

(b) The solution space and accepting path of Equa_intersect(τ_1, τ_2).

Fig. 3. The solution spaces and the accepting paths of CCon_intersect and Equa_intersect in deciding the non-emptiness of $\tau_1 \cap \tau_2$.

with these c-continuations simulating a transition of the identical symbol from positions used for calculating those c-continuations in both $M_{ccon}(E)/_{=_c}$.

Theorem 3. *Given two regular expressions E_1 and E_2, CCon_intersect returns true if and only if $L(E_1) \cap L(E_2) \neq \varnothing$.*

Proposition 5. *(See [13]).* $=_c \subseteq \equiv_c$.

This reveals $M_{ccon}(E)/_{\equiv_c}$ is a quotient of $M_{ccon}(E)/_{=_c}$, and also we have:

Proposition 6. *(See [13]).* $M_e(E) \simeq M_{ccon}(E)/_{\equiv_c}$.

From the fact above we know equation automaton is a quotient of its c-continuation automaton. We can improve Algorithm 2 by substituting the code in line 11 with **return** CCon_recur($E_1^\#, E_2^\#, \{(E_1^\natural, E_2^\natural)\}$), line 20 with condition $(c_1^\natural, c_2^\natural) \notin C$ and line 21 with CCon_recur($c_1, c_2, C \cup \{(c_1^\natural, c_2^\natural)\}$) = *true*. And algorithm Equa_intersect is obtained. By dropping the labels in c-continuations, each expression in the tuples stored in C corresponds to states in $M_{ccon}(E)/_{\equiv_c}$, the search space of the checking algorithm is reduced to simulating the search procedure on the states of the product automaton of two $M_{ccon}(E)/_{\equiv_c}$.

Theorem 4. *Given two regular expressions E_1 and E_2, Equa_intersect returns true if and only if $L(E_1) \cap L(E_2) \neq \varnothing$.*

Recall our example in Sect. 3, after the same preprocessing procedures. We have $\tau_1^\#$ and $\tau_2^\#$. The solution spaces and the accepting paths of CCon_intersect and Equa_intersect are shown in Fig. 3. Notice the solution space of CCon_inter-sect and Equa_intersect are identical for this example, since for both $\tau_1^\bullet$ and $\tau_2^\bullet$, $=_c = \equiv_c$, see Sect. 5 for more discussions.

Complexity. The computation of the first sets of c-continuations takes an $O(\|E_1\|^2|E_1| + \|E_2\|^2|E_2|)$ time and $O(\|E_1\|^2 + \|E_2\|^2)$ space complexity. The calculation of the intersection of two position sets can be done in linear time. The computation of c-continuations of both expressions costs $O(\|E_1\|\|E_1\|^2 +$

$\|E_2\|\|E_2|^2)$ time and space [13]. Computation of nullable on the resulted c-continuations costs $O(|E_1|^2 + |E_2|^2)$ time and $O(\|E_1\| + \|E_2\|)$ space as in the worst case, the size of a c-continuation of E is $|E|^2$ [23]. The identification of condition $(c_1, c_2) \notin C$ takes $O(\|E_1\|\|E_1|^2 + \|E_2\|\|E_2|^2)$ time, and $O(\|E_1\|\|E_1|^2 + \|E_2\|\|E_2|^2)$ space is required for representation of the list C of c-continuation tuples. Finally we have the time complexity of CCon_intersect: $O((\|E_1\|\|E_1|^2 + \|E_2\|\|E_2|^2) \times (\|E_1\|^2|E_1| + \|E_2\|^2|E_2|))$ and the space complexity: $O(|E_1|^2\|E_1\| + |E_2|^2\|E_2\|)$. In the case of deterministic regular expressions, the time complexity of CCon_intersect is $O((\|E_1\|\|E_1|^2 + \||E_2\|\|E_2|^2) \times (|\Sigma_{E_1}|\|E_1\|\|E_1| + |\Sigma_{E_2}|\|E_2\|\|E_2|))$ and space complexity is $O(|E_1|^2\|E_1\| + |E_2|^2\|E_2\|)$ because the first sets of c-continuation has an $O(|\Sigma_E|)$ size. The time and space complexity of Equa_intersect is exactly the same, since computing ♮ on c-continuations requires linear time and no additional space.

5 Experimental Evaluation

In this section, we evaluate the effectiveness and efficiency of our algorithms on regular expression datasets. In the following, Pos_intersect, Follow_intersect, CCon_intersect and Equa_intersect are abbreviated as PO, FO, CC and EQ respectively.

Benchmarks. SRE is a dataset of standard regular expressions randomly generated on alphabets of $1 \leq |\Sigma| \leq 10$ and symbol occurrence ranges from 1 to 1000 with step 10. For every step of symbol occurrences, we generate an expression as E_1. And generate 100 expressions as E_2 whose symbol occurrence ranges from 1 to 1000 with step 10, giving a total of 10000 pairs of expressions.

DRE is a dataset of 27129 pairs of deterministic regular expressions used in practical applications in [17], which are collected and normalized from XSD, DTD and Relax NG schema files. DRE is evaluated for deterministic inputs that can help in reducing the complexity of our algorithms.

Baselines. To evaluate the effectiveness and efficiency of our algorithms, we selected seven tools which take regular expressions as input for comparison: Z3str3 [5], Z3-Trau [1], Z3seq [39], Ostrich [21], CVC4 [33], Z3str3RE [4] and Brics library [36], since our algorithms avoid explicit automata construction.

Configurations. We implemented a prototype of our algorithms in Ocaml. Our experiments were run on a machine with 3.40GHz Intel i7-6700 8 CPU and 8G RAM, running Ubuntu 20. All baselines were configured in the settings reported in their original documents. A timeout of 20 s is used.

Efficiency and Effectiveness. In the following tables, True Positive denotes E_1 and E_2 intersect and the algorithm reported true. True Negative denotes E_1 and E_2 do not intersect and the algorithm reported false. False Positive denotes E_1 and E_2 do not intersect but the algorithm reported true. False Negative denotes E_1 and E_2 do not intersect but the algorithm reported true. Unknown is the sum of "unknown" responses, which can be resulted from when non-termination in

Table 1. Detailed results for the SRE benchmark.

	Z3-Trau	OSTRICH	Brics	Z3seq	CVC4	Z3str3	Z3str3RE	PO	FO	CC	EQ
True Positive	2	1	553	3486	1581	3740	4095	**4642**	**4642**	**4642**	**4642**
True Negative	386	38	35	2747	5288	137	1481	**5358**	**5358**	**5358**	**5358**
False Positive	0	0	0	0	0	0	0	0	0	0	0
False Negative	36	0	0	0	0	0	0	0	0	0	0
Program Crash	37	0	4489	0	0	9	0	0	0	0	0
Unknown	0	36	0	0	396	0	0	0	0	0	0
Timeout	9539	9925	4923	3767	3131	5727	4423	0	0	0	0
Time(s)	192353	199863	137076	95236	98283	126844	103611	**157**	171	340	348

Table 2. Detailed results for the DRE benchmark.

	Z3-Trau	OSTRICH	Brics	Z3seq	CVC4	Z3str3	Z3str3RE	PO	FO	CC	EQ
True Positive	972	11	12347	18536	12982	14226	14891	**19252**	**19252**	**19252**	**19252**
True Negative	484	108	703	1241	6995	889	1235	**7877**	**7877**	**7877**	**7877**
False Positive	0	0	0	0	0	0	0	0	0	0	0
False Negative	288	0	0	0	0	0	0	0	0	0	0
Program Crash	103	0	0	0	0	9	0	0	0	0	0
Unknown	0	4302	0	0	348	0	0	0	0	0	
Timeout	25282	22708	14079	7352	7152	11657	11003	0	0	0	0
Time(s)	518433	501129	283230	182877	185641	260525	263633	98.8	**98.6**	99.4	99.0

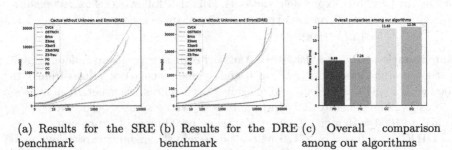

(a) Results for the SRE benchmark (b) Results for the DRE benchmark (c) Overall comparison among our algorithms

Fig. 4. Plots showing cumulative results for each benchmark.

their algorithms is detected or a resource limit is met. Program Crash denotes the sum of crashes. Timeout denotes the sum of reaching the time limit and Time is the total runtime of each algorithm. The best results achieved by the algorithms are shown in bold. In the cactus plots, algorithms that are further to the right and closer to the bottom of the plot have better performance.

As shown in Fig. 4(a) and 4(b), all the other tools have an extra cost from initializing of solvers/Java virtual machine etc., as also observed in [39].

The results for the SRE benchmark are shown in Table 1 and Fig. 4(a). All of our algorithms solved all of the instances correctly. Including timeouts, the fastest algorithm PO achieves a speedup of 606x over Z3seq, 626x over CVC4, 659x over Z3str3RE, 807x over Z3str3, 873x over Brics, 1225x over Z3-Trau, and 1273x over OSTRICH. The differences among curves of our algorithms are minor compared to the performance of the baselines on Fig. 4(a) and 4(b), thus close to coincide.

The results for the DRE benchmark are shown in Table 2 and Fig. 4(b). All of our algorithms solved all of the instances correctly and 7152 instances were uniquely solved by ours. Including timeouts, the fastest algorithm FO achieves a speedup of 1855x over Z3seq, 1883x over CVC4, 2642x over Z3str3, 2673x over Z3str3RE, 2873x over Brics, 5082x over OSTRICH and 5257x over Z3-Trau. The experimental results reveal that our algorithms are more efficient for deterministic regular expressions, since at line 16 of all our algorithms, the position tuple corresponding to a symbol is always unique for deterministic regular expressions.

Discussion. Z3-Trau [1] is based on Z3, which depends on parametric flat automata to handle string constraints, with both under- and over-approximations. The evaluation of Z3-Trau exposed 324 soundness errors and 140 crashes on our datasets. Similar observations are also revealed in literature [4,39]. OSTRICH [21] is a string solver implementing a transducer model and handling regular language intersection via cross product algorithm based on [36]. OSTRICH reported 4338 "unknown" responses in our benchmarks. Brics library [36] offers Boolean operation function interfaces which convert regular expressions into Thompson Automata [34] and perform product construction to handle regular expression intersection non-emptiness problem. Brics library reported 4489 program crashes caused by stack overflow errors in our benchmarks. Experimentally we found these three tools based on explicit automata construction are inefficient in solving regular expression intersection non-emptiness. Z3seq [39] is a hybrid solver which reasons on sequences of characters serving as the default string solver in current Z3. For regular language constraints, Z3seq uses symbolic Boolean derivatives based on Brzozowski's [10] and Antimirov's [2] derivatives without explicitly constructing symbolic Boolean finite automata. The decision procedure of CVC4 [33] for regular expression constraints extends Antimirov's partial derivatives [2] similar to [11]. We found CVC4's implementation of firstChars function is overapproximated when handling intersection between regular expressions, which partially explains their performance in our experiments. Experimentally derivative-based solvers show advantages over the other tools, however outperformed by our algorithms: we utilized derivatives in a different manner from the derivative-based solvers—firstly our algorithms are based on linearization technique, also we simulate cross product on derivatives instead of integrating intersection operation into derivatives. Z3str3 [5] handles Boolean combinations of regular expressions with reduction to word equations. On our benchmarks, Z3str3 reported unknown and crashes on 762 instances. Z3str3RE [4] is based on Z3str3 with the length-aware automata-based algorithm and heuristics. In the experiments we found Z3str3RE's optimizations and bug-fixes to Z3str3 are effective, however the cost from the intersection of automata has an adverse impact on its efficiency compared to our algorithms.

Relations Among Algorithms. To investigate the relation among our algorithms, relations among automata are necessary. From [12,18], we have:

Lemma 4. *For regular expressions in star normal form,* $=_c \subseteq \equiv_f \subseteq \equiv_c$.

In [26], authors showed mn states are sufficient and necessary for an NFA to accept the intersection of an m-state NFA and an n-state NFA in the worst case. According to the commutativity of intersection, denote ordering $M_1 \succeq M_2$ iff automaton M_1 has more or equal states than automaton M_2, then we can conclude:

Theorem 5. *For regular expressions $E_1, \ldots, E_m$ in star normal form, we have:*

$$\bigcap_{i=1}^{m} M_{pos}(E_i) \succeq \bigcap_{i=1}^{m} M_{ccon}(E_i)/_{=_c} \succeq \bigcap_{i=1}^{m} M_f(E_i) \succeq \bigcap_{i=1}^{m} M_e(E_i). \qquad (2)$$

From the theorem above, we can easily deduce the relations among the worst case search space of our algorithms. For our example in Sect. 3, from Fig. 2 and 3 we know the solution space of FO, CC and EQ are identical and smaller than that of PO, because for $\tau_1^{\bullet}$ and $\tau_2^{\bullet}$, $=_c = \equiv_f = \equiv_c$, which is a special case of Lemma 4. Besides, Fig. 4(c) shows the average time of our algorithms to solve an instance in all our benchmarks, where PO is the fastest and EQ is the slowest. Though the worst case complexity of our algorithms are much higher than the theoretical quadratic lower-bound, they perform better than explicit automata-based algorithms [1,21] in practice. We also observed the efficiency of PO and FO is higher than that of c-continuation-based algorithms. This is due to a position tuple (of PO) having constant size (recall in Sect. 1 when the number of input expressions is fixed as two) and position set tuples (of FO) having linear sizes while partial derivatives or c-continuations has sizes at worst-case quadratic [2,13,23]. This fact reveals smaller cost in the identification of states can significantly accelerate regular expression intersection non-emptiness checking algorithms. In general, FO is recommended for smaller solution space and average case performance.

Summary. Overall, all our algorithms outperform all baselines in both effectiveness and efficiency in solving intersection non-emptiness problems for regular expressions.

6 Related Work

Apart from tools mentioned in Sect. 5, the other related work is listed as follows. Mona [25] is a model checking tool using algorithms based on finite automata to check satisfiability of input monadic second order logic formulas. JAltImpact [43] reduces finite automata intersection non-emptiness problem into checking emptiness for alternating finite automata. VATA tree automata library [31] deploys antichains and simulation based inclusion checking among input tree automata. VATA can also be used to check intersection non-emptiness between tree automata. No Experimental comparison is made with tools taking automata or logic formulas as input since our algorithms directly check intersection non-emptiness between regular expressions without explicitly constructing automata.

7 Concluding Remarks

In this paper, we have given four algorithms based on online automata construction simulation to solve the intersection non-emptiness problem of regular expressions, which are compared against seven state-of-the-art tools over synthetic and real-world datasets. Overall we show that our algorithms outperformed all of the tools mentioned above.

Our algorithms also show high extension prospects: algorithms can be integrated into string solvers and be easily modified to output random witnesses of intersection non-emptiness to handle get-model constraints instead of only checking non-emptiness, add mechanisms for extended features in real-world regular expressions such as character classes, matching precedence and capturing groups, and introduce heuristics to find a locally optimal choice or conflict-driven strategies to backtrack non-chronologically and learn which state tuples are redundant to be recorded during the searching procedure for improving practical performance.

Acknowledgements. The authors would like to thank the anonymous reviewers for their helpful comments and suggestions. Work supported by the Natural Science Foundation of Beijing, China (Grant No. 4232038) and the National Natural Science Foundation of China (Grant No. 62372439).

References

1. Abdulla, P.A., et al.: Efficient handling of string-number conversion. In: PLDI 2020, pp. 943–957 (2020)
2. Antimirov, V.M.: Partial derivatives of regular expressions and finite automaton constructions. Theor. Comput. Sci. **155**, 291–319 (1996)
3. Berry, G., Sethi, R.: From regular expressions to deterministic automata. Theor. Comput. Sci. **48**, 117–126 (1986)
4. Berzish, M., et al.: Towards more efficient methods for solving regular-expression heavy string constraints. Theor. Comput. Sci. **943**, 50–72 (2023)
5. Berzish, M., Ganesh, V., Zheng, Y.: Z3str3: a string solver with theory-aware heuristics. In: FMCAD 2017, pp. 55–59 (2017)
6. Brüggemann-Klein, A.: Regular expressions into finite automata. Theor. Comput. Sci. **120**, 197–213 (1993)
7. Brüggemann-Klein, A., Wood, D.: One-unambiguous regular languages. Inf. Comput. **140**(2), 229–253 (1998)
8. Broda, S., Holzer, M., Maia, E., Moreira, N., Reis, R.: A mesh of automata. Inf. Comput. **265**, 94–111 (2019)
9. Broda, S., Machiavelo, A., Moreira, N., Reis, R.: Position automaton construction for regular expressions with intersection. In: Brlek, S., Reutenauer, C. (eds.) DLT 2016. LNCS, vol. 9840, pp. 51–63. Springer, Heidelberg (2016). https://doi.org/10.1007/978-3-662-53132-7_5
10. Brzozowski, J.A.: Derivatives of regular expressions. J. ACM **11**(4), 481–494 (1964)
11. Caron, P., Champarnaud, J.-M., Mignot, L.: Partial derivatives of an extended regular expression. In: Dediu, A.-H., Inenaga, S., Martín-Vide, C. (eds.) LATA 2011. LNCS, vol. 6638, pp. 179–191. Springer, Heidelberg (2011). https://doi.org/10.1007/978-3-642-21254-3_13

12. Champarnaud, J.M., Ouardi, F., Ziadi, D.: Normalized expressions and finite automata. Int. J. Algebra Comput. **17**, 141–154 (2007)
13. Champarnaud, J.M., Ziadi, D.: Canonical derivatives, partial derivatives and finite automaton constructions. Theor. Comput. Sci. **289**(1), 137–163 (2002)
14. Chang, C.-H., Paige, R.: From regular expressions to DFA's using compressed NFA's. In: Apostolico, A., Crochemore, M., Galil, Z., Manber, U. (eds.) CPM 1992. LNCS, vol. 644, pp. 90–110. Springer, Heidelberg (1992). https://doi.org/10.1007/3-540-56024-6_8
15. Chapman, C., Stolee, K.T.: Exploring regular expression usage and context in Python. In: ISSTA 2016, pp. 282–293 (2016)
16. Chen, H.: Finite automata of expressions in the case of star normal form and one-unambiguity. Technical report. ISCAS-LCS-10-11 (2010)
17. Chen, H., Li, Y., Dong, C., Chu, X., Mou, X., Min, W.: A large-scale repository of deterministic regular expression patterns and its applications. In: Yang, Q., Zhou, Z.-H., Gong, Z., Zhang, M.-L., Huang, S.-J. (eds.) PAKDD 2019. LNCS (LNAI), vol. 11441, pp. 249–261. Springer, Cham (2019). https://doi.org/10.1007/978-3-030-16142-2_20
18. Chen, H., Lu, P.: Derivatives and finite automata of expressions in star normal form. In: Drewes, F., Martín-Vide, C., Truthe, B. (eds.) LATA 2017. LNCS, vol. 10168, pp. 236–248. Springer, Cham (2017). https://doi.org/10.1007/978-3-319-53733-7_17
19. Chen, H., Xu, Z.: Inclusion algorithms for one-unambiguous regular expressions and their applications. Sci. Comput. Program. **193**, 102436 (2020)
20. Chen, H., Yu, S.: Derivatives of regular expressions and an application. In: Dinneen, M.J., Khoussainov, B., Nies, A. (eds.) WTCS 2012. LNCS, vol. 7160, pp. 343–356. Springer, Heidelberg (2012). https://doi.org/10.1007/978-3-642-27654-5_27
21. Chen, T., et al.: Solving string constraints with regex-dependent functions through transducers with priorities and variables. In: POPL 2022, vol. 6, pp. 1–31 (2022)
22. Glushkov, V.M.: The abstract theory of automata. Russ. Math. Surv. **16**, 1–53 (1961)
23. Gruber, H., Holzer, M.: Language operations with regular expressions of polynomial size. Theor. Comput. Sci. **410**(35), 3281–3289 (2009)
24. Guanciale, R., Gurov, D., Laud, P.: Private intersection of regular languages. In: PST 2014, pp. 112–120 (2014)
25. Henriksen, J.G., et al.: Mona: monadic second-order logic in practice. In: Brinksma, E., Cleaveland, W.R., Larsen, K.G., Margaria, T., Steffen, B. (eds.) TACAS 1995. LNCS, vol. 1019, pp. 89–110. Springer, Heidelberg (1995). https://doi.org/10.1007/3-540-60630-0_5
26. Holzer, M., Kutrib, M.: State complexity of basic operations on nondeterministic finite automata. In: Champarnaud, J.-M., Maurel, D. (eds.) CIAA 2002. LNCS, vol. 2608, pp. 148–157. Springer, Heidelberg (2003). https://doi.org/10.1007/3-540-44977-9_14
27. Hunt, H.B., Rosenkrantz, D.J., Szymanski, T.G.: On the equivalence, containment, and covering problems for the regular and context-free languages. J. Comput. Syst. Sci. **12**(2), 222–268 (1976)
28. Ilie, L., Yu, S.: Follow automata. Inf. Comput. **186**(1), 140–162 (2003)
29. Kozen, D.: Lower bounds for natural proof systems. In: SFCS 1977, pp. 254–266 (1977)
30. Le Glaunec, A., Kong, L., Mamouras, K.: Regular expression matching using bit vector automata. In: OOPSLA 2023, vol. 7, pp. 492–521 (2023)

31. Lengál, O., Šimáček, J., Vojnar, T.: VATA: a library for efficient manipulation of non-deterministic tree automata. In: Flanagan, C., König, B. (eds.) TACAS 2012. LNCS, vol. 7214, pp. 79–94. Springer, Heidelberg (2012). https://doi.org/10.1007/978-3-642-28756-5_7

32. Li, Y., et al.: ReDoSHunter: a combined static and dynamic approach for regular expression DoS detection. In: USENIX Security 2021, pp. 3847–3864 (2021)

33. Liang, T., Tsiskaridze, N., Reynolds, A., Tinelli, C., Barrett, C.: A decision procedure for regular membership and length constraints over unbounded strings. In: Lutz, C., Ranise, S. (eds.) FroCoS 2015. LNCS (LNAI), vol. 9322, pp. 135–150. Springer, Cham (2015). https://doi.org/10.1007/978-3-319-24246-0_9

34. McNaughton, R., Yamada, H.: Regular expressions and state graphs for automata. IRE Trans. Electron. Comput. 9, 39–47 (1960)

35. Middleton, J., Toro Icarte, R., Baier, J.: Real-time heuristic search with LTLf goals. In: IJCAI 2022, pp. 4785–4792 (2022)

36. Møller, A.: dk.brics.automaton. https://www.brics.dk/automaton/

37. de Oliveira Oliveira, M., Wehar, M.: On the fine grained complexity of finite automata non-emptiness of intersection. In: Jonoska, N., Savchuk, D. (eds.) DLT 2020. LNCS, vol. 12086, pp. 69–82. Springer, Cham (2020). https://doi.org/10.1007/978-3-030-48516-0_6

38. Rabin, M.O., Scott, D.: Finite automata and their decision problems. IBM J. Res. Dev. 3(2), 114–125 (1959)

39. Stanford, C., Veanes, M., Bjørner, N.: Symbolic Boolean derivatives for efficiently solving extended regular expression constraints. In: PLDI 2021, pp. 620–635 (2021)

40. Todd Wareham, H.: The parameterized complexity of intersection and composition operations on sets of finite-state automata. In: Yu, S., Păun, A. (eds.) CIAA 2000. LNCS, vol. 2088, pp. 302–310. Springer, Heidelberg (2001). https://doi.org/10.1007/3-540-44674-5_26

41. Wang, X., Hong, Y., Chang, H., Langdale, G., Hu, J.: Hyperscan: a fast multi-pattern regex matcher for modern CPUs. In: NSDI 2019, pp. 631–648 (2019)

42. Wehar, M.: Hardness results for intersection non-emptiness. In: Esparza, J., Fraigniaud, P., Husfeldt, T., Koutsoupias, E. (eds.) ICALP 2014. LNCS, vol. 8573, pp. 354–362. Springer, Heidelberg (2014). https://doi.org/10.1007/978-3-662-43951-7_30

43. Xu, X.: JAltImpact. https://github.com/cathiec/JAltImpact

44. Yu, S.: Regular languages. In: Handbook of Formal Languages, vol. 1: Word, Language, Grammar, pp. 41–110 (1997)

45. Yu, S., Zhuang, Q.: On the state complexity of intersection of regular languages. ACM SIGACT News 22(3), 52–54 (1991)

46. Ziadi, D., Ponty, J.L., Champarnaud, J.M.: Passage d'une expression rationnelle à un automate fini non-déterministe. Bull. Belg. Math. Soc. - Simon Stevin 4, 177–203 (1997)

Realisability of Global Models
of Interaction

Maurice H. ter Beek[1]([⊠]) [iD], Rolf Hennicker[2], and José Proença[3]([⊠]) [iD]

[1] ISTI-CNR, Pisa, Italy
`maurice.terbeek@isti.cnr.it`
[2] Ludwig-Maximilians-Universität München, Munich, Germany
`hennicker@ifi.lmu.de`
[3] CISTER & University of Porto, Porto, Portugal
`jose.proenca@fc.up.pt`

Abstract. We consider *global models* of communicating agents specified as transition systems labelled by *interactions* in which multiple senders and receivers can participate. A *realisation* of such a model is a set of local transition systems—one per agent—which are executed concurrently using synchronous communication. Our core challenge is how to check whether a global model is realisable and, if it is, how to synthesise a realisation. We identify and compare two variants to realise global interaction models, both relying on bisimulation equivalence. Then we investigate, for both variants, *realisability conditions* to be checked on global models. We propose a synthesis method for the construction of realisations by grouping locally indistinguishable states. The paper is accompanied by a tool that implements realisability checks and synthesises realisations.

1 Introduction

We deal with the development of systems of collaborating computing entities which interact by message exchange, like communicating component systems, multi-agent systems (MAS), collective adaptive systems (CAS), groupware systems, multi-party sessions, etc. Such systems are often presented by a set of components whose local behaviour is formally described by labelled transition systems (LTS) or process expressions. Their interaction behaviour is then captured by (synchronous or asynchronous) parallel composition of the local models.

Before designing such local models it is, however, safer to first model the interaction behaviour of the components from a *global* perspective. This led to the investigation of various forms of global models, like global (session) types [8,13, 23,24], global choreographies [35] and global languages [2]; also message sequence charts [20] and UML interaction diagrams [15,30] serve this purpose.

An important question is, of course, whether a global model $\mathcal{M}$ is indeed realisable by a system $\mathcal{S} = (\mathcal{M}_i)_{i \in \mathcal{I}}$ of local component models $\mathcal{M}_i$ (where $\mathcal{I}$ ranges over a set of component names). Possible solutions are investigated for global languages in [2] and, for global session types, in various papers (cf., e.g.,

E. Ábrahám et al. (Eds.): ICTAC 2023, LNCS 14446, pp. 236–255, 2023.
https://doi.org/10.1007/978-3-031-47963-2_15

[8,13,23,24]) by imposing syntactic restrictions on global types. These approaches use projections to generate local models from global ones.

A different idea is to provide, instead of a global model, a requirements specification Sp describing properties of the desired global interaction behaviour by means of some logical formalism like in [9,21,22]. Then local models $\mathcal{M}_i$ are constructed from scratch and their (synchronous) composition $\otimes(\mathcal{M}_i)_{i \in \mathcal{I}}$ must be proven to satisfy the requirements of Sp.

From Requirements to Realisations. We combine the advantages of logical specifications and global models for interaction-based systems by using both in a stepwise manner. Our development method is summarised in Fig. 1.

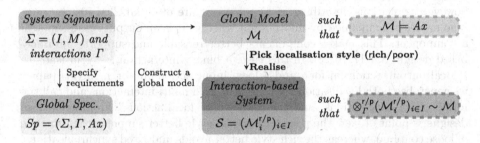

Fig. 1. Workflow for the development of interaction-based systems

We start by providing a *(system) signature* $\Sigma = (I, M)$, which determines finite sets I of component names and M of message names. Σ induces the set $\Gamma(\Sigma)$ of *(global) Σ-interactions* of the form out $\rightarrow$ in : m where out and in are disjoint sets of component names (such that out$\cup$in $\neq \varnothing$) and m $\in M$. The multi-interaction out $\rightarrow$ in : m expresses that all components of out send message m to all components of in such that all send and receive events occur simultaneously. Since usually not all interactions in $\Gamma(\Sigma)$ are desired in an application context (one may wish, e.g., to consider only binary or multicast communication) we consider pairs (Σ, Γ) where $\Gamma \subseteq \Gamma(\Sigma)$ is a user-defined *interaction set* which restricts the set of all Σ-interactions to admissible ones. For logical specifications of global interaction behaviour, we propose an action-based logic following a dynamic-logic style which has been successfully applied for specifying ensembles (cf., e.g., [22]). The logic uses the usual diamond and box modalities of dynamic logic ($\langle \alpha \rangle \, \varphi$ and $[\alpha] \, \varphi$, resp.) which range over (structured) interactions α built over Γ by sequential composition, choice and iteration. A *global interaction-behaviour specification* is then a triple $Sp = (\Sigma, \Gamma, Ax)$, where Ax is a set of formulas, called *axioms*, expressing requirements for the global interaction behaviour (e.g., safety and liveness properties and/or desired and forbidden interaction scenarios).

Given a (global) requirements specification $Sp = (\Sigma, \Gamma, Ax)$, we construct a global model $\mathcal{M}$ for the system's intended interaction behaviour. To formalise such models we use *global LTS* whose transitions are labelled by interactions according to Γ. If only binary interactions are admitted a global LTS is a choreography automaton as in [1]. Of course, we must check that the constructed global LTS $\mathcal{M}$ satisfies the requirements of the specification Sp, i.e. $\mathcal{M} \models Ax$.

The central part of our work concerns the realisation (decomposition) of a global LTS $\mathcal{M}$ in terms of a (possibly distributed) system of interacting components whose individual behaviour is modelled by *local LTS*. First we must determine, for each component name $i \in I$, which local actions component i should provide. To do so, any interaction in which i participates must be mapped to an appropriate local action for component i. We study two variants. The first follows approaches to multi-party session types and choreography languages where the names of the communication partners are kept in local actions. For instance, a binary interaction $i \rightarrow j$: m leads to a local output action $ij!$m for i and a local input action $ij?$m for j. In approaches to component-based development, however, transitions describing local behaviour are often labelled just by message names accompanied by information whether it is an output or an input of a component. This makes components better reusable and supports interface-based design [3,4,17,26,28]. In this case, a binary interaction $i \rightarrow j$: m leads to a local output action !m for i and a local input action ?m for j. In this paper, we generalise both localisation styles to deal with multi-interactions and call the former "rich local actions" and the latter "poor local actions". From a software designer's point of view the poor localisation style better supports the principle of loose coupling, whereas the rich style better avoids undesired synchronisations.

Once a localisation style $x \in \{r, p\}$ is chosen (r for "rich" and p for "poor") one can proceed with the actual construction of a realisation of $\mathcal{M}$ in terms of a system presented by a family $\mathcal{S} = (\mathcal{M}_i^x)_{i \in I}$ of local LTS. We say that $\mathcal{M}$ is *realisable* (with localisation style x) if such a system exists such that $\mathcal{M}$ is bisimilar (denoted by $\sim$) to the synchronous composition $\otimes_\Gamma^x (\mathcal{M}_i^x)_{i \in I}$ of all $\mathcal{M}_i^x$ taking into account the interactions Γ and the localisation style x. Hence, our realisation notion is generic w.r.t. Γ and parametrised by the chosen localisation style. We show that realisability with poor local actions implies realisability with rich local actions (Theorem 1) but the converse does not hold (Example 3). Since our realisability notion is based on bisimilarity we can deal with non-deterministic behaviour, differently from language-based approaches like [2,13].

Race Example. We illustrate our methodology outlined so far by developing a (small) system, called Race, which is meant to model the competition of two runner components R1 and R2 under the control of a third component Ctrl. To start, we provide a signature $\Sigma_{\mathsf{Race}} = (I_{\mathsf{Race}}, M_{\mathsf{Race}})$ with component names $I_{\mathsf{Race}} = \{\mathsf{R1}, \mathsf{R2}, \mathsf{Ctrl}\}$ and message names $M_{\mathsf{Race}} = \{\mathsf{start}, \mathsf{finish}\}$. The idea is that the controller starts the two runners simultaneously, while each runner signals individually to the controller when it has finished its run. Therefore, we use the interaction set on the left of Fig. 2. We do not model the actual running of a runner component, which would be an internal action (cf. [7]).

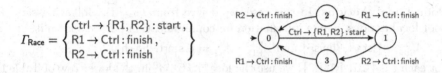

$$\Gamma_{\text{Race}} = \left\{ \begin{array}{l} \text{Ctrl} \rightarrow \{\text{R1}, \text{R2}\} : \text{start}, \\ \text{R1} \rightarrow \text{Ctrl} : \text{finish}, \\ \text{R2} \rightarrow \text{Ctrl} : \text{finish} \end{array} \right\}$$

Fig. 2. Interaction set Γ_{Race} (left) and global LTS $\mathcal{M}_{\text{Race}}$ (right); we write Ctrl for $\{\text{Ctrl}\}$ and similarly for R1, R2.

We require that no runner should finish before starting and that any started runner should be able to finish running. This will be expressed by dynamic logic formulas to be detailed in the requirements specification Sp_{Race} in Example 1.

Next we construct the global LTS $\mathcal{M}_{\text{Race}}$ shown on the right of Fig. 2, which models the required interaction behaviour of the system so that the requirements of the specification are satisfied. The system starts in the initial (global) state 0, where the controller starts both runners at once. Each runner separately sends a finish signal to the controller (in arbitrary order). After that a new run can start.

Finally, we want to realise the system by three local LTS such that their composition is bisimilar to the global LTS $\mathcal{M}_{\text{Race}}$. We distinguish the two variants.

Rich Local Actions. From Γ_{Race} we derive the following sets of rich local actions:

$\Lambda^r_{\text{Ctrl}} = \{\text{Ctrl}\,\{\text{R1}, \text{R2}\}\,!\,\text{start}, \text{R1}\,\text{Ctrl}\,?\,\text{finish}, \text{R2}\,\text{Ctrl}\,?\,\text{finish}\},$

$\Lambda^r_{\text{R1}} = \{\text{Ctrl}\,\{\text{R1}, \text{R2}\}\,?\,\text{start}, \text{R1}\,\text{Ctrl}\,!\,\text{finish}\},$ and

$\Lambda^r_{\text{R2}} = \{\text{Ctrl}\,\{\text{R1}, \text{R2}\}\,?\,\text{start}, \text{R2}\,\text{Ctrl}\,!\,\text{finish}\}.$

For each $i \in \{\text{Ctrl}, \text{R1}, \text{R2}\}$, we use the local LTS $\mathcal{M}^r_i$ in the upper row of Table 1 to build the system $\mathcal{S}^r_{\text{Race}} = \{\mathcal{M}^r_{\text{Ctrl}}, \mathcal{M}^r_{\text{R1}}, \mathcal{M}^r_{\text{R2}}\}$ with rich local actions. One can prove that the "rich" composition (Definition 4) of the three LTS by synchronisation w.r.t. Γ_{Race} is bisimilar (even isomorphic) to $\mathcal{M}_{\text{Race}}$; i.e., we have found a realisation with rich local actions.

Table 1. Local LTS for each localisation style and for each component

Localisation	Local Ctrl	Local R1	Local R2
Rich	R2 Ctrl?finish — 2 — R1 Ctrl?finish; 0 → Ctrl{R1,R2}!start → 1; R1 Ctrl?finish — 3 — R2 Ctrl?finish	Ctrl{R1,R2}?start; 0 ⇄ 1; R1 Ctrl!finish	Ctrl{R1,R2}?start; 0 ⇄ 1; R2 Ctrl!finish
Poor	?finish — 2 — ?finish; 0 → !start → 1	?start; 0 ⇄ 1; !finish	?start; 0 ⇄ 1; !finish

Poor Local Actions. In this case, we derive from Γ_{Race} the following sets of poor local actions, where information on communication partners is omitted:

$$\Lambda^{\mathsf{p}}_{\mathsf{Ctrl}} = \{!\mathsf{start}, ?\mathsf{finish}\} \text{ and } \Lambda^{\mathsf{p}}_{\mathsf{R1}} = \Lambda^{\mathsf{p}}_{\mathsf{R2}} = \{?\mathsf{start}, !\mathsf{finish}\}.$$

For each $i \in \{\mathsf{Ctrl}, \mathsf{R1}, \mathsf{R2}\}$, we use the local LTS $\mathcal{M}^{\mathsf{p}}_i$ in the lower row of Table 1 to build the system $\mathcal{S}^{\mathsf{p}}_{\mathsf{Race}} = \{\mathcal{M}^{\mathsf{p}}_{\mathsf{Ctrl}}, \mathcal{M}^{\mathsf{p}}_{\mathsf{R1}}, \mathcal{M}^{\mathsf{p}}_{\mathsf{R2}}\}$ with poor local actions. Also the "poor" composition (Definition 7) of the three LTS by synchronisation w.r.t. Γ_{Race} is bisimilar (even isomorphic) to $\mathcal{M}_{\mathsf{Race}}$.

Checking Realisability, Local Quotients, and System Synthesis. So far, we considered the case in which the realisation of a global interaction model $\mathcal{M}$ is "invented". However, there might be no realisation of $\mathcal{M}$ and it would be better to know this as soon as possible to align the global model. Next, we consider the following two important issues and proceed as shown in Fig. 3.

1. How to check whether a given global LTS $\mathcal{M}$ is realisable (rich/poor case)?
2. If it is, how can we build/synthesise a concrete realisation S (rich/poor case)?

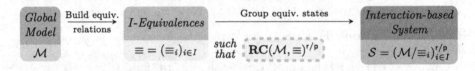

Fig. 3. Approach to check realisability and system synthesis

To tackle the first question we propose, similarly to [14], to find a family $\equiv \, = (\equiv_i)_{i \in I}$ of equivalence relations on the global state space Q of $\mathcal{M}$ such that, for each component name $i \in I$ and states $q, q' \in Q$, $q \equiv_i q'$ expresses that q and q' are not distinguishable from the viewpoint of i. This suggests that q and q', though globally different, can be locally interpreted as the same states. In particular, it is required that any two states q and q' which are related by a global transition $q \xrightarrow{\mathsf{out} \to \mathsf{in}:m}_{\mathcal{M}} q'$ should be indistinguishable for any $i \in I$ which does not participate in the interaction, i.e. $i \notin \mathsf{out} \cup \mathsf{in}$. On the basis of a given I-equivalence $\equiv$, we formulate realisability conditions $\mathsf{RC}(\mathcal{M}, \equiv)^{\mathsf{r}}$ and $\mathsf{RC}(\mathcal{M}, \equiv)^{\mathsf{p}}$ for both localisation styles. We show that in the rich and in the poor case our condition is sufficient for realisability (cf. Theorems 2 and 3).

In both cases, the principle idea how to synthesise a realisation is the same. Given a family $(\equiv_i)_{i \in I}$ of I-equivalences for which the realisability condition holds, we construct, for each $i \in I$, a local quotient $(\mathcal{M}/\equiv_i)^{\mathsf{r/p}}$ by identifying global states (in $\mathcal{M}$) which are i-equivalent. Thus we get the desired system (which might still benefit from minimisations w.r.t. bisimilarity).

Note that the I-equivalences found for satisfying the realisability condition in the rich case may not be the same as in the poor case and thus also the local quotients may show different behaviour. Moreover, the technique of building local quotients differs from projections used in the field of multi-party session types, since projections are partial operations depending on syntactic conditions (cf., e.g., [8]). A less syntactic and more expressive approach is proposed in [25].

As an example, recall the global LTS $\mathcal{M}_{\mathsf{Race}}$ shown in Fig. 2 (right). The three local LTS with *rich* local actions shown in the upper row of Table 1 are, up to renaming of states, local quotients of $\mathcal{M}_{\mathsf{Race}}$. To construct the local quotient for R1, global states 0 and 2 are identified, as well as states 1 and 3 (and symmetrically for the local quotient for R2). For Ctrl, no proper identification is applied (cf. Example 4 for details). Also the three local LTS with *poor* local actions in the lower row of Table 1 are, up to renaming of states, local quotients of $\mathcal{M}_{\mathsf{Race}}$. In this case, however, to construct the local quotient for Ctrl, two global states of $\mathcal{M}_{\mathsf{Race}}$ are identified, namely states 2 and 3 (cf. Example 6 for details).

Contributions and Related Work

1. We propose a rigorous discipline for developing interaction-based systems following a step-wise development method from dynamic-logic requirements specifications over global models of interaction down to systems of (possibly distributed) components. Thus our approach supplements approaches to realisations of global behaviour descriptions (in the form of global languages, e.g. [2], or global session types, e.g. [23]), by an abstract logical layer.
2. Our approach is driven by specified sets of multi-interactions supporting any kind of synchronous communication between multiple senders and multiple receivers. To the best of our knowledge, realisations of global models with arbitrary multi-interactions have not yet been studied in the literature.
3. Our correctness notion for realisation of global models by systems of communicating local components is based on bisimulation, thus letting us deal with non-determinism and going beyond language-based approaches like [2,13]. Bisimulation also fits well with global requirements specifications since dynamic logic formulas are invariant under bisimulation and therefore hold in any realisation of a global model of a global specification.
4. For constructing realisations we consider two localisation styles (rich and poor local actions) and analyse their relationship. This is a novel result.
5. A global interaction model may, in general, not be realisable. We provide conditions for realisability with respect to both localisation styles. Our conditions are related to the work in [14] which, however, does not deal with multi-interactions and uses a stronger condition ensuring realisation up to isomorphism of LTS; cf. our discussion in Sect. 5.1.
6. For realisable global models, we construct realisations in terms of systems of local quotients. Similar quotient constructions have been used in the proofs of [14], but not for multi-interactions and for different localisation styles. The technique of building local quotients differs from projections used in the field of multi-party session types, since projections are partial operations depending on syntactic conditions (cf., e.g., [8]). In our approach, no restrictions on the form of global models are assumed. However, it must be said that the syntactic restrictions used for global types guarantee some kind of communication properties of a resulting system which we do not consider.
7. We developed a prototypical tool Ceta which checks realisability conditions and, if they are satisfied, generates local quotients and hence realisations.

Outline. After some formal preliminaries in Sect. 2, we show how to specify requirements for global models of interaction in Sect. 3 and how to realise the latter in Sect. 4. The conditions that guarantee realisability are studied in Sect. 5. In Sect. 6, we present a tool that implements our analyses. It is available at https://lmf.di.uminho.pt/ceta and all examples of the paper are predefined in the tool, like $\mathcal{M}_{\mathsf{Race}}$ ⌴, including a hyperlink to open the tool with the specific example. Section 7 wraps up the paper. A companion report [6] includes all proofs of our results, more details of the tool, and a few additional examples.

2 Formal Preliminaries

LTS and Bisimulation. Let A be a finite set of actions. A *labelled transition system* (LTS) over A is a tuple $\mathcal{L} = (Q, q_0, A, T)$ such that Q is a finite set of states, $q_0 \in Q$ is the initial state, and $T \subseteq Q \times A \times Q$ is a transition relation. Note that we consider finite-state LTS, which makes the realisability conditions presented later *decidable*. We write $q \xrightarrow{a}_{\mathcal{L}} q'$ to denote $(q, a, q') \in T$. A state $q \in Q$ is *reachable* if there exists a finite sequence of transitions from initial state q_0 to q.

Let $\mathcal{L}_i = (Q_i, q_{i,0}, A, T_i)$ be two LTS (for $i = 1, 2$) over the same action set A. A *bisimulation relation* between $\mathcal{L}_1$ and $\mathcal{L}_2$ is a relation $B \subseteq Q_1 \times Q_2$ such that for all $(q_1, q_2) \in B$ and for all $a \in A$ the following holds:

1. if $q_1 \xrightarrow{a}_{\mathcal{L}_1} q_1'$ then there exist $q_2' \in Q_2$ and $q_2 \xrightarrow{a}_{\mathcal{L}_2} q_2'$ such that $(q_1', q_2') \in B$;
2. if $q_2 \xrightarrow{a}_{\mathcal{L}_2} q_2'$ then there exist $q_1' \in Q_1$ and $q_1 \xrightarrow{a}_{\mathcal{L}_1} q_1'$ such that $(q_1', q_2') \in B$.

$\mathcal{L}_1$ and $\mathcal{L}_2$ are *bisimilar*, denoted by $\mathcal{L}_1 \sim \mathcal{L}_2$, if there exists a bisimulation relation B between $\mathcal{L}_1$ and $\mathcal{L}_2$ such that $(q_{1,0}, q_{2,0}) \in B$.

Dynamic Logic. We use (test-free) propositional dynamic logic (PDL) [19] to formulate behavioural properties. Let A be a finite set of *(atomic) actions*. Let the grammar $\alpha := a \mid \alpha; \alpha \mid \alpha + \alpha \mid \alpha^*$, with $a \in A$, sequential composition ; , non-deterministic choice $+$, and iteration $*$, define the set $Act(A)$ of *structured actions* over A. If $A = \{a_1, \dots, a_n\}$, we write *some* for structured action $a_1 + \cdots + a_n$. We may also refer to all actions of A but one, say a, and express this by $-a$.

The set $Frm(A)$ of A-*formulas* is defined by the grammar

$$\varphi := \textit{true} \mid \neg\varphi \mid \varphi \vee \varphi \mid \langle\alpha\rangle\, \varphi \qquad\qquad \text{(formulas)}$$

where $\alpha \in Act(A)$. Formula $\langle\alpha\rangle\, \varphi$ expresses that at the current state it is possible to execute α such that φ holds in the next state.

Abbreviations. We use the usual abbreviations like *false*, $\varphi \wedge \varphi'$, $\varphi \to \varphi'$, and the modal box operator $[\alpha]\, \varphi$ which stands for $\neg\, \langle\alpha\rangle\, \neg\varphi$ and expresses that whenever in the current state α is executed, then φ holds afterwards.

For the interpretation of formulas we use LTS. Let $\mathcal{L} = (Q, q_0, A, T)$ be an LTS over A. First we extend the transition relation of $\mathcal{L}$ to structured actions:

$q \xrightarrow{\alpha_1;\alpha_2}_{\mathcal{L}} q'$ if there exists $\hat{q} \in Q$ such that $q \xrightarrow{\alpha_1}_{\mathcal{L}} \hat{q}$ and $\hat{q} \xrightarrow{\alpha_2}_{\mathcal{L}} q'$;

$q \xrightarrow{\alpha_1+\alpha_2}_{\mathcal{L}} q'$ if $q \xrightarrow{\alpha_1}_{\mathcal{L}} q'$ or $q \xrightarrow{\alpha_2}_{\mathcal{L}} q'$; and

$q \xrightarrow{\alpha^*}_{\mathcal{L}} q'$ if $q = q'$ or there exists $\hat{q} \in Q$ such that $q \xrightarrow{\alpha}_{\mathcal{L}} \hat{q}$ and $\hat{q} \xrightarrow{\alpha^*}_{\mathcal{L}} q'$.

The *satisfaction* of a formula $\varphi \in Frm(A)$ by $\mathcal{L}$ at a state $q \in Q$, denoted by $\mathcal{L}, q \models \varphi$, is inductively defined as follows:

$\mathcal{L}, q \models true$;

$\mathcal{L}, q \models \neg\varphi$ if not $\mathcal{L}, q \models \varphi$;

$\mathcal{L}, q \models \varphi_1 \vee \varphi_2$ if $\mathcal{L}, q \models \varphi_1$ or $\mathcal{L}, q \models \varphi_2$; and

$\mathcal{L}, q \models \langle\alpha\rangle \varphi$ if there exists $q' \in Q$ such that $q \xrightarrow{\alpha}_{\mathcal{L}} q'$ and $\mathcal{L}, q' \models \varphi$.

$\mathcal{L}$ *satisfies* a formula $\varphi \in Frm(A)$, denoted by $\mathcal{L} \models \varphi$, if $\mathcal{L}, q_0 \models \varphi$. Hence, for the satisfaction of a formula by an LTS the non-reachable states are irrelevant (deviating from the classical semantics of PDL [19]). We can express safety properties, like $[some^*] \varphi$, and some kinds of liveness properties like, e.g., $[some^*] \langle some^*; a\rangle \varphi$.

Satisfaction of formulas in PDL is invariant under bisimulation [10]: Let $\mathcal{L}_1, \mathcal{L}_2$ be two LTS over A. If $\mathcal{L} \sim \mathcal{L}'$ then, for any $\varphi \in Frm(A)$, $\mathcal{L} \models \varphi$ iff $\mathcal{L}' \models \varphi$.

3   Specifying Requirements for Global Models of Interaction

We focus on the stepwise development of systems whose components interact by synchronous message exchange. We support "multi-interactions", in which several senders and receivers may participate in a communication. Our starting point are *signatures* $\Sigma = (I, M)$, where I is a finite set of component names (also called participants) and M is a finite set of message names. Any signature Σ induces a set $\Gamma(\Sigma)$ of (global) Σ-*interactions* defined by

$$\Gamma(\Sigma) = \{\text{out} \to \text{in} : \text{m} \mid \text{out}, \text{in} \subseteq I, \text{out} \cup \text{in} \neq \varnothing, \text{m} \in M\}.$$

An interaction out $\to$ in : m expresses that all components whose name occurs in out send a message named m to all components whose name occurs in in. Such interactions involving arbitrarily many senders and receivers are also called *multi-interactions*. They will be interpreted by **synchronous** (handshake) communication. As a shorthand notation we write i for $\{i\}$. Special cases are binary interactions between two components i, j, denoted by $i \to j : \text{m}$, or multicast communication with one sender i and a group in of receivers, denoted by $i \to \text{in} : \text{m}$.

Usually not all Σ-interactions are meaningful for a certain application. Therefore our approach will be driven by user-definable *interaction sets* $\Gamma \subseteq \Gamma(\Sigma)$.

General Assumption. In the sequel, we assume that (Σ, Γ) denotes a system signature $\Sigma = (I, M)$ together with an interaction set Γ. When we talk about a signature we always mean a system signature.

We propose to use interactions as atomic actions in dynamic logic formulas for specifying desired and forbidden interaction properties from a global perspective.

Definition 1 (global Sp). A global interaction behaviour specification *is a triple* $Sp = (\Sigma, \Gamma, Ax)$ *where* $Ax \subseteq Frm(\Gamma)$ *is a set of* Γ-formulas, called axioms.

Example 1. A requirements specification for the interaction behaviour of the Race system is given by $Sp_{\mathsf{Race}} = (\Sigma_{\mathsf{Race}}, \Gamma_{\mathsf{Race}}, Ax_{\mathsf{Race}})$ where Σ_{Race} and Γ_{Race} are defined in Sect. 1 and Ax_{Race} consists of the following two dynamic logic formulas expressing the two informal requirements described in Sect. 1.

1. *"No runner should finish before it has been started by the controller".*
$$\left[\left(-(\mathsf{Ctrl} \to \{\mathsf{R1}, \mathsf{R2}\} : \mathsf{start})\right)^* ; \begin{pmatrix} \mathsf{R1} \to \mathsf{Ctrl} : \mathsf{finish} + \\ \mathsf{R2} \to \mathsf{Ctrl} : \mathsf{finish} \end{pmatrix}\right] \mathit{false}$$

2. *"For any started runner it should be possible to finish its run".*
$$\left[\mathit{some}^*; \mathsf{Ctrl} \to \{\mathsf{R1}, \mathsf{R2}\} : \mathsf{start}\right] \begin{pmatrix} \langle \mathit{some}^*; \mathsf{R1} \to \mathsf{Ctrl} : \mathsf{finish} \rangle \, \mathit{true} \, \wedge \\ \langle \mathit{some}^*; \mathsf{R2} \to \mathsf{Ctrl} : \mathsf{finish} \rangle \, \mathit{true} \end{pmatrix} \qquad \triangleright$$

Given a specification Sp, the goal of our next step is to model the global interaction behaviour of the intended system in accordance with Sp. For this purpose we use LTS with interactions from Γ on the transitions.

Definition 2 (global LTS). A global LTS *over* (Σ, Γ) *is defined as an LTS* $\mathcal{M} = (Q, q_0, \Gamma, T)$ *over* Γ.

To check that a global LTS satisfies the axioms of a specification, we may use the mCRL2 toolset [12] and, as explained in [7], the translation of LTS to process expressions as well as the translation of our dynamic logic formulas to the syntax used by mCRL2. For instance, the global LTS $\mathcal{M}_{\mathsf{Race}}$ provided for the race example in Sect. 1 satisfies the axioms of the specification Sp_{Race} above.

4   Realisations of Global Models of Interaction

A crucial step in our development method concerns the realisation of a global interaction model in terms of a system of (possibly distributed) components modelled by *local* LTS (cf. Fig. 1). In this section, we formally define what we mean by a realisation. For modelling local components we must first determine, for each component name $i \in I$, which are the local actions that component i is supposed to support. We study two variants obeying different localisation styles and leading to different instantiations of our realisability notion.

4.1   Realisations Using Rich Local Actions

It is common in approaches to global (session) types and choreography languages to preserve the names of communication partners when moving from global interactions to local actions. In [2], e.g., a binary interaction $i \to j : \mathsf{m}$ leads to a local output action $ij!\mathsf{m}$ for i and a local input action $ij?\mathsf{m}$ for j. We generalise this approach to multi-interactions and call the resulting local actions *rich*.

Definition 3 (rich local actions and local LTS). *For each $i \in I$, the set of rich local i-actions* derived from Γ is $\Lambda_i^r(\Gamma) = \Lambda_{i,out}^r(\Gamma) \cup \Lambda_{i,in}^r(\Gamma)$ where

$$\Lambda_{i,out}^r(\Gamma) = \{\text{out in}!\,m \mid \exists\,(\text{out} \rightarrow \text{in} : m) \in \Gamma \text{ such that } i \in \text{out}\} \text{ and}$$
$$\Lambda_{i,in}^r(\Gamma) = \{\text{out in}?\,m \mid \exists\,(\text{out} \rightarrow \text{in} : m) \in \Gamma \text{ such that } i \in \text{in}\}.$$

A local LTS for i with rich local actions is an LTS $\mathcal{M}_i^r = (Q_i, q_{i,0}, \Lambda_i^r(\Gamma), T_i)$.

A *system* over (Σ, Γ) with rich local actions is a family $\mathcal{S}^r = (\mathcal{M}_i^r)_{i \in I}$ of local LTS $\mathcal{M}_i^r$ over $\Lambda_i^r(\Gamma)$ for $i \in I$. The behaviour of such a system is modelled by the synchronous Γ-composition of its components $\mathcal{M}_i^r$ ($i \in I$) where for all interactions (out $\rightarrow$ in : m) $\in \Gamma$ a global transition exists (in a composed state) if for all $i \in$ out ($i \in$ in, resp.) there is a transition in $\mathcal{M}_i^r$ with the local action out in!m (out in?m, resp.) leaving the current local state of $\mathcal{M}_i^r$.

Definition 4 (synchronous Γ-composition with rich local actions). *Let $(\mathcal{M}_i^r)_{i \in I}$ be a family of local LTS $\mathcal{M}_i^r = (Q_i, q_{i,0}, \Lambda_i^r(\Gamma), T_i)$ with rich local actions. The synchronous Γ-composition of $(\mathcal{M}_i^r)_{i \in I}$ with rich local actions is the global LTS, denoted by $\otimes_\Gamma^r (\mathcal{M}_i^r)_{i \in I}$, over (Σ, Γ) with initial state $(q_{i,0})_{i \in I}$ and with (product) states $(q_i)_{i \in I}$ (with $q_i \in Q_i$ for all $i \in I$) and transitions generated from the initial state by the following rule:*

$$\frac{(\text{out} \rightarrow \text{in} : m) \in \Gamma \quad \forall i \in \text{out} : q_i \xrightarrow{\text{out in}!\,m}_{\mathcal{M}_i^r} q_i' \quad \forall i \in \text{in} : q_i \xrightarrow{\text{out in}?\,m}_{\mathcal{M}_i} q_i'}{(q_i)_{i \in I} \xrightarrow{\text{out} \rightarrow \text{in} : m}_{\otimes_\Gamma^r (\mathcal{M}_i^r)_{i \in I}} (q_i')_{i \in I} \text{ where } q_i' = q_i \text{ for all } i \in I \setminus (\text{out} \cup \text{in})}$$

Definition 5 (realisability with rich local actions). *Let $\mathcal{M}$ be a global LTS over (Σ, Γ). A system $\mathcal{S} = (\mathcal{M}_i^r)_{i \in I}$ over (Σ, Γ) with rich local actions is a (rich) realisation of $\mathcal{M}$, if $\mathcal{M} \sim \otimes_\Gamma^r (\mathcal{M}_i^r)_{i \in I}$ are bisimilar. $\mathcal{M}$ is realisable with rich local actions if such a realisation exists.*

Our realisability notion relies on bisimulation. Thus we are able to deal with non-determinism. In particular, according to the invariance of dynamic logic under bisimulation (cf. Sect. 2), we know that global models and their realisations satisfy the same formulas. Hence, once a global model of a global specification is provided, any realisation will be correct with respect to the global specification.

Example 2. Consider a non-deterministic example with two participants, a Person and a Coin, and tossing the Coin by the Person is modelled as a non-deterministic action that leads to either head or tail (cf. [29]). Formally, $\Sigma_{\text{Toss}} = (\{\text{Coin}, \text{Person}\}, \{\text{toss}, \text{head}, \text{tail}\})$ and $\Gamma_{\text{Toss}} = \{\text{Person} \rightarrow \text{Coin} : \text{toss}, \text{Coin} \rightarrow \text{Person} : \text{head}, \text{Coin} \rightarrow \text{Person} : \text{tail}\}$. The global LTS $\mathcal{M}_{\text{Toss}}$ [≥] and one of its realisations by the two LTS $\mathcal{M}_{\text{Person}}^r$ and $\mathcal{M}_{\text{Coin}}^r$ (with rich local actions) are shown in Table 2. Although $\mathcal{M}_{\text{Toss}} \sim \otimes_{\Gamma_{\text{Toss}}}^r \{\mathcal{M}_{\text{Person}}^r, \mathcal{M}_{\text{Coin}}^r\}$ there would be no bisimulation when considering a deterministic version for both Person and Coin. ▷

Table 2. Non-deterministic toss of a Coin by a Person

4.2 Realisations Using Poor Local Actions

We now consider a variant where we omit the communication partners when we move from a global interaction $(\text{out} \to \text{in}: \text{m}) \in \Gamma$ to local actions. In this case only the message name m is kept together with output information !m for $i \in \text{out}$ and input information ?m for $i \in \text{in}$. This complies with the idea of component automata used in teams [4,5,7] and many other approaches to component-based design (e.g., I/O automata [28] and interface automata [17]). We call the resulting local actions "poor" since they do not specify communication partners.

Definition 6 (poor local actions and local LTS). *For each* $i \in I$, *the set of poor local* i-*actions derived from* Γ *is given by* $\Lambda_i^{\text{p}}(\Gamma) = \Lambda_{i,out}^{\text{p}}(\Gamma) \cup \Lambda_{i,in}^{\text{p}}(\Gamma)$ *where*

$$\Lambda_{i,out}^{\text{p}}(\Gamma) = \{!\text{m} \mid \exists (\text{out} \to \text{in}: \text{m}) \in \Gamma \text{ such that } i \in \text{out}\} \text{ and}$$

$$\Lambda_{i,in}^{\text{p}}(\Gamma) = \{?\text{m} \mid \exists (\text{out} \to \text{in}: \text{m}) \in \Gamma \text{ such that } i \in \text{in}\}.$$

A local LTS for i *with poor local actions is an LTS* $\mathcal{M}_i^{\text{p}} = (Q_i, q_{i,0}, \Lambda_i^{\text{p}}(\Gamma), T_i)$ *over* $\Lambda_i^{\text{p}}(\Gamma)$.

The notion of a **system with poor local actions** is defined completely analogously to the rich case in Sect. 4.1. Γ-composition with poor local actions needs, however, special care since for matching local actions only the message name and input/output information is relevant.

Definition 7 (synchronous Γ-composition with poor local actions). *Let* $(\mathcal{M}_i^{\text{p}})_{i \in I}$ *be a family of local LTS* $\mathcal{M}_i^{\text{p}} = (Q_i, q_{i,0}, \Lambda_i^{\text{p}}(\Gamma), T_i)$ *with poor local actions. The synchronous* Γ-*composition of* $(\mathcal{M}_i^{\text{p}})_{i \in I}$ *with poor local actions is the global LTS, denoted by* $\otimes_\Gamma^{\text{p}}(\mathcal{M}_i^{\text{p}})_{i \in I}$, *over* (Σ, Γ) *with initial state* $(q_{i,0})_{i \in I}$ *and with (product) states* $(q_i)_{i \in I}$ *(such that* $q_i \in Q_i$ *for all* $i \in I$) *and transitions generated from the initial state by the following rule:*

$$\frac{(\text{out} \to \text{in}: \text{m}) \in \Gamma \qquad (\forall i \in \text{out}: q_i \xrightarrow{!\text{m}}_{\mathcal{M}_i^{\text{p}}} q_i') \qquad (\forall i \in \text{in}: q_i \xrightarrow{?\text{m}}_{\mathcal{M}_i^{\text{p}}} q_i')}{(q_i)_{i \in I} \xrightarrow{\text{out} \to \text{in}: \text{m}}_{\otimes_\Gamma^{\text{p}}(\mathcal{M}_i^{\text{p}})_{i \in I}} (q_i')_{i \in I} \text{ where } q_i' = q_i \text{ for all } i \in I \setminus (\text{out} \cup \text{in})}$$

The notion of **realisability with poor local actions** is defined completely analogously to the rich case (cf. Definition 5) replacing "rich (r)" by "poor (p)".

An obvious question is whether realisability with respect to the two different localisation styles can be formally compared. This is indeed the case.

Theorem 1 (poor realisation implies rich realisation). *Let $\mathcal{M}$ be a global LTS over (Σ, Γ) which is realisable by a system $\mathcal{S}^{\mathsf{p}} = (\mathcal{M}_i^{\mathsf{p}})_{i \in I}$ with poor local actions. Then there exists a system $\mathcal{S}^{\mathsf{r}} = (\mathcal{M}_i^{\mathsf{r}})_{i \in I}$ with rich local actions which is a realisation of $\mathcal{M}$.*

The converse of Theorem 1 is not true, as demonstrated by the next example.

Example 3 We consider a variant of the global LTS $\mathcal{M}_{\mathsf{Race}}$ [⌧] (Fig. 2) where the transitions $1 \xrightarrow{\text{R2} \to \text{Ctrl}\,:\,\text{finish}} 3 \xrightarrow{\text{R1} \to \text{Ctrl}\,:\,\text{finish}} 0$ are removed, enforcing R1 to finish before R2. Let us call the resulting LTS $\mathcal{M}'_{\mathsf{Race}}$ [⌧]. Moreover, consider the variant of the local controller $\mathcal{M}^{\mathsf{r}}_{\mathsf{Ctrl}}$ (upper row of Table 1, left) where the local transitions $1 \xrightarrow{\text{R2Ctrl?finish}} 3 \xrightarrow{\text{R1Ctrl?finish}} 0$ are removed and call it $\mathcal{M}''_{\mathsf{Ctrl}}$. Now let $\mathcal{S}'^{\mathsf{r}} = \{\mathcal{M}''_{\mathsf{Ctrl}}, \mathcal{M}^{\mathsf{r}}_{\mathsf{R1}}, \mathcal{M}^{\mathsf{r}}_{\mathsf{R2}}\}$ be the system with rich local actions (where $\mathcal{M}^{\mathsf{r}}_{\mathsf{R1}}$ and $\mathcal{M}^{\mathsf{r}}_{\mathsf{R2}}$ are shown in the upper row of Table 1, middle and right). It is easy to check that $\mathcal{S}'^{\mathsf{r}}$ is a realisation of $\mathcal{M}'_{\mathsf{Race}}$ with rich local actions, since $\mathcal{M}'_{\mathsf{Race}}$ is even isomorphic to the (rich) Γ_{Race}-composition of $\{\mathcal{M}''_{\mathsf{Ctrl}}, \mathcal{M}^{\mathsf{r}}_{\mathsf{R1}}, \mathcal{M}^{\mathsf{r}}_{\mathsf{R2}}\}$.

The situation is different if we consider the poor case with controller $\mathcal{M}^{\mathsf{p}}_{\mathsf{Ctrl}}$ (lower row of Table 1, left) which accepts two times in a row a "finish" signal but, due to the poor local actions, cannot fix an acceptance order. The only candidate for a realisation with poor local actions is then the system $\mathcal{S}'^{\mathsf{p}} = \{\mathcal{M}^{\mathsf{p}}_{\mathsf{Ctrl}}, \mathcal{M}^{\mathsf{p}}_{\mathsf{R1}}, \mathcal{M}^{\mathsf{p}}_{\mathsf{R2}}\}$ consisting of the local LTS with poor local actions shown in the lower row of Table 1. Obviously, the Γ_{Race}-composition of these local LTS with poor actions does allow a sequence of transitions $1 \xrightarrow{\text{R2} \to \text{Ctrl}\,:\,\text{finish}} 3 \xrightarrow{\text{R1} \to \text{Ctrl}\,:\,\text{finish}} 0$ and therefore cannot be bisimilar to $\mathcal{M}'_{\mathsf{Race}}$. ▷

5 Realisability Conditions

In general a global LTS may not be realisable. Therefore we are interested in (i) conditions that guarantee realisability and (ii) techniques to synthesise realisations from a global LTS $\mathcal{M}$. The notion of I-equivalence provides a helpful tool. The basic idea is to consider the source and target states of a global transition $q \xrightarrow{\text{out} \to \text{in}\,:\,\text{m}}_{\mathcal{M}} q'$ to be indistinguishable for a component $i \in I$ if i does not participate in the interaction, i.e. $i \notin \text{out} \cup \text{in}$ (cf. also [14] and the discussion below).

Definition 8 (I-equivalence). *Let $\mathcal{M} = (Q, q_0, \Gamma, T)$ be a global LTS over (Σ, Γ). An I-equivalence over $\mathcal{M}$ is a family $\equiv = (\equiv_i)_{i \in I}$ of equivalence relations $\equiv_i \subseteq Q \times Q$ (reflexive, symmetric, and transitive) such that $q \equiv_i q'$ holds whenever there exists a transition $q \xrightarrow{\text{out} \to \text{in}\,:\,\text{m}}_{\mathcal{M}} q'$ with $i \notin \text{out} \cup \text{in}$. The equivalence class of a state $q \in Q$ w.r.t. $\equiv_i$ is the set $[q]_{\equiv_i} = \{q' \in Q \mid q' \equiv_i q\}$.*

5.1 Condition for Realisability Using Rich Local Actions

First, we will formulate our realisability condition for the case of rich local actions. We consider a global LTS $\mathcal{M}$ over (Σ, Γ). Our goal is to find an I-equivalence $(\equiv_i)_{i \in I}$ over $\mathcal{M}$ such that for each interaction $(\text{out} \to \text{in}\,:\,\text{m}) \in \Gamma$ the following holds. Assume, for simplicity, that $\mathsf{out} \cup \mathsf{in} = \{1, \ldots, n\}$. Whenever there is a combination $q_1, \ldots, q_n$ of n (not necessarily different) global states together with a global *"glue"* state g, i.e. for each $j \in \mathsf{out} \cup \mathsf{in}$, $q_j \equiv_j g$, then we expect: if $\mathsf{out} \to \mathsf{in} : \mathsf{m}$ is enabled in each global state $q_1, \ldots, q_n$ then each $j \in \mathsf{out} \cup \mathsf{in}$ should also able to participate in $\mathsf{out} \to \mathsf{in} : \mathsf{m}$ when the global state is g, since j cannot distinguish g from q_j. Thus the global interaction $\mathsf{out} \to \mathsf{in} : \mathsf{m}$ should be enabled in g and preserve I-equivalences.

Definition 9 (realisability condition (rich case)). *Let $\mathcal{M}$ be a global LTS over (Σ, Γ). The realisability condition $RC(\mathcal{M})^r$ for $\mathcal{M}$ with respect to rich local actions says that there exists an I-equivalence $\equiv = (\equiv_i)_{i \in I}$ over $\mathcal{M}$ such that the following property $RC(\mathcal{M}, \equiv)^r$ holds.*
For all $\gamma = (\mathsf{out} \to \mathsf{in} : \mathsf{m}) \in \Gamma$ with $\mathsf{out} \cup \mathsf{in} = \{k_1, \ldots, k_n\}$ we have:

$$
\forall \left(\begin{array}{c} q_1 \xrightarrow{\gamma}_{\mathcal{M}} q_1' \quad \cdots \quad q_n \xrightarrow{\gamma}_{\mathcal{M}} q_n' \\ g \in \bigcap_{j=1}^n [q_j]_{\equiv_{k_j}} \end{array} \right) \qquad \exists g' : \left(\begin{array}{c} g \xrightarrow{\gamma}_{\mathcal{M}} g' \\ g' \in \bigcap_{j=1}^n [q_j']_{\equiv_{k_j}} \end{array} \right)
$$

Theorem 2 will provide a constructive argument why condition $RC(\mathcal{M})^r$ ensures realisability with rich local actions. Local quotients are crucial for this.

Definition 10 (local quotients with rich local actions). *Let $\mathcal{M} = (Q, q_0, \Gamma, T)$ be a global LTS over (Σ, Γ) and $\equiv = (\equiv_i)_{i \in I}$ an I-equivalence over $\mathcal{M}$. For each $i \in I$ the local i-quotient of $\mathcal{M}$ with rich local actions is the LTS $(\mathcal{M}/\equiv_i)^r = (Q/\equiv_i, [q_0]_{\equiv_i}, \Lambda_i^r(\Gamma), (T/\equiv_i)^r)$ where*

- $Q/\equiv_i = \{[q]_{\equiv_i} \mid q \in Q\}$,
- $(T/\equiv_i)^r$ *is the least set of transitions generated by the following rules:*

$$
\frac{q \xrightarrow{\mathsf{out} \to \mathsf{in} : \mathsf{m}}_{\mathcal{M}} q' \qquad i \in \mathsf{out}}{[q]_{\equiv_i} \xrightarrow{\mathsf{out}\,\mathsf{in}\,!\,\mathsf{m}}_{(\mathcal{M}/\equiv_i)^r} [q']_{\equiv_i}} \qquad \frac{q \xrightarrow{\mathsf{out} \to \mathsf{in} : \mathsf{m}}_{\mathcal{M}} q' \qquad i \in \mathsf{in}}{[q]_{\equiv_i} \xrightarrow{\mathsf{out}\,\mathsf{in}\,?\,\mathsf{m}}_{(\mathcal{M}/\equiv_i)^r} [q']_{\equiv_i}}
$$

Note that $[q]_{\equiv_i} \xrightarrow{\mathsf{out}\,\mathsf{in}\,!\,\mathsf{m}}_{(\mathcal{M}/\equiv_i)^r} [q']_{\equiv_i}$ implies that there exist $\hat{q} \in [q]_{\equiv_i}$, $\hat{q}' \in [q']_{\equiv_i}$ and a transition $\hat{q} \xrightarrow{\mathsf{out} \to \mathsf{in} : \mathsf{m}}_{\mathcal{M}} \hat{q}'$ with $i \in \mathsf{out}$ (and similarly for $\mathsf{out}\,\mathsf{in}\,?\,\mathsf{m}$).

Theorem 2. *Let $\mathcal{M}$ be a global LTS over (Σ, Γ) and let $\equiv = (\equiv_i)_{i \in I}$ be an I-equivalence over $\mathcal{M}$. If $RC(\mathcal{M}, \equiv)^r$ holds, then $\mathcal{M} \sim \otimes_\Gamma^r ((\mathcal{M}/\equiv_i)^r)_{i \in I}$.*

Example 4.
Consider the global LTS $\mathcal{M}_{\mathsf{Race}}$ (Fig. 2). We show that $RC(\mathcal{M}_{\mathsf{Race}})^r$ holds and how to construct, following Theorem 2, a realisation of $\mathcal{M}_{\mathsf{Race}}$. More concretely, we take the family of equivalences $\equiv = (\equiv_i)_{i \in \{\mathsf{Ctrl}, \mathsf{R1}, \mathsf{R2}\}}$ that obeys $RC(\mathcal{M}_{\mathsf{Race}}, \equiv)^r$ (see below) and partitions the state space Q as follows: $Q/\equiv_{\mathsf{Ctrl}} = \{\{0\}, \{1\}, \{2\}, \{3\}\}, Q/\equiv_{\mathsf{R1}} = \{\{0, 2\}, \{1, 3\}\}$, and $Q/\equiv_{\mathsf{R2}} = \{\{0, 3\}, \{1, 2\}\}$.

Using these equivalences, the local quotients for R1 and R2 are as follows:

$$(\mathcal{M}/\equiv_{R1})^r = \; \begin{array}{c} \text{Ctrl}\{R1,R2\}?\text{start} \\ \rightarrow \{0,2\} \underset{\text{R1 Ctrl!finish}}{\overset{}{\rightleftarrows}} \{1,3\} \end{array} \qquad (\mathcal{M}/\equiv_{R2})^r = \; \begin{array}{c} \text{Ctrl}\{R1,R2\}?\text{start} \\ \rightarrow \{0,3\} \underset{\text{R1 Ctrl!finish}}{\overset{}{\rightleftarrows}} \{1,2\} \end{array}$$

The local quotient for Ctrl is isomorphic to $\mathcal{M}_{\mathsf{Race}}$ but with local labels. Thus we have obtained a system which is a realisation with rich local actions of $\mathcal{M}_{\mathsf{Race}}$. The local quotients coincide, up to renaming of states, with the local LTS used in the system $\mathcal{S}^r_{\mathsf{Race}}$ considered in Sect. 1.

Now, we illustrate how to verify $RC(\mathcal{M}_{\mathsf{Race}}, \equiv)^r$ using, as an example, the interaction $\gamma = \mathsf{R1} \rightarrow \mathsf{Ctrl}:\mathsf{finish}$ which appears twice in $\mathcal{M}_{\mathsf{Race}}$: $t_{12} = (1 \overset{\gamma}{\rightarrow} 2)$ and $t_{30} = (3 \overset{\gamma}{\rightarrow} 0)$. There are two participants involved: R1 and Ctrl. Hence we need to consider four combinations: (t_{12}, t_{12}), (t_{12}, t_{30}), (t_{30}, t_{12}), and (t_{30}, t_{30}). For example, using the combination (t_{30}, t_{12}), we compute the glue $[3]_{\equiv_{R1}} \cap [1]_{\equiv_{Ctrl}} = \{1\}$. Then, trivially, there exists a transition $1 \overset{\gamma}{\rightarrow} 2$, and $2 \in [0]_{\equiv_{R1}} \cap [2]_{\equiv_{Ctrl}}$. The same can be shown for all the glues found for the other three combinations. $\qquad \triangleright$

In general it may happen that a global LTS $\mathcal{M}$ does not satisfy $RC(\mathcal{M})^r$ but nevertheless is realisable. We can prove that $RC(\mathcal{M})^r$ is a necessary condition to obtain a realisation which is related to a global model by a *functional* bisimulation. More interesting, however, would be to weaken $RC(\mathcal{M})^r$ such that it becomes necessary for realisability with respect to arbitrary bisimulations. This is an open and challenging question.

Example 5. Consider the signature $\Sigma = (I, M)$ with $I = \{\mathsf{a}, \mathsf{b}, \mathsf{c}\}$, $M = \{\mathsf{m}\}$ and the set $\Gamma = \{\mathsf{a} \rightarrow \mathsf{b}:\mathsf{m}, \mathsf{c} \rightarrow \mathsf{b}:\mathsf{m}, \mathsf{c} \rightarrow \mathsf{a}:\mathsf{m}\}$ of Σ-interactions. The global LTS $\mathcal{M}$ in Table 3 (left) is realisable by the system $\mathcal{S}^r = \{\mathcal{M}^r_a, \mathcal{M}^r_b, \mathcal{M}^r_c\}$. To see this, we compute the Γ-composition $\mathcal{M}' = \otimes^r_\Gamma \{\mathcal{M}^r_a, \mathcal{M}^r_b, \mathcal{M}^r_c\}$ shown in Table 3 (right). Obviously $\mathcal{M}$ is bisimilar to $\mathcal{M}'$ and hence $\mathcal{M}$ is realisable. However, $\mathcal{M}$ does not satisfy the realisability condition $RC(\mathcal{M})^r$.

We prove this by contradiction. Assume that $\equiv = \{\equiv_a, \equiv_b, \equiv_c\}$ is an I-equivalence such that $RC(\mathcal{M}, \equiv)^r$ holds. Now consider the interaction $\mathsf{a} \rightarrow \mathsf{b}:\mathsf{m}$, the global state 0 of $\mathcal{M}$ and the transition $0 \xrightarrow{\mathsf{a} \rightarrow \mathsf{b}:\mathsf{m}}_{\mathcal{M}} 1$. Obviously, $0 \equiv_a 1$

Table 3. Global LTS $\mathcal{M}$ not satisfying $RC(\mathcal{M})^r$ but with realisation $\mathcal{S}^r = \{\mathcal{M}^r_a, \mathcal{M}^r_b, \mathcal{M}^r_c\}$ where $\mathcal{M}' = \otimes^r\{\mathcal{M}^r_a, \mathcal{M}^r_b, \mathcal{M}^r_c\}$

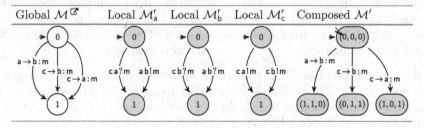

| Global $\mathcal{M}$ | Local $\mathcal{M}^r_a$ | Local $\mathcal{M}^r_b$ | Local $\mathcal{M}^r_c$ | Composed $\mathcal{M}'$ |

and $0 \equiv_b 1$ must hold since there is the transition $0 \xrightarrow{c \to b : m}_{\mathcal{M}} 1$ where a does not participate and the transition $0 \xrightarrow{c \to a : m}_{\mathcal{M}} 1$ where b does not participate. So we can take 1 as a glue state between the global states $q_1 = 0$ and $q_2 = 0$. Then we consider the transition $0 \xrightarrow{a \to b : m}_{\mathcal{M}} 1$ one time for q_1 and one time for q_2. Since we have assumed $RC(\mathcal{M}, \equiv)^r$, there must be a transition $1 \xrightarrow{a \to b : m}_{\mathcal{M}'}$ leaving the glue state which is, however, not the case. Contradiction! Note that nevertheless the bisimilar global LTS $\mathcal{M}'$ does satisfy $RC(\mathcal{M}')^r$. The example can be checked at $\mathcal{M}^{\mathbb{C}}$ and $\mathcal{M}'^{\mathbb{C}}$.   ▷

Discussion. Our realisability condition $RC(\mathcal{M})^r$, based on the notion of an I-equivalence $(\equiv_i)_{i \in I}$, is strongly related to a condition for implementability in [14, Theorem 3.1]. In fact, $RC(\mathcal{M})^r$ can be seen as a generalisation of [14] since we consider multi-interactions with distinguished sets of senders and receivers and also specifications for admissible interactions represented by Γ. Thus we get a generic realisability notion based on Γ-composition rather than full synchronisation. Moreover, our condition ensures realisability modulo bisimulation instead of isomorphism. Technically, implementability with respect to isomorphism is achieved in [14, Theorem 3.1] by requiring that whenever two global states q and q' are i-equivalent, i.e. $(q \equiv_i q')$, for all $i \in I$, then $q = q'$. We do not use this assumption and thus can get realisations modulo bisimilarity which do not realise a global LTS up to isomorphism (cf. [6, Example 8]). Note that [14, Theorem 6.2] also provides a proposal to deal with implementability modulo bisimulation under the assumption of "deterministic product transition systems". In the next section, we study a realisability condition for the case of poor local actions, which deviates significantly from [14].

5.2   Condition for Realisability Using Poor Local Actions

We return to the question of how to check realisability, now in the case of poor local actions. The notion of I-equivalence is again the key. Note, however, that the computation of an appropriate I-equivalence may differ from the rich case.

The realisability condition below is stronger than the one for rich local actions in Definition 9. Intuitively, the reason is that local LTS with poor local actions have, in general, more choices for synchronisation and therefore a global LTS must support these choices in order to be realisable. For each interaction (out → in : m) $\in \Gamma$, we require in more cases the enabledness in a glue state g. More concretely, out → in : m must be enabled in g already when in the j-equivalent states, say q_j, component j is able to output/input message m independently of the communication partners named in out $\cup$ in, since those would anyway not be known from a poor local action. This is formally reflected by considering the interactions $\gamma_1, \ldots, \gamma_n$ in the next definition.

Definition 11 (realisability condition (poor case)). *Let $\mathcal{M}$ be a global LTS over (Σ, Γ). The realisability condition $RC(\mathcal{M})^p$ for $\mathcal{M}$ with respect to poor local actions says that there exists an I-equivalence $(\equiv_i)_{i \in I}$ over $\mathcal{M}$ such that the following property $RC(\mathcal{M}, (\equiv_i)_{i \in I})^p$ holds.*

For all $\gamma = (\text{out} \rightarrow \text{in} : m) \in \Gamma$ *with participants* $\text{out} \cup \text{in} = \{k_1, \ldots, k_n\}$ *we get:*

$$
\forall \begin{pmatrix} \gamma_1 = (\text{out}_1 \rightarrow \text{in}_1 : m) \in \Gamma \\ k_1 \in (\text{out}_1 \cap \text{out}) \cup (\text{in}_1 \cap \text{in}) \\ \cdots \\ \gamma_n = (\text{out}_n \rightarrow \text{in}_n : m) \in \Gamma \\ k_n \in (\text{out}_n \cap \text{out}) \cup (\text{in}_n \cap \text{in}) \end{pmatrix} \forall \begin{pmatrix} q_1 \xrightarrow{\gamma_1}_{\mathcal{M}} q_1' \\ \cdots \\ q_n \xrightarrow{\gamma_n}_{\mathcal{M}} q_n' \\ g \in \bigcap_{j=1}^n [q_j]_{\equiv_{k_j}} \end{pmatrix} \exists g' : \begin{pmatrix} g \xrightarrow{\gamma}_{\mathcal{M}} g' \\ g' \in \bigcap_{j=1}^n [q_j']_{\equiv_{k_j}} \end{pmatrix}
$$

To prove that the condition $RC(\mathcal{M})^{\mathsf{p}}$ indeed guarantees realisability with poor local actions, the idea is again to consider local quotients. Their construction is, however, different from the rich case.

Definition 12 (local quotients with poor local actions). *Let* $\mathcal{M} = (Q, q_0, \Gamma, T)$ *be a global LTS over* (Σ, Γ) *and* $\equiv = (\equiv_i)_{i \in I}$ *an I-equivalence over* $\mathcal{M}$. *For each* $i \in I$ *the* local i-quotient *of* $\mathcal{M}$ *with poor local actions is the LTS* $(\mathcal{M}/\equiv_i)^{\mathsf{p}} = (Q/\equiv_i, [q_0]_{\equiv_i}, \Lambda_i^{\mathsf{p}}(\Gamma), (T/\equiv_i)^{\mathsf{p}})$ *where*

- $Q/\equiv_i = \{[q]_{\equiv_i} \mid q \in Q\}$,
- $(T/\equiv_i)^{\mathsf{p}}$ *is the least set of transitions generated by the following rules:*

$$
\frac{q \xrightarrow{\text{out} \rightarrow \text{in}:m}_{\mathcal{M}} q' \quad i \in \text{out}}{[q]_{\equiv_i} \xrightarrow{!m}_{(\mathcal{M}/\equiv_i)^{\mathsf{p}}} [q']_{\equiv_i}} \qquad \frac{q \xrightarrow{\text{out} \rightarrow \text{in}:m}_{\mathcal{M}} q' \quad i \in \text{in}}{[q]_{\equiv_i} \xrightarrow{?m}_{(\mathcal{M}/\equiv_i)^{\mathsf{p}}} [q']_{\equiv_i}}
$$

Theorem 3. *Let* $\mathcal{M}$ *be a global LTS over* (Σ, Γ) *and let* $\equiv = (\equiv_i)_{i \in I}$ *be an I-equivalence over* $\mathcal{M}$. *If* $RC(\mathcal{M}, \equiv)^{\mathsf{p}}$ *holds then* $\mathcal{M} \sim \otimes_\Gamma^{\mathsf{p}}((\mathcal{M}/\equiv_i)^{\mathsf{p}})_{i \in I}$.

Example 6. Consider the global LTS $\mathcal{M}_{\mathsf{Race}}$ ⧉ (Fig. 2). We show $RC(\mathcal{M}_{\mathsf{Race}})^{\mathsf{p}}$ holds and how, following Theorem 3, a realisation of $\mathcal{M}_{\mathsf{Race}}$ with poor local actions can be constructed. The situation differs from the rich case in Example 4, since the equivalence for Ctrl must be chosen differently. We use the family of equivalences $\equiv = (\equiv_i)_{i \in \{\mathsf{Ctrl}, \mathsf{R1}, \mathsf{R2}\}}$ that obeys $RC(\mathcal{M}_{\mathsf{Race}}, \equiv)^{\mathsf{p}}$ (see below) and partitions the state space Q as follows: $Q/\equiv_{\mathsf{Ctrl}} = \{\{0\}, \{1\}, \{2, 3\}\}$, $Q/\equiv_{\mathsf{R1}} = \{\{0, 2\}, \{1, 3\}\}$, and $Q/\equiv_{\mathsf{R2}} = \{\{0, 3\}, \{1, 2\}\}$. Using these equivalences, the local quotients for Ctrl, $\mathsf{R1}$ and $\mathsf{R2}$ are as follows:

Thus we have obtained a system which is a realisation with poor local actions of $\mathcal{M}_{\mathsf{Race}}$. The local quotients coincide, up to renaming of states, with the local LTS used in the system $\mathcal{S}_{\mathsf{Race}}^{\mathsf{p}}$ considered in Sect. 1.

Now, we illustrate how to verify $RC(\mathcal{M}_{\mathsf{Race}}, \equiv)^r$ using, as an example, the interaction $\mathsf{R1} \rightarrow \mathsf{Ctrl} : \mathsf{finish}$. We have $1 \xrightarrow{\mathsf{R1} \rightarrow \mathsf{Ctrl}:\mathsf{finish}}_{\mathcal{M}_{\mathsf{Race}}} 2$. We also have $1 \xrightarrow{\mathsf{R2} \rightarrow \mathsf{Ctrl}:\mathsf{finish}}_{\mathcal{M}_{\mathsf{Race}}} 3$ (we must consider the interaction $\mathsf{R2} \rightarrow \mathsf{Ctrl} : \mathsf{finish}$ as well since we are in the poor case). Taking 1 as a (trivial) glue state, we thus have, as required, the existence of $1 \xrightarrow{R1 \rightarrow Ctrl : finish}_{\mathcal{M}_{Race}} 2$ *but also* it is required that $2 \equiv_{Ctrl} 3$ must hold which is the case. Note that we wouldn't have succeeded here if we would have taken the identity for $\equiv_{Ctrl}$ as done for the rich case.   ▷

6   Tool Support: Ceta

We developed a supporting prototypical tool *Ceta* (Choreographic Extended Team Automata) to analyse global specifications and produce visualisations of state machines. It is open-source, available at https://github.com/arcalab/choreo/tree/ceta, and executable by browsing to https://lmf.di.uminho.pt/ceta.

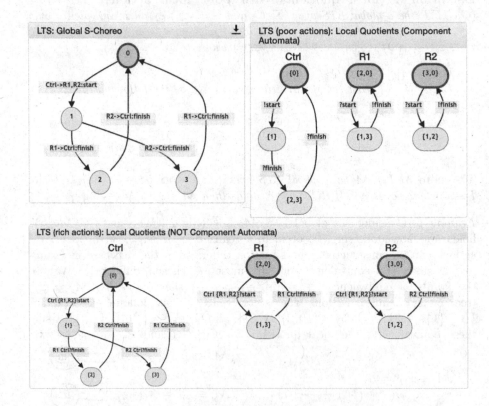

Fig. 4. Screenshots of the Ceta tool (http://lmf.di.uminho.pt/ceta)

Ceta starts with a web browser, opening a static webpage that uses our compiled JavaScript built with the Caos framework [32] (cf. screenshot in Fig. 4). The user input is a global protocol described in a choreographic language, resembling regular expressions of interactions. A set of examples with descriptions is also included, covering the examples presented in this paper. The analyses include graphical views of: (i) the global LTS; (ii) local LTS's with rich actions; and

(iii) local LTS's with poor actions. Other widgets provide further insights, such as the composition of the local LTS's, the intermediate equivalence classes for both the rich and poor case, the synchronous composition of local LTS's, and bisimulations between the global prototol and composed systems. Readable error messages are provided when the realisability conditions do not hold.

7 Conclusion

We have proposed a rigorous discipline for developing interaction-based systems. At the heart of our methodology lies the realisation of a global interaction model, i.e. its decomposition into a set of (possibly distributed) components with synchronous communication. We have investigated realisability conditions for two different localisation styles (rich and poor local actions) and techniques to synthesise realisations. Our approach is generic with respect to the choice of admissible interaction sets which may contain arbitrary interactions between multiple senders and receivers but may also be restricted, e.g., to various forms of communication, like multicast or peer-to-peer communication. Due to the generic nature of our notion of an interaction set, our results can be instantiated by different concrete coordination formalisms. For instance, synchronisation type specifications used in the framework of (extended) team automata [5] as well as interactions used in BIP [11] can be represented by interaction sets. Our results should then be directly applicable, to extend the team automata framework as well as BIP by global LTS and to generate distributed component systems for them on the basis of our realisation conditions.

In future research, we plan to (i) integrate the treatment of internal actions using weak bisimulation equivalence for the realisation notions; (ii) consider communication properties (like receptiveness and responsiveness, cf. [5]) when systems are generated from global models; (iii) study open global models (systems) and their composition; and (iv) investigate realisability conditions in the context of asynchronous communication. Moreover, we are still looking for a weaker version of our realisability condition for synchronous systems making it necessary for arbitrary (also non-functional) bisimulations.

Furthermore, we intend to investigate the relation with work in the literature on the decomposition of related formalisms like (Petri net or algebraic) processes into (indecomposable) components [27,31] used to parallelise (verification of) concurrent systems [16,18] or obtain better (optimised) implementations [33,34].

Acknowledgments. *Ter Beek* was supported by MUR PRIN 2020TL3X8X project T-LADIES (Typeful Language Adaptation for Dynamic, Interacting and Evolving Systems) and *Proença* by the CISTER Research Unit (UIDP/UIDB/04234/2020), financed by National Funds through FCT/MCTES (Portuguese Foundation for Science and Technology); by project IBEX (PTDC/CCI-COM/4280/2021) financed by national funds through FCT; and by project Route 25 (ref. TRB/2022/00061 – C645463824-00000063) funded by the EU/Next Generation, within the Recovery and Resilience Plan.

References

1. Barbanera, F., Lanese, I., Tuosto, E.: Choreography automata. In: Bliudze, S., Bocchi, L. (eds.) COORDINATION 2020. LNCS, vol. 12134, pp. 86–106. Springer, Cham (2020). https://doi.org/10.1007/978-3-030-50029-0_6
2. Barbanera, F., Lanese, I., Tuosto, E.: Formal choreographic languages. In: ter Beek, M.H., Sirjani, M. (eds.) COORDINATION 2022. LNCS, vol. 13271, pp. 121–139. Springer, Cham (2022). https://doi.org/10.1007/978-3-031-08143-9_8
3. Basile, D., Degano, P., Ferrari, G.-L., Tuosto, E.: Relating two automata-based models of orchestration and choreography. J. Log. Algebr. Meth. Program. **85**(3), 425–446 (2016). https://doi.org/10.1016/J.JLAMP.2015.09.011
4. ter Beek, M.H., Ellis, C.A., Kleijn, J., Rozenberg, G.: Synchronizations in team automata for groupware systems. Comput. Sup. Coop. Work **12**(1), 21–69 (2003). https://doi.org/10.1023/A:1022407907596
5. ter Beek, M.H., Hennicker, R., Kleijn, J.: Compositionality of safe communication in systems of team automata. In: Pun, V.K.I., Stolz, V., Simao, A. (eds.) ICTAC 2020. LNCS, vol. 12545, pp. 200–220. Springer, Cham (2020). https://doi.org/10.1007/978-3-030-64276-1_11
6. ter Beek, M.H., Hennicker, R., Proença, J.: Realisability of global models of interaction (extended version). Technical report, Zenodo (2023). https://doi.org/10.5281/zenodo.8377188
7. ter Beek, M.H., Cledou, G., Hennicker, R., Proença, J.: Can We communicate? Using dynamic logic to verify team automata. In: Chechik, M., Katoen, J.P., Leucker, M. (eds.) FM 2023. LNCS, vol. 14000, pp. 122–141. Springer, Cham (2023). https://doi.org/10.1007/978-3-031-27481-7_9
8. Bejleri, A., Yoshida, N.: Synchronous multiparty session types. ENTCS **241**, 3–33 (2008). https://doi.org/10.1016/j.entcs.2009.06.002
9. Ben-David, S., Chechik, M., Gurfinkel, A., Uchitel, S.: CSSL: a logic for specifying conditional scenarios. In: ESEC/FSE, pp. 37–47. ACM (2011). https://doi.org/10.1145/2025113.2025123
10. van Benthem, J., van Eijck, J., Stebletsova, V.: Modal logic, transition systems and processes. J. Log. Comput. **4**(5), 811–855 (1994). https://doi.org/10.1093/logcom/4.5.811
11. Bliudze, S., Sifakis, J.: The algebra of connectors: structuring interaction in BIP. IEEE Trans. Comput. **57**(10), 1315–1330 (2008). https://doi.org/10.1109/TC.2008.26
12. Bunte, O., et al.: The mCRL2 toolset for analysing concurrent systems. In: Vojnar, T., Zhang, L. (eds.) TACAS 2019. LNCS, vol. 11428, pp. 21–39. Springer, Cham (2019). https://doi.org/10.1007/978-3-030-17465-1_2
13. Castagna, G., Dezani-Ciancaglini, M., Padovani, L.: On global types and multiparty sessions. Log. Methods Comput. Sci. **8**(1), 24:1–24:45 (2012). https://doi.org/10.2168/LMCS-8(1:24)2012
14. Castellani, I., Mukund, M., Thiagarajan, P.S.: Synthesizing distributed transition systems from global specifications. In: Rangan, C.P., Raman, V., Ramanujam, R. (eds.) FSTTCS 1999. LNCS, vol. 1738, pp. 219–231. Springer, Heidelberg (1999). https://doi.org/10.1007/3-540-46691-6_17
15. Cengarle, M.V., Knapp, A., Mühlberger, H.: Interactions. In: Lano, K. (ed.) UML 2 Semantics and Applications, chap. 9, pp. 205–248. Wiley (2009). https://doi.org/10.1002/9780470522622
16. Corradini, F., Gorrieri, R., Marchignoli, D.: Towards parallelization of concurrent systems. RAIRO Theor. Inform. Appl. **32**(4–6), 99–125 (1998). https://doi.org/10.1051/ita/1998324-600991

17. de Alfaro, L., Henzinger, T.A.: Interface automata. In: ESEC/FSE, pp. 109–120. ACM (2001). https://doi.org/10.1145/503209.503226
18. Groote, J.F., Moller, F.: Verification of parallel systems via decomposition. In: Cleaveland, W.R. (ed.) CONCUR 1992. LNCS, vol. 630, pp. 62–76. Springer, Heidelberg (1992). https://doi.org/10.1007/BFb0084783
19. Harel, D., Kozen, D., Tiuryn, J.: Dynamic Logic. Foundations of Computing. MIT Press, Cambridge (2000). https://doi.org/10.7551/mitpress/2516.001.0001
20. Harel, D., Thiagarajan, P.S.: Message sequence charts. In: Lavagno, L., Martin, G., Selic, B. (eds.) UML for Real: Design of Embedded Real-Time Systems, pp. 77–105. Kluwer (2003). https://doi.org/10.1007/0-306-48738-1_4
21. Hennicker, R.: Role-based development of dynamically evolving esembles. In: Fiadeiro, J.L., Tutu, I. (eds.) WADT 2018. LNCS, vol. 11563, pp. 3–24. Springer, Cham (2019). https://doi.org/10.1007/978-3-030-23220-7_1
22. Hennicker, R., Wirsing, M.: Dynamic logic for ensembles. In: Margaria, T., Steffen, B. (eds.) ISoLA 2018. LNCS, vol. 11246, pp. 32–47. Springer, Cham (2018). https://doi.org/10.1007/978-3-030-03424-5_3
23. Honda, K., Yoshida, N., Carbone, M.: Multiparty asynchronous session types. In: POPL, pp. 273–284. ACM (2008). https://doi.org/10.1145/1328438.1328472
24. Hüttel, H., et al.: Foundations of session types and behavioural contracts. ACM Comput. Surv. 49(1), 3:1–3:36 (2016). https://doi.org/10.1145/2873052
25. Jongmans, S.S., Ferreira, F.: Synthetic behavioural typing: sound, regular multiparty sessions via implicit local types. In: ECOOP. LIPIcs, vol. 263, pp. 9:1–9:29. Dagstuhl (2023). https://doi.org/10.4230/LIPIcs.ECOOP.2023.9
26. Larsen, K.G., Nyman, U., Wąsowski, A.: Modal I/O automata for interface and product line theories. In: De Nicola, R. (ed.) ESOP 2007. LNCS, vol. 4421, pp. 64–79. Springer, Heidelberg (2007). https://doi.org/10.1007/978-3-540-71316-6_6
27. Luttik, B.: Unique parallel decomposition in branching and weak bisimulation semantics. Theor. Comput. Sci. 612, 29–44 (2016). https://doi.org/10.1016/j.tcs.2015.10.013
28. Lynch, N.A., Tuttle, M.R.: An introduction to Input/Output automata. CWI Q. 2(3), 219–246 (1989). https://ir.cwi.nl/pub/18164
29. Magee, J., Kramer, J.: Concurrency: State Models & Java Programming. Wiley, Hoboken (2006)
30. Micskei, Z., Waeselynck, H.: The many meanings of UML 2 sequence diagrams: a survey. Softw. Syst. Model. 10(4), 489–514 (2011). https://doi.org/10.1007/s10270-010-0157-9
31. Milner, R., Moller, F.: Unique decomposition of processes. Theor. Comput. Sci. 107(2), 357–363 (1993). https://doi.org/10.1016/0304-3975(93)90176-T
32. Proença, J., Edixhoven, L.: Caos: a reusable scala web animator of operational semantics. In: Jongmans, S.S., Lopes, A. (eds.) COORDINATION 2023. LNCS, vol. 13908, pp. 163–171. Springer, Cham (2023). https://doi.org/10.1007/978-3-031-35361-1_9
33. Teren, V., Cortadella, J., Villa, T.: Decomposition of transition systems into sets of synchronizing state machines. In: DSD, pp. 77–81. IEEE (2021). https://doi.org/10.1109/DSD53832.2021.00021
34. Teren, V., Cortadella, J., Villa, T.: Decomposition of transition systems into sets of synchronizing free-choice Petri Nets. In: DSD, pp. 165–173. IEEE (2022). https://doi.org/10.1109/DSD57027.2022.00031
35. Tuosto, E., Guanciale, R.: Semantics of global view of choreographies. J. Log. Algebr. Meth. Program. 95, 17–40 (2018). https://doi.org/10.1016/j.jlamp.2017.11.002

Efficient Reactive Synthesis Using Mode Decomposition

Matías Brizzio[1,2] and César Sánchez[1(✉)]

[1] IMDEA Software Institute, Madrid, Spain
cesar.sanchez@imdea.org
[2] Universidad Politécnica de Madrid, Madrid, Spain

Abstract. Developing critical components, such as mission controllers or embedded systems, is a challenging task. Reactive synthesis is a technique to automatically produce correct controllers. Given a high-level specification written in LTL, reactive synthesis consists of computing a system that satisfies the specification as long as the environment respects the assumptions. Unfortunately, LTL synthesis suffers from high computational complexity which precludes its use for many large cases.

A promising approach to improve synthesis scalability consists of decomposing a safety specification into a smaller specifications, that can be processed independently and composed into a solution for the original specification. Previous decomposition methods focus on identifying independent parts of the specification whose systems are combined via simultaneous execution.

In this work, we propose a novel decomposition algorithm based on *modes*, which consists on decomposing a complex safety specification into smaller problems whose solution is then composed *sequentially* (instead of simultaneously). The input to our algorithm is the original specification and the description of the modes. We show how to generate sub-specifications automatically and we prove that if all sub-problems are realizable then the full specification is realizable. Moreover, we show how to construct a system for the original specification from sub-systems for the decomposed specifications. We finally illustrate the feasibility of our approach with multiple cases studies using off-the-self synthesis tools to process the obtained sub-problems.

1 Introduction

Reactive synthesis [11] is the problem of constructing a reactive system automatically from a high-level description of its desired behavior. A reactive system interacts continuously with an uncontrollable external environment [12]. The specification describes both the assumptions that the environment is supposed

Funded by PRODIGY Project (TED2021-132464B-I00)—funded by MCIN/AEI/10.13039/501100011033 and the EU NextGenerationEU/PRTR—,by DECO Project (PID2022-138072OB-I00)—funded by MCIN/AEI/10.13039/501100011033 and by the ESF+—and by a research grant from Nomadic Labs and the Tezos Foundation.

E. Ábrahám et al. (Eds.): ICTAC 2023, LNCS 14446, pp. 256–275, 2023.
https://doi.org/10.1007/978-3-031-47963-2_16

to follow and the goal that the system must satisfy. Reactive synthesis guarantees that every execution of the system synthesized satisfies the specification as long as the environment respects the assumptions.

Linear-Time Temporal Logic (LTL) [47] is a widely used formalism in verification [44] and synthesis [48] of reactive systems. Reactive synthesis can produce controllers which are essential for various applications, including hardware design [6] and control of autonomous robotic systems [17,36].

Many reactive synthesis tools have been developed in recent years [19,25] in spite of the high complexity of the synthesis problem. Reactive synthesis for full LTL is 2EXPTIME-complete [48], so LTL fragments with better complexity have been identified. For example, GR(1)—general reactivity with rank 1—enjoys an efficient (polynomial) symbolic synthesis algorithm [6]. Even though GR(1) can express the safety fragment of LTL considered in this paper, translating our specifications into GR(1) involves at least an exponential blow-up in the worst case [32]. Better scalable algorithms for reactive synthesis are still required [38].

Model checking, which consists on deciding whether a *given system* satisfies the specification, is an easier problem than synthesis. Compositional approaches to model checking break down the analysis into smaller sub-tasks, which significantly improve the performance. Similarly, in this paper we aim to improve the scalability of reactive synthesis introducing a novel decomposition approach that breaks down the original specification into multiple sub-specifications.

There are theoretical compositional approaches [21,39], and implementations that handle large conjunctions [4,13,46]. For instance, Lisa [4] has successfully scaled synthesis to significant conjunctions of LTL formulas over finite traces (a.k.a. LTL_f [14]). Lisa is further extended to handling prominent disjunctions in Lydia [13]. These modular synthesis approaches rely heavily on the decomposition of the specification into simultaneous sub-specifications [24]. However, when sub-specifications share multiple variables, these approaches typically return the exact original specification, failing to generate smaller decompositions.

We tackle this difficulty by introducing a novel decomposition algorithm for safety LTL specifications. We chose the safety fragment of LTL [40,52] because it is a fundamental requirement language in many safety-critical applications. Extending our approach to larger temporal fragments of LTL is future work.

To break down a specification we use the concept of *mode*. A mode is a subset of the states in which the system can be during its execution which is of particular relevance for the designer of the system. At any given point in the execution, the system is in a single mode, and during an execution the system can transition between modes. In requirement design, the intention of modes is often explicitly expressed by the requirement engineers as a *high-level state machine*. Using LTL reactive synthesis these modes are boiled down into additional LTL requirements, which are then processed with the rest of the specification. In this paper, we propose to exploit modes to decompose the specification into multiple synthesis sub-problems.

Most previous decomposition methods [24,33] break specifications into independent *simultaneous* sub-specifications whose corresponding games are solved independently and the system strategies composed easily. In contrast, we propose *sequential* games, one for each mode. For each mode decomposition, we restrict the conditions under which each mode can "jump" into another mode based on the initial conditions of the arriving mode. From the point of local analysis of the game that corresponds to a mode, jumping into another mode is permanently winning. We show in this paper that our decomposition approach is sound—meaning that given a specification, system modes and initial conditions—if all the sub-specifications generated are realizable, then the original specification is realizable. Moreover, we show a synthesis method that efficiently constructs a system for the full specification from systems synthesized for the sub-specifications. An additional advantage of our method is that the automaton that encodes the solution is structured according to the modes proposed, so it is simpler to understand by the user.

Related Work. The problem of reactive synthesis from temporal logic specifications has been studied for many years [2,6,20,48]. Given its high complexity (2EXPTIME-complete [48]) easier fragments of LTL have been studied. For example, reactive synthesis for GR(1) specifications can be solved in polynomial time [6]. Safety-LTL has attracted significant interest due to its algorithmic simplicity compared to general LTL synthesis [53], but the construction of deterministic safety automaton presents a performance bottleneck for large formulas.

For the model-checking problem, compositional approaches improve the scalability significantly [50], even for large formulas. Remarkably, these approaches break down the analysis into smaller sub-tasks [48]. For model-checking, Dureja and Rozier [18] propose to analyze dependencies between properties to reduce the number of model-checking tasks. Recently, Finkbeiner et al. [24] adapt this idea to synthesis, where the dependency analysis is based on controllable variables, which makes the decomposition impossible when the requirements that form the specification share many system (controlled) variables. We propose an alternative approach for dependency analysis in the context of system specification, by leveraging the concept of *mode* to break down a specification into smaller components. This approach is a common practice in Requirements Engineering (*RE*) [27,28] where specifications typically contain a high-level state machine description (where states are called modes) and most requirements are specific to each mode. Furthermore, this approach finds widespread application in various industries, employing languages such as *EARS* [45] and *NASA*'s *FRET* language [26]. Recently, a notion of *context* is introduced by Mallozi et al [43] in their recent work on *assume-guarantee* contracts. Unlike modes, contexts depend solely on the environment and are not part of the elicitation process or the system specification.

Software Cost Reduction (SCR) [27,28,31] is a well-establish technique that structures specifications around *mode classes* and *modes*. A mode class refers to internally controlled variables that maintain state information with a set of possible values known as modes.

We use modes here provided by the user to accelerate synthesis, exploiting that in RE modes are comonly provided by the engineer during system specification. Recently, Balachander et al. [3] proposed a method to assist the synthesis process by providing a sketch of the desired Mealy machine, which can help to produce a system that better aligns with the engineer's intentions. This approach is currently still only effective for small systems, as it requires the synthesis of the system followed by the generation of example traces to guide the search for a reasonable solution. In contrast our interest is in the decomposition of the synthesis process in multiple synthesis sub-tasks.

Other compositional synthesis approaches aim to incrementally add requirements to a system specification during its design [39]. On the other hand, [23] and [24] rely extensively on dropping assumptions, which can restrict the ability to decompose complex real-world specifications.

2   Motivating Example

We illustrate the main ideas of our decomposition technique using the following running example of a counter machine (CM) with a reset. The system must count the number of ticks produced by an external agent, unless the reset is signaled—also by the environment—in which case the count is restarted. When the count reaches a specific limit, the count has to be restarted as well and an output variable is used to indicate that the bound has been reached. Figure 1 shows a specification for this system with a bound of 20. This example is written in TLSF (see [34]), a well-established specification language for reactive synthesis, which is widely used as a standard language for the synthesis competition, $SYNTCOMP$ [1]. Even for this simple specification, all state-of-the-art synthesis tools from the synthesis competition $SYNTCOMP$ [1], including $Strix$ [46], are unable to produce a system that satisfies CM.

Recent decomposition techniques [24,33] construct a dependency graph considering controllable variable relationships, but fail to decompose this specification due to the mutual dependencies among output variables. Our technique breaks down this specification into smaller sub-specifications, grouping the counter machine for those states with counter value 1 and 2 in a mode, states with counter 3 and 4 in a second mode, etc., as follows:

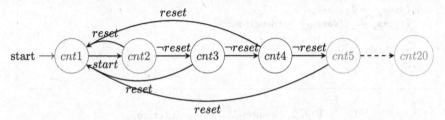

Smaller controllers are synthesized independently, which can be easily combined to satisfy the original specification Fig. 1. In the example, we group the states in pairs for better readability, but it is possible to use larger sizes. In fact, for

$N = 20$ the optimal decomposition considers modes that group four values of
the counter (see Sect. 5). The synthesis for each mode is efficient because in a
given mode we can ignore those requirements that involve valuations that belong
to other modes, leading to smaller specifications.

```
PARAMETERS { N = 20;}
INPUTS {reset;start;} OUTPUTS {counter[N+1];trigger;}
INITIALLY{ (!reset && !start);} ASSUMPTIONS{ G !(reset && start);}
PRESET{counter[0] && (&&[1 <= i <=N]!counter[i]);}
DEFINITIONS {
  mutual(b) = G ||[0 <= i < n](b[i] && &&[j IN {0, 1 .. (n-1)} (\) {i}] !
    b[j]);}}
GUARANTEES
  mutual(counter); G (reset → X counter[0]);
  G ((counter[0] &&  start) →  X (counter[1] || reset));
  G ((counter[1] && !reset) →  X (counter[2] || reset));
  ...
  G ((counter[N-1] && !reset) →  X (counter[N] || reset));
  G (counter[N] → X counter[0]);
  G (counter[N] → trigger);  G (!counter[N] → !trigger);
```

Fig. 1. Counter machine specification.

```
// common part to all projections.
INPUTS {reset;start;} INITIALLY (!reset && !start); ASSUMPTIONS G !(reset
     && start);

[Projection under m1]
OUTPUTS {counter_0, counter_1; trigger; jump₂; s_Oφ; done}
GUARANTEES
  G (!done → (counter_0 || counter_1));
  G (!done → (reset → X counter_0));
  G (!done → (counter_0 && start) → X (counter_1 || reset));
  G (!done → ((counter_1 && !reset) → s_Oφ));
  G (!done → (s_Oφ && !done) → X FALSE);
  G (!done → !trigger);
  G (done → X done);
  G (jump₂ → X done);
  G (!jump₂ → (!done → X !done));

  [Projection under m2]
  ...
```

Fig. 2. Counter-Machine projection.

In this work, we refer to these partitions of the state space as modes. In requirements engineering (RE) it is common practice to enrich reactive LTL specifications with a state transition system based on modes, which are also used to describe many constraints that only apply to specific modes.

Software cost reduction (SCR) uses modes in specifications and has been successfully applied in requirements for safety-critical systems, such as an aircraft's operational flight program [31], a submarine's communication system [30], nuclear power plant [51], among others [5,35]. SCR has also been used in the development of human-centric decision systems [29], and event-based transition systems derived from goal-oriented requirements models [41].

Despite the long-standing use of modes in SCR, state-of-the-art reactive synthesis tools have not fully utilized this concept. The approach that we introduce in this paper exploits mode descriptions to decompose specifications significantly reducing synthesis time. For instance, when decomposing our motivating example CM using modes, we were able to achieve 90% reduction in the specification size, measured as the number of clauses and the length of the specification (see Sect. 5). Figure 2 shows the projections with a bound $N = 4$ for mode $m_1 = (counter_0 \vee counter_1)$. In each sub-specification, we introduce new variables (controlled by the system). These variables encode mode transitions using *jump* variables. When the system transitions to a new mode, the current sub-specification automatically wins the ongoing game, encoded by the *done* variable A new game will start in the arriving mode. Furthermore, the system can only jump to new modes if the arriving mode is prepared, i.e., if its initial conditions—as indicated by the $s_{\bigcirc\varphi}$ variables—can satisfy the pending obligations. The semantics of these variables is further explained in the next section.

In this work, we assume that the initial conditions are also provided manually as part of the mode decomposition. While modes are common practice in requirement specification, having to manually provide initial conditions is the major current technical drawback of our approach. We will study in the future how to generate these initial conditions automatically. In summary, our algorithm receives the original specification S, a set of modes and their corresponding initial conditions. Then, it generates a sub-specification for each mode and discharges these to an off-the-self synthesis tool to decide their realizability. If all the sub-specifications are realizable, the systems obtained are then composed into a single system for the original specification, which also shares the structure of the mode decomposition.

3 Preliminaries

We consider a finite set of AP of atomic propositions. Since we are interested in reactive systems where there is an ongoing interaction between a system and its environment, we split AP into those propositions controlled by the environment $\mathcal{X}$ and those controlled by the system $\mathcal{Y}$, so $\mathcal{X} \cup \mathcal{Y} = $ AP and $\mathcal{X} \cap \mathcal{Y} = \emptyset$. The alphabet induced by the atomic propositions is $\Sigma = 2^{\mathsf{AP}}$. We use Σ^* for the set of finite words over Σ and Σ^ω for the set of infinite words over Σ. Given $\sigma \in \Sigma^\omega$

and $i \in \mathbb{N}$, $\sigma(i)$ represents the element of σ at position i, and σ^i represents the word σ' that results by removing the prefix $\sigma(0) \ldots \sigma(i-1)$ from σ, that is σ' s.t. $\sigma'(j) = \sigma(j-1)$ for $j \geq i$. Given $u \in \Sigma^*$ and $v \in \Sigma^\omega$, uv represents the ω-word that results from concatenating u and v. We use LTL [44,47] to describe specifications. The syntax of LTL is the following:

$$\varphi ::= true \mid a \mid \varphi \vee \varphi \mid \neg\varphi \mid \bigcirc\varphi \mid \varphi \, \mathcal{U} \, \varphi \mid \square\varphi$$

where $a \in \mathsf{AP}$, and $\vee$, $\wedge$ and $\neg$ are the usual Boolean disjunction, conjunction and negation, and $\bigcirc$ is the next temporal operator (a common derived operator is $false = \neg true$). A formula with no temporal operator is called a Boolean formula, or predicate. We say φ is in negation normal form (NNF), whenever all negation operators in φ are pushed only in front of atoms using dualities. The semantics of LTL associate traces $\sigma \in \Sigma^\omega$ with formulae as follows:

$$
\begin{aligned}
&\sigma \vDash true & &\text{always holds} \\
&\sigma \vDash a & &\text{iff } a \in \sigma(0) \\
&\sigma \vDash \varphi_1 \vee \varphi_2 & &\text{iff } \sigma \vDash \varphi_1 \text{ or } \sigma \vDash \varphi_2 \\
&\sigma \vDash \neg\varphi & &\text{iff } \sigma \nvDash \varphi \\
&\sigma \vDash \bigcirc\varphi & &\text{iff } \sigma^1 \vDash \varphi \\
&\sigma \vDash \varphi_1 \, \mathcal{U} \, \varphi_2 & &\text{iff for some } i \geq 0 \;\; \sigma^i \vDash \varphi_2, \text{ and for all } 0 \leq j < i, \sigma^j \vDash \varphi_1 \\
&\sigma \vDash \square\varphi & &\text{iff for all } i \geq 0 \;\; \sigma^i \vDash \varphi
\end{aligned}
$$

A Syntactic Fragment for Safety. A useful fragment of LTL is LTL_X where formulas only contain $\bigcirc$ as a temporal operator. In this work, we focus on a fragment of LTL we called $\mathsf{GX_0}$:

$$\alpha \rightarrow (\beta \wedge \square\psi)$$

where α, β and ψ are in LTL_X.

This fragment can only express safety properties [10,44] and includes a large fragment of all safety properties expressible in LTL. This format is supported by tools like Strix [46] and is convenient for our reactive problem specification.

Definition 1 (Reactive Specification). *A reactive specification $S = (A, G)$ is given by $A = (I_e, \varphi_e)$ and $G = (I_s, \varphi_s)$ (all LTL_X formulas), where I_e and I_s are the initial conditions of the environment and the system, and φ_e and φ_s are called assumptions and guarantees. The meaning of S is the $\mathsf{GX_0}$ formula:*

$$(I_e \rightarrow (I_s \wedge \square(\varphi_e \rightarrow \varphi_s)))$$

In TLSF I_e and I_s are represented as *INITIALLY* and *PRESET*, resp.

Reactive Synthesis. Consider a specification φ over $\mathsf{AP} = \mathcal{X} \cup \mathcal{Y}$. A trace σ is formed by the environment and the system choosing in turn valuations for their propositions. The specification φ is realizable with respect to $(\mathcal{X}, \mathcal{Y})$

if there exists a strategy $g : (2^{\mathcal{X}})^+ \rightarrow 2^{\mathcal{Y}}$ such that for an arbitrary infinite sequence $X = X_0, X_1, X_2, \ldots \in (2^{\mathcal{X}})^\omega$, φ is *true* in the infinite trace $\rho = (X_0 \cup g(X_0)), (X_1 \cup g(X_0, X_1)), (X_2 \cup g(X_0, X_1, X_2)), \ldots$ A play ρ is *winning* (for the system) if $\rho \models \varphi$.

Realizability is the decision problem of whether a specification has a winning strategy, and synthesis is the problem of computing one wining system (strategy). Both problems can be solved in double-exponential time for an arbitrary LTL formula [48]. If there is no winning strategy for the system, the specification is called *unrealizable*. In this scenario, the environment has at least one strategy to falsify φ for every possible strategy of the system. Reactive safety synthesis considers reactive synthesis for safety formulas.

We encode system strategies using a deterministic Mealy machine $W = (Q, s, \delta, L)$ where Q is the set of states, s is the initial state, $\delta : Q \times 2^{\mathcal{X}} \rightarrow Q$ is the transition function that given valuations of the environment variables it produces a successor state and $L : Q \times 2^{\mathcal{X}} \rightarrow 2^{\mathcal{Y}}$ is the output labeling that given valuations of the environment it produces valuations of the system. The strategy g encoded by a machine $W : (Q, s, \delta, L)$ is as follows:

- if $e \in 2^{\mathcal{X}}$, then $g(e) = L(s, e)$
- if $u \in (2^{\mathcal{X}})^+$ and $e \in 2^{\mathcal{X}}$ then $g(ue) = L(\delta^*(s, u), e)$ where δ^* is the usual extension of δ to $(2^{\mathcal{X}})^*$.

It is well known that if a specification is realizable then there is Mealy machine encoding a winning strategy for the system.

4   Mode Based Synthesis

We present now our mode-based solution to reactive safety synthesis. The starting point is a *reactive specification* as a $\mathsf{G}X_0$ formula written in TLSF. We define a mode m as a predicate over $\mathcal{X} \cup \mathcal{Y}$, that is $m \in 2^{\mathcal{X} \cup \mathcal{Y}}$. A mode captures a set of states of the system during its execution. Given a trace $\sigma = s_0, s_1, \ldots$, if $s_i \models m$ we say that m is the *active mode* at time i. In this paper, we consider mutually exclusive modes, so only one mode can be active at a given point in time. As part of the specification of synthesis problems the requirement engineer describes the modes $M = \{m_1, \ldots, m_n\}$, partially expressing the intentions of the structure of the intended system. A set of modes $M = \{m_1, m_2, \ldots, m_n\}$ is legal if it partitions the set of variable valuations, that is:

- **Disjointness:** for all $i \neq j$, $(m_i \rightarrow \neg m_j)$ is valid.
- **Completeness:** $\bigvee_i m_i$ is valid.

Within a trace σ there may be instants during execution there are transitions between modes. We will refer to the modes involved in this transition as *related modes*. Formally:

Definition 2 (Related Modes). *Consider a trace $\sigma = \sigma(0)\sigma(1)\sigma(2) \ldots$ and two modes $m_1, m_2 \in M$. We say that m_1 and m_2 as related, denoted as $m_1 \prec m_2$ if, at some point i: $(\sigma(i) \models m_1)$ and $(\sigma(i+1) \models m_2)$.*

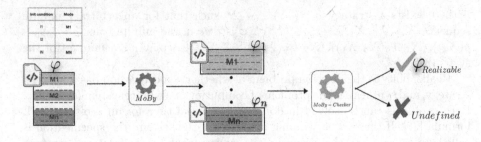

Fig. 3. Overview of MoBy

A key element of our approach is to enrich the specification of the synthesis sub-problem corresponding to mode m_i forbidding the system to jump to another mode m_j unless the initial condition of mode j satisfying the pending "obligations" at the time of jumping. To formally capture obligations we introduce fresh variables for future sub-formulas that appear in the specification.

Definition 3 (*Obligation Variables*). *For each sub-formula $\bigcirc\psi$ in the specification, we introduce a fresh variables $s_{\bigcirc\psi}$ to encodes that the system is obliged to satisfy ψ.*

These variables will be controlled by the system and their dynamics will be captured by $s_{\bigcirc\psi} \to \bigcirc\psi$ introduced in every mode (unless the system leaves the mode, which will be allowed only if the arriving system satisfy ψ). These variables are similar to temporal testers [49] and allow a simple treatment of obligations that are left pending after a mode jump. We also introduce variables $jump_j$ which will encode (in the game and sub-specification corresponding to mode m_i) whether the system decides to jump to mode m_j (see Algorithm 2 below).

4.1   Mode Based Decomposition

We present now the MoBy algorithm, which decomposes a reactive specification S into a set of (smaller) specifications $\Pi = \{S_1, \ldots, S_n\}$, using the provided system modes $M = \{m_1, \ldots, m_n\}$ and initial mode-conditions $I = \{I_1, \ldots, I_n\}$. Figure 3 shows an overview of MoBy. Particularly, MoBy receives a specification together with modes and one initial condition per mode. The algorithm decompose the specification into smaller sub-specifications one per mode.

The main result is that the decomposition that MoBy performs guarantees that if each projection $S_i \in \Pi$ is realizable then the original specification is also realizable, and that the systems synthesized independently for each sub-specification can be combined into an implementation for the original specification S (See Lemma 1 and Corollary 1).

We first introduce some useful notation before presenting the main algorithm. We denote by $\varphi[\phi\backslash\psi]$ the formula that is obtained by replacing in φ occurrences of ϕ by ψ. We assume that all formulas have been converted to *NNF*, where $\bigcirc$ operators have been pushed to the atoms. It is easy to see that a formula in

NNF is a Boolean combination of sub-formulas of the form $\bigcirc^i p$ where $p \in \mathsf{AP}$ and sub-formulas ψ that do not contain any temporal operator. We use some auxiliary functions:

- The first function is $ASF(\varphi)$, which returns the set of sub-formulas ψ of φ such that (1) ψ does not contain $\bigcirc$ (2) ψ is either φ or the father formula of ψ contains $\bigcirc$. We call these formulas maximal next-free sub-formulas of φ.
- The second function is $NSF(\varphi)$, which returns the set of sub-formulas ψ such that (1) the root symbol of ψ is $\bigcirc$ and (2) either ψ is φ, or the father of ψ does not start with $\bigcirc$. It is easy to see that all formulas returned by *NSF* are of the form $\bigcirc^i p$ for $i > 0$, and indeed are the sub-formulas of the form $\bigcirc^i p$ not contain in other formulas other sub-formulas of these forms. We call these formulas the maximal next sub-formulas of φ.

For example, let $\varphi = \bigcirc p \to (\bigcirc q \wedge r)$, which is in *NNF*. $ASF(\varphi) = \{r\}$, as r is the only formula that does not contain $\bigcirc$ but its father formula does. $NSF(\varphi) = \{\bigcirc p, \bigcirc q\}$. We also use the following auxiliary functions:

- SIMPL(φ), which performs simple Boolean simplifications, including *true* $\wedge$ $\varphi \mapsto \varphi$, *false* $\wedge \varphi \mapsto$ *false*, *true* $\vee \varphi \mapsto$ *true*, *false* $\vee \varphi \mapsto \varphi$, etc.
- RMNEXT, which takes a formula of the form $\bigcirc^i \varphi$ and returns $\bigcirc^{i-1} \varphi$.
- VAR, which takes a formula of the form $\bigcirc^i \varphi$ and returns the obligation variable $s_{\bigcirc^i \varphi}$. This function also accepts a proposition $p \in \mathsf{AP}$ in which case it returns p itself.

The output of SIMPL(φ) is either *true* or *false*, or a formula that does not contain *true* or *false* at all. The simplification performed by SIMPL is particularly useful simplifying (*false* $\to \psi$) to *true*, because given a requirement of the form $C \to D$, if C is simplified to false in a given mode then $C \to D$ will be simplified to *true* ignoring all sub-formulas within D. We introduce RMMODES(φ, m) on the left, which given a mode m and a formula φ simplifies φ under the assumption that the current state satisfies m, that is, specializes φ for mode m.

Algorithm 1. Simplify (remove)

1: **function** RMMODES(φ, m)
2:    **for** each $f \in ASF(\varphi)$ **do**
3:       **if** $(m \to f)$ is valid **then**
4:          $\varphi \leftarrow \varphi[f \setminus \textit{True}]$
5:       **if** $(m \to \neg f)$ is valid **then**
6:          $\varphi \leftarrow \varphi[f \setminus \textit{False}]$
7:    **return** SIMPL(φ)

Example 1. Consider $m_1 : (counter_1 \wedge \neg counter_2)$, and $\varphi_1 : \neg counter_2 \to$ $\neg trigger$ and $\varphi_2 : (counter_1 \wedge \neg reset) \to \bigcirc(counter_2 \vee reset)$. Then,

$$\text{RMMODES}(\varphi_1, m_1) = \neg trigger$$
$$\text{RMMODES}(\varphi_2, m_1) = \neg reset \to \bigcirc(counter_2 \vee reset)$$

Finally, $\text{VAR}(\bigcirc\psi) = s_{\bigcirc\psi}$.

4.2 The Mode-Base Projection Algorithm MoBy

As mentioned before our algorithm takes as a input a reactive specification S an indexed set $M = \{m_1, \ldots, m_n\}$ of modes and an indexed set $I = \{I_1, \ldots, I_n\}$ of initial conditions, one for each mode. We first add to each I_i the predicate $\neg done$, to encode that in its initial state a sub-system that solves the game for mode m_i has not jumped to another mode yet. For each mode m_i, MoBy specializes all guarantee formulas calling RMMODES, and then adds additional requirements for the obligation variables and to control when the system can exit the mode. Algorithm 2 presents MoBy in pseudo-code.

Line 5 simplifies all requirements specifically for mode m_i, that is, it will only focus on solving all requirements for states that satisfy m_i. Line 7 starts the goals for mode i establishing that unless the system has jumped to another mode, the mode predicate m_i must hold in mode i. Lines 8 to 10 substitute all temporal formulas in the requirements with their obligation variables, establishing that all requirements must hold unless the system has left the mode. Lines 11 to 12 establish the semantics of obligation variables, forcing their temporal behavior as long as the system stays within the mode ($\neg done$). Lines 13 to 15 precludes the system to jump to another mode m_j if m_j cannot fulfill pending promises. Lines 16 to 18 establish that once the system has jumped the game is considered finished, and that the system is only finished jumping to some other mode. Finally, line 19 limits to jump to at most one mode.

Algorithm 2. MoBy: Mode-Based Projections.

```
1:  Inputs: S : (A, G), M : {m₁,...,mₙ}, I : {I₁,...,Iₙ}.
2:  Outputs: Pr = [Π₁,...,Πₙ].
3:  function COMPUTEPROJECTION(S, M, I)
4:      for each mode index i ∈ {1...n} do
5:          G' ← REDUCE(G, mᵢ)
6:          Oblig ← NSF(G')
7:          Gᵢ = {¬done → mᵢ}
8:          for each requirement ψ ∈ G' do
9:              ψ' ← replace f for VAR(f) in ψ (for all f ∈ Oblig)
10:             Gᵢ.add((¬done) → ψ')
11:         for each obligation subformula f ∈ Oblig do
12:             Gᵢ.add((¬done ∧ VAR(f)) → ○VAR(RMNEXT(f)))
13:         for each mode j ≠ i such that mᵢ ≺ mⱼ and for every f ∈ Oblig do
14:             if (Iⱼ → RMNEXT(f)) is not valid then
15:                 Gᵢ.add(jumpⱼ → ¬VAR(f))
16:         Gᵢ.add(done → ○done)
17:         Gᵢ.add( (⋁ⱼ jumpⱼ) → ○done)
18:         Gᵢ.add((¬⋁ⱼ jumpⱼ) → (¬done → ○¬done))
19:         Gᵢ.add(⋀ⱼ≠ₖ jumpⱼ → ¬jumpₖ)
20:         Pr[i] ← (A, Gᵢ)
21:     return Pr
22: function REDUCE(Φ, m)
23:     return {RMMODES(φ, m) | φ ∈ Φ}
```

Example 2. We apply MoBy to the example in Fig. 1 for $N = 2$, with three modes $M = \{m_1 : \{counter_0\}, m_2 : \{counter_1\}, m_3 : \{counter_2\}\}$. The initial conditions only establish the variable of the mode is satisfied $I_1 = m_1$, $I_2 = m_2$, $I_3 = m_3$ (only forcing $\neg done$ as well). The MoBy algorithm computes the following projections:

```
INPUTS reset; start;
ASSUMPTIONS G !(reset && start); INITIALLY (!reset && !start) || reset
[Projection_1]
OUTPUTS counter_0; trigger; s_Oφ; jump_2; done
GUARANTEES
G (!done → (counter_0))
G (!done → (reset → X counter_0));
G (!done → (start → s_Oφ));
G (!done → ((s_Oφ && !done) → X FALSE));
G (!done → (!trigger));
G (done → X done);
G (jump_2 → X done);
G (!jump_2 → (!done →  X !done));


[Projection_2]
OUTPUTS counter_1; trigger; jump_1, jump_3 s_Oφ; s_Oφ1;
GUARANTEES
G !done → (counter_1)
G !done → (reset → s_Oφ);
G !done → (s_Oφ && !done → X FALSE);
G !done → (!reset → s_Oφ1);
G !done → (s_Oφ1 && !done → X FALSE);
G !done → (!trigger);
G ((s_Oφ || s_Oφ1) → X done);
G jump_1 → !s_Oφ1;
G jump_3 → !s_Oφ;
G (!(s_Oφ || s_Oφ1)  → (!done →  X !done));


[Projection_3]
OUTPUTS counter_2; trigger; jump_1; s_Oφ jump_1
GUARANTEES
G (!done → (counter_2))
G (!done → (reset → s_Oφ))
G (!done → (s_Oφ && !done → X FALSE));
G (!done → (counter_2 → s_Oφ));
G (!done → (trigger));
G (jump_1 → X done);
G (!jump_1 → (!done →  X !done));
```

4.3   Composing Solutions

After decomposing S into a set of projections $Pr = \{\Pi_1, \ldots, \Pi_n\}$ using MoBy, Algorithm 3 composes winning strategies for the system obtained for each mode into a single winning strategy for the original specification S.

Lemma 1 (Composition's correctness). *Let $M = \{m_1, \ldots, m_n\}$ and $I = \{I_1, \ldots, I_n\}$ be a set of valid mode descriptions for a specification S, and let $St = \{W_1, \ldots, W_n\}$ be a set of winning strategies for each projection $p \in Pr = \{\Pi_1, \ldots, \Pi_n\}$ Then, the composed winning strategy W obtained using Algorithm 3 is a winning strategy for S.*

Proof. Let S be a specification, $M = \{m_1, m_2, \ldots, m_n\}$ and $I = \{I_1, \ldots, I_n\}$ a mode description. Also, let's consider $Pr = \{\Pi_1, \ldots, \Pi_n\}$ be the projection generated by Algorithm 2. We assume that all sub-specifications are realizable. Let $St = \{W_1, \ldots, W_n\}$ be winning strategies for each of the sub-specifications and let $W : (Q, s, \delta, L)$ be the strategy for the original specifications generated by Algorithm 3. We will show now that W is a winning strategy. The essence of the proof is to show that if a mode m_j starts at position i and the system follows W, this corresponds to follow W_j. In turn, this guarantees that $Pr[j]$ holds until the next mode is entered (or ad infinitum if no mode change happens), which guarantees that S holds within the segment after the new mode enters in its initial state. By induction, the result follows.

By contradiction, assume that W is not winning and let $\rho \in 2^{\mathcal{X} \cup \mathcal{Y}}$ be a play that is played according to W that is loosing for the system. In other words, there is position i such that ρ^i violates some requirement in S. Let i be the first such position. Let m_j be the mode at position i and let $i' < i$ be the position at which m_j is the mode at position i' and either $i' = 0$ or the mode at position $i' - 1$ is not m_j.

Algorithm 3. Composition of Winning Strategies
***

1: **Input:** A winning strategy $W_i = (Q_i, s_i, \delta_i, L_i)$ for each projection $p_i \in Pr$.
2: **Output:** A composed winning strategy $W = (Q, s, \delta, L)$.
3: **function** COMPOSE($W_1, \ldots, W_n$)
4:     $Q \leftarrow \bigcup_{i=1}^{n} Q_i$
5:     $s \leftarrow s_1$
6:     $\delta \leftarrow \emptyset$
7:     **for** each mode index $i \in \{1 \ldots n\}$ **do**
8:         $(Q_i, s_i, \delta_i, L_i) \leftarrow W_i$
9:         **for** each $(q, a) \in Q_i \times 2^{\mathcal{X}}$ **do**
10:            $L(q, a) \leftarrow L_i(q, a)$
11:            **if** $\delta_i(s, a) \vDash jump_j$ for some j **then**
12:                $\delta(q, a) \leftarrow s_j$
13:            **else**   ▷ $jump_j \notin \delta_i(q, a)$ for any j
14:                $\delta(q, a) \leftarrow \delta_i(q, a)$
15:     **return** $W : (Q, s, \delta, L)$

- If $i' = 0$, between 0 and i, W coincides with W_j. Therefore, since W_j is winning $\Pi[j]$ must hold at i, which implies that S holds at i, which is contradiction.
- Consider now the case where $i' - 1$ is not m_j, but some other mode m_l. Then, since in m_l is winning W_l, it holds that $Pr[l]$ holds at $i' - 1$ so, in particular all pending obligations are implied by I_j. Therefore, the suffix trace $\rho^{i'}$ is winning for W_j. Again, it follows that S holds at i, which is a contradiction.

Hence, the lemma holds. $\square$

The following corollary follows immediately.

Corollary 1 (Semi-Realizability). *Given a specification S, a set M of valid system modes and a set I of initial conditions. If all projections generated by MoBy are realizable, then S is also realizable.*

5   Empirical Evaluation

We implemented MoBy in the *Java* programming language using the well-known *Owl* library [37] to manipulate LTL specifications. MoBy integrates the LTL satisfiability checker Polsat [42], a portfolio consisting of four LTL solvers that run in parallel. To perform all realizability checks, we discharge each sub-specification to *Strix* [46]. All experiments in this section were run on a cluster equipped with a Xeon processor with a clock speed of 2.6 GHz, 16 GB of RAM, and running the GNU/Linux operating system.

We report in this section an empirical evaluation of MoBy. We aim to empirically evaluate the following research questions:

- RQ1: *How effective is MoBy in decomposing mode-based specifications?*
- RQ2: *Does MoBy complement state of the art synthesis tools?*
- RQ3: *Can MoBy be used to improve the synthesis time?*

To address them, we analyzed specifications from published literature, evaluation of *RE* tools, and case studies on SCR specification and analysis:

Case	#A - #G	#Modes	#In	#Out
10-Counter-Machine	2-15	[2,5,10]	2	12
20-Counter-Machine	2-25	[2,5,10,20]	2	22
50-Counter-Machine	2-55	[2,5,10,50]	2	52
100-Counter-Machine	2-105	[2,5,10,50,100]	2	102
Minepump	3-4	[2]	300	5
Sis(n)	2-7	[3]	(2+n)	7
Thermostat(n)	3-4	[3]	(31+n)	4
Cruise(n)	3-15	[4]	(5+n)	8
AltLayer(n)	1-9	[3]	n	5
Lift(n)	1-187	[3]	n	(4+n)

Fig. 4. Assumptions (A), Guarantees (G), Modes, Variables

Specification	#Modes	Synthesis Time (s)		Specification Size			
		Monolithic	MoBy	Monolithic		MoBy	
				#Clauses	Length	#Clauses	Length
CM10	2	26	0.32	48	252	28	117
	5		0.67			8	30
	10		0.58			8	39
CM20	2	Timeout	3.62	88	672	48	252
	5		1.15			24	96
	10		2.06			16	60
	20		1.08			8	49
CM50	2	Timeout	2.56	208	3132	136	1036
	5		19			48	256
	10		3			28	117
	50		1.67			8	79
CM100	2	Timeout	Timeout	408	11232	208	3132
	5		5.12			88	672
	10		4			48	252
	50		9			19	57
	100		3.23			8	129
Minepump	2	140	90	11598	21365	5800	10685
Sis-250	3	18	2	521	1072	133	287
Sis-500	3	96	4	1021	2072	258	538
Sis-1000	3	Timeout	11	2021	4072	508	1035
Sis-1500	3	Timeout	20	3021	6072	758	1538
Sis-2000	3	Timeout	38	4021	8072	1258	2300
Sis-4000	3	Timeout	157	8021	16072	2678	3560
Sis-4500	3	Timeout	172	9020	18040	3006	4002
Sis-5000	3	Timeout	268	10020	20040	3340	4447
Thermostat-10	3	1	1	73	151	42	97
Thermostat-20	3	Timeout	1	172	276	75	152
Thermostat-100	3	Timeout	10	4032	4416	1375	1652
Thermostat-200	3	Timeout	48	12132	12916	4075	4619
Cruise-150	4	75	63	15339	15855	6824	7067
Cruise-200	4	132	100	30039	30756	10025	10294
Cruise-500	4	Timeout	770	118239	120153	39425	40097
AltLayer-50	3	15	9	3685	4147	1234	1395
AltLayer-100	3	41	25	8885	9747	2968	3269
AltLayer-150	3	153	100	30685	31947	10234	10699
AltLayer-200	3	Timeout	269	52485	54147	17500	18064
Lift-5	3	1	2	310	884	122	355
Lift-10	3	34	9	1585	4014	597	1522
Lift-15	3	Timeout	162	4560	10844	1672	3989
Lift-20	3	Timeout	789	6394	14948	3597	8255

Fig. 5. Comparision between MoBy and Monolithic

- our counter machine running example *CM* with varying bounds.
- Minepump: A mine pump controller [7,9,15,41], which manages a pump with sensors that detect high water levels and methane presence.
- Thermostat(n): A thermostat [22] that monitors a room temperature controls the heater and tracks heating duration.
- Lift(n): A simple elevator controller for n floors [1].
- Cruise(n): A cruise control system [35] which is in charge of maintaining the car speed on the occurrence of any event.
- Sis(n): A safety injection system [16], responsible for partially controlling a nuclear power plant by monitoring water pressure in a cooling subsystem.
- AltLayer(n): A communicating state machine model [8].

Figure 4 shows the number of input/output variables, assumptions (A), guarantees (G), and the number of modes for each case.

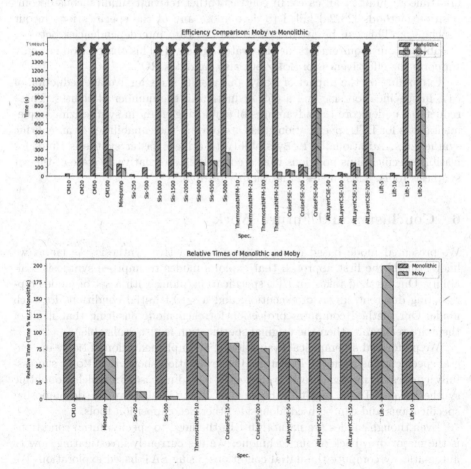

Fig. 6. Speed of MoBy vs monolithic synthesis. The figure above shows the time taken by a monolithic synthesis tool and the time taken by MoBy. The figure below normalizes the monolithic time to 100 for those that did not reach Timeout.

Experimental Results. To address RQ1 we compare the size of the original specification with the size of each projection measured by the number of clauses and the formula length. To determine the formula's length, we adopt the methodologies outlined in [7,9]. Additionally, we compared the running time required for synthesizing the original specification with the time taken for each projection, note that we report the aggregated time taken to synthesize the systems for each projection, when they can be solved independently and in parallel to potentially improve efficiency. The summarized results can be found in Fig. 5. We also provide additional insights in Fig. 6, which highlights the significance of MoBy in enhancing the synthesis time.

Our analysis demonstrates that MoBy successfully decomposes 100% of the specifications in our corpus, which indicates that MoBy is effective in handling complex specifications. Furthermore, MoBy consistently operates within the 25-min timeout limit in all cases. In contrast, other relevant simultaneous decomposition methods [23,24] failed to decompose any of the specifications in our benchmark. This can be attributed to the intricate interdependencies between variables in our requirements, as elaborated in Sect. 1. This observation not only supports the effectiveness of MoBy but also validates RQ2.

Expanding on the impact of MoBy, our results show an average reduction of 64% in specification size and a 65% reduction in the number of clauses. These reductions underscore the advantages of employing MoBy in synthesizing implementations for LTL specifications that are beyond the capabilities of monolithic synthesizers. Additionally, MoBy's ability to achieve faster synthesis times for feasible specifications positions it as a compelling alternative to state-of-the-art synthesis tools. This suggests the validity of RQ3.

6   Conclusion and Future Work

We presented mode based decomposition for reactive synthesis. As far as we know, this is the first approach that exploits modes to improve synthesis scalability. Our method takes an LTL specification, along with a set of modes representing different stages of execution, and a set of initial conditions for each mode. Our method computes projection for each mode ensuring that if all of them are realizable, then the original specification is also realizable.

We performed an empirical evaluation of an implementation of MoBy on several specifications from the literature. Our evaluation shows that MoBy successfully synthesizes implementations efficiently, including cases for which monolithic synthesis fails. These results indicate that MoBy is effective for decomposing specifications and can be used alongside other decomposition tools.

Even though modes are natural in RE, the need to specify initial conditions is the major drawback of our technique. We are currently investigating how to automatically compute the initial conditions, using SAT based exploration. We are also investigating the assessment of the quality of the specifications generated using MoBy.

References

1. The reactive synthesis competition. https://www.syntcomp.org/
2. Alur, R., Torre, S.L.: Deterministic generators and games for LTL fragments. In: Proceedings of the LICS'01, pp. 291–300. ACM (2001)
3. Balachander, M., Filiot, E., Raskin, J.F.: LTL reactive synthesis with a few hints. In: Sankaranarayanan, S., Sharygina, N. (eds.) Tools and Algorithms for the Construction and Analysis of Systems. TACAS 2023. LNCS, vol. 13994, pp. 309–328. Springer, Cham (2023). https://doi.org/10.1007/978-3-031-30820-8_20
4. Bansal, S., Li, Y., Tabajara, L.M., Vardi, M.Y.: Hybrid compositional reasoning for reactive synthesis from finite-horizon specifications. In: AAAI'20 (2020)
5. Bharadwaj, R., Heitmeyer, C.: Applying the SCR requirements method to a simple autopilot. In: NASA Conference Publication, pp. 87–102. NASA (1997)
6. Bloem, R., Jobstmann, B., Piterman, N., Pnueli, A., Sa'ar, Y.: Synthesis of reactive(1) designs. JCSS **78**(3), 911–938 (2012)
7. Brizzio, M., Cordy, M., Papadakis, M., Sánchez, C., Aguirre, N., Degiovanni, R.: Automated repair of unrealisable LTL specifications guided by model counting. In: Proceedings of the GECCO'23, pp. 1499–1507. ACM (2023)
8. Bultan, T.: Action language: a specification language for model checking reactive systems. In: In: Proceedings of the ICSE, pp. 335–344 (2000)
9. Carvalho, L., et al.: ACoRe: automated goal-conflict resolution. In: In: Proceedings of the FASE'23 (2023)
10. Chang, E., Manna, Z., Pnueli, A.: Characterization of temporal property classes. In: Kuich, W. (ed.) ICALP 1992. LNCS, vol. 623, pp. 474–486. Springer, Heidelberg (1992). https://doi.org/10.1007/3-540-55719-9_97
11. Church, A.: Logic, arithmetic, and automata (1962)
12. Church, A.: Application of recursive arithmetic to the problem of circuit synthesis. J. Symb. Log. **28**(4), 289–290 (1963). https://doi.org/10.2307/2271310
13. De Giacomo, G., Favorito, M.: Compositional approach to translate LTLf/LDLf into deterministic finite automata. In: Proceedings of the ICAPS'21, pp. 122–130 (2021)
14. De Giacomo, G., Vardi, M.Y.: Linear temporal logic and linear dynamic logic on finite traces. In: Proceedings of the IJCAI'13, pp. 854–860. AAAI Press (2013)
15. Degiovanni, R., Castro, P.F., Arroyo, M., Ruiz, M., Aguirre, N., Frias, M.F.: Goal-conflict likelihood assessment based on model counting. In: ICSE (2018)
16. Degiovanni, R., Ponzio, P., Aguirre, N., Frias, M.: Improving lazy abstraction for SCR specifications through constraint relaxation. STVR **28**(2), e1657 (2018)
17. D'ippolito, N., Braberman, V., Piterman, N., Uchitel, S.: Synthesizing nonanomalous event-based controllers for liveness goals. ACM Trans. Softw. Eng. Methodol. **22**(1) 1–36 (2013). https://doi.org/10.1145/2430536.2430543
18. Dureja, R., Rozier, K.Y.: More scalable LTL model checking via discovering design-space dependencies (D^3). In: Beyer, D., Huisman, M. (eds.) TACAS 2018. LNCS, vol. 10805, pp. 309–327. Springer, Cham (2018). https://doi.org/10.1007/978-3-319-89960-2_17
19. Ehlers, R., Raman, V.: Slugs: extensible GR(1) synthesis. In: Chaudhuri, S., Farzan, A. (eds.) CAV 2016. LNCS, vol. 9780, pp. 333–339. Springer, Cham (2016). https://doi.org/10.1007/978-3-319-41540-6_18
20. Emerson, E.A., Clarke, E.M.: Using branching time temporal logic to synthesize synchronization skeletons. Sci. Comput. Program. **2**(3), 241–266 (1982)

21. Esparza, J., Křetínský, J.: From LTL to deterministic automata: a safraless compositional approach. In: Biere, A., Bloem, R. (eds.) CAV 2014. LNCS, vol. 8559, pp. 192–208. Springer, Cham (2014). https://doi.org/10.1007/978-3-319-08867-9_13

22. Fifarek, A., Wagner, L., Hoffman, J., Rodes, B., Aiello, A., Davis, J.: SpeAR v2.0: formalized past LTL specification and analysis of requirements. In: NFM (2017)

23. Filiot, E., Jin, N., Raskin, J.-F.: Compositional algorithms for LTL synthesis. In: Bouajjani, A., Chin, W.-N. (eds.) ATVA 2010. LNCS, vol. 6252, pp. 112–127. Springer, Heidelberg (2010). https://doi.org/10.1007/978-3-642-15643-4_10

24. Finkbeiner, B., Geier, G., Passing, N.: Specification decomposition for reactive synthesis. ISSE (2022)

25. Finucane, C.P., Jing, G., Kress-Gazit, H.: Designing reactive robot controllers with LTLMoP. In: Proceedings of the AAAIWS'11 (2011)

26. Giannakopoulou, D., Mavridou, A., Rhein, J., Pressburger, T., Schumann, J., Nija, S.: Formal requirements elicitation with FRET. In: REFSQ'20 (2020)

27. Heitmeyer, C.: Requirements models for critical systems. In: Software and Systems Safety, pp. 158–181. IOS Press (2011)

28. Heitmeyer, C., Labaw, B., Kiskis, D.: Consistency checking of SCR-style requirements specifications. In: Proceedings of the RE'95, pp. 56–63. IEEE (1995)

29. Heitmeyer, C., et al.: Building high assurance human-centric decision systems. AuSE **22**, 159–197 (2015)

30. Heitmeyer, C.L., McLean, J.D.: Abstract requirements specification: a new approach and its application. IEEE TSE **5**, 580–589 (1983)

31. Heninger, K.L.: Software requirements for the a-7e aircraft. NRL Memorandum Report 3876, Naval Research Laboratory (1978)

32. Hermo, M., Lucio, P., Sánchez, C.: Tableaux for realizability of safety specifications. In: Proceedings of the FM'23, pp. 495–513 (2023)

33. Iannopollo, A., Tripakis, S., Vincentelli, A.: Specification decomposition for synthesis from libraries of LTL assume/guarantee contracts. In: DATE. IEEE (2018)

34. Jacobs, S., Klein, F., Schirmer, S.: A high-level LTL synthesis format: TLSF v1.1. EPTCS 229, 112–132, November 2016

35. Kirby, J.: Example NRL SCR software requirements for an automobile cruise control and monitoring system. Wang Inst. of Graduate Studies (1987)

36. Kress-Gazit, H., Wongpiromsarn, T., Topcu, U.: Correct, reactive, high-level robot control. IEEE Robot. Autom. Mag. **18**(3), 65–74 (2011)

37. Křetínský, J., Meggendorfer, T., Sickert, S.: Owl: a library for ω-words, automata, and LTL. In: Lahiri, S.K., Wang, C. (eds.) ATVA 2018. LNCS, vol. 11138, pp. 543–550. Springer, Cham (2018). https://doi.org/10.1007/978-3-030-01090-4_34

38. Kupferman, O.: Recent challenges and ideas in temporal synthesis. In: SOFSEM'12 (2012)

39. Kupferman, O., Piterman, N., Vardi, M.Y.: Safraless compositional synthesis. In: Ball, T., Jones, R.B. (eds.) CAV 2006. LNCS, vol. 4144, pp. 31–44. Springer, Heidelberg (2006). https://doi.org/10.1007/11817963_6

40. Kupferman, O., Vardi, M.Y.: Model checking of safety properties. Form. Methods Syst. Des. **19**, 291–314 (2001)

41. Letier, E., Kramer, J., Magee, J., Uchitel, S.: Deriving event-based transition systems from goal-oriented requirements models. AuSE **15**, 175–206 (2008)

42. Li, J., Pu, G., Zhang, L., Yao, Y., Vardi, M.Y., He, J.: Polsat: a portfolio LTL satisfiability solver (2013). http://arxiv.org/abs/1311.1602

43. Mallozzi, P., Incer, I., Nuzzo, P., Sangiovanni-Vincentelli, A.L.: Contract-based specification refinement and repair for mission planning. In: FormaliSE'23 (2023)

44. Manna, Z., Pnueli, A.: Temporal Verification of Reactive Systems: Safety. Springer-Verlag, New York, NY, USA (1995). https://doi.org/10.1007/978-1-4612-4222-2
45. Mavin, A., Wilkinson, P., Harwood, A., Novak, M.: Easy approach to requirements syntax (EARS), pp. 317–322, October 2009. https://doi.org/10.1109/RE.2009.9
46. Meyer, P.J., Sickert, S., Luttenberger, M.: Strix: explicit reactive synthesis strikes back! In: Chockler, H., Weissenbacher, G. (eds.) CAV 2018. LNCS, vol. 10981, pp. 578–586. Springer, Cham (2018). https://doi.org/10.1007/978-3-319-96145-3_31
47. Pnueli, A.: The temporal logic of programs. In: SFCS'77, pp. 46–57. IEEE (1977)
48. Pnueli, A., Rosner, R.: On the synthesis of a reactive module. In: Proceedings of the 16th ACM SIGPLAN-SIGACT Symposium on Principles of Programming Languages (POPL'89), pp. 179–190 (1989). https://doi.org/10.1145/75277.75293
49. Pnueli, A., Zaks, A.: PSL model checking and run-time verification via testers. In: Misra, J., Nipkow, T., Sekerinski, E. (eds.) FM 2006. LNCS, vol. 4085, pp. 573–586. Springer, Heidelberg (2006). https://doi.org/10.1007/11813040_38
50. de Roever, W.P., Langmaack, H., Pnueli, A. (eds.): Compositionality: The Significant Difference. Springer, Berlin, Heidelberg (1998). https://doi.org/10.1007/3-540-49213-5
51. van Schouwen, A.J., Parnas, D.L., Madey, J.: Documentation of requirements for computer systems. In: Proceedings of the ISRE, pp. 198–207. IEEE (1993)
52. Sistla, A.P.: Safety, liveness, and fairness in temporal logic. FAC **6**, 495–511 (1994)
53. Zhu, S., Tabajara, L.M., Li, J., Pu, G., Vardi, M.Y.: A symbolic approach to safety LTL synthesis. In: HVC 2017. LNCS, vol. 10629, pp. 147–162. Springer, Cham (2017). https://doi.org/10.1007/978-3-319-70389-3_10

A Categorical Approach to Synthetic Chemistry

Ella Gale[1], Leo Lobski[2]([⊠]), and Fabio Zanasi[2,3]

[1] University of Bristol, Bristol, UK
ella.gale@bristol.ac.uk
[2] University College London, London, UK
{leo.lobski.21,f.zanasi}@ucl.ac.uk
[3] University of Bologna, Bologna, Italy

Abstract. We introduce a mathematical framework for retrosynthetic analysis, an important research method in synthetic chemistry. Our approach represents molecules and their interaction using string diagrams in layered props – a recently introduced categorical model for partial explanations in scientific reasoning. Such principled approach allows one to model features currently not available in automated retrosynthesis tools, such as chirality, reaction environment and protection-deprotection steps.

Keywords: String diagrams · Chemistry · Retrosynthesis

1 Introduction

A chemical reaction can be understood as a rule which tells us what the outcome molecules (or molecule-like objects, such as ions) are when several molecules are put together. If, moreover, the reaction records the precise proportions of the molecules as well as the conditions for the reaction to take place (temperature, pressure, concentration, presence of a solvent etc.), it can be seen as a precise scientific prediction, whose truth or falsity can be tested in a lab, making the reaction reproducible. Producing complicated molecules, as required e.g. by the pharmaceutical industry, requires, in general, a chain of several consecutive reactions in precisely specified conditions. The general task of synthetic chemistry is to come up with reproducible reaction chains to generate previously unknown molecules (with some desired properties) [39]. Successfully achieving a given synthetic task requires both understanding of the chemical mechanisms and the empirical knowledge of existing reactions. Both of these are increasingly supported by computational methods [34]: rule-based and dynamical models are used to suggest potential reaction mechanisms, while database search is used to look for existing reactions that would apply in the context of interest [35]. The key desiderata for such tools are tunability and specificity. Tunability endows

E. Ábrahám et al. (Eds.): ICTAC 2023, LNCS 14446, pp. 276–294, 2023.
https://doi.org/10.1007/978-3-031-47963-2_17

a synthetic chemist with tools to specify a set of goals (e.g. adding or removing a functional group[1]), while by specificity we mean maximising yield and minimising side products.

In this paper, we focus on the area of synthetic chemistry known as *retrosynthesis* [16, 35, 38]. While reaction prediction asks what reactions will occur and what outcomes will be obtained when some molecules are allowed to interact, retrosynthesis goes backwards: it starts with a target molecule that we wish to produce, and it proceeds in the "reverse" direction by asking what potential reactants would produce the target molecule. While many automated tools for retrosynthesis exist (see e.g. [10, 13, 14, 19, 25, 26, 36]), there is no uniform mathematical framework in which the suggested algorithms could be analysed, compared or combined. The primary contribution of this paper is to provide such a framework. By formalising the methodology at this level of mathematical generality, we are able to provide insights into how to incorporate features that the current automated retrosynthesis tools lack: these include modelling chirality, the reaction environment, and the protection-deprotection steps (see for example [20]), which are all highly relevant to practical applications. Our formalism, therefore, paves the way for new automated retrosynthesis tools, accounting for the aforementioned features.

Mathematically, our approach is phrased in the algebraic formalism of *string diagrams*, and most specifically uses *layered props*. Layered props were originally introduced, in [27], as models for systems that have several interdependent levels of description. In the context of chemistry, the description levels play a threefold role: first, each level represents a reaction environment, second, the morphisms in different levels are taking care of different synthetic tasks, and third, the rules that are available in a given level reflect the structure that is deemed relevant for the next retrosynthetic step. The latter can be seen as a kind of coarse-graining, where by deliberately restricting to a subset of all available information, we reveal some essential features about the system. Additionally, organising retrosynthetic rules into levels allows us to include conditions that certain parts of a molecule are to be kept intact. While the presentation here is self-contained and, in particular, does not assume a background on layered props, we emphasise that our approach is principled in the sense that many choices we make are suggested by this more general framework. We point such choices out when we feel the intuition that comes from layered props is helpful for understanding the formalism presented in the present work.

The rest of the paper is structured as follows. In Sect. 2, we give a brief overview of the methodology of retrosynthetic analysis, as well as of the existing tools for automating it. Section 3 recalls the conceptual and mathematical ideas behind layered props. The entirety of Sect. 4 is devoted to constructing the labelled graphs that we use to represent molecular entities: these will be the objects of the monoidal categories we introduce in Sects. 6 and 7. Section 5 formalises retrosynthetic disconnection rules, while Sect. 6 formalises reactions. The culmination of the paper is the layered prop defined in Sect. 7, where we

---

[1] Part of a molecule that is known to be responsible for certain chemical function.

also describe how to reason about retrosynthesis within it. In Sect. 8 we sketch the prospects of future work.

2   Retrosynthetic Analysis

Retrosynthetic analysis starts with a target molecule we wish to produce but do not know how. The aim is to "reduce" the target molecule to known (commercially available) outcome molecules in such a way that when the outcome molecules react, the target molecule is obtained as a product. This is done by (formally) partitioning the target molecule into functional parts referred to as *synthons*, and finding actually existing molecules that are chemically equivalent to the synthons; these are referred to as *synthetic equivalents* [11,17,39]. If no synthetic equivalents can be found that actually exist, the partitioning step can be repeated, this time using the synthetic equivalents themselves as the target molecules, and the process can continue until either known molecules are found, or a maximum number of steps is reached and the search is stopped. Note that the synthons themselves do not refer to any molecule as such, but are rather a convenient formal notation for parts of a molecule. For this reason, passing from synthons to synthetic equivalents is a non-trivial step involving intelligent guesswork and chemical know-how of how the synthons *would* react if they were independent chemical entities.

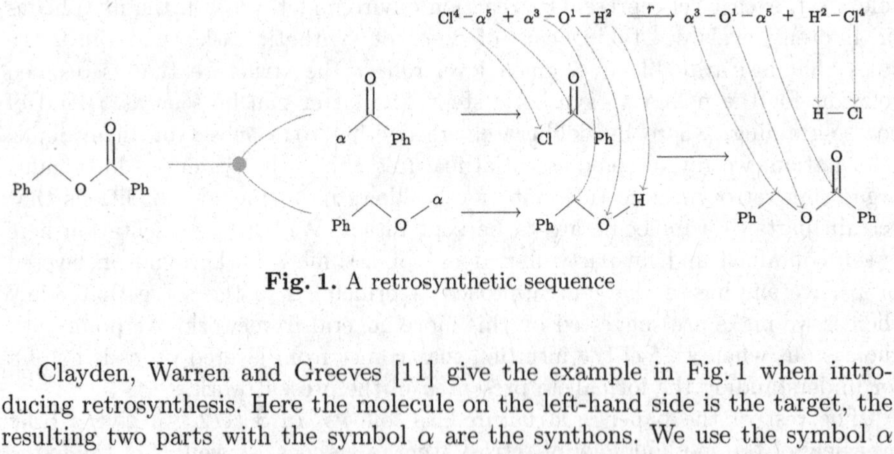

Fig. 1. A retrosynthetic sequence

Clayden, Warren and Greeves [11] give the example in Fig. 1 when introducing retrosynthesis. Here the molecule on the left-hand side is the target, the resulting two parts with the symbol α are the synthons. We use the symbol α to indicate where the cut has been made, and hence which atoms have unpaired electrons. Replacing the symbols α in the synthons with Cl and H, we obtain the candidate synthetic equivalents shown one step further to the right. Assuming existence of the reaction scheme r shown at the top, it can be shown that there is a reaction starting from the synthetic equivalents and ending with the target. This is the simplest possible instance of a retrosynthetic sequence. In general, the interesting sequences are much longer, and, importantly, contain information under what conditions the reactions will take place.

Existing Tools. Many tools for automatic retrosynthesis have been successfully developed starting from the 1960s [10, 14, 25, 26, 36]. They can be divided into two classes [35]: *template-based* [21, 40] and *template-free* [26, 33]. Template-based tools contain a rule database (the *template*), which is either manually encoded or automatically extracted. Given a molecule represented as a graph, the model checks whether any rules are applicable to it by going through the database and comparing the conditions of applying the rule to the subgraphs of the molecule [35]. Choosing the order in which the rules from the template and the subgraphs are tried are part of the model design. Template-free tools, on the other hand, are data-driven and treat the retrosynthetic rule application as a translation between graphs or their representations as strings: the suggested transforms are based on learning from known transforms, avoiding the need for a database of rules [35, 36].

While successful retrosynthesic sequences have been predicted by the computational retrosynthesis tools, they lack a rigorous mathematical foundation, which makes them difficult to compare, combine or modify. Other common drawbacks of the existing approaches include not including the reaction conditions or all cases of chirality as part of the reaction template [26, 35], as well as the fact that the existing models are unlikely to suggest protection-deprotection steps. Additionally, the template-free tools based on machine learning techniques sometimes produce output that does not correspond to molecules in any obvious way, and tend to reproduce the biases present in the literature or a data set [35].

For successful prediction, the reaction conditions are, of course, crucial. These include such factors as temperature and pressure, the presence of a solvent (a compound which takes part in the reaction and whose supply is essentially unbounded), the presence of a reagent (a compound without which the reaction would not occur, but which is not the main focus or the target), as well as the presence of a catalyst (a compound which increases the rate at which the reaction occurs, but is itself unaltered by the reaction). The above factors can change the outcome of a reaction dramatically [15, 30]. There have indeed been several attempts to include reaction conditions into the forward reaction prediction models [22, 28, 29, 37]. However, the search space in retrosynthesis is already so large that adding another search criterion should be done with caution. A major challenge for predicting reaction conditions is that they tend to be reported incompletely or inconsistently in the reaction databases [12].

Chirality (mirror-image asymmetery) of a molecule can alter its chemical and physiological properties, and hence constitutes a major part of chemical information pertaining to a molecule. While template-based methods have been able to successfully suggest reactions involving chirality (e.g. [14]), the template-free models have difficulties handling it [26]. This further emphasises usefulness of a framework which is able to handle both template-based and template-free models.

The protection-deprotection steps are needed when more than one functional group of a molecule A would react with a molecule B. To ensure the desired reaction, the undesired functional group of A is first "protected" by adding a molecule X, which guarantees that the reaction product will react with B in the required way. Finally, the protected group is "deprotected", producing the desired outcome of B reacting with the correct functional group of A. So, instead of having a direct reaction $A+B \to C$ (which would not happen, or would happen imperfectly, due to a "competing" functional group), the reaction chain is:

(1) $A+X \to A'$ (protection), (2) $A'+B \to C'$, (3) $C'+Y \to C$ (deprotection).

The trouble with the protection-deprotection steps is that they temporarily make the molecule larger, which means that an algorithm whose aim is to make a molecule smaller will not suggest them.

3   Layered Props

Layered props were introduced in [27] as categorical models for diagrammatic reasoning about systems with several levels of description. They have been employed to account for partial explanations and semantic analysis in the context of electrical circuit theory, chemistry, and concurrency. Formally, a layered prop is essentially a functor $\Omega : P \to \mathbf{StrMon}$ from a poset P to the category of strict monoidal categories, together with a right adjoint for each monoidal functor in the image of Ω. Given $\omega \in P$, we denote a morphism $\sigma : a \to b$ in $\Omega(\omega)$ by the box on the right. We think of σ as a *process* with an input a and an output b happening in the *context* ω. Note, however, that these diagrams are not merely a convenient piece of notation that capture our intuition: they are a completely formal syntax of string diagrams, describing morphisms in a certain subcategory of pointed profunctors [27].

The monoidal categories in the image of Ω are thought of as languages describing the same system at different levels of granularity, and the functors are seen as translations between the languages. Given $\omega \le \tau$ in P, let us write $f := \Omega(\omega \le \tau)$. Then, for each $a \in \Omega(\omega)$ we have the morphisms drawn on the right. The reason for having morphisms in both directions is that we want to be able to "undo" the action of a translation while preserving a linear reasoning flow. The two morphisms will not, in general, be inverse to each other: rather, they form an adjoint pair. This corresponds to the intuition that some information is gained by performing the translation, and that the translation in the reverse direction is our best guess, or an approximation, not a one-to-one correspondence.

There are two ways to compose morphisms in parallel in a layered prop: internally within a monoidal category $\Omega(\omega)$ using its own monoidal product (composition inside a context), and externally using the Cartesian monoidal structure of $\mathbf{StrMon}$ (doing several processes in different contexts in parallel). We represent the latter by stacking the boxes on top of each other. Additional morphisms of a layered prop ensure that the internal and the external monoidal structures interact in a coherent way. Finally, a layered prop comes with "deduction rules" (2-cells) which allow transforming one process into another one. We refer the reader to [27] for the details.

In this work, the processes in context will be the retrosynthetic disconnection rules (Sect. 5) and the chemical reactions (Sect. 6). The context describes the reaction environment as well as the level of granularity at which the synthesis is happening (i.e. what kinds of disconnection rules are available). The objects in the monoidal categories are given by molecular entities and their parts: this is the subject of the next section.

4   Chemical Graphs

We define a chemical graph as a labelled graph whose edge labels indicate the bond type (covalent, ionic), and whose vertex labels are either atoms, charges or unpaired electrons (Definitions 1 and 2). In order to account for chirality, we add spatial information to chemical graphs, making it an *oriented (pre-)chemical graph* (Definition 5).

Oriented chemical graphs form the objects of the layered props we suggest as a framework for synthetic chemistry. The morphisms of these layered prop correspond to retrosynthetic disconnection rules and chemical reactions; this is the topic of the next two sections.

Let us define the set of *atoms* as containing the symbol for each main-group element of the periodic table: $At := \{H, C, O, P, \ldots\}$. Define the function $\mathbf{v} :$ $At \sqcup \{+, -, \alpha\} \to \mathbb{N}$ as taking each element symbol to its valence[2], and define $\mathbf{v}(-) = \mathbf{v}(+) = \mathbf{v}(\alpha) = 1$, where $+$ and $-$ stand for positive and negative charge, while α denotes an unpaired electron. Let $\mathbf{Lab} := \{0, 1, 2, 3, 4, i\}$ denote the set of *edge labels*, where the integers stand for a covalent bond, and i for an ionic bond. We further define maps $\mathrm{cov}, \mathrm{ion} : \mathbf{Lab} \to \mathbb{N}$: for cov, assign to each edge label 0, 1, 2, 3, and 4 the corresponding natural number and let $i \mapsto 0$, while for ion, let $0, 1, 2, 3, 4 \mapsto 0$ and $i \mapsto 1$. Finally, let us fix a countable set $\mathbf{VN}$ of *vertex names*; we usually denote the elements of $\mathbf{VN}$ by lowercase Latin letters $u, v, w, \ldots$.

Definition 1 (Pre-chemical graph). *A pre-chemical graph is a triple (V, τ, m), where $V \subseteq \mathbf{VN}$ is a finite set of vertices, $\tau : V \to At \sqcup \{+, -, \alpha\}$ is a vertex labelling function, and $m : V \times V \to \mathbf{Lab}$ is an edge labelling function satisfying $m(v, v) = 0$ and $m(v, w) = m(w, v)$ for all $v, w \in V$.*

Thus, a pre-chemical graph is irreflexive (we interpret the edge label 0 as no edge) and symmetric, and each of its vertices is labelled with an atom, a charge or a placeholder variable α. Given a pre-chemical graph A, we write (V_A, τ_A, m_A) for its vertex set and the labelling functions. Further, we define the following special subsets of vertices: (1) α-*vertices* $\alpha(A) := \tau^{-1}(\alpha)$, (2) *chemical vertices*

---

[2] This is a bit of a naive model, as valence is, in general, context-sensitive. We leave accounting for this to future work.

$\mathsf{Chem}(A) := V_A \backslash \alpha(A)$, (3) *charged vertices* $\mathsf{Crg}(A) := \tau^{-1}(\{+,-\})$, and (4) *neutral vertices* $\mathsf{Neu}(A) := V_A \backslash \mathsf{Crg}(A)$.

Note that the collection of pre-chemical graphs has a partial monoid structure given by the disjoint union of labelled graphs, provided that the vertex sets are disjoint.

Definition 2 (Chemical graph). *A* chemical graph (V, τ, m) *is a pre-chemical graph satisfying the following additional conditions:*

1. *for all $v \in V$, we have $\sum_{u \in V} \mathsf{cov}(m(u,v)) = \mathbf{v}\tau(v)$,*
2. *for all $v, w \in V$ with $\tau(v) = \alpha$ and $m(v,w) = 1$, then $\tau(w) \in \mathrm{At} \sqcup \{-\}$,*
3. *if $v, w \in V$ such that $\tau(v) \in \{+,-\}$ and $m(v,w) = 1$, then $\tau(w) \in \mathrm{At} \sqcup \{\alpha\}$,*
4. *if $m(v,w) = \mathtt{i}$, then*
   (a) *$\tau(v), \tau(w) \in \{+,-\}$ and $\tau(v) \neq \tau(w)$,*
   (b) *for $a, b \in V$ with $m(v,a) = m(w,b) = 1$, we have $\tau(a), \tau(b) \in \mathrm{At}$,*
   (c) *if for some $w' \in V$ we have $m(v,w') = \mathtt{i}$, then $w = w'$.*

Condition 1 says that the sum of each row or column in the adjacency matrix formed by the integers $\mathsf{cov}(m(u,v))$ gives the valence of the (label of) corresponding vertex. Conditions 2 and 3 say that a vertex labelled by α, $+$ or $-$ has to be connected to an atom, with the exception that the vertices labelled α and $-$ are allowed to be connected to each other instead of atoms. Finally, conditions 4a–4c say that an edge with label $\mathtt{i}$ only connects vertices labelled with opposite charges ($+$ and $-$) that are themselves connected to atoms, such that each charge-labelled vertex is connected to at most one other such vertex.

A *synthon* is a chemical graph which is moreover connected. The collection of chemical graphs is, therefore, generated by the disjoint unions of synthons. A *molecular graph* is a chemical graph with no α-vertices. A *molecular entity* is a connected molecular graph.

When drawing a chemical graph, we simply replace the vertices by their labels, unless the precise vertex names play a role. We adopt the usual chemical notation for n-ary bonds by drawing them as n parallel lines. The ionic bonds are drawn as dashed lines.

Example 1. We give examples of a synthon on the left, and two moleculear entities on the right: a molecule (ethenone) and an ion (carbonate anion).

Chirality. Next, we introduce (rudimentary) spatial information into (pre-) chemical graphs. The idea is to record for each triple of atoms whether they are on the same line or not, and similarly, for each quadruple of atoms whether they are in the same plane or not.

Definition 3 (Triangle relation). *Let S be a set. We call a ternary relation $\mathcal{P} \subseteq S \times S \times S$ a triangle relation if the following hold for all elements A, B and C of S: (1) $ABB \notin \mathcal{P}$, and (2) if $\mathcal{P}(ABC)$ and $\mathfrak{p}(ABC)$ is any permutation of the three elements, then $\mathcal{P}(\mathfrak{p}(ABC))$.*

Definition 4 (Tetrahedron relation). *Let S be a set, and let $\mathcal{P}$ be a fixed triangle relation on S. We call a quaternary relation $\mathcal{T} \subseteq S \times S \times S \times S$ a tetrahedron relation if the following hold for all elements A, B, C and D of S: (1) if $\mathcal{T}(ABCD)$, then $\mathcal{P}(ABC)$, and (2) if $\mathcal{T}(ABCD)$ and $\mathfrak{p}(ABCD)$ is any even permutation of the four elements, then $\mathcal{T}(\mathfrak{p}(ABCD))$.*

Unpacking the above definitions, a triangle relation is closed under the action of the symmetric group S_3 such that any three elements it relates are pairwise distinct, and a tetrahedron relation is closed under the action of the alternating group A_4 such that if it relates some four elements, then the first three are related by some (fixed) triangle relation (this, inter alia, implies that any related elements are pairwise distinct, and their any 3-element subset is related by the fixed triangle relation).

The intuition is that the triangle and tetrahedron relations capture the spatial relations of (not) being on the same line or plane: $\mathcal{P}(ABC)$ stands for A, B and C not being on the same line, that is, determining a triangle; similarly, $\mathcal{T}(ABCD)$ stands for A, B, C and D not being in the same plane, that is, determining a tetrahedron. The tetrahedron is moreover oriented: $\mathcal{T}(ABCD)$ does not, in general, imply $\mathcal{T}(DABC)$. We visualise $\mathcal{T}(ABCD)$ in Fig. 2 by placing an "observer" at B who is looking at the edge AC such that A is above C for them. Then D is on the right for this observer. Placing an observer in the same way in a situation where $\mathcal{T}(DABC)$ (which is equivalent to $\mathcal{T}(CBAD)$), they now see D on their left.

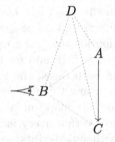

Fig. 2. Observer looking at the edge AC from B sees D on their right.

Remark 1. We chose not to include the orientation of the triangle, which amounts to the choice of S_3 over A_3 in the definition of a triangle relation (Definition 3). This is because we assume that our molecules float freely in space (e.g. in a solution), so that there is no two-dimensional orientation.

Definition 5 (Oriented pre-chemical graph). *An oriented pre-chemical graph is a tuple $(V, \tau, m, \mathcal{P}, \mathcal{T})$ where (V, τ, m) is a pre-chemical graph, $\mathcal{P}$ is a triangle relation on V and $\mathcal{T}$ is a tetrahedron relation on V with respect to $\mathcal{P}$, such that for all $a, b, c \in V$ we have: (1) if $\tau(a) \in \{+, -\}$, then $abc \notin \mathcal{P}$, and (2) if $\mathcal{P}(abc)$, then a, b and c are in the same connected component.*

An *oriented chemical graph* is an oriented pre-chemical graph, which is also a chemical graph. From now on, we adopt the convention that every pre-chemical graph is oriented: if the triangle and tetrahedron relations are not specified, we take them to be empty (meaning there are no constraints on the configuration).

Definition 6 (Preservation and reflection of orientation). *Let* $(M, \mathcal{P}_M, \mathcal{T}_M)$ *and* $(N, \mathcal{P}_N, \mathcal{T}_N)$ *be oriented pre-chemical graphs, and let* $f : M \to N$ *be a labelled graph isomorphism (an isomorphism on vertices which preserves the labelling). We say that* f *preserves orientation (or is* orientation-preserving*) if for all vertices A, B, C and D of M we have: (1)* $\mathcal{P}_M(ABC)$ *if and only if* $\mathcal{P}_N(fA, fB, fC)$*, and (2)* $\mathcal{T}_M(ABCD)$ *if and only if* $\mathcal{T}_N(fA, fB, fC, fD)$*.*

Similarly, we say that f *reflects orientation (or is* orientation-reflecting*) if for all vertices A, B, C and D of M we have: (1)* $\mathcal{P}_M(ABC)$ *if and only if* $\mathcal{P}_N(fA, fB, fC)$*, and (2)* $\mathcal{T}_M(ABCD)$ *if and only if* $\mathcal{T}_N(fD, fA, fB, fC)$*.*

Definition 7 (Chirality). *We say that two pre-chemical graphs are* chiral *if there is an orientation-reflecting isomorphism, but no orientation-preserving isomorphism between them.*

Example 2. Consider 2-butanol, whose molecular structure we draw in two different ways at the left of Fig. 3. Here we adopt the usual chemical convention for drawing spatial structure: a dashed wedge indicates that the bond points "into the page", and a solid wedge indicates that the bond points "out of the page". In this case, we choose to include the names of the vertices for some labels as superscripts. The spatial structure is formalised by defining the tetrahedron relation for the graph on the left-hand side as the closure under the action of A_4 of $\mathcal{T}(1234)$, and for the one on the right-hand side as (the closure of) $\mathcal{T}(4123)$. In both cases, the triangle relation is dictated by the tetrahedron relation, so that any three-element subset of $\{1, 2, 3, 4\}$ is in the triangle relation. Now the identity map (on labelled graphs) reflects orientation. It is furthermore not hard to see that every isomorphism restricts to the identity on the vertices labelled with superscripts, so that there is no orientation-preserving isomorphism. Thus the two molecules are chiral according to Definition 7.

By slightly modifying the structures, we obtain two configurations of isopentane, drawn at the right of Fig. 3. However, in this case we can find an orientation-preserving isomorphism (namely the one that swaps vertices 2 and 4), so that the molecules are not chiral.

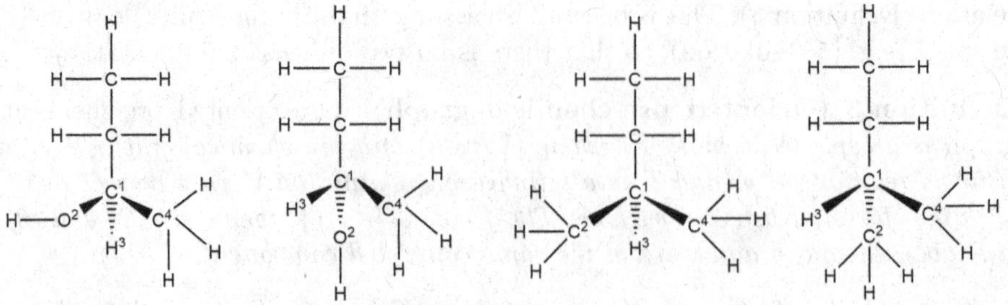

Fig. 3. Left: two configurations of 2-butanol. Right: two configurations of isopentane.

Example 3. Example 2 with 2-butanol demonstrated how to capture central chirality using Definition 7. In this example, we consider 1, 3-dichloroallene as an example of axial chirality. We draw two versions, as before:

The tetrahedron relation is generated by $T(1234)$ and $T(6123)$ for both molecules (note, however, that the vertices 4 and 6 have different labels). Now the isomorphism which swaps vertices 4 and 6 and is identity on all other vertices is orientation-reflecting, but not orientation-preserving. The only other isomorphism is $1 \mapsto 4, 2 \mapsto 5, 3 \mapsto 6, 4 \mapsto 3, 5 \mapsto 2, 6 \mapsto 1$, which does not preserve orientation. Thus the two molecules are indeed chiral.

5 Disconnection Rules

The backbone of retrosynthetic analysis are the *disconnection rules* that partition the target molecule into smaller parts. Formally, a disconnection rule is a partial endofunction on the set of chemical graphs. We define three classes of disconnection rules, all of which have a clear chemical significance: *electron detachment* (Definition 8), *ionic bond breaking* (Definition 9) and *covalent bond breaking* (Definition 10). These rules are chosen since they are used in the current retrosynthesis practice (e.g. [11, 39]). However, once the reverse "connection" rules are added, we also conjecture that the rules are complete in the sense that every reaction (Definition 12) can be decomposed into a sequence of disconnection rules.

Definition 8 (Electron detachment). *Let $u, v, a, b \in \mathbf{VN}$ be pairwise distinct vertex names. We define the* electron detachment *disconnection rule E_{ab}^{uv} as follows:*

- *a chemical graph $A = (V, \tau, m, \mathcal{P}, T)$ is in the domain of E_{ab}^{uv} if (1) $u, v \in V$, (2) $a, b \notin V$, (3) $\tau(u) \in \mathrm{At}$, (4) $\tau(v) = \alpha$, and (5) $m(u, v) = 1$,*
- *the chemical graph $E_{ab}^{uv}(A) = (V \cup \{a, b\}, \tau^E, m^E, \mathcal{P}^E, T^E)$ is defined by letting $\tau^E(a) = +, \tau^E(b) = -$ and letting τ^E agree with τ otherwise; further, define $m^E(u, v) = m^E(a, b) = 0, m^E(u, a) = m^E(v, b) = 1$ and let m^E agree with m otherwise; the relations $\mathcal{P}^E$ and T^E are defined by restricting $\mathcal{P}$ and T to $V \setminus \{v\}$.*

Example 4. The effect of the electron detachment is to detach an electron from a synthon, thus leaving it with a positive charge:

$$\mathrm{H}^u - \alpha^v \; \longrightarrow \; \boxed{E_{ab}^{uv}} \; \begin{array}{c} \diagup \; \mathrm{H}^u - +^a \\ \diagdown \; -^b - \alpha^v \end{array} \; .$$

Definition 9 (Ionic bond breaking). *Let $u, v \in \mathbf{VN}$ be distinct vertex names. We define the* ionic bond breaking *disconnection rule I^{uv} as follows:*

- a chemical graph $A = (V, \tau, m, \mathcal{P}, \mathcal{T})$ is in the domain of I^{uv} if (1) $u, v \in V$, (2) $\tau(u) = +$, (3) $\tau(v) = -$, and (4) $m(u, v) = \mathtt{i}$,
- the chemical graph $I^{uv}(A) = (V, \tau, m^I, \mathcal{P}^I, \mathcal{T}^I)$ is defined by letting $m^I(u, v) = 0$, and letting m^I agree with m on all other vertices; for the triangle and tetrahedron relations, define $\mathcal{P}^I(x, y, z)$ if and only if $\mathcal{P}(x, y, z)$ and x, y and z are in the same connected component of $I^{uv}(A)$, and similarly, define $\mathcal{T}^I(x, y, z, w)$ if and only if $\mathcal{T}(x, y, z, w)$ and x, y, z and w are in the same connected component of $I^{uv}(A)$.

Example 5. The effect of an ionic bond breaking is to remove an ionic bond between two specified charges:

Definition 10 (Covalent bond breaking). *Let $u, v, a, b \in$ **VN** be pairwise distinct vertex names. We define the covalent bond breaking disconnection rule C_{ab}^{uv} as follows:*

- a chemical graph $A = (V, \tau, m, \mathcal{P}, \mathcal{T})$ is in the domain of C_{ab}^{uv} if (1) $u, v \in V$, (2) $a, b \notin V$, (3) $\tau(u), \tau(v) \in \mathrm{At} \sqcup \{-\}$, and (4) $m(u, v) \in \{1, 2, 3, 4\}$,
- the chemical graph $C_{ab}^{uv}(A) = (V \cup \{a, b\}, \tau^C, m^C, \mathcal{P}^C, \mathcal{T}^C)$ is defined by letting $\tau^C(a) = \tau^C(b) = \alpha$ and letting τ^C agree with τ on all other vertices; further, let $m^C(u, v) = m(u, v) - 1$, $m^C(u, a) = m^C(v, b) = 1$ and let m^C agree with m on all other vertices; the triangle and tetrahedron relations are defined similarly to Definition 9 this time with respect to the connected components of $C_{ab}^{uv}(A)$.

Example 6. The effect of a covalent bond breaking is to reduce the number of electron pairs in a covalent bond by one. For a single bond this results in removing the bond altogether. We give two examples of this below:

Observe that each disconnection rule defined above is injective (as a partial function), and hence has an inverse partial function.

6 Reactions

After a disconnection rule has been applied and candidate synthetic equivalents have been found, the next step in a retrosynthetic analysis is to find an existing reaction that would transform the (hypothetical) synthetic equivalents to the target compound. In this section, we give one possible formalisation of chemical reactions using double pushout rewriting. Our approach is very similar, and inspired by, that of Andersen, Flamm, Merkle and Stadler [3], with some important differences, such as having more strict requirements on the graphs representing molecular entities, and allowing for the placeholder variable α.

Definition 11 (Morphism of pre-chemical graphs). *A morphism of pre-chemical graphs $f : A \to B$ is a function $f : V_A \to V_B$ such that its restriction to the chemical vertices $f|_{\text{Chem}(A)}$ is injective, and for all $v, u \in V_A$ we have (1) if $v \in \text{Chem}(A)$, then $\tau_B(fv) = \tau_A(v)$, (2) if $v \in \alpha(A)$, then $\tau_B(fv) \in \text{At} \sqcup \{\alpha\}$, (3) if $v, u \in \text{Chem}(A)$ and $m_A(v, u) \neq 0$, then $m_B(fv, fu) = m_A(v, u)$, and (4) if $v \in \alpha(A)$ and $\text{cov}(m_A(v, u)) \neq 0$, then*

$$\text{cov}(m_B(fv, fu)) = \sum_{w \in f^{-1}f(v), z \in f^{-1}f(u)} \text{cov}(m_A(w, z)).$$

Let us denote by **PChem** the category of pre-chemical graphs and their morphisms. This category has a partial monoidal structure given by the disjoint union: we can take the disjoint union of two morphisms provided that their domains as well as the codomains do not share vertex names. When the graphs are considered up to vertex renaming (as we shall do in the next section), this becomes an honest (strict) monoidal category.

The same reaction patterns are present in many individual reactions. A convenient way to represent this are spans whose left and right legs encode the preconditions for a reaction to occur and the effect of the reaction (outcome), respectively, while the centre denotes those parts that are unchanged.

Definition 12 (Reaction scheme). *A reaction scheme is a span $A \xleftarrow{f} K \xrightarrow{g} B$ in the category of pre-chemical graphs, whose boundaries A and B are chemical graphs with the same net charge, such that*

- *$f : V_K \to V_A$ and $g : V_K \to V_B$ are injective,*
- *f and g are surjective on neutral vertices: if $a \in \text{Neu}(A)$ and $b \in \text{Neu}(B)$, then there are $k, j \in V_K$ such that $f(k) = a$ and $g(j) = b$,*
- *f and g preserve all vertex labels: $\tau_A f = \tau_K = \tau_B g$,*
- *all vertices of K are neutral: $\text{Neu}(K) = V_K$,*
- *the span is terminal with respect to spans with the above properties.*

Example 7. The rule shown below appears in the equation describing glucose phosphorylation. It is a reaction scheme in the sense of Definition 12. We denote the morphisms by vertex superscripts: the vertex in the domain is mapped to the vertex in the codomain with the same superscript.

Definition 13 (Matching). *A* matching *is a morphism* $f : A \to C$ *in* **PChem** *whose domain and codomain are both chemical graphs, such that for all* $u, v \in$ Chem(A) *we have* $m_C(fu, fv) = m_A(u, v)$.

Proposition 1. *Given a matching and a reaction scheme as below left (all morphisms are in* **PChem***), there exist unique up to an isomorphism pre-chemical graphs* D *and* E *such that the diagram can be completed to the one on the right, where both squares are pushouts.*

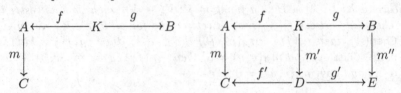

Moreover, E *is in fact a chemical graph, and if* $\alpha(C) = \varnothing$, *then also* $\alpha(E) = \varnothing$.

Definition 14. *A* reaction *is a span* $C \leftarrow D \to E$ *in* **PChem** *such that* C *and* D *are molecular graphs, there exist a reaction scheme and a matching as in Proposition 1 such that the diagram can be completed to a double pushout.*

Proposition 2. *The data of a reaction* $(V, \tau, m) \to (V', \tau', m')$ *can be equivalently presented as a tuple* (U, U', b, i) *where* $U \subseteq V$ *and* $U' \subseteq V'$ *are subsets with equal net charge,* $b : \text{Neu}(U) \to \text{Neu}(U')$ *is a labelled bijection, and* $i : V \backslash U \to V' \backslash U'$ *is an isomorphism of pre-chemical graphs.*

We denote by **React** the category whose objects are molecular graphs and whose morphisms are the reactions. The composition of $(U, U', b, i) : A \to B$ and $(W, W', c, j) : B \to C$ is given by $(U \cup b^{-1}(W) \cup i^{-1}(W), j(U' \backslash W) \cup W', jb * c, ji) : A \to C$, where $jb * c$ is defined by $a \mapsto cb(a)$ if $a \in b^{-1}(W)$, by $a \mapsto ci(a)$ if $a \in i^{-1}(W)$ and by $a \mapsto jb(a)$ if $a \in U \backslash b^{-1}(W)$.

7   Retrosynthesis in Layered Props

The main object of interest of this paper is the layered prop whose layers all share the same set of objects: namely, the chemical graphs up to a labelled graph isomorphism. The morphisms of a layer are either matchings, disconnection rules or reactions, parameterised by environmental molecules (these can act as solvents, reagents or catalysts). These layers are the main building blocks of our formulation of retrosynthesis.

Given a finite set M of molecular entities, let us enumerate the molecular entities in M as $M_1, \dots, M_k$. Given a list natural numbers $n = (n_1, \dots, n_k)$, we denote the resulting molecular graph $n_1 M_1 + \cdots + n_k M_k$ by (V_n, τ_n, m_n). We define three classes of symmetric monoidal categories parameterised by M as follows. The objects for all categories are the (equivalence classes of) chemical graphs, and the morphisms $A \to B$ are given below:

M-**Match**: a morphism $(m, b) : A \to B$ is given by a matching $m : A \to B$ together with a labelled injection $b : b_1 M_1 + \cdots + b_k M_k \to B$ such that im $(m) \cup$ im $(b) = B$, and im $(m) \cap$ im $(b) = m(\alpha(A)) \cap \mathbf{Chem}(B)$; the composite $A \xrightarrow{m,b} B \xrightarrow{n,c} C$ is given by $nm : A \to C$ and $nb+c : (b_1+c_1)M_1+\cdots+(b_k+c_k)M_k \to C$.

M-**React**: a generating morphism is a reaction $n_1 M_1 + \cdots + n_k M_k + A \xrightarrow{r} B$; given another reaction $m_1 M_1 + \cdots + m_k M_k + B \xrightarrow{s} C$, the composite $A \to C$ is given by

$$s \circ (r + \mathrm{id}_{m_1 M_1 + \cdots + m_k M_k}) : (n_1 + m_1)M_1 + \cdots + (n_k + m_k)M_k + A \to C.$$

M-**Disc**: for every disconnection rule d_{ab}^{uv} such that $d_{ab}^{uv}(n_1 M_1 + \cdots + n_k M_k + A) = B$, there are generating morphisms $d_{ab}^{uv} : A \to B$ and $\bar{d}_{ab}^{uv} : B \to A$, subject to the following equations: (1) $\bar{d}_{ab}^{uv} d_{ab}^{uv} = \mathrm{id}_A$ and $d_{ab}^{uv} \bar{d}_{ab}^{uv} = \mathrm{id}_B$, (2) $d_{ab}^{uv} h_{xy}^{wz} = h_{xy}^{wz} d_{ab}^{uv}$ whenever both sides are defined, and (3) $d_{u,v} + \mathrm{id}_C = d_{u,v}$ for every chemical graph C.

The idea is that the set M models the reaction environment: the parametric definitions above capture the intuition that there is an unbounded supply of these molecules in the environment.

In order to interpret sequences of disconnection rules as reactions, we need to restrict to those sequences whose domain and codomain are both molecular entities: we thus write M-**DiscMol** for the full subcategory of M-**Disc** on molecular entities. If $M = \varnothing$, we may omit the prefix. There are the following identity-on-object functors between the above parameterised categories:

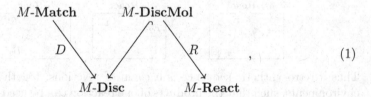

$$(1)$$

together with an inclusion functor for each of the three classes of categories whenever $M \subseteq N$. Given a morphism $(m, b) : A \to B$ in M-**Match**, the morphism $D(m, b) \in M$-**Disc** is given by first completely disconnecting (V_b, τ_b, m_b), and then "patching" the resulting bits to A to obtain B. The exact construction is somewhat technical, so we present it in the appendix. The functor R arises by noticing that every disconnection rule $d_{ab}^{uv} : A \to B$ gives rise to a pre-chemical graph isomorphism $A \backslash \{u, v\} \to B \backslash \{u, v, a, b\}$ and a labelled bijection between the *chemical* vertices in $\{u, v\}$ and $\{u, v, a, b\}$. Thus, a sequence of disconnection rules between molecular entities gives rise to a reaction.

Definition 15 (Retrosynthetic step). *A retrosynthetic step consists of*

- *a molecular graphs T and B, called the target, and the byproduct,*
- *a finite set of molecular entities $M \subseteq \mathcal{M}$, called the environment,*
- *a chemical graph S, whose connected components are called the synthons,*

– *a molecular graph* E, *whose components are called the* synthetic equivalents,
– *morphisms* $d \in \mathbf{Disc}(T, S)$, $m \in M\text{-}\mathbf{Match}(S, E)$, $r \in M\text{-}\mathbf{React}(E, T + B)$.

Proposition 3. *The data of a retrosynthetic step are equivalent to existence of the following morphism (1-cell) in the layered prop generated by the diagram (1):*

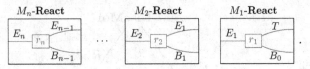

The morphism in the above proposition should be compared to the informal diagram in Fig. 1. The immediate advantage of presenting a retrosynthetic step as a morphism in a layered prop is that it illuminates how the different parts of the definition fit together in a highly procedural manner. Equally importantly, this presentation is fully compositional: one can imagine performing several steps in parallel, or dividing the tasks of finding the relevant morphisms (e.g. between different computers). Moreover, one can reason about different components of the step while preserving a precise mathematical interpretation (so long as one sticks to the rewrites (2-cells) of the layered prop).

Definition 16 (Retrosynthetic sequence). *A retrosynthetic sequence for a target molecular entity* T *is a sequence of morphisms* $r_1 \in M_1\text{-}\mathbf{React}(E_1, T + B_0)$, $r_2 \in M_2\text{-}\mathbf{React}(E_2, E_1 + B_1)$, ..., $r_n \in M_1\text{-}\mathbf{React}(E_n, E_{n-1} + B_{n-1})$ *such that the domain of* r_i *is a connected subgraph the codomain of* r_{i+1}:

Thus a retrosynthetic sequence is a chain of reactions, together with reaction environments, such that the products of one reaction can be used as the reactants for the next one, so that the reactions can occur one after another (assuming that the products can be extracted from the reaction environment, or one environment transformed into another one). In the formulation of a generic retrosynthesis procedure below, we shall additionally require that each reaction in the sequence comes from "erasing" everything but the rightmost cell in a retrosynthetic step.

We are now ready to formulate step-by-step retrosynthetic analysis. The procedure is a high-level mathematical description that, we suggest, is flexible enough to capture all instances of retrosynthetic algorithms. As a consequence, it can have various computational implementations. Let T be some fixed molecular entity. We initialise by setting $i = 0$ and $E_0 := T$.

1. Choose a subset $\mathcal{D}$ of disconnection rules,
2. Provide at least one of the following:
   (a) a finite set of reaction schemes $\mathcal{S}$,
   (b) a function $\mathfrak{F}$ from molecular graphs to finite sets of molecular graphs,

3. Search for a retrosynthetic step with $d \in \varnothing\text{-}\mathbf{Disc}(E_i, S)$, $m \in M\text{-}\mathbf{Match}(S, E)$, and $r \in M\text{-}\mathbf{React}(E, E_i + B_i)$ such that all disconnection rules in d and $D(m)$ are in $\mathcal{D}$, and we have at least one of the following:
   (a) there is an $s \in S$ such that the reaction r is an instance of s,
   (b) $E_i + B_i \in \mathfrak{F}(E)$;
   if successful, set $E_{i+1} := E$, $M_{i+1} := M$, $r_{i+1} := r$ and proceed to Step 4; if unsuccessful, stop,
4. Check if the molecular entities in E_{i+1} are known (commercially available): if yes, terminate; if no, increment $i \mapsto i + 1$ and return to Step 1.

Note how our framework is able to incorporate both template-based and template-free retrosynthesis, corresponding to the choices between (a) and (b) in Step 2: the set S is the template, while the function $\mathfrak{F}$ can be a previously trained algorithm, or other unstructured empirical model of reactions. We can also consider hybrid models by providing both S and $\mathfrak{F}$.

We take the output retrosynthetic sequence to always come with a specified reaction environment for each reaction. Currently existing tools rarely provide this information (mostly for complexity reasons), and hence, in our framework, correspond to the set M always being empty in Step 3.

Steps 1 and 2 both require making some choices. Two approaches to reduce the number of choices, as well as the search space in Step 3, have been proposed in the automated retrosynthesis literature: to use molecular similarity [14], or machine learning [26]. Chemical similarity can be used to determine which disconnection rules, reactions and environment molecules are actually tried: e.g. in Step 1, disconnection rules that appear in syntheses of molecules similar to T can be prioritised.

Ideally, each unsuccessful attempt to construct a retrosynthetic step in Step 3 should return some information on why the step failed: e.g. if the codomain of a reaction fails to contain E_i, then the output should be the codomain and a measure of how far it is from E_i. Similarly, if several reactions are found in Step 3, some of which result in products O that do not contain E_i, the step should suggest minimal alterations to E such that these reactions do not occur. This can be seen as a *deprotection* step: the idea is that in the next iteration the algorithm will attempt to construct (by now a fairly complicated) E, but now there is a guarantee this is worth the computational effort, as this prevents the unwanted reactions from occurring (*protection* step). Passing such information between the layers would take the full advantage of the layered prop formalism.

8   Discussion and Future Work

The main conceptual contributions of formulating retrosynthesis in layered props are the explicit mathematical descriptions of retrosynthetic steps (Definition 15) and sequences (Definition 16), which allows for a precise formulation of the entire process, as well as of more fine-grained concepts. While in the current article we showed how to account for the available disconnection rules, reactions and environmental molecules, the general formalism of layered props immediately suggests how to account for other environmental factors (e.g. temperature and pressure). Namely, these should be represented as posets which control the morphisms that are available between the chemical compounds. One idea for accounting for the available energy is via the disconnection rules: the higher the number of bonds that we are able to break in one step, the more energy is required to be present in the environment.

Apart from modelling retrosynthesis, another potential use of the reaction contexts is to capture context-dependent chemical similarity. While molecular similarity is a major research topic in computational chemistry [6], the current approaches are based on comparing the molecular structure (connectivity, number of rings etc.) of two compounds, and is therefore bound to ignore the reaction environment. Other advantages of our framework are representation of the protection-deprotection steps, and hard-wiring of chirality into the formalism.

At the level of the formalism, the next step is to model translations between the reaction environments as functors of the form M-**React** $\to N$-**React**. This would allow presenting a retrosynthetic sequence as a single, connected diagram, closely corresponding to actions to be taken in a lab. Similarly, we note that the informal algorithmic description in Sect. 7 could be presented internally in a layered prop: Steps 1 and 2 amount to choosing subcategories of **Disc** and **React**.

A theoretical issue that should be addressed in future work is the precise relation between reactions and disconnection rules. As was mentioned when introducing the disconnection rules, we believe that any reaction can be decomposed into a sequence of disconnection rules. This amounts to proving that the translation functor R is full, hence giving a completeness result for reactions with respect to the disconnection rules. In this way, the reactions can be seen as providing semantics for the disconnection rules. This also has a practical significance from the point of view of algorithm design: it would show that all computations, in principle, could be done with just using the disconnection rules.

On the practical side, the crucial next step is to take existing retrosynthesis algorithms and encode them in our framework. This requires implementing the morphisms of the layered prop in the previous section in some software. As the morphisms are represented by string diagrams, one approach is to use proof formalisation software specific to string diagrams and their equational reasoning, such as [32]. Alternatively, these morphisms could be coded into a programming language like python or Julia. The latter is especially promising, as there is a community writing category-theoretic modules for it [1]. As a lower level description, the disconnection rules and the reactions presented could be encoded in some graph rewriting language, such as Kappa [5,18,23,24], which is used to model systems of interacting agents, or MØD [2,4,5,31], which represents molecules as labelled graphs and generating rules for chemical transformations as spans of graphs (akin to this work). In order to formally represent reactions as disconnection rules, we need to rewrite string diagrams, the theory for which has been developed in a recent series of articles [7–9].

Acknowledgements. F. Zanasi acknowledges support from EPSRC EP/V002376/1.

References

1. AlgebraicJulia. https://www.algebraicjulia.org/
2. Andersen, J.L., Flamm, C., Merkle, D., Stadler, P.F.: Chemical transformation motifs - modelling pathways as integer hyperflows. IEEE/ACM Trans. Comput. Biol. Bioinform. **16**(2), 510–523 (2019)
3. Andersen, J., Flamm, C., Merkle, D., Stadler, P.: Inferring chemical reaction patterns using rule composition in graph grammars. J. Syst. Chem. **4**(1), 1–4 (2013)
4. Andersen, J., Flamm, C., Merkle, D., Stadler, P.: An intermediate level of abstraction for computational systems chemistry. Philos. Trans. R. Soc. A **375**(2109), 20160354 (2017)
5. Behr, N., Krivine, J., Andersen, J.L., Merkle, D.: Rewriting theory for the life sciences: a unifying theory of CTMC semantics. Theor. Comput. Sci. **884**(C), 68–115 (2021)
6. Bender, A., Glen, R.C.: Molecular similarity: a key technique in molecular informatics. Org. Biomol. Chem. **2**, 3204–3218 (2004)
7. Bonchi, F., Gadducci, F., Kissinger, A., Sobociński, P., Zanasi, F.: String diagram rewrite theory I: rewriting with frobenius structure. J. ACM **69**(2), 1–58 (2022)
8. Bonchi, F., Gadducci, F., Kissinger, A., Sobociński, P., Zanasi, F.: String diagram rewrite theory II: rewriting with symmetric monoidal structure. Math. Struct. Comput. Sci. **32**(4), 511–541 (2022)
9. Bonchi, F., Gadducci, F., Kissinger, A., Sobociński, P., Zanasi, F.: String diagram rewrite theory III: confluence with and without frobenius. Math. Struct. Comput. Sci. **32**(7), 829–869 (2022)
10. Chen, S., Jung, Y.: Deep retrosynthetic reaction prediction using local reactivity and global attention. JACS Au **1**(10), 1612–1620 (2021)
11. Clayden, J., Greeves, N., Warren, S.: Organic Chemistry. OUP (2012)
12. Coley, C.W., Barzilay, R., Jaakkola, T.S., Green, W.H., Jensen, K.F.: Prediction of organic reaction outcomes using machine learning. ACS Cent. Sci. **3**(5), 434–443 (2017)
13. Coley, C.W., Green, W.H., Jensen, K.F.: Machine learning in computer-aided synthesis planning. Acc. Chem. Res. **51**(5), 1281–1289 (2018)
14. Coley, C.W., Rogers, L., Green, W.H., Jensen, K.F.: Computer-assisted retrosynthesis based on molecular similarity. ACS Cent. Sci. **3**(12), 1237–1245 (2017)
15. Cook, A.G., Feltman, P.M.: Determination of solvent effects on keto-enol equilibria of 1, 3-dicarbonyl compounds using NMR. J. Chem. Educ. **84**(11), 1827 (2007)
16. Corey, E.J.: Robert Robinson lecture. Retrosynthetic thinking - essentials and examples. Chem. Soc. Rev. **17**, 111–133 (1988)
17. Corey, E.J., Cheng, X.-M.: The Logic of Chemical Synthesis. Wiley, Hoboken (1989)
18. Danos, V., Laneve, C.: Formal molecular biology. Theor. Comput. Sci. **325**(1), 69–110 (2004)
19. Dong, J., Zhao, M., Liu, Y., Su, Y., Zeng, X.: Deep learning in retrosynthesis planning: datasets, models and tools. Brief. Bioinform. **23**(1), bbab391 (2022)
20. Filice, M., Guisan, J.M., Palomo, J.M.: Recent trends in regioselective protection and deprotection of monosaccharides. Curr. Org. Chem. **14**(6), 516–532 (2010)

21. Fortunato, M.E., Coley, C.W., Barnes, B.C., Jensen, K.F.: Data augmentation and pretraining for template-based retrosynthetic prediction in computer-aided synthesis planning. J. Chem. Inf. Model. **60**(7), 3398–3407 (2020)

22. Gao, H., Struble, T.J., Coley, C.W., Wang, Y., Green, W.H., Jensen, K.F.: Using machine learning to predict suitable conditions for organic reactions. ACS Cent. Sci. **4**(11), 1465–1476 (2018)

23. Kappa language. https://kappalanguage.org/

24. Krivine, J.: Systems biology. ACM SIGLOG News **4**(3), 43–61 (2017)

25. Law, J., et al.: Route designer: a retrosynthetic analysis tool utilizing automated retrosynthetic rule generation. J. Chem. Inf. Model. **49**(3), 593–602 (2009)

26. Lin, K., Xu, Y., Pei, J., Lai, L.: Automatic retrosynthetic route planning using template-free models. Chem. Sci. **11**(12), 3355–3364 (2020)

27. Lobski, L., Zanasi, F.: String diagrams for layered explanations. In: Master, J., Lewis, M. (eds.) Proceedings Fifth International Conference on Applied Category Theory. EPTCS, vol. 380, pp. 362–382 (2023)

28. Marcou, G., et al.: Expert system for predicting reaction conditions: the Michael reaction case. J. Chem. Inf. Model. **55**(2), 239–250 (2015)

29. Maser, M.R., Cui, A.Y., Ryou, S., DeLano, T.J., Yue, Y.: Multilabel classification models for the prediction of cross-coupling reaction conditions. J. Chem. Inf. Model. **61**(1), 156–166 (2021)

30. Matwijczuk, A., et al.: Effect of solvent polarizability on the keto/enol equilibrium of selected bioactive molecules from the 1, 3, 4-thiadiazole group with a 2, 4-hydroxyphenyl function. J. Phys. Chem. A **121**(7), 1402–1411 (2017)

31. MØD. https://cheminf.imada.sdu.dk/mod/

32. Sobocinski, P., Wilson, P., Zanasi, F.: CARTOGRAPHER: a tool for string diagrammatic reasoning. In: Roggenbach, M., Sokolova, A. (eds.) 8th Conference on Algebra and Coalgebra in Computer Science, pp. 20:1–20:7. Schloss Dagstuhl-Leibniz-Zentrum fuer Informatik (2019)

33. Somnath, V.R., Bunne, C., Coley, C.W., Krause, A., Barzilay, R.: Learning graph models for template-free retrosynthesis. arXiv:2006.07038 (2020)

34. Strieth-Kalthoff, F., Sandfort, F., Segler, M.H.S., Glorius, F.: Machine learning the ropes: principles, applications and directions in synthetic chemistry. Chem. Soc. Rev. **49**(17), 6154–6168 (2020)

35. Sun, Y., Sahinidis, N.V.: Computer-aided retrosynthetic design: fundamentals, tools, and outlook. Curr. Opin. Chem. Eng. **35**, 100721 (2022)

36. Ucak, U.V., Ashyrmamatov, I., Ko, J., Lee, J.: Retrosynthetic reaction pathway prediction through neural machine translation of atomic environments. Nat. Commun. **13**(1), 1186–1186 (2022)

37. Walker, E., Kammeraad, J., Goetz, J., Robo, M.T., Tewari, A., Zimmerman, P.M.: Learning to predict reaction conditions: relationships between solvent, molecular structure, and catalyst. J. Chem. Inf. Model. **59**(9), 3645–3654 (2019)

38. Warren, S.: Designing Organic Syntheses: A Programmed Introduction to the Synthon Approach. Wiley, Hoboken (1991)

39. Warren, S., Wyatt, P.: Organic Synthesis: The Disconnection Approach, 2nd edn. Wiley, Hoboken (2008)

40. Yan, C., Zhao, P., Lu, C., Yu, Y., Huang, J.: RetroComposer: composing templates for template-based retrosynthesis prediction. Biomolecules **12**(9), 1325 (2022)

Closure and Decision Properties for Higher-Dimensional Automata

Amazigh Amrane[1], Hugo Bazille[1], Uli Fahrenberg[1(✉)],
and Krzysztof Ziemiański[2]

[1] EPITA Research Laboratory (LRE), Paris, France
uli@lrde.epita.fr
[2] University of Warsaw, Warsaw, Poland

Abstract. In this paper we develop the language theory of higher-dimensional automata (HDAs). Regular languages of HDAs are sets of finite interval partially ordered multisets (pomsets) with interfaces (iiPoms). We first show a pumping lemma which allows us to expose a class of non-regular languages. We also give an example of a regular language with unbounded ambiguity. Concerning decision and closure properties, we show that inclusion of regular languages is decidable (hence is emptiness), and that intersections of regular languages are again regular. On the other hand, complements of regular languages are not regular. We introduce a width-bounded complement and show that width-bounded complements of regular languages are again regular.

1 Introduction

Higher-dimensional automata (HDAs), introduced by Pratt and van Glabbeek [16,18], are a general geometric model for non-interleaving concurrency which subsumes, for example, event structures and Petri nets [19]. HDAs of dimension one are standard automata, whereas HDAs of dimension two are isomorphic to asynchronous transition systems [2,11,17]. As an example, Fig. 1 shows Petri net and HDA models for a system with two events, labelled a and b. The Petri net and HDA on the left side model the (mutually exclusive) interleaving of a and b as either $a.b$ or $b.a$; those to the right model concurrent execution of a and b. In the HDA, this independence is indicated by a filled-in square.

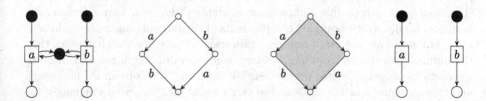

Fig. 1. Petri net and HDA models distinguishing interleaving (left) from non-interleaving (right) concurrency. Left: models for $a.b + b.a$; right: models for $a \parallel b$.

E. Ábrahám et al. (Eds.): ICTAC 2023, LNCS 14446, pp. 295–312, 2023.
https://doi.org/10.1007/978-3-031-47963-2_18

Recent work defines languages of HDAs [4], which are sets of partially ordered multisets with interfaces (ipomsets) [6] that are closed under subsumptions. Follow-up papers introduce a language theory for HDAs, showing a Kleene theorem [5], which makes a connection between rational and regular ipomset languages (those accepted by finite HDAs), and a Myhill-Nerode theorem [8] stating that regular languages are precisely those that have finite prefix quotient. Here we continue to develop this nascent higher-dimensional automata theory.

Our first contribution, in Sect. 4, is a pumping lemma for HDAs, based on the fact that if an ipomset accepted by an HDA is long enough, then there is a cycle in the path that accepts it. As an application we can expose a class of non-regular ipomset languages. We also show that regular languages are closed under intersection, both using the Myhill-Nerode theorem and an explicit product construction.

The paper [8] introduces deterministic HDAs and shows that not all HDAs are determinizable. As a weaker notion in-between determinism and non-determinism, one may ask whether all regular languages may be recognized by finitely ambiguous HDAs, *i.e.*, HDAs in which there is an upper bound for the number of accepting paths on any ipomset. We show that the answer to this question is negative and that there are regular languages of unbounded ambiguity.

In Sect. 5 we introduce a translation from HDAs to ordinary finite automata over an alphabet of discrete ipomsets, called ST-automata. The translation forgets some of the structure of the HDA, and we leave open the question if, and in what sense, it would be invertible. Nevertheless, this translation allows us to show that inclusion of regular ipomset languages is decidable. This immediately implies that emptiness is decidable; universality is trivial given that the universal language is not regular.

Finally, in Sect. 6, we are interested in a notion of complement. This immediately raises two problems: first, complements of ipomset languages are generally not closed under subsumption; second, the complement of the empty language, which is regular, is the universal language, which is non-regular. The first problem is solved by taking subsumption closure, turning complement into a pseudocomplement in the sense of lattice theory.

As to the second problem, we can show that complements of regular languages are non-regular. Yet if we restrict the width of our languages, *i.e.*, the number of events which may occur concurrently, then the so-defined width-bounded complement has good properties: it is still a pseudocomplement; its skeletal elements (the ones for which double complement is identity) have an easy characterisation; and finally width-bounded complements of regular languages are again regular. The proof of that last property again uses ST-automata and the fact that the induced translation from ipomset languages to word languages over discrete ipomsets has good algebraic properties. We note that width-bounded languages and (pseudo)complements are found in other works on concurrent languages, for example [9,14,15].

Another goal of this work was to obtain the above results using automata-theoretic means as opposed to category-theoretic or topological ones. Indeed we do not use presheaves, track objects, cylinders, or any other of the categorical or topological constructions employed in [5,8]. Categorical reasoning would have simplified proofs in several places, and we do make note of this in several footnotes, but no background in category theory or algebraic topology is necessary to understand this paper.

To sum up, our main contributions to higher-dimensional automata theory are as follows:

- a pumping lemma (Lemma 11);
- regular languages of unbounded ambiguity (Proposition 16);
- closure of regular languages under intersection (Proposition 15);
- closure of regular languages under width-bounded complement (Theorem 33);
- decidability of inclusion of regular languages (Theorem 22).

Due to space constraints, some proofs had to be omitted from this paper. These can be found in the long version [1].

2   Pomsets with Interfaces

HDAs model systems in which (labelled) events have duration and may happen concurrently. Notably, as seen in the introduction, concurrency of events is a more general notion than interleaving. Every event has an interval in time during which it is active: it starts at some point in time, then remains active until it terminates, and never appears again. Events may be concurrent, in which case their activity intervals overlap: one of the two events starts before the other terminates. Executions are thus isomorphism classes of partially ordered intervals. For reasons of compositionality we also consider executions in which events may be active already at the beginning or remain active at the end.

Any time point of an execution defines a *concurrency list* (or *conclist*) of currently active events. The relative position of any two concurrent events on such lists does not change during passage of time; this equips events of an execution with a partial order which we call *event order*. The temporal order of non-concurrent events (one of two events terminating before the other starts) introduces another partial order which we call *precedence*. An execution is, then, a collection of labelled events together with two partial orders.

To make the above precise, let Σ be a finite alphabet. We define three notions, in increasing order of generality:

- A *concurrency list*, or *conclist*, $U = (U, \dashrightarrow_U, \lambda_U)$ consists of a finite set U, a strict total order $\dashrightarrow_U \subseteq U \times U$ (the event order),[1] and a labelling $\lambda_U : U \to \Sigma$.

---

[1] A strict *partial* order is a relation which is irreflexive and transitive; a strict *total* order is a relation which is irreflexive, transitive, and total. We may omit the "strict".

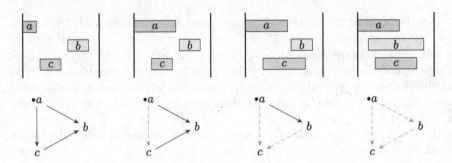

Fig. 2. Activity intervals of events (top) and corresponding ipomsets (bottom), *cf.* Example 1. Full arrows indicate precedence order; dashed arrows indicate event order; bullets indicate interfaces.

- A *partially ordered multiset*, or *pomset*, $P = (P, <_P, \dashrightarrow_P, \lambda_P)$ consists of a finite set P, two strict partial orders $<_P, \dashrightarrow_P \subseteq P \times P$ (precedence and event order), and a labelling $\lambda_P : P \to \Sigma$, such that for each $x \neq y$ in P, at least one of $x <_P y$, $y <_P x$, $x \dashrightarrow_P y$, or $y \dashrightarrow_P x$ holds.
- A *pomset with interfaces*, or *ipomset*, $(P, <_P, \dashrightarrow_P, S_P, T_P, \lambda_P)$ consists of a pomset $(P, <_P, \dashrightarrow_P, \lambda_P)$ together with subsets $S_P, T_P \subseteq P$ (*source* and *target interfaces*) such that elements of S_P are $<_P$-minimal and those of T_P are $<_P$-maximal.

We will omit the subscripts $_U$ and $_P$ whenever possible.

Conclists may be regarded as pomsets with empty precedence (*discrete* pomsets); the last condition above enforces that $\dashrightarrow$ is then total. Pomsets are ipomsets with empty interfaces, and in any ipomset P, the substructures induced by S_P and T_P are conclists. Note that different events of ipomsets may carry the same label; in particular we do *not* exclude autoconcurrency. Figure 2 shows some simple examples. Source and target events are marked by "•" at the left or right side, and if the event order is not shown, we assume that it goes downwards.

An ipomset P is *interval* if $<_P$ is an interval order [10], that is, if it admits an interval representation given by functions b and e from P to real numbers such that $b(x) \leq e(x)$ for all $x \in P$ and $x <_P y$ iff $e(x) < b(y)$ for all $x, y \in P$. Given that our ipomsets represent activity intervals of events, any of the ipomsets we will encounter will be interval, and we omit the qualification "interval". We emphasise that this is *not* a restriction, but rather induced by the semantics, see also [21]. We let iiPoms denote the set of (interval) ipomsets.

Ipomsets may be *refined* by shortening activity intervals, potentially removing concurrency and expanding precedence. The inverse to refinement is called *subsumption* and defined as follows. For ipomsets P and Q we say that Q subsumes P and write $P \sqsubseteq Q$ if there is a bijection $f : P \to Q$ for which

(1) $f(S_P) = S_Q$, $f(T_P) = T_Q$, and $\lambda_Q \circ f = \lambda_P$;
(2) $f(x) <_Q f(y)$ implies $x <_P y$;
(3) $x \not<_P y$, $y \not<_P x$ and $x \dashrightarrow_P y$ imply $f(x) \dashrightarrow_Q f(y)$.

That is, f respects interfaces and labels, reflects precedence, and preserves essential event order. (Event order is essential for concurrent events, but by transi-

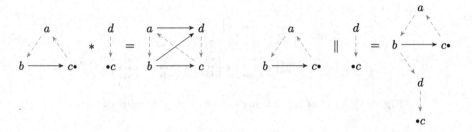

Fig. 3. Gluing and parallel composition of ipomsets.

tivity, it also appears between non-concurrent events. Subsumptions ignore such non-essential event order.) This definition adapts the one of [12] to event orders and interfaces. Intuitively, P has more order and less concurrency than Q.

Example 1. In Fig. 2 there is a sequence of subsumptions from left to right:

$$\bullet acb \sqsubseteq \begin{bmatrix} \bullet a \\ {\scriptstyle \succ} b \\ c \end{bmatrix} \sqsubseteq [\bullet a \!\to\! b] \sqsubseteq \begin{bmatrix} \bullet a \\ b \\ c \end{bmatrix}$$

An event e_1 is smaller than e_2 in the precedence order if e_1 is terminated before e_2 is started; e_1 is smaller than e_2 in the event order if they are concurrent and e_1 is above e_2 in the respective conclist.

Isomorphisms of ipomsets are invertible subsumptions, *i.e.*, bijections f for which items (2) and (3) above are strengthened to

$(2')$ $f(x) <_Q f(y)$ iff $x <_P y$;

$(3')$ $x \not<_P y$ and $y \not<_P x$ imply that $x \dashrightarrow_P y$ iff $f(x) \dashrightarrow_Q f(y)$.

Due to the requirement that all elements are ordered by $<$ or $\dashrightarrow$, there is at most one isomorphism between any two ipomsets. Hence we may switch freely between ipomsets and their isomorphism classes. We will also call these equivalence classes ipomsets and often conflate equality and isomorphism.

Compositions. The standard serial and parallel compositions of pomsets [12] extend to ipomsets. The *parallel* composition of ipomsets P and Q is $P \parallel Q = (P \sqcup Q, <, \dashrightarrow, S, T, \lambda)$, where $P \sqcup Q$ denotes disjoint union and

- $x < y$ if $x <_P y$ or $x <_Q y$;
- $x \dashrightarrow y$ if $x \dashrightarrow_P y$, $x \dashrightarrow_Q y$, or $x \in P$ and $y \in Q$;
- $S = S_P \cup S_Q$ and $T = T_P \cup T_Q$;
- $\lambda(x) = \lambda_P(x)$ if $x \in P$ and $\lambda(x) = \lambda_Q(x)$ if $x \in Q$.

Note that parallel composition of ipomsets is generally not commutative, see [6] or Example 28 below for details.

Serial composition generalises to a *gluing* composition which continues interface events across compositions and is defined as follows. Let P and Q be ipomsets such that $T_P = S_Q$, $x \dashrightarrow_P y$ iff $x \dashrightarrow_Q y$ for all $x, y \in T_P = S_Q$, and the restrictions $\lambda_{P \restriction T_P} = \lambda_{Q \restriction S_Q}$, then $P * Q = (P \cup Q, <, \dashrightarrow, S_P, T_Q, \lambda)$, where

$$\text{Sparse:} \begin{bmatrix} {\bullet}a{\bullet} \\ c{\bullet} \\ d{\bullet} \end{bmatrix} * \begin{bmatrix} {\bullet}a \\ {\bullet}c{\bullet} \\ {\bullet}d{\bullet} \end{bmatrix} * \begin{bmatrix} b{\bullet} \\ {\bullet}c{\bullet} \\ {\bullet}d{\bullet} \end{bmatrix} * \begin{bmatrix} {\bullet}b \\ {\bullet}c \\ {\bullet}d \end{bmatrix}$$

$$\text{Dense:} \begin{bmatrix} {\bullet}a{\bullet} \\ c{\bullet} \end{bmatrix} * \begin{bmatrix} {\bullet}a{\bullet} \\ {\bullet}c{\bullet} \\ d{\bullet} \end{bmatrix} * \begin{bmatrix} {\bullet}a \\ {\bullet}c{\bullet} \\ {\bullet}d{\bullet} \end{bmatrix} * \begin{bmatrix} b{\bullet} \\ {\bullet}c{\bullet} \\ {\bullet}d{\bullet} \end{bmatrix} * \begin{bmatrix} {\bullet}b \\ {\bullet}c{\bullet} \\ {\bullet}d{\bullet} \end{bmatrix} * \begin{bmatrix} {\bullet}c{\bullet} \\ {\bullet}d \end{bmatrix} * {\bullet}c$$

Fig. 4. Ipomset of size 3.5 and two of its step decompositions.

- $x < y$ if $x <_P y$, $x <_Q y$, or $x \in P - T_P$ and $y \in Q - S_Q$;[2]
- $\dashrightarrow$ is the transitive closure of $\dashrightarrow_P \cup \dashrightarrow_Q$;
- $\lambda(x) = \lambda_P(x)$ if $x \in P$ and $\lambda(x) = \lambda_Q(x)$ if $x \in Q$.

Gluing is, thus, only defined if the targets of P are equal to the sources of Q *as conclists*. If we would not conflate equality and isomorphism, we would have to define the carrier set of $P * Q$ to be the disjoint union of P and Q quotiented out by the unique isomorphism $T_P \to S_Q$. We will often omit the "$*$" in gluing compositions. Figure 3 shows some examples.

An ipomset P is a *word* (with interfaces) if $<_P$ is total. Conversely, P is *discrete* if $<_P$ is empty (hence $\dashrightarrow_P$ is total). Conclists are discrete ipomsets without interfaces. The relation $\sqsubseteq$ is a partial order on iiPoms with minimal elements words and maximal elements discrete ipomsets. Further, gluing and parallel compositions respect $\sqsubseteq$.

Special Ipomsets. A *starter* is a discrete ipomset U with $T_U = U$, a *terminator* one with $S_U = U$. The intuition is that a starter does nothing but start the events in $A = U - S_U$, and a terminator terminates the events in $B = U - T_U$. These will be so important later that we introduce special notation, writing $_A{\uparrow}U$ and $U{\downarrow}_B$ for the above. Starter $_A{\uparrow}U$ is *elementary* if A is a singleton, similarly for $U{\downarrow}_B$. Discrete ipomsets U with $S_U = T_U = U$ are identities for the gluing composition and written id_U. Note that $\mathrm{id}_U = {}_\emptyset{\uparrow}U = U{\downarrow}_\emptyset$.

The *width* $\mathrm{wid}(P)$ of an ipomset P is the cardinality of a maximal $<$-antichain. For $k \geq 0$, we let $\text{iiPoms}_{\leq k} \subseteq \text{iiPoms}$ denote the set of ipomsets of width at most k. The *size* of an ipomset P is $\mathrm{size}(P) = |P| - \frac{1}{2}(|S_P| + |T_P|)$. Identities are exactly the ipomsets of size 0. Elementary starters and terminators are exactly the ipomsets of size $\frac{1}{2}$.

Any ipomset can be decomposed as a gluing of starters and terminators [6], see also [13]. Such a presentation we call a *step decomposition*. If starters and terminators are alternating, the step decomposition is called *sparse*; if they are all elementary, then it is *dense*.

Example 2. Figure 4 illustrates two step decompositions. The sparse one first starts c and d, then terminates a, starts b, and terminates b, c and d together. The dense one first starts c, then starts d, terminates a, starts b, and finally terminates b, d, and c in order.

Lemma 3 ([8]). *Every ipomset P has a unique sparse step decomposition.*

---

[2] We use "$-$" for set difference instead of the perhaps more common "$\backslash$".

Dense step decompositions are generally not unique, but they all have the same length.

Lemma 4. *Every dense step decomposition of ipomset P has length $2\,\mathsf{size}(P)$.*

Rational Languages. For $A \subseteq \mathsf{iiPoms}$ we let

$$A{\downarrow} = \{P \in \mathsf{iiPoms} \mid \exists Q \in A : P \sqsubseteq Q\}.$$

Note that $(A \cup B){\downarrow} = A{\downarrow} \cup B{\downarrow}$ for all $A, B \subseteq \mathsf{iiPoms}$, but for intersection this does *not* hold. For example it may happen that $A \cap B = \emptyset$ but $A{\downarrow} \cap B{\downarrow} \neq \emptyset$. A *language* is a subset $L \subseteq \mathsf{iiPoms}$ for which $L{\downarrow} = L$. The set of all languages is denoted $\mathscr{L} \subseteq 2^{\mathsf{iiPoms}}$.

The *width* of a language L is $\mathsf{wid}(L) = \sup\{\mathsf{wid}(P) \mid P \in L\}$. For $k \geq 0$ and $L \in \mathscr{L}$, denote $L_{\leq k} = \{P \in L \mid \mathsf{wid}(P) \leq k\}$. L is *k-dimensional* if $L = L_{\leq k}$. We let $\mathscr{L}_{\leq k} = \mathscr{L} \cap \mathsf{iiPoms}_{\leq k}$ denote the set of k-dimensional languages.

The *singleton ipomsets* are $[a]$ $[{\bullet}a]$, $[a{\bullet}]$ and $[{\bullet}a{\bullet}]$, for all $a \in \Sigma$. The *rational operations* $\cup$, $*$, $\|$ and (Kleene plus) $^+$ for languages are defined as follows.

$$L * M = \{P * Q \mid P \in L,\, Q \in M,\, T_P = S_Q\}{\downarrow},$$
$$L \parallel M = \{P \parallel Q \mid P \in L,\, Q \in M\}{\downarrow},$$
$$L^+ = \bigcup_{n \geq 1} L^n, \qquad \text{for } L^1 = L, L^{n+1} = L * L^n.$$

The class of *rational languages* is the smallest subset of $\mathscr{L}$ that contains

$$\{\emptyset, \{\epsilon\}, \{[a]\}, \{[{\bullet}a]\}, \{[a{\bullet}]\}, \{[{\bullet}a{\bullet}]\} \mid a \in \Sigma\}$$

(ϵ denotes the empty ipomset) and is closed under the rational operations.

Lemma 5 ([5]). *Any rational language has finite width.*

It immediately follows that the universal language iiPoms is *not* rational.

The *prefix quotient* of a language $L \in \mathscr{L}$ by an ipomset P is $P{\backslash}L = \{Q \in \mathsf{iiPoms} \mid PQ \in L\}$. Similarly, the *suffix quotient* of L by P is $L/P = \{Q \in \mathsf{iiPoms} \mid QP \in L\}$. Denoting

$$\mathsf{suff}(L) = \{P{\backslash}L \mid P \in \mathsf{iiPoms}\}, \qquad \mathsf{pref}(L) = \{L/P \mid P \in \mathsf{iiPoms}\},$$

we may now state the central result of [8].

Theorem 6 ([8]). *A language $L \in \mathscr{L}$ is rational iff $\mathsf{suff}(L)$ is finite, iff $\mathsf{pref}(L)$ is finite.*

3   Higher-Dimensional Automata

An HDA is a collection of *cells* which are connected by *face maps*. Each cell contains a conclist of events which are active in it, and the face maps may

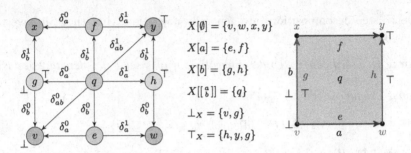

Fig. 5. A two-dimensional HDA X on $\Sigma = \{a, b\}$, see Example 7.

terminate some events (*upper* faces) or "unstart" some events (*lower* faces), *i.e.*, map a cell to another in which the indicated events are not yet active.

To make this precise, let $\square$ denote the set of conclists. A *precubical set*

$$X = (X, \mathsf{ev}, \{\delta^0_{A,U}, \delta^1_{A,U} \mid U \in \square, A \subseteq U\})$$

consists of a set of cells X together with a function $\mathsf{ev} : X \to \square$. For a conclist U we write $X[U] = \{x \in X \mid \mathsf{ev}(x) = U\}$ for the cells of type U. Further, for every $U \in \square$ and $A \subseteq U$ there are face maps $\delta^0_A, \delta^1_A : X[U] \to X[U - A]$ which satisfy $\delta^\nu_A \delta^\mu_B = \delta^\mu_B \delta^\nu_A$ for $A \cap B = \emptyset$ and $\nu, \mu \in \{0, 1\}$. The upper face maps δ^1_A transform a cell x into one in which the events in A have terminated, whereas the lower face maps δ^0_A transform x into a cell where the events in A have not yet started. The *precubical identity* above expresses the fact that these transformations commute for disjoint sets of events.

A *higher-dimensional automaton* (HDA) $X = (X, \bot_X, \top_X)$ is a precubical set together with subsets $\bot_X, \top_X \subseteq X$ of *start* and *accept* cells. While HDAs may have an infinite number of cells, we will mostly be interested in finite HDAs. Thus, in the following we will omit the word "finite" and will be explicit when talking about infinite HDAs. The *dimension* of an HDA X is $\dim(X) = \sup\{|\mathsf{ev}(x)| \mid x \in X\} \in \mathbb{N} \cup \{\infty\}$.[3]

A standard automaton is the same as a one-dimensional HDA X with the property that for all $x \in \bot_X \cup \top_X$, $\mathsf{ev}(x) = \emptyset$: cells in $X[\emptyset]$ are states, cells in $X[\{a\}]$ for $a \in \Sigma$ are a-labelled transitions, and face maps $\delta^0_{\{a\}}$ and $\delta^1_{\{a\}}$ attach source and target states to transitions. In contrast to ordinary automata we allow start and accept *transitions* instead of merely states, so languages of one-dimensional HDAs may contain words with interfaces.

Example 7. Figure 5 shows a two-dimensional HDA as a combinatorial object (left) and in a geometric realisation (right). It consists of nine cells: the corner cells $X_0 = \{x, y, v, w\}$ in which no event is active (for all $z \in X_0$, $\mathsf{ev}(z) = \emptyset$), the transition cells $X_1 = \{g, h, f, e\}$ in which one event is active ($\mathsf{ev}(f) = \mathsf{ev}(e) = a$ and $\mathsf{ev}(g) = \mathsf{ev}(h) = b$), and the square cell q where $\mathsf{ev}(q) = \begin{bmatrix} a \\ b \end{bmatrix}$.

---

[3] Precubical sets are presheaves over a category on objects $\square$, and then HDAs form a category with the induced morphisms, see [5].

The arrows between the cells on the left representation correspond to the face maps connecting them. For example, the upper face map δ^1_{ab} maps q to y because the latter is the cell in which the active events a and b of q have been terminated. On the right, face maps are used to glue cells together, so that for example $\delta^1_{ab}(q)$ is glued to the top right of q. In this and other geometric realisations, when we have two concurrent events a and b with $a \dashrightarrow b$, we will draw a horizontally and b vertically.

Regular Languages. *Computations* of HDAs are *paths*, i.e., sequences $\alpha = (x_0, \phi_1, x_1, \ldots, x_{n-1}, \phi_n, x_n)$ consisting of cells x_i of X and symbols ϕ_i which indicate face map types: for every $i \in \{1, \ldots, n\}$, (x_{i-1}, ϕ_i, x_i) is either

- $(\delta^0_A(x_i), \nearrow^A, x_i)$ for $A \subseteq \mathsf{ev}(x_i)$ (an *upstep*)
- or $(x_{i-1}, \searrow_A, \delta^1_A(x_{i-1}))$ for $A \subseteq \mathsf{ev}(x_{i-1})$ (a *downstep*).

Downsteps terminate events, following upper face maps, whereas upsteps start events by following inverses of lower face maps. Both types of steps may be empty, and $\nearrow^\emptyset = \searrow_\emptyset$.

The *source* and *target* of α as above are $\mathsf{src}(\alpha) = x_0$ and $\mathsf{tgt}(\alpha) = x_n$. The set of all paths in X starting at $Y \subseteq X$ and terminating in $Z \subseteq X$ is denoted by $\mathsf{Path}(X)^Z_Y$. A path α is *accepting* if $\mathsf{src}(\alpha) \in \bot_X$ and $\mathsf{tgt}(\alpha) \in \top_X$. Paths α and β may be concatenated if $\mathsf{tgt}(\alpha) = \mathsf{src}(\beta)$. Their concatenation is written $\alpha * \beta$ or simply $\alpha\beta$.

Path equivalence is the congruence $\simeq$ generated by $(z \nearrow^A y \nearrow^B x) \simeq (z \nearrow^{A \cup B} x)$, $(x \searrow_A y \searrow_B z) \simeq (x \searrow_{A \cup B} z)$, and $\gamma\alpha\delta \simeq \gamma\beta\delta$ whenever $\alpha \simeq \beta$. Intuitively, this relation allows to assemble subsequent upsteps or downsteps into one bigger step. A path is *sparse* if its upsteps and downsteps are alternating, so that no more such assembling may take place. Every equivalence class of paths contains a unique sparse path.

The observable content or *event ipomset* $\mathsf{ev}(\alpha)$ of a path α is defined recursively as follows:

- if $\alpha = (x)$, then $\mathsf{ev}(\alpha) = \mathsf{id}_{\mathsf{ev}(x)}$;
- if $\alpha = (y \nearrow^A x)$, then $\mathsf{ev}(\alpha) = {}_A{\uparrow}\mathsf{ev}(x)$;
- if $\alpha = (x \searrow_A y)$, then $\mathsf{ev}(\alpha) = \mathsf{ev}(x){\downarrow}_A$;
- if $\alpha = \alpha_1 * \cdots * \alpha_n$ is a concatenation, then $\mathsf{ev}(\alpha) = \mathsf{ev}(\alpha_1) * \cdots * \mathsf{ev}(\alpha_n)$.

Note that upsteps in α correspond to starters in $\mathsf{ev}(\alpha)$ and downsteps correspond to terminators. Path equivalence $\alpha \simeq \beta$ implies $\mathsf{ev}(\alpha) = \mathsf{ev}(\beta)$ [5]. Further, if $\alpha = \alpha_1 * \cdots * \alpha_n$ is a sparse path, then $\mathsf{ev}(\alpha) = \mathsf{ev}(\alpha_1) * \cdots * \mathsf{ev}(\alpha_n)$ is a sparse step decomposition.

The *language* of an HDA X is $\mathsf{L}(X) = \{\mathsf{ev}(\alpha) \mid \alpha \text{ accepting path in } X\}$.[4]

Example 8. The HDA X of Fig. 5 admits several accepting paths with target h, for example $v \nearrow^{ab} q \searrow_a h$. This is a sparse path and equivalent to the non-sparse paths $v \nearrow^a e \nearrow^b q \searrow_a h$ and $v \nearrow^b g \nearrow^a q \searrow_a h$. Their event ipomset

---

[4] Every ipomset P may be converted into a *track object* $\square^P$, see [5], which is an HDA with the property that for any HDA X, $P \in \mathsf{L}(X)$ iff there is a morphism $\square^P \to X$.

is $[^a_{b\bullet}]$. In addition, since g is both a start and accept cell, we have also g and $v \nearrow^b g$ as accepting paths, with event ipomsets $\bullet b \bullet$ and $b \bullet$, respectively. We have $\mathsf{L}(X) = \{b\bullet, \bullet b\bullet, [^a_{b\bullet}], [^a_{\bullet b\bullet}], [^a_b], [^a_{\bullet b}]\}\downarrow$.

Lemma 9. *Let X be an HDA, $P \in \mathsf{L}(X)$ and $P = P_1 * \cdots * P_n$ be any decomposition (not necessarily a step decomposition). Then there exists an accepting path $\alpha = \alpha_1 * \cdots * \alpha_n$ in X such that $\mathsf{ev}(\alpha_i) = P_i$ for all i. If $P = P_1 * \cdots * P_n$ is a sparse step decomposition, then $\alpha = \alpha_1 * \cdots * \alpha_n$ is sparse.*

Languages of HDAs are sets of (interval) ipomsets which are closed under subsumption [5], *i.e.*, languages in our sense. A language is *regular* if it is the language of a finite HDA.

Theorem 10 ([5]). *A language is regular iff it is rational.*

4 Regular and Non-regular Languages

Pumping Lemma. The next lemma is similar to the pumping lemma for word languages.

Lemma 11. *Let L be a regular language. There exists $k \in \mathbb{N}$ such that for any $P \in L$, any decomposition $P = Q_1 * \cdots * Q_n$ with $n > k$ and any $0 \le m \le n - k$ there exist i, j such that $m \le i < j \le m + k$ and $Q_1 * \cdots * Q_i * (Q_{i+1} * \cdots * Q_j)^+ * Q_{j+1} * \cdots * Q_n \subseteq L$.*

Proof. Let X be an HDA accepting L and $k > |X|$. By Lemma 9 there exists an accepting path $\alpha = \alpha_1 * \cdots * \alpha_n$ such that $\mathsf{ev}(\alpha_i) = Q_i$ for all i, and $\mathsf{ev}(\alpha) = P$. Denote $x_i = \mathsf{tgt}(\alpha_i) = \mathsf{src}(\alpha_{i+1})$. Amongst the cells $x_m, \ldots, x_{m+k}$ there are at least two equal, say $x_i = x_j$, $m \le i < j \le m + k$. As a consequence, $\mathsf{src}(\alpha_{i+1}) = \mathsf{tgt}(\alpha_j)$, and for every $r \ge 1$

$$\alpha_1 * \cdots * \alpha_i * (\alpha_{i+1} * \cdots * \alpha_j)^r * \alpha_{j+1} * \cdots * \alpha_n$$

is an accepting path that recognises $Q_1 * \cdots * Q_i * (Q_{i+1} * \cdots * Q_j)^r * Q_{j+1} * \cdots * Q_n$. $\square$

Corollary 12. *Let L be a regular language. There exists $k \in \mathbb{N}$ such that any $P \in L$ with $\mathsf{size}(P) > k$ can be decomposed into $P = Q_1 * Q_2 * Q_3$ such that Q_2 is not an identity and $Q_1 * Q_2^+ * Q_3 \subseteq L$.*

The proof follows by applying Lemma 11 to a dense step decomposition $P = Q_1 * \cdots * Q_{2\,\mathsf{size}(P)}$, *cf.* Lemma 4. We may now expose a language which is not regular.

Proposition 13. *The language $L = \{[^a_a]^n * a^n \mid n \ge 1\}\downarrow$ is not regular.*

Note that the restriction $L_{\le 1} = (aaa)^+$ *is regular, showing that regularity of languages may not be decided by restricting to their one-dimensional parts.*

Proof (Proof of Proposition 13). We give two proofs. The first uses Theorem 6: for every $k \geq 1$, $[{a \atop a}]^k \backslash L = \{[{a \atop a}]^n * a^{n+k} \mid n \geq 0\}\downarrow$, and these are different for different k, so suff(L) is infinite.

The second proof uses Lemma 11. Assume L to be regular, let k be the constant from the lemma, and take $P = [{a \atop a}]^k * a^k = Q_1 * \cdots * Q_k * Q_{k+1}$, where $Q_1 = \cdots = Q_k = [{a \atop a}]$ and $Q_{k+1} = a^k$. For $m = 0$ we obtain that $[{a \atop a}]^{k+(j-i)r} a^k \in L$ for all r and some $j - i > 0$: a contradiction. □

We may strengthen the above result to show that regularity of languages may not be decided by restricting to their k-dimensional parts for any $k \geq 1$. For $a \in \Sigma$ let $a^{\|_1} = a$ and $a^{\|_k} = a \parallel a^{\|_{k-1}}$ for $k \geq 2$: the k-fold parallel product of a with itself. Now let $k \geq 1$ and

$$L = \{(a^{\|_{k+1}})^n * P^n \mid n \geq 0, P \in \{a^{\|_{k+1}}\}\downarrow - \{a^{\|_{k+1}}\}\}\downarrow.$$

The idea is to remove from the right-hand part of the expression precisely the only ipomset of width $k + 1$. Using the same arguments as above one can show that L is not regular, but $L_{\leq k} = ((\{a^{\|_{k+1}}\}\downarrow - \{a^{\|_{k+1}}\})^2)^+$ is.

Yet the k-restriction of any regular language remains regular:

Proposition 14. *Let $k \geq 0$. If $L \in \mathscr{L}$ is regular, then so is $L_{\leq k}$.*

Intersection. By definition, the regular languages are closed under union, parallel composition, gluing composition, and Kleene plus. Here we show that they are also closed under intersection. (For complement this is more complicated, as we will see later.)

Proposition 15. *The regular languages are closed under $\cap$.*

Proof. We again give two proofs, one algebraic using Theorem 6 and another, constructive proof using Theorem 10. For the first proof, let L_1 and L_2 be regular, then suff(L_1) and suff(L_2) are both finite. Now

$$\begin{aligned}
\text{suff}(L_1 \cap L_2) &= \{P\backslash(L_1 \cap L_2) \mid P \in \text{iiPoms}\} \\
&= \{\{Q \in \text{iiPoms} \mid PQ \in L_1 \cap L_2\} \mid P \in \text{iiPoms}\} \\
&= \{\{Q \in \text{iiPoms} \mid PQ \in L_1\} \cap \{Q \in \text{iiPoms} \mid PQ \in L_2\} \mid P \in \text{iiPoms}\} \\
&= \{P\backslash L_1 \cap P\backslash L_2 \mid P \in \text{iiPoms}\} \\
&\subseteq \{M_1 \cap M_2 \mid M_1 \in \text{suff}(L_1),\ M_2 \in \text{suff}(L_2)\}
\end{aligned}$$

which is thus finite.

For the second, constructive proof, let X_1 and X_2 be HDAs. We construct an HDA X with $\mathsf{L}(X) = \mathsf{L}(X_1) \cap \mathsf{L}(X_2)$:[5]

$$\begin{aligned}
X &= \{(x_1, x_2) \in X_1 \times X_2 \mid \mathsf{ev}_1(x_1) = \mathsf{ev}_2(x_2)\}, \quad \delta_A^\nu(x_1, x_2) = (\delta_A^\nu(x_1), \delta_A^\nu(x_2)), \\
\mathsf{ev}((x_1, x_2)) &= \mathsf{ev}_1(x_1) = \mathsf{ev}_2(x_2), \qquad \perp = \perp_1 \times \perp_2, \qquad \top = \top_1 \times \top_2.
\end{aligned}$$

---

[5] This is the product in the category of HDAs. Using track objects, the lemma follows immediately.

For the inclusion $L(X) \subseteq L(X_1) \cap L(X_2)$, any accepting path α in X projects to accepting paths β in X_1 and γ in X_2, and then $ev(\beta) = ev(\gamma) = ev(\alpha)$. For the reverse inclusion, we need to be slightly more careful to ensure that accepting paths in X_1 and X_2 may be assembled to an accepting path in X.

Let $P \in L(X_1) \cap L(X_2)$ and $P = P_1 * \cdots * P_n$ the sparse step decomposition. Let $\beta = \beta_1 * \cdots * \beta_n$ and $\gamma = \gamma_1 * \cdots * \gamma_n$ be sparse accepting paths for P in X_1 and X_2, respectively, such that $ev(\alpha_i) = ev(\beta_i) = P_i$ for all i, cf. Lemma 9.

Let $i \in \{1, \ldots, n\}$ and assume that $P_i = {_A}{\uparrow}U$ is a starter, then $\beta_i = (\delta_A^0 x_1, \nearrow^A, x_1)$ and $\gamma_i = (\delta_A^0 x_2, \nearrow^A, x_2)$ for $x_1 \in X_1$ and $x_2 \in X_2$ such that $ev(x_1) = ev(x_2) = U$. Hence we may define a step $\alpha_i = (\delta_A^0(x_1, x_2), \nearrow^A, (x_1, x_2))$ in X. If P_i is a terminator, the argument is similar. By construction, $tgt(\alpha_i) = src(\alpha_{i+1})$, so the steps α_i assemble to an accepting path $\alpha = \alpha_1 * \cdots * \alpha_n \in Path(X)_\perp^\top$, and $ev(\alpha) = P$. $\qquad\square$

Ambiguity. It is shown in [8] that not all languages are determinizable, that is, there exist regular languages which cannot be recognised by deterministic HDAs. We have not introduced deterministic HDAs here and will not need them in what follows, instead we prove a strengthening of that result. Say that an HDA X is *k-ambiguous*, for $k \geq 1$, if every $P \in L(X)$ is the event ipomset of at most k sparse accepting paths in X. (Deterministic HDAs are 1-ambiguous.) A language L is said to be *of bounded ambiguity* if it is recognised by a k-ambiguous HDA for some k.

Proposition 16. *The regular language $L = (\left[\begin{smallmatrix}a\\b\end{smallmatrix}\right] cd + ab \left[\begin{smallmatrix}c\\d\end{smallmatrix}\right])^+$ is of unbounded ambiguity.*

5   ST-Automata

We define a variant of a construction from [5] which translates HDAs into finite automata over an alphabet of starters and terminators. This will be useful for showing properties of HDA languages. Let $\Omega = \{{_A}{\uparrow}U, U{\downarrow}_A \mid U \in \square, A \subseteq U\}$ be the (infinite) set of starters and terminators over Σ and, for any $k \geq 0$, $\Omega_{\leq k} = \Omega \cap \text{iiPoms}_{\leq k}$. Note that the sets $\Omega_{\leq k}$ are all finite.

Let X be an HDA and $k \geq \dim(X)$. The ST_k-*automaton* pertaining to X is the finite automaton $G_k(X) = (\Omega_{\leq k}, Q, I, F, E)$ with $Q = X \cup \{x_\perp \mid x \in \perp_X\}$, $I = \{x_\perp \mid x \in \perp_X\}$, $F = \top_X$, and

$$E = \{(\delta_A^0(x), {_A}{\uparrow}U, x) \mid x \in X[U], A \subseteq U\} \cup \{(x_\perp, id_U, x) \mid x \in \perp_X \cap X[U]\}$$
$$\cup \{(x, U{\downarrow}_A, \delta_A^1(x)) \mid x \in X[U], A \subseteq U\}.$$

We add extra copies of start cells in $G_k(X)$ in order to avoid runs on the empty word ϵ. Note that only the alphabet of $G_k(X)$ changes for different k.

In what follows, we consider languages of nonempty words over Ω, which we denote by W etc. and the class of such languages by $\mathscr{W}$. Further, $W(\mathcal{A})$ denotes the set of words accepted by a finite automaton $\mathcal{A}$.

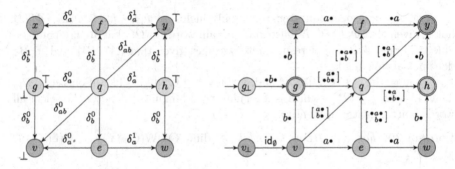

Fig. 6. HDA of Fig. 5 and its ST-automaton (identity loops not displayed).

Example 17. Figure 6 displays the ST-automaton $G_2(X)$ pertaining to the HDA X in Fig. 5, with the identity loops $(z, \mathsf{id}_{\mathsf{ev}(z)}, z)$ for all states z omitted. Notice that the transitions between a cell and its lower face are opposite to the face maps in X. Further, this example illustrates the necessity to duplicate initial states: without that, the empty word would be accepted by $G_2(X)$, while the empty ipomset is *not* in $\mathsf{L}(X)$ (see Example 8). We have $\mathsf{W}(G_2(X)) = \{\mathsf{id}_\emptyset b\bullet, \bullet b\bullet, \mathsf{id}_\emptyset \left[\begin{smallmatrix} a\bullet \\ b\bullet \end{smallmatrix}\right] \left[\begin{smallmatrix} \bullet a \\ \bullet b\bullet \end{smallmatrix}\right], \bullet b\bullet \left[\begin{smallmatrix} a\bullet \\ \bullet b\bullet \end{smallmatrix}\right] \left[\begin{smallmatrix} \bullet a \\ \bullet b\bullet \end{smallmatrix}\right], \dots\}$.

Define functions $\Phi : \mathscr{L} \to \mathscr{W}$ and $\Psi : \mathscr{W} \to \mathscr{L}$ by

$$\Phi(L) = \{P_1 \cdots P_n \in \Omega^* \mid P_1 * \cdots * P_n \in L, \ n \geq 1, \ \forall i : P_i \in \Omega\},$$
$$\Psi(W) = \{P_1 * \cdots * P_n \in \mathsf{iiPoms} \mid P_1 \cdots P_n \in W, \ n \geq 1, \ \forall i : T_{P_i} = S_{P_{i+1}}\}\!\downarrow.$$

Φ translates ipomsets into concatenations of their step decompositions, and Ψ translates words of composable starters and terminators into their ipomset composition (and takes subsumption closure). Hence Φ creates "coherent" words, *i.e.*, nonempty concatenations of starters and terminators with matching interfaces. Conversely, Ψ disregards all words which are not coherent in that sense. Every ipomset is mapped by Φ to infinitely many words over Ω (because ipomsets $\mathsf{id}_U \in \Omega$ are not units in $\mathscr{W}$). This will not be a problem for us later. It is clear that $\Psi(\Phi(L)) = L$ for all $L \in \mathscr{L}$, since every ipomset has a step decomposition. For the other composition, neither $\Phi(\Psi(W)) \subseteq W$ nor $W \subseteq \Phi(\Psi(W))$ hold:

Example 18. If $W = \{a\bullet \bullet b\}$ (the word language containing the concatenation of $a\bullet$ and $\bullet b$), then $\Psi(W) = \emptyset$ and thus $\Phi(\Psi(W)) = \emptyset \not\supseteq W$. If $W = \{\left[\begin{smallmatrix} a\bullet \\ b\bullet \end{smallmatrix}\right]\left[\begin{smallmatrix} \bullet a \\ \bullet b \end{smallmatrix}\right]\}$, then $\Psi(W) = \{\left[\begin{smallmatrix} a \\ b \end{smallmatrix}\right], ab, ba\}$ and $\Phi(\Psi(W)) \not\subseteq W$.

Lemma 19. Φ *respects boolean operations: for all* $L_1, L_2 \in \mathscr{L}$, $\Phi(L_1 \cap L_2) = \Phi(L_1) \cap \Phi(L_2)$ *and* $\Phi(L_1 \cup L_2) = \Phi(L_1) \cup \Phi(L_2)$. Ψ *respects regular operations: for all* $W_1, W_2 \in \mathscr{W}$, $\Psi(W_1 \cup W_2) = \Psi(W_1) \cup \Psi(W_2)$, $\Psi(W_1 W_2) = \Psi(W_1) * \Psi(W_2)$, *and* $\Psi(W_1^+) = \Psi(W_1)^+$.

Φ does *not* respect concatenations: only inclusion $\Phi(L * L') \subseteq \Phi(L) * \Phi(L')$ holds, given that $\Phi(L) * \Phi(L')$ also may contain words in Ω^* that are not composable in iiPoms. Ψ does not respect intersections, given that $(A \cap B)\!\downarrow = A\!\downarrow \cap B\!\downarrow$ does not always hold.

Let $\mathsf{Id} = \{\mathrm{id}_U \mid U \in \square\} \subseteq \Omega$ and, for any $k \geq 0$, $\mathsf{Id}_{\leq k} = \mathsf{Id} \cap \mathsf{iiPoms}_{\leq k} \subseteq \Omega_k$. Then $\mathsf{Id}_{\leq k}\, \Omega^*_{\leq k} \subseteq \Omega^*_{\leq k}$ (which is a regular word language) denotes the set of all words starting with an identity.

Lemma 20. *For any HDA X and $k \geq \dim(X)$, $\mathsf{W}(G_k(X)) = \Phi(\mathsf{L}(X)) \cap \mathsf{Id}_{\leq k}\, \Omega^*_{\leq k}$.*

Proof. There is a one-to-one correspondence between the accepting paths in X and $G_k(X)$:

$$\alpha = (x_0, \phi_1, x_1, \phi_2, \ldots, \phi_n, x_n) \mapsto \left((x_0)\!\perp \to x_0 \xrightarrow{\psi_1} x_1 \xrightarrow{\psi_2} \cdots \xrightarrow{\psi_n} x_n\right) = \omega$$

where ψ_i is the starter or terminator corresponding to the step ϕ_i. If $P_0 P_1 \cdots P_n \in \mathsf{W}(G_k(X))$, then there is an accepting path ω such that $P_0 = \mathrm{id}_{\mathsf{ev}(x_0)}$ and $P_i = \mathsf{ev}(x_{i-1}, \varphi_i, x_i)$. The corresponding path α in X is accepting. Hence $P_0 * P_1 * \cdots * P_n = P_1 * \cdots * P_n = \mathsf{ev}(\alpha) \in \mathsf{L}(X)$, and $P_0 P_1 \cdots P_n \in \Phi(\mathsf{L}(X))$. Further, P_0 is an identity, which shows the inclusion $\subseteq$.

Now let $P_0 P_1 \cdots P_n \in \Phi(\mathsf{L}(X)) \cap \mathsf{Id}_{\leq k}\, \Omega^*_{\leq k}$. Thus P_0 is an identity and $P_0 * P_1 * \cdots * P_n \in \mathsf{L}(X)$. Using Lemma 9 we conclude that the exists an accepting path $\alpha = \beta_1 * \cdots * \beta_n$ in X such that $\mathsf{ev}(\beta_i) = P_i$. The path ω corresponding to α recognises $P_0 P_1 \cdots P_n$, which shows the inclusion $\supseteq$. $\square$

Lemma 21. *Let $k \geq 0$. For all $L_1, L_2 \in \mathscr{L}_{\leq k}$, $L_1 \subseteq L_2$ iff $\Phi(L_1) \cap \mathsf{Id}_{\leq k}\, \Omega^*_{\leq k} \subseteq \Phi(L_2) \cap \mathsf{Id}_{\leq k}\, \Omega^*_{\leq k}$.*

Proof. The forward implication is immediate from Lemma 19. Now if $L_1 \not\subseteq L_2$, then also $\Phi(L_1) \cap \mathsf{Id}_{\leq k}\, \Omega^*_{\leq k} \not\subseteq \Phi(L_2) \cap \mathsf{Id}_{\leq k}\, \Omega^*_{\leq k}$, since every ipomset admits a step decomposition starting with an identity. $\square$

Theorem 22. *Inclusion of regular languages is decidable.*

Proof. Let L_1 and L_2 be regular and recognised respectively by X_1 and X_2, and let $k = \max(\dim(X_1), \dim(X_2))$. By Lemmas 20 and 21,

$$L_1 \subseteq L_2 \iff \Phi(L_1) \cap \mathsf{Id}_{\leq k}\, \Omega^*_{\leq k} \subseteq \Phi(L_2) \cap \mathsf{Id}_{\leq k}\, \Omega^*_{\leq k}$$
$$\iff \mathsf{W}(G_k(X_1)) \subseteq \mathsf{W}(G_k(X_2)).$$

Given that these are finite automata, the latter inclusion is decidable. $\square$

6   Complement

The *complement* of a language $L \subseteq \mathsf{iiPoms}$, *i.e.*, $\mathsf{iiPoms} - L$, is generally not down-closed and thus not a language. If we define $\overline{L} = (\mathsf{iiPoms} - L)\!\downarrow$, then $\overline{L}$ *is* a language, but a *pseudocomplement* rather than a complement: because of down-closure, $L \cap \overline{L} = \emptyset$ is now false in general. The following additional problem poses itself.

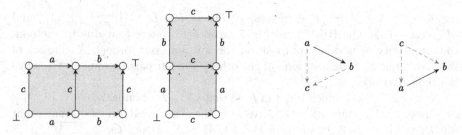

Fig. 7. HDA X which accepts language L of Example 28 and the two generating ipomsets in L.

Proposition 23. *If L is regular, then $\overline{L}$ has infinite width, hence is not regular.*

Proof. By Lemma 5, $\operatorname{wid}(L)$ is finite. For any $k > \operatorname{wid}(L)$, $\mathsf{iiPoms} - L$ contains all ipomsets of width k, hence $\{\operatorname{wid}(P) \mid P \in \overline{L}\}$ is unbounded. $\qquad\square$

To remedy this problem, we introduce a width-bounded version of (pseudo) complement. We fix an integer $k \geq 0$ for the rest of the section.

Definition 24. The *k-bounded complement* of $L \in \mathscr{L}$ is $\overline{L}^k = (\mathsf{iiPoms}_{\leq k} - L)\!\downarrow$.

Lemma 25. *Let L and M be languages.*

1. $\overline{L}^0 = \{\mathrm{id}_\emptyset\} - L$.
2. $L \subseteq M$ implies $\overline{M}^k \subseteq \overline{L}^k$.
3. $\overline{\overline{L}^k}^k \subseteq L_{\leq k} \subseteq L$.
4. $\overline{L}^k = \overline{L_{\leq k}}^k$.

Proposition 26. *For any $k \geq 0$, $\overline{\cdot}^k$ is a pseudocomplement on the lattice $(\mathscr{L}_{\leq k}, \supseteq)$, that is, for any $L, M \in \mathscr{L}_{\leq k}$, $L \cup M = \mathsf{iiPoms}_k$ iff $\overline{L}^k \subseteq M$.*

Proof. Let $L, M \in \mathscr{L}_{\leq k}$ such that $L \cup M = \mathsf{iiPoms}_k$ and $P \in \overline{L}^k$. There exists $Q \in \mathsf{iiPoms}_{\leq k}$ such that $P \sqsubseteq Q$ and $Q \notin L$. Thus, $Q \in M$ and since M is closed by subsumption, $P \in M$.

Conversely, let $L, M \in \mathscr{L}_{\leq k}$ such that $\overline{L}^k \subseteq M$ and $P \in \mathsf{iiPoms}_{\leq k} - M$. Then $P \in \overline{M}^k$, and we have that $\overline{M}^k \subseteq \overline{\overline{L}^k}^k \subseteq L$ by Lemma 25(3). Thus, $P \in L$ and then $L \cup M = \mathsf{iiPoms}_k$. $\qquad\square$

The pseudocomplement property immediately gets us the following.

Corollary 27. *Let $k \geq 0$ and $L, M \in \mathscr{L}_{\leq k}$. Then $L \cup \overline{L}^k = \mathsf{iiPoms}_{\leq k}$, $\overline{\overline{\overline{L}^k}^k}^k = \overline{L}^k$, $\overline{L \cap M}^k = \overline{L}^k \cup \overline{M}^k$, $\overline{L \cup M}^k \subseteq \overline{L}^k \cap \overline{M}^k$, and $\overline{\overline{L \cup M}^k}^k = \overline{\overline{L}^k}^k \cup \overline{\overline{M}^k}^k$. Further, $\overline{L}^k = \emptyset$ iff $L = \mathsf{iiPoms}_{\leq k}$.*

For $k = 0$ and $k = 1$, $\overline{\cdot}^k$ is a complement on $\mathsf{iiPoms}_{\leq k}$, but for $k \geq 2$ it is not: in general, neither $L = \overline{\overline{L}^k}^k$, $L \cap \overline{L}^k = \emptyset$, nor $\overline{L \cup M}^k = \overline{L}^k \cap \overline{M}^k$ hold:

Example 28. Let $A = \{P \in \text{iiPoms}_{\leq 2} \mid abc \sqsubseteq P\}$, $L = \{[\begin{smallmatrix} a \to b \\ c \end{smallmatrix}], [\begin{smallmatrix} c \\ a \to b \end{smallmatrix}]\}{\downarrow}$ and $M = (A - L){\downarrow}$. The HDA X in Fig. 7 accepts L. Notice that due to the non-commutativity of parallel composition (because of event order), X consists of two parts, one a "transposition" of the other. The left part accepts $[\begin{smallmatrix} a \to b \\ c \end{smallmatrix}]$, while the right part accepts $[\begin{smallmatrix} c \\ a \to b \end{smallmatrix}]$.

Now $abc \sqsubseteq [\begin{smallmatrix} a \to c \\ b \end{smallmatrix}]$ which is not in L, so that $abc \in \overline{L}^2$. Similarly, $abc \sqsubseteq [\begin{smallmatrix} a \to b \\ c \end{smallmatrix}] \notin M$, so $abc \in \overline{M}^2$. Thus, $abc \in \overline{L}^2 \cap \overline{M}^2$. On the other hand, for any P such that $\text{wid}(P) \leq 2$ and $abc \sqsubseteq P$, we have $P \in L \cup M = A{\downarrow}$. Hence $abc \notin \overline{L \cup M}^2$.

Finally, $\overline{L}^3$ contains every ipomset of width 3, hence $\overline{L}^3 = \text{iiPoms}_{\leq 3}$, so that $L \cap \overline{L}^3 = L \neq \emptyset$ and $\overline{\overline{L}^3}^3 = \emptyset \neq L$. This may be generalised to the fact that $\overline{L}^k{}^k = \emptyset$ as soon as $\text{wid}(L) < k$.

We say that $L \in \mathscr{L}$ is *k-skeletal* if $L = \overline{\overline{L}^k}^k$. Let $\mathscr{S}_k$ be the set of all k-skeletal languages. We characterise $\mathscr{S}_k$ in the following. By $\overline{\overline{\overline{L}^k}^k}^k = \overline{L}^k$ (Corollary 27), $\mathscr{S}_k = \{\overline{L}^k \mid L \in \mathscr{L}\}$, i.e., $\mathscr{S}_k$ is the image of $\mathscr{L}$ under $^{-k}$. (This is a general property of pseudocomplements.)

Define $\mathsf{M}_k = \{P \in \text{iiPoms}_{\leq k} \mid \forall Q \in \text{iiPoms}_{\leq k} : Q \neq P \implies P \not\sqsubseteq Q\}$, the set of all $\sqsubseteq$-maximal elements of $\text{iiPoms}_{\leq k}$. In particular, $\mathsf{M}_k{\downarrow} = \text{iiPoms}_{\leq k}$. Note that $P \in \mathsf{M}_k$ does not imply $\text{wid}(P) = k$: for example, $[\begin{smallmatrix} a \\ b \end{smallmatrix}] \in \mathsf{M}_3$.

Lemma 29. *For any $L \in \mathscr{L}$, $\overline{L}^k = (\mathsf{M}_k - L){\downarrow}$.*

Proof. We have

$$\begin{aligned} Q \in \overline{L}^k &\iff \exists P \in (\text{iiPoms}_{\leq k} - L) : Q \sqsubseteq P \\ &\iff \exists P \in (\text{iiPoms}_{\leq k} - L) \cap \mathsf{M}_k : Q \sqsubseteq P \\ &\iff \exists P \in \mathsf{M}_k - L : Q \sqsubseteq P \iff Q \in (\mathsf{M}_k - L){\downarrow}. \end{aligned}$$

$\square$

Corollary 30. *Let $L \in \mathscr{L}$ and $k \geq 0$, then $\overline{L}^k = \text{iiPoms}_{\leq k}$ iff $L \cap \mathsf{M}_k = \emptyset$.*

Proposition 31. $\mathscr{S}_k = \{A{\downarrow} \mid A \subseteq \mathsf{M}_k\}$.

Proof. Inclusion $\subseteq$ follows from Lemma 29. For the other direction, $A \subseteq \mathsf{M}_k$ implies

$$\overline{A{\downarrow}^k}^k = \overline{(\mathsf{M}_k - A{\downarrow}){\downarrow}}^k = \overline{(\mathsf{M}_k - A){\downarrow}}^k = (\mathsf{M}_k - (\mathsf{M}_k - A)){\downarrow} = A{\downarrow}.$$

$\square$

If $A \neq B \subseteq \mathsf{M}_k$, then also $A{\downarrow} \neq B{\downarrow}$, since all elements of M_k are $\sqsubseteq$-maximal. As a consequence, $\mathscr{S}_k$ and the powerset $\mathcal{P}(\mathsf{M}_k)$ are isomorphic lattices, hence $\mathscr{S}_k$ is a distributive lattice with join $L \vee M = L \cup M$ and meet $L \wedge M = (L \cap M \cap \mathsf{M}_k){\downarrow}$.

Corollary 32. *For $L, M \in \mathscr{L}$, $\overline{L}^k = \overline{M}^k$ iff $L \cap \mathsf{M}_k = M \cap \mathsf{M}_k$.*

We can now show that bounded complement preserves regularity.

Theorem 33. *If $L \in \mathscr{L}$ is regular, then for all $k \geq 0$ so is $\overline{L}^k$.*

Proof. By Proposition 14, $L_{\leq k}$ is regular. Let X be an HDA such that $\mathsf{L}(X) = L_{\leq k}$ and $k = \dim(X)$. The $\Omega_{\leq k}$-language $\mathsf{Id}_{\leq k}\, \Omega_{\leq k}^* \cap \Phi(\mathsf{L}(X))$ is regular by Lemma 20, hence so is $\mathsf{Id}_{\leq k}\, \Omega_{\leq k}^* - \Phi(\mathsf{L}(X))$. $\overline{\Psi}$ preserves regularity, so $\Psi(\mathsf{Id}_{\leq k}\, \Omega_{\leq k}^* - \Phi(\mathsf{L}(X)))$ is a regular ipomset language. Now for $P \in \mathsf{iiPoms}_{\leq k}$ we have

$$
\begin{aligned}
P \in \Psi(\mathsf{Id}_{\leq k}\, &\Omega_{\leq k}^* - \Phi(L_{\leq k})) \\
&\iff \exists Q \sqsupseteq P, \exists Q_0 Q_1 \cdots Q_n \in \mathsf{Id}_{\leq k}\, \Omega_{\leq k}^* - \Phi(L_{\leq k}) : Q = Q_0 * Q_1 * \cdots * Q_n \\
&\iff \exists Q_0 Q_1 \cdots Q_n \in \mathsf{Id}_{\leq k}\, \Omega_{\leq k}^* : P \sqsubseteq Q_0 * Q_1 * \cdots * Q_n \notin L_{\leq k} \\
&\iff P \in \overline{L_{\leq k}}^k,
\end{aligned}
$$

hence $\overline{L_{\leq k}}^k = \Psi(\mathsf{Id}_{\leq k}\, \Omega_{\leq k}^* - \Phi(L_{\leq k}))$. Lemma 25(4) allows us to conclude. □

Corollary 34. *$\mathsf{iiPoms}_{\leq k}$ is regular for every $k \geq 0$.*

7 Conclusion and Further Work

We have advanced the theory of higher-dimensional automata (HDAs) along several lines: we have shown a pumping lemma, exposed a regular language of unbounded ambiguity, introduced width-bounded complement, shown that regular languages are closed under intersection and width-bounded complement, and shown that inclusion of regular languages is decidable.

A question which is still open is if it is decidable whether a regular language is deterministic or of bounded ambiguity and, related to that, whether HDAs are learnable. On a more general level, two things which are missing are a Büchi-type theorem on a logical characterisation of regular languages and a notion of recognizability. The latter is complicated by the fact that ipomsets do not form a monoid but rather a 2-category with lax tensor [6].

Even more generally, a theory of weighted and/or timed HDAs would be called for, with a corresponding Kleene-Schützenberger theorem. For timed HDAs, some initial work is available in [3]. For weighted HDAs, the convolution algebras of [7] provide a useful framework.

Acknowledgement. We are in debt to Emily Clement, Thomas Colcombet, Christian Johansen, Georg Struth, and Safa Zouari for numerous discussions regarding the subjects of this paper. Any errors, however, are exclusively ours.

References

1. Amrane, A., Bazille, H., Fahrenberg, U., Ziemiański, K.: Closure and decision properties for higher-dimensional automata. CoRR, abs/2305.02873 (2023)
2. Bednarczyk, M.A.: Categories of Asynchronous Systems. PhD thesis, University of Sussex, UK (1987)

3. Fahrenberg, U.: Higher-dimensional timed and hybrid automata. Leibniz Trans. Embed. Syst. **8**(2), 03:1–03:16 (2022)

4. Fahrenberg, U., Johansen, C., Struth, G., Ziemianski, K.: Languages of higher-dimensional automata. Math. Struct. Comput. Sci. **31**(5), 575–613 (2021). http://arxiv.org/2103.07557

5. Fahrenberg, U., Johansen, C., Struth, G., Ziemianski, K.: A Kleene theorem for higher-dimensional automata. In: Klin, B., Lasota, S., Muscholl, A. (eds.), CONCUR, volume 243 of Leibniz International Proceedings in Informatics, pp. 29:1–29:18. Schloss Dagstuhl - Leibniz-Zentrum für Informatik (2022). https://doi.org/10.4230/LIPIcs.CONCUR.2022.29

6. Fahrenberg, U., Johansen, C., Struth, G., Ziemianski, K.: Posets with interfaces as a model for concurrency. Inf. Comput. **285**(B), 104914 (2022). http://arxiv.org/2106.10895

7. Fahrenberg, U., Johansen, C., Struth, G., Ziemianski, K.: Catoids and modal convolution algebras. Algebra Univ. **84**(10) (2023)

8. Fahrenberg, U., ZiemiaNski, K.: A myhill-nerode theorem for higher-dimensional automata. In: Gomes, L., Lorenz, R. (eds.) Application and Theory of Petri Nets and Concurrency. PETRI NETS 2023. LNCS, vol. 13929, pp. 167–188. Springer, Cham (2023). https://doi.org/10.1007/978-3-031-33620-1_9, http://arxiv.org/2210.08298

9. Fanchon, J., Morin, R.: Regular sets of pomsets with autoconcurrency. In: Brim, L., Křetínský, M., Kučera, A., Jančar, P. (eds.) CONCUR 2002. LNCS, vol. 2421, pp. 402–417. Springer, Heidelberg (2002). https://doi.org/10.1007/3-540-45694-5_27

10. Fishburn, P.C.: Interval Orders and Interval Graphs: A Study of Partially Ordered Sets. Wiley, Hoboken (1985)

11. Goubault, E.: Labelled cubical sets and asynchronous transition systems: an adjunction. In: CMCIM (2002). http://www.lix.polytechnique.fr/~goubault/papers/cmcim02.ps.gz

12. Grabowski, J.: On partial languages. Fundam. Inform. **4**(2), 427 (1981)

13. Janicki, R., Koutny, M.: Operational semantics, interval orders and sequences of antichains. Fundam. Inform. **169**(1–2), 31–55 (2019)

14. Jipsen, P., Moshier, M.A.: Concurrent Kleene algebra with tests and branching automata. J. Log. Algebraic Methods Program. **85**(4), 637–652 (2016)

15. Lodaya, K., Weil, P.: Series-parallel languages and the bounded-width property. Theor. Comput. Sci. **237**(1–2), 347–380 (2000)

16. Pratt, V.R.: Modeling concurrency with geometry. In: POPL, pp. 311–322. ACM Press, New York City (1991)

17. Mike, W.: Shields. Concurrent machines. Comput. J. **28**(5), 449–465 (1985)

18. van Glabbeek, R.J.: Bisimulations for higher dimensional automata. Email message, June 1991. http://theory.stanford.edu/~rvg/hda

19. van Glabbeek, R.J.: On the expressiveness of higher dimensional automata. Theor. Comput. Sci. **356**(3), 265–290 (2006). See also [20]

20. van Glabbeek, R.J.: Erratum to "On the expressiveness of higher dimensional automata". Theor. Comput. Sci. **368**(1–2), 168–194 (2006)

21. Wiener, N.: A contribution to the theory of relative position. Proc. Camb. Philos. Soc. **17**, 441–449 (1914)

Robustness in Metric Spaces over Continuous Quantales and the Hausdorff-Smyth Monad

Francesco Dagnino[1], Amin Farjudian[2]($\boxtimes$), and Eugenio Moggi[1]

[1] DIBRIS, Università di Genova, Genova, Italy
{francesco.dagnino,moggi}@unige.it
[2] School of Mathematics, University of Birmingham, Birmingham, UK
A.Farjudian@bham.ac.uk

Abstract. Generalized metric spaces are obtained by weakening the requirements (e.g., symmetry) on the distance function and by allowing it to take values in structures (e.g., quantales) that are more general than the set of non-negative real numbers. Quantale-valued metric spaces have gained prominence due to their use in quantitative reasoning on programs/systems, and for defining various notions of behavioral metrics.

We investigate imprecision and robustness in the framework of quantale-valued metric spaces, when the quantale is continuous. In particular, we study the relation between the robust topology, which captures robustness of analyses, and the Hausdorff-Smyth hemi-metric. To this end, we define a preorder-enriched monad P_S, called the Hausdorff-Smyth monad, and when Q is a continuous quantale and X is a Q-metric space, we relate the topology induced by the metric on $\mathsf{P}_S(X)$ with the robust topology on the powerset $\mathsf{P}(X)$ defined in terms of the metric on X.

Keywords: Quantale · Robustness · Monad · Topology · Enriched category

Introduction

In the 1970s, Lawvere [21] proposed viewing metric spaces as small categories enriched over the monoidal category $\mathbb{R}_+$, whose objects are the extended non-negative real numbers, where there is an arrow $x \to y$ if and only if $x \geq y$, and $+$ and 0 provide the monoidal structure. In this way, one recovers most notions and results about metric spaces as instances of those about enriched categories [19].

Enrichment over arbitrary monoidal categories, however, is unnecessarily general for studying metric phenomena. Indeed, the base of enrichment for Lawvere's metric spaces belongs to the class of small (co)complete posetal categories, where the tensor commutes with colimits. These categories are called *quantales* and small categories enriched over a quantale Q are dubbed *Q-metric spaces*. Quantales are a useful compromise between arbitrary monoidal categories and the specific case of $\mathbb{R}_+$ [5,10,16]. Beside a substantial simplification of the theory,

E. Ábrahám et al. (Eds.): ICTAC 2023, LNCS 14446, pp. 313–331, 2023.
https://doi.org/10.1007/978-3-031-47963-2_19

restricting to quantales allows to use well-known order-theoretic notions which do not have obvious counterparts in arbitrary monoidal categories, but are crucial to relating Q-metric spaces to other structures such as topological spaces.

Quantale-valued metric spaces are also increasingly used for *quantitative reasoning* on programs/systems, and for defining various notions of *behavioral metrics* [3,8,11,12,26,28]. The use of quantitative methods is important in coping with the uncertainty/imprecision that arises in the analysis of, e.g., probabilistic programs or systems interacting with physical processes. In these contexts, quantales provide a flexible framework which allows choosing the most suitable notion of distance for the specific analysis one is interested in.

Quantales arise naturally also in analysis of algorithms, namely, *costs* are values in certain quantales (see Example 2), but researchers in this area usually consider only subsets of these quantales and their partial order.

Motivations. The notions of imprecision and robustness are relevant in the context of software tools for analysis of hybrid/continuous systems. These tools manipulate (formal descriptions of) mathematical models. A mathematical model is usually a simplified description of the system (and its environment), with the requirement that the simplification should be *safe*, i.e., if the analysis says that the model satisfies a property, then the system also satisfies that property. Usually, safe simplification is achieved by injecting *non-determinism* in the model (non-determinism is useful also to model *known unknowns* in the environment and *don't care* in the model). For hybrid/continuous systems there is another issue: *imprecision* in observations. In fact, predictions based on a mathematical model and observations on a real system can be compared only up to the precision of measurements on the real system. We say that an analysis is *robust* when it can cope with *small amounts* of imprecision in the model, i.e., if a robust analysis says that a model M has a property, then it says so also for models that have a bit more non-determinism than M. Working with metric spaces makes it possible to define imprecision formally and to quantify the amount of non-determinism added to a model.

Following [23], given a metric space X, we can identify analyses with monotonic maps on the complete lattice $P(X)$ of subsets of X ordered by reverse inclusion.[1] However, even when imprecision is made arbitrarily small, two subsets with the same closure are *indistinguishable*. Therefore, analyses should be considered over the complete lattice $C(X)$ of closed subsets, rather than that of arbitrary subsets, and should cope with *small amounts* of imprecision in the input. Formally, this property was defined as continuity with respect to the *robust topology* [22, Def. A.1] on $C(X)$. This yields a functor from metric spaces to T_0-topological spaces, which maps a metric on X to the robust topology on $C(X)$. An anonymous referee suggested that the robust topology might be related to the *Hausdorff-Smyth hemi-metric* in [14, Proposition 1], and thus the functor from metric spaces to topological spaces might be replaced with an endofunctor on *hemi-metric spaces* (aka, Lawvere's metric spaces).

---

[1] The category of complete lattices and monotonic maps is the framework proposed in [6] for abstract interpretations.

Contributions. This paper studies the link between the robust topology and the Hausdorff-Smyth hemi-metric—as suggested by an anonymous referee of [9]—and in doing so, addresses also more general issues, namely:

1. The notion of *imprecision* and the definition of *robust topology* are generalized to Q-metric spaces when Q is a *continuous quantale*, and the results in [23] are extended to this wider setting (see Sect. 4.1).
2. *Indistinguishability* is investigated in the context of *Po*-enriched categories[2] and the notion of *separated object* is introduced. In Sect. 5, we prove that, under certain conditions, every *Po*-enriched monad can be *transformed* into one that factors through the full sub-category of separated objects. The conditions that allow this transformation hold in many *Po*-enriched categories, such as that of Q-metric spaces and that of topological spaces.
3. The *Hausdorff-Smyth Po-enriched monad* P_S is defined on the category of Q-metric spaces, with Q an arbitrary quantale (see Sect. 6). When Q is a continuous quantale, the topology induced by the metric on $\mathsf{P}_S(X)$ is shown to coincide with a topology on $\mathsf{P}(X)$, called **-robust*, defined in terms of the metric on X. In general, the *-robust topology is included in the robust topology, but they coincide when Q is *linear and non-trivial* (e.g., $\mathbb{R}_+$).

Although we apply the construction in Sect. 5 only to the monad defined in Sect. 6, it is applicable to other monads definable on Q-metric spaces (see Sect. 7) or on other *Po*-enriched categories.

Summary. The rest of the paper is organized as follows:

- Section 1 contains the basic notation and mathematical preliminaries.
- Section 2 introduces the category Qnt of quantales and lax-monoidal maps, and states some properties of continuous quantales.
- Section 3 defines the *Po*-enriched category Met_Q of Q-metric spaces and short maps for a quantale Q, and gives some of its properties.
- Section 4 introduces two topologies associated with a Q-metric space when Q is continuous, and characterizes the open and closed subsets.
- Section 5 defines separated objects in a *Po*-enriched category $\mathcal{A}$, and shows that, under certain assumptions on $\mathcal{A}$ satisfied by Met_Q, every *Po*-enriched monad on $\mathcal{A}$ can be transformed (in an optimal way) into one that factors through the full sub-category of separated objects.
- Section 6 defines the Hausdorff-Smyth distance d_S and a related *Po*-enriched monad on Met_Q, characterizes the preorder induced by d_S and, when Q is continuous, also the topology induced by d_S.
- Section 7 contains an overview of related work and some concluding remarks.

Proofs are omitted due to page limit, but they can be found in the extended version of the paper [7].

---

[2] *Po* denotes the category of preorders and monotonic maps.

1   Mathematical Preliminaries

In this section, we present the basic mathematical notation used throughout the paper. We assume basic familiarity with order theory [15]. We write $\sqcup S$ to denote the join (aka lub) of a set S, and write $\sqcap S$ to denote the meet (aka glb) of S. Binary join and meet of two elements x and y are written as $x \sqcup y$ and $x \sqcap y$, respectively. We write $\bot$ and $\top$ to denote the bottom and top element of a partial order Q, respectively, when they exist.

We also assume basic familiarity with category theory [4]. In this article:

- *Set* denotes the category of sets and functions (alias maps).
- *Po* denotes the category of preorders and monotonic maps.
- *Po$_0$* denotes the full (reflective) sub-category of *Po* consisting of posets.
- *Top* denotes the category of topological spaces and continuous maps.
- *Top$_0$* denotes the full (reflective) sub-category of *Top* consisting of T_0-spaces.

All categories above have small limits and colimits. *Set*, *Po* and *Po$_0$* have also exponentials, thus they are examples of *symmetric monoidal closed* categories [19]. *Po* and *Top* (and their sub-categories) can be viewed as *Po*-enriched categories [19], e.g., the hom-set *Po*(X, Y) of monotonic maps from X to Y can be equipped with the pointwise preorder induced by the preorder Y.

Other categories introduced in subsequent sections are *Po*-enriched, and this additional structure is relevant when defining adjunctions and equivalences between two objects of a *Po*-enriched category.

Definition 1. (Adjunction). *Given a pair of maps* $X \underset{\longleftarrow g}{\overset{f \longrightarrow}{\rule{0pt}{0pt}}} Y$ *in a Po-enriched category $\mathcal{A}$, we say that they form:*

1. *an **adjunction** (notation $f \dashv g$)* $\overset{\triangle}{\Longleftrightarrow}$ $f \circ g \leq \mathsf{id}_Y$ *and* $\mathsf{id}_X \leq g \circ f$, *in which f and g are called left- and right-adjoint, respectively.*
2. *an **equivalence*** $\overset{\triangle}{\Longleftrightarrow}$ $\mathsf{id}_Y \leq f \circ g \leq \mathsf{id}_Y$ *and* $\mathsf{id}_X \leq g \circ f \leq \mathsf{id}_X$.

We use '$\in$' for set membership (e.g., $x \in X$), but we use ':' for membership of function types (e.g., $f : X \to Y$) and to denote objects and arrows in categories (e.g., $X : Top$ and $f : Top(X, Y)$). The powerset of a set X is denoted by $\mathsf{P}(X)$. Subset inclusion is denoted by $\subseteq$, whereas strict (proper) subset inclusion is denoted by $\subset$. The finite powerset (i.e., the set of finite subsets) of X is denoted by $\mathsf{P}_f(X)$, and $A \subseteq_f B$ denotes that A is a finite subset of B.

We denote with ω the set of natural numbers, and identify a natural number with the set of its predecessors, i.e., $0 = \emptyset$ and $n = \{0, \ldots, n-1\}$, for any $n \geq 1$.

2   Quantales

Conceptually, a quantale [2, 24, 25] is a degenerate case of monoidal category [19], in the same way that a partial order is a degenerate case of category.

Definition 2. (Quantale). *A **quantale** $(Q, \sqsubseteq, \otimes)$ is a complete lattice $(Q, \sqsubseteq)$ with a monoid structure $(Q, \otimes, u)$ satisfying the following distributive laws:*

$$x \otimes (\sqcup S) = \sqcup\{x \otimes y \mid y \in S\} \quad \text{and} \quad (\sqcup S) \otimes x = \sqcup\{y \otimes x \mid y \in S\},$$

*for any $x \in Q$ and $S \subseteq Q$. A quantale is **trivial** when $\bot = u$ (which implies that $\forall x \in Q. \ \bot = x$), **affine** when $u = \top$, **linear** when $\sqsubseteq$ is a linear order, and **commutative** when $\otimes$ is commutative (in this case the two distributive laws are inter-derivable). A **frame**[3] is a quantale where $\otimes = \sqcap$ (thus, necessarily commutative and affine).*

The complete lattice $(Q, \sqsubseteq)$ amounts to a complete and cocomplete category, while the distributivity laws imply that:

- $\otimes$ is monotonic. Thus, $(Q, \otimes, u)$ makes $(Q, \sqsubseteq)$ a (strict) monoidal category.
- $\otimes$ (viewed as a functor) preserves colimits, in particular $\bot \otimes x = \bot = x \otimes \bot$.

These properties imply that the functors $x \otimes -$ and $- \otimes y$, have right-adjoints $x \backslash -$ and $-/y$, i.e., $x \otimes y \sqsubseteq z \iff y \sqsubseteq x \backslash z$ and $x \otimes y \sqsubseteq z \iff x \sqsubseteq z/y$, called left- and right-residual, respectively. In commutative quantales (i.e., degenerate examples of symmetric monoidal closed categories) $x \backslash z = z/x$ is denoted as $[x, z]$ and is given by $[x, z] = \sqcup\{y \mid x \otimes y \sqsubseteq z\}$.

Example 1. We present some examples of quantales. The first four examples describe linear, commutative and affine quantales (some are frames). The last two items (excepts in degenerate cases) give non-linear, non-commutative and non-affine quantale. The construction Q/u always returns an affine quantale and preserves the linearity and commutative properties, while $\prod_{j \in J} Q_j$ and Q^P preserve the affine and commutative properties.

1. The quantale $\mathbb{R}_+$ of [21] is the set of non-negative real numbers extended with ∞, with $x \sqsubseteq y \overset{\triangle}{\iff} x \geq y$ and $x \otimes y \overset{\triangle}{=} x + y$. Therefore, $\sqcup S = \inf S$, $\sqcap S = \sup S$, $\bot = \infty$, $u = \top = 0$, $[x, z] = z - x$ if $x \leq z$ else 0.
2. $\mathbb{R}_\sqcap$ is similar to $\mathbb{R}_+$, but $x \otimes y \overset{\triangle}{=} x \sqcap y = \max(x, y)$. Thus, $\mathbb{R}_\sqcap$ is a frame, $u = 0$, $[x, z] = z$ if $x \leq z$ else 0 ($\top$, $\bot$, $\sqcup S$, and $\sqcap S$ are the same as in $\mathbb{R}_+$).
3. $\mathbb{N}_+$ is the *sub-quantale* of $\mathbb{R}_+$ whose carrier is the set of natural numbers extended with ∞. $\mathbb{N}_\sqcap$ is the *sub-frame* of $\mathbb{R}_\sqcap$ with the same carrier as $\mathbb{N}_+$.
4. Σ is the *sub-quantale* of $\mathbb{R}_+$ whose carrier is $\{0, \infty\}$. Σ is a frame.
5. Q/u is the *sub-quantale* of Q whose carrier is $\{x \in Q \mid x \sqsubseteq u\}$. Thus, u is the top element of Q/u.
6. $\prod_{j \in J} Q_j$ is the product of the quantales Q_j, with $\sqsubseteq$ and $\otimes$ defined pointwise.
7. Q^P is the quantale of monotonic maps from the poset P to the quantale Q, with $\sqsubseteq$ and $\otimes$ defined pointwise.
8. $(P(M), \subseteq, \otimes)$ is the quantale (actually a boolean algebra) of subsets of the monoid $(M, \cdot, e)$, with $u = \{e\}$ and $A \otimes B \overset{\triangle}{=} \{a \cdot b \mid a \in A, b \in B\}$.

---

[3] Alternative names for frame are locale and Heyting algebra, see [18].

9. $(\mathsf{P}(X^2), \subseteq, \otimes)$ is the quantale (boolean algebra) of relations on the set X, with $\mathsf{u} = \{(x,x) \mid x \in X\}$ and:

$$R \otimes S \overset{\triangle}{=} \{(x,z) \mid \exists y \in X.(x,y) \in R, (y,z) \in S\}.$$

Example 2. We consider some quantales arising in the analysis of algorithms. We identify algorithms with multi-tape deterministic Turing Machines (TM), which accept/reject strings written in a finite input alphabet A. In this context, one is interested in quantale-valued cost functions $X \to Q$, rather than distances.

- The size $s(w)$ of an input w for a TM is a value in the quantale $\mathbb{N}_+$, namely the length of the string w. In particular, the size of an infinite string is ∞, and the size of the concatenation of two strings is the sum of their sizes.
- The time (i.e., the number of steps) taken by a TM on a specific input w is again a value in $\mathbb{N}_+$. In particular, a TM failing to terminate on w takes time ∞, and the time taken for executing sequentially two TMs on w is the sum of the times taken by each TM (plus a linear overhead for copying w on two separate tapes, so that the two TMs work on disjoint sets of tapes).

The time complexity associated to a TM typically depends on the input (or its size), thus it cannot be a cost in $\mathbb{N}_+$. Such cost should be drawn from a quantale reflecting this dependency, namely a *higher-order* quantale.[4] We now describe some of such quantales from the most precise to the most abstract.

1. The most precise quantale is $\mathbb{N}_+^{A^*}$ (i.e., the product of A^* copies of $\mathbb{N}_+$). A $t \in \mathbb{N}_+^{A^*}$ maps each finite input $w \in A^*$ to the time taken by a TM on w.
2. A first abstraction is to replace $t \in \mathbb{N}_+^{A^*}$ with $T \in \mathbb{N}_+^{\omega}$, where $T(n)$ is the best upper-bound for the time taken by a TM on inputs of size n, i.e., $T(n) = \max\{t(w) \mid s(w) = n\}$.
3. In practice (by the linear speed-up theorem), time complexity is given in O-notation, i.e., $T \in \mathbb{N}_+^{\omega}$ is replaced with the subset $O(T)$ of $\mathbb{N}_+^{\omega}$ such that $T' \in O(T) \iff \forall n \geq n_0.T'(n) \leq C * T(n)$ for some n_0 and C in ω.
   If we replace $\mathbb{N}_+^{\omega}$ with the partial order L_O of O-classes $O(T)$ ordered by reverse inclusion, we get a distributive lattice (i.e., binary meets distribute over finite joins, and conversely): the top is $O(0)$, the bottom is $O(\infty)$, the join $O(T_1) \sqcup O(T_2)$ is $O(T_1) \cap O(T_2) = O(T_1 \sqcup T_2) = O(\min(T_1, T_2))$, the meet $O(T_1) \sqcap O(T_2)$ is $O(T_1 \sqcap T_2) = O(\max(T_1, T_2)) = O(T_1 + T_2)$.
   The lattice L_O is distributive, because the complete lattice underlying $\mathbb{N}_+^{\omega}$ is distributive, but it is not a frame (as it fails to have arbitrary joins). However, there is a general construction, see [18, page 69], which turns a distributive lattice L into the *free frame* $I(L)$ over L. More precisely, $I(L)$ is the poset of *ideals* in L ordered by inclusion, and the embedding $x \mapsto \downarrow x$ from L to $I(L)$ preserves finite meets and joins.
4. A simpler way to obtain a frame is to take the subset of L_O consisting of the $O(n^k)$ with $k \in [0, \infty]$. This linear frame is isomorphic to $\mathbb{N}_\sqcap$, namely $k \in \mathbb{N}_\sqcap$ corresponds to $O(n^k)$.

---

[4] This resembles higher-order distances used to compare functional programs [8, 26].

There are several notions of morphism between quantales, we consider those corresponding to lax and strict monoidal functors.

Definition 3. *A monotonic map* $h : Q \to Q'$ *between quantales is called:*

- **lax-monoidal** $\stackrel{\Delta}{\iff}$ $u' \sqsubseteq' h(u)$ *and* $\forall x, y \in Q.h(x) \otimes' h(y) \sqsubseteq h(x \otimes y)$;
- **strict-monoidal** $\stackrel{\Delta}{\iff}$ $u' = h(u)$ *and* $\forall x, y \in Q.h(x) \otimes' h(y) = h(x \otimes y)$.

$\mathcal{Q}nt$ *denotes the* $\mathcal{P}o_0$*-enriched category of quantales and lax-monoidal maps, where* $\mathcal{Q}nt(Q, Q')$ *has the pointwise order induced by the order on* Q'.

We give some examples of monotonic maps between quantales.

Example 3. In the following diagram we write $\dashrightarrow$ for lax- and $\longrightarrow$ for strict-monoidal maps, 1 for the trivial quantale (with only one element $*$), $!_Q$ for the unique map from Q to 1, and $f \dashv g$ for "f is left-adjoint to g":

$$1 \underset{!_Q}{\overset{\top_Q}{\dashrightarrow}} Q \underset{f}{\overset{g}{\dashrightarrow}} Q/u \underset{f'}{\overset{g'}{\dashrightarrow}} \Sigma \quad \mathbb{N}_+ \overset{c}{\underset{i}{\dashleftarrow}} \mathbb{R}_+ \overset{id}{\dashleftarrow} \mathbb{R}_\sqcap$$

- $\top_Q$ maps $*$ to $\top$;
- f is the inclusion of Q/u into Q, and g maps x to $x \sqcap u$;
- f' maps $\bot$ to $\bot$ and $\top$ to $\top$, and g' maps $\top$ to $\top$ and $x \sqsubset \top$ to $\bot$;
- i is the inclusion, $c(x) = \lceil x \rceil$ is integer round up, and id is the identity.

The frames for measuring the time complexity of TMs (see Example 2) are related by obvious monoidal maps going from the more precise to the more abstract frame:

$$\mathbb{N}_+^{A^*} \overset{f}{\dashrightarrow} \mathbb{N}_+^\omega \overset{g}{\longrightarrow} I(L_O) \overset{h}{\dashrightarrow} \mathbb{N}_\sqcap$$

- f maps $t \in \mathbb{N}_+^{A^*}$ to $T \in \mathbb{N}_+^\omega$ such that $T(n) = \max\{t(w) \mid s(w) = n\}$;
- g maps $T \in \mathbb{N}_+^\omega$ to the principal ideal $\downarrow O(T) \in I(L_O)$;
- h maps $X \in I(L_O)$ to $n \in \mathbb{N}_\sqcap$ such that $n = \min\{k \mid \forall A \in X.A \subseteq O(n^k)\}$.

2.1 Continuous Quantales

To reinterpret in quantale-valued metric spaces the common ϵ-δ definition of continuous maps, and relate such spaces to topological spaces, we restrict to *continuous quantales*, i.e., quantales whose underlying lattices are continuous. Note that linear quantales are always continuous. We recall the definition of a continuous lattice and related notions. More details may be found in [1,13,15].

Definition 4. *Given a complete lattice* $(Q, \sqsubseteq)$ *and* $x, y \in Q$, *we say that:*

1. $D \subseteq Q$ *is directed* $\stackrel{\Delta}{\iff}$ $\forall x, y \in D.\exists z \in D.x \sqsubseteq z$ *and* $y \sqsubseteq z$.
2. x *is* **way-below** y *(notation* $x \ll_Q y$, *or* $x \ll y$ *when* Q *is clear from the context)* $\stackrel{\Delta}{\iff}$ *for any directed subset* D *of* Q, $y \sqsubseteq \sqcup D \implies \exists d \in D.x \sqsubseteq d$.

3. x is compact $\overset{\triangle}{\Longleftrightarrow} x \ll x$.

We write $\downarrow\!\!\downarrow y$ for $\{x \in Q \mid x \ll y\}$, and Q_0 for the set of compact elements in Q.

The following are some basic properties of the way-below relation.

Proposition 1. *In any complete lattice* $(Q, \sqsubseteq)$, *and for all* $x, x_0, x_1 \in Q$:

1. $x_0 \ll x_1 \implies x_0 \sqsubseteq x_1$.
2. $x_0' \sqsubseteq x_0 \ll x_1 \sqsubseteq x_1' \implies x_0' \ll x_1'$.
3. $\bot \ll x$.
4. $\downarrow\!\!\downarrow x$ *is directed. In particular,* $x_0, x_1 \ll x \implies x_0 \sqcup x_1 \ll x$.

Definition 5 (Continuous Lattice). *Given a complete lattice* Q, *we say that:*

1. Q *is continuous* $\overset{\triangle}{\Longleftrightarrow} \forall x \in Q.x = \bigsqcup\downarrow\!\!\downarrow x$.
2. $B \subseteq Q$ *is a base for* $Q \overset{\triangle}{\Longleftrightarrow} \forall x \in X.B \cap \downarrow\!\!\downarrow x$ *is directed and* $x = \bigsqcup(B \cap \downarrow\!\!\downarrow x)$.
3. Q *is* ω-*continuous* $\overset{\triangle}{\Longleftrightarrow} Q$ *has a countable base.*
4. Q *is algebraic* $\overset{\triangle}{\Longleftrightarrow} Q_0$ *is a base for* Q.

A complete lattice Q is continuous exactly when it has a base. Any base for Q must includes Q_0. The set Q_0 is a base only when Q is algebraic and the bottom element $\bot$ is always compact. Continuous lattices enjoy the following interpolation property (see [1, Lemma 2.2.15]):

Lemma 1. *For any continuous lattice* Q *and* $q_1, q_2 \in Q$, $q_1 \ll q_2 \implies \exists q \in Q.q_1 \ll q \ll q_2$.

Continuous quantales enjoy a further interpolation property:

Lemma 2. *In every continuous quantale,* $q_1 \ll q_2 \implies \exists q \ll \mathsf{u}.q_1 \ll q_2 \otimes q$ *and* $q_1 \ll q_2 \implies \exists q \ll \mathsf{u}.q_1 \ll q \otimes q_2$.

Example 4. The quantales in Example 1 have the following properties:

- N_+, $\mathsf{N}_\sqcap$, and Σ are ω-algebraic. More precisely, all elements in these quantales are compact, and $x \ll y \iff x \geq y$ (or equivalently $x \sqsubseteq y$).
- $\mathbb{R}_+$ and $\mathbb{R}_\sqcap$ are ω-continuous, e.g., the set of rational numbers with ∞ is a base, $x \ll y \iff (x = \infty \vee x > y)$, and ∞ is the only compact element.
- $\mathsf{P}(M)$ and $\mathsf{P}(X^2)$ are algebraic, the sets of compact elements are $\mathsf{P}_f(M)$ for $\mathsf{P}(M)$ and $\mathsf{P}_f(X^2)$ for $\mathsf{P}(X^2)$, and $A \ll B \iff A \subseteq_f B$.

Continuous lattices (and quantales) have the following closure properties:

Proposition 2. *Continuous (algebraic) lattices are closed under small products.* ω-*continuous lattices are closed under countable products.*

We conclude by observing that linear quantales are always continuous.

Proposition 3. *Every linear quantale is continuous.*

3   Quantale-Valued Metric Spaces

In [21], Lawvere views metric spaces as $\mathbb{R}_+$-enriched categories, and shows that several definitions and results on metric spaces are derivable from general results on $\mathcal{V}$-enriched categories, where $\mathcal{V}$ is a symmetric monoidal closed category (see [19]). We replace $\mathbb{R}_+$ with a quantale Q, and consider the $\mathcal{P}o$-enriched category of Q-metric spaces and short maps, whose objects are Q-enriched small categories and whose arrows are Q-enriched functors.

Definition 6 ($\mathcal{M}et_Q$). *Given a quantale Q, the $\mathcal{P}o$-enriched category $\mathcal{M}et_Q$ of Q-metric spaces and **short maps** is given by:*

objects *are pairs (X, d) with $d : X^2 \to Q$ satisfying $d(x, y) \otimes d(y, z) \sqsubseteq d(x, z)$ and $\mathsf{u} \sqsubseteq d(x, x)$; d induces on X the d-**preorder** $x \leq_d y \overset{\Delta}{\Longleftrightarrow} \mathsf{u} \sqsubseteq d(x, y)$.*
arrows *in $\mathcal{M}et_Q((X, d), (X', d'))$ are $f : X \to X'$ satisfying $\forall x, y \in X. d(x, y) \sqsubseteq d'(f(x), f(y))$ with **hom-preorder** $f \leq f' \overset{\Delta}{\Longleftrightarrow} \forall x \in X. f(x) \leq_{d'} f'(x)$.*

*An arrow $f : \mathcal{M}et_Q((X, d), (X', d'))$ is said to be an **isometry** when $\forall x, y \in X. d(x, y) = d'(f(x), f(y))$.*

In comparison with the properties of a standard metric d, we have that:

- the triangular inequality $d(x, z) \leq d(x, y) + d(y, z)$ becomes $d(x, y) \otimes d(y, z) \sqsubseteq d(x, z)$. Note that, in $\mathbb{R}_+$, the order $\sqsubseteq$ is $\geq$, and $\otimes = +$;
- $d(x, y) = 0 \iff x = y$ is replaced by the weaker property $\mathsf{u} \sqsubseteq d(x, x)$, which corresponds to $d(x, x) = 0$. Note that in $\mathbb{R}_+$, we have $\mathsf{u} = 0 = \top$;
- symmetry $d(x, y) = d(y, x)$ is unusual in (enriched) category theory.

In the absence of symmetry, *separation*, i.e., $d(x, y) = 0 \implies x = y$, should be recast as $(d(x, y) = 0 \wedge d(y, x) = 0) \implies x = y$, which in a quantale setting becomes $(\mathsf{u} \sqsubseteq d(x, y) \wedge \mathsf{u} \sqsubseteq d(y, x)) \implies x = y$. The objects with this property are exactly the (X, d) such that the preorder $\leq_d$ is a poset. Section 5 gives a more abstract definition of separated object in a $\mathcal{P}o$-enriched category.

Example 5. We relate $\mathcal{M}et_Q$ for some quantales Q to more familiar categories:

1. $\mathbb{R}_\sqcap$-metric spaces generalize ultrametric spaces, i.e., spaces where the metric satisfies $d(x, z) \leq \max(d(x, y), d(y, z))$.
2. $\mathcal{M}et_\Sigma$ is (isomorphic to) the $\mathcal{P}o$-enriched category $\mathcal{P}o$ of preorders and monotonic maps, and the *separated objects* of $\mathcal{M}et_\Sigma$ are the posets.
3. $\mathcal{M}et_1$ is the category $\mathcal{S}et$ of sets and functions, with the chaotic preorder on $\mathcal{S}et(X, Y)$, i.e., $f \leq g$ for every $f, g; \mathcal{S}et(X, Y)$, and the *separated objects* of $\mathcal{M}et_1$ are the sets with at most one element.

We summarize some properties of $\mathcal{M}et_Q$, which ignore the $\mathcal{P}o$-enrichment, proved in [19] for a generic complete and cocomplete symmetric monoidal closed category in place of a quantale Q.

Proposition 4. *For any quantale Q, the category $\mathcal{M}et_Q$ has small products, small sums, equalizers and coequalizers.*

Lax-monoidal maps induce $\mathcal{P}o$-enriched functors.

Definition 7. *Given a lax monoidal map $h : \mathcal{Q}nt(P, Q)$, the $\mathcal{P}o$-enriched functor $h : \mathcal{M}et_P \to \mathcal{M}et_Q$ is such that $h(X, d) \triangleq (X, h \circ d)$ and is the identity on arrows.*

4 Topologies on Q-Metric Spaces

When Q is a continuous quantale, one can establish a relation between $\mathcal{M}et_Q$ and $\mathcal{T}op$, thereby generalizing the open ball topology induced by a standard metric. In general, to a Q-metric d on X one can associate at least two topologies on X. When Q is ω-continuous—a restriction desirable from a computational viewpoint (see [27])—convergence can be defined in terms of sequences.

Definition 8. *Given a continuous quantale Q and $(X, d) : \mathcal{M}et_Q$, the **open ball** with center $x \in X$ and radius $\delta \ll u$ is $B(x, \delta) \triangleq \{y \in X \mid \delta \ll d(x, y)\}$. The **open ball topology** τ_d is the topology generated by the family of open balls.*

*One can define also the **dual open ball** $B^o(x, \delta) \triangleq \{y \in X \mid \delta \ll d(y, x)\}$, and the corresponding **dual open ball topology** τ_d^o.*

When d is symmetric, i.e., $d(x, y) = d(y, x)$, the two notions of open ball agree. In the rest of this section, we focus on open balls only, but the results hold *mutatis mutandis* also for the dual notion. The following proposition implies that open balls form a *base* for τ_d, i.e., every open in τ_d is a union of open balls.

Proposition 5. *Open balls satisfy the following properties:*

1. $x \in B(x, \delta)$.
2. $\delta \sqsubseteq \delta' \implies B(x, \delta') \subseteq B(x, \delta)$.
3. $y \in B(x, \delta) \implies \exists \delta' \ll u.B(y, \delta') \subseteq B(x, \delta)$.
4. $y \in B(x_1, \delta_1) \cap B(x_2, \delta_2) \implies \exists \delta' \ll u.\ B(y, \delta') \subseteq B(x_1, \delta_1) \cap B(x_2, \delta_2)$.

We show that, for continuous quantales, continuity with respect to the open ball topology can be recast in terms of the usual *epsilon-delta* formulation:

Lemma 3. *If $(X, d) : \mathcal{M}et_Q$, with Q continuous, and $O \subseteq X$, then $O \in \tau_d \iff$*

$$\forall x \in O.\exists \delta \ll u.B(x, \delta) \subseteq O. \tag{1}$$

The following result characterizes the closed subsets for the topology τ_d. Informally, the closure of a subset A can be described as the set of points *from* which one can reach a point in A within any arbitrarily small distance.

Lemma 4. *If $(X, d) : \mathcal{M}et_Q$, with Q continuous, and $A \in \mathsf{P}(X)$, then the closure of A in the topological space (X, τ_d) is given by:*

$$\overline{A} = \{y \in X \mid \forall \delta \ll u.\exists x \in A.\delta \ll d(y, x)\}. \tag{2}$$

Theorem 1. *Given a continuous quantale Q_i and an object $(X_i, d_i) : \mathcal{M}et_{Q_i}$ for each $i \in \{1, 2\}$, if $f : X_1 \to X_2$, then $f : \mathcal{T}op((X_1, \tau_{d_1}), (X_2, \tau_{d_2})) \iff$*

$$\forall x \in X_1. \forall \epsilon \ll \mathsf{u}_2. \exists \delta \ll \mathsf{u}_1. f(B(x, \delta)) \subseteq B(f(x), \epsilon). \tag{3}$$

The above characterization of continuous maps suggests a variant of $\mathcal{T}op$ in which the objects are Q-metric spaces (for some continuous quantale Q) instead of topological spaces, while the rest is unchanged (see [5]):

Definition 9. *The $\mathcal{P}o$-enriched category $\mathcal{M}et_c$ of metric spaces and continuous maps is given by:*

objects *are the triples (X, d, Q) with Q continuous quantale and $(X, d) : \mathcal{M}et_Q$;*
arrows *in $\mathcal{M}et_c((X, d, Q), (X', d', Q'))$ are $f : \mathcal{T}op((X, \tau_d), (X', \tau_{d'}))$, or equivalently $f : X \to X'$ satisfying $\forall x \in X. \forall \epsilon \ll \mathsf{u}'. \exists \delta \ll \mathsf{u}. f(B(x, \delta)) \subseteq B(f(x), \epsilon)$.*

Similarly, one can define the sub-category $\mathcal{M}et_u$ of $\mathcal{M}et_c$ with the same objects, but whose arrows are the *uniformly continuous* maps, i.e., $f : X \to X'$ satisfying $\forall \epsilon \ll \mathsf{u}'. \exists \delta \ll \mathsf{u}. \forall x \in X. f(B(x, \delta)) \subseteq B(f(x), \epsilon)$.

4.1 Imprecision and Robustness

We extend the notions of imprecision and robustness, that in [22,23] are defined for standard metric spaces, to Q-metric spaces for a continuous quantale Q[5]. Since a Q-metric may fail to be symmetric, we must consider the "direction" along which the distance is measured. In particular, in the presence of imprecision, two subsets are indistinguishable when they have the same closure in the dual topology τ_d^o, rather than in the topology τ_d (Proposition 7). This difference cannot be appreciated when d is symmetric, because the two topologies coincide.

Definition 10. *Given a Q-metric space (X, d), with Q continuous, the notions introduced in [23, Definition 1] can be recast as follows:*

1. $B_R(A, \delta) \triangleq \{y \in X \mid \exists x \in A. \delta \ll d(x, y)\} = \cup_{x \in A} B(x, \delta) \subseteq X$ *is the set of points belonging to $A \subseteq X$ with precision greater than $\delta \ll \mathsf{u}$.*[6]
2. $A_\delta \triangleq \overline{B_R(A, \delta)} \subseteq X$ *is the δ-flattening of $A \subseteq X$ with $\delta \ll \mathsf{u}$, where $\overline{A}^o$ is the closure of A in τ_d^o (see Lemma 4).*

Proposition 6. *The subsets $B_R(A, \delta)$ have the following properties:*

1. $A \subseteq B_R(A, \delta) \subseteq B_R(A', \delta')$ *when $A \subseteq A' \subseteq X$ and $\delta' \sqsubseteq \delta \ll \mathsf{u}$.*
2. $B_R(B_R(A, \delta_1), \delta_2) \subseteq B_R(A, \delta)$ *when $\delta_1, \delta_2 \ll \mathsf{u}$ and $\delta \ll \delta_1 \otimes \delta_2 [\sqsubseteq \delta_i]$.*
3. $\overline{A}^o = \cap_{\delta \ll \mathsf{u}} B_R(A, \delta)$ *for every $A \subseteq X$.*
4. $B_R(\overline{A}^o, \delta) = B_R(A, \delta)$ *for every $A \subseteq X$ and $\delta \ll \mathsf{u}$, i.e., A and $\overline{A}^o$ are indistinguishable in the presence of imprecision.*
5. $B_R(A, \delta) \subseteq A_\delta \subseteq B_R(A, \delta')$ *when $A \subseteq X$ and $\delta' \ll \delta \ll \mathsf{u}$.*

Example 6. Consider the Q-metric space (X, d), where $Q = X = \mathbb{R}_+$ and $d(x, y) \triangleq y - x$ if $x \leq y$ else 0. If $A = [a, b]$ and $\delta \in (0, +\infty)$, then $\overline{A} = [a, +\infty]$, $\overline{A}^o = [0, b]$, and $B_R(\overline{A}^o, \delta) = B_R(A, \delta) = [0, b + \delta]$, as depicted in Fig. 1.

---

[5] It is possible to relax the assumption of continuity of Q along the lines of [5].
[6] The terminology used in [23] is "with imprecision less than δ".

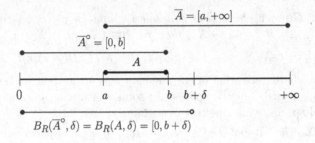

Fig. 1. Graphic recast of Example 6.

We can generalize to this wider setting also the definition of robust topology in [22, Definition A.1]. We define such topology on $\mathsf{P}(X)$, rather than on the set of closed subsets in the topology τ_d^o, since the restriction to the set of closed subsets amounts to replacing a topological space with an equivalent *separated* topological space (see Sect. 5).

Definition 11. *Given a Q-metric space (X, d), with Q continuous, the* **robust topology** $\tau_{d,R}$ *on $\mathsf{P}(X)$ is given by:*

$$U \in \tau_{d,R} \overset{\triangle}{\Longleftrightarrow} \forall A \in U. \exists \delta \ll \mathsf{u}. \mathsf{P}(B_R(A, \delta)) \subseteq U.$$

Finally, we characterize the specialization preorder $\leq_{\tau_{d,R}}$ induced by the robust topology $\tau_{d,R}$ on $\mathsf{P}(X)$. As a consequence, we have that two subsets are indistinguishable in $\tau_{d,R}$ exactly when they have the same closure in τ_d^o.

Proposition 7. *Let (X, d) be a Q-metric space with Q continuous, and $A, B \subseteq X$. Then, we have $A \leq_{\tau_{d,R}} B \iff B \subseteq \overline{A}^o$.*

5   Separation in Preorder-Enriched Categories

Structures like preorders and topologies have a notion of *indistinguishability* between elements. Informally, in such structures, *separation* can be understood as the property requiring that indistinguishable elements are equal.

In this section, we define and study this notion in the setting of $\mathcal{P}o$-enriched categories. We also show that the definition of separation in this abstract setting subsumes many *set-theoretic* definitions within specific categories, in particular the category of Q-metric spaces.

Definition 12 (Separation). *Given a $\mathcal{P}o$-enriched category $\mathcal{A}$, we say that:*

1. *$f, g \in \mathcal{A}(X, Y)$ are* **equivalent** *(notation $f \sim g$) $\overset{\triangle}{\Longleftrightarrow} f \leq g \wedge g \leq f$.*
2. *the hom-preorder $\mathcal{A}(X, Y)$ is separated $\overset{\triangle}{\Longleftrightarrow}$ it is a poset.*
3. *the object $Y \in \mathcal{A}$ is separated $\overset{\triangle}{\Longleftrightarrow} \mathcal{A}(X, Y)$ is separated for every $X \in \mathcal{A}$.*
4. *$\mathcal{A}$ is separated $\overset{\triangle}{\Longleftrightarrow} Y$ is separated for every $Y \in \mathcal{A}$, i.e., $\mathcal{A}$ is $\mathcal{P}o_0$-enriched.*

Remark 1. The definition of "$\mathcal{A}(X,Y)$ is separated" can be recast in terms of equivalence, i.e., $f \sim g \implies f = g$, for every $f, g : \mathcal{A}(X,Y)$. There is a similar recast also for the definition of "$\mathcal{A}$ is separated", i.e., $f \sim g \implies f = g$, for every pair (f, g) of parallel arrows in $\mathcal{A}$. In some $\mathcal{P}o$-enriched categories, separated objects have a set-theoretic characterization that does not refer to arrows:

1. In $\mathcal{P}o$, separated objects are posets.
2. In $\mathcal{T}op$, separated objects are T_0-spaces.
3. In $\mathcal{M}et_Q$, separated objects are separated Q-metric spaces (see Sect. 3).

Recall from [19] that a $\mathcal{P}o$-enriched functor $F : \mathcal{A} \longrightarrow \mathcal{B}$ is **full&faithful** (notation $F : \mathcal{A} \longhookrightarrow \mathcal{B}$) when the maps $F_{X,Y} : \mathcal{A}(X,Y) \to \mathcal{B}(FX, FY)$ are iso in $\mathcal{P}o$, and a $\mathcal{P}o$-enriched sub-category $\mathcal{A}$ of $\mathcal{B}$ is full when the $\mathcal{P}o$-enriched inclusion functor is full&faithful.

Definition 13. *If $\mathcal{A}$ is a $\mathcal{P}o$-enriched category, then $\mathcal{A}_0$ denotes the full subcategory of separated objects in $\mathcal{A}$.*

If every object in $\mathcal{A}$ is separated, then $\mathcal{A}_0$ is equal to $\mathcal{A}$. A weaker property is that every object in $\mathcal{A}$ is *equivalent* (in the sense of Definition 1) to one in $\mathcal{A}_0$. This weaker property holds in $\mathcal{P}o$, $\mathcal{T}op$, and $\mathcal{M}et_Q$.

Proposition 8. *In $\mathcal{M}et_Q$, every object is equivalent to a separated one.*

If every object in $\mathcal{A}$ is equivalent to a separated one, then every $\mathcal{P}o$-enriched endofunctor on $\mathcal{A}$ can be *transformed* into one that factors through $\mathcal{A}_0$. This *transformer* lifts to the category of $\mathcal{P}o$-enriched monads on $\mathcal{A}$.

Definition 14. *Given a $\mathcal{P}o$-enriched category $\mathcal{A}$, we denote by $\mathsf{Mon}(\mathcal{A})$ the category of $\mathcal{P}o$-enriched **monads** on $\mathcal{A}$ and **monad maps**, i.e.*

objects: *$\mathcal{P}o$-enriched monads on $\mathcal{A}$, i.e., triples $\hat{M} = (M, \eta, -^*)$, where:*
  - *M is a function on the objects of $\mathcal{A}$,*
  - *η is a family of arrows $\eta_X : \mathcal{A}(X, MX)$ for $X : \mathcal{A}$,*
  - *$-^*$ is a family of monotonic maps $\mathcal{A}(X, MY) \to \mathcal{A}(MX, MY)$ between hom-preorders for $X, Y : \mathcal{A}$,*
  and satisfy the equations:

$$\eta_X^* = \mathsf{id}_{MX} \quad , \quad f^* \circ \eta_X = f \quad , \quad g^* \circ f^* = (g^* \circ f)^*. \tag{4}$$

arrows: *θ from $\hat{M}$ to $\hat{M}'$ are families of maps $\theta_X : \mathcal{A}(MX, M'X)$ for $X : \mathcal{A}$ satisfying the equations:*

$$\theta_X \circ \eta_X = \eta_X' \quad , \quad \theta_Y \circ f^* = (\theta_Y \circ f)^{*'} \circ \theta_X. \tag{5}$$

A basic **monad transformer** on $\mathsf{Mon}(\mathcal{A})$ is a pair $(\mathsf{T}, \mathsf{in})$, where T is function on the objects of $\mathsf{Mon}(\mathcal{A})$ and in is a family of monad maps $\mathsf{in}_{\hat{M}}$ from $\hat{M}$ to $\mathsf{T}\hat{M}$.

Remark 2. The category $\mathsf{Mon}(\mathcal{A})$ can be made $\mathcal{P}o$-enriched. The enrichment is relevant for defining equivalence of monads. For our purposes, however, it suffices to relate (by a monad map) a generic $\mathcal{P}o$-enriched monad on $\mathcal{A}$ to one that factors through $\mathcal{A}_0$.

We use the simplest form of monad transformer among those in the taxonomy of [17], i.e., *basic transformer*. However, the monad transformer described in the following theorem can be shown to be a *monoidal transformer*.

Theorem 2. *If $\mathcal{A}$ is a $\mathcal{P}o$-enriched category and $(r_X : X \to RX \mid X : \mathcal{A})$ is a family of arrows in $\mathcal{A}$ such that:*

$$RX : \mathcal{A}_0 \text{ and } (r_X, s_X) \text{ is an equivalence for some } s_X : RX \to X, \qquad (6)$$

then $(\mathsf{T}, \mathsf{in})$ defined below is a monad transformer on $\mathsf{Mon}(\mathcal{A})$:

- T *is the function mapping $\hat{M} = (M, \eta, -^*)$ to $\mathsf{T}\hat{M} = (M', \eta', -^{*'})$, where*
  - $M'X \triangleq R(MX)$
  - $\eta'_X \triangleq r_{MX} \circ \eta_X : \mathcal{A}(X, M'X)$
  - *if $f : \mathcal{A}(X, M'Y)$, then $f^{*'} \triangleq r_{MY} \circ (s_{MY} \circ f)^* \circ s_{MX} : \mathcal{A}(M'X, M'Y)$.*
- in *is the family of monad maps such that $\mathsf{in}_{\hat{M},X} \triangleq r_{MX} : \mathcal{A}(MX, M'X)$.*

Moreover, the definition of T is independent of the choice of s_X.

6   The Hausdorff-Smyth Monad

In this section, we introduce a $\mathcal{P}o$-enriched monad P_S on $\mathcal{M}et_Q$, related to the Hausdorff-Smyth hemi-metric in [14], which *extends* the powerset monad P on $\mathcal{S}et$ to Q-metric spaces. By applying the monad transformer T defined in Sect. 5, one obtains a separated version of P_S, which amounts to partitioning $\mathsf{P}(X)$ into equivalence classes, for which we define canonical representatives. Finally, we investigate the relation between P_S and the robust topology in Definition 11.

Recall that the monad $(\mathsf{P}, \eta, -^*)$ on $\mathcal{S}et$ is given by $\eta_X : \mathcal{S}et(X, \mathsf{P}(X))$ and $-^* : \mathcal{S}et(X, \mathsf{P}(X')) \to \mathcal{S}et(\mathsf{P}(X), \mathsf{P}(X'))$, where:

$$\eta(x) = \{x\},$$
$$f^*(A) = \bigcup_{x \in A} f(x).$$

Definition 15 (The P_S monad). *Let P_S be the function on Q-metric spaces such that $\mathsf{P}_S(X, d) = (\mathsf{P}(X), d_S)$, where $d_S : \mathsf{P}(X)^2 \to Q$ is given by:*

$$d_S(A, B) = \sqcap_{y \in B} \sqcup_{x \in A} d(x, y).$$

The rest of the monad structure for P_S, i.e., the unit η and the Kleisli extension $-^*$, is inherited from that for P. In particular, $\eta_{(X,d)} = \eta_X$.

We now prove that what we have defined is a $\mathcal{P}o$-enriched monad on $\mathcal{M}et_Q$.

Proposition 9. *The triple* $(\mathsf{P}_S, \eta, -^*)$ *is a* $\mathcal{P}o$-*enriched monad on* $\mathcal{M}et_Q$, *i.e.*

1. $(\mathsf{P}(X), d_S) : \mathcal{M}et_Q$, *i.e.*, $\mathsf{u} \sqsubseteq d_S(A, A)$ *and* $d_S(A, B) \otimes d_S(B, C) \sqsubseteq d_S(A, C)$.
2. $\eta : \mathcal{M}et_Q(X, \mathsf{P}_S(X))$.
3. $f : \mathcal{M}et_Q(X, \mathsf{P}_S(X'))$ *implies* $f^* : \mathcal{M}et_Q(\mathsf{P}_S(X), \mathsf{P}_S(X'))$.
4. $f \leq g$ *in* $\mathcal{M}et_Q(X, \mathsf{P}_S(X'))$ *implies* $f^* \leq g^*$ *in* $\mathcal{M}et_Q(\mathsf{P}_S(X), \mathsf{P}_S(X'))$.

Moreover, $(\mathsf{P}_S, \eta, -^*)$ *satisfies the equations (4) for a monad.*

The Hausdorff-Smyth metric d_S induces a preorder $\leq_{d_S}$ and an equivalence $\sim_{d_S}$ on $\mathsf{P}(X)$. In the following, we define the canonical representative for the equivalence class of $A \subseteq X$ with respect to $\sim_{d_S}$, called the *-closure of A, which turns out to be the biggest subset of X in the equivalence class.

Definition 16. *Given a Q-metric space* (X, d), *we define:*

1. $d(A, y) \triangleq \bigsqcup_{x \in A} d(x, y) \in Q$ *the* ***-distance** *from* $A \subseteq X$ *to* $y \in X$.
2. $\widetilde{A} \triangleq \{y \in X \mid \mathsf{u} \sqsubseteq d(A, y)\}$ *the* ***-closure** *of* $A \subseteq X$.

Proposition 10. *For every Q-metric space* (X, d) *the following properties hold:*

1. $d_S(A, B) = \bigsqcap_{y \in B} d(A, y)$ *and* $d(A, y) = d_S(A, \{y\})$.
2. $A \leq_{d_S} B \iff B \subseteq \widetilde{A}$.
3. $A \sim_{d_S} B \iff \widetilde{A} = \widetilde{B}$.

6.1 Hausdorff-Smyth and *-Robust Topology

We give a characterization of the topology τ_{d_S} on $\mathsf{P}(X)$ using a topology $\tau_{d,S}$ defined by analogy with the robust topology $\tau_{d,R}$ of Sect. 4.1. In summary, we have that $\tau_{d_S} = \tau_{d,S} \subseteq \tau_{d,R}$ when Q is continuous, and $\tau_{d,S} = \tau_{d,R}$ when Q is linear and non-trivial.

Definition 17. *Given a Q-metric space* (X, d), *with Q continuous, we define the topology* $\tau_{d,S}$ *on* $\mathsf{P}(X)$:

1. $B_S(A, \delta) \triangleq \{y \in X \mid \delta \ll d(A, y)\} \subseteq X$ *is the set of points belonging to* $A \subseteq X$ *with *-precision greater than* $\delta \ll \mathsf{u}$.
2. *the* ***-robust topology** $\tau_{d,S}$ *on* $\mathsf{P}(X)$ *is given by:*
   $$U \in \tau_{d,S} \stackrel{\triangle}{\iff} \forall A \in U. \exists \delta \ll \mathsf{u}. \mathsf{P}(B_S(A, \delta)) \subseteq U.$$

Lemma 5. *The subsets* $B_S(A, \delta)$ *have the following properties:*

1. $B_R(A, \delta) \subseteq B_S(A, \delta) \subseteq B_S(A', \delta')$ *when* $A \subseteq A' \subseteq X$ *and* $\delta' \sqsubseteq \delta \ll \mathsf{u}$.
2. $\delta \sqsubseteq d_S(A, B_S(A, \delta))$ *for every* $A \subseteq X$ *and* $\delta \ll \mathsf{u}$.

Proposition 11. *For every Q-metric space* (X, d) *with Q continuous:*

$$\tau_{d_S} = \tau_{d,S} \subseteq \tau_{d,R}.$$

Lemma 6. *For every* $(X, d) : \mathbf{Met}_Q$ *with* Q *continuous,* $A \subseteq X$, $y \in X$, *and* $\delta \in Q$:

$$\delta \ll d(A, y) \iff \exists A_0 \subseteq_f A.\delta \ll d(A_0, y).$$

Moreover, if Q *is linear and* $\bot \neq \delta$, *then:*

$$\delta \ll d(A, y) \iff \exists x \in A.\delta \ll d(x, y).$$

Proposition 12. *If* Q *is a linear non-trivial quantale, then* $\tau_{d,R} = \tau_{d,S}$.

Remark 3. Propositions 12 and 7 ensure that, when Q is linear and non-trivial, by applying the monad transformer T of Sect. 5, we get a monad mapping a Q-metric space (X, d) to the separated Q-metric space of closed subsets of X with respect to the dual topology τ_d^o with the Hausdorff-Smyth metric. In this way, we recover the setting of [23] as a special case.

Example 7. When the quantale Q is not linear, the robust topology $\tau_{d,R}$ can be strictly finer than the *-robust topology $\tau_{d,S}$. For instance, consider the Q-metric space (X, d), in which $Q = \mathbb{R}_+ \times \mathbb{R}_+$, $X = \mathbb{R}^2$, and the distance is given by $d((x, y), (x', y')) = (|x - x'|, |y - y'|)$. Let $\delta_0 \triangleq (1, 1)$ and note that $u = (0, 0)$. Take $A \triangleq \{(0, 2), (2, 0)\} \subseteq \mathbb{R}^2$, $p \triangleq (2, 2) \in \mathbb{R}^2$, and consider the set $O \triangleq \bigcup_{\delta_0 \ll \delta' \ll u} \mathsf{P}(B_R(A, \delta'))$. The set O is in $\tau_{d,R}$, but it is not open in the *-robust topology $\tau_{d,S}$. The reason is that $d(A, p) = (0, 0) = u$. Hence, for any $\delta \ll u$, the set $B_S(A, \delta)$ must contain p. But, the point p is not included in any set in O, because $\forall p' \in A.\ (1, 1) \not\ll d(p', p)$.

7   Concluding Remarks

Related work. Flagg and Kopperman define $\mathcal{V}$-continuity spaces [10, Def 3.1] and $\mathcal{V}$-domains, with $\mathcal{V}$ a *value quantale* [10, Def 2.9], i.e., the dual $\mathcal{V}^o$ of $\mathcal{V}$ is (in our terminology) a commutative affine quantale, whose underlying complete lattice is completely distributive—hence, by [1, Thm. 7.1.1], continuous—and satisfies additional properties formulated using a stronger variant $\lll$ of the way-below relation $\ll$, called the *totally-below* relation, namely $p \lll q$ iff for any $A \subseteq Q$, if $q \sqsubseteq \sqcup A$, then $\exists a \in A.p \sqsubseteq a$ (in contrast with the definition of $\ll$, the set A is not required to be directed). Thus, a $\mathcal{V}$-continuity space (X, d) is what we call a $\mathcal{V}^o$-metric space, while a $\mathcal{V}$-domain is a separated $\mathcal{V}^o$-metric space satisfying further properties. The metric d_U in [10, Sec 6] corresponds to our d_S, and [10, Thm 6.1] characterizes those B such that $d_U(A, B) = 0$ as the subsets of the closure of A in the topology τ_d^o, under the stronger assumption that $\mathcal{V}$ is a value quantale. The upper powerdomain $U(X)$ defined in [10, Sec 6] is almost the separated object equivalent to $\mathsf{P}_S(X)$, as its carrier consists of the closed subsets in the topology τ_d^o, except the empty one.

Although not every topology is induced by a classical metric, Kopperman [20] showed that all topologies come from generalized metrics. Cook and Weiss [5] present a more nuanced discussion of this fact, with constructions that avoid the shortcomings of Kopperman's original construction. Their focus, however, is on comparing various topologies that arise from a given generalized metric, i.e., those generated by open sets, closed sets, interior, and exterior systems. Although the four topologies coincide in classical metric spaces, they may be different in quantale valued metric spaces. In particular, they consider three conditions on a quantale, which are named Kuratowski, Sierpiński, and triangularity conditions [5, Def. 3]. When a commutative affine quantale Q satisfies these three conditions, it can be shown that all the four topologies coincide for the metric spaces valued in Q. Cook and Weiss [5] use the totally-below relation $\lll$, which is included in the way-below relation $\ll$. Under the three conditions they impose on quantales, one can show that for every $\delta \ll u$ there exists $\delta' \lll u$ such that $\delta \sqsubseteq \delta'$. Therefore, the topology generated by open balls with radius $\delta' \lll u$ coincide with that generated by the open balls with radius $\delta \ll u$.

The main drawback of value quantales and the quantales considered in [5] is that they are not closed under product, which is crucial for multi-dimensional quantitative analyses. On the other hand, a continuous quantale Q may not satisfy the Kuratowski condition, and therefore the four topologies considered in [5] for a Q-metric space may not coincide. Specifically, $d_S(A, \{x\}) = u$ may not entail that x is in the closure of A under the open ball topology.

Future Work. The results of the current article may be regarded as the first steps towards a framework for robustness analysis with respect to perturbations that are measured using generalized metrics. As such, more remains to be done for development of the framework. Our future work will include study of effective structures on Q-metric spaces.

In [14], Goubault-Larrecq defines the Hausdorff-Hoare and the Hutchinson hemi-metrics. We plan to investigate if they scale-up to $\mathcal{P}o$-enriched monads (or endofunctors) on the category of Q-metric spaces, and in this case apply to them the monad transformer defined in Sect. 5.

We also plan to study the impact of imprecision on probability distributions on $(Q\text{-})$metric spaces, i.e., to which extent they are indistinguishable in the presence of imprecision, by applying our monad transformer to probability monads.

References

1. Abramsky, S., Jung, A.: Domain theory. In: Abramsky, S., Gabbay, D.M., Maibaum, T.S.E. (eds.) Handbook of Logic in Computer Science, vol. 3, pp. 1–168. Clarendon Press, Oxford (1994)
2. Abramsky, S., Vickers, S.: Quantales, observational logic and process semantics. Math. Struct. Comput. Sci. **3**(2), 161–227 (1993). https://doi.org/10.1017/S0960129500000189
3. Bonchi, F., König, B., Petrisan, D.: Up-to techniques for behavioural metrics via fibrations. In: Schewe, S., Zhang, L. (eds.) 29th International Conference on Concurrency Theory, CONCUR 2018. LIPIcs, vol. 118, pp. 17:1–17:17. Schloss Dagstuhl - Leibniz-Zentrum für Informatik (2018). https://doi.org/10.4230/LIPIcs.CONCUR.2018.17

4. Borceux, F.: Handbook of Categorical Algebra: Volume 1, Basic Category Theory, vol. 1. Cambridge University Press, Cambridge (1994)

5. Cook, D.S., Weiss, I.: The topology of a quantale valued metric space. Fuzzy Sets Syst. **406**, 42–57 (2021). https://doi.org/10.1016/j.fss.2020.06.005

6. Cousot, P., Cousot, R.: Abstract interpretation frameworks. J. Log. Comput. **2**(4), 511–547 (1992)

7. Dagnino, F., Farjudian, A., Moggi, E.: Robustness in metric spaces over continuous quantales and the Hausdorff-Smyth monad (2023). https://arxiv.org/abs/2309.06968

8. Dal Lago, U., Gavazzo, F., Yoshimizu, A.: Differential logical relations, part I: the simply-typed case. In: Baier, C., Chatzigiannakis, I., Flocchini, P., Leonardi, S. (eds.) 46th International Conference on Automata, Languages and Programming, ICALP 2018. LIPIcs, vol. 132, pp. 111:1–111:14. Schloss Dagstuhl - Leibniz-Zentrum für Informatik (2019). https://doi.org/10.4230/LIPIcs.ICALP.2019.111

9. Farjudian, A., Moggi, E.: Robustness, Scott continuity, and computability. Math. Struct. Comput. Sci. 1–37 (2023). https://doi.org/10.1017/S0960129523000233

10. Flagg, B., Kopperman, R.: Continuity spaces: reconciling domains and metric spaces. Theoret. Comput. Sci. **177**(1), 111–138 (1997). https://doi.org/10.1016/S0304-3975(97)00236-3

11. Gavazzo, F.: Quantitative behavioural reasoning for higher-order effectful programs: applicative distances. In: Dawar, A., Grädel, E. (eds.) Proceedings of the 33rd Annual ACM/IEEE Symposium on Logic in Computer Science, LICS 2018, pp. 452–461. ACM (2018). https://doi.org/10.1145/3209108.3209149

12. Gavazzo, F., Florio, C.D.: Elements of quantitative rewriting. Proc. ACM Program. Lang. **7**(POPL), 1832–1863 (2023). https://doi.org/10.1145/3571256

13. Gierz, G., Hofmann, K.H., Keimel, K., Lawson, J.D., Mislove, M.W., Scott, D.S.: A Compendium of Continuous Lattices. Springer, Heidelberg (1980). https://doi.org/10.1007/978-3-642-67678-9

14. Goubault-Larrecq, J.: Simulation hemi-metrics between infinite-state stochastic games. Lect. Notes Comput. Sci. **4962**, 50–65 (2008)

15. Goubault-Larrecq, J.: Non-Hausdorff Topology and Domain Theory. Cambridge University Press, Cambridge (2013)

16. Hofmann, D., Seal, G.J., Tholen, W.: Monoidal Topology: A Categorical Approach to Order, Metric, and Topology, vol. 153. Cambridge University Press, Cambridge (2014)

17. Jaskelioff, M., Moggi, E.: Monad transformers as monoid transformers. Theoret. Comput. Sci. **411**(51–52), 4441–4466 (2010)

18. Johnstone, P.T.: Stone Spaces. Cambridge Studies in Advanced Mathematics, vol. 3. Cambridge University Press, Cambridge (1986)

19. Kelly, M.: Basic Concepts of Enriched Category Theory, vol. 64. CUP Archive (1982). Reprints in Theory and Applications of Categories, no. 10 (2005)

20. Kopperman, R.: All topologies come from generalized metrics. Am. Math. Mon. **95**(2), 89–97 (1988)

21. Lawvere, F.W.: Metric spaces, generalized logic, and closed categories. Rendiconti seminario matématico fisico Milano **43**, 135–166 (1973). Reprints in Theory and Applications of Categories (1), 1–37 (2002)

22. Moggi, E., Farjudian, A., Duracz, A., Taha, W.: Safe & robust reachability analysis of hybrid systems. Theor. Comput. Sci. **747**, 75–99 (2018). https://doi.org/10.1016/j.tcs.2018.06.020

23. Moggi, E., Farjudian, A., Taha, W.: System analysis and robustness. In: Cherubini, A., Sabadini, N., Tini, S. (eds.) Proceedings of the 20th Italian Conference on Theoretical Computer Science, ICTCS 2019, Como, Italy, 9–11 September 2019. CEUR Workshop Proceedings, vol. 2504, pp. 1–7. CEUR-WS.org (2019), http://ceur-ws.org/Vol-2504/paper1.pdf
24. Mulvey, C.J.: Second topology conference (Taormina, 1984). Rend. Circ. Mat. Palermo 2(Suppl 12), 99–104 (1986)
25. Niefield, S.B., Rosenthal, K.I.: Constructing locales from quantales. Math. Proc. Cambridge Philos. Soc. 104(2), 215–234 (1988)
26. Pistone, P.: On generalized metric spaces for the simply typed lambda-calculus. In: 36th Annual ACM/IEEE Symposium on Logic in Computer Science, LICS 2021, pp. 1–14. IEEE (2021). https://doi.org/10.1109/LICS52264.2021.9470696
27. Smyth, M.B.: Effectively given domains. Theor. Comput. Sci. 5(3), 257–274 (1977)
28. Sprunger, D., Katsumata, S., Dubut, J., Hasuo, I.: Fibrational bisimulations and quantitative reasoning: extended version. J. Log. Comput. 31(6), 1526–1559 (2021). https://doi.org/10.1093/logcom/exab051

Synchronous Agents, Verification, and Blame—A Deontic View

Karam Kharraz[1]([✉])[ID], Shaun Azzopardi[2][ID], Gerardo Schneider[2][ID],
and Martin Leucker[1][ID]

[1] ISP, University of Lübeck, Lübeck, Germany
{kharraz,leucker}@isp.uni-luebeck.de
[2] University of Gothenburg, Gothenburg, Sweden
{shauna,gersch}@chalmers.se

Abstract. A question we can ask of multi-agent systems is whether the agents' collective interaction satisfies particular goals or specifications, which can be either individual or collective. When a collaborative goal is not reached, or a specification is violated, a pertinent question is whether any agent is to blame. This paper considers a two-agent synchronous setting and a formal language to specify when agents' collaboration is required. We take a *deontic* approach and use *obligations*, *permissions*, and *prohibitions* to capture notions of non-interference between agents. We also handle *reparations*, allowing violations to be corrected or compensated. We give trace semantics to our logic, and use it to define blame assignment for violations. We give an automaton construction for the logic, which we use as the base for model checking and blame analysis. We also further provide quantitative semantics that is able to compare different interactions in terms of the required reparations.

1 Introduction

Interaction between agents can be adversarial, where each agent pursues its own set of individual goals, or cooperative where the agents collaborate to achieve a collective goal. Verification techniques can help us detect whether such goals may be achieved. Agents may also interfere or not cooperate, at which point the failure to achieve a goal could be attributed to some agent. In this paper, we develop a *deontic* logic allowing us to specify the anticipated interaction of two agents in the presence of such aspects.

A deontic logic [16,21] includes norms as first-class concepts, with *obligations*, *permissions*, and *prohibitions* as basic norms. These concepts are crucial in legal documents and contractual relationships, where the agents are the parties to a contract.[1] Norms are parameterised by actions/events or propositions and are used to specify what *ought to be*, or the parties *ought to do*.

In this paper, interaction or cooperation of the agents is modelled as the interplay of the individual actions performed by each agent, leading to the concept

---

[1] We use *party* and *agent* interchangeably throughout.

E. Ábrahám et al. (Eds.): ICTAC 2023, LNCS 14446, pp. 332–350, 2023.
https://doi.org/10.1007/978-3-031-47963-2_20

of cooperative actions. Cooperative actions could be synchronous, i.e., actions at each time point of each agent are meant to describe the possible cooperation, or asynchronous, meaning that actions for cooperation may happen a different time points.[2] We choose synchrony as an abstraction to simplify the concept of cooperation and non-interference between parties. We also study only the setting with two rather than many parties. As such, we are concerned with *two-party synchronous systems*, leaving extensions as future work.

We re-purpose and extend the syntax of a deontic language from literature [3, 4] into a new deontic logic with denotational semantics appropriate for this two-party setting. Our semantics depends on two notions of *informative* satisfaction or violation, which talk about the exact point in time a contract is satisfied or violated. Other features of the logic include the ability to make contracts trigger on matching a regular language, requiring the satisfaction of a contract while one is still within the prefix language of a regular language, and a recursion operator to allow the definition of persistent contracts and repetition.

We extend the semantics with a notion of *blame assignment*, to identify which party is responsible for a certain violation. We further use this to define quantitative semantics that counts the number of violations caused by a certain party, which can be used to compare different traces or behaviour of a party.

We give an exponential automata construction for the logic, transforming a contract specification into an automaton capable of identifying satisfaction, and violation as specified in our semantics. We also provide a model checking algorithm, which is quadratic in the size of the contract automaton, hence exponential in the size of the contract. We re-use this construction for blame analysis, but leave analysis for the quantitative semantics for future work.

The paper organisation follows. Section 2 lays out preliminaries, Sect. 3 presents our logic, and Sect. 4 presents algorithms for model checking and blame analysis through automata constructions. Related work is considered in Sect. 5, and we conclude in Sect. 6.

2 Preliminaries

We write $\mathbb{N}_\infty$ for $\mathbb{N} \cup \{\infty\}$. Given a finite alphabet Σ, we write Σ_0, and Σ_1 for re-labellings of Σ with party identifiers 0 and 1, and $\Sigma_{0,1}$ for $\Sigma_0 \cup \Sigma_1$. We use $P[x/y]$ to refer to the syntactic replacement of x in P with y, where P can be an automaton (x and y are states), or a specification (x and y are syntactic objects in the language). We write $(*, s)$ to refer to all state pairs with s in the second position, and similarly for $(s, *)$.

Traces. For $i \in \mathbb{N}$, $j \in \mathbb{N}_\infty$, and an infinite trace w over sets of actions from a finite alphabet Σ, we denote the trace between positions i and j by $w[i..j]$, including the values at both positions. If $j < i$ then $w[i..j]$ is the empty trace. When $j = \infty$ then $w[i..j]$ is the suffix of w from i. We write $w[i]$ for $w[i...i]$, and $w \cdot w'$ for concatenation of w and w', which is only defined for a finite word w.

---

[2] Observe similarities with synchronous and asynchronous communication.

Given two traces w, w' over 2^{Σ}, we define stepwise intersection: $(w \sqcap w')[i] \overset{\text{def}}{=}$ $w[i] \cap w'[i]$, union $(w \sqcup w')[i] \overset{\text{def}}{=} w[i] \cup w'[i]$, and union with party labelling: $(w \sqcup_1^0 w')[i] \overset{\text{def}}{=} w[i] \sqcup_1^0 w'[i]$, where $E \cup_1^0 E' \overset{\text{def}}{=} \{a_0 \mid a \in E\} \cup \{a_1 \mid a \in E'\}$, i.e. the left actions are labeled by 0 and the right actions by 1. This gives a trace in $\Sigma_{0,1}$. For instance, given $w = \langle \{a\}, \{b\}, \{c, d\}\rangle$ and $w' = \langle\{a\}, \{e\}, \{d, e\}\rangle$, we have that $w[2] \cap w'[2] = \{c, d\} \cap \{d, e\} = \{d\}$ and $w[2] \sqcup_1^0 w'[2] = \{c, d\} \sqcup_1^0 \{d, e\} = \{c_0, d_0, d_1, e_1\}$.

Given two traces w_0 and w_1, over 2^{Σ}, we write $\boldsymbol{w}_i^j$ for the pair $(w_0[i..j], w_1[i..j])$. $\boldsymbol{w}_i^j$ is said to be an *interaction*, and when $j \in \mathbb{N}$ a *finite interaction*. Sometimes we abuse notation and treat $\boldsymbol{w}_i^j$ as a trace in $\Sigma_{0,1}$, since it can be projected into such a trace through $\sqcup_1^0$.

Automata. A tuple $A = \langle \Sigma, Q, q_0, Rej, \rightarrow \rangle$ is an *automaton*, where Σ is a finite alphabet, S is a finite set of states, $s_0 \in S$ is the initial state, $Rej \subseteq S$ is a set of rejecting states, and $\rightarrow \in S \times 2^{\Sigma} \rightarrow (2^S \setminus \emptyset)$ is the transition function ($\rightarrow \in S \times 2^{\Sigma} \rightarrow S$ when the automaton is deterministic). The language $L(A)$ of automaton A is the set of infinite traces with no prefix reaching a rejecting state. The rejecting language $RL(A)$ of automaton A is the set of infinite traces with a prefix reaching a rejecting state. We write $RL_s(A)$ for the rejecting language through a specific rejecting state $s \in Rej$.

The *synchronous product* of automata A and B over the same alphabet Σ, denoted by $A\|B$, is the automaton: $(\Sigma, S_A \times S_B, (s_{0_A}, s_{0_B}), (Rej_A \times S_B) \cup (S_A \times Rej_B), \rightarrow)$ where $\rightarrow$ is the minimal relation such that: for any $E \subseteq \Sigma$, if $s_1 \xrightarrow{E}_A s_1'$ and $s_2 \xrightarrow{E}_B s_2'$ then $(s_1, s_2) \xrightarrow{E} (s_1', s_2')$.

The *relaxed synchronous product* of automata A and B over the same alphabet Σ, denoted by $A\|^r B$ includes $A\|B$ but allows moving independently when there is no match: if $s_1 \xrightarrow{E}_A s_1'$ and $\nexists s_2' \cdot s_2 \xrightarrow{E}_B s_2'$, then $(s_1, s_2) \xrightarrow{E} (s_1', s_2)$; and symmetrically.

Moore Machines. A Moore machine is a 5-tuple $M = (S, s_0, \Sigma_I, \Sigma_O, \delta, \lambda)$ where S is a finite set of states, $s_0 \in S$ is the initial state, Σ_I and Σ_O are respectively the finite set of input and output actions, $\delta : S \times 2^{\Sigma_I} \rightarrow 2^S$ is a transition function that maps each state and inputs to a next state, and $\lambda : S \rightarrow 2^{\Sigma_O}$ is an output function that maps each state to a set of outputs.

The *product* of a Moore machine M_1 over input alphabet Σ_I and output alphabet Σ_O, and Moore machine M_2 with flipped input and output alphabets is the automaton: $M_1 \otimes M_2 \overset{\text{def}}{=} (\Sigma_I \cup \Sigma_O, S_1 \times S_2, (s_{0_1}, s_{0_2}), \emptyset, \rightarrow)$ where $\rightarrow$ is the minimal relation such that: for any states $s_1 \in S_1$ and $s_2 \in S_2$, where $s_1 \xrightarrow{\lambda_2(s_2)} s_1'$ and $s_2 \xrightarrow{\lambda_1(s_1)} s_2'$ then $(s_1, s_2) \xrightarrow{\lambda_1(s_1) \cup \lambda_2(s_2)} (s_1', s_2')$.

Regular Expressions. We use standard syntax for regular expressions. We treat as atomic boolean combinations of actions from $\Sigma_{0,1}$. The operators are standard: choice, $re + re$ (match either); sequence, $re; re$ (match the first then the second) and the Kleene plus, re^+ (match a non-zero finite amount of times in sequence). The language of a regular expression re is a set of finite traces: $L(re) \subseteq (2^{\Sigma_{0,1}})^*$. We abuse notation and write $\boldsymbol{w}_i^j \in L(re)$ for $w_0[i...j] \sqcup_1^0 w_1[i...j] \in L(re)$.

We restrict attention to the *tight language* of a regular expression, containing matching finite traces that have no matching strict prefix: $TL(re) \overset{\text{def}}{=} \{\boldsymbol{w}_i^j \in L(re) \mid \nexists k : k < j \wedge \boldsymbol{w}_i^k \in L(re)\}$. The *prefix closure* of the tight language is the set of finite prefixes of the tight language up to a match: $cl(re) \overset{\text{def}}{=} \{\boldsymbol{w}_i^k \mid \exists j : \boldsymbol{w}_i^j \in TL(re) \wedge i \leq k < j\}$. We define the *complement of the prefix closure* as the set of finite traces that do not tightly match the regular expression but whose maximal strict prefix is in the closure of the expression: $\overline{cl}(re) \overset{\text{def}}{=} \{\boldsymbol{w}_i^j \mid (\boldsymbol{w}_i^{j-1} \in cl(re) \wedge \boldsymbol{w}_i^j \notin cl(re) \wedge \boldsymbol{w}_i^j \notin TL(re))\}$.

We denote by $A(re, s_0, s_\checkmark, s_\times)$ the deterministic finite automaton corresponding to regular expression re, with s_0, and $s_\times$ respectively as the initial and rejecting states and, $s_\checkmark$ as a sink state, s.t. $\forall \boldsymbol{w}_i^j \in TL(re) : s_0 \overset{\boldsymbol{w}_i^j}{\Longrightarrow} s_\checkmark$, $\forall \boldsymbol{w}_i^j \in cl(re) : \exists s : s_0 \overset{\boldsymbol{w}_i^j}{\Longrightarrow} s \wedge s \neq s_\checkmark \wedge s \neq s_\times$, and $\forall \boldsymbol{w}_i^j \in \overline{cl}(re) : s_0 \overset{\boldsymbol{w}_i^j}{\Longrightarrow} s_\times$.

3   A Deontic Logic for Collaboration

In this section, we present the syntax and semantics of $c\mathcal{DL}$, a deontic logic able to express the extent to which parties should cooperate and non-interfere.

Definition 3.1 ($c\mathcal{DL}$ **Syntax**). *A $c\mathcal{DL}$ contract C is given by the following grammar, given an alphabet Σ, regular expressions re, a set of variables $\mathbb{X}$, and party labels p from $\{0,1\}$:*

$$a \in \Sigma_0 \cup \Sigma_1$$
$$N := O_p(a) \mid F_p(a) \mid P_p(a) \mid \top \mid \bot$$
$$C := N \mid C \wedge C \mid C; C \mid C \blacktriangleright C \mid$$
$$\langle re \rangle C \mid re \triangleright C \mid \mathbb{X} \mid recX.C$$

Our setting is that of two-party systems, with one party indexed with 0 and the other with 1. As the basic atoms of the language, we have *norms*. These norms are labeled by the party that is the main subject of the norm, and the action that is normed: $O_p(a)$ denotes an obligation for party p to achieve a; $F_p(a)$ denotes a prohibition for party p from achieving a, and $P_p(a)$ denotes a permission/right for party p to achieve a.

We call $c\mathcal{DL}$ specifications *contracts*. Contracts include norms, the atomic satisfied ($\top$), and the transgressed ($\bot$) contract. Contracts can be *conjuncts* ($\wedge$) and *sequentially composed* (;). A contract may repair the violation of another ($C \blacktriangleright C'$ means that C' is the *reparation* applied when C is violated).

Contracts can be triggered when a regular expression matches tightly ($\langle re \rangle C$). A regular expression can also guard $\triangleright$ a contract C, such that an unrecoverable mismatch with it removes the need to continue complying with C in $(re \triangleright C)$.

We allow *recursive* definitions of contracts ($rec\ X.C$), where $X \in \mathbb{X}$, with some restrictions. First, we do not allow a contract to have two recursive sub-contracts using the same variable name. Secondly, we have some syntactic restrictions on the contract C appearing inside of the recursion: C's top-level operator is always a sequence, or a regular expression trigger contract, with X only appearing once and on the right-hand side of a sequence, i.e., the expression must be tail recursive. We also require an additional restriction for recursion with the reparation operator: the reparation has to either not be the last operation before X or the whole recursion should be guarded with $re \triangleright$, the reason behind it is to avoid the procrastination dilemma [14]. For example, $rec\ X.\langle re \rangle((C \blacktriangleright C'); X)$ and $re \triangleright (rec\ X.C \blacktriangleright X)$ are valid, unlike $rec\ X.X$, $rec\ X.C; (C' \wedge X)$, $rec\ X.\langle re \rangle((C; X); C')$, and $rec\ X.C \blacktriangleright X$. Moreover, a recursion variable $X \in \mathbb{X}$ must always be bound when it appears in a contract.

In our setting, we want to be able to talk about collaborative actions (actions that require both parties to be achieved successfully) and non-interference between the parties (a party not being allowed to interfere with the other party carrying out a certain action). We model both of these using a notion of synchronicity. We will later represent parties as Moore machines; here we talk just about their traces.

We assume two traces over 2^Σ, one for each party: w_0 and w_1. A party's trace is a record of which actions were enabled (or attempted) by that party. The step-wise intersection of these traces, $w_0 \sqcap w_1$, is the trace of *successful* actions. Restricting attention to the successful actions misses information about attempts that were not successful. Instead, we give semantics over pairs of party traces, an *interaction*, rather than over $w_0 \sqcap w_1$, allowing us to localise interference. This setting allows us to model both collaboration and non-interference between the parties in the same way. If the parties are required to collaborate on an action, then they must both propose it (*obligation*). If instead, the parties should ensure an action is not successful, then at least one of them must not enable it (*prohibition*). If a party is required to not interfere with another party's action, then they must also enable it (*permission*). We refer to actions of one party variously as *proposed*, *attempted*, or *enabled* by that party. We consider an example specification in our language.

Example 3.1. *Consider two possibly distinct robots, 0 and 1, working on a factory floor, with their main goal being to cooperate in placing incoming packages on shelves. Each robot has sensors to identify when a new package is in the queue (detectProd), and they must lift the package together (lift), and place it on a shelf (putOnShelf). Between iterations of this process, the robots are individually allowed to go to their charging ports (charge0 or charge1). If a robot does not help in lifting, it is given another chance:*

$$permitCharge \stackrel{\text{def}}{=} P_0(charge0) \wedge P_1(charge1)$$

$$lift(p) \stackrel{\text{def}}{=} O_p(lift) \blacktriangleright O_p(lift)$$

$$detect\&Lift(p) \stackrel{\text{def}}{=} \langle detectProd_p \rangle lift(p)$$

$$detect\&Place \stackrel{\text{def}}{=} (detect\&Lift(0) \wedge detect\&Lift(1)) \,;$$
$$(O_0(putOnShelf) \wedge O_1(putOnShelf))$$

$$collabRobot \stackrel{\text{def}}{=} rec\ X.permitCharge;\ detect\&Place;\ X.$$

$$
\begin{aligned}
\boldsymbol{w}_i^j \models_s \top &\stackrel{\text{def}}{=} i = j \\
\boldsymbol{w}_i^j \models_s \bot &\stackrel{\text{def}}{=} false \\
\boldsymbol{w}_i^j \models_s O_p(a) &\stackrel{\text{def}}{=} i = j \wedge a \in w_0[i] \text{ and } a \in w_1[i] \\
\boldsymbol{w}_i^j \models_s F_p(a) &\stackrel{\text{def}}{=} i = j \wedge a \notin w_p[i] \text{ or } a \notin w_{1-p}[i] \\
\boldsymbol{w}_i^j \models_s P_p(a) &\stackrel{\text{def}}{=} i = j \wedge a \in w_p[i] \text{ implies } a \in w_{1-p}[i]) \\
\boldsymbol{w}_i^j \models_v N &\stackrel{\text{def}}{=} i = j \wedge \boldsymbol{w}_i^j \not\models_s N
\end{aligned}
$$

$$
\begin{aligned}
\boldsymbol{w}_i^j \models_s \langle re \rangle C &\stackrel{\text{def}}{=} \boldsymbol{w}_i^j \in \overline{cl}(re) \text{ or } (\exists k < j : \boldsymbol{w}_i^k \in TL(re) \text{ and } \boldsymbol{w}_{k+1}^j \models_s C) \\
\boldsymbol{w}_i^j \models_v \langle re \rangle C &\stackrel{\text{def}}{=} \exists k < j : \boldsymbol{w}_i^k \in TL(re) \text{ and } \boldsymbol{w}_{k+1}^j \models_v C \\
\boldsymbol{w}_i^j \models_s re \flat C &\stackrel{\text{def}}{=} (\boldsymbol{w}_i^j \in \overline{cl}(re) \cup TL(re) \text{ and } \nexists k < j : (\boldsymbol{w}_i^k \models_v C)) \\
&\quad \text{or } (\boldsymbol{w}_i^j \in cl(re) \text{ and } \boldsymbol{w}_i^j \models_s C) \\
\boldsymbol{w}_i^j \models_v re \flat C &\stackrel{\text{def}}{=} \boldsymbol{w}_i^j \in cl(re) \text{ and } \boldsymbol{w}_i^j \models_v C \\
\boldsymbol{w}_i^j \models_s C \wedge C' &\stackrel{\text{def}}{=} \boldsymbol{w}_i^k \models_s C \text{ and } \boldsymbol{w}_i^l \models_s C' \text{ and } j = max(k, l) \\
\boldsymbol{w}_i^j \models_v C \wedge C' &\stackrel{\text{def}}{=} (\boldsymbol{w}_i^j \models_v C \text{ or } \boldsymbol{w}_i^j \models_v C') \text{ and } \nexists k < j : \boldsymbol{w}_i^k \models_v C \wedge C' \\
\boldsymbol{w}_i^j \models_s C; C' &\stackrel{\text{def}}{=} \exists k < j : \boldsymbol{w}_i^k \models_s C \text{ and } \boldsymbol{w}_{k+1}^j \models_s C' \\
\boldsymbol{w}_i^j \models_v C; C' &\stackrel{\text{def}}{=} (\exists k < j : \boldsymbol{w}_i^k \models_s C \text{ and } \boldsymbol{w}_{k+1}^j \models_v C') \text{ or } \boldsymbol{w}_i^j \models_v C \\
\boldsymbol{w}_i^j \models_s C \blacktriangleright C' &\stackrel{\text{def}}{=} \boldsymbol{w}_i^j \models_s C \text{ or } (\exists k < j : \boldsymbol{w}_i^k \models_v C \text{ and } \boldsymbol{w}_{k+1}^j \models_s C') \\
\boldsymbol{w}_i^j \models_v C \blacktriangleright C' &\stackrel{\text{def}}{=} \exists k < j : \boldsymbol{w}_i^k \models_v C \text{ and } \boldsymbol{w}_{k+1}^j \models_v C' \\
\boldsymbol{w}_i^j \models_s rec\ X.C &\stackrel{\text{def}}{=} \boldsymbol{w}_i^j \models_s C[X\backslash rec\ X.C] \\
\boldsymbol{w}_i^j \models_v rec\ X.C &\stackrel{\text{def}}{=} \boldsymbol{w}_i^j \models_v C[X\backslash rec\ X.C]
\end{aligned}
$$

$$\boldsymbol{w}_i^j \models_? C \quad \stackrel{\text{def}}{=} \quad \nexists k \leq j : \boldsymbol{w}_i^k \models_s C \text{ or } \boldsymbol{w}_i^k \models_v C$$

Fig. 1. Informative semantics rules over a finite interaction $\boldsymbol{w}_i^j$.

3.1 Informative Semantics

The semantics of our language is defined on an *interaction*, i.e. a pair of traces w_0 and w_1, restricting our view to a slice with a minimal position i and maximal one j. For the remainder of this paper, we will refer to this interaction with $\boldsymbol{w}_i^j$.

In Fig. 1, we introduce the semantic relations for *informative* satisfaction ($\models_s$) and violation ($\models_v$). These capture the moment of satisfaction and violation of a contract in a finite interaction. We use this to later define when an infinite interaction models a contract. In Fig. 1 we also capture with $\models_?$, when the interaction slice neither informatively satisfies nor violates the contract.

We give some intuition and mention interesting features of the semantics. Note how we only allow the status of atomic contracts to be informatively decided in one time-step (when $i = j$), given they only talk about one action. When it comes to the trigger contract, our goal is to confirm its fulfillment only when we no longer closely align with the specified trigger language. Alternatively, we consider it satisfied if we've matched it previously and subsequently maintained compliance with the contract. Conversely, we would classify a violation if we achieved a close match but then deviated from the contract's terms. Regarding the regular expression guard, we have two scenarios for evaluating satisfaction. First, we ensure satisfaction when either we have precisely matched the language or have taken actions preventing any future matching of the guard, with no prior violations or the guarded contract. Second, we verify satisfaction when there's still a possibility of a precise match of the guard, and the guarded contract has already been satisfied. In contrast, a violation occurs when there remains a chance for a precise match in the future of the guard, and a violation of the sub-contract occurs.

The definitions for conjunction and sequence are relatively simple. Note that for conjunction we take the maximum index at which both contracts have been satisfied. Sequence and reparation are similar, except in reparation we only continue in the second contract if the first is violated, while we violate it if both contracts end up being violated. For recursion, we simply re-write variable X as needed to determine satisfaction or violation.

Example 3.2. *Note how the semantics ensure that, given traces w_0 and w_1 such that $w_0[0] = w_1[1] = \{charge0, charge1\}$ then $\boldsymbol{w}_0^0 \models_s permitCharge$, i.e. both robots try to charge and allow each other to charge. But if further $w_0[1..3] = \langle \{detectProd\}, \{lift\}, \{lift\} \rangle$ and $w_1[1..3] = \langle \{\}, \{\}.\{\} \rangle$, then $\boldsymbol{w}_0^3 \models_v CollabRobot$, since robot 0 attempted a lift but robot 1 declined helping in lifting.*

Then, we show that if a contract is informatively satisfied (violated), then any suffix or prefix of the interaction cannot also be informatively satisfied (violated):

Lemma 3.1 (Unique satisfaction and violation). *If there exists j and k such that $\boldsymbol{w}_i^j \models_s C$ and $\boldsymbol{w}_i^k \models_s C$, then $j = k$. Similarly, if there exists j and k such that $\boldsymbol{w}_i^j \models_v C$ and $\boldsymbol{w}_i^k \models_v C$ then $j = k$.*

Proof (sketch). For the atomic contracts, this is clear. By structural induction, the result follows for conjunction, sequence, and reparation. For the trigger operations, the definition of TL ensures the result. For recursion, note how given a finite interaction there is always a finite amount of times the recursion can be unfolded (with an upper bound of $j - i$) so that we can determine satisfaction or violation in finite time.

If an interaction is not informative for satisfaction, it is not necessarily informative for violation, and vice-versa. But we can show that if there is a point of informative satisfaction then there is no point of informative violation.

Lemma 3.2 (Disjoint satisfaction and violation). *Informative satisfaction and violation are disjoint: there are no j, k s.t. $\boldsymbol{w}_i^j \models_s C$ and $\boldsymbol{w}_i^k \models_v C$.*

Proof (sketch). The proof follows easily by induction on the structure of C.

We can then give semantics to infinite interactions.

Definition 3.2 (Models). *For an infinite interaction $\boldsymbol{w}_0^\infty$, and a cDL contract C, we say $\boldsymbol{w}_0^\infty$ models a contract C, denoted by $\boldsymbol{w}_0^\infty \models C$, when there is no prefix of the interaction that informatively violates C:* $\boldsymbol{w}_0^\infty \models C \stackrel{\text{def}}{=} \nexists k \in \mathbb{N} \cdot \boldsymbol{w}_0^k \models_v C.$

$$\boldsymbol{w}_i^j \models_v^p \top \stackrel{\text{def}}{=} false$$

$$\boldsymbol{w}_i^j \models_v^p \bot \stackrel{\text{def}}{=} false$$

$$\boldsymbol{w}_i^j \models_v^p O_{1-p}(a) \stackrel{\text{def}}{=} i = j \wedge a \in w_{1-p}[i] \text{ and } a \notin w_p[i]$$

$$\boldsymbol{w}_i^j \models_v^p O_p(a) \stackrel{\text{def}}{=} i = j \wedge a \notin w_p[i]$$

$$\boldsymbol{w}_i^j \models_v^p F_{1-p}(a) \stackrel{\text{def}}{=} false$$

$$\boldsymbol{w}_i^j \models_v^p F_p(a) \stackrel{\text{def}}{=} i = j \wedge a \in w_p[i] \text{ and } a \in w_{1-p}[i]$$

$$\boldsymbol{w}_i^j \models_v^p P_{1-p}(a) \stackrel{\text{def}}{=} i = j \wedge a \in w_{1-p}[i] \text{ and } a \notin w_p[i]$$

$$\boldsymbol{w}_i^j \models_v^p P_p(a) \stackrel{\text{def}}{=} false$$

$$\boldsymbol{w}_i^j \models_v^p \langle re \rangle C \stackrel{\text{def}}{=} \exists k < j : \boldsymbol{w}_i^k \models_s TL(re) \text{ and } \boldsymbol{w}_{k+1}^j \models_v^p C$$

$$\boldsymbol{w}_i^j \models_v^p re \natural C \stackrel{\text{def}}{=} \boldsymbol{w}_i^j \in cl(re) \text{ and } \boldsymbol{w}_i^j \models_v^p C$$

$$\boldsymbol{w}_i^j \models_v^p C \wedge C' \stackrel{\text{def}}{=} (\boldsymbol{w}_i^j \models_v^p C \text{ or } \boldsymbol{w}_i^j \models_v^p C') \text{ and}$$
$$(\nexists k < j : \boldsymbol{w}_i^k \models_v^{1-p} C \wedge C') \text{ and}$$
$$\neg(conflict(C, C', \boldsymbol{w}_i^{j-1}))$$

$$\boldsymbol{w}_i^j \models_v^p C \blacktriangleright C' \stackrel{\text{def}}{=} \exists k : \boldsymbol{w}_i^k \models_v C \text{ and } \boldsymbol{w}_{k+1}^j \models_v^p C'$$

$$\boldsymbol{w}_i^j \models_v^p rec\ X.C \stackrel{\text{def}}{=} \boldsymbol{w}_i^j \models_v^p C[X \backslash rec\ X.C]$$

Fig. 2. Blame semantics rules over a finite interaction $\boldsymbol{w}_i^j$

3.2 Blame Assignment

We are not interested only in whether a contract is satisfied or violated, but also on *causation* and *responsibility* [9,10,12]. Here we give a relation that identifies when a party is responsible for a violation at a certain point in an interaction. Blame assignment could be specified following multiple criteria, we assign blame when an agent neglects to perform an action it is obliged to do or that another agent is obliged to do (passive blame), or for attempting to do an action it is forbidden from doing (active blame). The blame is forward looking where we identify the earliest cause of violation. Furthermore, we are only interested in causation and not on more advanced features such as "moral responsibility" or "intentionality". The blame semantics is only defined as a violation by party p relation as in $\models_v^p$. This semantics is defined in Fig. 2.

For blame assignment, the labeling of norms with parties is crucial. Here we give meaning to these labels in terms of who is the main subject of the norm in question. For example, consider that $O_0(a)$ can be violated in three ways: either (i) both parties do not attempt a, (ii) party 0 does not attempt a but party 1 does, or (iii) party 0 attempts a but party 1 does not. Our interpretation is that since party 0 is the main subject of the obligation, party 0 is blamed when it does not attempt a (cases (i) and (ii)), but party 1 is blamed when it does not attempt a (case (iii)). The intuition is that by not attempting a, party 0 violated the contract, thus relieving party 1 of any obligation to cooperate or non-interfere (given party 0 knows there is no hope for the norm to be satisfied if they do not attempt a). We use similar interpretations for the other norms.

Another crucial observation is that violations of a contract are not necessarily caused by a party. For example, the violated contract $\perp$ cannot be satisfied. Moreover, norms can conflict, e.g., $O_p(a) \wedge F_p(a)$. Conflicts are not immediately obvious without some analysis, e.g., $\langle re \rangle O_p(a) \wedge \langle re' \rangle F_p(a)$ (where there is some interaction for which re and re' tightly match at the same time). We provide machinery to talk about conflicts, to avoid unsound blaming, by characterising two contracts to be conflicting when there is no way to satisfy them together.

Definition 3.3 (Conflicts). *Two contracts C and C' are in conflict after a finite interaction $\boldsymbol{w}_i^j$ if at that point their conjunction has not been informatively satisfied or violated yet, but all possible further steps lead to its violation:*
$$conflict(C, C', \boldsymbol{w}_i^j) \stackrel{\text{def}}{=} \nexists \boldsymbol{w}' : \boldsymbol{w'}_i^j = \boldsymbol{w}_i^j \wedge \boldsymbol{w'}_i^{j+1} \not\models_v C \wedge C'.$$

Another instance of a conflict can be observed between $C_1 = O_0(a); F_1(c)$ and $C_2 = O_0(b) \blacktriangleright O_0(c)$ at the second position. This can be demonstrated with a trace of length one, $\langle a_0; a_1 \rangle$, where the obligation to achieve c for party 0 and the prohibition to achieve c for party 1 have to be enforced simultaneously.

Example 3.3. *Recall the violating example in Example. 3.2, where robot 1 declines in helping lifting, twice. Clearly in that case $\boldsymbol{w}_0^3 \models_v^1$ collabRobot . However, if robot 0 did not attempt a lift in position 3 (i.e., to attempt to satisfy the reparation), the blame would be on the other agent.*

From the definition of blame it easily follows that a party is blamed for a violation only when there is a violation:

Proposition 3.1. *If a party p is blamed for the violation of C then C has been violated: $\exists p \cdot \boldsymbol{w}_i^j \models_v^p C$ implies $\boldsymbol{w}_i^j \models_v C$.*

Proof. Note how each case of $\models_v^p$ implies its counterpart in $\models_v$.

But the opposite is not true:

Proposition 3.2. *A contract may be violated but both parties be blameless: $\boldsymbol{w}_i^j \models_v C$ does not imply $\exists p \cdot \boldsymbol{w}_i^j \models_v^p C$.*

Proof. Consider their definitions on $\perp$, and given conjunction and the presence of conflicts.

Proposition 3.3 (Satisfaction implies no blame). *Satisfaction of contract C means that no party will get blamed:* $\boldsymbol{w}_i^j \models_s C$ *implies* $\nexists p \cdot \boldsymbol{w}_i^j \models_v^p C$

Proof. Assume the contrary, i.e. that C is satisfied but party p is blamed. By Proposition 3.1 then there is a violation, but Lemma 3.2 implies we cannot both have a satisfaction or violation.

Observation 3.1. *For any contract $C^{\perp}$ defined on cDL free of $\perp$ and free of conflicts, the violation of a contract $C^{\perp}$ leads to blame.*

Observation 3.2 (Double blame). *Double blame in cDL for both parties p and $1-p$ is possible. Consider $C = O_p(a) \wedge O_p(b)$. Violation of the left-hand side by p and the violation of the right-hand side by $1 - p$ can happen at the same time.*

3.3 Quantitative Semantics

While it is possible to assign blame to one party for violating a contract, other qualitative metrics can provide additional information about the violation. These metrics can determine the number of violations caused by each party, as well as the level of satisfaction with the contract. To assess responsibility for contract violations, we introduce the notion of a mistake score, ρ, for each party, enabling us to calculate a *responsibility degree*. It is important to note that our language permits reparations, whereby violations can be corrected in the next time step. However, interactions that are satisfied with reparations are not considered ideal. We present quantitative semantics to compare satisfying interactions based on the number of repaired violations a party incurs. We define relations that track the number of repaired violations attributed to each party with a mistake score, ρ, written $\models_s^p$ for informative satisfaction and $\models_v^p$ for informative violation of the contract. We can also keep track of the number of violations when the trace is not informative through $\models_?^p$. Figure 3 provides a definition of this semantics. Note this definition intersects the previous semantic definitions, and due to space constraints, we do not re-expand that further. The addition is that we are disambiguating some cases to identify when to add to the score to identify a violation caused by p. For example, see the definition of $\models_v^p$ for a norm.

Example 3.4. *Consider again Example 3.1, and consider the finite interaction $(\langle \{charge0\}, \{detectProd\}, \{\}, \{lift\}\rangle$ and $\langle \{charge0\}, \{\}, \{lift\}, \{lift\}\rangle$. Note how this will lead to robot 0 being given a score of one since on the third step there is a violation that is repaired subsequently.*

Lemma 3.3 (Soundness and completeness). *The quantitative semantics is sound and complete with regard to the informative semantics:* $\boldsymbol{w}_i^j \models_\gamma C \iff \exists \rho_1, \rho_2 : \boldsymbol{w}_i^j, \rho_1 \models_v^p C$ *and* $\boldsymbol{w}_i^j, \rho_2 \models_v^{1-p} C$ *with $\gamma \in \{s, v, ?\}$.*

Proof (sketch). By induction on the quantitative semantics and informative semantics.

$$w_i^j, \rho \models_s^p N \quad \stackrel{def}{=} \quad \rho = 0 \wedge w_i^j \models_s N$$

$$w_i^j, \rho \models_v^p N \quad \stackrel{def}{=} \quad \begin{cases} \rho = 1 & \text{if } w_i^i \models_v^p N \\ \rho = 0 & \text{if } N = \perp \vee w_i^i \models_v^{1-p} N \end{cases}$$

$$w_i^j, \rho \models_?^p N \quad \stackrel{def}{=} \quad false$$

$$w_i^j, \rho \models_s^p \langle re \rangle C \quad \stackrel{def}{=} \quad \begin{cases} \rho = 0 & \text{if } w_i^j \in \overline{cl}(re) \\ w_{k+1}^j, \rho \models_s^p C & \text{if } \exists k : w_i^k \in TL(re) \end{cases}$$

$$w_i^j, \rho \models_v^p \langle re \rangle C \quad \stackrel{def}{=} \quad \exists k : w_i^k \in TL(re) \text{ and } w_{k+1}^j, \rho \models_v^p C$$

$$w_i^j, \rho \models_?^p \langle re \rangle C \quad \stackrel{def}{=} \quad \begin{cases} \rho = 0 & \text{if} \quad \nexists k \leq j : w_i^k \in TL(re) \\ w_{k+1}^j, \rho \models_?^p C & \text{else } \exists k \leq j : w_i^k \in TL(re) \end{cases}$$

$$w_i^j, \rho \models_s^p re \!\restriction\! C \quad \stackrel{def}{=} \quad \begin{cases} w_i^{j-1}, \rho \models_?^p C \text{ if } w_i^j \in \overline{cl}(re) \cup TL(re) \\ \qquad \text{and } \nexists \rho', k < j : w_i^k, \rho' \models_v^p C \\ w_i^j, \rho \models_s^p C & \text{if } w_i^j \in cl(re) \end{cases}$$

$$w_i^j, \rho \models_v^p re \!\restriction\! C \quad \stackrel{def}{=} \quad w_i^j \in cl(re) \text{ and } w_i^j, \rho \models_v^p C$$

$$w_i^j, \rho \models_?^p re \!\restriction\! C \quad \stackrel{def}{=} \quad w_i^j \in cl(re) \text{ and } w_i^j, \rho \models_?^p C$$

$$w_i^j, (\rho_1 + \rho_2) \models_s^p C \wedge C' \quad \stackrel{def}{=} \quad \exists k, l : w_i^k, \rho_1 \models_s^p C \text{ and } w_i^l, \rho_2 \models_s^p C' \\ \text{and } j = max(k, l)$$

$$w_i^j, (\rho_1 + \rho_2) \models_v^p C \wedge C' \quad \stackrel{def}{=} \quad ((w_i^j, \rho_2 \models_v^p C' \text{ or } w_i^j, \rho_2 \models_s^p C') \\ \text{and } w_i^j, \rho_1 \models_v^p C) \\ \text{or } ((w_i^j, \rho_1 \models_v^p C' \text{ or } w_i^j, \rho_1 \models_s^p C') \\ \text{and } w_i^j, \rho_2 \models_v^p C') \\ \text{or } (w_i^j, \rho_1 \models_v^p C \text{ and } w_i^j, \rho_2 \models_v^p C' \\ \text{and } \neg conflict(C, C', w_i^{j-1})) \\ \text{or } (w_i^{j-1}, \rho_1 \models_?^p C \text{ and } w_i^{j-1}, \rho_2 \models_?^p C' \\ \text{and } conflict(C, C', w_i^{j-1}))$$

$$w_i^j, (\rho_1 + \rho_2) \models_?^p C \wedge C' \quad \stackrel{def}{=} \quad (w_i^j, \rho_1 \models_s^p C \text{ and } w_i^j, \rho_2 \models_?^p C') \\ \text{or } (w_i^j, \rho_1 \models_?^p C \text{ and } w_i^j, \rho_2 \models_s^p C')$$

$$w_i^j, (\rho_1 + \rho_2) \models_s^p C; C' \quad \stackrel{def}{=} \quad \exists k < j : w_i^k, \rho_1 \models_s^p C \text{ and } w_{k+1}^j, \rho_2 \models_s^p C'$$

$$w_i^j, \rho \models_v^p C; C' \quad \stackrel{def}{=} \quad \begin{cases} \rho = \rho_1 + \rho_2 \text{ if } & \exists k < j : w_i^k, \rho_1 \models_s^p C \\ & \text{and } w_{k+1}^j, \rho_2 \models_v^p C' \\ w_i^j, \rho \models_v^p & \text{else} \end{cases}$$

$$w_i^j, (\rho_1 + \rho_2) \models_?^p C \ ; \ C' \quad \stackrel{def}{=} \quad w_i^j, \rho \models_?^p C \\ \text{or } (w_i^k, \rho_1 \models_s^p C \text{ and } w_{k+1}^j, \rho_2 \models_?^p C')$$

$$w_i^j, \rho \models_s^p C \blacktriangleright C' \quad \stackrel{def}{=} \quad w_i^j, \rho \models_s^p C \\ \text{or } (\exists k < j : w_i^k, \rho_1 \models_s^p C \\ \text{and } w_{k+1}^j, \rho_2 \models_s^p C' \wedge \rho = \rho_1 + \rho_2)$$

$$w_i^j, (\rho_1 + \rho_2) \models_v^p C \blacktriangleright C' \quad \stackrel{def}{=} \quad (\exists k < j : w_i^k, \rho_1 \models_v^p C \text{ and } w_{k+1}^j, \rho_2 \models_v^p C')$$

$$w_i^j, \rho \models_?^p C \blacktriangleright C' \quad \stackrel{def}{=} \quad \begin{cases} \rho = \rho_1 + \rho_2 \text{ if } & w_i^k, \rho_1 \models_v^p C \\ & \text{and } w_{k+1}^j, \rho_2 \models_?^p C' \\ w_i^j, \rho \models_?^p C \text{ else} \end{cases}$$

$$w_i^j, \rho \models_\gamma^p rec \ X.C \quad \stackrel{def}{=} \quad w_i^j, \rho \models_\gamma^p C[X \setminus rec \ X.C] \qquad \text{for } \gamma \in \{s, v, ?\}$$

Fig. 3. Quantitative semantics rules over a finite interaction w_i^j.

Lemma 3.4 (Fairness of the Quantitative semantics). *The quantitative semantic is fair, meaning that if the score of a player p is ρ then p is to be blamed for non-fulfilling ρ norms of the contract: $\boldsymbol{w}_i^j, \rho \models_\gamma^p C \implies \exists N_1 \ldots N_\rho \in$ subcontracts$(C) : \boldsymbol{w}_i^j \models_\gamma^p N_i$ with $\gamma \in \{s, v, ?\}$, where subcontracts(C) is a multiset containing the subcontracts of C, up to how often they appear.*

Proof (sketch). We prove, this by structural induction, noting that the score only increases when p is blamed for the violation of a norm, while the inductive case easily follows from the inductive hypothesis.

4 Analysis

In this section, we define an automata-theoretic approach to analyzing $c\mathcal{DL}$ contracts, through a construction to a safety automaton. We use this for model checking and blame analysis, but leave the application for quantitative analysis for future work.

4.1 Contracts to Automata

We give a construction from $c\mathcal{DL}$ contracts to automata that recognize interactions that are informative for satisfaction or violation. For brevity, we keep the definition of the automata symbolic, with transitions tagged by propositions over party actions, representing a set of concrete transitions. The automaton is over the alphabet $\Sigma_{0,1}$ since it requires information about the parties.

Definition 4.1. *The deterministic automaton of contract C is:*

$$aut(C) \stackrel{\text{def}}{=} \langle \Sigma_{0,1}, S, s_0, \{s_B\}, \rightarrow \rangle.$$

We define $\rightarrow$ through the below function $\tau(C, s_0, s_G, s_B, \{\})$ that computes a set of transitions, given a contract, an initial state (s_0), a state denoting satisfaction (s_G), a state denoting violation (s_B), and a partial function V from recursion variables $(\mathbb{X})$ to states, characterised by (with s as a fresh state):

$$\tau(\top, s_0, s_G, s_B, V) \stackrel{\text{def}}{=} \{s_0 \xrightarrow{true} s_G\}$$

$$\tau(\bot, s_0, s_G, s_B, V) \stackrel{\text{def}}{=} \{s_0 \xrightarrow{true} s_B\}$$

$$\tau(O_p(a), s_0, s_G, s_B, V) \stackrel{\text{def}}{=} \{s_0 \xrightarrow{a_p \wedge a_{1-p}} s_G, s_0 \xrightarrow{\neg(a_p \wedge a_{1-p})} s_B\}$$

$$\tau(F_p(a), s_0, s_G, s_B, V) \stackrel{\text{def}}{=} \{s_0 \xrightarrow{\neg(a_p \wedge a_{1-p})} s_G, s_0 \xrightarrow{a_p \wedge a_{1-p}} s_B\}$$

$$\tau(P_p(a), s_0, s_G, s_B, V) \stackrel{\text{def}}{=} \{s_0 \xrightarrow{a_p \implies a_{1-p}} s_G, s_0 \xrightarrow{\neg(a_p \implies a_{1-p})} s_B\}$$

$$\tau(\langle re \rangle C, s_0, s_G, s_B, V) \stackrel{\text{def}}{=} A(re, s_0, s, s_G) \cup \tau(C, s, s_G, s_B, V)$$

$$\tau(re \!\!\upharpoonright\!\! C, s_0, s_G, s_B, V) \stackrel{\text{def}}{=} (A(re, s_0, s_G, s_G) \| \tau(C, s_0, s_G, s_B, V))$$
$$[(s_G, *)/s_G][(*, s_B)/s_B][(*, s_G)/s_G]$$

$$\tau(C \wedge C', s_0, s_G, s_B, V) \stackrel{\text{def}}{=} (\tau(C, s_0, s_G, s_B, V) \|^r \tau(C', s_0, s_G, s_B, V))$$
$$[(s_G, s_G)/s_G][(s_B, *)/s_B][(*, s_B)/s_B]$$

$$\tau(C; C', s_0, s_G, s_B, V) \stackrel{\text{def}}{=} \tau(C, s_0, s, s_B, V) \cup \tau(C', s, s_G, s_B, V)$$

$$\tau(C \blacktriangleright C', s_0, s_G, s_B, V) \stackrel{\text{def}}{=} \tau(C, s_0, s_G, s, V) \cup \tau(C', s, s_G, s_B, V)$$

$$\tau(X, s_0, s_G, s_B, V) \stackrel{\text{def}}{=} \{s_G \stackrel{\epsilon}{\to} V(X)\}$$

$$\tau(recX.C, s_0, s_G, s_B, V) \stackrel{\text{def}}{=} \tau(C, s_0, s_G, s_B, V[X \mapsto s_0])$$

We define $\to'$ as $\tau(C, s_0, s_G, s_B, \{\})$ *without all transitions outgoing from* s_G *and* S_B, *and define* $\to \stackrel{\text{def}}{=} \to' \cup \{s_B \xrightarrow{true} s_B\} \cup \{s_G \xrightarrow{true} s_G\}$, *where* S *is the set of states used in* $\to$. *We assume the ϵ-transitions are removed using standard methods.*

We give some intuition for the construction. The transitions for the atomic contracts follow quite clearly from their semantics. For the trigger contracts, we use a fresh state s to connect the automaton for the regular expression, with that of the contract, ensuring the latter is only entered when the former tightly matches. For the guard contract, we instead synchronously compose ($\|$) both automata (i.e., intersect their languages), getting a set of transitions. Here we also relabel tuples of states to single states. Recall we use $(*, s)$ to match any pair, where the second term is s, and similarly for $(s, *)$. Through the sequence of re-labellings, we ensure: first that reaching s_G in the acceptance of the first means; (2) reaching s_B in the second means violation; and (3) if the previous two situations are not the case, reaching s_G in the second means acceptance.

For conjunction, instead of using the synchronous product, we use the relaxed variant ($\|^r$), since the contracts may require traces of different lengths for satisfaction. This relaxed product allows the 'longer' contract to continue after the status of the other is determined. For sequence, we use the fresh state s to move between the automata, once the first contract has been satisfied. For reparation this is similar, except we move between the contracts at the moment the first is violated. For recursion, we simply loop back to the initial state of the recursed contract with an ϵ-transition once the corresponding recursion variable is encountered.

Note how analyzing states without viable transitions, after applying τ, can be used for *conflict analysis* of cDL contracts. For example, when there is a conflict, e.g., $O_p(a) \wedge F_p(a)$, there will be a state with all outgoing transitions to s_B.

Theorem 4.1 (Correctness). *An infinite interaction is a model of C, iff it never reaches a rejecting state in* $aut(C)$:
$$\forall w_0^\infty \cdot w_0^\infty \models C \iff w_0 \sqcup_1^0 w_1 \in L(aut(C)).$$

Proof (sketch). For the atomic contracts, the correspondence should be clear. By structural induction on the rest: triggering, sequence, and reparation should also be clear from the definition. For conjunction, the relaxed synchronous product makes sure the contract not yet satisfied continues being executed, as required, while the replacements ensure large nestings of conjunctions do not lead to large tuples of accepting or rejecting states. For $\flat$, using the synchronous product ensures the path ends when either is satisfied/violated, as required.

Corollary 4.1. *An infinite interaction is not a model of C, iff it reaches a rejecting state in $aut(C)$:* $\forall (w_0, w_1) \not\models C \iff \exists j \in \mathbb{N} \cdot s_0 \xrightarrow{(w_0 \sqcup_1^0 w_1)[0...j]} s_B$.

Proof (sketch). Follows from Theorem. 4.1 and completeness (up to rejection) of $aut(C)$.

Complexity From the translation note that without regular expressions the number of states and transitions is linear in the number of sub-clauses and operators in the contract, but is exponential in the presence of regular expressions.[3]

4.2 Model Checking

We represent the behaviour of each party as a Moore machine (M_0, and M_1). For party 0, the input alphabet is Σ_1 and the output alphabet is Σ_0, and vice-versa for party 1. We characterise their composed behaviour by using the product of the two dual Moore machines: $M_0 \otimes M_1$, getting an automaton over $\Sigma_0 \cup \Sigma_1$.

We can then compose this automaton that represents the interactive behaviour of the parties with the contract's automaton, $(M_0 \otimes M_1) \| aut(C)$. Then, if no rejecting state is reachable in this automaton, the composed party's behaviour respects the contract.

Theorem 4.2 (Model Checking Soundness and Completeness). $\emptyset = RL((M_0 \otimes M_1) \| aut(C))$ *iff* $\nexists \boldsymbol{w}_0^\infty : w_0 \sqcup_1^0 w_1 \in L(M_0 \otimes M_1) \wedge \boldsymbol{w}_0^\infty \models_v C$.

Proof. Consider that $\|$ computes the intersection of the languages, while Theorem 4.1 states that $L(aut(C))$ contains exactly the traces satisfying C (modulo a simple technical procedure to move between labelled traces and pairs of traces). Then it follows easily that $RL((M_0 \otimes M_1) \| aut(C))$ is empty only when there is no trace in $(M_0 \otimes M_1)$ that leads to a rejecting state in $aut(C)$. The same logic can be taken in the other direction.   □

4.3 Blame Assignment

For the blame assignment, we can modify the automaton construction by adding two other violating states: s_B^0 and s_B^1, and adjust the transitions for the basic norms accordingly.

---

[3] For example, a contract $recX.\top; (O_0(a) \wedge P_1(b)); X$ has size 8 (note normed actions are not counted).

Definition 4.2. *The deterministic* blame automaton *of contract* C *is:*

$$blAut(C) \stackrel{\text{def}}{=} \langle \Sigma_{0,1}, S, s_0, \{s_B, s_B^0, s_B^1, (s_B^0, s_B^1)\}, \to \rangle$$

We define $\to$ *through the function* $\tau(C, s_0, s_G, s_B^0, s_B^1, V)$ *that computes a set of transitions, as in Definition 4.1 but now assigning blame by transitioning to the appropriate state. We focus on a subset of the rules, given limited space, where there are substantial changes[4]:*

$$\tau(O_p(a), s_0, s_G, s_B^0, s_B^1, V) \stackrel{\text{def}}{=} \{s_0 \xrightarrow{a_p \wedge a_{1-p}} s_G, s_0 \xrightarrow{\neg a_p} s_B^p, s_0 \xrightarrow{a_p \wedge \neg a_{1-p}} s_B^{1-p}\}$$

$$\tau(F_p(a), s_0, s_G, s_B^0, s_B^1, V) \stackrel{\text{def}}{=} \{s_0 \xrightarrow{\neg(a_p \wedge a_{1-p})} s_G, s_0 \xrightarrow{a_p \wedge a_{1-p}} s_B^p\}$$

$$\tau(P_p(a), s_0, s_G, s_B^0, s_B^1, V) \stackrel{\text{def}}{=} \{s_0 \xrightarrow{a_p \implies a_{1-p}} s_G, s_0 \xrightarrow{a_p \wedge \neg a_{1-p}} s_B^{1-p}\}$$

$$\tau(C \blacktriangleright C', s_0, s_G, s_B^0, s_B^1, V) \stackrel{\text{def}}{=} \tau(C, s_0, s_G, s^0, s^1, V)$$
$$\cup \tau(C', s^0, s_G, s_B^0, V) \cup \tau(C', s^1, s_G, s_B^1, V)$$

Given $\to' = \tau(C, s_0, s_G, s_B, \{\})$, $\to$ *is defined as* $\to'$ *with the following transformations, in order: (1) any tuple of states containing both* s_B^0 *and* s_B^1 *is relabelled as* (s_B^0, s_B^1); *(2) any tuple of states containing* s_B^0 *(s_B^1) is relabelled as* s_B^0 *(s_B^1); (3) any state for which all outgoing transitions go to a bad state are redirected to* s_B; *(4) any tuple of states containing* s_G *is relabelled as* s_G; *and (5) all bad states and* s_G *become sink states.* S *is the set of states used in* $\to$. *We assume the ϵ-transitions are removed using standard methods.*

Note how this automata simply refines the bad states of the original automata construction, by assigning blame for the violation of norms through a transition to an appropriate new state. While the post-processing (see (3)), allows violations caused by conflicts to go instead to state s_B, where no party is blamed.

Then we prove correspondence with the blame semantics:

Theorem 4.3 (Blame Analysis Soundness and Completeness). *Where* RL_p, *for* $p \in \{0,1\}$, *is the rejecting language of the automaton through states that pass through* s_B^p *or the tuple state* (s_B^0, s_B^1):

$$\emptyset = RL_p((M_0 \otimes M_1) \| blAut(C)) \text{ iff } \nexists w_0, w_1 \in (2^\Sigma)^* : w_0 \sqcup_1^0 w_1 \in L(M_0 \otimes M_1) \wedge (w_0, w_1) \models_v^p C.$$

Proof. This follows from a slight modification of Corollary 4.1 (since here we just refine the bad states of $aut(C)$) with the replacement of s_B by party-tagged bad states, and from a similar argument to Theorem 4.2.

---

[4] The missing rules essentially mirror the previous construction with the added states, and the different domains.

This automaton can be used for model checking as before, but it can also answer queries about who is to blame.

Example 4.1. *We illustrate in Fig. 4 an example of two Moore machines representing the behaviour of two parties (Figs. 4a and 4b). Note these are deterministic, therefore their composition (Fig. 4) is just a trace. Note the same theory applies even when the Moore machines are non-deterministic. In Figs. 4d and 4e we show the automaton and blame automaton for the contract $recX.(O_1(c) \blacktriangleright O_0(b); X)$. Our model checking procedure (without blame) will compose Fig. 4 and Fig. 4d, and identify that the trace reaches the bad state. Consider that the reparation consisting of an obligation to perform an action b was not satisfied. Similarly (not shown here) blame automaton would blame party 1 for the violation.*

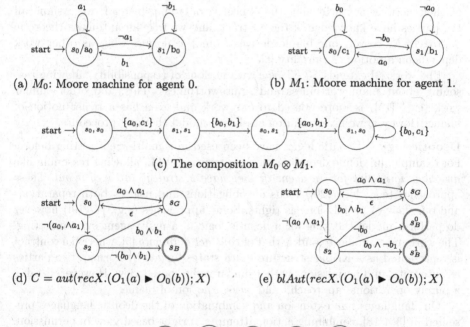

(a) M_0: Moore machine for agent 0.

(b) M_1: Moore machine for agent 1.

(c) The composition $M_0 \otimes M_1$.

(d) $C = aut(recX.(O_1(a) \blacktriangleright O_0(b)); X)$

(e) $blAut(recX.(O_1(a) \blacktriangleright O_0(b)); X)$

(f) $(M_0 \otimes M_1) \| C$

Fig. 4. Example of the model checking approach.

5 Related Work

Multi-agent systems. Several logics can express properties about multi-agent systems. For example, ATL can express the existence of a strategy for one or more agents to enforce a certain specification [2], while strategy logic makes strategies first-class objects [7]. Checking for the existence of strategies is in 2EXPTIME. Our logic is not concerned with the existence of strategies, but with analyzing the party strategies to ensure they respect a contract. So, our approach is more comparable to LTL than to game-based logic, limited to (co-)safety properties and with a notion of norms that allows us to talk about blame natively.

Concerning blame, [11] considers the notion of *blameworthiness*. They use structural equations to represent agents, but the approach is not temporal, and each agent performs only one action. Work in this area (e.g., [9,11,13]) tends to be in a different setting than ours.

They consider the cost of actions and agents' beliefs about the probability of their actions not achieving the expected outcome. Instead, we assume all the parties have knowledge of the contract, and we take an automata-theoretic approach. Moreover, our blame derives from the norms, whereas other work depends on a notion of causality [8].

The work [1] extends *STIT logic* with notions of responsibility, allowing reasoning about blameworthiness and praiseworthiness. This, and other similar work (e.g., [15]) is more related to our work and even has a richer notion of blame. However, we give an automata-based model checking procedure.

Deontic logics. Deontic logics have been used in a multi-agent setting before. For example, [6] define deontic notions in terms of ATL, allowing reasoning like *an obligation holds for an agent iff they have a strategy to carry it out*. These approaches (e.g., [6,17,20]) focus on obligations and neglect both reparations and our view of permissions as rights. Some approaches (e.g., [17,19]) however do perform model checking for a deontic logic in a multi-agent system setting. The work most similar to ours is that of *contract automata* [5], wherein a contract is represented as a Kripke structure (with states tagged by norms), two parties as automata, and permissions with a similar rights-based view. However, it takes a purely operational approach, and lacks a notion of blame.

Our language is an extension and combination of the deontic languages presented in [3,4,18], combining action attempts, a right-based view of permission, a two-party setting, and regular expressions as conditions.

Besides maintaining all these, we give denotational trace semantics, and provide blame and model checking algorithms.

6 Conclusions

In this paper we have introduced a deontic logic for reasoning about a two-party synchronous setting. This logic allows one to define constraints on when parties should support or non-interfere with the carrying out of a certain action or protocol. Using a pair of party traces, we can talk about attempts and success to perform collaborative actions. We consider automata constructions describing both the set of all satisfying and violating sequences. Given the behavior of the agents in the form of suitable automata, we have also provided algorithms for model checking and for blame assignment. To differentiate between satisfying a formula in the expected manner or by fullfilling the exceptional case, we introduce a quantitative semantics. This allows ordering satisfying traces depending on how often they use these exceptions.

This work may be extended in many directions. First, we could consider asynchronous interaction, distinguishing between sending and receiving. The syntax and semantics can also be extended easily to handle multi-party agents rather than just a two-party setting. Different quantitative semantics could be given, for example considering the *costs of actions* to reason when it is better to pay a fine rather than to behave as expected. We plan to study how to synthesise strategies for the different parties, for instance to ensure the optimal behaviour of agents.

References

1. Abarca, A.I.R., Broersen, J.M.: A STIT logic of responsibility. In: Faliszewski, P., Mascardi, V., Pelachaud, C., Taylor, M.E. (eds.) 21st International Conference on Autonomous Agents and Multiagent Systems, AAMAS 2022, Auckland, New Zealand, 9-13 May 2022, pp: 1717–1719. International Foundation for Autonomous Agents and Multiagent Systems (IFAAMAS) (2022). https://www.ifaamas.org/Proceedings/aamas2022/pdfs/p1717.pdf
2. Alur, R., Henzinger, T.A., Kupferman, O.: Alternating-time temporal logic. J. ACM (JACM) **49**(5), 672–713 (2002)
3. Azzopardi, S., Gatt, A., Pace, G.J.: Reasoning about partial contracts. In: JURIX 2016. Frontiers in Artificial Intelligence and Applications, vol. 294, pp. 23–32. IOS Press (2016). https://doi.org/10.3233/978-1-61499-726-9-23
4. Azzopardi, S., Pace, G.J., Schapachnik, F.: On observing contracts: deontic contracts meet smart contracts. In: JURIX 2018. Frontiers in Artificial Intelligence and Applications, vol. 313, pp. 21–30. IOS Press (2018). https://doi.org/10.3233/978-1-61499-935-5-21
5. Azzopardi, S., Pace, G.J., Schapachnik, F., Schneider, G.: Contract automata. Artif. Intell. Law **24**(3), 203–243 (2016). https://doi.org/10.1007/s10506-016-9185-2
6. Broersen, J.: Strategic deontic temporal logic as a reduction to ATL, with an application to Chisholm's scenario. In: Goble, L., Meyer, J.-J.C. (eds.) DEON 2006. LNCS (LNAI), vol. 4048, pp. 53–68. Springer, Heidelberg (2006). https://doi.org/10.1007/11786849_7
7. Chatterjee, K., Henzinger, T.A., Piterman, N.: Strategy logic. In: Caires, L., Vasconcelos, V.T. (eds.) CONCUR 2007. LNCS, vol. 4703, pp. 59–73. Springer, Heidelberg (2007). https://doi.org/10.1007/978-3-540-74407-8_5
8. Chockler, H.: Causality and responsibility for formal verification and beyond. In: CREST@ETAPS 2016. EPTCS, vol. 224, pp. 1–8 (2016). https://doi.org/10.4204/EPTCS.224.1

9. Chockler, H., Halpern, J.Y.: Responsibility and blame: a structural-model approach. In: Gottlob, G., Walsh, T. (eds.) IJCAI-03, Proceedings of the Eighteenth International Joint Conference on Artificial Intelligence, Acapulco, Mexico, 9-15 August 2003, pp. 147–153. Morgan Kaufmann (2003). http://ijcai.org/Proceedings/03/Papers/021.pdf

10. Chockler, H., Halpern, J.Y.: Responsibility and blame: a structural-model approach. J. Artif. Intell. Res. **22**, 93–115 (2004)

11. Friedenberg, M., Halpern, J.Y.: Blameworthiness in multi-agent settings. In: Proceedings of the AAAI Conference on Artificial Intelligence vol. 33, no. 01, pp. 525–532 (2019). https://doi.org/10.1609/aaai.v33i01.3301525

12. Halpern, J.Y.: Cause, responsibility and blame: a structural-model approach. Law, Probab. Risk **14**(2), 91–118 (2015)

13. Halpern, J.Y., Kleiman-Weiner, M.: Towards formal definitions of blameworthiness, intention, and moral responsibility. In: AAAI/IAAI/EAAI 2018. AAAI Press (2018)

14. Jackson, F.: On the semantics and logic of obligation. Mind **94**(374), 177–195 (1985)

15. Lorini, E., Longin, D., Mayor, E.: A logical analysis of responsibility attribution: emotions, individuals and collectives. J. Logic Comput. **24**(6), 1313–1339 (2013). https://doi.org/10.1093/logcom/ext072

16. McNamara, P.: Deontic logic. In: Gabbay, D.M., Woods, J. (eds.) Logic and the Modalities in the Twentieth Century, Handbook of the History of Logic, vol. 7, pp. 197–288. Elsevier (2006). https://doi.org/10.1016/S1874-5857(06)80029-4

17. Penczek, W., Lomuscio, A.: Verifying epistemic properties of multi-agent systems via bounded model checking. In: Proceedings of the Second International Joint Conference on Autonomous Agents and Multiagent Systems, pp. 209–216. AAMAS 2003, Association for Computing Machinery, New York, NY, USA (2003). https://doi.org/10.1145/860575.860609

18. Prisacariu, C., Schneider, G.: $\mathcal{CL}$: an action-based logic for reasoning about contracts. In: Ono, H., Kanazawa, M., de Queiroz, R. (eds.) WoLLIC 2009. LNCS (LNAI), vol. 5514, pp. 335–349. Springer, Heidelberg (2009). https://doi.org/10.1007/978-3-642-02261-6_27

19. Raimondi, F., Lomuscio, A.: Automatic verification of deontic properties of multi-agent systems. In: Lomuscio, A., Nute, D. (eds.) DEON 2004. LNCS (LNAI), vol. 3065, pp. 228–242. Springer, Heidelberg (2004). https://doi.org/10.1007/978-3-540-25927-5_15

20. Shea-Blymyer, C., Abbas, H.: A deontic logic analysis of autonomous systems' safety. In: HSCC 2020, pp. 26:1–26:11. ACM (2020). https://doi.org/10.1145/3365365.3382203

21. Von Wright, G.H.: Deontic logic. Mind **60**(237), 1–15 (1951)

Store Locally, Prove Globally

Nadine Karsten and Uwe Nestmann[(✉)] [ID]

Technische Universität Berlin, Berlin, Germany
{n.karsten,uwe.nestmann}@tu-berlin.de

Abstract. The use of message-passing process calculi for the verification of distributed algorithms requires support for state-based reasoning that goes beyond their traditional action-based style: knowledge about (local) states is at best provided implicitly. Therefore, we propose a distributed process calculus with locations, the units of distribution, which we equip with explicit state information in the form of memories. On top, we provide a simple formal model for location failure and failure detection such that we can deal with the verification of *fault-tolerant* distributed algorithms. We exhibit the use of our calculus by formalizing a simple algorithm to solve Distributed Consensus and prove its correctness. The proof exploits global invariants by direct access to the local memories.

1 Introduction

Distributed Algorithms. Traditionally [17], distributed algorithms are often described by means of pseudo code for its local processes: sequences of statements may manipulate local variables or trigger the exchange of messages with other participating processes. The following code [23, 9] describes the intended behavior of a single so-called *participant* i (one out of n) which is meant to solve the problem of Distributed Consensus [17] in a system where processes may fail.

```
x_i := input;
for r := 1 to n do { if r = i then  broadcast x_i;
                     if alive(p_r) then  x_i := input from broadcast };
output x_i;
```

An understanding of such a distributed algorithm requires to precisely fix the underlying assumptions of the system model, e.g., the meaning of send (broadcast) and receive (input) actions in the context of failures. In the above algorithm, an essential ingredient is the alive-test whose passing is subject to subtle guarantees. In the following, we explain the intuition behind alive-tests in the context of fault tolerance and the correctness of Distributed Consensus in more detail.

Fault Tolerance. In the so-called *fail-stop* model of distributed systems, processes may fail; and when they do so, they do not recover from this state. A failed process does no longer contribute to the system evolution, i.e., it can neither

E. Ábrahám et al. (Eds.): ICTAC 2023, LNCS 14446, pp. 351–369, 2023.
https://doi.org/10.1007/978-3-031-47963-2_21

send nor receive messages. A process that does not fail in a run, is called *correct* (in that run). Failure *detection* provides processes with the permission to *suspect* other processes to *have failed* and, thus, to no longer wait for their messages to arrive. Perfect (i.e., always reliable) failure detection is not implementable in purely asynchronous systems, since it is impossible to distinguish the processes that have failed from those that are just slow. Here, Chandra and Toueg [6] proposed the concept of *unreliable* failure detection, whose degree of reliability is expressed by means of temporal constraints on runs. For example, for the above Consensus algorithm, a property called *Weak Accuracy* suffices: "*Some* correct process is never suspected by *any* (correct) process".

Correctness. Specifications for distributed algorithms typically consist of properties of some temporal logic flavor that capture the intended safety and liveness guarantees. For Distributed Consensus, all participants shall agree on the decision for some value, while every participant starts with a private input value as proposal. In the above algorithm, this input value is initially assigned to the local variable x_i, which may then be updated due to knowledge acquired by learning about the values kept by other participants via communication. Three temporal properties then capture in how far an algorithm works correctly. • *Validity*: Every decision must be for some initial proposal. • *Agreement*: No two correct processes decide differently. • *Termination*: Every correct process eventually decides. The verification of these properties is dominated by *state-based reasoning* techniques, often referring to global state invariants about the values that are memorized in the respective local variables x_i of every (alive) participant.

In the above example algorithm, each participant gets its turn to propose a value in the role of the *coordinator* of "its" round. In every other round, each participant is to adopt the value proposed by *that* round's coordinator ... unless it cannot detect that it is still "alive". The algorithm satisfies Termination, as it runs a for-loop and never deadlocks. It satisfies Validity, as values are never invented, but only passed on. It satisfies Agreement, as (at least) in the round of the process that—by Weak Accuracy—is *never* suspected, every other process will have to adopt this proposal. Afterwards, there is no way to decide otherwise.

Using Process Calculi. Process calculi provide a wealth of proof methods and their syntactic nature allows for concise formal models that are nevertheless close to executable code in programming languages. A great variety of process calculi have been developed in the past, most of them for general purposes, some of them rather domain-specific. In the above case, the domain prompts two choices: (i) It is natural to employ *distributed* process calculi [12], where so-called *locations* represent units of distribution, possibly subject to failure. (ii) As message-passing models are prevalent for distributed systems, it is obvious to also use *message passing calculi*, as opposed to distributed process calculi that are based on the migration among and within so-called ambients [5].

Most of the existing process calculi (often descendants of CSP [13], CCS [19], ACP [3], or the π-calculus family [20]), however, are based on notions of action, thus essentially supporting just *action-based reasoning*. The main observations in the above-mentioned attempts to use process calculi to verify distributed algorithms are that (i) even if action-based reasoning—often using bisimulation techniques—is employed on the outside, it still heavily relies on state-based reasoning inside to construct the required bisimulations [9], and (ii) classical process calculi do not at all support state-based reasoning. This was also the main problem in [22, 15], where the respective authors applied process calculus machinery to the specification and verification of fault-tolerant algorithms that solve Distributed Consensus. In [24], the authors propose a method to systematically (re)construct state information for the reachable global states of an example Distributed Consensus algorithm (which was formalized in a tailor-made process calculus) and to capture this information within a dedicated data structure outside of the calculus. The lesson learned from [24] was that this method is too tedious and highly error-prone; it simply did not scale. This is the motivation to, instead of reconstructing implicit state information, make it explicit from the outset and provide linguistic support and structure within the process calculus itself. In this paper, we report on some of our recent results in this endeavor.

Our Approach. We use a reasonably standard and widespread notion of memory: mappings from variables to values. In our calculus, processes are threads that are associated with its local memories. Threads may declare variables and assign the value of complex expressions to them, resulting in updates to their own memory. Threads can be defined recursively, and they may run concurrently. In a fault-tolerant scenario, locations are "named processes" such that failures can be named. Parallel processes, together with "message in transit", form networks.

In the operational semantics of our calculi, we let transitions operate between structural equivalence classes (equipped with some convenient congruence properties) of states. In a fault-tolerant scenario, global configurations keep track of failures and their detection. Executions of failure-aware networks, and their reachable configurations, can be analyzed via induction on transition sequences.

Related Work. Next to the above-mentioned work [22, 15, 9] using process calculi, we also used a state-machine approach [14], which suffers from the fact its global view on algorithms slightly obfuscating the locality of behaviors.

There are only few other related approaches using process calculi. In several contexts, process calculi have been equipped with notions of location or locality [4, 12 ,5], but there they have different meaning; in particular, locations were not equipped with memories. In calculi with reversibility (e.g., [7]), process-local memories are used to store back-tracking information, i.e., a history of steps of a process that led it to the current state, which can be exploited to undo these steps in a causally consistent manner. Closest to our approach is the work of Garavel [10] on LNT, which is a programming language in the spirit of LOTOS that was developed to be easier to use for engineers [11]. Our treatment of write-many variables, which is uncommon for most process calculi, was partly inspired by them. However, the context of LOTOS/LNT is different from our distributed world, as it mainly addresses concurrent algorithms without support for fault-tolerance. More detailed comparisons are found later on in Sect. 3.

Structure and Contributions. In Sect. 2, we introduce memories and expression evaluation. In Sect. 3, we define syntax and semantics of a novel calculus of distributed processes that dispose of local memories. We provide a reasonably simple operational semantics for this calculus and discuss the impact of α-conversion arising from the role of memories as binders for variables. In Sect. 4, we equip the calculus with awareness for locations and failures, which allows for completely new ways to model messages in transit and to deal with failure suspicions. In Sect. 5, we demonstrate the use of the calculus in a case study, where the advantage of direct access to local memories of processes is apparent. In Sect. 6, we summarize our contributions and conclude with a glimpse on future work.

2   Memories

We employ the widely-used idea that *states*, in the simplest possible way, are just variable assignments, which are often also called *memories*. This follows the tradition of research on state-based reasoning (see the ABZ conference series [2]).

We assume a set $\mathbb{V}$ of *values* v, for example, booleans or natural numbers. We also assume a countably infinite set $\mathcal{X}$ of *variables* x. A *memory* is modeled as a total function $M : \mathcal{X} \to \mathbb{V} \cup \{\top, \bot\}$, by which variables may be associated with values or otherwise have the status of being just *initialized* ($\top$) or *undefined* ($\bot$). The set $\mathrm{dom}(M) \triangleq \{x \in \mathcal{X} \mid M(x) \neq \bot\}$ denotes all variables *defined* in M. Accordingly, $M_\bot$ denotes an initial memory, thus without any defined variables.

By their mutable nature, memories may be *updated*, which can be defined as follows: a memory $M\langle x \mapsto \mathsf{w}\rangle$, where x is updated to map to $\mathsf{w} \in \mathbb{V} \cup \{\top\}$, behaves just like memory M unless we access the entry of the updated variable x:

$$M\langle x \mapsto \mathsf{w}\rangle(y) \triangleq \begin{cases} \mathsf{w} & \text{if } x = y \\ M(y) & \text{if } x \neq y \end{cases}$$

Note that also the cases with $M(y) \in \{\top, \bot\}$ are properly covered.

We assume a set $\mathcal{E}$ of *expressions* e with $\mathbb{V} \cup \mathcal{X} \subseteq \mathcal{E}$. One may consider arbitrarily complex expressions with vectors and function symbols, as given by:

$$e ::= \mathsf{v} \mid x \mid (e, \ldots, e) \mid \mathsf{f}(e)$$

The intended application will decide the respective range of allowed expressions.

We define the set $\mathrm{fv}(e)$ of *(free) variables of* e inductively by $\mathrm{fv}(\mathsf{v}) \triangleq \emptyset$, $\mathrm{fv}(x) \triangleq \{x\}$, $\mathrm{fv}((e_1, \ldots, e_n)) \triangleq \bigcup_{i \in \{1, \ldots, n\}} \mathrm{fv}(e_i)$, and $\mathrm{fv}(\mathsf{f}(e)) \triangleq \mathrm{fv}(e)$.

We assume that expressions can be "reduced" to values by terminating computations. As expressions $e \in \mathcal{E}$ may contain variables, we should *evaluate* them within the context of a memory M with $\mathrm{fv}(e) \subseteq \mathrm{dom}(M)$. We let the function $\mathrm{fetch}_M : \mathcal{E} \to \mathcal{E} \cup \{\bot\}$ for memory M replace the variables in $\mathrm{fv}(e)$ with their M-value; if a variable is only initialized, the result will yield undefined (see Definition 3 in the Appendix). To model the evaluation of expressions that include function symbols f, we assume a homomorphic function $\mathrm{eval}(\cdot) : \mathcal{E} \cup \{\bot\} \to \mathbb{V} \cup \{\bot\}$

to be employed *after* fetch$_M(e)$ has fetched from M—if possible—current values for the variables contained in e. The obvious idea then is that eval applies the semantics of each application of the function symbol f. Thus, we define eval$_M(e) \triangleq$ eval(fetch$_M(e)$).

3   A Distributed Process Calculus with Local Memories

As we intend to use this calculus in the context of *distributed* systems, we have to rely on a concept of distributable units. We propose to use *threads* that dispose of their own private memory, which we call *processes*, as the units of distribution. In physically distributed systems, messages take time to travel from one process to another. Therefore, the *asynchronous* variant of message passing is to be preferred, in which send and receive actions are decoupled, as they cannot happen at the same time. Causally evident, send actions must always occur strictly before their corresponding receive action, which we model via a representation of "messages in travel". All local memory states together with all messages in travel then provide us with the global state of a system.

In this section, we fix all of the these concepts as a calculus with two-level syntax for threads and (networks of distributed) processes.

In our calculus, the standard issues of bindings of variables as well as the notion of α-conversion inevitably pop up and get proper treatment. Note in advance that this treatment is just necessary in order to provide a sound operational semantics for the calculus. When it comes to the use of the calculus for verification, we better avoid the need for α-conversion *during* executions.

Syntax. We assume the set $\mathcal{X}$ of variables, the set $\mathbb{V}$ of values, and the set $\mathcal{E}$ of expressions with $\mathcal{X} \cup \mathbb{V} \subseteq \mathcal{E}$. Let $\mathbb{B} = \{t, f\}$ be the set of booleans with $\mathbb{B} \subseteq \mathbb{V}$. Let $\mathbb{C} \subseteq \mathbb{V}$ denote the set of available channels where $c \in \mathcal{E}$ is a metavariable for an expression that has to be evaluated to a channel $c \in \mathbb{C}$.

We use $\wr \cdot \int$ to denote multisets/bags and $\uplus$ to denote their disjoint union.

The following figure defines the syntax of our calculus with local memories. The right column represents designators for the respective syntactic categories.

$O ::= \emptyset \mid \wr \overline{c}\langle e \rangle \int \mid O \uplus O$	outgoing bag	
$\cancel{E} ::= \emptyset \mid \wr \overline{c}\langle v \rangle \int \mid \cancel{E} \uplus \cancel{E}$	message aether	$\cancel{E}$
$\mu ::= \text{var } x \mid \langle x := e \rangle \mid c(x) \mid O$	actions	$\mathcal{A}$
$G ::= \mathbf{0} \mid \mu.T \mid G + G$	guards	$\mathcal{G}$
$T ::= G \mid \text{if } e \text{ then } T \text{ else } T \mid I^{x_1,\dots,x_n} \mid T \mid T$	threads	$\mathcal{T}$
$P ::= [M \triangleleft T]$	processes	$\mathcal{P}$
$N ::= P \mid \cancel{E} \mid N \| N$	networks	$\mathcal{N}$

The syntax defines two layers, threads ($\mathcal{T}$) and networks ($\mathcal{N}$).

We first explain threads T, which assemble guards G, which in turn perform actions μ. Action var x *declares* variable x, action $\langle x := e \rangle$ *assigns* (the value of) expression e to variable x, action $c(x)$ receives a value over a channel c to store it in variable x; messages $\bar{c}\langle e \rangle$ that each send some payload e over some channel c are collected in action O which resembles a multicast operation sending a multiset of messages in one go. A guard G can be $\mathbf{0}$ which does nothing, an action prefix $\mu.T$, or an (external) choice $G + G$. Threads can be guards G, conditionals if e then T else T, or refer to *thread identifiers* $I \in \mathcal{I}$ that are equipped with a list of variables $x_1, \ldots, x_n$ for which they need access. We require a defining equation $I^{x_1, \ldots, x_n} \stackrel{\text{def}}{=} G$ with $\mathrm{fv}(G) \subseteq \{x_1, \ldots, x_n\}$ (see Definition 1) for every used thread identifier. Threads may also run in parallel $T \mid T$.

A *process* $[M \triangleleft T]$ associates a memory M (introduced in Sect. 2) with a thread T. Multisets $\mathbb{E}$ collect messages $\bar{c}\langle v \rangle$ in travel, where c and v $\in \mathbb{V}$ are concrete channels and values, respectively, as determined by expression evaluation. A *network* N is composed of parallel processes together with the message aether.

Our calculus allows for *concurrent* threads *within* processes. This is often required, because concurrent activities support a natural modeling principle for node-local code of distributed algorithms. Unless restrictions are imposed, the memory M is *shared*. For example, in process $[M \triangleleft T_1 \mid T_2]$, both T_1 and T_2 have access to the memory M and can manipulate its variables, i.e., both threads can declare new variables and assign values to them. Thus, we get the usual and well-known problems of potentially competing reads and writes, which we do not intend to repeat in this paper. We also do not intend to discuss potential solutions to race conditions. We do, however, intend to be precise about the semantic implications of such an extension concerning variable bindings.

Binders. Our calculus contains *two* binders for variables. (i) The thread var $x.T$ acts as a binder for x with scope T. (ii) The process $[M \triangleleft T]$ acts as a binder for the variables in $\mathrm{dom}(M)$ with scope T. As usual, we must carefully deal with free and bound variables. This can be done in a mostly straightforward way.

Definition 1 (Bound and Free Variables). *We define the functions* bv/fv *on actions, threads and processes as follows. For actions:*

$$\mathrm{bv}(\mu) \triangleq \begin{cases} \{x\} & \textit{if } \mu = \mathrm{var}\, x \\ \emptyset & \textit{otherwise} \end{cases} \qquad \mathrm{fv}(\mu) \triangleq \begin{cases} \{x\} \cup \mathrm{fv}(e) & \textit{if } \mu = \langle x := e \rangle \\ \{x\} \cup \mathrm{fv}(c) & \textit{if } \mu = c(x) \\ \bigcup_{\bar{c}\langle e \rangle \in O} \mathrm{fv}((c, e)) & \textit{if } \mu = O \\ \emptyset & \textit{otherwise} \end{cases}$$

For threads, the full version can be consulted as Definition 4 in the Appendix. Here, we just point out the case for identifiers:

$$\mathrm{bv}(I^{x_1, \ldots, x_n}) \triangleq \emptyset \qquad\qquad \mathrm{fv}(I^{x_1, \ldots, x_n}) \triangleq \{x_1, \ldots, x_n\}$$

The other cases are defined homomorphically.

For processes, the interpretation of memories as binders yields:

$$\mathrm{bv}([M \triangleleft T]) \triangleq \mathrm{bv}(T) \cup \mathrm{dom}(M)$$
$$\mathrm{fv}([M \triangleleft T]) \triangleq \mathrm{fv}(T) \setminus \mathrm{dom}(M)$$

A variable x is called fresh w.r.t. process P *if* $x \notin \mathrm{bv}(P) \cup \mathrm{fv}(P)$. *An occurrence of a variable is* bound *if it occurs within the scope of a binder for it. (Note that* var $x.T$ *is a binder for x, so the x in "var x" itself does* not *qualify as an occurrence of x.) An occurrence of a variable is* free *if it is not bound.*

For example, in thread (var $x.T_1 \mid \langle x := e \rangle.T_2$), variable x is both free and bound, as $x \in \mathrm{bv}(\mathrm{var}\, x.T_1)$ and $x \in \mathrm{fv}(\langle x := e \rangle.T_2)$.

As usual, we may employ the concept of α-*conversion* to identify processes that only differ in the concrete naming of variables. Likewise, we may rename bound variables, when needed, by consistently replacing all bound occurrences together with the respective binders with appropriately fresh variables. We write $T_1 =_\alpha T_2$, if T_1 and T_2 differ only in consistent renamings of var-bound variables.

Here, we also apply this principle to processes $[M \triangleleft T]$. We may rename variables in T that are bound by M with fresh variables: We do so by consistently replacing them in M—i.e., in $\mathrm{dom}(M)$, as the values associated by M do *not* contain variables—together with all of the respective bound occurrences in T. Formally, replacing a binding for x in M (i.e., with $x \in \mathrm{dom}(M)$) by a binding for a sufficiently fresh y to the M-value of x, can be defined as

$$\{y/x\}M \triangleq (M{\upharpoonright}_{\mathrm{dom}(M) \setminus \{x\}}) \langle y \mapsto M(x) \rangle$$

by first removing the binding for x ($M{\upharpoonright}_{\mathrm{dom}(M) \setminus \{x\}}$), then updating $\langle y \mapsto M(x) \rangle$. Let $\{y/x\}T$ denotes the standard substitution of free occurrences of x in T with y. Assuming $x \in \mathrm{dom}(M)$ and y fresh for $[M \triangleleft T]$, we then define:

$$[M \triangleleft T] =_\alpha [\, \{y/x\}M \triangleleft \{y/x\}T \,]$$

The reflexive, symmetric and transitive closure of $=_\alpha$ is of course an equivalence. As it just involves consistent in-place renamings of variables, it also satisfies congruence properties. For example, we define $[M \triangleleft T] =_\alpha [M \triangleleft T']$ if $T =_\alpha T'$.

Sanity Conventions. Processes shall provide sufficient knowledge about their local variables. Therefore, a process P is called *closed* if $\mathrm{fv}(P) = \emptyset$. It is practically useful to always require closedness, as the intuitive meaning of an "open" process referring to free variables would be rather dubious: Where should such variables, not bound to their process, refer to? We generalize closedness of processes to networks by stating: A network N is called *legal*, if all its processes are closed.

For verification purposes, we use memories with the intention to access specifically-named local variables. Allowing the application of α-conversion during the course of execution obviously defeats this purpose.[1] Thus, we require that, in any given application, variable names will be chosen such that there is no need to refer to α-conversion when declaring new variables. One ingredient in this respect is that we only permit defining equations $I^{x_1,\ldots,x_n} \stackrel{\text{def}}{=} G$ with $\mathrm{bv}(G) = \emptyset$.

---

[1] The same problem was observed by the authors of [8] when doing invariant proofs.

$$(\text{T-Alpha})\ \frac{T_1 =_\alpha T_2}{T_1 \equiv T_2} \qquad\qquad (\text{T-Out})\ \frac{}{\emptyset.T \equiv T}$$

$$(\text{T-Par})\ \frac{T_1 \equiv T_2 \qquad T \in \mathcal{T}}{T_1 \mid T \equiv T_2 \mid T}$$

$$(\text{P-Alpha})\ \frac{P_1 =_\alpha P_2}{P_1 \equiv P_2} \qquad\qquad (\text{P-Mem})\ \frac{T_1 \equiv T_2 \qquad M \in {'}\mathcal{M}}{[M \triangleleft T_1] \equiv [M \triangleleft T_2]}$$

$$(\text{N-Chem})\ \frac{}{\mathcal{E}_1 \parallel \mathcal{E}_2 \equiv \mathcal{E}_1 \uplus \mathcal{E}_2} \qquad\qquad (\text{N-Par})\ \frac{N_1 \equiv N_2 \qquad N \in \mathcal{N}}{N_1 \parallel N \equiv N_2 \parallel N}$$

Fig. 1. Structural Equivalence[s]

$$(\text{Str})\ \frac{N \equiv \widehat{N} \qquad \widehat{N} \to \widehat{N'} \qquad \widehat{N'} \equiv N'}{N \to N'} \qquad\qquad (\text{Par})\ \frac{N \to N' \qquad \widehat{N} \in \mathcal{N}}{N \parallel \widehat{N} \to N' \parallel \widehat{N}}$$

Fig. 2. Structure I

Definition 2 (Structural Equivalence).

We define the equivalence $\equiv$ for threads $(\mathcal{T})$, processes $(\mathcal{P})$ and networks $(\mathcal{N})$ by the rules in Fig. 1.[2]

For threads, we assume that both $(\mathcal{G}, +, \mathbf{0})$ and $(\mathcal{T}, \mid, \mathbf{0})$ are commutative monoids. In addition, we include α-conversion by rule T-Alpha, *while rule* T-Out *gets rid of empty outgoing bags.*

For processes, we also include α-conversion by rule P-Alpha, *while rule* P-Mem *simply embeds thread congruence.*

For networks, we assume that $(\mathcal{N}, \parallel, \emptyset)$ is a commutative monoid. Moreover, rule N-Chem *allows us to combine and separate multisets of traveling messages.*

Let $\equiv_{\alpha\!\!\!/}$ denote structural equivalence in which rules T-Alpha *and* P-Alpha *are not allowed.*

Note that the equivalence $\equiv$ preserves the set of free variables and satisfies some useful congruence properties, due to the inclusion of the rules T-Par and N-Par. Note further that we will only consider closed processes in spite of rule P-Mem leaving this aspect open.

Operational Semantics. We define the notion of execution of networks as an unlabeled transition relation on $\mathcal{N}$. As usual, we exploit the structural equivalence relation $\equiv$ via the rule Str in Fig. 2. Rule Par allows us to focus on the actions of individual processes: these are captured by the rules in Fig. 3 and 4. Rules Decl, Assign, and Rcv are *memory-changing*. Rules Snd, True, False, and Ident are *not memory-changing*. Rules Snd and Rcv are *global-state-changing*.

---

[2] For simplicity, we use the symbol $\equiv$ with heavy overloading. The use of metavariables and the respective context will act like an implicit typing scheme.

$$(\text{Decl})\ \frac{x \notin \text{dom}(M) \cup \text{fv}(\widehat{T})}{[\ M\ \lhd\ \text{var } x.T\ |\ \widehat{T}\ ] \to [\ M\langle x \mapsto \top\rangle\ \lhd\ T\ |\ \widehat{T}\ ]}$$

$$(\text{Assign})\ \frac{x \in \text{dom}(M) \qquad \text{eval}_M(e) = \mathsf{v} \in \mathbb{V}}{[\ M\ \lhd\ \langle x := e\rangle.T\ |\ \widehat{T}\ ] \to [\ M\langle x \mapsto \mathsf{v}\rangle\ \lhd\ T\ |\ \widehat{T}\ ]}$$

$$(\text{Rcv})\ \frac{\text{eval}_M(c) = \mathsf{c} \in \mathbb{C} \qquad x \in \text{dom}(M) \qquad \mathsf{v} \in \mathbb{V}}{[\ M\ \lhd\ c(x).T\ |\ \widehat{T}\ ]\ \|\ \wr\overline{\mathsf{c}}\langle\mathsf{v}\rangle\wr \to [\ M\langle x \mapsto \mathsf{v}\rangle\ \lhd\ T\ |\ \widehat{T}\ ]}$$

Fig. 3. Local Memory-Changing Steps

Rule DECL declares a *new* variable for memory M, so $x \notin \text{dom}(M)$ is clear. We also require $x \notin \text{fv}(\widehat{T})$, as $M\langle x \mapsto \top\rangle$ is a binder for x. Note that for closed processes, $x \notin \text{dom}(M)$ implies $x \notin \text{fv}(\widehat{T})$. Rule ASSIGN evaluates expression e and updates variable x in memory M, but only if it is already defined in M. It is not allowed to reset the variable to $\bot$ (undefined) or $\top$ (initialized).[3]

Rule RCV defines the reception of message $\mathsf{c}\langle\mathsf{v}\rangle$. Just like assignment, the received value v updates variable x in memory M; we only need to further check whether expression c evaluates to channel c. Note, however, that reception may overwrite previous values; this imperative style [10] distinguishes our approach from the "classical" functional style of input, as in CCS [19].

Rule SND selects one of the messages $\overline{c}\langle e\rangle$ in the outgoing bag O; it then evaluates both c and e and checks whether they fit the requirement of resulting in a channel c and a value v. In case of success, the message is removed from O (where $\backslash$ denotes multiset removal), and its evaluated counterpart $\overline{\mathsf{c}}\langle\mathsf{v}\rangle$ is placed into the network as "message in travel".[4] Rule IDENT describes the insertion of threads via identifiers. The premises ensure that the variables $x_1, \ldots, x_n$ of I are captured—as with dynamic scoping—by the associated memory M and that no other variables are accessed from within the defined body G. The rules TRUE and FALSE for evaluating conditionals are standard.

---

[3] Our treatment of variables, the declaration and evaluation is similar to Garavel's [10] who argues that it is important to have variables not only be declared, but initialized. Garavel [10] suggests to have a static semantics check whether uninitialized variables would be used "too early". We propose to have the eval()-function take care of this: for uninitialized variables, it returns $\bot$ and prevents the application of rule ASSIGN.

[4] In the spirit of asynchronous communication, a thread T shall not be blocked by $O.T$. At least, it shall not be blocked by the non-availability of some matching receiver. Here, the potential blocking is fully caused on the sending side, as the outgoing messages must be evaluated, before the thread T may continue. We consider this OK.

$$(\textsc{Snd}) \frac{\bar{c}\langle e \rangle \in O \qquad O' = O \setminus \{\bar{c}\langle e \rangle\}}{[\, M \vartriangleleft O.T \mid \widehat{T} \,] \to [\, M \vartriangleleft O'.T \mid \widehat{T} \,] \parallel \bar{c}\langle \mathsf{v}\rangle}$$

$$(\textsc{Ident}) \frac{I^{x_1,\ldots,x_n} \overset{\text{def}}{=} G \qquad \mathrm{fv}(G) = \{x_1,\ldots,x_n\} \qquad \{x_1,\ldots,x_n\} \subseteq \mathrm{dom}(M)}{[\, M \vartriangleleft I^{x_1,\ldots,x_n} \mid \widehat{T} \,] \to [\, M \vartriangleleft G \mid \widehat{T} \,]}$$

$$(\textsc{True}) \frac{\mathrm{eval}_M(e) = \mathsf{t}}{[\, M \vartriangleleft \text{ if } e \text{ then } T_1 \text{ else } T_2 \mid \widehat{T} \,] \to [\, M \vartriangleleft T_1 \mid \widehat{T} \,]}$$

$$(\textsc{False}) \frac{\mathrm{eval}_M(e) = \mathsf{f}}{[\, M \vartriangleleft \text{ if } e \text{ then } T_1 \text{ else } T_2 \mid \widehat{T} \,] \to [\, M \vartriangleleft T_2 \mid \widehat{T} \,]}$$

Fig. 4. Local Non-Memory-Changing Steps

Example. As we require processes to be closed, let $x \in \mathrm{dom}(M)$ for:

$$[\, M \vartriangleleft \text{var } x.T_1 \mid \langle x := e \rangle.T_2 \,]$$

With $x \in \mathrm{bv}(\text{var } x.T_1)$ and $x \in \mathrm{fv}(\langle x := e \rangle.T_2)$, the occurrence of x in $\langle x := e \rangle.T_2$ is bound by M, whereas var $x.T_1$ declares x as a "private" variable with scope T_1.[5] Note how the premise of rule DECL ensures to require an α-conversion before the variable can actually be declared.[6]

The following lemma states that α-conversion and transitions get along well.

Lemma 1 (Preservation). *Let N be a legal network.*
If $N \to N'$, then N' is legal.

Proof (Sketch). Variables are never removed from memories M. They can only be changed via α-conversions, but then their bound occurrences in the associated process will be changed accordingly. Otherwise, memories can only grow.

Variables that are bound within the scope of a declaration will remain bound when rule (DECL) is applied, but then by the associated memory M.

---

[5] LNT [10] uses var-environments to delimit the scope of variables. Semantically, LNT introduces *stores* (similar to our memories) to keep track of associated values.

[6] In [10], Garavel suggests to even "prohibit shared variables" and states that in Occam [18] and LOTOS-successor LNT [11] "*a parallel composition is considered to be invalid if any of its branches may change the value of a variable used in another branch*". While Occam tries to prevent this at run time, LNT "*adds static semantic constraints that forbid at compile time all (syntactically correct) behaviors involving shared variables*" [10]. Such considerations can be added on top of our formalization.

$$\text{(TRIM)} \frac{\text{trim} \in \mathcal{L}}{\emptyset \blacktriangleright N \longmapsto \emptyset \blacktriangleright_{\text{trim}} N} \qquad \text{(FAIL)} \frac{\text{trim} \neq k \notin F}{F \blacktriangleright_{\text{trim}} N \longmapsto F \cup k \blacktriangleright_{\text{trim}} N}$$

Fig. 5. Failures

4   Location Failures and Their Detection

Syntax. We follow the approach of [21] and introduce a set $\mathbb{L} \subseteq \mathbb{V}$ of *location names*. In our calculus, we then let the processes $[M \lhd T]$ of Sect. 3 evolve into *locations* $\ell[M \lhd T]$, where $\ell \in \mathbb{L}$, so locations are simply *located processes* [12]. Conveniently, locations may also serve as a natural unit of failure.

We adapt the communication actions of Sect. 3 to become "location-aware":

- Output $\bar{c}@l\langle e \rangle$ adds the name of the intended target;
- Input $c@l(x)$ adds the name of the intended source;

where l represents an expression that is expected to be evaluated to a location name, so we should require that $\text{eval}_M(l) \in \mathbb{L}$. This has two concrete advantages: (i) Location-aware send actions fit to the intended application domain. (ii) Location-aware receive actions conveniently support suspicions. Message in travel, the elements of bags Æ, now take the form $c_{\text{src} \to \text{trg}}\langle v \rangle$, with $\text{src}, \text{trg} \in \mathbb{L}$ indicating the source and target of the message.

Structural Equivalence. We adapt the rules of Definition 2 to the extended syntax. The changes from processes to locations and the location-aware forms of communication actions and the messages in transit are orthogonal to the rules.

Operational Semantics. In order to track the failures of locations, we again follow [21] and identify a so-called *trusted-immortal* location trim that cannot fail and will never be suspected. With this abstraction, it is almost trivial to model systems that satisfy *Weak Accuracy* (see Sect. 1). We use global configurations of the form $F \blacktriangleright_{\text{trim}} N$, in which (i) $F \subseteq \mathbb{L}$ indicates which locations *have* failed (so far); (ii) trim is the dynamically determined trusted immortal; (iii) N is a network running in the context of (i) and (ii). For Weak Accuracy, it is required [21] that the very first transition of an execution randomly chooses the trusted immortal from the set of available location names. Rule TRIM in Fig. 5 shows how we represent this behavior starting out from an initial configuration. Rule FAIL then allows any location to fail at any time, unless it has already failed or is immortal. Note that, in case of a location failure, we allow that the associated memory may still be inspected in spite of the location no longer contributing.

Figure 6 embeds the steps of the (adapted) semantics of the location-free calculus into the location-aware setting. Assuming that those steps now carry a label $@\ell$ (see Figs. 8 and 9), rule N-STEP allows such steps only if their responsible location ℓ has not (yet) failed. Rule N-SUSP relies on the label $\text{susp}(k)@\ell$

$$(\text{N-STEP}) \frac{N \xrightarrow{@\ell} N' \quad \ell \notin F}{F \blacktriangleright_{\mathsf{trim}} N \longmapsto F \blacktriangleright_{\mathsf{trim}} N'}$$

$$(\text{N-SUSP}) \frac{N \xrightarrow{\mathsf{susp}(k)@\ell} N' \quad k \neq \mathsf{trim} \quad \ell \notin F}{F \blacktriangleright_{\mathsf{trim}} N \longmapsto F \blacktriangleright_{\mathsf{trim}} N'}$$

Fig. 6. Located Steps

$$(\text{L-PAR}) \frac{N \xrightarrow{\eta} N' \quad \widehat{N} \in \mathcal{N}}{N \parallel \widehat{N} \xrightarrow{\eta} N' \parallel \widehat{N}}$$

$$(\text{L-STR}) \frac{N \equiv \widehat{N} \quad \widehat{N} \xrightarrow{\eta} \widehat{N'} \quad \widehat{N'} \equiv N'}{N \xrightarrow{\eta} N'}$$

Fig. 7. Structure II

to govern suspicions: it indicates that (a thread at) location ℓ would like suspect location k to have failed. This is generously permitted, unless it applies to the trusted location trim and unless the suspector itself has failed. As a consequence, every run generated with these rules satisfies Weak Accuracy.

Figure 7 is the counterpart to Fig. 2, but now adapted to deal with location-aware labels $\eta \in \{@\ell, \mathsf{susp}(k)@\ell \mid \ell, k \in \mathbb{L}\}$.

Figure 8 contains the location-aware variants of the rules in Fig. 3. Rules L-DECL and L-ASSIGN now take place in locations as opposed to just processes. However, rule L-RCV will now only allow a thread inside a location at ℓ to receive a message $c_{\mathsf{src} \to \ell} \langle v \rangle$ if two conditions are satisfied: it must be explicitly addressed to ℓ and it also must originate from the expected source location at src.

Figure 9 contains the location-aware variants of the rules in Fig. 4. In addition, rule L-SUSP allows a thread to ignore a reception by launching a suspicion request for the intended source location of the sender. Rule L-SND differs from rule SND of Fig. 4 mainly in the formation of the message in travel: now, mes-

$$(\text{L-DECL}) \frac{x \notin \mathrm{dom}(M) \cup \mathrm{fv}(\widehat{T})}{\ell[\ M \ \triangleleft \ \mathsf{var}\ x.T \mid \widehat{T}\ ] \xrightarrow{@\ell} \ell[\ M\langle x \mapsto T\rangle \ \triangleleft \ T \mid \widehat{T}\ ]}$$

$$(\text{L-ASSIGN}) \frac{x \in \mathrm{dom}(M) \quad \mathrm{eval}_M(e) = v \in \mathbb{V}}{\ell[\ M \ \triangleleft \ \langle x := e\rangle.T \mid \widehat{T}\ ] \xrightarrow{@\ell} \ell[\ M\langle x \mapsto v\rangle \ \triangleleft \ T \mid \widehat{T}\ ]}$$

$$(\text{L-RCV}) \frac{\mathrm{eval}_M(c) = c \in \mathbb{C} \quad \mathrm{eval}_M(l) = \mathsf{src} \in \mathbb{L} \quad x \in \mathrm{dom}(M)}{\ell[\ M \ \triangleleft \ c@l(x).T \mid \widehat{T}\ ] \parallel \mathfrak{L}c_{\mathsf{src} \to \ell}\langle v\rangle\mathfrak{f} \xrightarrow{@\ell} \ell[\ M\langle x \mapsto v\rangle \ \triangleleft \ T \mid \widehat{T}\ ]}$$

Fig. 8. Located Memory-Changing Steps

$$(\text{L-Susp}) \frac{\text{eval}_M(l) = \text{src} \in \mathbb{L}}{\ell[\ M\ \triangleleft\ c@l(x).T\ |\ \widehat{T}\ ] \xrightarrow{@\ell} \ell[\ M\ \triangleleft\ T\ |\ \widehat{T}\ ]}$$

$$(\text{L-Snd}) \frac{\overline{c}@l\langle e\rangle \in O \qquad\qquad O' = O\backslash\{\overline{c}@l\langle e\rangle\}}{\text{eval}_M(c) = \text{c} \in \mathbb{C} \qquad \text{eval}_M(l) = \text{trg} \in \mathbb{L} \qquad \text{eval}_M(e) = \text{v} \in \mathbb{V}}$$
$$\overline{\ell[\ M\ \triangleleft\ O.T\ |\ \widehat{T}\ ] \xrightarrow{@\ell} \ell[\ M\ \triangleleft\ O'.T\ |\ \widehat{T}\ ]\ \|\ \langle c_{\ell\to\text{trg}}\langle v\rangle\rangle}$$

$$(\text{L-Ident}) \frac{I^{x_1,\ldots,x_n} \stackrel{\text{def}}{=} G \qquad \text{fv}(G) \subseteq \{x_1,\ldots,x_n\} \qquad \{x_1,\ldots,x_n\} \subseteq \text{dom}(M)}{\ell[\ M\ \triangleleft\ I^{x_1,\ldots,x_n}\ |\ \widehat{T}\ ] \xrightarrow{@\ell} \ell[\ M\ \triangleleft\ G\ |\ \widehat{T}\ ]}$$

$$(\text{L-True}) \frac{\text{eval}_M(e) = \text{t}}{\ell[\ M\ \triangleleft\ \text{if}\ e\ \text{then}\ T_1\ \text{else}\ T_2\ |\ \widehat{T}\ ] \xrightarrow{@\ell} \ell[\ M\ \triangleleft\ T_1\ |\ \widehat{T}\ ]}$$

$$(\text{L-False}) \frac{\text{eval}_M(e) = \text{f}}{\ell[\ M\ \triangleleft\ \text{if}\ e\ \text{then}\ T_1\ \text{else}\ T_2\ |\ \widehat{T}\ ] \xrightarrow{@\ell} \ell[\ M\ \triangleleft\ T_2\ |\ \widehat{T}\ ]}$$

Fig. 9. Located Non-Memory-Changing Steps

sage $c_{\ell\to\text{trg}}\langle v\rangle$ explicitly mentions its source ℓ and target trg. Rules L-Ident, L-True, and L-False now take place in locations as opposed to just processes.

Normalized Derivations. Due to the design of our semantics rules, every derivation of a transition on configurations $F \blacktriangleright_{\text{trim}} N$ can be normalized. Either, the root of the derivation tree is generated by one of the rules in Fig. 5; then nothing else needs to be considered, as the premises do only depend on F and trim. Or, the root is derived by one of the rules in Fig. 6. Then, the transition premise can be always be derived with an application of rule L-Str of Fig. 7. Its purpose is to rearrange the structure of N as well as the internals of its locations such that rule L-Par can be applied (possibly multiple times). The goal is to identify a *single* location $\ell[\ M\ \triangleleft\ T\ |\ \widehat{T}\ ]$, possibly together with a suitable *singleton* "travel bag" in order to enable the application of one of the rules in Figs. 8 and 9. An application of rule L-Str can support this by shifting the identified location to the left, if needed (by L-Rcv) together with a suitable message, and also shift the intended thread T to the left inside this location.

5 Case Study: Distributed Consensus

In this section, we formalize the algorithm that we presented in the Introduction within our distributed process calculus and prove that it correctly solves Distributed Consensus, i.e., that it satisfies Validity, Agreement and Termination.

As the algorithm uses booleans and natural numbers, we define our sets of expressions and values accordingly: $\mathbb{B} \cup \mathbb{N} \subseteq \mathbb{V}$. We also need operations on numbers and comparisons among them, so $\mathcal{E}$ shall include $e_1 + e_2$, $e_1 = e_2$,

$$\text{Consensus}_{(\text{input}_1,\ldots,\text{input}_n)} \quad \stackrel{\text{def}}{=}$$

$$\prod_{\ell \in \{1,\ldots,n\}} \ell \Bigg[\quad M_\perp \ \langle \text{chan} \mapsto c \rangle$$

$$\langle x \mapsto \text{input}_\ell \rangle$$

$$\langle r \mapsto 0 \rangle$$

$$\langle \text{output} \mapsto \top \rangle$$

$$\vartriangleleft \ \text{❶} \ L_\ell^{\text{chan},x,r,\text{output}} \ \Bigg]$$

$$L_\ell^{\text{chan},x,r,\text{output}} \quad \stackrel{\text{def}}{=}$$

❷ $\langle r := r + 1 \rangle$.

❸ if $r \leq n$

   then ❹ if $\ell = r$

        then ❺ $\Big(\biguplus_{\ell \neq j \in \{1,\ldots,n\}} \overline{\text{chan}}@j\langle x \rangle \Big)$. ❶ $L_\ell^{\text{chan},x,r,\text{output}}$

        else ❻ $\Big(\text{chan}@r(x) \Big)$. ❶ $L_\ell^{\text{chan},x,r,\text{output}}$

   else ❼ $\langle \text{output} := x \rangle$. ❽ 0

Fig. 10. Algorithm

$e_1 \leq e_2$ for $e_1, e_2 \in \mathcal{E}$. We assume that the evaluation function eval (see Sect. 2) takes care for ill-formed and ill-typed cases by then yielding $\perp$.

In addition, we use a single channel c for the message exchanges; as our calculus fixes source and target location names in communication actions, it will always be unambiguous for which round a message is intended by simply identifying the sender as the respective coordinator of a round: $\mathbb{C} \triangleq \{c\} \subseteq \mathbb{V}$. Likewise, we let $\mathbb{L} \triangleq \{1, \ldots, n\} \subseteq \mathbb{N}$, as this is the convention provided by the algorithm. On may (and should!) criticize the abuse of natural numbers for this purpose, which intentionally confuses location names and round numbers, but in order to remain as close to the pseudo code as possible, we follow this convention.

For the vector $(\text{input}_1, \ldots, \text{input}_n)$ of initial proposals for the n participants, the code in Fig. 10 represents the algorithm, as formalized in our calculus. We instrument the code with tags ❶ ... ❽ to refer to positions in the code. (Tag ❶ is used several times, but always with the same thread identifier).

$\text{Consensus}_{(\text{input}_1,\ldots,\text{input}_n)}$ defines a network of locations, one for each participant $\ell \in \{1, \ldots, n\}$. Each location is equipped with an initial memory, where we directly set the four variables chan, x, r, output to their initial values. Note that all participants dispose of the same channel vector. Note also that their initial memories only potentially differ in their initial proposals. We could also use dedicated var -declarations and assignment steps; the effect would be the same, but at the expense of $4 * 2 * n$ additional execution steps. Note that all locations are closed, so the defined network $\text{Consensus}_{(\text{input}_1,\ldots,\text{input}_n)}$ is legal.

On each location, the same code is run, as represented by the thread definition for $\mathsf{L}_\ell^{\mathrm{chan,x,r,output}}$. Note that the code does not include any variable declarations, so no α-conversion will ever be needed during execution. The increment of the round number (❷) together with the break condition (❸) simulate the for-loop of the pseudo code. Apart from this deviation, the code only essentially differs from its pseudo variant in that we do not need to check for "alive(p_r)", as in our calculus suspicion is, except for the trusted immortal, always allowed (❻). Note that the command broadcast x_i is explicit in our code as multiple output (❺). Here, we deviate from the pseudo code in that we have a coordinator *not* send a message to itself and then wait for its reception; therefore, we use an if-then-else instead of the two if-then constructs in the pseudo code. Finally, note that the thread is completely sequential; there are no parallel threads.

The execution of the algorithm then starts from $\emptyset \blacktriangleright \mathsf{Consensus}_{(\mathsf{input}_1,\ldots,\mathsf{input}_n)}$ with no failed processes, and with a trusted immortal yet to be determined. By the design of our semantics, every reachable configuration can be represented in a standard form, up to structural congruence $\equiv_\alpha$, as follows:

$$\emptyset \blacktriangleright \mathsf{Consensus}_{(\mathsf{input}_1,\ldots,\mathsf{input}_n)} \longmapsto^+ \; F \blacktriangleright_{\mathsf{trim}} \text{\AE} \parallel \prod_{\ell \in \{1,\ldots,n\}} \ell[\, M_\ell \lhd \mathbf{O}_\ell \, T_\ell \,]$$

where we use $\prod_{\ell \in L} \ell[M_\ell \lhd T_\ell]$ for $L \subseteq \mathbb{L}$ as abbreviation for the parallel composition of locations $\ell[M_\ell \lhd T_\ell]$ modulo associativity and commutativity.

Therefore, for every reachable configuration, we can now simply inspect (i) the messages in transit ($\text{\AE}$), (ii) the individual local states M_ℓ of all participants, and (iii) the "program counters" $\mathbf{O}_\ell$ (to be understood as a location-specific metavariable) for all participants. Using this direct access, we can now state an informative (global state) invariant. On the one hand, it is very close to the intuitive reasoning that we sketched in Sect. 1. On the other hand, it is formal and can be checked with precise reference to our operational semantics.

Lemma 2 (Invariant). *Let* $(\mathsf{input}_1,\ldots,\mathsf{input}_n)$ *be a valid vector of proposals. Let* $\mathsf{Undecided} \triangleq \{\mathsf{input}_1,\ldots,\mathsf{input}_n\}$.

If $\emptyset \blacktriangleright \mathsf{Consensus}_{(\mathsf{input}_1,\ldots,\mathsf{input}_n)} \longmapsto^+ F \blacktriangleright_{\mathsf{trim}} \text{\AE} \parallel \prod_{\ell \in \{1,\ldots,n\}} \ell[\, M_\ell \lhd \mathbf{O}_\ell \, T_\ell \,]$, *then* $\forall \ell \in [1,n]$.

$$
\begin{aligned}
\Big(\quad & M_\ell(\mathrm{r}) < \mathsf{trim} & \to \; & M_\ell(\mathrm{x}) \in \mathsf{Undecided} \\
\wedge \; & \mathsf{c}_{\mathsf{trim} \to \ell}\langle \mathsf{v} \rangle \in \text{\AE} & \to \; & \mathsf{v} = M_{\mathsf{trim}}(\mathrm{x}) \\
\wedge \; & M_\ell(\mathrm{r}) = \mathsf{trim} \wedge \ell \ne \mathsf{trim} \to \; & & \Big((\mathbf{O}_\ell \in \{❸,❹,❻\} \to M_\ell(\mathrm{x}) \in \mathsf{Undecided}) \\
& & & \wedge \, (\mathbf{O}_\ell \in \{❼,❶,❷\} \to M_\ell(\mathrm{x}) = M_{\mathsf{trim}}(\mathrm{x})) \Big) \\
\wedge \; & M_\ell(\mathrm{r}) > \mathsf{trim} & \to \; & M_\ell(\mathrm{x}) = M_{\mathsf{trim}}(\mathrm{x}) \\
\wedge \; & \mathsf{c}_{\ell \to \mathsf{k}}\langle \mathsf{v} \rangle \in \text{\AE} \wedge \ell > \mathsf{trim} \to \; & & \mathsf{v} = M_{\mathsf{trim}}(\mathrm{x}) \\
\wedge \; & M_\ell(\mathrm{r}) > n \wedge \mathbf{O}_\ell = ❽ & \to \; & M_\ell(\mathsf{output}) = M_\ell(\mathrm{x}) \; \Big)
\end{aligned}
$$

Note that we use the convention of TLA+ on the use of *conjunction lists* [16], in which the enlisted conjuncts internally have stronger operator precedence.

The invariant of Lemma 2 points out that for every participant ℓ, depending on their respective round $M_\ell(\mathrm{r})$, the content of its current proposal $M_\ell(\mathrm{x})$ can be constrained. Before round trim, not much can be guaranteed (conjunct 1), as suspicions may be applied at will. However, within round trim, it is precisely the passage of *all* non-coordinators from ❻ to ❶ that changes the situation (conjuncts 2 and 3), as none of them may suspect the coordinator trim to have failed. Afterwards, this value will be uniformly proposed by all later coordinators (conjuncts 4 and 5). In the invariant, the statements on messages in Æ just strengthen the statement in order to make the induction go through, as the information of the decision value is passed on from locations to messages in transit, from where they will be received by the target locations. Finally, note that if the conditions of the constraints are met in a configuration, then this means that a participant was non-failing for long enough in order to reach this state.

Proof (Sketch). We proceed by induction on the length of the sequence $\longmapsto^+$ (note that this induction starts after the first step to determine trim). The invariant is initially trivially satisfied, as all processes are in round 0 and $Æ = \emptyset$.

The induction step addresses

$$F \blacktriangleright_{\mathsf{trim}} Æ \parallel \prod_{\ell \in \{1,\ldots,n\}} \ell[\, M_\ell \lhd \mathbf{O}_\ell\, T_\ell\,]$$
$$\longmapsto F' \blacktriangleright_{\mathsf{trim}} Æ' \parallel \prod_{\ell \in \{1,\ldots,n\}} \ell[\, M'_\ell \lhd \mathbf{O}'_\ell\, T'_\ell\,]$$

for which we check all possibilities of deriving such a transition. Note that every derivation that results from an application of the rules FAIL (only changes F to F'), L-TRUE, L-FALSE, L-IDENT, L-SUSP (only change $\mathbf{O}_\ell\, T_\ell$ to $\mathbf{O}'_\ell\, T'_\ell$) will keep the invariant valid, as they neither change Æ nor any of the M_ℓ. The changes to the position must be checked, but are harmless (e.g., ❸ to ❹ to ❻, or ❶ to ❷). Rule L-DECL will never be applied, as there are no variable declarations in the code. Otherwise, we only have to deal with applications of the rules L-ASSIGN, L-SND and L-RCV, appearing in the following cases (in which $\ell \notin F$):

1. participant ℓ moving from ❷ to ❸: rule L-ASSIGN
2. participant ℓ moving from ❺ to (either again ❺ or) ❶: rule L-SND
3. participant ℓ moving from ❻ to ❶: rule L-RCV
4. participant ℓ moving from ❼ to ❽: rule L-ASSIGN

As an example of case 2, consider $\ell = \mathsf{trim}$ with $M_{\mathsf{trim}}(\mathrm{r}) = \mathsf{trim}$ for the first time in position ❺. If the induction step applies L-SND, then the message $c_{\mathsf{trim} \to j}\langle v \rangle$ appearing in Æ is the first one originating from trim such that for the induction step afterwards conjunct 2 must be checked. It is satisfied, as rule L-SND will use $\mathrm{eval}_{M_{\mathsf{trim}}}(\mathrm{x}) = M_{\mathsf{trim}}(\mathrm{x})$ as the payload v for this message.

As another example, consider a non-coordinator ℓ ($\neq \mathsf{trim}$) in just the round $M_\ell(\mathrm{r}) = \mathsf{trim}$ in position ❻. By induction (conjunct 3, subconjunct 1), $M_\ell(\mathrm{x}) \in$ Undecided. If the induction step applies L-RCV, then the message $c_{\mathsf{trim} \to \ell}\langle v \rangle \in Æ$ must be available. After the step, participant ℓ will be in position ❶, so the second subconjunct of conjunct 3 must be satisfied. This holds, as conjunct 2 is true in the hypothesis, because rule L-RCV updates the memory with the received v.

Note how this proof makes heavy use of the direct access to the values of local variables $M_\ell(\mathrm{r})$ for the various $\ell \in \mathbb{L}$ at each reachable configuration of an execution. After all, it is this possibility of access to local variables in our calculus that makes the proof doable and thus satisfies the title of this paper.

Theorem 1. *The algorithm of Fig. 10 solves Distributed Consensus.*

Proof (Sketch). Termination holds, as the only potentially blocking operation is in input position (❺). Participants may always suspect, though, unless they wait for trim. In this case, there will eventually be a message, as trim cannot fail.

Validity holds, as the invariant never uses a value that is not in Undecided.

Agreement holds with conjunct 6 of the invariant and *Termination*.

6 Conclusion

We provide linguistic support for state-based reasoning in distributed process calculi. We do so by equipping located processes, the units of distribution in such calculi, with local memories. We develop syntax and operational semantics for this calculus in two steps, starting with a fault-free version. We demonstrate the applicability of our calculus on the formalization of a fault-tolerant algorithm to solve Distributed Consensus. The correctness proof highlights the proximity of our formalization with the widely-used intuitive correctness arguments.

We conjecture that our calculus (or slight extensions of it) is applicable to the large class of fault-tolerant distributed algorithms, which use typical pseudo code with global asynchronous message passing and reference to local variables, next to simple control structures like loops and conditionals. It is rare in this domain that (channel) name passing, as known from the (Applied) Pi Calculus [20, 1], is needed in algorithms. We see, however, no problem at all to also include a restriction operator in our calculus to govern the scope of channel names.

Further work consists of applying our approach to other Distributed Consensus algorithms and mechanizing the reasoning about the invariant and the correctness proof. In [14], we used state machines and checked their correctness in Isabelle. We plan to develop a similar formalization of our calculus.

A Definitions

Definition 3 (Fetching Values for Variables in Memories).

$$
\mathrm{fetch}_M(e) \triangleq \begin{cases} e & \textit{if } e \in \mathbb{V} \\ M(e) & \textit{if } e \in \mathcal{X} \wedge M(e) \in \mathbb{V} \\ (\mathrm{fetch}_M(e_1), \dots, \mathrm{fetch}_M(e_n)) & \textit{if } e = (e_1, \dots, e_n) \\ \mathrm{f}(\mathrm{fetch}_M(e')) & \textit{if } e = \mathrm{f}(e') \\ \bot & \textit{else} \end{cases}
$$

Definition 4 (Bound and Free Variables). *We define the functions* bv/fv *on threads as follows:*

$$\mathrm{bv}(\mathbf{0}) \triangleq \emptyset$$

$$\mathrm{bv}(\mu.T) \triangleq \mathrm{bv}(\mu) \cup \mathrm{bv}(T)$$

$$\mathrm{bv}(G_1 + G_2) \triangleq \mathrm{bv}(G_1) \cup \mathrm{bv}(G_2)$$

$$\mathrm{bv}(I^{x_1,\dots,x_n}) \triangleq \emptyset$$

$$\mathrm{bv}(\text{if } e \text{ then } T_1 \text{ else } T_2) \triangleq \mathrm{bv}(T_1) \cup \mathrm{bv}(T_2)$$

$$\mathrm{bv}(T_1 \mid T_2) \triangleq \mathrm{bv}(T_1) \cup \mathrm{bv}(T_2)$$

$$\mathrm{fv}(\mathbf{0}) \triangleq \emptyset$$

$$\mathrm{fv}(\mu.T) \triangleq (\mathrm{fv}(\mu) \cup \mathrm{fv}(T)) \setminus \mathrm{bv}(\mu)$$

$$\mathrm{fv}(G_1 + G_2) \triangleq \mathrm{fv}(G_1) \cup \mathrm{fv}(G_2)$$

$$\mathrm{fv}(I^{x_1,\dots,x_n}) \triangleq \{x_1,\dots,x_n\}$$

$$\mathrm{fv}(\text{if } e \text{ then } T_1 \text{ else } T_2) \triangleq \mathrm{fv}(e) \cup \mathrm{fv}(T_1) \cup \mathrm{fv}(T_2)$$

$$\mathrm{fv}(T_1 \mid T_2) \triangleq \mathrm{fv}(T_1) \cup \mathrm{fv}(T_2)$$

References

1. Abadi, M., Blanchet, B., Fournet, C.: The applied pi calculus: mobile values, new names, and secure communication. J. ACM **65**(1), 1–41 (2017)
2. ABZ—Rigorous State Based Methods. https://abz-conf.org/. A conference series dedicated to the use of state-based formal methods
3. Bergstra, J., Klop, J.W.: Algebra of communicating processes with abstractions. Theoret. Comput. Sci. **37**(1), 77–121 (1985)
4. Boudol, G., Castellani, I., Hennessy, M., Kiehn, A.: A theory of processes with localities. Formal Aspects Comput. **6**(2), 165–200 (1994)
5. Cardelli, L., Gordon, A.: Mobile ambients. Theor. Comput. Sci. **240**(1), 177–213 (2000)
6. Chandra, T.D., Toueg, S.: Unreliable failure detectors for reliable distributed systems. J. ACM **43**(2), 225–267 (1996)
7. Danos, V., Krivine, J.: Reversible communicating systems. In: Gardner, P., Yoshida, N. (eds.) CONCUR 2004. LNCS, vol. 3170, pp. 292–307. Springer, Heidelberg (2004). https://doi.org/10.1007/978-3-540-28644-8_19
8. Fehnker, A., van Glabbeek, R.J., Höfner, P., McIver, A., Portmann, M., Tan, W.L.: A process algebra for wireless mesh networks used for modelling, verifying and analysing AODV (2013). http://arxiv.org/abs/1312.7645. See also ESOP 2012
9. Francalanza, A., Hennessy, M.: A fault tolerance bisimulation proof for consensus (extended abstract). In: De Nicola, R. (ed.) ESOP 2007. LNCS, vol. 4421, pp. 395–410. Springer, Heidelberg (2007). https://doi.org/10.1007/978-3-540-71316-6_27
10. Garavel, H.: Revisiting sequential composition in process calculi. J. Log. Algebraic Methods Program. **84**(6), 742–762 (2015)

11. Garavel, H., Lang, F., Serwe, W.: From LOTOS to LNT. In: Katoen, J.-P., Langerak, R., Rensink, A. (eds.) ModelEd, TestEd, TrustEd. LNCS, vol. 10500, pp. 3–26. Springer, Cham (2017). https://doi.org/10.1007/978-3-319-68270-9_1

12. Hennessy, M.: A Distributed Pi-Calculus. Cambridge University Press, Cambridge (2007)

13. Hoare, C.A.R.: Communicating Sequential Processes. Prentice-Hall, Hoboken (1985)

14. Küfner, P., Nestmann, U., Rickmann, C.: Formal verification of distributed algorithms. In: Baeten, J.C.M., Ball, T., de Boer, F.S. (eds.) TCS 2012. LNCS, vol. 7604, pp. 209–224. Springer, Heidelberg (2012). https://doi.org/10.1007/978-3-642-33475-7_15

15. Kühnrich, M., Nestmann, U.: On process-algebraic proof methods for fault tolerant distributed systems. In: Lee, D., Lopes, A., Poetzsch-Heffter, A. (eds.) FMOODS/-FORTE -2009. LNCS, vol. 5522, pp. 198–212. Springer, Heidelberg (2009). https://doi.org/10.1007/978-3-642-02138-1_13

16. Lamport, L.: Specifying Systems. Addison-Wesley Professional, Boston (2002)

17. Lamport, L., Lynch, N.: Distributed computing: models and methods. In: van Leeuwen, J. (ed.) Handbook of Theoretical Computer Science, vol. B: Formal Models and Semantics, chap. 18, pp. 1157–1199. Elsevier (1990)

18. May, D.: Occam. SIGPLAN Not. 18(4), 69–79 (1983). https://doi.org/10.1145/948176.948183

19. Milner, R.: Communication and Concurrency. Prentice Hall, Hoboken (1989)

20. Milner, R.: Communicating and Mobile Systems: The π-Calculus. Cambridge University Press, Cambridge (1999)

21. Nestmann, U., Fuzzati, R.: Unreliable failure detectors via operational semantics. In: Saraswat, V.A. (ed.) ASIAN 2003. LNCS, vol. 2896, pp. 54–71. Springer, Heidelberg (2003). https://doi.org/10.1007/978-3-540-40965-6_5

22. Nestmann, U., Fuzzati, R., Merro, M.: Modeling consensus in a process calculus. In: Amadio, R., Lugiez, D. (eds.) CONCUR 2003. LNCS, vol. 2761, pp. 399–414. Springer, Heidelberg (2003). https://doi.org/10.1007/978-3-540-45187-7_26

23. Tel, G.: Introduction to Distributed Algorithms. Cambridge University Press, Cambridge (1994)

24. Wagner, C., Nestmann, U.: States in process calculi. In: Borgström, J., Crafa, S. (eds.) Proceedings of EXPRESS/SOS 2014. EPTCS, vol. 160, pp. 48–62 (2014). https://doi.org/10.4204/EPTCS.160.6

Denotational Semantics for Symbolic Execution

Erik Voogd[(✉)] [iD], Åsmund Aqissiaq Arild Kløvstad[iD],
and Einar Broch Johnsen[iD]

Department of Informatics, University of Oslo, Oslo, Norway
{erikvoogd,aaklovst,einarj}@ifi.uio.no

Abstract. Symbolic execution is a technique to systematically explore all possible paths through a program. This technique can be formally explained by means of small-step transition systems that update symbolic states and compute a precondition corresponding to the taken execution path (called the path condition). To enable swift and robust compositional reasoning, this paper defines a denotational semantics for symbolic execution. We prove the correspondence between the denotational semantics and both the small-step execution semantics and a concrete semantics. The denotational semantics is a function defined piecewise using a partitioning of the input space. Each part of the input space is a path condition obtained from symbolic execution, and the semantics of this part is the corresponding symbolic substitution interpreted as a function on the initial state space. Correctness and completeness of symbolic execution is encapsulated in a graceful identity of functions. We provide mechanizations in Coq for our main results.

Keywords: Formal methods · Programming semantics · Denotational semantics · Symbolic execution

1 Introduction

Major successes in program analysis, particularly for debugging, test case generation, and verification, have been achieved by *symbolic execution* [2–6, 8–10]: a powerful simulation technique in which symbolic states represent a wide range of concrete program states. It has only recently been formalized and proven correct [2] with respect to a concrete operational semantics.

With symbolic execution, program states associate program variables to symbolic expressions rather than concrete values. Assignments in the program can then be understood as updating the symbolic state through substitutions σ. When encountering control-flow statements guarded by Boolean expressions, no concrete choice can be made. Instead, the transition system modeling symbolic execution branches in both possible directions (theoretically using nondeterminism, in practice exploring both branches), and updates its own state by storing the Boolean guard under substitution. It thus generates the *path condition* ϕ: an aggregation of all Boolean control-flow guards under substitution. If a program

E. Ábrahám et al. (Eds.): ICTAC 2023, LNCS 14446, pp. 370–387, 2023.
https://doi.org/10.1007/978-3-031-47963-2_22

p has a finite trace in the symbolic execution system that ends in a symbolic state (σ, ϕ), then the final state of a concrete execution of p on an initial state satisfying ϕ can also be obtained by performing the substitution σ on that initial state. Thus, symbolic execution is really a way to partition program behavior into different branches, where behavior of the branch is tracked by the symbolic substitution σ, and the path conditions ϕ are preconditions specifying the branch that is taken.

Symbolic execution is a compelling technique for verification purposes: given a postcondition ψ and a terminated symbolic execution (σ, ϕ) of a program p, the formula $\phi \wedge \sigma \psi$ is a precondition for ψ. The path condition ϕ ensures that program behavior corresponds to σ, and applying σ to the postcondition ψ – this is done variable-wise – is a way of inverting program behavior corresponding to σ on the set specified by ψ—this inversion is made formal later in (3). Ranging over the (possibly infinite) set of terminated symbolic executions, taking the disjunction of all the formulae $\phi \wedge \sigma \psi$ yields the *weakest* precondition in disjunctive normal form.

All this and more can be reasoned about more effectively when symbolic execution is equipped with a denotational semantics, which is the goal of this work. To this end, two seemingly obvious, yet crucial observations are in order:

- The symbolic substitutions σ are syntactic objects representing functions that denotationally transform concrete initial states (cf. (1) in Sect. 4).
- The path conditions ϕ are syntactic objects representing subsets of the initial state space, and form a *subpartition* for it. For programs that terminate on all inputs, the path conditions form a *partition* of the input space.

It is well-understood that syntactically performing a substitution within a substitution means to do function composition. This means that symbolic execution traces can be denotationally composed by performing nested substitutions. A natural question to ask now is: what happens to the path condition when we compose symbolic execution traces?

Example. As a simple example, consider a program[1] that stipulates the behavior of the *absolute value* function for real numbers:

$$p_{\text{abs}} \equiv \text{if } (\text{x<0}) \ \{ \ \text{x := -x; } \} \text{ else } \{ \text{ Skip; } \}$$

Symbolically executing a program is usually done starting from the *initial* configuration $(\sigma_0, \top)$: the identity substitution σ_0 along with the path condition $\top$ (true) specifying the entire input space. The program p_{abs} above has two symbolic executions, both terminating. One of these executions is

$$(p_{\text{abs}}, \sigma_0, \top) \rightsquigarrow (\text{x:=-x}, \sigma_0, \top \wedge \text{x} < 0) \rightsquigarrow (\text{Skip}, (\text{x} \mapsto -\text{x}), \top \wedge \text{x} < 0)$$

where Skip is the terminated program. The first step analyzes the *if* statement, in this case picks the *true* branch, and updates the path condition accordingly

---

[1] Symbolic execution may seem to be a trivial exercise for this simple program, but note that, as programs grow, it is highly effective in several areas of program analysis.

with the conjunct $x < 0$. The second step analyzes the assignment $x := -x$ and updates the substitution accordingly. Hence, we have $(p_{\text{abs}}, \sigma_0, \top) \overset{*}{\rightsquigarrow} (\texttt{Skip}, \sigma, \phi)$ where σ and ϕ are as above, and $\overset{*}{\rightsquigarrow}$ is a reflexive-transitive closure.

Suppose now that we have analyzed two programs p and q and obtained

$$(p, \sigma_0, \top) \overset{*}{\rightsquigarrow} (\texttt{Skip}, \sigma_p, \phi_p) \qquad \text{and} \qquad (q, \sigma_0, \top) \overset{*}{\rightsquigarrow} (\texttt{Skip}, \sigma_q, \phi_q)$$

It is not straightforward from the usual small-step symbolic operational semantics how these two traces compose to the sequenced program $p \, ; q$. This is because the second execution does not continue from the configuration where the first one left off; it used the usual initial configuration. One would *expect* to obtain a symbolic trace

$$(p \, ; q, \sigma_0, \top) \overset{*}{\rightsquigarrow} (\texttt{Skip}, \sigma, \phi)$$

where σ is σ_p *within* σ_q (syntactically), meaning σ_q *after* σ_p when interpreted as functions. Regarding the path condition, one will expect to obtain $\phi = \phi_p \wedge \sigma_p \phi_q$ (i.e., σ_p applied to all the variables occurring in ϕ_q), since executing p yields ϕ_p, and executing q yields ϕ_q, but this time we started from σ_p instead of σ_0.

Contribution. These and similar facts regarding compositionality of symbolic execution traces are not easily proven using small-step transition systems. In this paper, we introduce *denotational semantics for symbolic execution* to support such compositional reasoning. Historically, denotational semantics have been very effective for compositional reasoning, enabling swift and potent reasoning about programs. Our experience in reasoning about symbolic execution for, e.g., concurrent or probabilistic programs [19], has shown us that this novel view of symbolic execution is fruitful and, for some proofs, even necessary. Example 6 in Sect. 4 illustrates how compositionality of sequencing in symbolic execution can be applied using our denotational semantics.

This new denotational semantics for symbolic execution formalizes the ideas described above: symbolic substitutions σ are interpreted as functions $|\sigma|$ on the initial state space, and the collection of path conditions ϕ are interpreted as a partition of the initial state space where execution terminates. The denotational semantics (presented in Definition 1) then *selects* the right partition ϕ_i of the initial state space, and picks the corresponding function $|\sigma_i|$. This selection process is informally denoted by $\bigoplus$ in the pictorial representation of the denotational semantics in Fig. 1 (right).

To introduce this new semantics, we use the toy language While, presented in Sect. 2, which supports unbounded loops. We describe its concrete denotational semantics as a recursively defined function. After that, in Sect. 3, we introduce our main contribution: a denotational semantics for symbolic execution. This semantics corresponds to the concrete semantics given in Sect. 2, as stated in Theorem 1. This result, which is simply a very graceful identity of functions, trickles down to correctness and completeness of the transition systems implementing concrete and symbolic execution.

In Sect. 4, we present symbolic execution in two equivalent ways: first, as done by De Boer and Bonsangue [2], we extract *traces*—finite lists of assignments and Boolean assertions—from programs, and define the substitutions and path

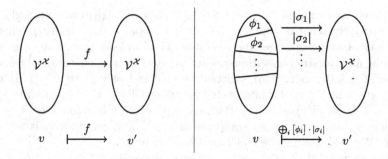

Fig. 1. Pictorial representations of denotational semantics (left concrete, right symbolic execution). $\mathcal{V}$ is the value space; $\mathcal{X}$ the set of variables

conditions on these traces. Every trace constitutes a part of the denotational semantics presented in Sect. 3, as stated in Theorem 2. Second, the substitutions and path conditions can be directly generated by a transition system—this is more in line with implementation practice. We provide a proof of correspondence between these two approaches to symbolic execution in Proposition 1. Most results up until Sect. 4 have been mechanized[2] in the Coq theorem prover [7]— they are labeled with the symbol 🐓. In Sect. 5, we discuss a straightforward extension of our work to procedure calls, with support for mutual recursion.

2   The Language While

In the language While, programs p are generated by means of assignments $\mathbf{x}:=e$ of expressions e to variables $\mathbf{x}$ (free of side-effects), sequencing, conditional branching and unbounded loops. Expressions $e \in \mathbb{E}$ are generated by operators $\mathtt{op}$ over the variables $\mathbf{x} \in \mathcal{X}$. Zero-arity operators can be considered constants (in $\mathbb{Q}$, for example). There is a distinct subset $\mathbb{BE} \subseteq \mathbb{E}$ of *Boolean expressions* $b \in \mathbb{BE}$ that are used for branching and loops.

$$e \in \mathbb{E} \quad ::= \mathbf{x}$$
$$\mid \quad \mathtt{op}(e_1, \ldots, e_n)$$

$$p \in \mathbb{P} \quad ::= \mathtt{Skip}$$
$$\mid \quad \mathbf{x} := e$$
$$\mid \quad p \, \mathbf{\mathring{,}} \, p$$
$$\mid \quad \mathtt{if} \ b \ p \ p$$
$$\mid \quad \mathtt{while} \ b \ p$$

There are at least the following three distinguished operators: the constant *truth* $\top \in \mathbb{BE}$, the unary operator $\neg$ for negation, and the binary operator $\wedge$ for conjunction.

Concrete Semantics. Variables $\mathbf{x} \in \mathcal{X}$ take values in a value space $\mathcal{V}$. To evaluate Boolean expressions $b \in \mathbb{BE}$, we assume there is a distinguished *truth value* $1 \in \mathcal{V}$. A (concrete) program state is a *valuation* $v : \mathcal{X} \to \mathcal{V}$, or $v \in \mathcal{V}^{\mathcal{X}}$ that assigns a value to each program variable. The *updated* valuation $v[\mathbf{y} \mapsto a]$ (some $a \in \mathcal{V}$) denotes the valuation v' for which $v'(\mathbf{x}) = v(\mathbf{x})$ if $\mathbf{x} \neq \mathbf{y}$ and $v'(\mathbf{y}) = a$.

---

[2] The mechanized theory is available at https://doi.org/10.5281/zenodo.8096802.

Expressions e are functions $|e| : \mathcal{V}^{\mathcal{X}} \to \mathcal{V}$ such that $|\mathbf{x}|(v) = v(\mathbf{x})$, and evaluated recursively. That is, $|\mathsf{op}(e_1, \ldots, e_n)|(v) = \overline{\mathsf{op}}(|e_1|(v), \ldots, |e_n|(v))$, where $\overline{\mathsf{op}}$ denotes the interpretation of the operator. The Boolean expressions $b \in \mathbb{BE}$ of branching and iteration conditions are interpreted as an indicator function. That is, v satisfies b (by definition), written $v \vDash b$, if and only if $|b|(v) = 1$. Boolean expressions b may thus be interpreted as *subsets* $|b| \subseteq \mathcal{V}^{\mathcal{X}}$ of the state space, where $v \in |b|$ iff $|b|(v) = 1$. The Boolean expression $\top$ is defined as $|\top| = \mathcal{V}^{\mathcal{X}}$. Negation is interpreted as set complement in $\mathcal{V}^{\mathcal{X}}$ and conjunction is set intersection. We sometimes write e or b in lieu of $|e|$ or $|b|$.

The semantics of programs $p \in \mathbb{P}$ are partial functions $f_p : \mathcal{V}^{\mathcal{X}} \rightharpoonup \mathcal{V}^{\mathcal{X}}$ defined inductively as:

$$f_p : v \mapsto \begin{cases} v & \text{if } p = \mathtt{Skip} \\ v[\mathbf{x} \mapsto e(v)] & \text{if } p = \mathtt{x} := e \\ (f_{p_2} \circ f_{p_1})(v) & \text{if } p = p_1 \,\mathring{,}\, p_2 \\ f_{p_1}(v) & \text{if } p = \mathtt{if}\ b\ p_1\ p_2 \text{ and } v \vDash b \\ f_{p_2}(v) & \text{if } p = \mathtt{if}\ b\ p_1\ p_2 \text{ and } v \nvDash b \\ f_q^m(v) & \text{if } p = \mathtt{while}\ b\ q, \text{ where } m := \min\{j \in \mathbb{N} : f_q^j(v) \nvDash b\} \end{cases}$$

Here, f^m denotes m-fold iterated applications of f (and identity for $m = 0$). Partiality of a function arises when *while* loops diverge: there may not exist $j \in \mathbb{N}$ such that $f_q^j(v) \notin b$. If p is undefined for input v, we write $f_p(v)\!\uparrow$. On the other hand, if p *is* defined for v, we write $f_p(v)\!\downarrow$.

The definition of the partial function for the while case is equivalent to a least fixed point construction using total functions, extending the codomain with *undefinedness* ($\bot$). The partial order of functions is pointwise, and the relation on $\mathcal{V}^{\mathcal{X}} \cup \{\bot\}$ is the identity unioned with $\{\bot \leq v \mid v \in \mathcal{V}^{\mathcal{X}}\}$.

Example 1. Consider the program p_{abs} from Sect. 1, and let $\mathcal{V} = \mathbb{Z}$ and $\mathcal{X} = \{\mathbf{x}\}$, so $\mathcal{V}^{\mathcal{X}} = \mathbb{Z}$. We have, e.g., $f_{p_{\mathrm{abs}}} : -2 \mapsto 2$ and $f_{p_{\mathrm{abs}}} : 42 \mapsto 42$.

3   Symbolic Execution Semantics

We now turn to the central definition in this work. The denotational semantics for symbolic execution is defined using the subset $\mathbb{F}_p \subseteq (\mathcal{V}^{\mathcal{X}} \to \mathcal{V}^{\mathcal{X}}) \times \mathcal{P}(\mathcal{V}^{\mathcal{X}})$, defined inductively below over the structure of p. The semantics of a program p will then be a piecewise definition of pairs $(F, B) \in \mathbb{F}_p$. We therefore refer to an element $(F, B) \in \mathbb{F}_p$ as a *piece* of p; F is the piece *behavior* and B is the piece *precondition*. Every piece corresponds to a symbolic execution, as we will show later.

- For *inaction*, the state remains unaltered and there is no restriction on the precondition:

$$\mathbb{F}_{\mathtt{Skip}} := \{(v \mapsto v, \mathcal{V}^{\mathcal{X}})\}$$

- An *assignment* has no restriction on the precondition, but the state is updated according to the assignment:

$$\mathbb{F}_{\mathtt{x:=}e} := \{(v \mapsto v[\mathtt{x} \mapsto e(v)], \mathcal{V}^{\mathcal{X}})\}$$

- When *sequencing* two programs p and q, range over all pairs of executions and compose them. The first precondition should be satisfied and, after executing the first component, the second precondition should be satisfied:

$$\mathbb{F}_{p\,\S\,q} := \{(F_2 \circ F_1, B_1 \cap F_1^{-1}[B_2]) : (F_1, B_1) \in \mathbb{F}_p, (F_2, B_2) \in \mathbb{F}_q\}$$

  For later use, we will also denote this structure by $\mathbb{F}_q \odot \mathbb{F}_p$.
- The two branches of an *if* statement are put together in a union of sets—the precondition is updated accordingly ($-^{\mathsf{C}}$ denotes complement):

$$\mathbb{F}_{\mathtt{if}\ b\ p\ q} := \{(F, B \cap b\ ) : (F, B) \in \mathbb{F}_p\} \cup \{(F, B \cap b^{\mathsf{C}}) : (F, B) \in \mathbb{F}_q\}$$

- In a *while* statement, the disjoint union is for every possible number of iterations m. For $m = 0$, the behavior is that of $\mathtt{Skip}$, $v \mapsto v$, and the pre-condition is the negation of the Boolean formula. Every next number $m+1$ of loop iterations takes all possible executions of m iterations, pre-composes all possible additional iterations, and updates the preconditions accordingly:

$$\mathbb{F}_{\mathtt{while}\ b\ p} := \bigcup_{m=0}^{\infty} (\Omega_{b,p})^m \{(v \mapsto v, b^{\mathsf{C}})\},$$

where $(\Omega_{b,p})^m$ denotes m applications of the mapping $\Omega_{b,p}$ from $(\mathcal{V}^{\mathcal{X}} \to \mathcal{V}^{\mathcal{X}}) \times \mathcal{P}(\mathcal{V}^{\mathcal{X}})$ to itself that pre-composes an additional iteration of the loop:

$$\Omega_{b,p} : \mathbb{F} \mapsto \{(F \circ F_p, b \cap B_p \cap F_p^{-1}[B]) : (F, B) \in \mathbb{F}, (F_p, B_p) \in \mathbb{F}_p\}$$

Example 2. For the program p_{abs} from Sect. 1, with $\mathcal{V}^{\mathcal{X}} = \mathbb{Z}$, we have $\mathbb{F}_{p_{abs}} = \{(F_1, B_1), (F_2, B_2)\}$, where $F_1 : x \mapsto -x$ and $B_1 = \mathbb{Z}_{<0}$; $F_2 : x \mapsto x$ and $B_2 = \mathbb{N}$.

The preconditions form a *subpartition* of the input space; they may not cover the whole input space due to non-termination:

Lemma 1 (Pairwise Disjoint Preconditions). *Let* $(F, B), (F', B') \in \mathbb{F}_p$. *If* $B \cap B' \neq \emptyset$ *then* $(F, B) = (F', B')$.

Proof (Sketch). By induction on the structure of p. The base cases vacuously hold because the $\mathbb{F}_p$ are singletons. The inductive steps are mechanically verified.

The lemma justifies the following definition, where a unique (F, B), if it exists, is picked:

Definition 1 (Denotational Semantics of Symbolic Execution). *Let* p *be a program. The symbolic semantics of* p *is the partial function* $\mathcal{F}_p : \mathcal{V}^{\mathcal{X}} \rightharpoonup \mathcal{V}^{\mathcal{X}}$ *defined by*

$$\mathcal{F}_p : v \mapsto \begin{cases} F(v) & \text{if } (F, B) \in \mathbb{F}_p \text{ s.t. } v \in B \\ \text{undefined} & \text{otherwise} \end{cases}$$

With this semantics, correctness and completeness of symbolic execution with respect to concrete execution are encapsulated in one elegant identity:

Theorem 1 (Concrete Correspondence 🐚). *For all p, $f_p = \mathcal{F}_p$.*

4   Symbolic Execution

The semantics described in Sect. 3 is a denotational semantics for symbolic execution systems, such as the one described by De Boer and Bonsangue [2]. We will provide a detailed proof of this in the sequel, by defining *traces through a program* and showing that each $(F, B) \in \mathbb{F}_p$ corresponds to a trace. Every such trace corresponds to a final substitution and path condition obtained from symbolic execution.

Traces form a subclass of programs that are free of branching and loops. The syntax of traces is generated by the following grammar:

$$\mathbb{T} \ni t ::= (\quad \texttt{x:=}e \quad | \quad b \quad)^*$$

They are finite lists of assignments and Boolean assertions.

Traces are extracted from a program p through a nondeterministic transition relation $\longrightarrow \, \subseteq (\mathbb{P} \times \mathbb{T}) \times (\mathbb{P} \times \mathbb{T})$. The following symbolic transition rules implement the extraction of traces; we write $\cdot$ to attach an element at the end of the list (and later also overload it to denote concatenation of traces, and furthermore for deconstruction):

$(\texttt{if } b\ p_1\ p_2, t) \longrightarrow (p_1, t \cdot b)$	$(\texttt{x:=}e, t) \longrightarrow (\texttt{Skip}, t \cdot \texttt{x:=}e)$
$(\texttt{if } b\ p_1\ p_2, t) \longrightarrow (p_2, t \cdot \neg b)$	$(\texttt{Skip ⨾ } p, t) \longrightarrow (p, t)$
$(\texttt{while } b\ p, t) \longrightarrow (p \texttt{ ⨾ while } b\ p, t \cdot b)$	$\dfrac{(p, t) \longrightarrow (p', t')}{(p \texttt{ ⨾ } q, t) \longrightarrow (p' \texttt{ ⨾ } q, t')}$
$(\texttt{while } b\ p, t) \longrightarrow (\texttt{Skip}, t \cdot \neg b)$	

Fig. 2. Inductive transition rules for trace extraction

The reflexive-transitive closure $\xrightarrow{*}$, starting from the empty trace ε, produces all finite traces through a program p:

$$\mathcal{T}_p := \{t \in \mathbb{T} : (p, \varepsilon) \xrightarrow{*} (\texttt{Skip}, t)\}.$$

The unfolding of while loops produces infinite traces (not considered in $\mathcal{T}_p$). The system is progressive; the program $\texttt{Skip}$ is the only one that cannot make a transition, and is considered the terminated program. Nondeterminism arises only from the outgoing transitions from *if* and *while* statements.

Example 3. The program p_{abs} from Sect. 1 has two traces: $(\texttt{x} < 0) \cdot (\texttt{x:=} - \texttt{x})$ and $\neg(\texttt{x} < 0)$.

If $(p, s) \xrightarrow{*} (q, u)$ then s is a prefix of u, i.e., $u = s \cdot t$ for some trace t. Moreover, $(p, s) \xrightarrow{*} (q, s \cdot t)$ if and only if $(p, \varepsilon) \xrightarrow{*} (q, t)$. Sequencing of programs is concatenation of traces: $u \in T_{p\,\S\,q}$ if and only if there are $s \in T_p$ and $t \in T_q$ such that $u = s \cdot t$.

4.1 Final Substitutions

Below we will show how to extract *substitutions* from traces. A (symbolic) substitution is a map $\sigma : \mathcal{X} \to \mathbb{E}$ from variables to expressions over variables. Expressions $e \in \mathbb{E}$ should be interpreted *symbolically*; the denotation $|e|$ will always be made explicit from now on.

The *updated* substitution $\sigma[\mathsf{x} \mapsto e]$ for some $e \in \mathbb{E}$ maps $\mathsf{x} \mapsto e$ and leaves every other variable y unchanged: $\mathsf{y} \mapsto \sigma\,\mathsf{y}$ for $\mathsf{y} \neq \mathsf{x}$. A substitution σ can be naturally extended to expressions $e \in \mathbb{E}$ by $\sigma\,\mathsf{op}(e_1, \ldots, e_n) := \mathsf{op}(\sigma\,e_1, \ldots, \sigma\,e_m)$. The identity, or *initial* substitution $\{\mathsf{x} \mapsto \mathsf{x}\}_{\mathsf{x} \in \mathcal{X}}$ is denoted σ_0.

Semantically, expression evaluation, as in $|e| : \mathcal{V}^{\mathcal{X}} \to \mathcal{V}$, extends naturally to symbolic substitutions σ. In fact, $|\sigma|$, given a concrete state $v \in \mathcal{V}^{\mathcal{X}}$, provides the evaluations of the expressions associated to the variables by the substitution. That is,

$$|\sigma| : \mathcal{V}^{\mathcal{X}} \to \mathcal{V}^{\mathcal{X}}, \quad v \mapsto (\mathsf{x} \mapsto |\sigma\,\mathsf{x}|(v)) \tag{1}$$

In other words, $|\sigma|$ is a concrete state transformer. Note that we overload the notation $|\cdot|$ here: on the left, it interprets a substitution; on the right, it interprets an expression.

We have $|\sigma_0|(v) = v$ for all $v \in \mathcal{V}^{\mathcal{X}}$, which corresponds to the behavior of Skip. Induction over expressions (not unexpectedly) shows that evaluating expressions after the semantic effect of a substitution is denotationally the same as performing the substitution within the expression:

$$(|e| \circ |\sigma|)(v) = |\sigma\,e|(v) \tag{2}$$

for every expression $e \in \mathbb{E}$ and every $v \in \mathcal{V}^{\mathcal{X}}$. This holds in particular for Boolean expressions $b \in \mathbb{BE}$, so that, for $v \in \mathcal{V}^{\mathcal{X}}$, it holds that $|\sigma|(v) \vDash b$ if and only if $v \vDash \sigma\,b$, and so

$$|\sigma\,b| = |\sigma|^{-1}[|b|] \tag{3}$$

Behaviors of traces are extracted as a symbolic substitution as follows:

Definition 2 (Trace Substitution). *The function* $\mathsf{Sub} : \mathbb{T} \to \mathbb{E}^{\mathcal{X}} \to \mathbb{E}^{\mathcal{X}}$ *is defined inductively over the structure of traces* $t \in \mathbb{T}$ *as follows:*

$$\mathsf{Sub}(\varepsilon, \sigma) = \sigma$$
$$\mathsf{Sub}(\mathsf{x} \mathbin{:=} e \cdot t, \sigma) = \mathsf{Sub}(t, \sigma[\mathsf{x} \mapsto \sigma\,e])$$
$$\mathsf{Sub}(b \cdot t, \sigma) = \mathsf{Sub}(t, \sigma)$$

The substitution of a trace t, *denoted* $\mathsf{Sub}(t)$, *is defined to be* $\mathsf{Sub}(t, \sigma_0)$.

In this definition, the notation Sub is overloaded: a trace and a substitution define a new substitution, but if only a trace is specified, the substitution is taken to be the initial one, σ_0. If $t \in \mathcal{T}_p$ (meaning $(p, \varepsilon) \xrightarrow{*} (\text{Skip}, t)$), the substitution $\text{Sub}(t)$ is called a *final substitution* of p. Final substitutions $\text{Sub}(t)$ of a program p are thus interpreted as functions $|\text{Sub}(t)|$ that transform inputs according to the trace t through p.

Example 4. The final substitution of the trace $t = (\text{x} < 0) \cdot (\text{x} := -\text{x}) \in \mathcal{T}_{p_{\text{abs}}}$ is

$$\text{Sub}(t) = \text{Sub}((\text{x} < 0) \cdot (\text{x} := -\text{x}), \sigma_0) = \text{Sub}(\text{x} := -\text{x}, \sigma_0) = \text{Sub}(\varepsilon, \sigma_0[\text{x} \mapsto -\text{x}])$$

and this is just $\text{x} \mapsto -\text{x}$. Note the distinction in font typesetting between this substitution and the function F_1 in Example 2. The substitution here is really the syntactic object $\text{x} \mapsto -\text{x}$ whose denotation is F_1. This distinction is crucial for understanding symbolic execution from a denotational perspective.

Concatenation of traces is composition of the substitutions:

Lemma 2 (Composition of Substitutions ✿). *For all traces $s, t \in \mathbb{T}$:* $|\text{Sub}(s \cdot t)| = |\text{Sub}(t)| \circ |\text{Sub}(s)|$ *as functions.*

Proof. We have $\text{Sub}(s \cdot t, \sigma) = \text{Sub}(t, \text{Sub}(s, \sigma))$ by induction on s. Also $|\text{Sub}(s, \sigma)| = |\text{Sub}(s, \sigma_0)| \circ |\sigma|$, where the interesting inductive step is

$$
\begin{aligned}
|\text{Sub}(\text{x} := e \cdot s, \sigma)| &= |\text{Sub}(s, \sigma[\text{x} \mapsto \sigma\, e])| \\
&\overset{\text{IH}}{=} |\text{Sub}(s)| \circ |\sigma[\text{x} \mapsto \sigma\, e]| \\
&\overset{*}{=} |\text{Sub}(s)| \circ |\text{Sub}(\text{x} := e)| \circ |\sigma| \\
&\overset{\text{IH}}{=} |\text{Sub}(s, \text{Sub}(\text{x} := e))| \circ |\sigma| \\
&= |\text{Sub}(\text{x} := e \cdot s)| \circ |\sigma|
\end{aligned}
$$

where, at (*), one uses $|\text{Sub}(\text{x} := e)| \circ |\sigma| = |\sigma[\text{x} \mapsto \sigma\, e]|$. Indeed, for $\text{y} \neq \text{x}$ and arbitrary input v, both sides reduce to $|\sigma\, \text{y}|(v)$, and for $\text{y} = \text{x}$, where x is the variable used in the assignment, the left-hand side reduces to $|e|(|\sigma|(v))$; the right-hand side to $|\sigma\, e|(v)$—these are equal as mentioned (2). Now

$$|\text{Sub}(s \cdot t, \sigma_0)| = |\text{Sub}(t, \text{Sub}(s, \sigma_0))| = |\text{Sub}(t, \sigma_0)| \circ |\text{Sub}(s, \sigma_0)|,$$

which was to be shown.

4.2   Path Conditions

Given a program p and a final substitution $\text{Sub}(t)$ of some trace $t \in \mathcal{T}_p$, how do we know for which inputs p behaves like $|\text{Sub}(t)|$? To answer this question, we extract a precondition from the Boolean assertions in the trace. This precondition is called the *path condition* in symbolic execution, and represents the unique part of the input space that triggers p to behave like $\text{Sub}(t)$. The Boolean conditions have to be taken under appropriate substitutions; this makes their definition somewhat intricate.

Definition 3 (Trace Path Condition). *The function* $\mathsf{PC} : \mathbb{T} \to \mathbb{E}^{\mathcal{X}} \to \mathbb{E}$ *is defined inductively over the structure of traces* $t \in \mathbb{T}$ *as follows:*

$$\mathsf{PC}(\varepsilon, \sigma) = \top$$
$$\mathsf{PC}(\mathsf{x}{:=}e \cdot t, \sigma) = \mathsf{PC}(t, \sigma[\mathsf{x} \mapsto \sigma\,e])$$
$$\mathsf{PC}(b \cdot t, \sigma) = \sigma\,b \wedge \mathsf{PC}(t, \sigma)$$

The path condition *of a trace* t, *denoted* $\mathsf{PC}(t)$, *is defined to be* $\mathsf{PC}(t, \sigma_0)$.

The notation PC is again overloaded: if only a trace is provided, the substitution is taken to be the initial one. Interestingly, PC treats assignments in the same way as Sub. Whereas Sub ignores Boolean assertions, PC uses them to generate the Boolean precondition. Being a Boolean expression, the path condition has an interpretation (denoted $|\cdot|$) as a subset of the initial state space $\mathcal{V}^{\mathcal{X}}$.

Example 5. Suppose now that p_{abs} is preceded by an assignment $\mathsf{x}{:=}\mathsf{x}{+}2$, so let $q_{\mathrm{abs}} = \mathsf{x}{:=}\mathsf{x} + 2 \,\mathring{,}\, p_{\mathrm{abs}}$. This q_{abs} has a trace $t = (\mathsf{x}{:=}\mathsf{x}{+}2) \cdot (\mathsf{x} < 0) \cdot (\mathsf{x}{:=} -\mathsf{x})$ in $\mathcal{T}_{q_{\mathrm{abs}}}$. Its path condition is

$$\mathsf{PC}(t, \sigma_0) = \mathsf{PC}((\mathsf{x} < 0) \cdot (\mathsf{x}{:=} -\mathsf{x}), \sigma_0[\mathsf{x} \mapsto \mathsf{x} + 2])$$
$$= (\mathsf{x} + 2 < 0) \wedge \mathsf{PC}(\mathsf{x}{:=} -\mathsf{x}, (\mathsf{x} \mapsto \mathsf{x} + 2))$$

and this is $(\mathsf{x} + 2 < 0) \wedge \top$.

Similar to substitutions (Lemma 2), path conditions can be composed (backwards) when traces are sequenced:

Lemma 3 (Backward-Composition of Path Conditions ●). *For all traces* $s, t \in \mathbb{T} :$ $|\mathsf{PC}(s \cdot t)| = |\mathsf{PC}(s)| \cap F^{-1}\big[|\mathsf{PC}(t)|\big]$ *where* $F = |\mathsf{Sub}(s)|$.

Proof. By induction on s, for every substitution σ, $\mathsf{PC}(s \cdot t, \sigma) \equiv \mathsf{PC}(s, \sigma) \wedge \mathsf{PC}(t, \mathsf{Sub}(s, \sigma))$, where $\equiv$ denotes the equivalence $b \equiv b'$ defined by $|b| = |b'|$. Syntactic equality fails due to extra truth conjuncts in the base case. By induction on t, one also shows that $|\mathsf{PC}(t, \sigma)| = |\sigma|^{-1}\big[|\mathsf{PC}(t)|\big]$, where one crucially uses the fact (3) that $|\sigma\,b| = |\sigma|^{-1}\big[|b|\big]$ for all b. Now

$$|\mathsf{PC}(s \cdot t, \sigma_0)| = |\mathsf{PC}(s, \sigma_0) \wedge \mathsf{PC}(t, \mathsf{Sub}(s, \sigma_0))| = |\mathsf{PC}(s)| \cap |\mathsf{Sub}(s)|^{-1}\big[|\mathsf{PC}(t)|\big]$$

A trace $t \in \mathcal{T}_p$ is *feasible* if $|\mathsf{PC}(t)| \neq \emptyset$.

Theorem 2 (Trace Correspondence ●). *Let* p *be a program. There is a one-to-one correspondence between feasible traces* $t \in \mathcal{T}_p$ *and pieces* $(F, B) \in \mathbb{F}_p$ *with* $B \neq \emptyset$.

Proof (Sketch). The bijection is $\Phi_p : \mathcal{T}_p \to \mathbb{F}_p, t \mapsto (|\mathsf{Sub}(t)|, |\mathsf{PC}(t)|)$. For all p, there are three things to show: well-definedness, surjectivity, and injectivity. Well-definedness here means $(|\mathsf{Sub}(t)|, |\mathsf{PC}(t)|) \in \mathbb{F}_p$ for $t \in \mathcal{T}_p$. These three things are proven by induction on the structure of p.

Unfeasible traces are not considered in the correspondence, because they have no semantic contribution to the program. They are moreover semantically hard to identify, because one is forced to reason about the nature of F. On the other hand, two pieces $(F, B), (F', B')$ for *feasible* traces can easily be distinguished by their path conditions, since they have to be disjoint (Lemma 1).

$$
\begin{array}{ll}
(\text{if } b \ p_1 \ p_2, \sigma, \phi) \rightsquigarrow (p_1, \sigma, \phi \wedge \sigma b) & (\mathbf{x}:=e, \sigma, \phi) \rightsquigarrow (\text{Skip}, \sigma[\mathbf{x} \mapsto \sigma e], \phi) \\
(\text{if } b \ p_1 \ p_2, \sigma, \phi) \rightsquigarrow (p_2, \sigma, \phi \wedge \neg \sigma b) & (\text{Skip} \ \mathbin{\mathring{,}} \ p, \sigma, \phi) \rightsquigarrow (p, \sigma, \phi) \\
(\text{while } b \ p, \sigma, \phi) \rightsquigarrow (p \ \mathbin{\mathring{,}} \text{while } b \ p, \sigma, \phi \wedge \sigma b) & (p, \sigma, \phi) \rightsquigarrow (p', \sigma', \phi') \\
(\text{while } b \ p, \sigma, \phi) \rightsquigarrow (\text{Skip}, \sigma, \phi \wedge \neg \sigma b) & \overline{(p \ \mathbin{\mathring{,}} \ q, \sigma, \phi) \rightsquigarrow (p' \ \mathbin{\mathring{,}} \ q, \sigma', \phi')}
\end{array}
$$

Fig. 3. Inductive transition rules for direct symbolic execution

4.3 Direct Symbolic Execution

We have extracted traces from a program and defined the final substitutions and path conditions for them. Instead, we could have extracted these directly, as is done in practice. For the rules of a transition system that does exactly this, see Fig. 3. Again, $\overset{*}{\rightsquigarrow}$ denotes the transitive closure of $\rightsquigarrow$. Note that every rule here has a corresponding rule in Fig. 2, and a simple analysis will show that both systems produce the same results:

Proposition 1 (Symbolic Execution via Traces ✿). *Let p be a program.*

- *If $(p, \varepsilon) \overset{*}{\longrightarrow} (p', t)$ then $(p, \sigma_0, \top) \overset{*}{\rightsquigarrow} (p', \mathsf{Sub}(t), \phi)$ where $|\phi| = |\mathsf{PC}(t)|$.*
- *If $(p, \sigma_0, \top) \overset{*}{\rightsquigarrow} (p', \sigma, \phi)$ then there is a trace t such that $(p, \varepsilon) \overset{*}{\longrightarrow} (p', t)$ with $\mathsf{Sub}(t) = \sigma$ and $|\mathsf{PC}(t)| = |\phi|$.*

This proposition holds in particular for $p' = \text{Skip}$, yielding a correspondence between $\mathcal{T}_p$ and pairs of final substitutions and path conditions obtained from direct symbolic execution.

Proof (Sketch). By induction on the length of the transition chains. The inductive step consists of a case analysis of all single-step transitions, which is a straightforward unfolding of definitions.

The following are immediate corollaries of Theorems 1 and 2 and the above proposition.

Corollary 1 (Correctness ✿). *If $(p, \sigma_0, \top) \overset{*}{\rightsquigarrow} (\text{Skip}, \sigma, \phi)$ then $f_p(v) = |\sigma|(v)$ for all v such that $v \vDash \phi$.*

Corollary 2 (Completeness ✿). *If $f_p(v) \!\downarrow$ then there is a symbolic execution $(p, \sigma_0, \top) \overset{*}{\rightsquigarrow} (\text{Skip}, \sigma, \phi)$ such that $v \vDash \phi$ which is unique in this property.*

Example 6. Consider the program q_{abs} from Example 5. The program p_{abs} has the two terminating symbolic executions $(\mathbf{x} \mapsto -\mathbf{x}, \mathbf{x} < 0)$ and $(\sigma_0, \mathbf{x} \geq 0)$, whose denotations are respectively $(\alpha : x \mapsto -x, \mathbb{Z}_{<0})$ and $(\mathrm{id}_{\mathbb{Z}} : x \mapsto x, \mathbb{Z}_{\geq 0})$. The assignment $\mathbf{x}:=\mathbf{x} + 2$ has one symbolic execution $(\mathbf{x} \mapsto \mathbf{x} + 2, \top)$ with denotation $(\beta : x \mapsto x + 2, \mathbb{Z})$. The denotational semantics immediately says that the sequence $q_{\text{abs}} = \mathbf{x}:=\mathbf{x} + 2 \ \mathbin{\mathring{,}} \ p_{\text{abs}}$ has two symbolic executions with denotations

$$
\begin{array}{ll}
(\alpha \mathbin{\mathring{\circ}} \beta, \ \mathbb{Z} \cap \beta^{-1}[\mathbb{Z}_{<0}]) = (x \mapsto -(x+2), \mathbb{Z}_{<-2}), \\
(\mathrm{id} \circ \beta, \ \mathbb{Z} \cap \beta^{-1}[\mathbb{Z}_{\geq 0}]) = (x \mapsto x + 2, \quad \mathbb{Z}_{\geq -2}),
\end{array}
$$

This example illustrates a more general potential of denotational semantics for symbolic execution. Indeed, consider again the two symbolic executions

$$(p, \sigma_0, \top) \overset{*}{\rightsquigarrow} (\text{Skip}, \sigma_p, \phi_p) \quad \text{and} \quad (q, \sigma_0, \top) \overset{*}{\rightsquigarrow} (\text{Skip}, \sigma_q, \phi_q)$$

from Sect. 1. Then, using the denotational semantics of symbolic executions, it follows naturally that $(p \, \mathring{,} \, q, \sigma_0, \top) \overset{*}{\rightsquigarrow} (\text{Skip}, \sigma, \phi)$ for some (σ, ϕ) with

$$|\sigma| = |\sigma_q| \circ |\sigma_p| \quad \text{and} \quad |\phi| = |\phi_p| \cap |\sigma_p|^{-1}[|\phi_q|]$$

That is, σ is denotationally equivalent to σ_p *within* σ_q – formally $\{x \mapsto \sigma_p(\sigma_q \, x)\}$ – and ϕ is denotationally equivalent to $\phi_p \wedge \sigma_p \phi_q$.

5 Extension to Procedure Calls

In this section we extend While with procedure calls. Let $P, Q, \ldots$ range over procedure names and extend the syntax of program statements with

$$p ::= \quad \ldots \quad | \quad P(\vec{e})$$

Here, $\vec{e}$ denotes a finite list $e_1, \ldots, e_n$ of expressions that are passed as arguments. They are evaluated to a list of values written $|\vec{e}|(v)$, accordingly. For a finite ordered set of variables $\mathcal{U} = \{u_1, \ldots, u_n\}$, write $\mathcal{U} := \vec{e}$ for the sequence of assignments $u_1 := e_1 \, \mathring{,} \, \ldots \, \mathring{,} \, u_n := e_n$. Its semantics $v \mapsto v[\mathcal{U} \mapsto |\vec{e}|(v)]$ is clear.

It is assumed that procedures are always declared; a *procedure declaration* $P :: p$ binds the procedure name P to the program p. A *structured program* $[P :: p]^* p$ is then a list of procedure declarations followed by a single main program statement. For notational simplicity, we assume that the names of declared procedures in a structured program are distinct and let *every* local variable in a procedure be a parameter. Moreover, *one* finite set $\mathcal{U} = \{u_1, \ldots, u_n\}$ of local variables is used for *all* procedures. Then, for a procedure declaration $P :: p$, p contains variables from $\mathcal{X}$ and $\mathcal{U}$. The main function only uses variables in $\mathcal{X}$—the set of *global* variables. $\mathcal{X}$ is disjoint from $\mathcal{U}$. Every procedure call always passes n—the size of $\mathcal{U}$—arguments $\vec{e}$ for the parameters. We use *void* procedures without return values; these can be encoded using a global return variable.

5.1 Concrete Semantics

A parameter k is used to track the recursion depth. Following the terminology of Owens et al. [15], we refer to this k as the *clock*. The clock is only instantiated by the main function and carried across different procedures, allowing for arbitrarily long chains of nested procedure calls and even mutual recursion.

Let $\mathcal{Y}$ be an infinite set of variables used to substitute the local variables $\mathcal{U}$, and let $\mathcal{Y}$ be disjoint from $\mathcal{X}$. For a procedure call $P(\vec{e})$ with clock value k, there is always a finite set $\mathcal{Y}_k \subseteq \mathcal{Y}$ of fresh variables available. We substitute $\mathcal{Y}_k$ for the local variables $\mathcal{U}$ in the body p of a procedure P to avoid overwriting local variables in calls from lower depths. This is written $p[\mathcal{U}/\mathcal{Y}_k]$. A state during procedure calls is an evaluation $w \in \mathcal{V}^{\mathcal{X} \cup \mathcal{Y}}$. Write $w = (v, u)$, where $v : \mathcal{X} \to \mathcal{V}$ is the *global* component and $u : \mathcal{Y} \to \mathcal{V}$ contains the *local* states.

The semantics $g_{p,k} : \mathcal{V}^{\mathcal{X} \cup \mathcal{Y}} \rightharpoonup \mathcal{V}^{\mathcal{X} \cup \mathcal{Y}}$ of *procedure statements p with clock value $k \in \mathbb{N}$* is defined inductively over k and p as:

$$g_{p,k} : w \mapsto \begin{cases} \quad \vdots \\ g_{q[\mathcal{U}/\mathcal{Y}_{k-1}],k-1}(w[\mathcal{Y}_{k-1} \mapsto |\overrightarrow{e}|(w)]) & \text{if } p = \mathtt{P}(\overrightarrow{e}), \ k > 0, \text{ and } \mathtt{P} :: q \\ \text{undefined} & \text{if } p = \mathtt{P}(\overrightarrow{e}) \text{ and } k = 0 \end{cases}$$

The semantics of all other cases is the same as in the concrete semantics of Sect. 2, with the exception that the clock value k is passed around; it is never altered except at procedure calls. At a procedure call, the local state is prepared, i.e., w is updated with $\mathcal{Y}_{k-1} \mapsto |\overrightarrow{e}|(w)$, and $\mathcal{Y}_{k-1}$ substitutes the set $\mathcal{U}$ of local variables occurring in q, which is the body of the procedure labeled $\mathtt{P}$. For this reason, we have either $\mathtt{x} \in \mathcal{X}$ or $\mathtt{x} \in \mathcal{Y}_k$ for all variables $\mathtt{x}$ occurring in assignments and Boolean expressions in the definitions at clock value k, since q only contains variables from $\mathcal{X}$ and $\mathcal{U}$. Hence, expressions in a local environment at clock value k are over $\mathcal{X} \cup \mathcal{Y}_k$ and can be evaluated accordingly.

We let the semantics of the main program follow that of Sect. 2, extended to procedure calls as follows: if $p = \mathtt{P}(\overrightarrow{e})$ and $\mathtt{P} :: q$ is a declaration then

$$f_p(v) := v', \quad \text{where } (v', u') = g_{q[\mathcal{U}/\mathcal{Y}_k],k}(v, u_0[\mathcal{Y}_k \mapsto |\overrightarrow{e}|(v)]),$$

Here, k is the minimum clock value such that the right-hand side is defined, and $u_0 \in \mathcal{V}^{\mathcal{Y}}$ is some initialized local state; e.g., $u_0(\mathtt{y}) = \mathtt{1}$ for all $\mathtt{y} \in \mathcal{Y}$. To take the minimum clock value k such that the computation is defined is an approach similar to while loops, where we chose the minimum integer such that the state violated the loop guard. Like before, this integer may not exist.

If a clock value *does* exist, one can choose *any* sufficiently large one:

Lemma 4. *Let p be a statement and $w \in \mathcal{V}^{\mathcal{X} \cup \mathcal{Y}}$.*

- *If $g_{p,k}(w)\uparrow$ then for all $j < k$: $g_{p,j}(w[\mathcal{Y}_j \mapsto \mathcal{Y}_k])\uparrow$.*
- *If $g_{p,k}(w)\downarrow$ then for all $\ell > k$ and $\mathtt{x} \in \mathcal{X}$: $g_{p,\ell}(w[\mathcal{Y}_\ell \mapsto \mathcal{Y}_k])(\mathtt{x}) = g_{p,k}(w)(\mathtt{x})$.*

The proof is by induction over the clock value ℓ, with base case $k + 1$, and induction over p.

5.2 Symbolic Semantics

The denotational semantics for symbolic execution of procedure call statements is presented in Fig. 4. The definition follows Sect. 3 for general statements, with the exception that a parameter k for recursion depth is passed around. For sequencing, recall the notation $\odot$ introduced in Sect. 3. The while case is an infinite union of m-fold applications of the operator $\Omega_{b,q,k}$, which is the same as $\Omega_{b,q}$ as introduced in Sect. 3, but uses $\mathbb{G}_{q,k}$ instead of $\mathbb{F}_q$.

p	$\mathbb{G}_{p,k}$
Skip	$\{(\mathrm{id}_{\mathcal{V}^{\mathcal{X} \cup \mathcal{Y}}}, \mathcal{V}^{\mathcal{X} \cup \mathcal{Y}})\}$
x:=e	$\{(w \mapsto w[\mathbf{x} \mapsto |e|(w)], \mathcal{V}^{\mathcal{X} \cup \mathcal{Y}})\}$
$q \mathbin{;} r$	$\mathbb{G}_{r,k} \odot \mathbb{G}_{q,k}$
if b q r	$\{(G, B \cap |b|) : (G, B) \in \mathbb{G}_{q,k}\} \cup \{(G, B \cap |b|^{\complement}) : (G, B) \in \mathbb{G}_{r,k}\}$
while b q	$\bigcup_{m=0}^{\infty} (\Omega_{b,q,k})^{m} \{(\mathrm{id}_{\mathcal{V}^{\mathcal{X} \cup \mathcal{Y}}}, |b|^{\complement})\}$
P($\vec{e}$)	$\begin{cases} \mathbb{G}_{q[\mathcal{U}/\mathcal{Y}_{k-1}],k-1} \odot \mathbb{G}_{\mathcal{Y}_{k-1}:=\vec{e},0} & \text{if } k > 0 \text{ where P} :: q \\ \{(\mathrm{id}_{\mathcal{V}^{\mathcal{X} \cup \mathcal{Y}}}, \emptyset)\} & \text{if } k = 0 \end{cases}$

Fig. 4. Denotational semantics for symbolic execution with procedure calls

In case $k = 0$, the function becomes undefined at a procedure call. This is reflected in the fact that the piece precondition is set to the emptyset.

The semantics of the main program statement is extended to procedure calls in a way similar to while loops. For a procedure declaration P $::$ p, we define

$$\mathbb{F}_{\text{P}(\vec{e})} := \bigcup_{k=0}^{\infty} \mathbb{G}_{p,k} \odot \mathbb{G}_{\mathcal{Y}_k:=\vec{e},0}$$

Since the resulting global state is independent of the choice of k, Lemma 1 still holds and Definition 1 is still justified.

5.3 Symbolic Execution Traces

To extract symbolic traces we simply add the rule

$$(\text{P}(\vec{e}), t) \longrightarrow (p[\mathcal{U}/\mathcal{Y}_k], t)$$

for declarations P $::$ p, where $\mathcal{Y}_k$ is the fresh set of variables that we may assume to correspond to the k-th recursive call in the denotational semantics of symbolic execution and the concrete semantics. Theorems 1 and 2 still hold for While extended with procedure calls.

6   Related Work

We have drawn inspiration from earlier formal descriptions of symbolic execution [2], where de Boer and Bonsangue proved correctness and completeness of symbolic executions with respect to an operational-style semantics modeling concrete execution. Whereas their proofs work directly by induction on the execution chains, it is interesting to note that correctness and completeness in our setting arise as straightforward corollaries of the correspondence between the denotational and concrete semantics. Moreover, de Boer and Bonsangue used substitutions to define *evaluation after substitution*; we have semanticized this by interpreting substitutions as mathematical functions on the state space $\mathcal{V}^{\mathcal{X}}$. Although crucial to our work, this semantics of substitutions is far from unexpected, as substitutions are syntactic objects describing mathematical functions. However, we feel this fact is easily overlooked when reasoning about symbolic execution. Defining a denotational semantics for symbolic execution amends this.

De Boer and Bonsangue [2] described two ways of obtaining the final symbolic substitutions and path conditions. These are exactly the two methods we described in Sect. 4. Proving that they are equivalent (Proposition 1) could not be done syntactically: the conjuncts appearing in the corresponding path conditions are different, but equivalent. Having a denotational semantics here was essential for the proof.

Kneuper [12] gives a denotational semantics of symbolic execution based on sets of sequences of symbolic states and a function extending these sequences. Steinhöfel [17, Ch. 3] describes a more general approach based on *concretization* of symbolic states. A similar approach is taken by Porncharoenwase et al. [16] who describe symbolic execution of a Scheme dialect through big-step semantics. Whereas the present work defines symbolic semantics for a language and relates them to concrete semantics, these works describe semantics for the *exploration* of symbolic states.

Owens et al. [15] mechanize what they call a *functional* big-step semantics for a toy language called FOR, which is similar to ours, but has *for* loops instead of *while* loops, and models assignments as side-effects of expressions. Their functional big-step semantics is essentially identical to our concrete semantics, and we have drawn inspiration from their work for our proof mechanizations in Coq, but our work is the first to approach *symbolic execution* from a denotational perspective.

Nakata and Uustalu [14] explored four different trace-based coinductive operational semantics for the While language: big-step and small-step, functional and relational—all of them for *concrete* execution, whereas we include *symbolic*. In the terminology of [14,15], the present work could have been titled: *Functional Big-Step Semantics for Symbolic Execution*. We deemed "denotational" more appropriate, as the purpose of our work is to elucidate the *denotation* of the syntactic objects generated in symbolic execution, and to enable compositional reasoning; this has historically been the use of denotational semantics in formal methods.

7   Conclusions and Future Work

We have defined a denotational semantics for symbolic execution as a function defined piecewise on a partition of the input space. Each part is the interpretation of the path condition in symbolic execution, and the piecewise definition on this part is the corresponding symbolic substitution, interpreted as a function on the input space. The correspondence between this denotational semantics and a concrete semantics (Theorem 1), which is a simple identity of functions, has correctness (or *coverage*) and completeness (or *precision*) of the symbolic semantics as immediate corollaries, as formulated in Corollaries 1 and 2. Having this denotational semantics allows for compositional reasoning about symbolic executions, which can be particularly unintuitive for the path condition.

These results have been mechanized in the theorem prover Coq. The proofs are all constructive; we have used the *constructive definite description axiom* (consistent but not constructively provable) to assume we can find the minimum integer regarding while loops and recursive procedure calls. This assumption is not surprising or unrealistic, as symbolic execution in practice deals with finite traces only. A reason to consider infinite symbolic executions (which we aim for in future work by using a *stream* semantics) is to allow *arbitrarily long but finite* symbolic executions.

The denotational semantics extends easily to more language constructs, such as procedures (Sect. 5). Other work [19] illustrates the use of a denotational semantics for proof techniques involving *probabilistic* language constructs such as sampling and observe statements. A denotational semantics for such language constructs are straightforward extensions of the work presented here.

A highly interesting extension of the work in this paper is to incorporate parallelization; compositional correctness and completeness of a small-step symbolic semantics for parallel programs has recently been mechanized in [11]. In a denotational setting, parallelization can be addressed by means of a trace semantics and corresponding coinductive techniques (see, e.g., [18]); furthermore, concurrency is very context-sensitive, which makes assigning a denotational (or functional big-step) semantics challenging. In future work we plan to study a trace-based denotational semantics of symbolic execution, allowing parallelization as well as non-termination. We further consider describing a language-independent approach to symbolic execution using coalgebras. This has previously been studied coinductively [13] (but without coalgebras). Finally, having both an *operational* and a *denotational* semantics, a natural follow-up question is: can we show a correspondence between our denotational semantics and an *axiomatic* semantics for symbolic execution (e.g., in the style of the rules of the KeY verification system [1, Chap. 3])? We believe such a correspondence could be used to enrich verification techniques based on symbolic execution.

References

1. Ahrendt, W., Beckert, B., Bubel, R., Hähnle, R., Schmitt, P.H., Ulbrich, M. (eds.): Deductive Software Verification - The KeY Book - From Theory to Practice. LNCS, vol. 10001. Springer, Cham (2016). https://doi.org/10.1007/978-3-319-49812-6

2. de Boer, F.S., Bonsangue, M.: Symbolic execution formally explained. Formal Aspects Comput. **33**(4), 617–636 (2021)
3. Cadar, C., Dunbar, D., Engler, D.R.: KLEE: unassisted and automatic generation of high-coverage tests for complex systems programs. In: Draves, R., van Renesse, R. (eds.) Proceedings of the 8th USENIX Symposium on Operating Systems Design and Implementation (OSDI 2008), pp. 209–224. USENIX Association (2008)
4. Cadar, C., Ganesh, V., Pawlowski, P.M., Dill, D.L., Engler, D.R.: EXE: automatically generating inputs of death. In: Juels, A., Wright, R.N., di Vimercati, S.D.C. (eds.) Proceedings of the 13th ACM Conference on Computer and Communications Security (CCS 2006), pp. 322–335. ACM (2006)
5. Cadar, C., et al.: Symbolic execution for software testing in practice: preliminary assessment. In: Taylor, R.N., Gall, H.C., Medvidovic, N. (eds.) Proceedings of the 33rd International Conference on Software Engineering (ICSE 2011), pp. 1066–1071. ACM (2011)
6. Cadar, C., Sen, K.: Symbolic execution for software testing: three decades later. Commun. ACM **56**(2), 82–90 (2013)
7. Coq Development Team: The Coq proof assistant (2022). https://doi.org/10.5281/zenodo.7313584
8. Godefroid, P., Klarlund, N., Sen, K.: DART: directed automated random testing. In: Sarkar, V., Hall, M.W. (eds.) Proceedings of the ACM SIGPLAN Conference on Programming Language Design and Implementation (PLDI 2005), pp. 213–223. ACM (2005)
9. de Gouw, S., Rot, J., de Boer, F.S., Bubel, R., Hähnle, R.: OpenJDK's Java.utils.Collection.sort() is broken: the good, the bad and the worst case. In: Kroening, D., Puasuareanu, C.S. (eds.) CAV 2015. LNCS, vol. 9206, pp. 273–289. Springer, Cham (2015). https://doi.org/10.1007/978-3-319-21690-4_16
10. Hentschel, M., Bubel, R., Hähnle, R.: The symbolic execution debugger (SED): a platform for interactive symbolic execution, debugging, verification and more. Int. J. Softw. Tools Technol. Transf. **21**(5), 485–513 (2019)
11. Kløvstad, Å.A.A., Kamburjan, E., Johnsen, E.B.: Compositional correctness and completeness for symbolic partial order reduction. In: Proceedings of the 34th International Conference on Concurrency Theory (CONCUR 2023). LIPIcs, Schloss Dagstuhl - Leibniz-Zentrum für Informatik (2023, to appear)
12. Kneuper, R.: Symbolic execution: a semantic approach. Sci. Comput. Program. **16**(3), 207–249 (1991)
13. Lucanu, D., Rusu, V., Arusoaie, A.: A generic framework for symbolic execution: a coinductive approach. J. Symb. Comput. **80**, 125–163 (2017)
14. Nakata, K., Uustalu, T.: Trace-based coinductive operational semantics for while. In: Berghofer, S., Nipkow, T., Urban, C., Wenzel, M. (eds.) TPHOLs 2009. LNCS, vol. 5674, pp. 375–390. Springer, Heidelberg (2009). https://doi.org/10.1007/978-3-642-03359-9_26
15. Owens, S., Myreen, M.O., Kumar, R., Tan, Y.K.: Functional big-step semantics. In: Thiemann, P. (ed.) ESOP 2016. LNCS, vol. 9632, pp. 589–615. Springer, Heidelberg (2016). https://doi.org/10.1007/978-3-662-49498-1_23
16. Porncharoenwase, S., Nelson, L., Wang, X., Torlak, E.: A formal foundation for symbolic evaluation with merging. Proc. ACM Program. Lang. **6**(POPL) (2022). https://doi.org/10.1145/3498709
17. Steinhöfel, D.: Abstract execution: automatically proving infinitely many programs. Ph.D. thesis, Technische Universität Darmstadt (2020)

18. Uustalu, T.: Coinductive big-step semantics for concurrency. In: Yoshida, N., Van-derbauwhede, W. (eds.) Proceedings of the 6th Workshop on Programming Language Approaches to Concurrency and Communication-cEntric Software (PLACES 2013), EPTCS, vol. 137, pp. 63–78 (2013)
19. Voogd, E., Johnsen, E.B., Silva, A., Susag, Z.J., Wąsowski, A.: Symbolic semantics for probabilistic programs. In: Jansen, N., Tribastone, M. (eds.) QEST 2023. LNCS, vol. 14287, pp. 329–345. Springer, Cham (2023). https://doi.org/10.1007/978-3-031-43835-6_23

TeSSLa-ROS-Bridge – Runtime Verification of Robotic Systems

Marian Johannes Begemann, Hannes Kallwies[✉] ⓘ, Martin Leucker ⓘ,
and Malte Schmitz ⓘ

University of Lübeck, Lübeck, Germany
kallwies@isp.uni-luebeck.de

Abstract. Runtime Verification is a formal method to check a run of a
system against a specification. To this end, a monitor is generated from
the specification checking the system under scrutiny. Typically, runtime
verification is used for checking executions of programs. However, it may
equally be well suited for runs of robotic systems, most of which are built
and controlled on top of the Robot Operating System (ROS). In stream
runtime verification the specifications are given as stream transformations and this approach has become popular recently with several stream
runtime verification systems starting from LOLA having emerged. This
paper introduces the TeSSLa-ROS-Bridge, which allows to interact with
ROS-based robotic systems via the temporal stream-based specification
language TeSSLa.

1 Introduction

Runtime verification (RV) is a lightweight formal dynamic verification technique
analyzing single executions of systems wrt. given correctness properties. RV has
been studied both in theory and practical applications [4,20]. The starting point
is a formal specification of the property to verify, from which typically a monitor
is generated checking the run of the system under scrutiny.

Originally, runtime verification is used to verify (partially) program executions. A common specification language is Linear-time Temporal Logic (LTL) [28]
restricted to traces of atomic propositions.

Cyber-physical systems (CPS) [3,18] are computer-based systems in which
software typically controls and monitors the overall system and its execution.
To this extent, physical and software components are deeply intertwined. Their
correct behaviour requires to reason on different spatial and temporal scales
and complex interactions. Hence, correctness specifications for CPS require new
specification formalisms. The most prominent formalism patterned after LTL is
STL which comes with a qualitative [21] and quantitative semantics [14]. STL has
been used in many different application contexts for CPS, especially automotive
systems [22]. It has also been used in the CPS subfield of robotics [23].

An alternative family of formalisms for runtime verification is stream-based
runtime verification (SRV), pioneered by Lola [7]. The basic idea is to understand

E. Ábrahám et al. (Eds.): ICTAC 2023, LNCS 14446, pp. 388–398, 2023.
https://doi.org/10.1007/978-3-031-47963-2_23

the run of the underlying system (formally a word) as a stream and to specify stream transformations translating input streams to output streams which may cast errors according to the specification. If the output is sent back to the underlying system, the specification may also compute measures to correct the run, or, e.g. to steer the robot. Modern SRV systems (both synchronous and asynchronous) including RTLola [5], Lola2.0 [9], CoPilot [26], TeSSLa [6] and Striver [13] follow this approach.

The Robot Operating System (ROS) [29] is an open-source framework that provides a collection of software libraries and tools for building robot applications. ROS was developed to simplify the process of creating and controlling robots by providing a flexible and modular architecture. ROS has a large and active community of developers, researchers, and enthusiasts. This community contributes to the development and maintenance of ROS, shares code and packages, and provides support and resources for new users.[1]

Large and heavy robots may cause serious hazards, especially when operating in environments with humans. As such, a significant number of robotic systems can be classified as safety critical. Therefore, providing runtime verification capabilities for monitoring and controlling robots is beneficial, and this is what this paper is about: It presents a solution allowing to check and control ROS-based systems with the stream runtime verification language TeSSLa, i.e. a TeSSLa-ROS-Bridge, which allows a TeSSLa monitor to run as part of the ROS-based system (available open source, see https://git.tessla.io/ros/tesslarosbridge).

We explain that using the TeSSLa-ROS-Bridge (TRB) allows to program a robot facilitating the pattern of separation of concerns [24]. The robot may be programmed as usual, e.g. using machine learning techniques, while safety checks and e.g. emergency stops may be specified in TeSSLa. Using the TRB, the resulting monitor will run in parallel to the actual robot code and ensure the given safety conditions.

Related Work and Contribution. Since the first release of ROS in 2007, ROS bindings have been developed for several stand-alone tools to allow them to be easily integrated into the framework, supporting its emergence as the standard development platform for robotic systems. E.g. Carla ROS bridge[2], which integrates a tool for simulation of autonomous driving (CARLA [8]) with ROS, or Mathwork's ROS Toolbox[3] to connect ROS with Matlab/Simulink, just to name a few. The idea of embedding monitoring and runtime verification components into a ROS system has also been explored in recent years. There are several tools for running RV monitors on ROS, such as [23], which allows a user to build and run monitors from STL specifications. The Ogma [27] tool allows execution of the languages CoPilot, FRET and Lustre as ROS components, for example to monitor and control the robot system. Similarly, ROS Monitoring [11] provides a formalism agnostic platform to connect the ROS system to a monitor.

---

[1] See http://ros.org.
[2] See https://github.com/carla-simulator/ros-bridge.
[3] See https://de.mathworks.com/products/ros.html.

In this paper we present a tool for execution of the asynchronous SRV language TeSSLa on a ROS system. In contrast to synchronous SRV languages, TeSSLa is characterized by the fact that input and output events of the monitor can occur independently of each other not in a fixed time grid but at arbitrary time stamps, which is particularly suitable for monitoring CPS. Furthermore, the TeSSLa-ROS-Bridge enables the use of TeSSLa's rich standard library and other existing TeSSLa libraries for various runtime verification purposes on robotic systems. Thereby, the handling for the user takes place most comfortably via the use of so called annotations. In detail the paper covers the following sub-aspects: 1. We present the design and implementation details of the TeSSLa-ROS-Bridge. 2. We show by means of an example how to enrich a robotic system with a safety envelope for checking given properties formulated in TeSSLa.

Structure of the Paper. The paper is structured as follows: Sect. 2 gives a brief introduction to ROS and the specification language TeSSLa. Section 3 presents the concept and implementation of the TeSSLa-ROS-Bridge and Sect. 4 demonstrates its usage and the concept of creating a safety-envelope for a robotic system on basis of a practical example. Section 5 contains the conclusion and hints at future work.

2   Preliminaries

ROS. The open-source Robot Operating System (ROS) [29] was developed to simplify the process of creating and controlling robots by providing a flexible and modular architecture. ROS offers a hardware abstraction layer that allows developers to write robot applications without worrying about the specific details of the underlying hardware. This abstraction makes it easier to develop portable and reusable code that can work with different robot platforms.

Most important in our setting, ROS uses a publish-subscribe messaging system, where different components of a robot system can communicate with each other by publishing and subscribing to message channels or topics. This decoupled communication model allows for modular development and easy integration of different components. In fact, the TeSSLa-ROS-Bridge and the compiled TeSSLa monitor will be a component of the ROS system communicating via the publish-subscribe messaging system with the underlying robot system, as described in detail in the next section.

TeSSLa. TeSSLa, short for Temporal Stream Based Specification language, names a specification language [6] and belonging tool chain [16] developed as a community-driven open source project[4]. The basic concept behind TeSSLa is that a specification describes a stream transformation from input to output streams. This enables its usage for Runtime Verification, where the input streams originate from the system under scrutiny and comprise data about events that occurred in the system (like memory values, notification about function calls or

---

[4] https://www.tessla.io.

sensor readings). A TeSSLa specification can then be used to define a boolean output stream, indicating whether a certain property over the inputs (and thus the system) is met. However, TeSSLa's streams are not restricted to boolean domains and thus specifications can also define more advanced output streams, bearing e.g. statistical data about the observed system. Furthermore all events of TeSSLa streams have a timestamp attached which enables simple specification of timing properties in TeSSLa.

TeSSLa's tool chain allows the compilation of a specification to a monitor in different backend languages (Rust, Scala among others) into which input stream events can iteratively be fed and which in turn computes the events on the output streams. In addition to logging or notifying the user, these monitor outputs can be fed directly back to the monitored system and influence it, e.g. by triggering an emergency stop, or even be used to control the system.

A TeSSLa specification consists of a number of input stream declarations with their corresponding types. Further derived streams can be defined by applying certain operators on the input stream and other defined streams. Some of the derived streams can then be marked as output streams of the specification.

While all TeSSLa specifications can in theory be defined with use of six core operators [6], the TeSSLa implementation also allows the definition of so-called macros, i.e. user defined stream-operations built on other core operations or other macros, to make specification of complex properties more convenient. A selection of belonging macros can be grouped into a module, which makes it easy to share and reuse them in other specifications. There are for example modules for monitoring AUTOSAR Timing constraints [12, 25] or Timed Dyadic Deontic Logic [17] with TeSSLa. The TeSSLa compiler also comes with a standard library, containing macros and modules for frequently needed operations and typical use-cases, e.g. a module with Past LTL operators.

Furthermore, TeSSLa contains an annotation system. It is possible to define global or local annotations, which can be used inside a specification. These annotations are intended to contain meta information about the specification that is used to configure other tools, which interact with the monitor (e.g. instrumentation tools or output visualization). While global annotations (starting with two @ signs) can be placed anywhere in the specification and relate to the specification as a whole, local annotations (starting with a single @ sign) refer to a single input or output stream. Annotations from a specification can be extracted by the compiler and passed to connected tools.

```
module MyModule {
    import StreamFunctions
    def cntTimeReset[A](cnt: Events[A], resetTime: Int) =
        resetCount(cnt, delay(const(resetTime, cnt), cnt))
}
import MyModule
in x: Events[Int]
def c = cntTimeReset(x, 10s)
@VisBubbles out c
```

Listing 1. Example TeSSLa specification

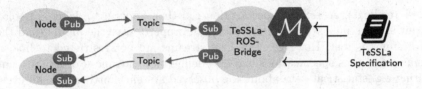

Fig. 1. Generalized ROS graph showing how the TeSSLa-ROS-Bridge is connected to an existing ROS system. Messages on subscribed topics are fed to the monitor as events on its input streams and derived events on the monitor's output streams are made available to other nodes as messages on topics.

A simple example of a TeSSLa specification can be found in Listing 1. The specification contains the declaration of an input stream x with events of type integer and defines a derived stream c, which is also marked as output. Stream c is defined by the application of the macro cntTimeReset on stream x and the value 10 s as second parameter. Note at this point that TeSSLa natively supports the usage of time units in specifications. The utilized macro cntTimeReset is defined on the top of the specification inside the module MyModule. It counts the number of events on stream cnt (with generic event type A), but resets to 0, if for the time period passed via parameter resetTime no new cnt event has appeared. Therefore it utilizes the core operator **delay** and the standard library macros const and resetCount. The module is imported in the outermost scope to make the macro directly available there. Finally, stream c is further annotated with @VisBubbles. This annotation (also defined in the standard library) is intended to signal a visualization frontend for the output log in which style to draw the corresponding stream.

3   TeSSLa-ROS-Bridge

As motivated in the introduction, the TeSSLa-ROS-Bridge allows the integration of TeSSLa monitors into a ROS computation graph. The TeSSLa monitor is encapsulated in a ROS node that subscribes to existing topics of the graph and publishes monitoring output to topics.

Figure 1 shows a generalized ROS computation graph. A ROS computation graph consists of nodes, visualized as round blue shapes. A node can encapsulate hardware actuators and sensors, or computational logic. Nodes communicate through topics, shown as green boxes in the diagram. A node can have multiple publishers and subscribers, represented as Pup and Sub respectively. Publishers send messages to a topic and subscribers receive messages from a topic.

The TeSSLa-ROS-Bridge is shown to the right of the Fig. 1. It is implemented as a ROS node (runnable on ROS 2), and like any other ROS node, the TeSSLa-ROS-Bridge can subscribe to topics and use the information provided on those topics as input. This approach allows TeSSLa monitors to be added to existing ROS systems. The monitor is clearly separated from the monitored system and does not manipulate the monitored system in any way other than by publishing to topics. This separation of concerns between sensors, actuators, control logic and monitoring fits well with the ROS approach. A practical example illustrating this idea is given in the next section.

The TeSSLa monitor $\mathcal{M}$ and the corresponding TeSSLa-ROS-Bridge are automatically compiled from a TeSSLa specification. TeSSLa's annotation system is used to map streams to topics: Input streams annotated with the ROS annotation `@RosSubscription` are connected to a subscriber in the TeSSLa-ROS-Bridge that is subscribed to the given topic. Output streams annotated with the ROS annotation `@RosPublisher` are connected to a publisher in the TeSSLa-ROS-Bridge that publishes to the given topic.

The `@RosSubscription` and `@RosPublisher` annotations take three arguments each: The topic's name, its type and its quality of service. The quality of service indicates the queue size, which limits the amount of queued messages if a subscriber is not receiving them fast enough. Predefined profiles for special use cases such as sensor values are also available. For example, `qos_profile_sensor_data` uses best effort reliability and a smaller queue size.

At runtime, the compiled TeSSLa monitor is provided with every message received on the subscribed topics. The monitor computes the events on the derived TeSSLa output streams of the specification. These new events are published to the topics connected to the TeSSLa-ROS-Bridge publishers, and those annotated as output are additionally written to a log file for further offline analysis.

The TeSSLa-ROS-Bridge is written in Python using the ROS client library for the Python language rclpy[5]. The TeSSLa specification is compiled into a Rust library which is included in the TeSSLa-ROS-Bridge using the PyO3[6] Rust bindings for Python. This approach allows us to integrate the widely used Python library for ROS 2 with the fast, natively compiled TeSSLa monitor.

In detail, the automated compilation process performs the following steps: 1. Compile the TeSSLa specification into a Rust monitoring library using the TeSSLa Rust compiler. 2. Compile the annotations in the TeSSLa specification into a JSON configuration using the TeSSLa core compiler. 3. Configure the TeSSLa-ROS-Bridge using the JSON configuration: Add publishers and subscribers and generate Python code to connect them to the monitor's input and output streams. 4. Package the TeSSLa-ROS-Bridge with the TeSSLa monitor as a ROS 2 package using the ROS 2 toolchain.

Evaluation and Limitations. We have evaluated the tool both in a practical case study on a ROS 1 robot system (see the following section) using a ROS1/ROS2 bridge, and in a synthetic example on a personal computer with Intel Core i7 CPU and 8GB RAM inside a virtual machine. In particular, we used artificial specifications with 10 to 2500 core operations and a single ROS node that generated dummy events and received events from the TeSSLa monitor. We also used this ROS node to record the latency between sending events to the monitor and receiving responses. We measured a latency of about 15 milliseconds per

---

[5] https://github.com/ros2/rclpy.

[6] https://github.com/PyO3/pyo3.

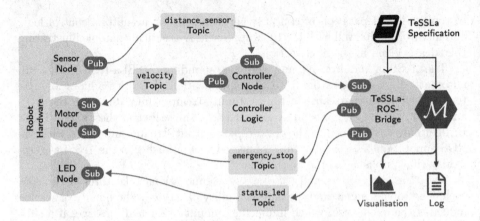

Fig. 2. Simplified ROS graph of the example discussed in Sect. 4. The diagram shows the ROS nodes with their publishers and subscribers to topics. Each node is integrated with either some real hardware, the controller logic or the TeSSLa monitor.

event. In our case studies, the measurement was not noticeably affected by the size of the specification, and was therefore mainly caused by the message passing between the ROS nodes and the bridge.

An input event rate that is too high, causing the monitor to lag behind the input values, can cause the monitor to produce safety-relevant outputs too late, and is thus a potential threat to the correctness of the tool. In addition, incorrect or incomplete sensor readings can cause the monitor to cast incorrect and potentially fatal verdicts. However, solutions have been developed for monitoring TeSSLa specifications in the presence of imprecise or missing inputs that can partially remedy the situation [19]. Similarly, [15] discusses sound and perfect LOLA monitoring in the presence of uncertainty, but it is an open problem how to transfer this strategy to the asynchronous SRV language TeSSLa. However, both approaches suffer from rather high execution time overheads, which makes them only partially applicable for the described use cases. Finally, components that do not report correctly to the monitor, or that do not behave according to its output, can also undermine the safety layer generated by the monitor.

Security is an important aspect in the context of safety-critical applications. Since the TeSSLa-ROS-Bridge integrates the monitor as a regular node into the ROS computation graph, the usual security considerations for ROS apply[7]: ROS nodes communicate over networks which are by default shared resources. However, attacks over the network are impossible, as long as all nodes are in the same physical network that is not connected to any other network. In more complex environments firewalls and routing rules can be used to isolate the network of the ROS nodes. ROS2 is based on the Data Distribution Service (DDS) [1] specification and can therefore take advantage of the security enhancements provided by the DDS security specification [2], such as authentication, access control and

---

[7] See http://wiki.ros.org/Security.

encryption [10]. These can easily be enabled in our approach since the TeSSLa-ROS-Bridge provides a standard ROS2 node.

4   TeSSLa-ROS-Bridge in Action

In this section we discuss how a robot system can be shielded by a runtime verification layer by means of a practical example. In our setting we have a driving robot with distance sensor and status LED running ROS. The simplified ROS computation graph is shown in Fig. 2.

The robot's hardware is accessed directly by dedicated ROS nodes: the sensor, motor and LED nodes on the left are connected to the actual robot hardware and provide sensor values in the form of messages to topics or subscribe to topics in order to execute command messages on actuators. The node `controller` contains the control logic steering the robot. This node subscribes to values and publishes new values based on the information it receives. Similarly, but separately, the TeSSLa-ROS-Bridge monitors the robot by subscribing and publishing to topics.

We now want to assure two safety criteria on the system: (1) The system may not drive whenever there is something too close to the sensor. (2) The system has to stop completely if there were more than five near-collisions within a period of 30 s (usually an indication of a human or animal in the robot's movement range or the robot being stuck somewhere).

```
include "TesslaROSBridge.tessla"
def RED = 0; def YELLOW = 1; def GREEN = 2

@RosSubscription("/distance_sensor", "int64", "10") in distance: Events[Int]

def tooClose = default(distance < 20, false)
def tooManyErrors = MyModule.cntTimeReset(rising(tooClose), 30s) > 5
def stop = tooClose || LTL.once(tooManyErrors)
def ledCode = if tooClose then RED else if stop then YELLOW else GREEN

@RosPublisher("/emergency_stop", "bool", "10") @VisBool out stop
@RosPublisher("/status_led", "int64", "10") @VisSignal out ledCode
@VisSignal out tooClose
```

Listing 2. Example TeSSLa specification with ROS interaction

Listing 2 shows a TeSSLa specification for this property. The specification defines an input stream `distance` with events of type `Int`. Further it marks the streams `stop`, `ledCode` and `tooClose` as outputs. All of these streams are annotated. On the one hand with visualization annotations in case the TeSSLa-ROS-Bridge log shall be viewed in a graphical backend. On the other hand `distance` is connected to the robot's distance sensor and `stop` and `ledCode` to the corresponding driver units of the robot via TeSSLa-ROS-Bridge annotations (defined in the imported `TesslaROSBridge.tessla`).

Further the specification defines a stream `tooClose`, which is true if the value from `distance` falls below 20 (with default set to false). The stream `tooManyErrors` turns true if there were more than five `tooClose` events during the last 30 s (defined via macro from Listing 1). The stream `stop` is true if either `tooClose` is currently true or once in the past `tooManyErrors` was true (realized by standard

Fig. 3. Jackal stops after obstacle is too close, as identified in TeSSLa. Full video at https://www.tessla.io/blog/rosBridge/

library macro LTL.once implementing Past-LTL's once operator). Stream ledCode finally determines a numeric code for the status LED, red if something is currently too close to the robot, yellow if the robot stopped because of too many errors and green otherwise. The color codes for this purpose are defined in the upper part of the specification. With the TeSSLa-ROS-Bridge it is possible to run an additional monitor node on the ROS system, executing the specification.

As motivated in the previous section, by the chosen design we reach a separation of concerns: while the control logic is responsible for the robot to fulfill its potentially complex task, the enforcement of a safe driving behavior is fully outsourced to the TeSSLa monitor. This is an advantage in terms of formally verified development of safety critical software: For the guarantee that the robot behaves according to the specification (i.e. not driving when something is too close and stop moving after too many close contacts) it is not necessary to prove anything about the (arbitrarily complex) control logic but just to prove that the motor really stops whenever it receives an emergency_stop event from the monitor node. This can usually be done, for example with help of static verification methods. We implemented and tested (see Fig. 3) the core of the example and executed it on Jackal robots, running ROS.

5   Conclusions and Future Work

In this paper, we describe the TeSSLa-ROS-Bridge allowing to fuse runtime verification and programming robots. It allows to monitor ROS-based robot applications, especially for safety properties. By means of an example, we show that we have laid the foundation for such combinations, while sophisticated experiences still have to be gained. We plan mainly two directions of future work. Using TeSSLa's module system, it is possible to provide domain specific specification routines. We plan to develop a control library simplifying to issue mitigation actions once violations to specifications have been detected. However, as a precursor of this work, we plan to study monitoring aware programming patterns for robots. Besides checking and managing safety properties and respectively violations, this will allow for more elaborated monitoring of robots, especially health parameters such as energy availability etc. while at the same time supporting the concept of separation of concerns.

References

1. OMG Data Distribution Service (DDS), Version 1.4. Standard, Object Management Group (2015)
2. DDS Security, Version 1.1. Standard, Object Management Group (2018)
3. Baheti, R., Gill, H.: Cyber-physical systems. .Impact Control Technol. **12**(1), 161–166 (2011)
4. Bartocci, E., Falcone, Y. (eds.): Lectures on Runtime Verification - Introductory and Advanced Topics. Lecture Notes in Computer Science, vol. 10457. Springer, Cham (2018). https://doi.org/10.1007/978-3-319-75632-5
5. Baumeister, J., Finkbeiner, B., Schirmer, S., Schwenger, M., Torens, C.: RTLola cleared for take-off: monitoring autonomous aircraft. In: Lahiri, S.K., Wang, C. (eds.) CAV 2020. LNCS, vol. 12225, pp. 28–39. Springer, Cham (2020). https://doi.org/10.1007/978-3-030-53291-8_3
6. Convent, L., Hungerecker, S., Leucker, M., Scheffel, T., Schmitz, M., Thoma, D.: TeSSLa: temporal stream-based specification language. In: Massoni, T., Mousavi, M.R. (eds.) SBMF 2018. LNCS, vol. 11254, pp. 144–162. Springer, Cham (2018). https://doi.org/10.1007/978-3-030-03044-5_10
7. D'Angelo, B., et al.: LOLA: runtime monitoring of synchronous systems. In: 12th International Symposium on Temporal Representation and Reasoning (TIME 2005), 23–25 June 2005, Burlington, Vermont, USA, pp. 166–174. IEEE Computer Society (2005). https://doi.org/10.1109/TIME.2005.26
8. Dosovitskiy, A., Ros, G., Codevilla, F., López, A.M., Koltun, V.: CARLA: an open urban driving simulator. In: CoRL. Proceedings of Machine Learning Research, vol. 78, pp. 1–16. PMLR (2017)
9. Faymonville, P., et al.: StreamLAB: stream-based monitoring of cyber-physical systems. In: Dillig, I., Tasiran, S. (eds.) CAV 2019. LNCS, vol. 11561, pp. 421–431. Springer, Cham (2019). https://doi.org/10.1007/978-3-030-25540-4_24
10. Fazzari, K.: ROS 2 DDS-security integration (2020). https://design.ros2.org/articles/ros2_dds_security.html. Accessed 16 Sept 2023
11. Ferrando, A., Cardoso, R.C., Fisher, M., Ancona, D., Franceschini, L., Mascardi, V.: ROSMonitoring: a runtime verification framework for ROS. In: Mohammad, A., Dong, X., Russo, M. (eds.) TAROS 2020. LNCS (LNAI), vol. 12228, pp. 387–399. Springer, Cham (2020). https://doi.org/10.1007/978-3-030-63486-5_40
12. Friese, M.J., Kallwies, H., Leucker, M., Sachenbacher, M., Streichhahn, H., Thoma, D.: Runtime verification of AUTOSAR timing extensions. In: Abdeddaïm, Y., Cucu-Grosjean, L., Nelissen, G., Pautet, L. (eds.) RTNS 2022: The 30th International Conference on Real-Time Networks and Systems, Paris, France, 7–8 June 2022, pp. 173–183. ACM (2022). https://doi.org/10.1145/3534879.3534898
13. Gorostiaga, F., Sánchez, C.: Stream runtime verification of real-time event streams with the Striver language. Int. J. Softw. Tools Technol. Transfer **23**, 157–183 (2021). https://doi.org/10.1007/s10009-021-00605-3
14. Jaksic, S., Bartocci, E., Grosu, R., Nguyen, T., Nickovic, D.: Quantitative monitoring of STL with edit distance. Formal Methods Syst. Des. **53**(1), 83–112 (2018). https://doi.org/10.1007/s10703-018-0319-x

15. Kallwies, H., Leucker, M., Sánchez, C.: Symbolic runtime verification for monitoring under uncertainties and assumptions. In: Bouajjani, A., Holík, L., Wu, Z. (eds.) ATVA 2022. LNCS, vol. 13505, pp. 117–134. Springer, Cham (2022). https://doi.org/10.1007/978-3-031-19992-9_8

16. Kallwies, H., Leucker, M., Schmitz, M., Schulz, A., Thoma, D., Weiss, A.: TeSSLa - an ecosystem for runtime verification. In: Dang, T., Stolz, V. (eds.) RV 2022. LNCS, vol. 13498, pp. 314–324. Springer, Cham (2022). https://doi.org/10.1007/978-3-031-17196-3_20

17. Kharraz, K.Y., Leucker, M., Schneider, G.: Timed dyadic deontic logic. In: Erich, S. (ed.) Legal Knowledge and Information Systems - JURIX 2021: The Thirty-fourth Annual Conference, Vilnius, Lithuania, 8–10 December 2021. Frontiers in Artificial Intelligence and Applications, vol. 346, pp. 197–204. IOS Press (2021). https://doi.org/10.3233/FAIA210336

18. Lee, E.A.: The past, present and future of cyber-physical systems: a focus on models. Sensors **15**(3), 4837–4869 (2015)

19. Leucker, M., Sánchez, C., Scheffel, T., Schmitz, M., Thoma, D.: Runtime verification for timed event streams with partial information. In: Finkbeiner, B., Mariani, L. (eds.) RV 2019. LNCS, vol. 11757, pp. 273–291. Springer, Cham (2019). https://doi.org/10.1007/978-3-030-32079-9_16

20. Leucker, M., Schallhart, C.: A brief account of runtime verification. J. Logic Algebr. Progr. **78**(5), 293–303 (2009)

21. Maler, O., Nickovic, D.: Monitoring temporal properties of continuous signals. In: Lakhnech, Y., Yovine, S. (eds.) FORMATS/FTRTFT -2004. LNCS, vol. 3253, pp. 152–166. Springer, Heidelberg (2004). https://doi.org/10.1007/978-3-540-30206-3_12

22. Nguyen, T., Nickovic, D.: Assertion-based monitoring in practice - checking correctness of an automotive sensor interface. Sci. Comput. Program. **118**, 40–59 (2016). https://doi.org/10.1016/j.scico.2015.11.002

23. Ničković, D., Yamaguchi, T.: RTAMT: online robustness monitors from STL. In: Hung, D.V., Sokolsky, O. (eds.) ATVA 2020. LNCS, vol. 12302, pp. 564–571. Springer, Cham (2020). https://doi.org/10.1007/978-3-030-59152-6_34

24. Painter, R.R.: Software plans: multi-dimensional fine-grained separation of concerns. A Dissertation Proposal (2006)

25. AUTOSAR, Development, Partnership: Specification of Timing Extensions, Version 1.0.0, Release 4.0.1 (2009)

26. Perez, I., Dedden, F., Goodloe, A.: Copilot 3. Technical report NASA/TM-2020-220587, NASA Langley Research Center (2020)

27. Perez, I., Mavridou, A., Pressburger, T., Will, A., Martin, P.J.: Monitoring ROS2: from requirements to autonomous robots. In: FMAS/ASYDE@SEFM. EPTCS, vol. 371, pp. 208–216 (2022)

28. Pnueli, A.: The temporal logic of programs. In: Proceedings of the 18th IEEE Symposium on the Foundations of Computer Science (FOCS-77), pp. 46–57. IEEE Computer Society Press, Providence (1977)

29. Quigley, M., et al.: ROS: an open-source robot operating system. In: ICRA Workshop on Open Source Software, Kobe, Japan, vol. 3, p. 5 (2009)

Simplifying Process Parameters
by Unfolding Algebraic Data Types

Anna Stramaglia$^{(\boxtimes)}$, Jeroen J. A. Keiren, and Thomas Neele

Eindhoven University of Technology, Eindhoven, The Netherlands
{a.stramaglia,j.j.a.keiren,t.s.neele}@tue.nl

Abstract. Complex abstract data types are often used to facilitate creating concise models of the behavior of realistic systems. However, static analysis techniques that aim to optimize such models often consider variables of complex types as a single indivisible unit. The use of complex data types thus negatively affects the optimizations that can be performed. In this paper we revisit and extend a technique by Groote and Lisser that can be used to replace a single, complex variable by multiple variables of simpler data types, improving the effectiveness of other static analyzes. We describe the technique in the context of the process algebraic specification language mCRL2, and establish its correctness. We demonstrate using an implementation in the mCRL2 toolset that it sometimes reduces the size of the underlying state spaces, and it typically reduces the verification times when using symbolic model checking.

1 Introduction

The mCRL2 language [7] is a process algebraic specification language with an associated toolset to model, validate and verify complex systems [3]. Models in mCRL2 typically consist of a number of (communicating) parallel processes that are parameterized with data. As preprocessing for further analysis, mCRL2 specifications are transformed into *linear process equations* (LPEs). In this step, parallelism and communication are removed from the process definition. Therefore, an LPE consists of a single (recursive) process definition, parameterized with data, and a number of condition-action-effect rules referred to as *summands*.

The mCRL2 toolset, among other features, offers several manipulation tools for LPEs (e.g. constant elimination and unused parameter elimination, see [6]). The transformations applied by these tools mainly operate on process parameters and aim to reduce the complexity of the LPE under consideration. They can result in a reduction (under bisimilarity) of the underlying state space.

To facilitate the modeling of realistic processes, mCRL2 supports complex algebraic data types. However, since the LPE transformations do not consider the structure within the data type of a process parameter, using complex data types reduces the effectiveness of these transformations. Thus, in order to benefit from their full potential, we need to simplify these complex data structures.

To address this, Groote and Lisser [6] originally introduced a technique for flattening the structure of process parameters and implemented this under the

© The Author(s), under exclusive license to Springer Nature Switzerland AG 2023
E. Ábrahám et al. (Eds.): ICTAC 2023, LNCS 14446, pp. 399–416, 2023.
https://doi.org/10.1007/978-3-031-47963-2_24

name `structelm` in μCRL [1] (the precursor of mCRL2). The idea behind this approach is to replace a given parameter p by multiple parameters $p_1, \ldots, p_n$ that together encode the data type of p, effectively exposing its internal structure. This enables the application of the aforementioned LPE simplification techniques to $p_1, \ldots, p_n$, which would otherwise not be possible [6]. This same technique was implemented in the mCRL2 tool `lpsparunfold`.

In this paper, we revisit the transformation behind `lpsparunfold` and identify several constructions that occur often in LPEs, but are not dealt with adequately, limiting the practical applicability of `lpsparunfold`. We extend this technique to enable further simplifications and preserve bisimilarity of the LPE. Our contributions are:

- we identify an alternative way of placing the functions that reconstruct the original parameter p from its unfolded constituents $p_1, \ldots, p_n$,
- we allow the technique to preserve global variables in such a way that they can be effectively used by other static analysis techniques,
- we simplify complex state update expressions by locally eliminating functions that are defined using *pattern matching*, and
- we experimentally demonstrate that our extensions are effective at enabling other LPE transformations and speeding up the model checker.

In particular, our experiments show that our extensions enable larger reductions of the underlying state space, directly benefiting explicit-state model checking. For symbolic reachability we observe that, even if no state space reduction is possible, the flattening achieved by `lpsparunfold` reduces the execution time.

Related Work. Our work is most closely related to various analysis and transformation techniques for LPEs that have been developed over the years. The aforementioned elimination techniques from [6] are a prime example. A more advanced algorithm is *liveness analysis* [16], which reconstructs a control flow graph from a given LPE and uses knowledge of relevant data parameters to reduce the size of the underlying state space.

Similar ideas have been developed for *Parameterized Boolean Equation Systems* (PBES) [8]. For example, redundant and constant parameter elimination for PBES is presented in [13], liveness analysis in [10]; a generalization of constant elimination occurs in [12].

The implementation of symbolic reachability used in our experiments is based on the techniques from [2,11], and uses the decision diagrams from Sylvan [17].

Overview. Section 2 introduces an example that is used throughout the paper. Next, preliminaries are provided in Sect. 3. Parameter unfolding from [6] is presented in Sect. 4. Our extensions to [6] are presented in Sect. 5. Finally, we validate our ideas with experiments in Sect. 6 and conclude in Sect. 7.

2   Motivating Example

As a running example we use an mCRL2 specification of a simple system, shown in Fig. 1, inspired by the mCRL2 models generated from OIL specifications [4].

sort $Sys = $ **struct** $uninit \mid sys(get\_state : State, get\_ip : \mathbb{N})$;
      $State = $ **struct** $p\_on \mid p\_off$;
map $set\_state\colon Sys \times State \to Sys$;
      $set\_ip\colon Sys \times \mathbb{N} \to Sys$;
var $s\colon Sys; p_1, p_2\colon State; n, m\colon \mathbb{N}$;
eqn $set\_state(uninit, p_1) = uninit$;
      $set\_state(sys(p_1, n), p_2) = sys(p_2, n)$;
      $set\_ip(uninit, m) = uninit$;
      $set\_ip(sys(p_1, n), m) = sys(p_1, m)$;
act $on, off, initialize$;
glob $dc1, dc2 : \mathbb{N}$;
proc $P(s\colon Sys) =$
      $(s \approx uninit) \to initialize \cdot P(sys(p\_off, dc1))$
   $+ \sum_{n : \mathbb{N}}(s \not\approx uninit \wedge get\_state(s) \approx p\_off)$
      $\to on \cdot P(set\_state(set\_ip(s, n), p\_on))$
   $+(s \not\approx uninit \wedge get\_state(s) \approx p\_on) \to off \cdot P(set\_state(set\_ip(s, dc2), p\_off))$;
init $P(uninit)$;

Fig. 1. Linear process specification of a simple system

The system starts out *uninitialized* (**init** $P(uninit)$). If the system is *initialized*, it can be in one of two states, *off* or *on*, and can be toggled between them. Moreover, an IP address, abstracted as natural number, is assigned to the system.

The LPE is given after the **proc** keyword. The definition of the process consists of (possibly recursive) summands, that, essentially, describe a set of condition-action-effect rules. When *uninitialized*, it can be *initialized* to *off*, where the IP address is irrelevant. This is modeled using a global variable *dc1* (*dc* stands for don't-care). When the system is *off*, it can be switched *on*, and the IP address is set to an arbitrary value using the sum operator $\sum_{n : \mathbb{N}}$. If the system is *on*, the system can be switched *off*. Again the IP address is immaterial.

The LPE is defined in the context of the data specification, which consists of several parts. First, **sort** specifies two sorts. Structured sort *Sys* has two constructors, *uninit*: *Sys* and *sys*: *State* $\times \mathbb{N} \to Sys$. For this, standard operations such as equality ($\approx$) and inequality ($\not\approx$) are predefined, e.g., that $sys(p, n) \not\approx uninit$ for all p: *State*, n: $\mathbb{N}$. Also, the projection functions *get_state*: *Sys* $\to$ *State* and *get_ip*: *Sys* $\to \mathbb{N}$ are defined such that, $get\_state(sys(p, n)) = p$ and $get\_ip(sys(p, n)) = n$. The *State* argument indicates the status of the system which can be set to *p_on* or *p_off*, e.g., given s: *Sys*, function $set\_state(s, p\_on)$ sets the state of s to *p_on*. Similarly, $set\_ip(s, 1)$ sets the IP address of s to 1.

Note that the labeled transition system underlying this process has an infinite state space due to the use of natural numbers for IP addresses. However, this parameter does not affect the behavior of the system: the behavior of the system when it is *on*, *i.e.*, it is in a state $sys(p\_on, n)$, is bisimilar for all values of n. Yet, static analysis tools such as parameter elimination and constant elimination are not able to simplify the LPE because the real structure of the process is hidden in process parameter s.

3   Preliminaries

The mCRL2 language is a modeling language based on process algebra with data [7]. In general, the language allows the specification of communicating, parallel processes. However, the first step in any automated analysis using the mCRL2 toolset [3] is to *linearize* the specification. In this process, parallel composition operators are eliminated, and replaced by sequential composition and choice, effectively making the allowed interleavings explicit. This results in a standardized format for processes, the *linear process equations* (LPEs). The technique we study in this paper operates on such LPEs. In the remainder of this section we first introduce the data, and subsequently the LPEs.

3.1   Data

The language for data types in mCRL2 is based on an algebraic specification. We here give a brief overview. For details, we refer to the treatment in [7]. A *signature* is a triple $\Sigma = (\mathcal{S}, \mathcal{C}_\mathcal{S}, \mathcal{M}_\mathcal{S})$ where $\mathcal{S}$ is a set of sorts, $\mathcal{C}_\mathcal{S}$ and $\mathcal{M}_\mathcal{S}$ are disjoint sets of function symbols over $\mathcal{S}$, called *constructors*, and *mappings*, respectively. Such function symbols are of the form $f \colon D_1 \times \cdots \times D_n \to D$ such that $D_i, D \in \mathcal{S}$ for $1 \le i \le n$. If $n = 0$, we say f is a constant. We generally assume that the signature contains Booleans and standard numeric types along with their constructors and operations. With a slight abuse of notation we use their semantic sets $\mathbb{B}, \mathbb{N}, \ldots$ and operations such as $\wedge$ and $+$ also for the syntactic counterparts. For any sort D, we assume sort $List(D)$ is defined, with constructors $[]$ for the empty list, and $\triangleright$ for the constructor that adds an element in front of a list. Sorts constructed using $\to$, such as $D_1 \times \cdots \times D_n \to D$ are called function sorts. If $D = D_1 \times \cdots \times D_n \to D'$ we write $range(D)$ for its range D'.

Constructors are used to inductively define the elements of a sort. We write $\mathcal{C}_\mathcal{S}(D) = \{f \colon D' \in \mathcal{C}_\mathcal{S} \mid range(D') = D\}$ for the constructors of sort D. We assume a bijection ι_D between $\mathcal{C}_\mathcal{S}(D)$ and $0..|\mathcal{C}_\mathcal{S}(D)| - 1$ ordering the constructors, and write ι if D is clear from the context. We say that D is a *constructor sort* if, and only if, $\mathcal{C}_\mathcal{S}(D) \ne \emptyset$. A constructor sort D is syntactically non-empty if there is a constructor $f \colon D_1 \times \cdots \times D_n \to D$ such that if D_i is a constructor sort, then D_i is syntactically non-empty, for $1 \le i \le n$. We require all constructor sorts to be non-empty, and for $f \colon D \in \mathcal{C}_\mathcal{S}$, $range(D)$ must not be a function sort.

Expressions in the data language are referred to as *data expressions* or *terms* over a set $\mathcal{X}_\mathcal{S}$ of $\mathcal{S}$-sorted variables. They are syntactically described by the following grammar:

$$t ::= x \mid f \mid t(t, \ldots, t)$$

where $x \in \mathcal{X}_\mathcal{S}$ are variables, $f \in \mathcal{C}_\mathcal{S} \cup \mathcal{M}_\mathcal{S}$ are function symbols, and $t(t, \ldots, t)$ describes the application of a term to its arguments. We write $e[x := e']$ for the syntactic substitution of x with e' in e. The mCRL2 language additionally supports quantification and lambda expressions. Our technique straightforwardly extends to this setting, so we omit those constructs for the sake of simplicity. With every sort D, we associate a default expression, def_D.

Equality of terms is defined using a *data specification* $\mathcal{D} = (\Sigma, E)$, where Σ is a signature and E is a set of conditional equations of the form $\langle \mathcal{X}, c \rightarrow t = u \rangle$, where $\mathcal{X} \subseteq \mathcal{X}_\mathcal{S}$, and c, t, u are terms over $\mathcal{X}$. We typically write $\langle \mathcal{X}, t = u \rangle$, when $c = true$ and $c \rightarrow t = u$ or $t = u$, if $\mathcal{X}$ is clear from the context.

The semantics of data types is described using *model class semantics* [7]. Sorts are mapped into their semantic counterpart using applicative structures. A set $\{M_D \mid D \in \mathcal{S}\}$ is an applicative structure if, and only if, $M_\mathbb{B} = \{\mathbf{true}, \mathbf{false}\}$, and if $D = D_1 \times \cdots \times D_n \rightarrow D'$, then M_D contains all (semantic) functions from $M_{D_1} \times \cdots \times M_{D_n} \rightarrow M_{D'}$. Function $[\![-]\!]$ maps every function symbol in the data specification into its semantic counterpart, that is, for all $f \in \mathcal{C}_\mathcal{S} \cup \mathcal{M}_\mathcal{S}$ of sort D, $[\![f]\!] \in M_D$. This is generalized to arbitrary terms as follows:

$$[\![x]\!]^\sigma = \sigma(x) \qquad\qquad \text{if } x \in \mathcal{X}_\mathcal{S}$$
$$[\![f]\!]^\sigma = [\![f]\!] \qquad\qquad \text{if } f \in \mathcal{C}_\mathcal{S} \cup \mathcal{M}_\mathcal{S}$$
$$[\![t(t_1, \ldots, t_n)]\!]^\sigma = [\![t]\!]^\sigma([\![t_1]\!]^\sigma, \ldots, [\![t_n]\!]^\sigma)$$

where $\sigma \colon \mathcal{X}_\mathcal{S} \rightarrow \bigcup_{D \in \mathcal{S}} M_D$ is a valuation that ensures that $\sigma(x) \in M_D$ for all $x \colon D$. We write $\sigma[v/d]$ for the valuation that assigns v to d and otherwise behaves as σ. The model $\mathbb{M}$ of a data specification is an applicative structure together with an interpretation function, that in addition ensures that for equations $\langle \mathcal{X}, c \rightarrow t = u \rangle \in E$ and valuations σ, if $[\![c]\!]^\sigma = \mathbf{true}$ then $[\![t]\!]^\sigma = [\![u]\!]^\sigma$; $[\![true]\!]^\sigma = \mathbf{true}$, $[\![false]\!]^\sigma = \mathbf{false}$, for all valuations σ; and if D is a constructor sort, then every $v \in M_D$ is a *constructor element*. Element $v \in M_D$ is a constructor element if a constructor function $f \in \mathcal{C}_\mathcal{S}$ of sort $D_1 \times \cdots \times D_n \rightarrow D$ exists such that $v = [\![f]\!](v_1, \ldots, v_n)$ where v_i is either a constructor element of sort D_i, or sort D_i is not a constructor sort. We write $t \equiv t'$ for terms t and t' if for all models, $[\![t]\!]^\sigma = [\![t']\!]^\sigma$ for all valuations σ.

3.2 Linear Processes

A Linear Process Equation (LPE) defines the name of a recursive process, whose definition is a set of summands that are, essentially, condition-action-effect rules that may refer to local variables. An LPE is typically defined in the context of a data specification $\mathcal{D}$, that specifies algebraic data types, and a set of global variables $\mathcal{X}_g$. The combination of an LPE with a data specification and its global variables is a Linear Process Specification (LPS).

Definition 1. *A linear process specification (LPS) L is a tuple $(\mathcal{D}, \mathcal{X}_g, P, \vec{e})$ where $\mathcal{D}$ is a data specification describing the data types used in the LPS, $\mathcal{X}_g$ is a set of global variables, P is a linear process equation (LPE), and $\vec{e}$ is a vector of expressions of sort $\vec{D}$ that may refer to variables in $\mathcal{X}_g$. We typically say that $P(\vec{e})$ is the initial process. LPE P is described as follows:*

$$P(\vec{d} \colon \vec{D}) = \sum_{i \in I} \sum_{\vec{e}_i \colon \vec{E}_i} c_i \rightarrow a_i(f_i) \cdot P(g_i) + \sum_{j \in J} \sum_{\vec{e}_j \colon \vec{E}_j} c_j \rightarrow a_{\delta j}(f_j)$$

where $\vec{d}$ is a vector of process parameters whose types are $\vec{D}$. I and J are disjoint, finite index sets, such that for $i \in I$ and $j \in J$ we have that c_i and c_j are boolean expressions, a_i and $a_{\delta j}$ are actions, f_i and f_j are terms that form the action parameters, and g_i is the next state, providing the vector of terms assigned to the parameters of process P in the recursive call to P. Terms c_i, f_i, g_i (c_j, f_j) range over $\vec{d}$, $\mathcal{X}_g$, and $\vec{e_i}$ $(\vec{e_j})$.

In their full generality, LPEs can use timestamps on the actions. These timestamps are treated by our transformation in the same way as action parameters. For the sake of simplicity, we restrict ourselves to untimed LPEs in this paper. For the same reason, we will henceforth only consider recursive summands.

Transformations of LPEs are correct if they are behavior preserving. For this, we use a generalization of strong bisimulation to linear processes [6]. Two LPEs P and P' with initial values e and e', respectively, are strongly bisimilar if and only if the labeled transition systems induced by $P(e)$ and $P'(e')$ are strongly bisimilar. In this case, we write $P(e) \leftrightarrow P'(e')$.

4   Parameter Unfolding

Parameter unfolding was introduced by Groote and Lisser under the name `structelm` [6], and has later been implemented in the mCRL2 toolset in a tool called `lpsparunfold`. The idea behind parameter unfolding is that a term from a constructor sort whose head symbol is a constructor can be replaced by separate terms for the name of the constructor and each of the arguments. For instance, in our running example, the single process parameter s is then replaced by three process parameters: $e: U_{Sys}$, $s_1: State$ and $s_2: \mathbb{N}$, where e represents the constructor at the head of s, and s_1 and s_2 are the arguments of the first constructor. The term $sys(p\_off, dc1)$ in the first summand of our running example can be replaced by the terms $\overline{c}_{sys}$, p_off, and $dc1$; the Sys constructor $uninit$ in the initialization is replaced by the value $\overline{c}_{uninit}$. As $uninit$ does not have any parameter, the new parameters s_1 and s_2 can be set to a default value.

Unfolding of process parameters happens in two steps. First, the data specification is extended with a new sort to represent constructors, and mappings to move between the sort that is unfolded, and newly introduced parameters. Next, the parameters in the linear process are unfolded.

4.1   Extending the Data Specification

Our improvements to Groote and Lisser's technique concern the unfolding of the parameters in the linear process. The extension of the data specification is, in essence, left unchanged, and its formal definition can be found in [6]. We therefore only introduce the unfolding of the data type using our running example.

When unfolding a sort D, a new data specification is constructed that extends $\mathcal{D}$ with a new sort U_D, to represent the constructors of D, constructors for this new sort, as well as case functions, determinizers and projection functions and the associated equations.

Example 1. Recall the data specification from Fig. 1. We unfold sort *Sys*. Note that $\mathcal{C}_S(Sys) = \{sys\colon State \times \mathbb{N} \to Sys, uninit\colon Sys\}$, that is it has two constructors, *sys* and *uninit*. The data specification of the running example is extended with the following.

sort U_{Sys};
cons $\overline{c}_{sys}, \overline{c}_{uninit}\colon U_{Sys}$;
map $C_{Sys}\colon U_{Sys} \times Sys \times Sys \to Sys$
$\quad det_{Sys}\colon Sys \to U_{Sys}$;
$\quad \pi^1_{sys}\colon Sys \to State$;
$\quad \pi^2_{sys}\colon Sys \to \mathbb{N}$;
var $x, x_1, x_2\colon Sys; e\colon U_{Sys}$;
$\quad y_1\colon State; y_2\colon \mathbb{N}$;

eqn $C_{Sys}(\overline{c}_{uninit}, x_1, x_2) = x_1$;
$\quad C_{Sys}(\overline{c}_{sys}, x_1, x_2) = x_2$;
$\quad C_{Sys}(e, x, x) = x$;
$\quad det_{Sys}(uninit) = \overline{c}_{uninit}$;
$\quad det_{Sys}(sys(y_1, y_2)) = \overline{c}_{sys}$;
$\quad \pi^1_{sys}(uninit) = p\_on$;
$\quad \pi^2_{sys}(uninit) = 0$;
$\quad \pi^1_{sys}(sys(y_1, y_2)) = y_1$;
$\quad \pi^2_{sys}(sys(y_1, y_2)) = y_2$;

The explanation of the additions is as follows. We add constructor sort U_{Sys}, with constructors $\overline{c}_{sys}, \overline{c}_{uninit}$, i.e., we introduce one new constructor in sort U_{Sys} for every constructor in the unfolded sort. Case function C_{Sys} is used in the unfolding of processes to reconstruct an expression of sort *Sys* from the unfolded parts, e.g., $C_{Sys}(\overline{c}_{sys}, uninit, sys(p\_on, 3)) = sys(p\_on, 3)$. The case $C_{sys}(e, x, x) = x$ is used to facilitate simplifications in the implementation even when the arguments do not yet have a concrete value. We add determinizer functions det_{Sys} that are used to recognize the head symbol of an expression of sort *Sys*, and map it onto the corresponding constructor in U_{Sys}, e.g., $det_{Sys}(sys(p\_on, 3)) = \overline{c}_{sys}$. Projection functions π^1_{sys} and π^2_{sys} are added to extract the arguments of an expression with head symbol *sys*, e.g., $\pi^2_{sys}(sys(p\_on, 3)) = 3$; if this projection function is applied to *uninit* it returns a default value. Since constructor *uninit* has no arguments, there are no projection functions π_{uninit}.

To be effective in practice, the projection and determinizer functions need to distribute over if-then-else and the case functions. Therefore, also the following distribution laws are added.

var $x_1, x_2\colon Sys; e\colon U_{Sys}; b\colon \mathbb{B}$
eqn $\pi^1_{sys}(C_{Sys}(e, x_1, x_2)) = C_{Sys}(e, \pi^1_{sys}(x_1), \pi^1_{sys}(x_2))$;
$\quad \pi^1_{sys}(if(b, x_1, x_2)) = if(b, \pi^1_{sys}(x_1), \pi^1_{sys}(x_2))$;
$\quad \pi^2_{sys}(C_{Sys}(e, x_1, x_2)) = C_{Sys}(e, \pi^2_{sys}(x_1), \pi^2_{sys}(x_2))$;
$\quad \pi^2_{sys}(if(b, x_1, x_2)) = if(b, \pi^2_{sys}(x_1), \pi^2_{sys}(x_2))$;
$\quad det_{Sys}(C_{Sys}(e, x_1, x_2)) = C_{Sys}(e, det_{Sys}(x_1), det_{Sys}(x_2))$;
$\quad det_{Sys}(if(b, x_1, x_2)) = if(b, det_{Sys}(x_1), det_{Sys}(x_2))$;

4.2   Unfolding Process Parameters in an LPE

We next describe how to unfold a process parameter d in an LPE, and how to split expressions e that were assigned to d into expressions that can be assigned to the new process parameters. As our extensions modify these definitions, we present them in more detail. For the sake of simplicity, we describe the unfolding in the setting of an LPE with a single process parameter. For processes with multiple process parameters, this generalizes in the obvious way.

Definition 2. *Let $d\colon D$ be a variable of constructor sort D, with $C_S(D) = \{f_0, \ldots, f_n\}$. Let D be such that for all constructors $f\colon D_1 \times \cdots \times D_n \to D \in C_S(D)$, and terms $t_1, \ldots, t_n, t'_1, \ldots, t'_n$, if $f(t_1, \ldots, t_n) \equiv f(t'_1, \ldots, t'_n)$ then $t_i \equiv t'_i$ for all i.*

We first define how process parameters are manipulated.

– *First, if we unfold parameter d, new parameters need to be introduced to store the arguments for each of the constructors of sort d. For $f_i\colon D_i^1 \times \cdots \times D_i^{n_i} \to D \in C_S(D)$, this is the vector* $\mathsf{params}(d, f_i) = d_i^1\colon D_i^1, \ldots, \ldots d_i^{n_i}\colon D_i^{n_i}$. *Note that if f_i is a constant, $\mathsf{params}(d, f_i)$ is the empty vector.*
– *To define the parameters unfolding d we need one variable that represents the constructor, and parameters for the arguments of each of the constructors.*

$$\mathsf{params}(d) = e_d\colon U_D, \mathsf{params}(d, f_1), \ldots, \mathsf{params}(d, f_n)$$

Note $e_d\colon U_D$ determines the constructor of sort D, with U_D the corresponding constructor sort.

– *If d is replaced by $\mathsf{params}(d)$, any use of d needs to be reconstructed using an equivalent expression in terms of the new parameters. We abbreviate this by $\mathsf{reconstruct}(d)$.*

$$\mathsf{reconstruct}(d) = C(e_d, f_0(\mathsf{params}(d, f_0)), \ldots, f_n(\mathsf{params}(d, f_n)))$$

If originally e was assigned to d, after d has been replaced by $\mathsf{params}(d)$, expression e also needs to be split into expressions that can be assigned to these new parameters. We define the following. Let e be an expression of type D. Then

$$\mathsf{unfold}(e) = det_D(e), \pi_{f_0}^1(e), \ldots, \pi_{f_0}^{m_0}(e), \ldots, \pi_{f_n}^1(e), \ldots, \pi_{f_n}^{m_n}(e)$$

where m_i denotes the index of the last argument of constructor f_i.

The unfolding of process parameters described in [6] is as follows. In the rest of this paper, we will refer to this as using *default case placement*.

Definition 3 (Unfolding of process parameters [6]). *Let $L = (\mathcal{D}, \mathcal{X}_g, P, e)$ be an LPS, where P is the following LPE.*

$$P(d\colon D) = \sum_{i \in I} \sum_{\vec{e_i}\colon \vec{E_i}} c_i \to a_i(f_i) \cdot P(g_i)$$

The result of unfolding process parameter $d\colon D$ in L, denoted $\mathsf{parunfold}(d)(L)$ is the LPS $(\mathcal{D}', \mathcal{X}_g, P', \mathsf{unfold}(e))$, where $\mathcal{D}'$ is data specification $\mathcal{D}$ in which sort D is unfolded, and LPE P' is as follows:

$$P'(\mathsf{params}(d)) = \sum_{i \in I} \sum_{\vec{e_i}\colon \vec{E_i}} c_i[d := \mathsf{reconstruct}(d)]$$

$$\to a_i(f_i[d := \mathsf{reconstruct}(d)]) \cdot P'(\mathsf{unfold}(g_i[d := \mathsf{reconstruct}(d)]))$$

So, essentially, unfolding parameter d replaces d by the vector $\mathsf{params}(d)$. In the right hand side of the equation, every occurrence of d is replaced syntactically by $\mathsf{reconstruct}(d)$, i.e., an application of the corresponding case function. Finally, in the recursive calls to P, the expression that after the previous step has become $g_i[d := \mathsf{reconstruct}(d)]$, is unfolded using $\mathsf{unfold}(g_i[d := \mathsf{reconstruct}(d)])$. Similarly, using $\mathsf{unfold}(e)$, the initial process is unfolded.

Example 2. Recall our motivating example, for which we have described the unfolding of sort *Sys* in the data specification in Example 1. If we unfold parameter s, we get the LPE and initialization shown below.

proc $P(e\colon U_{Sys}, s_1\colon State, s_2\colon \mathbb{N})$
$\quad = C(e, uninit, sys(s_1, s_2)) \approx uninit)$
$\qquad \rightarrow initialize \cdot$
$\qquad\qquad P(det_{Sys}(sys(p\_off, dc1)), \pi^1_{sys}(sys(p\_off, dc1)), \pi^2_{sys}(sys(p\_off, dc1)))$
$\quad + \sum_{n:\mathbb{N}}(!(C(e, uninit, sys(s_1, s_2)) \approx uninit) \wedge$
$\qquad\qquad get\_state(C(e, uninit, sys(s_1, s_2))) \approx p\_off)$
$\qquad \rightarrow on \cdot P(det_{Sys}(set\_state(set\_ip(C(e, uninit, sys(s_1, s_2)), n), p\_on)),$
$\qquad\qquad\qquad \pi^1_{sys}(set\_state(set\_ip(C(e, uninit, sys(s_1, s_2)), n), p\_on)),$
$\qquad\qquad\qquad \pi^2_{sys}(set\_state(set\_ip(C(e, uninit, sys(s_1, s_2)), n), p\_on)))$
$\quad + (!(C(e, uninit, sys(s_1, s_2)) \approx uninit) \wedge$
$\qquad\qquad get\_state(C(e, uninit, sys(s_1, s_2))) \approx p\_on)$
$\qquad \rightarrow off \cdot P(det_{Sys}(set\_state(set\_ip(C(e, uninit, sys(s_1, s_2)), dc2), p\_off)),$
$\qquad\qquad\qquad \pi^1_{sys}(set\_state(set\_ip(C(e, uninit, sys(s_1, s_2)), dc2), p\_off)),$
$\qquad\qquad\qquad \pi^2_{sys}(set\_state(set\_ip(C(e, uninit, sys(s_1, s_2)), dc2), p\_off)));$
init $\quad P(det_{Sys}(uninit), \pi^1_{sys}(uninit), \pi^2_{sys}(uninit));$

It has three parameters. Parameter e keeps track of the constructor of the expression in s, e.g., initially s is $uninit$, so the corresponding value in e is $\overline{c}_{uninit}$. Parameters s_1 and s_2 are used to track the arguments of the constructor sys. If e is $\overline{c}_{sys}$, then $sys(s_1, s_2)$ is equivalent to s (the orginal parameter that is unfolded). As $uninit$ does not have arguments, no parameters need to be introduced for its arguments. The original expression s is then reconstructed in the process by replacing s with $C(e, uninit, sys(s_1, s_2))$. The functions det_{Sys}, π^1_{sys} and π^2_{sys} are used to move from an expression of sort Sys to expressions of sort U_{Sys}, $State$ and $\mathbb{N}$.

Using the equations for det_{Sys}, π^1_{sys} and π^2_{sys} for rewriting, this can be simplified slightly. The recursion of the first summand then becomes $P(\overline{c}_{sys}, p\_off, dc1)$ and the initialization becomes **init** $P(\overline{c}_{uninit}, p\_on, 0)$, as per the default values of $\pi^i_{sys}(uninit)$. The resulting LPE cannot be simplified further. Since parameters s_1 and s_2 appear in the conditions of each of the summands, existing static analysis tools for constant elimination and parameter elimination are not able to remove any of the parameters from this process.

Correctness of the unfolding is established by the following theorem.

Theorem 1 ([6]). *Let $L = (\mathcal{D}, \mathcal{X}_g, P, e)$ and $\mathsf{parunfold}(d)(L) = (\mathcal{D}', \mathcal{X}_g, P', \mathsf{unfold}(e))$ be the LPSs as in Definition 3. Then $P(e) \leftrightarrow P'(\mathsf{unfold}(e))$.*

5   Improving Parameter Unfolding

In this section we present three improvements to parameter unfolding: we alter the way case functions are placed in the processes, we explicitly take global variables into account during the transformation, and we show how pattern matching rules in the data specification can be used to simplify the data in the resulting process expressions.

5.1   Alternative Case Placement

In our standard definition of unfolding, each occurrence of d is replaced by reconstruct(d), and thus case functions are placed at an *innermost* level. This can limit simplification by rewriting; e.g., expression $C(e, uninit, sys(s_1, s_2)) \approx uninit$ in the condition of the first summand in Example 2 cannot be simplified.

In many cases, placing the case function at an *outermost* level aids rewriting and subsequent analysis of the LPE. Formally, every condition c_i now becomes $C(e_d, c_i[d := f_0(\mathsf{params}(d, f_0))], \ldots, c_i[d := f_n(\mathsf{params}(d, f_n))])$. However, this may lead to an exponential blow-up in the size of the conditions if multiple parameter unfoldings are performed successively. Therefore, we propose an intermediate approach that places case functions at the level where subexpressions are no longer Boolean. We call this *alternative case placement*. Intuitively, starting from the outermost placement, we distribute the case function over the standard Boolean operators.

Definition 4. *Given a data expression c and a variable d, the* alternative case placement *is the expression* $\mathsf{acp}(c, d)$, *where* acp *is the recursive function:*

$$
\begin{aligned}
\mathsf{acp}(b, d) \quad &= C(e, b[d := f_1(\mathsf{params}(d, f_1))], \ldots, b[d := f_n(\mathsf{params}(d, f_n))]) \\
\mathsf{acp}(\neg \varphi, d) \quad &= \neg \mathsf{acp}(\varphi, d) \\
\mathsf{acp}(\varphi \wedge \psi, d) &= \mathsf{acp}(\varphi, d) \wedge \mathsf{acp}(\psi, d) \\
\mathsf{acp}(\varphi \vee \psi, d) &= \mathsf{acp}(\varphi, d) \vee \mathsf{acp}(\psi, d) \\
\mathsf{acp}(\varphi \Rightarrow \psi, d) &= \mathsf{acp}(\varphi, d) \Rightarrow \mathsf{acp}(\psi, d)
\end{aligned}
$$

Here, φ and ψ are arbitrary terms and b is a data expression that does not have $\neg, \wedge, \vee, \Rightarrow$ as its top-level operator.

Note that in the first case of the definition of acp, $\mathsf{acp}(b, d)$ is equivalent to b if d does not occur in b, by the rule $C(e, x, x) = x$. Under alternative case placement, the unfolded LPE of Definition 3 becomes:

$$
P'(\mathsf{params}(d)) = \sum_{i \in I} \sum_{\vec{e_i}\, :\, \vec{E_i}} \mathsf{acp}(c_i, d) \rightarrow a_i(\mathsf{acp}(f_i, d)) \cdot P'(\mathsf{acp}(\mathsf{unfold}(g_i), d))
$$

Correctness follows immediately from the observation that $\mathsf{acp}(b, d) \equiv b[d := \mathsf{reconstruct}(d)]$ (by case analysis on e). We next discuss the benefits of alternative case placement on our running example.

Example 3. Recall our motivating example, for which we have described the unfolding of sort *Sys* in Examples 1 and 2. We show the result of the unfolding using the alternative case placement. As all summands are changed in a similar way, we focus on the last summand of the LPE:

$$(!C(e, uninit \approx uninit, sys(s_1, s_2) \approx uninit) \wedge$$
$$C(e, get\_state(uninit) \approx p\_on, get\_state(sys(s_1, s_2)) \approx p\_on))$$
$$\rightarrow off \cdot P(C(e, det_{Sys}(set\_state(set\_ip(uninit, dc2), p\_off)),$$
$$det_{Sys}(set\_state(set\_ip(sys(s_1, s_2), dc2), p\_off))),$$
$$C(e, \pi^1_{sys}(set\_state(set\_ip(uninit, dc2), p\_off)),$$
$$\pi^1_{sys}(set\_state(set\_ip(sys(s_1, s_2), dc2), p\_off))),$$
$$C(e, \pi^2_{sys}(set\_state(set\_ip(uninit, dc2), p\_off)),$$
$$\pi^2_{sys}(set\_state(set\_ip(sys(s_1, s_2), dc2), p\_off))))$$

Compared to the LPE using default case placement, observe that the case functions now appear at a higher level. For instance, the second conjunct of the condition was changed from $get\_state(C(e, uninit, sys(s_1, s_2))) \approx p\_on$ to $C(e, get\_state(uninit) \approx p\_on, get\_state(sys(s_1, s_2)) \approx p\_on)$. In the original, the case function cannot be simplified further, as the first argument e is a variable, and it cannot be matched to any of the rewrite rules; also, there are no rules that allow distributing equality over the case function. When applying alternative case placement, the equality appears within the scope of the arguments of the case function, and the (implicit) equations for $\approx$ can be used to simplify the individual arguments.

Similar changes can be seen in the arguments of the recursive processes. Using the equations for $\approx$, det_{Sys}, π^1_{sys}, π^2_{sys}, set_ip and set_state, the last summand is simplified to:

$$(!C(e, true, false) \wedge C(e, get\_state(uninit) \approx p\_on, s_1 \approx p\_on))$$
$$\rightarrow off \cdot P(C(e, \overline{c}_{uninit}, \overline{c}_{sys}), C(e, p\_on, p\_off), C(e, 0, dc2))$$

We thus obtained more concise expressions than those in Example 2. In particular, this summand no longer contains any reference to unfolded parameter s_2. The same applies to the other two summands, hence parameter s_2 can be eliminated. As a result, the sum over n in the second summand can be eliminated as well, and the final LPE we obtain is:

proc $P(e: U_{Sys}, s_1: State)$
$= C(e, true, false)$
$\quad \rightarrow initialize \cdot P(\overline{c}_{sys}, p\_off)$
$+(!C(e, true, false) \wedge C(e, get\_state(uninit) \approx p\_off, s_1 \approx p\_off))$
$\quad \rightarrow on \cdot P(C(e, \overline{c}_{uninit}, \overline{c}_{sys}), p\_on)$
$+(!C(e, true, false) \wedge C(e, get\_state(uninit) \approx p\_on, s_1 \approx p\_on))$
$\quad \rightarrow off \cdot P(C(e, \overline{c}_{uninit}, \overline{c}_{sys}), C(e, p\_on, p\_off))$
init $P(\overline{c}_{uninit}, p\_on)$;

Note that the original state space before the unfolding is infinite while after unfolding with alternative case placement the state space has only three states.

5.2   Global Variables

Other static analysis techniques use global variables to more effectively simplify the process. For instance, when constant elimination observes that the only change to a parameter is assigning a global variable to that parameter, the global variable can be replaced by a constant. This is safe since all values for global variables lead to bisimilar processes.

When unfolding a process parameter, the value assigned to it in the initialization or recursion may be a global variable $dc \in \mathcal{X}_g$. Applying the unfoldings described so far results in $unfold(dc)$, which contains expressions such as $det_D(dc)$ and $\pi_{f_i}^j(dc)$ that cannot be rewritten further. Other static analysis techniques cannot directly use such expressions, leaving the resulting LPE more complicated than it needs to be, resulting in longer verification times.

We illustrate the issue using an example that is based on the representation of the board in the specifications of games such as tic-tac-toe.

Example 4. Process P is initialized with a singleton list $[o]$ of sort $List(Piece)$ representing the board. It also has parameters p, keeping track of the player whose turn it is, and *done* to indicate that the game ends. As long as *done* is false, and l contains a piece of player p whose turn it is, p is updated to the next player. If l contains a piece of the other player, a τ transition is taken, the values of l and p are set to global variables, and *done* is set to true. If *done* is true, the process deadlocks. This resembles what happens in models of board games such as tic-tac-toe when the game ends.

$$
\begin{aligned}
&\textbf{sort} \quad Piece = \textbf{struct } x \mid o; \\
&\textbf{map} \quad other: Piece \rightarrow Piece; \\
&\textbf{eqn} \quad other(x) = o; other(o) = x; \\
&\textbf{act} \quad is: Piece; \\
&\textbf{glob} \quad dc1: List(Piece); dc2: Piece; \\
&\textbf{proc} \quad P(l: List(Piece), p: Piece, done: Bool) \\
&\qquad = (\neg done \wedge l \approx [other(p)]) \rightarrow \tau.P(dc1, dc2, true) \\
&\qquad\quad +(\neg done \wedge l \approx [p]) \rightarrow is(p).P([p], other(p), done); \\
&\textbf{init} \quad P([o], o, false);
\end{aligned}
$$

Unfolding parameter l yields the following LPE.

$$
\begin{aligned}
&\textbf{proc} \quad P(e: U_{Piece}, l_p: Piece, l_l: List(Piece), p: Piece, done: Bool) \\
&\qquad = \neg done \wedge C_{List(Piece)}(e, [], l_p \triangleright l_l) \approx [other(p)] \\
&\qquad\quad \rightarrow \tau.P(det_{List(Piece)}(dc1), \pi_\triangleright^1(dc1), \pi_\triangleright^2(dc1), dc2, true) \\
&\qquad\quad +(\neg done \wedge C_{List(Piece)}(e, [], l_p \triangleright l_l) \approx [p]) \\
&\qquad\quad \rightarrow is(p).P(det_{List(Piece)}([p]), \pi_\triangleright^1([p]), \pi_\triangleright^2([p]), other(p)); \\
&\textbf{init} \quad P(det_{List(Piece)}([o]), \pi_\triangleright^1([o]), \pi_\triangleright^2([o]), o, false);
\end{aligned}
$$

The recursion in the first summand cannot be simplified further, and constant- and redundant parameter elimination cannot remove any parameters.

Since the behavior of a process is not affected by (the value of) a global variable, the individual arguments of the expression assigned to that global variable also do not affect the behavior of the process. Therefore, instead of applying projection functions to a global variable, fresh global variables can be introduced for each of the new process parameters when unfolding a global variable. We extend the definition of unfold from Definition 2 as follows.

Definition 5. *Let e be an expression of constructor sort D. Then*

$$\mathsf{unfold}_g(e) = \begin{cases} dc_e, dc_{f_0}^1, \ldots, dc_{f_0}^{m_0}, \ldots, dc_{f_n}^1, \ldots, dc_{f_n}^{m_n} & \text{if } e \in \mathcal{X}_g \\ \mathsf{unfold}(e) & \text{otherwise} \end{cases}$$

where $dc_e, dc_{f_0}^1, \ldots, dc_{f_0}^{m_0}, \ldots dc_{f_n}^1, \ldots, dc_{f_n}^{m_n}$ are fresh global variables, and m_i denotes the index of the last argument of constructor f_i.

The unfolded LPE taking global variables is obtained by using unfold_g instead of unfold in Definition 3.[1] We apply this improved definition to the specification in Example 4.

Example 5. Recall the specification from Example 4. When using unfold_g instead of unfold, the recursion in the first summand becomes $P(dc_e, dc_{lp}, dc_{ll}, dc2, true)$.

This allows further simplification using constant elimination and parameter elimination and simplification using rewriting to the LPE below.

> **proc** $P(l_p: Piece, p: Piece, done: Bool)$
> $= (\neg done \wedge l_p \approx p) \rightarrow is(p).P(p, other(p), done)$
> $+(\neg done \wedge l_p \approx other(p)) \rightarrow \tau.P(dc_{lp}, dc2, true);$
> **init** $P(o, o, false);$

In particular, all case functions, determinizers and projection functions are fully removed. The transformation now essentially replaced the (fixed-length) list in the original process by its individual elements.

5.3   Simplifications for Pattern Matching Rules

In the recursion $P(\mathsf{unfold}(g_i[d := \mathsf{reconstruct}(d)]))$, we regularly obtain expressions of the shape $det_D(h(a_1, \ldots, a_n))$ or $\pi_{f_k}^l(h(a_1, \ldots, a_n))$ for some function symbol h that is not a constructor. Both of these cannot be rewritten any further, often due to the fact that there is insufficient information to apply the pattern matching in the equations for h. Therefore, we propose a method to perform one unfolding of the function h, allowing us to achieve the necessary simplifications. Let us first consider an example.

Example 6. Suppose we have a function *plusone*, which is defined using pattern matching, that increments every element of a list. Our linear process P updates the elements of its argument $l : List(\mathbb{N})$ using this function as follows:

> **map** $plusone : List(\mathbb{N}) \rightarrow List(\mathbb{N});$
> **var** $x : \mathbb{N};\ xs : List(\mathbb{N});$
> **eqn** $plusone([]) = [];$
> $plusone(x \rhd xs) = (x + 1) \rhd plusone(xs);$
> **proc** $P(l : List(\mathbb{N})) = a \cdot P(plusone(l));$
> **init** $P([7]);$

---

[1] The definition using alternative case placement can be modified to take global variables into account in the same way.

If we unfold l (default case placement), we obtain as first argument update in the summand the expression $det_{List(N)}(plusone(C_{List(N)}(e, [], s_1 \triangleright s_2)))$, which cannot be rewritten any further.

Intuitively, since $det_{List(N)}$ considers only its argument's constructor, and *plusone* does not modify the constructor, $det_{List(N)}(l) = det_{List(N)}(plusone(l))$ for all l. However, due to the pattern matching nature of *plusone*, we can only eliminate the application of $det_{List(N)}$ by means of term rewriting if l is of the shape $[]$ or $x \triangleright xs$. Thus, the tools are not able to deduce that the update in the example above is in fact equal to e, and that the summand does not modify e. To facilitate further static analysis in the above example, it would be helpful to have a general technique for further simplification in such situations.

Our approach is to compute a single non-pattern-matching rewrite rule for each mapping that is equivalent to its original pattern-matching-based definition. The pattern matching logic will instead be encoded in a tree of case functions. We will apply the new singly-defined rule in selected places in order to eliminate determinizer and projection functions by means of ordinary rewriting. At its core, our transformation is based on the following observation, which follows by case analysis on the top-level constructor in a_i.

Lemma 1. *Let* $h : D_1 \times \ldots D_n \to D$ *be a mapping and* $a_1, \ldots, a_n$ *arbitrary expressions. Then we have for any* σ *and any* $1 \le i \le n$:

$$\begin{aligned}
[\![h(a_1, \ldots, a_n)]\!]^\sigma = [\![C_{D_i}(det_{D_i}(a_i), \\
h(a_1, \ldots, a_{i-1}, f_1(\pi^1_{f_1}(a_i), \ldots, \pi^{n_1}_{f_1}(a_i)), a_{i+1}, \ldots, a_n), \ldots, \\
h(a_1, \ldots, a_{i-1}, f_{|\mathcal{C}_S(D)|}(\pi^1_{f_{|\mathcal{C}_S(D)|}}(a_i), \ldots, \pi^{n_{|\mathcal{C}_S(D)|}}_{f_{|\mathcal{C}_S(D)|}}(a_i)), a_{i+1}, \ldots, a_n))]\!]^\sigma
\end{aligned}$$

We repeatedly apply this equality until each application of h can be rewritten, leading to nested case function applications. Furthermore, we add the rewrite rule $C_D(e, \bar{c}_{f_1}, \ldots, \bar{c}_{f_{|\mathcal{C}_S(D)|}}) = e$ to aid simplification. Using the distribution laws, the surrounding determinizer/projection functions can often be eliminated.

Example 7. We revisit the expression $det_{List(N)}(plusone(C_{List(N)}(e, [], s_1 \triangleright s_2)))$ obtained from unfolding in Example 6. Applying Lemma 1 on *plusone*, we obtain the following expression that can be rewritten to just e.

$$\begin{aligned}
det_{List(N)}(C_{List(N)}(det_{List(N)}(C_{List(N)}(e, [], s_1 \triangleright s_2)), \\
plusone([]), \\
plusone(\pi^1_{List(N)}(C_{List(N)}(e, [], s_1 \triangleright s_2)) \triangleright \pi^2_{List(N)}(C_{List(N)}(e, [], s_1 \triangleright s_2)))))
\end{aligned}$$

6 Experiments

The original parameter unfolding technique from [6] has been available in the tool `lpsparunfold` in the mCRL2 toolset [3] for over a decade. We have extended the C++ implementation with the ideas described. The tool allows selecting

Table 1. Experimental results for symbolic reachability, reporting size of the underlying labeled transition system, and the mean total time of each of the tool executions out of 10 runs.

Models	Sizes (# states)				Times (s)			
	standard	original	new.def	new.alt	standard	original	new.def	new.alt
cylinder			1 593 209		30.2	16.8	16.9	17.4
fourinarow3-4			12 305		63.9	59.2	1.5	1.5
fourinarow3-5	t-o		171 243		t-o	1 437.6	10.5	10.5
fourinarow4-3			6 214		15.3	32.3	1.0	1.0
fourinarow4-4	t-o		187 928		t-o	1 790.0	10.6	10.4
fourinarow4-5	t-o		5 464 759		t-o	t-o	350.5	350.1
fourinarow5-3			44 131		832.8	400.7	3.4	3.3
fourinarow5-4	t-o		2 788 682		t-o	t-o	166.0	164.9
fourinarow5-5	t-o				t-o	t-o	t-o	t-o
onoff	t-o			3	t-o	t-o	t-o	0.1
sla7			7 918		2.0	2.5	2.6	2.4
sla10			238 931		31.9	19.1	18.8	15.6
sla13	t-o		6 693 054		t-o	432.7	418.3	324.2
swp2-2			14 064		1.2	1.2	1.2	1.2
swp2-4			140 352		2.4	2.5	2.4	2.4
swp2-6			598 320		3.2	3.5	3.1	3.2
swp2-8			1 731 840		4.1	4.8	3.9	4.0
swp4-2			2 589 056		5.9	9.8	7.4	7.3
swp4-4			292 878 336		132.4	173.6	110.4	111.7
swp4-6			5 729 304 960		3 072.5	1 146.3	716.9	725.5
swp4-8	t-o		50 128 191 488		t-o	t-o	2 968.2	3 010.4
swp8-2	t-o				t-o	t-o	t-o	t-o
tictactoe3-3			5 479		14.1	9.6	1.5	1.5
wms			155 034 776		17.0	17.0	16.8	16.2

which parameters to unfold, and the number of times that parameter should be unfolded using command-line options. Multiple parameters can be unfolded in a single run; this is achieved by iterating the unfolding of a single parameter.

To evaluate the effect of our improvements on further analysis of LPEs and the generation of the underlying state space using symbolic reachability, we compare the following workflows:

- **standard**: standard static analysis workflow: instantiate finite summations, eliminate constant and redundant parameters and superfluous summation variables [6] (tools lpssuminst, lpsconstelm, lpsparelm and lpssumelm). Finally, perform symbolic reachability (lpsreach). No parameter unfolding.
- **original**: before **standard**, perform the original parameter unfolding.
- **new.def**: before **standard**, perform parameter unfolding with our extension for global variables and pattern matching rules with default case placement.
- **new.alt**: same as **new.def** but use alternative case placement.

The workflows are executed on various models translated to mCRL2, including our running example (onoff). Models of two-player games, often used to teach formal methods: *four-in-a-row*, with varying numbers of rows and columns and *tic-tac-toe* on a standard 3×3 board, in which the board is encoded using fixed length lists of lists. First, the board is unfolded, and then each of the rows resulting from this first unfolding. Models of a *sliding window protocol* [5], that forms the basis of the TCP protocol used for reliable in-order delivery of packets, as it occurs in [7], with window size n and m messages (swp-n-m) for different values of n and m. The send and receive windows are unfolded. Moreover, we include models based on industrial applications: a UML state machine diagram of an industrial pneumatic cylinder (cylinder) [15]; the protocol negotiating a *service level agreement* (sla) between two parties communicating via message passing along reliable channels encoded using fixed length lists [9]; and a model of the Workload Management System (wms) of the DIRAC Community Grid Solution for the LHCb experiment at CERN [14]. Note that the use of complex data structures for industrial case studies is wide-spread, allowing the creation of concise and elegant models.

All experiments were run 10 times, on a machine with 4 Intel 6136 CPUs and 3 TB of RAM, running Ubuntu 20.04. A reproduction package is available from https://github.com/astramaglia/lpsparunfold-experiments. The results are presented in Table 1. We used a time-out of 1 h (3600 s), and a memory limit of 64 GB. We report the size of the explored state space (in number of states, or 't-o' in case of a time-out) and the mean total running time of ten runs in seconds. For most of the experiments, the standard deviation is below 10% of the mean.[2] If workflows result in the same state space for a model, we report the size only once in the table.

The experiments show that our improvements typically reduce the total running time of the verification. In particular, our extension for global variables reduces the running time for *four-in-a-row* and *tic-tac-toe*. The simplifications for pattern matching rules show a reduction in the running time for the sliding window protocol (swp). Alternative case placement reduces the infinite state space of our running example (onoff) to only three states; for the service-level-agreement protocol (sla) it reduces the total running time.

Even when the size of the state space is not changed, our improvements often reduce the running time of symbolic reachability. This is due to the simplification of data in the processes, and the reduction of dependencies between process parameters. Although in theory alternative case placement could lead to an exponential blow-up of the expressions in the LPE, this is not observed in our experiments.

7   Conclusion

In this paper we described and revisited the static analysis technique for flattening the structure of process parameters in LPEs, in the context of mCRL2. The extensions improve the effectiveness of parameter unfolding in two ways. First,

---

[2] The SDs for the only cases where it exceeds 10% of the mean are: *fourinarow4-3* standard 1.7, *sla7* new.def: 0.3, *tictactoe3-3* standard: 2.0, *wms* standard: 2.5, original: 2.2, new.def: 1.9.

it improves the effectiveness of other static analysis tools. Our experiments show that this can result in large reductions of the underlying state space, directly improving explicit-state model checking. Second, for symbolic model checking, and symbolic reachability in particular, our improvements reduce the execution times even if the size of the state space is not reduced.

We believe the effect of `lpsparunfold` should be investigated in relation to other static analysis techniques such as dead variable analysis. Together these have the potential to speed up the model checking of industrial systems, e.g., described by OIL models [4] and Cordis models [15] using mCRL2. Furthermore, the effect of `lpsparunfold` could be investigated in the context of PBESs.

Acknowledgements. Michel Reniers and Frank Stappers previously described Groote and Lisser's original definition of parameter unfolding in an unpublished note. Some of our notation is inspired by their note.

References

1. Blom, S., Fokkink, W., Groote, J.F., van Langevelde, I., Lisser, B., van de Pol, J.: μCRL: a toolset for analysing algebraic specifications. In: Berry, G., Comon, H., Finkel, A. (eds.) CAV 2001. LNCS, vol. 2102, pp. 250–254. Springer, Heidelberg (2001). https://doi.org/10.1007/3-540-44585-4_23

2. Blom, S., van de Pol, J.: Symbolic reachability for process algebras with recursive data types. In: Fitzgerald, J.S., Haxthausen, A.E., Yenigun, H. (eds.) ICTAC 2008. LNCS, vol. 5160, pp. 81–95. Springer, Heidelberg (2008). https://doi.org/10.1007/978-3-540-85762-4_6

3. Bunte, O., et al.: The mCRL2 toolset for analysing concurrent systems. In: Vojnar, T., Zhang, L. (eds.) TACAS 2019. LNCS, vol. 11428, pp. 21–39. Springer, Cham (2019). https://doi.org/10.1007/978-3-030-17465-1_2

4. Bunte, O., Gool, L.C.M., Willemse, T.A.C.: Formal verification of OIL component specifications using mCRL2. In: ter Beek, M.H., Ničković, D. (eds.) FMICS 2020. LNCS, vol. 12327, pp. 231–251. Springer, Cham (2020). https://doi.org/10.1007/978-3-030-58298-2_10

5. Cerf, V., Kahn, R.: A protocol for packet network intercommunication. IEEE Trans. Commun. **22**(5), 637–648 (1974). https://doi.org/10.1109/TCOM.1974.1092259

6. Groote, J.F., Lisser, B.: Computer assisted manipulation of algebraic process specifications. Technical report SEN-R0117, CWI (2001). https://ir.cwi.nl/pub/4326/

7. Groote, J.F., Mousavi, M.R.: Modeling and Analysis of Communicating Systems. The MIT Press, Cambridge (2014)

8. Groote, J.F., Willemse, T.A.C.: Parameterised Boolean equation systems. Theoret. Comput. Sci. **343**(3), 332–369 (2005). https://doi.org/10.1016/j.tcs.2005.06.016

9. Groote, J.F., Willemse, T.A.C.: A symmetric protocol to establish service level agreements. Log. Methods Comput. Sci. **16**(3) (2020). https://doi.org/10.23638/LMCS-16(3:19)2020

10. Keiren, J.J.A., Wesselink, W., Willemse, T.A.C.: Liveness analysis for parameterised Boolean equation systems. In: Cassez, F., Raskin, J.-F. (eds.) ATVA 2014. LNCS, vol. 8837, pp. 219–234. Springer, Cham (2014). https://doi.org/10.1007/978-3-319-11936-6_16

11. Meijer, J., Kant, G., Blom, S., van de Pol, J.: Read, write and copy dependencies for symbolic model checking. In: Yahav, E. (ed.) HVC 2014. LNCS, vol. 8855, pp. 204–219. Springer, Cham (2014). https://doi.org/10.1007/978-3-319-13338-6_16

12. Neele, T.: (Re)moving quantifiers to simplify parameterised Boolean equation systems. In: ARQNL 2022, vol. 3326, pp. 64–80. CEUR-WS (2022)

13. Orzan, S., Wesselink, W., Willemse, T.A.C.: Static analysis techniques for parameterised Boolean equation systems. In: Kowalewski, S., Philippou, A. (eds.) TACAS 2009. LNCS, vol. 5505, pp. 230–245. Springer, Heidelberg (2009). https://doi.org/10.1007/978-3-642-00768-2_22

14. Remenska, D., Willemse, T.A.C., Verstoep, K., Templon, J., Bal, H.: Using model checking to analyze the system behavior of the LHC production grid. Futur. Gener. Comput. Syst. **29**(8), 2239–2251 (2013). https://doi.org/10.1016/j.future.2013.06.004

15. Stramaglia, A., Keiren, J.J.A.: Formal verification of an industrial UML-like model using mCRL2. In: Groote, J.F., Huisman, M. (eds.) FMICS 2022. LNCS, vol. 13487, pp. 86–102. Springer, LNCS (2022). https://doi.org/10.1007/978-3-031-15008-1_7

16. van de Pol, J., Timmer, M.: State space reduction of linear processes using control flow reconstruction. In: Liu, Z., Ravn, A.P. (eds.) ATVA 2009. LNCS, vol. 5799, pp. 54–68. Springer, Heidelberg (2009). https://doi.org/10.1007/978-3-642-04761-9_5

17. Van Dijk, T., van de Pol, J.: Sylvan: multi-core framework for decision diagrams. Int. J. Softw. Tools Technol. Transf. **19**(6), 675–696 (2017). https://doi.org/10.1007/s10009-016-0433-2

Modular Soundness Checking of Feature Model Evolution Plans

Ida Sandberg Motzfeldt[1], Ingrid Chieh Yu[2], Crystal Chang Din[3]([✉]) [iD],
Violet Ka I Pun[4][iD], and Volker Stolz[4][iD]

[1] FINN.no, Oslo, Norway
ida.s.motzfeldt@gmail.com
[2] University of Oslo, Oslo, Norway
ingridcy@ifi.uio.no
[3] University of Bergen, Bergen, Norway
crystal.din@uib.no
[4] Western Norway University of Applied Sciences, Bergen, Norway
{violet.ka.i.pun,volker.stolz}@hvl.no

Abstract. A software product line (SPL) is a family of closely related
software systems which capitalizes on the variability and reusability of
the software products and can be formalised by a feature model. Feature
model evolution plans (FMEP) capture the current SPL as well as the
planned evolution of the SPL to ensure successful long-term development.
As business requirements often change, FMEPs should support intermediate update. This modification may cause paradoxes in an FMEP, e.g.,
a node left without a parent, making the plan impossible to realise. Current tools exist to validate FMEPs, but require analysing the entire plan
even when a modification affects only small parts of it. Hence, there is a
need for a method that detects such paradoxes in a more efficient way.
In this paper, we present an interval based feature model (IBFM), a representation for FMEPs, that allows local reasoning to validates only the
parts of the plan affected by changes. We define operations for updating
the FMEPs and the preconditions under which they preserve soundness,
i.e., absence of paradoxes, and show the correctness of the method.

Keywords: Software Product Line · Evolution Planning ·
Interval-based Feature Models · Operational Semantics

1 Introduction

A software product line (SPL) capitalizes on the similarity and variability of
closely related software products [23]. The similarities and variability are captured by features, which are customer-visible characteristics of a system [23].
Each product in the product line (called a *variant*) comprises a selection of
these features, resulting in a flexible and customisable set of variants available
to customers. To model an SPL it is common to use a *feature model* (FM), a
tree-like structure with nodes representing features. From this model, a variant
can be derived by selecting features. The structure of the feature model specifies

E. Ábrahám et al. (Eds.): ICTAC 2023, LNCS 14446, pp. 417–437, 2023.
https://doi.org/10.1007/978-3-031-47963-2_25

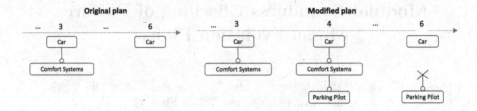

Fig. 1. Simple paradox

restrictions for which variants are allowed, while also making it possible to model all possible variants at once [3]. Due to the size and complexity of software systems, SPLs constitute a major investment with long-term strategic value. Over time, SPLs have to be adapted as part of software evolution to address new or changing requirements, which is particularly complicated as an entire software family has to be adapted [15, 20].

Long Term Evolution Planning. Complex projects require planning [7], where a plan may contain many changes to a feature model, which describes how the feature model should look at a future point in time. For instance, new technology may emerge that the manager wishes to incorporate into the product line but which she believes will take a year to implement. One can then plan how the feature model will look at that point and at some earlier stages where the new technology is partly included. On the other hand, as requirements may change over time, existing plans must *evolve* accordingly, for instance, some features may need to be added or removed. These retroactive changes can affect later parts of the plan, causing *paradoxes* that make the plan impossible to realise [14].

We illustrate in Fig. 1 how a paradox can be introduced through making changes to an existing plan. In the original evolution plan on the left of Fig. 1, a feature `Comfort Systems` exists at time 3 and is removed at time 6; and on the right we have the modified plan in which a child feature `Parking Pilot` is added to `Comfort Systems` at time 4. This change eventually causes a paradox at time 6 since feature `Parking Pilot` is left without a parent feature. In this case, it is straightforward to detect this paradox manually, but infeasible for a plan with hundreds of features and points in time. Thus, there is a need for tooling that supports safe retroactive change to *feature model evolution plans*. Notice also the difference between *feature model change*, i.e., planning to remove `Comfort Systems` at time 6, and *plan change*, i.e., modifying the original plan by introducing `Parking Pilot` at time 4. In this paper, we focus on plan changes.

Formalisation of feature model evolution plans (FMEPs) and methods for verifying soundness of FMEPs has been introduced in [10]. However, *changes* to FMEPs have not been addressed formally. The method in [10] requires analysis of the *entire plan* each time a change is made to the plan, even though much of the plan will often not be affected by a change.

This paper aims to remedy this by providing local reasoning of *plan change* instead of entire plans, leveraging the knowledge that a change may only affect parts of the plan, in both *spatial* (i.e., which parts of the feature model a change affects) and *temporal* dimensions (i.e., which points in time in the plan are affected by the change). As part of this challenge, we establish operations for modifying feature model evolution plans and a modular rule-based analysis method that can determine each operation's scopes and effects. We introduce the notion of intervals, enabling the lookup of information about specific parts of the feature models at a specific time. Changing an intermediate stage of a feature model evolution plan may cause *paradoxes*—structural violations of the feature model—at a later stage of the plan. Such paradoxes should be discovered, and the rule-based analysis must be sound. For this, we need to take into account the corresponding properties, namely, modularity, well-formedness, and correctness of model modification. An implementation of the resulting soundness checker for interval-based feature model evolution plans with an example is available at [18].

The rest of the paper is organised as follows: Sect. 2 provides the background knowledge, Sect. 3 introduces the interval-based feature models and presents the operational semantics rules of update operations. Section 4 shows the soundness of the rule system presented in Sect. 3. Finally, we discuss related work in Sect. 5 and conclude the paper in Sect. 6.

2   Background

In this section, we will first briefly recall the background of software product lines and feature model evaluation plans. Then, we use a simple example to describe the spatial and temporal scopes of update operations introduced in this paper.

2.1   Software Product Lines

A software product line (SPL) is a family of closely related software systems. These systems will often have several features in common, as well as variations that make each piece of software unique. SPLs are used to make highly configurable systems, where each product in the SPL, called a *variant*, is defined by the combination of features chosen.

Variants of a software product line can be defined in terms of a feature model. These models play a central role in planning and are also used as a communication tool. A feature model is a tree structure of features and groups. Features represent a concrete aspect in an SPL. They can be mandatory or optional and will contain zero or more groups. Each group has a set of features and the type of the group dictates which features in the group can be selected. For example, in an *and* group, all the mandatory features have to be chosen, while *or* groups have to select at least one feature and *alternative* groups have to select exactly one feature. Therefore, groups with types *or* or *alternative* must not contain mandatory features. A visual representation of a feature model can be seen in Fig. 2. The small filled dot above Infotainment System indicates

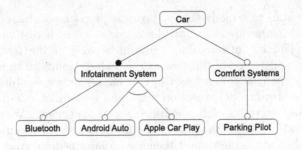

Fig. 2. Vehicle feature model

that the feature is mandatory, whereas the white dot above Comfort Systems represents an optional feature. Each feature (except the root) is in a group. The Infotainment System feature is in an *and* group below Car. The features Android Auto and Apple Car Play are in an *alternative* group, indicated by the arc between the features, meaning that each valid variant has exactly one of the two features. This vehicle feature model does not contain any *or* group, which can be indicated by a filled arc between the features if needed.

Well-Formedness Requirements. In addition to the described tree structure, a feature model is considered to be *sound* if it satisfies the following well-formedness requirements:

WF1 A feature model has exactly one root feature.
WF2 The root feature must be mandatory.
WF3 Each feature has exactly one unique name, variation type and (potentially empty) collection of subgroups.
WF4 Features are organised in groups that have exactly one variation type.
WF5 Each feature, except the root feature, must be part of exactly one group.
WF6 Each group must have exactly one parent feature.
WF7 ALTERNATIVE or OR groups must not contain MANDATORY features.
WF8 A feature model must not contain cycles.

Definition 1 (Paradox, Sound Plan). *A* paradox *is a violation of well-formedness requirements* **WF1–WF8**; *a plan without paradoxes is called* sound.

2.2 Planning Feature Model Evolution

Feature models let engineers capture all variants of the current software product line, but it can be beneficial to model future versions as well. Changing the SPL may potentially influence many configurations. Thus, it is paramount to thoroughly plan SPL evolution in advance, e.g., to perform analyses and to have enough time for implementing new or adapted features.

Feature Model Evolution Plans (FMEPs) [10], or Evolution Plans (EPs), allow us to model a sequence of feature models representing the current and

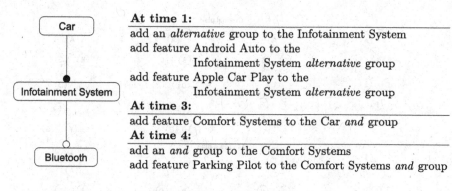

At time 1:

add an *alternative* group to the Infotainment System
add feature Android Auto to the
    Infotainment System *alternative* group
add feature Apple Car Play to the
    Infotainment System *alternative* group

At time 3:

add feature Comfort Systems to the Car *and* group

At time 4:

add an *and* group to the Comfort Systems
add feature Parking Pilot to the Comfort Systems *and* group

Fig. 3. Vehicle evolution plan

all planned future versions of an SPL. Each feature model in an EP represents the product line at a point in time, which could have varying validity, from a week from now to a year or more. Since the next feature model is derived from the previous one, we can represent the EP by means of an initial feature model as well as a sequence of time points, where each time point specifies a set of operations to be performed on the previous feature model to derive the next. The operations will either add, remove, move, rename, or change types of feature and/or groups in the feature model.

An example of an EP can be seen in Fig. 3, where the initial feature model containing three features is shown on the left, while a sequence of three time points together with the corresponding set of operations is on the right. At time 1, a group and two features are added to the initial feature model, at time 3, one feature is added, and at time 4, another group and a feature are added. Performing all the operations at these three time points results in a feature model that is identical to the one in Fig. 2.

For an EP to be sound, all of the feature models in the plan must uphold the structural requirements **WF1–WF8** described in Sect. 2.1. While the soundness can be verified automatically in [10], it requires verifying the entire plan, which is a sequence of feature models, each time a change is made, even though the majority of the plan may not be affected. To improve the efficiency of soundness checking for modified plans, we propose interval-based feature models (IBFMs), whose explicit representation of intervals for features and groups allow us to check the soundness of the corresponding affected parts of the plans. To achieve such local reasoning with IBFMs, we first introduce the notion of scopes of an update operation below.

2.3   Spatial and Temporal Scopes of Update Operations

The scopes of an update operation consist of two parts, *spatial* and *temporal*, indicating the parts of a plan that *may* be affected by the operation. The spatial scope refers to the parts of a feature model that may be influenced by the change performed by an operation, while the temporal scope corresponds to the time points that may be affected by applying an operation. We illustrates these two

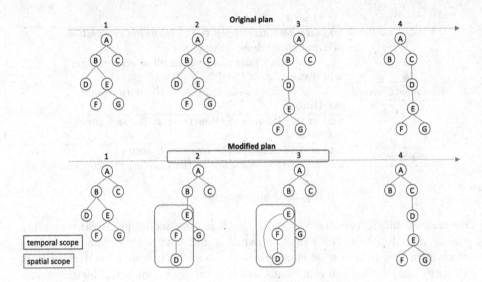

Fig. 4. Visualisation of the scopes for a move-feature operation

scopes of a move-feature operation in Fig. 4. For simplicity, only features are presented while groups are implicit in the visualisation.

In the original plan, feature E is moved to the group below feature D at time 3, and feature D to the group below feature C at time 4. In the modified EP at the bottom part of Fig. 4, a *move-feature* operation is introduced to the original plan, by which the feature D is moved to the group below feature F at time 2 and all the other operations remain the same as in the original plan. Note that moving a feature includes moving its entire subtree, as shown in the figure.

Although the feature model might be sound at the point the feature is moved, it might become invalid due to other operations applied at a later point in time. In this example, the feature model is sound at time 2 when feature D is moved to the group below feature F, but becomes unsound at time 3 when feature E is moved to the group below feature D according to the original plan, creating a cycle (details about cycle detection will be discussed in the next section). Since feature D is moved under the group of feature C at time 4 as in the original plan, the temporal scope for the soundness checking of this newly added move-feature operation is from time 2 to time 3. Since the operation only affects features D, E and F, the spatial scope contains only these three features. Observe that features A, B, C and G are not in the scope, nor are the time points 1 and 4, for which we can rely on the soundness of the original plan and do not need to perform the soundness checking again.

For each of the update operations, we define the scope in the spatial and temporal dimensions of an EP. By assuming that the original plan is sound, we can analyse only within the corresponding scope that may cause a paradox. We reformalise the tree-based feature model into an interval-based feature model (IBFM) in Sect. 3.

3   Formalisation of IBFMs

In this section we present the interval-based feature model as our representation for feature model evolution plans, and the requisite data structures.

A feature model evolution plan has two dimensions: the spatial dimension and the temporal dimension. The spatial dimension consists of the feature models—which features and groups exist, what their names and types are, and how they are related. The temporal dimension concerns time, i.e., which points in time appear in the feature model evolution plan. To store the information about the spatial dimension, we have decided to use maps, which are useful for looking up information about a specific element. Looking up a feature ID in such a map will give us the information about that feature.

Definition 2 (Map). *A* map *is a set of entries on the form* $[k \mapsto v]$, *where each key* k *uniquely defines a value* v. *The query* MAP $[k]$ *would give us* v *if* $[k \mapsto v] \in$ MAP. *Assigning (or overwriting) a value* v *to key* k *is denoted by* MAP $[k] \leftarrow v$. *To remove a mapping with key* k, *we use* MAP$\backslash k$. *For maps with set values, we define the operator* $\overset{\cup}{\leftarrow}$. *If* MAP $[k] = S$ *then* MAP $[k] \overset{\cup}{\leftarrow} v =$ MAP $[k] \leftarrow S \cup \{v\}$. *We additionally define* $\backslash^v$, *to remove a specific value* v *from a set at key* k.

Definition 3 (Interval). *We define an interval as a set of time points (members of a set* T *such that* $<$ *is a strict total order on* T*) between a lower bound and an upper bound, where the lower and upper bounds are time points. We denote the interval using the familiar mathematical notation* $[t_{start}, t_{end})$, *where* t_{start} *is the lower bound, and* t_{end} *is the upper bound. These intervals are left-closed and right-open, meaning that* t_{start} *is contained in the interval, and all time points until but not including* t_{end}. *To allow us to use intervals that have no end, we define the time point* ∞ *as upper bound, such that* $t_n < \infty$ *for all* t_n.

Definition 4 (Interval map). *An* interval map *is a map where the key is an interval. Lookups are performed using intervals (returning values in the overlap) or a timepoint in a straight-forward manner.*

Furthermore, IM $[t_n]_{\leq}$ *returns the set of keys containing time point* t_n. *For interval maps with set values, we define an additional function* IM $[t_n]^v_{\leq}$ *where* v *is some value, returning the set of the keys containing* t_n *and associated with a set containing* v. *The function* IM $[[t_n, t_m)]_{\lessgtr}$ *returns all the interval keys in the map* IM *overlapping the interval* $[t_n, t_m)$.

Hence for interval maps with non-overlapping keys, the resulting set will contain at most one element.

To describe an entire feature model evolution plan, we define the *interval-based feature model*. It consists of three maps: NAMES, FEATURES, and GROUPS.

The NAMES map contains *all* of the names used in the feature model, and which features they belong to during which times. Similarly, the FEATURES and GROUPS maps rely on interval maps to store all of the information about features and groups throughout the plan, respectively. The information is retrieved by looking up a name, a feature ID, or a group ID, which promotes the modularity of plan change verification. The reason for this choice is mainly modularity. As previously mentioned, the goal of this paper is to minimize which parts of the plan are checked for paradoxes, as a change rarely affects more than a small part of the plan. Representing an updated plan either as a sequence of trees associated with time points or as an initial model followed by a sequence of operations is suboptimal for the reasoning of plan change, since to add a new feature to the plan, both representations would require us to look through the entire plan to check that the feature ID and name are unique at all times.

To add or rename a feature, a soundness checker must verify that no other feature is using the name during the affected part of the plan. We therefore include the NAMES map in the representation for efficient verification of aforementioned issue. A feature or group ID may not already be in use when we add it, so the FEATURES and GROUPS maps support efficient lookup for IDs.

Definition 5 (Interval-based feature model). *An interval-based feature model (IBFM) is defined as a triple* (NAMES, FEATURES, GROUPS) *where* NAMES *is a map from names to interval maps with feature ID values,* FEATURES *is a map from feature IDs to feature entries, and* GROUPS *is a map from group IDs to group entries.*

The NAMES *map has entries of the form* $[\textbf{name} \mapsto \text{IM}]$*, where the interval map* IM *contains mappings on the form* $[[t_{start}, t_{end}) \mapsto \textbf{featureID}]$*, where* **featureID** *is the ID of some feature in the interval-based feature model. This should be interpreted as "The name* **name** *belongs to the feature with ID* **featureID** *from* t_{start} *to* t_{end}*".*

The FEATURES *map has entries of the form* $[\textbf{featureID} \mapsto feature\ entry]$*. A feature entry has a name, a type, a parent group, and zero or more child groups. This information is collected into a 5-tuple* $(F_e, F_n, F_t, F_p, F_c)$*, where* F_e *is an interval set denoting when the feature exists,* F_n *is an interval map with name values,* F_t *is an interval map with the feature's variation types,* F_p *is an interval map with group ID values, and* F_c *is an interval map where the values are sets containing group IDs, the interval keys possibly overlapping.*

The GROUPS *map has entries of the form* $[\textbf{groupID} \mapsto group\ entry]$*. A group entry has a type, a parent feature, and zero or more child features, which we define in terms of intervals and collected into a 4-tuple* (G_e, G_t, G_p, G_c) *similarly to the feature entries, where* G_e *is an interval set denoting when the group exists,* G_t *is an interval map with the group's types,* G_p *is an interval map with parent feature IDs, and* G_c *is an interval map with child feature ID set values, the interval keys possibly overlapping.*

Figure 5 shows an example IBFM-triple. Lookups for missing elements return (tuples of) $\emptyset$. The root feature's ID is constant for a interval-based feature

$(\{\ [\,\text{Car} \mapsto [[t_0, \infty) \mapsto 0]]$
$,\ [\text{Infotainment System} \mapsto [[t_0, \infty) \mapsto 1]]$
$,\ [\text{Comfort Systems} \mapsto [[t_3, t_6) \mapsto 2]]\ \}$
$,\{\ [0 \mapsto$

$(\{[t_0, \infty)\},$
$\{[[t_0, \infty) \mapsto \text{Car}]\},$
$\{[[t_0, \infty) \mapsto \text{MANDATORY}]\},$
$\emptyset,$
$\{[[t_0, \infty) \mapsto 10]\})]$

$,[1 \mapsto$

$(\{[t_0, \infty)\},$
$\{[[t_0, \infty) \mapsto \text{Infotainment System}]\},$
$\{[[t_0, \infty) \mapsto \text{MANDATORY}]\},$
$\{[[t_0, \infty) \mapsto 10]\},$
$\emptyset)]$

$,[2 \mapsto$

$(\{[t_3, t_6)\},$
$\{[[t_3, t_6) \mapsto \text{Comfort Systems}]\},$
$\{[[t_3, t_6) \mapsto \text{OPTIONAL}]\},$
$\{[[t_3, t_6) \mapsto 10]\},$
$\emptyset)]\}$

$,\{\ [10 \mapsto$

$(\{[t_0, \infty)\},$
$\{[[t_0, \infty) \mapsto \text{AND}]\},$
$\{[[t_0, \infty) \mapsto 0]\},$
$\{[[t_0, \infty) \mapsto 1], [[t_3, t_6) \mapsto 2]\})]$

$\})$

Fig. 5. Example interval-based feature model

model. We assume that it has been computed and represent it by referring to *RootID*. This is to avoid cluttering the representation with information that never changes.

Operations

The following operations cover the changes that are likely to be desired for a feature model evolution plan. The choice of operations is largely based on the edit operations defined in our earlier work [10]. We adapt them by adding a temporal dimension, letting us specify both *where* an operation should be applied in the feature model, and *when*, i.e., at which stage of the plan.

In the following, we discuss the **ADD-FEATURE** and **MOVE-FEATURE** operations in detail by showing the semantics rules as well as the corresponding helper functions, and briefly describe the rest of the operations. We refer the reader to Chap. 4 in [17] for the semantics rules of the remaining operations.

Helper Functions. In these two operations, five straight-forward helper functions are used: `compatibleTypes`, `setFeatureAttributes`, `addChildFeature`, `clampInterval` and `removeFeatureAt` (see Appendix).

The `compatibleTypes` function takes a group type (AND, OR or ALTERNATIVE) and a feature type (MANDATORY or OPTIONAL) and checks whether they are compatible. The types should belong to a parent group and its child feature. The only combination which is not allowed is a MANDATORY feature with an ALTERNATIVE or OR parent group.

The `setFeatureAttributes` function takes a feature entry, an interval, a name, a type, and a group ID, and returns the feature entry with the information included. It modifies the existence set by adding the interval, maps the interval to the name in the names map, to the type in the types map, and to the parent group ID in the parent groups map.

The `addChildFeature` function takes a group entry, an interval, and a feature ID, and adds the feature ID to the group's child feature map during the interval. The `clampInterval` function takes an interval map and a time point, and shortens containing this time point to end at this point. The `removeFeatureAt` function takes a group entry, a feature ID, and a time point and removes the feature ID from its parent group's child feature map.

The operational rules update a state of the interval-based feature plan of the form **operation** $\triangleright$ (NAMES, FEATURES, GROUPS), where **operation** denotes the change we intend to make to the interval-based feature model (NAMES, FEATURES, GROUPS). The new state is of the form (NAMES′, FEATURES′, GROUPS′), where the maps have been updated according to the semantics of the operation.

addFeature(`featureID`, `name`, `featureType`, `parentGroupID`) from t_n to t_m:

$$
\frac{
\begin{array}{c}
[t_n, t_m) \not\in_{\lessgtr} F_e \qquad [t_n, t_m) \in_{\leq} G_e \qquad \text{NAMES}\,[\text{name}]\,[[t_n, t_m)] = \emptyset \qquad t_n < t_m \\
\text{FEATURES}\,[\text{featureID}] = (F_e, F_n, F_t, F_p, F_c) \\
\text{GROUPS}\,[\text{parentGroupID}] = (G_e, G_t, G_p, G_c) \\
\forall \text{gt} \in G_t\,[[t_n, t_m)] : \texttt{compatibleTypes(gt, type)}
\end{array}
}{
\begin{array}{c}
\textbf{addFeature}(\text{featureID}, \text{name}, \text{type}, \text{parentGroupID}) \text{ from } t_n \text{ to } t_m \triangleright \\
(\text{NAMES}, \text{FEATURES}, \text{GROUPS}) \\
\longrightarrow (\text{NAMES}\,[\text{name}]\,[[t_n, t_m)] \leftarrow \text{featureID}, \\
\text{FEATURES}\,[\text{featureID}] \leftarrow \texttt{setFeatureAttributes}(\text{FEATURES}\,[\text{featureID}], [t_n, t_m), \\
\text{name}, \text{type}, \text{parentGroupID}), \\
\text{GROUPS}\,[\text{parentGroupID}] \leftarrow \texttt{addChildFeature}(\text{GROUPS}\,[\text{parentGroupID}], [t_n, t_m), \text{featureID}))
\end{array}
} \text{(ADD-FEATURE)}
$$

Rule **ADD-FEATURE** checks that when adding a feature during the interval $[t_n, t_m)$, its ID cannot be in use during the interval ($[t_n, t_m) \not\in_{\lessgtr} F_e$). The parent group must exist ($[t_n, t_m) \in_{\leq} G_e$), and the types it has during the interval must be compatible with the type of the added feature ($\forall \text{gt} \in G_t\,[[t_n, t_m)]$: `compatibleTypes(gt, type)`). The name of the feature must not be in use during the interval (NAMES $[\text{name}]\,[[t_n, t_m)] = \emptyset$), and the interval must start before it ends ($t_n < t_m$).

If applied, this rule adds feature with ID `featureID`, name `name`, and feature variation type `featureType` to the group with ID `parentGroupID` in the interval $[t_n, t_m)$. Notice that the default value in the FEATURES map lets us treat a failed lookup as a feature. We choose to let this operation affect the plan only within an interval so as to enable the adding of features to groups that are planned to be removed, and to add flexibility. **Temporal scope:** $[t_n, t_m)$. **Spatial scope:** self, parent, name.

moveFeature(`featureID`, `targetGroupID`) at t_n: Moves the feature with ID `featureID` to the group with ID `targetGroupID` at t_n. The operation does not affect future moves planned for the feature. The feature's subtree is moved along with the feature.

$$\neg\texttt{createsCycle} \quad F_p\,[t_n]_{\leq} = \{[t_{p_1}, t_{p_2})\}$$
$$F_p\,[[t_n, t_{p_2})] = \{\texttt{oldParentID}\} \quad [t_n, t_{p_2}) \in_{\leq} G_e$$
$$\forall [t_{f_1}, t_{f_2}) \in F_t\,[[t_n, t_{p_2})]_{\lessgtr} \; \forall [t_{g_1}, t_{g_2}) \in G_t\,\Big[\langle[t_{f_1}, t_{f_2})\rangle_{t_n}^{t_{p_2}}\Big]_{\lessgtr}$$
$$\forall \texttt{ft} \in F_t\,[[t_{f_1}, t_{f_2})] \; \forall \texttt{gt} \in G_t\,[[t_{g_1}, t_{g_2})] \, (\texttt{compatibleTypes(gt, ft)})$$
$$\text{FEATURES}\,[\texttt{featureID}] = (F_e,\, F_n,\, F_t,\, F_p,\, F_c)$$
$$\text{GROUPS}\,[\texttt{newParentID}] = (G_e,\, G_t,\, G_p,\, G_c)$$

————————————————————————————— (MOVE-FEATURE)

$$\texttt{moveFeature}(\texttt{featureID, newParentID}) \text{ at } t_n \, \triangleright$$
$$(\text{NAMES, FEATURES, GROUPS})$$
$$\longrightarrow (\text{NAMES},$$
$$\text{FEATURES}\,[\texttt{featureID}] \leftarrow \quad (F_e,\, F_n,\, F_t,\, \texttt{clampInterval}(F_p, t_n)\,[[t_n, t_{p_2})]$$
$$\leftarrow \texttt{newParentID},\, F_c),$$
$$((\text{GROUPS}\,[\texttt{oldParentID}] \leftarrow \texttt{removeFeatureAt}\,(\text{GROUPS}\,[\texttt{oldParentID}]\,, \texttt{featureID}, t_n))$$
$$[\texttt{newParentID}]\,)$$
$$\leftarrow \texttt{addChildFeature}(\text{GROUPS}\,[\texttt{newParentID}]\,, [t_n, t_{p_2}), \texttt{featureID}))$$

The premise ¬createsCycle invokes a cycle detection algorithm (see Sect. 4.5.1 in [17]), making sure that within the temporal scope no structural cycles occur, by looking up only the ancestors of both the feature and the target group during the temporal scope. The premise $F_p\,[t_n]_{\leq} = \{[t_{p_1}, t_{p_2})\}$ indicates the scope of the operation, namely $[t_n, t_{p_2})$, while the premise $F_p\,[[t_n, t_{p_2})] = \{\texttt{oldParentID}\}$ identifies the ID of the feature's former parent group for updating the GROUPS map. The premise $[t_n, t_{p_2}) \in_{\leq} G_e$ ensures that the new parent exists during the entire temporal scope.

As the plan may contain several type changes for both the feature being moved and its new parent, we check that the types they have at the same time are compatible through compatibleTypes: for each interval key overlapping the temporal scope in the feature's type map, then for each interval in the group's type map overlapping the aforementioned key and restricted by the temporal scope, then for all types mapped to by those keys, those types must be compatible. This ensures that the rule is not too strict, because it check only those combinations of types which the feature and its new parent group have at the same time, further restricted by the temporal scope.

If applied, the feature's parent group map is updated by shortening the interval mapped to the former parent's ID to end at t_n, and adding a new mapping $[[t_n, t_{p_2}) \mapsto \texttt{newParentID}]$. The feature is removed from the previous parent's (oldParentID) set of child features during the temporal scope, and the feature is added to the new parent's set of child features during the same interval. **Temporal scope, Spatial scope:** implicit/computed.

addGroup(groupID, groupType, parentFeatureID) from t_n to t_m: Adds group with ID groupID and type groupType to the feature with ID parentFeatureID during the interval $[t_n, t_m)$. The group ID cannot be in use during the interval, and the parent feature must exist during the entire interval. **Temporal scope:** $[t_n, t_m)$. **Spatial scope:** group groupID, parent feature parentFeatureID.

removeFeature(featureID) at t_n: Removes the feature with ID featureID from the feature model at t_n. If the plan contains a removal of the feature and a subsequent reintroduction, removing the feature at an earlier stage does not affect the reintroduction, but rather moves the point of removal to an earlier point in time. The feature must exist at t_n in the original plan for the modification to be valid. The feature must not have any child groups that are left orphaned after removal. **Temporal scope:** $[t_n, t_k)$, with $t_m \leq t_n \leq t_k$, where $[t_m, t_k)$ in which the feature exists inside the feature model. **Spatial scope:** Self, parent, children, name.

removeGroup(groupID) at t_n: Very similar to **removeFeature**. Removes the group with ID groupID from the feature model at t_n, not affecting potential later reintroductions. The group must exist at t_n in the original plan, and the group must not have any child features that are left orphaned after removal. **Temporal scope:** $[t_n, t_k)$, where t_k is the time at which the group was originally planned to be removed. **Spatial scope:** Self, parent, children, name.

moveGroup(groupID, targetFeatureID) at t_n: Very similar to **moveFeature**; moves the group with ID groupID to the feature with ID targetFeatureID at t_n. The operation does not affect future moves planned for the group. The group's subtree is moved along with the group. If the move causes a cycle, then the modification should not be applied. **Temporal scope:** $[t_n, t_m)$, where t_m is the time at which the group is next moved or removed in the original plan. **Spatial scope:** self, parent, children.

changeFeatureVariationType(featureID, newType) at t_n: Changes the feature variation type of the feature with ID featureID to newType at time t_n. The change does not affect planned type changes to the feature. If the new type is MANDATORY, the parent group type must be AND, or else the operation cannot be applied. **Temporal scope:** $[t_n, t_m)$ where t_m is the next time point at which the feature's type changes next or when the feature is (next) removed. **Spatial scope:** self, parent.

changeGroupVariationType(groupID, newType) at t_n: Changes the group variation type of the group with ID groupID to newType. If the new type is OR or ALTERNATIVE, and a child feature has type MANDATORY, then the operation cannot be applied. **Temporal scope:** $[t_n, t_m)$, where t_m is the next time point at which the group's type changes next or when the group is (next) removed. **Spatial scope:** self, children.

changeFeatureName(featureID, name) at t_n: Changes the name of the feature with ID featureID to name. It does not affect future renaming operations to the feature. No other feature may have the same name. **Temporal scope:** $[t_n, t_m)$ where t_m is the next time point at which the feature's name changes next or when the feature is (next) removed. **Spatial scope:** name, feature, previous name.

4   Soundness

In this section, we are going to show the soundness of the rule system presented in Sect. 3. Given a *sound* plan, i.e., containing no paradoxes, we show that applying a rule will result in a sound plan, and that the rules operate within the operation's scope and updates the model correctly. For the rest of the section, we will first present the well-formedness for interval-based feature models, and we sketch the soundness proof of the two representative rules **ADD-FEATURE** and **MOVE-FEATURE**, and consequently the soundness of the rule system. We refer the interested readers to [17] for the complete proofs.

4.1   Well-Formedness of Interval-Based Feature Models

To show the resulting modified plan, that is, an interval-based feature model, is sound, we will have to show the absence of paradoxes. In other words, we have to show the model respects the well-formedness requirements. Assuming the first time point in the plan is t_0, we formalise the well-formedness requirements listed in Sect. 2.1 for interval-based feature models (NAMES, FEATURES, GROUPS) as follows:

IBFM1. An interval-based feature model has exactly one root feature. Let *RootID* be the root of the model, and assume that FEATURES [*RootID*] = $(R_e, R_n, R_t, R_p, R_c)$. This requirement means that the root always exists, i.e., $R_e = \{[t_0, \infty)\}$, and it does not have a parent group, i.e., $R_p = \emptyset$.

IBFM2. The root feature must be MANDATORY, i.e., $R_t = \{[[t_0, \infty) \mapsto \text{MANDATORY}]\}$ where R_t is the types map of the root feature.

IBFM3. At any time $t_n \geq t_0$, each feature has exactly one unique name, variation type and (potentially empty) collection of child groups. Given a feature ID featureID, if FEATURES [featureID] = $(F_e, F_n, F_t, F_p, F_c)$ and $t_n \in_\leq F_e$, then

  (i) $F_n[t_n] = \{\text{name}\}$—the feature has exactly one name,
  (ii) NAMES [name] $[t_n] = \{\text{featureID}\}$—the name is unique *at the time point* t_n,
  (iii) $F_t[t_n] = \{\text{type}\}$ with type $\in \{\text{MANDATORY, OPTIONAL}\}$—the feature has exactly one type, and
  (iv) $F_c[t_n] = C$, such that $\bigcup C$ is a set of the group IDs, and if groupID $\in \bigcup C$ and GROUPS [groupID] = (G_e, G_t, G_p, G_c), then $G_p[t_n] = \{\text{featureID}\}$—if a group is listed as a child group of a feature, then the feature is listed as the parent of the group at the same time.

IBFM4. At any time $t_n \geq t_0$, each group has exactly one variation type. Given a group ID groupID, this means that if GROUPS [groupID] = (G_e, G_t, G_p, G_c) and $t_n \in_\leq G_e$, then $G_t[t_n] = \{\text{type}\}$ for type $\in \{\text{AND, OR, ALTERNATIVE}\}$.

IBFM5. At any time $t_n \geq t_0$, each feature, except for the root feature, must be part of exactly one group. Formally, given a feature ID featureID $\neq$ *RootID*, if FEATURES [featureID] = $(F_e, F_n, F_t, F_p, F_c)$ and $t_n \in_\leq F_e$, then $F_p[t_n] = \{\text{groupID}\}$ with GROUPS [groupID] = (G_e, G_t, G_p, G_c), $t_n \in_\leq G_e$, and featureID $\in \bigcup G_c[t_n]$. Conversely, if featureID $\in \bigcup G_c[t_n]$, then $F_p[t_n] = $ groupID.

IBFM6. At any time $t_n \geq t_0$, each group must have exactly one parent feature. Formally, given a group ID groupID, if GROUPS [groupID] = (G_e, G_t, G_p, G_c)

and $t_n \in_{\leq} G_e$, then $G_p[t_n] = \{\texttt{featureID}\}$, and FEATURES $[\texttt{featureID}] = (F_e, F_n, F_t, F_p, F_c)$ with $\texttt{groupID} \in \bigcup F_c[t_n]$.

IBFM7. At any time t_n, a group with types ALTERNATIVE or OR must not contain MANDATORY features. Formally, given a group ID $\texttt{groupID}$ with GROUPS $[\texttt{groupID}] = (G_e, G_t, G_p, G_c)$, if $G_t[t_n] = \{\texttt{type}\}$ with $\texttt{type} \in \{\text{ALTERNATIVE}, \text{OR}\}$, and if $\texttt{featureID} \in \bigcup G_c[t_n]$ and FEATURES $[\texttt{featureID}] = (F_e, F_n, F_t, F_p, F_c)$, then $F_t[t_n] = \{\text{OPTIONAL}\}$.

IBFM8. The interval-based feature model contains no cycles, which means that at any time point $t_n \geq t_0$, for any feature or group that exists at t_n, if we follow the parent chain upwards, we never encounter the same feature or group twice. In other words, no feature or group is its own ancestor.

IBFM9. Consider a feature with ID $\texttt{featureID}$ where FEATURES $[\texttt{featureID}] = (F_e, F_n, F_t, F_p, F_c)$, if $t_n \notin_{\leq} F_e$, then $F_n[t_n] = F_t[t_n] = F_p[t_n] = F_c[t_n] = \emptyset$, and for all keys $\texttt{name}$ in NAMES, $\texttt{featureID} \notin \text{NAMES}[\texttt{name}][t_n]$, i.e., no name belongs to the feature. Similarly, for a group with ID $\texttt{groupID}$ such that GROUPS $[\texttt{groupID}] = (G_e, G_t, G_p, G_c)$, if $t_n \notin_{\leq} G_e$, then $G_t[t_n] = G_p[t_n] = G_c[t_n] = \emptyset$, i.e., a feature or a group which does not exist cannot have a name, a type, a parent, or a child.

Since our IBFM representation does not enforce structural requirements, we need **IBFM9** in addition to the original eight well-formedness requirements.

4.2   Soundness of the Rule System

In the following, we prove the soundness of the rule system by showing the soundness of each rule in the system. We assume that the original plan is sound, i.e., well-formed. The soundness proof of each rule consists of three parts: (i) *modularity*: the rule operates strictly within the previously defined temporal and spatial scopes (see Sect. 2.3); (ii) *well-formedness preservation*: the rule preserves the well-formedness requirements defined in Sect. 4.1; and (iii) *correctness of model modification*: the rule updates the model correctly, preserves soundness as well as respects the semantics of the operation.

Soundness of rule **ADD-FEATURE**. Let the initial state be

$$\text{addFeature}(\texttt{featureID}, \texttt{name}, \texttt{type}, \texttt{parentGroupID}) \text{ from } t_n \text{ to } t_m \vartriangleright$$
$$(\text{NAMES}, \text{FEATURES}, \text{GROUPS})$$

and $(\text{NAMES}', \text{FEATURES}', \text{GROUPS}')$ the resulting state after rule **ADD-FEATURE** is applied. Recall that this operation adds the feature with ID $\texttt{featureID}$ to the well-formed interval-based feature model $(\text{NAMES}, \text{FEATURES}, \text{GROUPS})$ from t_n to t_m.

Proof. Firstly, we are going to show the rule is modular, i.e., to prove that the rule operates strictly within the temporal and spatial scopes of the **addFeature** operation. It is straightforward to see that the rule operates within the spatial scope of the operation since the rule just looks up the feature ID, the parent group ID, and the name, and only updates the name, feature, and parent group in the model. Furthermore, the only interval looked up or assigned to in model's interval maps and sets is $[t_n, t_m)$, which corresponds to the temporal scope of the rule. Thus, the rule is modular.

Next, we are going to show that the rule preserves well-formedness, i.e., the updated interval-based feature model (NAMES', FEATURES', GROUPS') is well-formed. **IBFM1** and **IBFM2** obviously hold since featureID $\neq$ *RootID* due to the rule guarantees that the feature does not exist during the temporal scope in the original model.

Since **IBFM9** holds for the original model, the feature does not exist during the temporal scope $[t_n, t_m)$, and therefore has no name, type, or child groups in the original plan. The rule uses setFeatureAttributes to add the feature with exactly one name and one type during the temporal scope, and with an empty set of child groups. The temporal scope is also added to the feature's existence set, so only the new feature has the ID featureID during the temporal scope. Hence, we conclude that **IBFM3** holds.

It is straightforward for **IBFM4** as the rule does not modify the parent group's variation type. The argument for **IBFM5** is similar to **IBFM3**. In addition, no other feature IDs are removed from the parent group's feature set, and we have already established that featureID $\neq$ *RootID*, which consequently justify **IBFM5**.

It is easy to see **IBFM6** and **IBFM7** hold: for **IBFM6**, the new feature does not have any child groups during the temporal scope, and the parent group's parent feature does not change; and for **IBFM7**, the rule ensures that all of the parent group's types are compatible with the added feature's type during the temporal scope.

Since the new feature has no child groups, adding the feature cannot create a cycle; and by assumption, **IBFM8** holds in the original plan, thus, **IBFM8** also holds in the modified plan. **IBFM9** is also preserved as the rule adds the temporal scope to the new feature's existence table, and since the parent group exists in the original plan.

As the rule is modular, it does not affect any other part of the plan, thus, preserves well-formedness. Finally, it is straightforward to see that the NAMES map is modified correctly, i.e., NAMES' [name] $[t_k]$ = {featureID} where $t_n \leq t_k < t_m$.

To show that the **addFeature** operation updates the FEATURES map in the feature model correctly with the rule, we have to show that for all time points t_k with $t_n \leq t_k < t_m$, the feature exists ($t_k \in_{\leq} F'_e$), the features has the expected name, type and parent group, i.e., $F'_n[t_k]$ = {name}, $F'_t[t_k]$ = {type} and $F'_p[t_k]$ = {parentGroupID}, respectively, and the feature has no child groups, i.e., $F'_c[t_k] = \emptyset$. These statements hold due to both premises in the rule and the definition of function setFeatureAttributes. For example, $t_k \in_{\leq} F'_e$ is true due to the function updates F_e with $F_e \cup \{[t_n, t_m)\}$.

As for the modified GROUPS map, we have to show that the child features of the group is updated correctly. Since the map is updated with the function addChildFeature which ensures that featureID $\in \bigcup G_c'\,[t_k]$ for all t_k with $t_n \le t_k < t_m$, where GROUPS$'$ [parentGroupID] $= (G_e',\, G_t',\, G_p',\, G_c')$, the feature is in the parent group's set of child features in the updated model during the entire temporal scope.

As a result, we conclude that the rule is sound by showing the modularity, the well-formedness and the correctness of modification.

Soundness of rule **MOVE-FEATURE**. Let the initial state be

moveFeature(featureID, newParentID) at $t_n \triangleright$ (NAMES, FEATURES, GROUPS)

and the state resulting from the rule application (NAMES$'$, FEATURES$'$, GROUPS$'$). Recall that this operation moves the feature with identity featureID in the original well-formed IBFM to the group with identity newParentID at time t_n.

Proof. Similar to the previous case, we first show the rule is modular, i.e., to prove that the rule operates strictly within the temporal and spatial scopes of the **moveFeature** operation. The premise $F_p\,[t_n]_< = \{[t_{p_1}, t_{p_2})\}$ of rule indicates that in the original plan, the feature being moved has a parent group during the temporal scope $[t_{p_1}, t_{p_2})$. As the rule moves this feature at time t_n, the temporal scope for this rule is $[t_n, t_{p_2})$. We can easily see that the rule only modifies the plan within this temporal scope, and detects cycles for each feature model at each time point in this interval.

The spatial scope in this rule refers to the new ancestors of the feature after the rule application. We can see that only the feature with ID featureID and its new parent group with ID newParentID are looked up in the rule. As for the cycle detection algorithm used in the rule, it looks up only the ancestors of both the feature and the target group during the temporal scope. Thus, the rule operates within the defined spatial scope, and consequently is modular.

Next, we are going to show that the rule preserves well-formedness. *IBFM1* and *IBFM2* immediately hold because the rule can only be applied if the feature to be moved has a parent group, thus, not the root. The rule neither updates the name, type and child groups of the feature, nor modifies the target group's type and parent feature. Hence, *IBFM3*, *IBFM4* and *IBFM6* hold for the updated model.

With the functions clampInterval, removeFeatureAt and addChildFeature, the rule ensures that the feature is removed from the old parent group at t_n. The ID of the feature is then added to the new parent group at t_n, which guarantees that the feature always has exactly one parent group during the temporal scope. Hence, *IBFM5* holds.

IBFM7 follows immediately as the function compatibleTypes to ensure that each type the feature has during the time scope is compatible with the type of the parent group. As for *IBFM8*, since the original plan is sound, the modified one will only contain a cycle if the feature being moved is part of this cycle, i.e., occurs in its own list of ancestors. *IBFM8* therefore holds since the cycle detection algorithm guarantees that the modified interval-based feature model does not contain any cycle by checking the *new* ancestors of the moved feature. It is easy to see that ***IBFM9*** holds as it holds for the orignal plan and the feature exists in the temporal scope in the modified plan.

As the rule is modular, it does not affect any other part of the plan, thus, preserves well-formedness. Finally, the rule correctly modifies the original model since during the temporal scope, the feature's parent group should be `newParentID`, and the feature should only appear in the new parent group's set of child features. By the definition of function `clampInterval`, the feature belongs to the old parent group `oldParentID` is shortened to end at t_n, and a new mapping $[[t_n, t_{p_2}) \mapsto$ `newParentID`$]$ is inserted. Thus, it is clear that for all t_i with $t_n \le t_i < t_{p_2}$, $F'_p[t_i] = \{$`newParentID`$\}$. Together with ***IBFM5*** from the well-formedness of the modified feature model, we can easily see that the feature appears in the new parent group's set of child features.

As a result, we conclude that the rule is sound.

Corollary 1 (Soundness of the rule system). *Given a sound plan in a form of interval-based feature model and an operation, if the operation is applied by a rule in the rule system, the resulting model is sound: it does not contain paradoxes, and is well-formed.*

Proof. This holds immediately by the soundness of each rule in the system.

5 Related Work

Due to changes in product requirements, SPL evolution is often crucial and has been investigated in the context such as refactoring [1,11], catalog of change operators and modification operations on feature models with various levels of granularity [7,19,24], diagram differences detection and model transformation [8,22]. The conflict and dependency analysis field for graph transformation systems proposed methods for detecting incompatibilities between general graph modifications [2,12,13]. Such procedures could be utilised to prevent incompatibilities between operations within a feature model evolution plan, thus ensure its structural consistency. Compared to these procedures, our work additionally focuses on the semantical consistency and detection of paradoxes of plans for evolution planning.

DeltaEcore [26] is a tool suite for generating custom delta languages for arbitrary meta models of the source languages. DeltaEcore addresses temporal variability in terms of Hyper Feature Models, which capture feature versions which can be mapped to different implementation artefacts. However, it is not possible to model evolution of feature models themselves. DarwinSPL [20] is a tool suite for modeling SPLs with spatial, contextual and temporal variability but it does not address the issues related to the updates of FMEPs. EvoFM [7] supports long-term feature-oriented planning and analysis of evolution plans but it also does not support plan changes. Other tools for planning the evolution of SPLs include Feature-Driven Versioning [16], FORCE [9], EvolPL [6] and SuperMod [25]. Even though the need and principle feasibility for SPL evolution planning has been recognized before [6,21], most existing concepts and tools do not tackle the issues resulted from the modification of evolution plans.

A term rewriting system for soundness checking for FMEPs was introduced and integrated [10]. It validates FMEPs but requires analysis of the entire plan, even when a modification affects only small parts of the FMEPs. Other works on the formal side of product line evolution include [24] where safe evolution scenarios are formalised through a notion of partial refinement and [4,5] a language-independent theory of product line refinement for stepwise and compositional product line evolution, including soundness of several refinement transformation templates. We provide a solution to the challenge of supporting feature model evolution planning while ensuring consistent feature model evolution plans through modular rule-based analysis.

6   Conclusion

In this paper, we present a set of update operations for changing feature model evolution plans. Furthermore, we define the scope of each of these operations, meaning that we deduce exactly which parts of a plan may be affected by each operation. A representation for feature model evolution plans is devised with the aim to easily isolate the scope of an operation for analysis. Based on the scope and representations, we create an analysis method for validation and application of the update operations. The analysis is formalised as a set of rules, giving a detailed specification of when an operation may be applied to the evolution plan, and how to apply the modification. We implement a prototype of the analysis as proof of concept. Finally, we give a proof that the rule set is sound by showing that each rule preserves well-formedness of the structure of the feature model, that the application of each rule affects only a specified scope within the feature model evolution plan, and that each rule updates the evolution plan correctly according to the semantics of the operation applied.

The implementation of the soundness checker in Haskell published at [18] provides methods for validating the result of applying an operation to an interval-based feature model. It also makes it possible to convert from a simple feature model evolution plan to an interval-based feature model. Models and operations are specified in straight-forward datatypes, and the tool executes the soundness checks and updates the model.

A future improvement of this work could be the formalisation within a theorem proving framework, as we already have an implementation in a functional language and we expect verification of all properties of data structures and operations to be amenable to mechanisation. We also plan to provide more examples to practically explore the complexity of the operations beyond the example provided in the artefact.

Acknowledgements. This paper is partially supported by the CroFlow project: Enabling Highly Automated Cross-Organisational Workflow Planning (grant no. 326249).

A   Helper Functions [17]

Here we show the helper functions that are used in the two operational rules **addFeature** and **moveFeature** in Sect. 3.

```
compatibleTypes(AND, _) = True
compatibleTypes(_, MANDATORY) = False
compatibleTypes(_, _) = True
```

$\texttt{setFeatureAttributes}((F_e, F_n, F_t, F_p, F_c), [t_{start}, t_{end}), \texttt{name}, \texttt{type}, \texttt{parentGroupID})$
$= (\ F_e \cup \{[t_{start}, t_{end})\}$
$\quad , F_n\, [[t_{start}, t_{end})] \leftarrow \texttt{name}$
$\quad , F_t\, [[t_{start}, t_{end})] \leftarrow \texttt{type}$
$\quad , F_p\, [[t_{start}, t_{end})] \leftarrow \texttt{parentGroupID}$
$\quad , F_c\ )$

$\texttt{addChildFeature}((G_e, G_t, G_p, G_c), [t_{start}, t_{end}), \texttt{fid})$
$= \Big(G_e, G_t, G_p, G_c\, [[t_{start}, t_{end})] \overset{\cup}{\leftarrow} \texttt{fid}\Big)$

$\texttt{removeFeatureAt}(\, (G_e, G_t, G_p, G_c), \texttt{featureID}, t_c)$
$= \big(G_e, G_t, G_p, \texttt{clampIntervalValue}\,(G_c, t_c, \texttt{featureID})\, \big)$

$\texttt{clampInterval}\,(\textsc{map}, t_c)$
$= \textsc{map}'\,[[t_{start}, t_c)] \leftarrow v$
$\textbf{where}\ \ \{[t_{start}, t_{end})\} = \textsc{map}\,[t_c]_{\leq}$
$\qquad\quad \{v\} = \textsc{map}\,[t_c]$
$\qquad\quad \textsc{map}' = \textsc{map} \setminus [t_{start}, t_{end})$

$\texttt{clampIntervalValue}\,(\textsc{map}, t_c, v)$
$= \textsc{map}'\,[[t_{start}, t_c)] \overset{\cup}{\leftarrow} v$
$\textbf{where}\ \ \{[t_{start}, t_{end})\} = \textsc{map}\,[t_c]_{\leq}^v$
$\qquad\quad \textsc{map}' = \textsc{map} \setminus^v [t_{start}, t_{end})$

References

1. Alves, V., Gheyi, R., Massoni, T., Kulesza, U., Borba, P., de Lucena, C.J.P.: Refactoring product lines. In: Jarzabek, S., Schmidt, D.C., Veldhuizen, T.L. (eds.) 5th International Conference on Generative Programming and Component Engineering GPCE 2006, pp. 201–210. ACM (2006). https://doi.org/10.1145/1173706.1173737
2. Azzi, G.G., Corradini, A., Ribeiro, L.: On the essence and initiality of conflicts. In: Lambers, L., Weber, J. (eds.) ICGT 2018. LNCS, vol. 10887, pp. 99–117. Springer, Cham (2018). https://doi.org/10.1007/978-3-319-92991-0_7
3. Batory, D.: Feature models, grammars, and propositional formulas. In: Obbink, H., Pohl, K. (eds.) SPLC 2005. LNCS, vol. 3714, pp. 7–20. Springer, Heidelberg (2005). https://doi.org/10.1007/11554844_3
4. Borba, P., Teixeira, L., Gheyi, R.: A theory of software product line refinement. In: Cavalcanti, A., Deharbe, D., Gaudel, M.-C., Woodcock, J. (eds.) ICTAC 2010. LNCS, vol. 6255, pp. 15–43. Springer, Heidelberg (2010). https://doi.org/10.1007/978-3-642-14808-8_2
5. Borba, P., Teixeira, L., Gheyi, R.: A theory of software product line refinement. Theor. Comput. Sci. **455**, 2–30 (2012). https://doi.org/10.1016/j.tcs.2012.01.031
6. Botterweck, G., Pleuss, A.: Evolution of software product lines. In: Mens, T., Serebrenik, A., Cleve, A. (eds.) Evolving Software Systems, pp. 265–295. Springer, Heidelberg (2014). https://doi.org/10.1007/978-3-642-45398-4_9
7. Botterweck, G., Pleuss, A., Dhungana, D., Polzer, A., Kowalewski, S.: EvoFM: feature-driven planning of product-line evolution. In: Rubin, J., Botterweck, G., Mezini, M., Maman, I., Pleuss, A. (eds.) Proceedings of the 2010 ICSE Workshop

on Product Line Approaches in Software Engineering, PLEASE 2010, pp. 24–31. ACM (2010). https://doi.org/10.1145/1808937.1808941

8. Bürdek, J., Kehrer, T., Lochau, M., Reuling, D., Kelter, U., Schürr, A.: Reasoning about product-line evolution using complex feature model differences. In: Jürjens, J., Schneider, K. (eds.) Software Engineering 2017, Fachtagung des GI-Fachbereichs Softwaretechnik, 21–24. February 2017, Hannover, Deutschland. LNI, vol. P-267, pp. 67–68. GI (2017). https://dl.gi.de/20.500.12116/1274

9. Hinterreiter, D., Prähofer, H., Linsbauer, L., Grünbacher, P., Reisinger, F., Egyed, A.: Feature-oriented evolution of automation software systems in industrial software ecosystems. In: 23rd IEEE International Conference on Emerging Technologies and Factory Automation, ETFA, pp. 107–114. IEEE (2018). https://doi.org/10.1109/ETFA.2018.8502557

10. Hoff, A., et al.: Consistency-preserving evolution planning on feature models. In: Lopez-Herrejon, R.E. (ed.) 24th ACM International Systems and Software Product Line Conference, Volume A, SPLC 2020, pp. 8:1–8:12. ACM (2020). https://doi.org/10.1145/3382025.3414964

11. Laguna, M.A., Crespo, Y.: A systematic mapping study on software product line evolution: from legacy system reengineering to product line refactoring. Sci. Comput. Program. **78**(8), 1010–1034 (2013). https://doi.org/10.1016/j.scico.2012.05.003

12. Lambers, L., Strüber, D., Taentzer, G., Born, K., Huebert, J.: Multi-granular conflict and dependency analysis in software engineering based on graph transformation. In: ICSE 2018, pp. 716–727. Association for Computing Machinery, New York (2018). https://doi.org/10.1145/3180155.3180258

13. Machado, R., Ribeiro, L., Heckel, R.: Characterizing conflicts between rule application and rule evolution in graph transformation systems. In: Parisi-Presicce, F., Westfechtel, B. (eds.) ICGT 2015. LNCS, vol. 9151, pp. 171–186. Springer, Cham (2015). https://doi.org/10.1007/978-3-319-21145-9_11

14. Mauro, J., Nieke, M., Seidl, C., Yu, I.C.: Anomaly detection and explanation in context-aware software product lines. In: ter Beek, M.H., et al. (eds.) 21st International Systems and Software Product Line Conference, SPLC 2017, Volume B, pp. 18–21. ACM (2017). https://doi.org/10.1145/3109729.3109752

15. Mauro, J., Nieke, M., Seidl, C., Yu, I.C.: Context-aware reconfiguration in evolving software product lines. Sci. Comput. Program. **163**, 139–159 (2018). https://doi.org/10.1016/j.scico.2018.05.002

16. Mitschke, R., Eichberg, M.: Supporting the evolution of software product lines. In: ECMDA Traceability Workshop (2008). http://tubiblio.ulb.tu-darmstadt.de/34815/

17. Motzfeldt, I.S.: Modular Soundness Checking of Feature Model Evolution Plans. Master's thesis, University of Oslo (2021). http://urn.nb.no/URN:NBN:no-91791

18. Motzfeldt, I.S., Yu, I.C., Din, C.C., Pun, V.K.I, Stolz, V.: Software artefact for: modular soundness checking of feature model evolution plans. In: Motzfeldt, I.S., et al., ICTAC 2023 (2023). https://doi.org/10.5281/zenodo.8362683, original source at: https://github.com/idamotz/Master/tree/master/soundness-checker

19. Neves, L., Teixeira, L., Sena, D., Alves, V., Kulesza, U., Borba, P.: Investigating the safe evolution of software product lines. In: 10th ACM International Conference on Generative Programming and Component Engineering, GPCE 2011, pp. 33–42. Association for Computing Machinery, New York (2011). https://doi.org/10.1145/2047862.2047869

20. Nieke, M., Engel, G., Seidl, C.: DarwinSPL: an integrated tool suite for modeling evolving context-aware software product lines. In: ter Beek, M.H., Siegmund, N., Schaefer, I. (eds.) 11th International Workshop on Variability Modelling of Software-Intensive Systems, VaMoS 2017, pp. 92–99. ACM (2017). https://doi.org/10.1145/3023956.3023962

21. Passos, L., Czarnecki, K., Apel, S., Wąsowski, A., Kästner, C., Guo, J.: Feature-oriented software evolution. In: VaMoS 2013. Association for Computing Machinery, New York (2013). https://doi.org/10.1145/2430502.2430526

22. Pleuss, A., Botterweck, G., Dhungana, D., Polzer, A., Kowalewski, S.: Model-driven support for product line evolution on feature level. J. Syst. Softw. **85**(10), 2261–2274 (2012). https://doi.org/10.1016/j.jss.2011.08.008

23. Pohl, K., Böckle, G., van der Linden, F.: Software Product Line Engineering - Foundations, Principles, and Techniques. Springer, Cham (2005). https://doi.org/10.1007/3-540-28901-1

24. Sampaio, G., Borba, P., Teixeira, L.: Partially safe evolution of software product lines. J. Syst. Softw. **155**, 17–42 (2019). https://doi.org/10.1016/j.jss.2019.04.051

25. Schwägerl, F.: Version Control and Product Lines in Model-Driven Software Engineering. Ph.D. thesis, University of Bayreuth, Germany (2018). https://epub.uni-bayreuth.de/3554/

26. Seidl, C., Schaefer, I., Aßmann, U.: DeltaEcore - A model-based delta language generation framework. In: Fill, H., Karagiannis, D., Reimer, U. (eds.) Modellierung 2014, 19.-21. März 2014, Wien, Österreich. LNI, vol. P-225, pp. 81–96. GI (2014). https://dl.gi.de/20.500.12116/17067

Author Index

A

Accattoli, Beniamino   196
Amrane, Amazigh   295
Attala, Ziggy   15
Azzopardi, Shaun   332

B

Bazille, Hugo   295
Begemann, Marian Johannes   388
Bereczky, Péter   139
Brizzio, Matías   256
Butler, Michael   178

C

Cavalcanti, Ana   15
Chen, Haiming   216
Cimini, Matteo   100

D

D'Argenio, Pedro R.   1
Dagnino, Francesco   313
Din, Crystal Chang   417
Dorfhuber, Florian   55

E

Eisentraut, Julia   55

F

Fahrenberg, Uli   295
Farjudian, Amin   313
Franken, Tom T. P.   158

G

Gale, Ella   276
Groote, Jan Friso   158
Guerrieri, Giulio   196

H

Hennicker, Rolf   236
Heule, Marijn J. H.   4

Hoang, Thai Son   178
Horpácsi, Dániel   139

J

Johnsen, Einar Broch   370

K

Kallwies, Hannes   388
Karsten, Nadine   351
Keiren, Jeroen J. A.   399
Kharraz, Karam   332
Kløvstad, Åsmund Aqissiaq Arild   370
Křetínský, Jan   55
Kuznetsov, Stepan L.   83

L

Leberle, Maico   196
Leucker, Martin   332, 388
Li, Rongchen   216
Lobski, Leo   276

M

Moggi, Eugenio   313
Morris Wright, Karla Vanessa   178
Motzfeldt, Ida Sandberg   417

N

Nakanishi, Rindo   36
Neele, Thomas   158, 399
Nestmann, Uwe   351

P

Peng, Chengyao   216
Pombo, Carlos G. Lopez   119
Proença, José   236
Pun, Violet Ka I   417

R

Ruangwises, Suthee   74

E. Ábrahám et al. (Eds.): ICTAC 2023, LNCS 14446, pp. 439–440, 2023.
https://doi.org/10.1007/978-3-031-47963-2

S
Sánchez, César   256
Schmitz, Malte   388
Schneider, Gerardo   332
Seki, Hiroyuki   36
Snook, Colin   178
Stolz, Volker   417
Stramaglia, Anna   399
Su, Weihao   216
Suñé, Agustín E. Martinez   119

T
Takata, Yoshiaki   36
ter Beek, Maurice H.   236

Tuosto, Emilio   119
Tušil, Jan   139

V
Voogd, Erik   370

W
Woodcock, Jim   15

Y
Yu, Ingrid Chieh   417

Z
Zanasi, Fabio   276
Ziemiański, Krzysztof   295

Printed in the United States
by Baker & Taylor Publisher Services

Printed in the United States
by Baker & Taylor Publisher Services